Contaminated Land

AUSTRALIA
The Law Book Company
Brisbane – Sydney – Melbourne – Perth

CANADA
Carswell
Ottawa – Toronto – Calgary – Montreal – Vancouver

Agents
Steimatzky's Agency Ltd., Tel Aviv
N.M. Tripathi (Private) Ltd., Bombay
Eastern Law House (Private) Ltd., Calcutta
M.P.P. House, Bangalore
Universal Book Traders, Delhi
Aditya Books, Delhi
MacMillan Shuppan KK, Tokyo
Pakistan Law House, Karachi, Lahore

Contaminated Land

Stephen Tromans, M.A.(Cantab.)

*Partner and Head of Environmental Law
Department, Simmons & Simmons*

and

Robert Turrall-Clarke, M.A.(Oxon.)

Environmental Group, Beachcroft Stanleys, Solicitors

London
Sweet & Maxwell
1994

Published in 1994 by
Sweet & Maxwell Limited of
South Quay Plaza
183 Marsh Wall
London E14 9FT
Phototypeset by LBJ Enterprises Ltd. of Aldermaston and Chilcompton
Printed in Great Britain by The Bath Press, Bath, Avon

No natural forests were destroyed to make this product;
only farmed timber was used and replanted

A CIP catalogue record for this book is
available from the British Library

ISBN 0-421-50920-1

PREFACE

Our aim in writing this book has been to tackle, from a legal viewpoint, the myriad problems presented by land which is, or which may be, subject to contamination. Many of these problems are only now emerging, having laid dormant for many years, in some cases decades. For solicitors and other professionals who may have no specialist knowledge of contaminated land, these issues may seem daunting. Even for those with practical experience, the lack of clear policy guidance and legislative standards presents grave uncertainties.

We have tried to make this book both accessible to the non-expert and useful to the specialist. As well as the predictable issue of liability, we have addressed other areas such as prevention of contamination, redevelopment and clean-up. We have included chapters dealing with property and corporate transactions and the use of consultants; various Appendices deal with issues such as valuation, insurance, information sources and precedents.

Policy on contaminated land is at a sensitive and formative stage in the UK and EC—particularly so in relation to issues such as registers, clean-up standards and the design of any liability régime. We have therefore included a significant amount of material on policy, including comparative material, and our own concluding recommendations as to a possible way forward.

Producing the text was made all the more interesting and challenging by a number of significant developments which occurred during its gestation period. The House of Lords' decision in the *Cambridge Water Company* case was handed down in time for incorporation at manuscript stage. The consultation paper, "Paying for Our Past", and the implementation of the waste management system under Part II of the Environmental Protection Act 1990 were significant developments between manuscript and galley proof stage, and have been assimilated into the text. Generally the position is stated as at April 22, 1994.

Many friends and colleagues from various professional disciplines have assisted greatly by providing technical advice, by reading parts of the text, and by stimulating helpful lines of thought or enquiry. A list of those to whom we are indebted follows this preface.

We hope that lawyers and others dealing (willingly or reluctantly) with contaminated land, in whatever context, will find this book a useful guide.

Stephen Tromans	Robert Turrall-Clarke
Simmons & Simmons	Beachcroft Stanleys
14 Dominion Street	20 Furnival Street
London EC2M 2RJ	London EC4A 1BN

ACKNOWLEDGMENTS

We are grateful to the following for their help and encouragement in the writing of this book:

Martin Beckett	Mott McDonald
Peter Brazel	Beachcroft Stanleys
John Cowan	Consulting Engineer
Tom Elliott	Black Country Development Corporation
Sue Herbert	Rendel Science & Environment
Alyson Howells	Simmons & Simmons
John Hurdley	Beachcroft Stanleys
Neil Jackson	Department of Environment
Andrew Kennedy	Beachcroft Stanleys
Philip Lawrence	Beachcroft Stanleys
Tony Lennon	ECS Underwriters
Albert Mumma	Simmons & Simmons
Kathy Mylrea	Simmons & Simmons
Mark Plenderleith	Pembroke College, Oxford
Gary Smith	Solicitor, NRA
John Spencer	Selwyn College, Cambridge
Brian Street	ECS Underwriters
Phillip Vallance	Queen's Counsel
Martin Whiteland	Hunting Land and Environment
Peter Young	Aspinwall & Co.

Additionally, various colleagues from other jurisdictions assisted greatly in providing material on which Chapter 13 (Contaminated Land in other jurisdictions) is based. They are named at the appropriate part of the Chapter and their contribution is gratefully acknowledged.

CONTENTS

Preface v
Acknowledgements vii
Table of Cases xvii
Table of Statutes xxxvii
Table of Statutory Instruments xlvii

Preamble 1

Discussion: What is Contaminated Land? 3
    The Government's view 3
    The harm test 5
    Derelict land and contaminated land 5

Chapter 1
INTRODUCTION
    Causes of contaminated land 7
    Consequences of contamination 8
    Contamination: interests and concerns 11
    How big a problem? 14
    Examples of problems 16
    UK policy approaches 20
    Naturally occurring contamination: radon 23
    Identifying contaminated land 25
    Institutions dealing with contaminated land 25
    The European Community dimension 27
    Comparative approaches 28

Chapter 2
LIABILITY
    Introduction 30
    Nature of liability 31
  Civil Liability
    Civil liability generally 32
    Direct or immediate damage: trespass 34
    Rylands v. Fletcher 36
  Nuisance
    Generally 42
    Public nuisance 43
    Possible defences 48
    Pollution of surface waters 48
    Pollution of groundwater 49

Negligence
Generally 53

Breach of Statutory Duty
General principles 56

Occupiers' Liability
Duty to visitors 58
Duty to trespassers 58

General Issues
Causation and proof 60
Concurrent causes 61
Remedies 62
Joint and several liability 67
Limitation of actions 69

Liability Under the Environmental Protection Act 1990, Part I
Generally 72

Water Pollution
Criminal liability for water pollution: principle offences 74
Causing or knowingly permitting 79
Anti-pollution works and operations 81
NRA: Enforcement Policy 83

Waste Related Contamination
Generally 86
Removal of waste unlawfully deposited: section 59 88
Harmful waste deposits: section 61 90

Statutory Nuisance
Relevant statutory nuisances 96
Abatement by local authority and cost recovery 98
Who is liable? 100

Planning Powers
Section 215 notices 102

Powers of Criminal Courts
Compensation orders 107
Power to deprive offender of property 108
EC Proposals 110
Council of European Convention 112

Chapter 3
INFORMATION
Generally 115

Proposal for Registers of Contaminative Uses
Section 143 registers 116
The proposed register 119
Alternative proposals 121
Further consultation—"Paying for Our Past" 124

Other Functions Relating to Information
Powers to obtain information 127
Limitation on investigative powers 130
Information held on registers 133

Public Access to Information

The European Directive 136
The Environmental Information Regulations 1992 138
Access to information 144
Relationship to statutory restrictions 145
Personal information and volunteered information 145
Local Government meetings: information 146

Chapter 4
INVESTIGATION AND APPRAISAL

Investigation in Context 147
Sources of Guidance 148
Site History: Problematic Issues 151
Interpretation of Information 157
Sampling 159
Analysis 165
Assessment of Findings 169
Risk Assessment 175

Chapter 5
PREVENTION

Generally 183

Town and Country Planning

Generally 184
Development plan policies 185
Planning conditions and obligations 188

Integrated Pollution Control

IPC generally 195
The need for authorisation 198
The relationship of IPC to soil contamination 198
Air pollution control 200
EC proposals for integrated pollution control 201

Waste Management Law

Generally 202
The Deposit of Poisonous Waste Act 1972 203
The Control of Pollution Act 1974 205
The Environmental Protection Act 1990, Part II 210
Controlled waste and "Directive waste" 212
Waste other than controlled waste 216
Relevance of "fit and proper person" 217
Licence conditions 218

Special Waste

Generally 221
Regulation of special waste 224
Registers and site records 225

Radioactive Substances

Generally 226
Application of control 227
Site records 227

Agriculture
Generally 228
Codes of Practice 231

EC Waste Legislation
"The Framework Directives" 232
The proposed Landfill Directive 233

Chapter 6
WATER

Introduction
Contaminated land and water pollution 237
Relevant domestic and EC legislation 239
The functions of the National Rivers Authority 241

Groundwater
Introduction 244
EC Policy on Groundwater 245
UK Implementation of EC Groundwater Policy 247
Groundwater protection responsibilities: the NRA 248
Statutory water quality objectives 253
Basis of classifying groundwater: vulnerability and risk 255
National Rivers Authority 257

Surface Water Quality
Generally 269
Classification of surface waters and quality objectives 269
Dangerous substances 270
NRA policy 272

Clean Water Supply and Abstraction
Water undertakers generally 273
Water quality: generally 274
The drinking water directives 276
Drinking water quality 277
Contamination of water sources 281
Abstraction of water 282

Foul Water Sewage
Prevention of contamination by foul water 286
Discharge into sewers 287
Sewage treatment 291
Contamination, beaches and bathing 292

Chapter 7
CLEAN-UP

Clean-Up Methodologies
Introduction 294
Forms of remedial action 296
Seclection of remedial techniques 304
How clean is clean? 305
Validation and monitoring 306

Health and Safety Law Relating to Development of Contaminated Land
General requirements 309

General statutory duties 310
Risk assessment 312
Control of substances hazardous to health 313
Contractual matters and design management 323

Waste Disposal
Licensing: the definition of waste 324
Exemptions from licensing 326
The duty of care 333
Waste carrier registration 336

Building Contract Aspects
Generally 338
Development under JCT '80 339
JCT '81—"design & build" contracts 342

Chapter 8
DEVELOPMENT
Introduction 348

Town and Country Planning Controls
The need for planning permission 348
Policy Guidance on the development of contaminated land ... 349
Development plan policies 352
Environmental assessment 354
Landfill gas 356
Relevant appeal decisions 361
Water protection issues 366
Planning conditions 367
Planning obligations 370
"Overall advantage" issues 371
The problems of clean-up 373

Building Control
The Building Regulations 1991 374

Annex
EXAMPLES OF DEVELOPMENT PLAN POLICIES
.... 379

Chapter 9
FUNDING
Generally 385
The Urban Regeneration Agency 387
Urban Development Corporations 390
The "Action for Cities" Initiative 394
Derelict Land Grant 395
City Grant 407
Urban Programme 410
Information on unused and under-used land 412

European Community Initiatives
LIFE Programme 416
Structural Funds 417

Chapter 10
CONSULTANTS

Introduction 421
Selection of consultant 421
Terms of contract 426
Reliance on report 431
Extension of duty to third parties 435
sub-contractors 436
Insurance 437

Chapter 11
PROPERTY TRANSACTIONS

Introduction 439

Sale
Generally 440
Local authority enquiries 442
Enquiries of other bodies 443
Disclosure of information by the vendor 444
Standard contract provisions 448
Warranties and indemnities 450
Criticisms of the *caveat emptor* rule 454
Contamination surveys 455
The use of conditional contracts 456

Leases
General Issues 457
Selection of tenant 457
Drafting and construing leases 458
Protecting the landlord 461
Fitness for purpose 462
Safeguarding the tenant 463

Mortgages
Generally 464
Lending policy 465
Mortgage documentation

Chapter 12
CORPORATE TRANSACTIONS AND INSOLVENCY

Corporate transaction: general issues 467
Investigations and information 468
Risk Allocation 469
Warranties 470
Indemnities 471
Common drafting problems 472
Company accounts and listing particulars 479

Corporate Insolvency
Receivership 480
Insolvency Act administrators 483
Liquidators 484

Chapter 13
CONTAMINATED LAND LEGISLATION IN OTHER JURISDICTIONS

A. Scotland 486
B. USA 490
C. Canada 504
D. The Netherlands 507
E. Germany 512
F. Denmark 517
G. Australia 519

Chapter 14
RECOMMENDATIONS

Generally 524
Identification of contaminated land 524
Prioritisation of sites 525
Spill reporting and response 526
Past contamination 526
Joint compensation funds 529
Contingent problems 530
How clean is clean? 531
The decision making process 532
Anti-avoidance measures 533

Appendix A
PRECEDENTS

PRECEDENTS 535

Appendix B
VALUATION OF CONTAMINATED LAND

VALUATION OF CONTAMINATED LAND 585

Appendix C
INFORMATION SOURCES

INFORMATION SOURCES 596

Appendix D
ASSESSMENT OF CONTAMINATION

ASSESSMENT OF CONTAMINATION 606

Appendix E
CURRENT RESEARCH

CURRENT RESEARCH 611

Appendix F
INSURANCE

INSURANCE 619

Index 625

TABLE OF CASES

(All references are to paragraph numbers)

AB v. Southwest Water Services [1993] Q.B. 507; [1993] 2 W.L.R. 507;
    [1993] 1 All E.R. 609; [1993] P.I.Q.R. 167; [1992] N.P.C. 146;
    (1993) 143 New L.J. 235; [1993] I.C.R............ 2.14, 2.37, 6.27, 6.31
Abrams v. Ancliffe [1978] 2 N.Z.L.R. 420, N.Z. Sup. Ct................ 10.07
Achusnet River and New Bedford Harbor : Proceedings Re Alleged PCB
    Pollution. Re (Achusnet VIII) 725 F.Supp. 1264 (D. Mass. 1989).. 13.09
Acton v. Blundell (1843) 12 M & W 324; 13 LJEx. 289; 1 LTOS 207; 152
    E.R. 1223, Ex. Ch.. 2.22
Albacruz (Cargo Owners) v. Albazero (Owners) [1977] A.C. 774; [1976]
    3 W.L.R. 419; [1976] 3 All E.R. 129; [1976] 2 Lloyd's Law Rep.
    467; 120 S.J. 570, H.L...................................... 10.08
Albazero, The. See Albacruz (Cargo Owners) v. Albazero (Owners)
Alphacell v. Woodward [1972] A.C. 824; [1972] 2 W.L.R. 1320; 116 S.J.
    431; [1972] 2 All E.R. 475; 70 L.G.R. 455; [1972] Crim.L.R. 41,
    H.L.; affirming [1972] 1 Q.B. 127; [1971] 3 W.L.R. 445; 115 S.J.
    464; [1971] 2 All E.R. 910; 69 L.G.R. 561, D.C................... 2.48
Adams v. Southern Electricity Board The Times, October 21, 1993........ 2.33
Anglican Water Services v. H.G. Thurston & Co. [1993] E.G.C.S. 162
    (C.A.)... 2.23, 10.06
Ashland Oil Inc. v. Sonford Products Corp. 810 F. Supp. 1057 (D. Minn.
    1993)... 13.09
Astra Trust v. Adams and Williams [1969] 1 Lloyd's Rep. 81............ 11.13
Atkinson v. Secretary of State for the Environment and Leeds City
    Council [1983] J.P.L. 599..................................... 8.12
Att.-Gen. v. Tod Heatley [1897] 1 Ch. 560; [1895–9] All E.R. 636; 66
    L.J. Ch. 275; 76 L.T. 174; 61 J.P.Jo. 164; 45 WR 394; 13 T.L.T.
    220; 41 S.J. 311, C.A.. 2.14
Att.-Gen. (Gambia) v. N'Jie [1961] A.C. 617; [1961] 2 W.L.R. 845; 105
    S.J. 421; [1961] 2 All E.R. 504. P.C............................ 2.70
Att.-Gen. (Ontario) v. Tyre King Tyre Recycling (1992) 8 C.E.L.R.
    (N.S.) 202.. 12.10, 13.17
Att.-Gen.'s Reference (No. 2 of 1988) [1990] 1 Q.B. 77; [1989] 3 W.L.R.
    397; (1989) 153 J.P. 574; (1989) 133 S.J. 978; (1989) 89 Cr.App.R.
    314; (1989) 153 J.P.N. 577; (1989) 153 L.G.Rev. 787; [1990] L.S.
    Gaz. Januray 31, 67, C.A................................ 5.20, 5.28

B.L. HOLDINGS v. Wood (Roberts J.) and Partners (1979) 123 S.J. 570;
    (1979) 12 Build L.R. 1, C.A.; reversing [1978] J.P.L. 833; (1978)
    10 Build L.R. 48; (1978) 122 S.J. 525.......................... 10.07
Backup Corporation v. Smith [1890] 44 Ch.D. 395.................... 12.10
Balabel v. Air India [1988] Ch. 317; [1988] 2 W.L.R. 1036; (1988) 132
    S.J. 699; [1988] 2 All E.R. 246; (1988) 138 New L.J. 85, C.A..... 3.09A
Ballard v. Tomlinson (1885) 29 Ch.D. 115.......................... 2.22
Bar-Gur v. Squire [1993] E.G.C.S. 151............................. 2.36

Bell v. Midland Ry. Co. (1861) 30 L.J.C.P. 273; (1861) 10 C.B.N.S. 287. .   2.37
Benning v. Wong (1969) 43 A.L.J.R. 467; (1969) 122 C.L.R. 249. . . . . 2.09
Berridge Incinerators v. Nottinghamshire County Council, Nottingham
    Crown Court, June 12, 1992, unreported. 2.59, 5.20, 5.21, 5.24
Berton v. Alliance Economic Investment Co. [1922] 1 K.B. 742; 91
    LJKB 748; 127 L.T. 422; 38 T.L.R. 435; 66 S.J. 487, C.A. 2.48
Betts v. Penge U.D.C. [1942] 2 K.B. 154; [1942] 2 All E.R. 61; 111
    LJKB 565; 167 L.T. 205; 106 J.P. 203; 58 T.L.R. 283, 86 S.J. 313;
    40 L.G.R. 199, D.C. 2.66
Bevan Investments v. Blackhall & Struthers (1977) 11 Building L.R. 78,
    N.Z.C.A. 10.07
Beyfus v. Lodge [1925] 1 Ch. 350; [1925] All E.R. 552; 95 L.J. Ch. 27;
    133 L.T. 265; 41 T.L.R. 429; 69 S.J. 507. . . . . 11.06
Bilboe (J.F.) v. Secretary of State for the Environment and West
    Lancashire District Council; Bilboe (J.F.) and Bilboe (J.F.)
    (Junior) v. Secretary of State for the Environment and West
    Lancashire District Council (1980) 39 P. & C.R. 495; [1980] J.P.L.
    330; (1980) 78 L.G.R. 357; (1980) 254 E.G. 607, C.A.; reversing
    [1979] J.P.L. 100; (1978) E.G. 229, D.C. 5.08
Blackwood (Hugh) (Farms) v. Motherwell District Council 1988 G.W.D.
    30–1290. . . . . 13.02
Blundell v. Caterall (1821) 5 B & A 268; 106 E.R. 1190. . . . . 6.41
Boehm v. Goodall [1911] 1 Ch. 155; [1908–10] All E.R. 485; 80 L.J. Ch.
    86; 103 L.T. 717; 27 T.L.R. 106; 55 S.J. 108. 12.10
Bonnington Castings v. Wardlaw [1956] 1 A.C. 613; [1956] 2 W.L.R.
    707; 100 S.J. 207; [1956] 1 All E.R. 615; 54 L.G.R. 153; sub nom.
    Wardlaw v. Bonnington Castings, 1956 S.C. (H.L.) 26; 1956
    S.L.T. 135, H.L.; affirming sub nom. Wardlaw v. Bonnington
    Castings, 1955 S.C. 320; 1955 S.L.T. 225; [1955] C.L.Y. 1075. . . . . . 2.35
Bower v. Peate (1876) 1 Q.B.D. 321; [1874–80] All E.R. 905; 45 L.J.Q.B.
    446; 35 L.T. 321; 40 J.P. 789. . . . . 2.17
Bradford Corporation v. Ferrand [1902] 2 Ch. 655; 71 L.J. Ch. 859; 87
    L.T. 388; 67 J.P. 21; 51 W.R. 122; 18 T.L.R. 830, D.C. 2.22
Brew Bros. v. Snax (Ross) [1970] 1 Q.B. 612; [1969] 3 W.L.R. 657; 113
    S.J. 795; [1970] 1 All E.R. 587; 20 P. & C.R. 829, C.A.; affirming
    (1968) 19 P. & C.R. 702; 207 E.G. 341. . . . . 2.18, 2.19, 11.16
British Celanese v. Hunt (A.H.) (Capacitors) [1969] 1 W.L.R. 959;
    [1969] 2 All E.R. 1252; sub nom. British Celanese v. Hunt (A.M.)
    (Capacitors) (1969) 113 S.J. 368. Petition for Leave to appeal to
    the House of Lords allowed. 2.07
British Railway Board v. Herrington [1972] A.C. 877; [1972] 2 W.L.R.
    537; 116 S.J. 178; [1972] 1 All E.R. 749, H.L.; affirming sub nom.
    Herrington v. British Railways Board [1971] 2 Q.B. 107; [1971] 2
    W.L.R. 477; (1970) 114 S.J. 954; [1971] 1 All E.R. 897, C.A.;
    affirming (1970) 214 E.G. 561. . . . . 2.33
——— v. Secretary of State for the Environment [1994] J.P.L. 32. . . . . 8.12
British Waterways Board v. National Rivers Authority, sub nom. British
    Waterways Board v. Anglian Water Authority [1992] NPC 100;
    The Times, August 4, 1992, C.A.; affirming [1991] E.G.C.S. 44. . . . . . 6.34
Broder v. Saillard (1876) 3 Ch.D. 692; 45 L.J. Ch. 414; 40 J.P. 644; 24
    W.R. 1011. . . . . 2.18

Broderick *v.* Gale and Ainslie [1993] Water Law, Vol. 4, Issue 4, p. 127. . 2.21
Bromsgrove District Council *v.* Carthy (1975) 30 P. & C.R. 34, D.C.. . . . . 2.48
Brown *v.* Raphael [1958] Ch. 636; [1958] 2 W.L.R. 647; 102 S.J. 269;
    [1958] 2 All E.R. 79; C.A. 11.07
Buccleuch (Duke of) *v.* Cowan (1866) 4 M 475; 5 Macph (Ct. of
    Sessions) 214; 39 Sc. Jur. 152. . . . . 13.02
Buckland *v.* MacKesy; Buckland *v.* Watts (1968) 112 S.J. 841; 208 E.G.
    969; 118 New L.J. 1009, C.A.. . . . . 10.05

CADDER LOCAL AUTHORITY *v.* Lang (1879) 6 R. 1242; 16 Sc. L.R. 737. . . . . 13.04
Caledonia (E.E.) *v.* Orbit Valve Company Europe, Q.B.D. May 18, 1993 12.07
Caledonian Railway *v.* Greenock Corporation 1917 S.C. (H.L.) 56; 54 Sc.
    L.R. 600. . . . . 13.02
Cambridge Water Co. *v.* Eastern Counties Leather plc [1994] 2 W.L.R.
    53; [1993] Env.L.R. 287; [1992] Env.L.R. 116. . . . . 2.03, 2.05, 2.07, 2.08,
          2.09, 2.10, 2.11, 2.18, 2.20, 2.22, 2.23, 2.24, 2.26, 2.34, 6.30, 13.02
Campbell *v.* Kennedy (1864) 3 M. 121; 37 Sc. Jur. 62. . . . . 13.02
Canada Steamship Lines *v.* R [1952] A.C. 192; [1952] 1 T.L.R. 261; 96
    S.J. 72; [1952] 1 All E.R. 305; [1952] 1 Lloyd's Rep. 1, P.C. 12.07
Canada Trust Co. *v.* Bulora Corporation (1980) 34 C.B.R. (N.S.) 145;
    affirmed 39 C.B.R. (N.S.) 152. . . . . 12.10
Candler *v.* Crane, Christmas & Co. [1951] 2 K.B. 164; [1951] 1 T.L.R.
    371; 95 S.J. 171; [1951] 1 All E.R. 426, C.A. 10.09
Cann *v.* Willson (1888) 39 Ch.D. 39; 57 L.J.Ch. 1034; 59 L.T. 723; 37
    W.R. 23; 4 T.L.R. 588; 32 S.J. 542. . . . . 10.09
Capro Industries *v.* Dickman [1990] 2 A.C. 605; [1990] 2 W.L.R. 358;
    [1990] 1 All E.R. 568; (1990) 134 S.J. 494; [1990] BCC 164; [1990]
    BCLC 273; [1990] E.C.C. 313; [1990] L.S.Gaz, March 28, 42;
    (1990) 140 New L.J. 248, H.L.; reversing [1989] Q.B. 653; [1989]
    2 W.L.R. 316; (1989) 133 S.J. 221; [1989] 1 All E.R. 798; (1989) 5
    BCC 105; [1989] BCLC 154; 1989 PCC 125, C.A.; reversing in
    part. 10.09
Carlish *v.* Salt [1906] 1 Ch. 335; 75 L.J.Ch. 175; 94 L.T. 58. . . . . 11.06
Carradine Properties *v.* D.J. Freeman (1982) 126 S.J. 157; *The Times,*
    February 19, 1982, C.A.. . . . . 10.05
Carrick District Council *v.* Taunton Vale Meat Traders, *The Times,*
    February 15, 1994. . . . . 3.08
Cartwright *v.* G.K.N. Sankey (1973) 14 K.I.R. 349, C.A.; reversing 116
    S.J. 433; (1972) 12 K.I.R. 453. . . . . 2.26
Cassell & Co. *v.* Broome [1972] A.C. 1027; [1972]2 W.L.R. 645; 116 S.J.
    199; [1972] 1 All E.R. 801, H.L.; affirming *sub nom.* Broome *v.*
    Cassell & Co. [1971] 2 Q.B. 354; [1971] 2 W.L.R. 853; 115 S.J.
    289; [1971] 2 All E.R. 187, C.A.; affirming [1971] 1 All E.R. 262. . . 2.37
Caswell *v.* Powell Duffryn Associated Collieries [1940] A.C. 152; [1939] 3
    All E.R. 722; 108 L.J.K.B. 779; 161 L.T. 374; 55 T.L.R. 1004; 83
    S.J. 976, H.L.. . . . . 2.20
Chasemore *v.* Richards (1859) 7 H.L. Cas. 349. . . . . 2.22
Cheminova II, Danish Weekly Law Report 1992 575H. 13.27
Chu *v.* District of North Vancouver (1982) 139 D.L.R. (3rd) 201. . . . . 2.07
Citytowns *v.* Bohemian Properties [1986] 2 E.G.L.R. 258. . . . . 11.06
Clayton *v.* Sale U.D.C. [1926] 1 K.B. 415; [1925] All E.R. 279; 95
    L.J.K.B. 178; 134 L.T. 147; 90 J.P. 5; 42 T.L.R. 72; 24 L.G.R. 34,
    D.C.. . . . . 2.71

Clydebank District Council v. Monaville Estates 1982 S.L.T. (Sh. Ct.) 2
App.Ct. (Scotland)..................................... 2.71, 13.04
Callard v. Saunders (Paul A.) (Trading as Saunders (W.G.R.) & Son)
[1971] C.L.Y. 116.. 10.05
Columbus Co. v. Clowes [1903] 1 K.B. 244; 72 L.J.K.B. 330; 51 W.R.
366.. 10.07
Container Transport International Inc. v. Oceanus Mutual Underwrit-
ing Association (Burmuda) [1984] 1 Lloyd's Rep. 476, C.A.;
reversing [1982] 2 Lloyd's Rep. 178; [1982] Com.L.R. 68........ F–02
Corbett v. Hill (1870) L.R. 9 Eq. 671; 39 L.J.Ch. 547; 22 L.T. 263...... 2.04
Corisand Investments Limited v. Druce & Co. (1978) 248 E.G. 315, 407,
504... B–03
Coventry City Council v. Cartwright [1975] 1 W.L.R. 845; 119 S.J. 235;
[1975] 2 All E.R. 99; 73 L.G.R. 218, D.C...................... 2.66
Crump v. Lambert (1867) L.R. 3 Eq. 409; 15 L.T. 600; 31 J.P. 485; 15
W.R. 417... 2.36
Cumberland Consolidated Holdings v. Ireland [1946] K.B. 264; [1946] 1
All E.R. 284; 115 L.J.K.B. 301; 174 L.T. 257; 62 T.L.R. 215, C.A. 11.08
Cunard v. Antifyre [1953] 1 K.B. 551......................... 2.16, 2.36

DES Daughters—Supreme Court of the Netherlands, October 9, 1992,
Case No. 1466 7 (Rud W 1992 No. 219) [1993] Env. Liab. C525;
[1993] Env. Liab. 72..................................... 2.35
D. & F. Estates v. Church Commissioners [1989] A.C. 177; [1988] 2
E.G.L.R. 213; 15 Con.L.R. 35, H.L.......................... 10.09
Darley Main Colliery Co. v. Mitchell (1886) 11 App.Cas. 127; 55
L.J.Q.B. 529; 54 L.T. 882; 51 J.P. 148; 2 T.L.R. 301, H.L........ 2.41
Davy v. Guy Salmon (Service) June 9, 1993, reported Chartered
Surveyor Weekly, July 23, 1992............................. 11.17
Department of the Environment v. Thomas Bates [1991] 1 A.C. 499;
[1990] 3 W.L.R. 457; [1990] 2 All E.R. 943; [1990] 46 E.G. 115;
(1990) 134 S.J. 1077; 50 BLR 61; 21 Con.L.R. 54, H.L.; affirming
[1989] 1 All E.R. 1075; [1989] 26 E.G. 121; 13 Con.L.R. 1; 44
BLR 88; (1989) 139 New L.J. 39, C.A......................... 10.09
Devon Lumber Co. v. MacNeill (1987) 45 D.L.R. (4th)............... 2.16
Dougherty v. Chandler (1946) 46 S.R. (N.S.W.) 370............... 2.40
Dunlop v. Lambert (1839) 6 Cl. & F. 600; Macl & Rob 663; 7 E.R. 824,
H.L... 10.08
Dunne v. North Western Gas Board; Lambert v. Same; Doyle v. Same
[1964] 2 Q.B. 806; [1964] 2 W.L.R. 164; 107 S.J. 890; [1963] 3 All
E.R. 916; 62 L.G.R. 197; C.A............................... 2.06

Eagle-Picher Industries v. EPA 759 F. 2d 905 (D.C. Cir. 1985)........ 13.07
Eames London Estates v. North Hertfordshire District Council (1981)
259 E.G. 491; [1982] Build.L.R. 50........................... 10.07
EcKersley v. Binnie & Partners, 1988 Court of Appeal, February 18.
Unreported... 2.28, 10.07
Edler v. Averbach [1950] 1 K.B. 359; 65 T.L.R. 645; 93 S.J. 727; [1949]
2 All E.R. 692; 1 P. & C.R. 10.............................. 11.06
Emhart Indus. Inc. v. Duracell International Incorporated 665 F. Supp.
549 (M.D. Tenn 1987)..................................... 3.10

Englefield Holdings and Sinclair's Contract, *Re,* Rosslyn and Lorimer
   Estates *v.* Englefield Holdings [1962] 1 W.L.R. 1119; 106 S.J. 721;
   [1962] 3 All E.R. 503. . . . . 11.06
Esso Petroleum Co. *v.* Southport Corporation [1956] A.C. 218; [1956] 2
   W.L.R. 81; 120 J.P.54; 100 S.J. 32; [1955] 3 All E.R. 864; 54
   L.G.R. 91; *sub nom.* Southport Corporation *v.* Esso Petroleum Co.
   [1955] 2 Lloyd's Rep. 665, H.L.; reversing *sub nom.* Southport
   Corporation *v.* Esso Petroleum Co. [1954] 2 Q.B. 182; [1954] 3
   W.L.R. 200; 188 J.P. 411; 98 S.J. 472; [1954] 2 All E.R. 561; 52
   L.G.R. 404; [1954] 1 Lloyd's Rep. 446; [1954] C.L.Y. 2302, C.A.;
   restoring [1953] 3 W.L.R. 773; 118 J.P. 1; 97 S.J. 764; [1952] 2 All
   E.R. 1204; 52 L.G.R. 22; [1953] 2 Lloyd's Rep. 414; [1953] C.L.Y.
   2567. . . . . 2.04

FARLOW *v.* Stevenson [1900] 1 Ch. 128; 69 L.J.Ch. 106; 81 L.T. 589; 48
   W.R. 213; 16 T.L.R. 57; 44 S.J. 73, C.A. 11.16
Fay *v.* Prentice (1845) 1 C.B. 828; 14 L.J.C.P. 298; 5 L.T.O.S. 216; 9 Jur.
   876; 135 E.R. 769. . . . . 2.36
Fayrewood Fish Farms *v.* Secretary of State for the Environment and
   Hampshire [1984] J.P.L. 267. . . . . 8.02
Fitzgerald *v.* Firbank [1897] 2 Ch. 96; [1895–9] All E.R. 415; 66 L.J.Ch.
   529; 76 L.T. 584; 13 T.L.R. 390; 41 S.J. 490, C.A. 2.21
Fleming *v.* Hislop (1886) 11 A.C. 686; 2 T.L.R. 360; 13 R. (H.L.) 43; 23
   Sc. L.R. 491, H.L. 13.05
Flight *v.* Booth (1834) 1 Bing N.C. 370; 1 Scott 190; 4 L.J.C.P. 66; 131
   E.R. 1160. . . . . 11.06
Florida Power & Light Co. *v.* Allis-Chalmers Corp. 893 F. 2d 1313 (11th
   Cir. 1990). 13.09
Foliejohn Establishment *v.* Gain S.A. (Ch.D. July 7, 1993). . 2.34, 11.07, 11.10,
                                                                                                             11.13
Forte & Co. *v.* General Accident Life Assurance (1987) 54 P. & C.R. 9;
   [1986] 2 E.G.L.R. 115; (1986) 279 E.G. 1227. . . . . 11.18

G.U.S. PROPERTY MANAGEMENT *v.* Littlewoods Mail Order, 1982 S.C.
   (H.L.) 157. . . . . 10.08
Gateshead Metropolitan Borough Council *v.* Secretary of State for the
   Environment and Northumbrian Water Group plc [1994] J.P.L.
   255. . . . . 5.05
Gebhardt *v.* Saunders [1892] 2 Q.B.D. 452; 67 L.T. 684; 56 J.P. 741; 40
   W.R. 571; 36 S.J. 524, D.C. 2.71
Gertsen *v.* Municipality of Metropolitan Toronto (1973) 41 D.L.R. (3d)
   646, Ontario High Ct. 2.06, 2.07, 2.17, 2.27, 2.36
Gibbons and Others *v.* South West Water Services, *see* A.B. *v.* South
   West Water Services
Gillingham Borough Council *v.* Medway (Chatham) Dock Co. [1992] 3
   W.L.R. 449; [1992] 3 All E.R. 923; (1991) 63 P. & C.R. 205;
   [1992] 1 PLR 113; [1992] J.P.L. 458; [1991] E.C.G.S. 101; [1991]
   NPC 97; *The Independent,* September 20, 1991; *The Times,* October
   10, 1991. . . . . 2.15, 2.20
Glasgow District Council, City of *v.* Carroll, 1991 S.L.T. (Sh.Ct.) 46;
   1991 S.C.L.R. 199. . . . . 13.04

Goldman (Allan William) v. Hargrave (Rupert William Edeson) [1967]
1 A.C. 645; [1966] 3 W.L.R. 513; 110 S.J. 527; [1966] 2 All E.R.
989; [1966] 2 Lloyd's Rep. 65, P.C.; affirming sub nom. Hargrave v.
Goldman (1963) 37 A.L.J.R. 277; [1964] C.L.Y. 3538. . . . .   2.18
Gomba Holdings UK v. Homan: Same v. Johnson Matthey Bankers
[1986] 1 W.L.R. 1301; [1986] 130 S.J. 821; [1986] 3 All E.R. 94;
1986 PCC 49; (1987) 84 L.S.Gaz 36. . . . .   12.10
Gordon v. Selico Co. [1986] 1 E.G.L.R. 71; (1986) 18 H.L.R. 219; (1986)
278 E.G. 53, C.A.; affirming (1985) 129 S.J. 347; [1985] 2
E.G.L.R. 79; (1984) 275 E.G. 841; (1985) 82 L.S.Gaz 2087. . . . . . .   11.06
Govan Police Commissioners v. MacKinnan (1885) 22 S.L.R. 843. . . . . . .   13.04
Government of State of Penang v. Beng Hong Oon [1972] A.C. 425;
[1972] 2 W.L.R. 1; 115 S.J. 889; [1971] 3 All E.R. 1163, P.C. 6.41
Grampian Regional Council v. City of Aberdeen District Council (1984)
47 P. & C.R. 633; [1984] F.S.R. 590, H.L. 8.12
Greaves & Co. Contractors v. Baynham Meikle & Partners [1975] 1
W.L.R. 1095; 119 S.J. 372; [1975] 3 All E.R. 99; [1975] 2 Lloyd's
Rep. 325, C.A.; affirming [1974] 1 W.L.R. 1261; 118 S.J. 595;
[1974] 3 All E.R. 666; [1975] 1 Lloyd's Rep. 31. . . . .   10.07
Greenhalgh v. Brindley [1901] 2 Ch. 324; 70 L.J.Ch. 740; 84 L.T. 763; 49
W.R. 597; 17 T.L.R. 574; 45 S.J. 576. . . . .   11.06
Grieg (David) v. Goldfinch (1961) 105 S.J. 367; 59 L.G.R. 304, D.C. 6.31
Grigsby v. Melville [1974] 1 W.L.R. 80; 117 S.J. 632; [1973] 3 All E.R.
455; 26 P. & C.R. 182, C.A.; affirming [1972] 1 W.L.R. 1355; 116
S.J. 784; [1973] 1 All E.R. 385; (1972) 24 P. & C.R. 191. . . . .   11.16
Guild v. Gateway Foodmarkets, 1991 S.L.T. 578; 1990 J.C. 277; 1990
S.C.C.R. 179. . . . .   6.31
Gunn v. Wallsend Slipway and Engineering Co., The Times, January 23,
1989. . . . .   2.26
Guppys (Bridport) v. Brookling; Guppys (Bridport) v. James (1984) 14
H.L.R. 1; (1984) 269 E.G. 846; (1984) 269 E.G. 942, C.A. 2.37

HADDON v. Black Country Development Corporation (REF/166/1991;
March 15, 1993, unreported). B–06
Hadley v. Baxendale (1854) 9 Ex. 341; [1843–60] All E.R. 461; 23
L.J.Ex. 179; 23 L.T.O.S. 69; 18 Jur. 358; 2 W.R. 302; 2 C.L.R.
517; 156 E.R. 145. . . . .   10.08
Halsey v. Esso Petroleum Co. [1961] 1 W.L.R. 683; [1961] 2 All E.R.
145; 105 S.J. 209. . . . .   2.15, 2.36
Hancock v. Brazier (B.W.) (Anerley) [1966] 1 W.L.R. 1317; [1966] 2 All
E.R. 901, C.A.; affirming 110 S.J. 368; [1966] 2 All E.R. 1. . . . .   11.06
Hanrahan v. Merck Sharp & Dohme (Ireland) [1988] I.L.R.M. 629. . . . .   2.03,
                                                                              2.04, 2.05
Hargraves Transport v. Lynch [1969] 1 W.L.R. 215; 112 S.J. 54; [1969]
1 All E.R. 455; 20 P. & C.R. 143, C.A. 11.13
Harris v. Wyre Forest District Council. See Smith v. Eric S. Bush; Harris
v. Wyre Forest District Council. 10.09
Hedley Byrne & Co. v. Heller & Partners [1964] A.C. 465; [1963] 3
W.L.R. 101; 107 S.J. 454; [1963] 2 All E.R. 575; [1963] 1 Lloyd's
Rep. 485, H.L.; affirming [1962] 1 Q.B. 396; [1961] 3 W.L.R.
1225; 105 S.J. 910; [1961] 3 All E.R. 891; [1961] C.L.Y. 518, C.A.;
affirming The Times, December 21, 1960; [1960] C.L.Y. 186. . . . . . .   10.09

Herbert *v.* Lambeth London Borough Council, *The Times,* November 27, 1991, D.C... 2.78

Heywood *v.* Mallalieu [1883] 25 Ch.D. 357; 53 L.J.Ch. 492; 49 L.T. 658; 32 W.R. 538.. 11.07

Highland Insurance Co. *v.* Continental Insurance Co. [1987] 1 Lloyd's Rep. 109... F–02

Hill *v.* Harris [1965] 2 Q.B. 601; [1965] 2 W.L.R. 1331; 109 S.J. 333; [1965] 2 All E.R. 358, C.A..................................... 11.06

Home Brewery Co. *v.* Davis (William) & Co. (Leicester) [1987] Q.B. 339; [1987] 2 W.L.R. 117; [1987] 1 All E.R. 637; (1987) 84 L.S.Gaz 657; (1987) 131 S.J. 102.............................. 2.23

Home Brewery Co. *v.* Davis (William) & Co. (Loughborough). *See* Home Brewery Co. (Leicester)

Hone *v.* Benson (1978) 248 E.G. 1013, February 17, 1978.............. 11.06

Horner *v.* Franklin [1905] 1K.B. 479; 74 L.J.K.B. 291; 92 L.T. 178; 69 J.P. 117; 21 T.L.R. 225; 3 L.G.R. 423, C.A................. 2.71, 11.16

Horton's Estate *v.* James Beattie [1927] 1 Ch. 75; 96 L.J.Ch. 15; 136 L.T. 218; 42 T.L.R. 701; 70 S.J. 917............................ 2.15

Hotson *v.* East Berkshire Health Authority *sub nom.* Hotson *v.* Fitzgerald [1987] A.C. 750; [1987] 3 W.L.R. 232; (1987) 131 S.J. 975; [1987] 2 All E.R. 909; (1987) 84 L.S.Gaz. 2365, H.L.; reversing [1987] 2 W.L.R. 287; [1987] 1 All E.R. 210; (1986) 130 S.J. 925; (1986) 136 New L.J. 1163; (1987) 84 L.S.Gaz 37, C.A.; affirming [1985] 1 W.L.R. 1036; (1985) 129 S.J. 558; [1985] 3 All E.R. 167; (1985) 82 L.S.Gaz 2818.. 2.34

Hubbs *v.* Prince Edward County, Boyd and Boyd *v.* Prince Edward County and Preston (1957) 8 D.L.R. (2d) 394.................... 2.22

Hughes *v.* Advocate (Lord) [1963] A.C. 837; [1963] 2 W.L.R. 779; 107 S.J. 232; [1963] 1 All E.R. 705; 1963 S.C. (H.L.) 31; 1963 S.L.T. 150, H.L.; reversing 1961 S.C. 310; 1962 S.L.T. 90; [1962] C.L.Y. 2332.. 2.26

Hynes *v.* Vaughan (1985) 50 P. & C.R. 444, D.C..................... 11.08

I.B.A. *v.* E.M.I. and B.I.C.C. (1980) 14 BLR 1....................... 10.07

Idaho *v.* Bunker Hill Co. 635 F. Supp. 665 (D. Idaho 1986)........... 13.09

Impress (Worcester) *v.* Rees, 115 S.J. 245; [1971] 2 All E.R. 357; 69 L.G.R. 305, D.C.. 2.48

Investors in Industry Commercial Properties *v.* South Bedfordshire District Council; Ellison & Partners and Hamilton Associates (Third Parties) [1986] Q.B. 1034; [1986] 2 W.L.R. 937; [1986] 1 All E.R. 787; (1985) 5 Con.L.R. 1; [1986] 1 E.G.L.R. 252; (1986) 2 Const.L.J. 108; (1985) 32 Build.L.R. 1; (1986) 83 L.S.Gaz 441; (1986) 136 New L.J. 118, C.A........................ 10.07, 10.11

Ivon Trades Mutual Insurance Co. *v.* J.K. Buckenham [1990] 1 All E.R. 808; [1989] 2 Lloyd's Rep. 85, D.C........................... 2.42

Istel (A.T. & T.) *v.* Tully, *The Times,* July 24, 1992 (H.L.)............. 3.09A

JEB FASTENERS *v.* Marks, Bloom & Co. [1983] 1 All E.R. 583, C.A.; affirming [1982] Com.L.R. 226; [1981] 3 All E.R. 289............ 10.09

James & Son *v.* Smee; Green *v.* Burnett [1955] 1 Q.B. 78; [1954] 3 W.L.R. 631; 118 J.P. 536; 98 S.J. 771; [1954] 3 All E.R. 273; 52 L.G.R. 545, D.C.. 2.48

Janmohamed *v.* Hassam (1976) 241 E.G. 609......................... 11.13

Johnston *v.* Courtney [1920] 2 W.W.R. 459 (Can)..................... 12.10
Johnson *v.* Moreton [1980] A.C. 37; [1978] 3 W.L.R. 538; (1978) 122
    S.J. 697; [1978] 3 All E.R. 37; (1978) 37 P. & C.R. 243; (1978) 247
    E.G. 895, H.L.; affirming (1977) 35 P. & C.R. 378; 241 E.G. 759,
    C.A... A–11
Jones *v.* Llanrwst Urban District Council [1911] 1 Ch. 893; (1911) 27
    T.L.R. 33.. 2.04
—— *v.* Williams (1843) 11 M. & W. 176; 12 L.J.Ex. 249; 152 E.R. 764.. 2.39
Jones (R.T.) *v.* Secretary of State for Wales and Ogwr Borough Council
    [1990] 3 PLR 102; 88 L.G.R. 942; (1990) 61 P. & C.R. 238; [1990]
    C.O.D. 466; [1990] J.P.L. 907; (1991) 155 L.G.Rev. 69; *The Times*,
    June 13, 1990, C.A.; reversing [1990] J.P.L. 493................. 8.12
Joslyn Mfg. Co. *v.* T.L. James & Co., Inc. 893 F. 2d 80 (5th Cir. 1990)
    cert. denied 111 S.Ct. 1017 (1991)............................ 13.09

KAISER ALUMINIUM AND CHEMICAL CORP. *v.* Catellus Development Corp.
    92 Daily Journal D.A.R. 13871 (1992)......................... 13.09
Kelly *v.* EPA and Others 1994 WL 278881 (D.C. Cir. February 4,
    1994)... 13.09, 13.13
Kelly *v.* Norwich Union Fire and Life Insurance [1990] 1 W.L.R. 139;
    (1990) 134 S.J. 49; [1989] 2 All E.R. 888; [1989] 2 Lloyd's Rep.
    333; (1989) 5 Const.L.J. 215; 1989 Fin.L.R. 331; [1990] L.S.Gaz,
    January 10, 32, C.A.. F–06
Kent County Council *v.* Beaney [1993] Env.L.R. 225.................. 2.48
—— *v.* Queenborough Rolling Mill Co. 89 L.G.R. 306; (1990) 154 J.P.
    530; [1990] Crim.L.R. 813; (1990) 154 J.P.N. 442, D.C...... 5.21, 5.24
Kerr *v.* Orkney (Earl of) (1857) 20 D. 298......................... 13.02
Kessler *v.* Tarrats 194 N.J.Super. 136, 476A 2d 326 (N.J.Super. Ct. App.
    Div. 1984)... 13.14
Khorasandijian *v.* Bush [1993] Q.B. 727; [1993] 3 W.L.R. 476; [1993] 3
    All E.R. 669; (1993) 25 H.L.R. 392; (1993) 137 S.J. (LB) 88;
    [1993] 2 FLR 66; *The Times*, February 18, 1993, C.A............. 2.16

LANFORD FOREST PRODUCTS, *Re* (1992) 86 D.L.P.; 8 C.E.L.R. (2d) 186... 12.10,
                                                                    13.17
Lansford—Coaldale Joint Water Authority *v.* Tonolli Corporation 4 F.
    3d 1209 (3rd Cir. 1993)..................................... 13.09
Leakey *v.* National Trust for Places of Historic Interest and Natural
    Beauty [1980] Q.B. 485; [1980] 2 W.L.R. 65; (1979) 123 S.J. 606;
    [1980] 1 All E.R. 17; (1979) 78 L.G.R. 100, C.A.; affirming [1978]
    Q.B. 849; [1978] 2 W.L.R. 774; (1978) 122 S.J. 231; [1978] 3 All
    E.R. 234; (1978) 76 L.G.R. 488..................... 2.18, 2.24, 2.38
Lee-Parker *v.* Izzet (No. 2) [1972] 1 W.L.R. 775; 116 S.J. 446; [1972] 2
    All E.R. 800; 23 P. & C.R. 301.............................. 11.13
Leicester City Council *v.* Barratt (East Midlands)..................... 8.07
Leigh Land Reclamation *v.* Walsall Metropolitan Borough Council
    [1991] J.P.L. 867; [1991] C.O.D. 152; (1991) 155 J.P. 547; [1991]
    Crim.L.R. 298; [1991] 155 L.G.Rev. 507; (1991) 155 J.P.N. 332;
    The Independent, November 2, 1990, D.C.................... 5.20, 5.22
Linden Garden Trust *v.* Lenesta Sludge Disposals; St. Martin's Property
    Corp. *v.* Sir Robert McAlpine & Sons 57 BLR 57; *Financial Times*,
    February 20, 1992; *The Times*, February 27, 1992; *The Independent*,
    March 6, 1992, C.A.; reversing 52 BLR 93; 25 Con.L.R. 28; [1991]
    E.G.C.S. 11.. 10.06, 10.08

Logan v. Wang (U.K.), 1991 S.L.T. 580............................ 13.02
Lomas v. Peek, 63 T.L.R. 593; 112 J.P. 13; [1947] 2 All E.R. 574; 46
    L.G.R. 15, D.C.. 2.48
Long v. Brooke [1980] Crim.L.R. 109, Bradford Crown Ct.......... 5.21, 5.24
Longlands Farm, Long Common, Botley, Hants, Re, Alford v. Superior
    Developments [1968] 3 All E.R. 552; 20 P. & C.R. 25............ 11.13
Lonrho v. Shell Petroleum Co. (No. 2) [1982] A.C. 173; [1980] 1 W.L.R.
    627; (1980) 124 S.J. 412, H.L.; affirming [1980] Q.B. 358; [1980] 2
    W.L.R. 367; (1980) 124 S.J. 205, C.A.; affirming The Times,
    February 1, 1978... 2.30
Lord Advocate v. Aero Technologies (in receivership) 1991 S.L.T. 134.. 12.10,
                                                                      13.05
Lurcott v. Wakely and Wheeler [1911] 1 K.B. 905; [1911–13] All E.R.
    41; 80 L.J.K.B. 713; 104 L.T. 290; 55 S.J. 290, C.A............. 11.16

McDonald v. Associated Fuels [1954] 3 D.L.R. 775.................. 2.04
McGhee v. National Coal Board [1973] 1 W.L.R. 1; 116 S.J. 967; [1972]
    3 All E.R. 1008; 13 K.I.R. 471, H.L.; reversing 1972 S.L.T.
    (Notes) 61, Court of Session.................................. 2.34
McLeod (or Houston) v. Buchanan [1940] 2 All E.R. 179; 84 S.J. 452,
    H.L.. 2.48
Maguire v. Leigh-on-Sea Urban District Council (1906) 95 L.T. 319; 70
    J.P. 479; 34 L.G.R. 979...................................... 11.20
Mailer v. Austin Rover Group [1989] 2 All E.R. 1087, H.L.......... 7.19
Malone v. Laskey [1907] 2 K.B. 141; [1904-7] All E.R. 304; 76 L.J.K.B.
    1134; 97 L.T. 324; 23 T.L.R. 399; 51 S.J. 356, C.A.............. 2.16
Mancetter Developments v. Garmanson and Givertz [1986] Q.B. 1212;
    [1986] W.L.R. 871; (1986) 130 S.J. 129; [1986] 1 All E.R. 449;
    [1986] 1 E.G.L.R. 240; (1985) 83 L.S.Gaz. 612, C.A............. 11.16
Manchester Corporation v. Farnworth [1930] A.C. 171; [1929] All E.R.
    90; 99 L.J.K.B. 83; 94 J.P. 62; 46 T.L.R. 85; 73 S.J. 818; 27 L.G.R.
    709.. 2.20
Mareva Compania Naviera S.A. of Panama v. International Bulk
    Carriers S.A. (1975) 119 S.J. 660; [1975] 2 Lloyd's Rep. 509, C.A. 11.10
Marks v. Board (1930 46 T.L.R. 424; 74 S.J. 354.................... 11.13
Maryon (John) International v. New Brunswick Telephone Co. (1982)
    141 D.L.R. (3d) 193... 10.07
Masters v. Brent London Borough Council [1978] Q.B. 841; [1978] 2
    W.L.R. 768; (1977) 122 S.J. 300; [1978] 2 All E.R. 664; (1977) 76
    L.G.R. 379; (1977) 245 E.G. 483............................. 2.16
Matania v. National Provincial Bank [1936] 2 All E.R. 633; 106 L.J.K.B.
    113; 155 L.T. 74; 80 S.J. 532, C.A............................ 11.16
Mayor and Corporation of High Wycombe v. The Conservators of the
    River Thames (1898) 78 L.T. 463............................. 2.48
Mayor and Corporation of Scarborough v. The Rural Sanitary Authority
    of the Scarborough Poor Law Union (1876) 34 L.T. 768.......... 2.71
Meadows and Morley v. Homer Properties Q.B.D., February 12, 1993... 11.16
Medina Borough Council v. Probevum [1991] J.P.L. 159............. 8.12
Meigh v. Wickenden [1942] 2 K.B. 160; [1942] 2 ALL E.R. 68; 112
    L.J.K.B. 76; 167 L.T. 135; 106 J.P. 207; 58 T.L.R. 260; 86 S.J.
    218; 40 L.G.R. 191, D.C..................................... 12.10
Mellor v. Walmesley [1905] 2 Ch. 164; 74 L.J.Ch. 475; 93 L.T. 574; 53
    W.R. 581; 21 T.L.R. 591; 49 S.J. 566, C.A..................... 6.41

Midland Bank *v.* Bardgrove Property Services and John Willmott (W.B.)
   [1992] 37 E.G. 126; (1993) 9 Const.L.J. 49; [1992] NPC 83; [1992]
   E.G.C.S. 87, C.A.; affirming 24 Con.L.R. 98; [1991] 2 E.G.L.R.
   283... 2.39
—— *v.* Conway Corporation [1965] 1 W.L.R. 1165; 129 J.P. 466; 109
   S.J. 494; [1965] 2 All E.R. 972; 63 L.G.R. 346, D.C........ 11.20, 12.10
Miles *v.* Forest Rock Granite Co. (1918) 34 T.L.R. 500; 62 S.J. 634, C.A... 2.09
Mint *v.* Good [1951] 1 K.B. 517; 94 S.J. 822; [1950] 2 All E.R. 1159; 49
   L.G.R. 495, C.A.; reversing 155 E.G. 409......................... 2.20
Monk *v.* Arnold [1902] 1 K.B. 761; 71 L.J.K.B. 441; 86 L.T. 580; 50
   W.R. 667; 46 S.J. 340, D.C.............................. 2.71, 11.16
Montgomery & Fleming *v.* Buchanan's Trustees (1853) 15 D. 853....... 13.02
Moresk Cleaners *v.* Hicks [1966] 2 Lloyd's Rep. 338; 116 New L.J. 1546 10.11
Morris *v.* Martin (C.W.) & Sons [1966] 1 Q.B. 716; [1965] 3 W.L.R.
   276; 109 S.J. 451; [1965] 2 All E.R. 725; [1965] 2 Lloyd's Rep. 63,
   C.A... 10.11
—— *v.* Redland Bricks. *See* Redland Bricks *v.* Morris
Morris-Thomas *v.* Petticoat Lane Rentals (1987) 53 P. & C.R. 238, C.A. 11.18
Moses *v.* Midland Railway Co. (1915) 84 L.J.K.B. 2181; 113 L.T. 451;
   79 J.P. 367; 31 T.L.R. 440; 14 L.G.R. 91........................ 2.48
Motherwell *v.* Motherwell (1976) 73 D.L.R. (3d) 62.................. 2.16
Mullaney *v.* Maybourne Grange (Croydon) Management Co. [1986] 1
   E.G.L.R. 70; (1985) 277 E.G. 1350............................. 11.16
Munro *v.* Lord Burghclere [1918] 1 K.B. 291; 87 L.J.K.B. 366; 118 L.T.
   343; 82 J.P. 86; 34 T.L.R. 131; 62 S.J. 231; 16 L.G.R. 210, D.C.... 2.71,
                                                                     11.16
Murphy *v.* Brentwood District Council [1991] 1 A.C. 398; [1990] 3
   W.L.R. 414; [1990] 2 All E.R. 908; (1990) 22 H.L.R. 502; (1990)
   134 S.J. 1076; 21 Con.L.R. 1; 89 L.G.R. 24; (1990) 6 Const.L.J.
   304; (1990) 154 L.G.Rev. 1010; 50 BLR 1; (1991) 3 Admin.L.R.
   37, H.L.; reversing [1990] 2 W.L.R. 944; [1990] 2 All E.R. 269; 88
   L.G.R. 333; (1990) 134 S.J. 458; [1990] L.S.Gaz, February 7, 42,
   C.A.; affirming 13 Con.L.R. 96.............................. 10.09

NRA *v.* Harcros Timber and Building Supplies (1992) 156 J.P. 743;
   (1992) 156 J.P.N.S. 88, *The Times,* April 2, 1992, D.C.......... 3.09A
—— *v.* Yorkshire Water Services [1993] NPC 157; *The Times,* November
   24, 1993; *The Independent,* November 24, 1993................. 6.39
Nalder *v.* Ilford Corporation [1951] 1 K.B. 22; 66 T.L.R. (Pt. 2) 949; 114
   J.P. 594; 94 S.J. 840; [1950] 2 All E.R. 903; 1 P. & C.R. 413....... 2.04
Nash and Others *v.* Eli Lilly & Co. [1993] 1 W.L.R. 782; [1993] 4 All
   E.R. 383, C.A... 2.41
National Coal Board *v.* Neath Borough Council [1976] 2 All E.R. 478,
   D.C.. 2.66, 4.78
National Justice Compania Naviera S.A. *v.* Prudential Assurance Co.
   Ikarian Reefer, The, [1993] 2 Lloyd's Rep. 68; [1993] 37 E.G. 158;
   The Times, March 5, 1993... 2.34
National Rivers Authority *v.* Egger U.K. Newcastle upon Tyne, Crown
   Court, June 15, 1992, unreported................................ 2.46
—— *v.* McAlpine (Alfred) Homes East [1994] NPC 6; *The Independent,*
   February 3, 1994; *The Times,* February 3, 1994................. 2.48
—— *v.* Welsh Development Agency (1994) 158 J.P. 137; [1993]
   E.G.C.S. 160; [1993] C.O.D. 211; *The Times,* December 29, 1992.... 2.48

National Rivers Authority *v*. Wright Engineering, *The Independent*,
    November 19, 1993.. 2.48
—— *v*. Yorkshire Water Services, *The Independent*, November 15/19??,
    1993; *The Times*, November 24, 1993.......................... 2.48
Neushul *v*. Mellish & Harkary (1987) 111 S.J. 399; 203 E.G. 27; 117 New
    L.J. 546, C.A.; affirming (1966) 110 S.J. 792; 200 E.G. 685; [1966]
    C.L.Y. 11473. Petition for Leave to appeal to the House of Lords
    dismissed... 10.05
New Zealand Shipping Co. *v*. Satterthwaite (A.M.) & Co. [1975] A.C.
    154; [1974] 2 W.L.R. 865; 118 S.J. 387; [1974] 1 All E.R. 105; *sub
    nom*. New Zealand Shipping Co. *v*. Satterthwaite (A.M.) & Co.;
    Eurymedon, The [1974] 1 Lloyd's Rep. 534, P.C................. 10.11
Newbury District Council *v*. Secretary of State for the Environment;
    Same *v*. International Synthetic Rubber Co. [1981] A.C. 578;
    [1980] 2 W.L.R. 379; (1980) 124 S.J. 186; [1980] 1 All E.R. 731;
    (1980) 78 L.G.R. 306; (1980) 40 P. & C.R. 148; [1980] J.P.L. 325,
    H.L.; reversing [1978] 1 W.L.R. 1241; (1978) 122 S.J. 524; [1979]
    1 All E.R. 243; (1978) 37 P. & C.R. 73; (1978) 77 L.G.R. 60;
    (1978) 248 E.G. 223; [1979] J.P.L. 26; (1978) 248 E.G. 1017, C.A.;
    reversing (1977) 121 S.J. 254; (1977) 75 L.G.R. 608; [1977] J.P.L.
    373, 640; (1977) 242 E.G. 377; (1977) 35 P. & C.R. 170, D.C...... 8.12
Newham London Borough *v*. Taylor Woodrow-Anglian (1982)
    Build.L.R. 99, C.A.. 10.07
Nicholls *v*. Ely Beet Sugar Factory [1936] 1 Ch. 343; 105 L.J.Ch. 279;
    154 L.T. 531; 80 S.J. 127, C.A................................ 2.21
Nitrigin Eireann Teoranta *v*. Inco Alloys [1992] 1 W.L.R. 498; [1992] 1
    All E.R. 854; (1992) 135 S.J. (LB) 213; 60 BLR 65; [1992] *Gazette*,
    January 22, 34; [1991] NPC 17; (1991) 141 New L.J. 1518; *The
    Times*, November 4, 1991...................................... 10.09
Noble's Trustees *v*. Economic Forestry (Scotland) 1988 S.L.T. 662...... 13.02
Northern Wood Preservers *v*. Ministry of the Environment, May 3, 1991,
    Div. Ct. Ontario.. 13.17
Nottinghamshire Patent Brick and Tile Co. *v*. Butler (1886) 16 Q.B.D.
    778; 55 L.J.Q.B. 280; 54 L.T. 444; 34 W.R. 405; 2 T.L.R. 391,
    C.A... 11.06
Nunn *v*. Parkes & Co. (1924) 59 L. Jo 806......................... 2.04
Nurad, Inc. *v*. William E. Hooper & Sons Company 966 F. 2d 837 (4th
    Cir. 1992) Cert. denied 113 S.Ct. 33 (1992)................... 13.09

O'Gorman *v*. Brent London Borough Council, 91 L.G.R. 555; *The Times*,
    May 20, 1993.. 2.71
O'Neil *v*. Picillo 883 F 2d 176 (1st Cir. 1989).................. 13.09
Osman *v*. Moss (J. Ralph) [1970] 1 Lloyd's Rep. 313, C.A............ 10.08
Overseas Tankship (U.K.) *v*. Miller Steamship Co. Pty. [1967] 1 A.C.
    617; [1966] 3 W.L.R. 498; 110 S.J. 447; [1966] 2 All E.R. 709;
    [1966] 1 Lloyd's Rep. 657, P.C.; reversing *sub nom*. Miller Steam-
    ship Co. Pty. *v*. Overseas Tankship (U.K.); Miller (R.W.) & Co. *v*.
    Same. The Wagon Mound (No. 2) [1963] 1 Lloyd's Rep. 402;
    [1963] C.L.Y. 969... 2.23

Pan Antlantic Insurance Co. *v*. Pine Top Insurance Co. [1992] 1
    Lloyd's Rep. 120; *Financial Times*, November 8, 1991, C.A........ F–02
Panamericana de Bienes Y Servicios, S.A. *v*. Northern Badger Oil and
    Gas (1991) 81 D.L.R. 4d 280.......................... 12.10, 13.17

Pedgrift v. Oxfordshire County Council (1991) 63 P. & C.R. 246; [1992]
    J.P.L. 731; [1991] E.G.C.S. 89, C.A........................... 8.12
Performance Cars v. Abraham [1962] 1 Q.B. 33; [1961] 3 W.L.R. 749;
    105 S.J. 748; [1961] 3 All E.R. 413, C.A...................... 2.40
Pirelli General Cable Works v. Faber (Oscar) & Partners [1983] 2 A.C.
    1; [1983] 2 W.L.R. 6; (1983) 127 S.J. 16; [1983] 1 All E.R. 65;
    (1983) 265 E.G. 979; (1983) 133 New L.J. 63, H.L.; reversing
    (1982) 263 E.G. 879, C.A.............................. 2.41, 10.09
Philips v. Ward [1956] 1 W.L.R. 471; 100 S.J. 317; [1956] 1 All E.R. 874,
    C.A.. B–03
Phoenix v. Garbage Services Company, U.S. District court for District of
    Arizona, April 16, 1993.................................... 13.09
Port Jackson Stevedoring Pty. v. Salmond & Spraggon (Australia) Pty.;
    New York Star, The [1981] 1 W.L.R. 138; (1980) 124 S.J. 756;
    [1980] 3 All E.R. 257, P.C.; reversing sub nom. Salmond &
    Spraggon (Australia) Pty. v. Joint Cargo Services Pty.; New York
    Star, The [1979] 1 Lloyd's Rep. 298, Aust. High Ct.; affirming
    [1979] 1 Lloyd's Rep. 445, N.S.W., C.A....................... 10.11
Post Office v. Aquarius Properties (1987) 54 P. & C.R. 61; [1987] 1 All
    E.R. 1055; (1987) 281 E.G. 789; [1987] 1 E.G.L.R. 40; (1987) 84
    L.S.Gaz. 820, C.A.; [1985] 2 E.G.L.R. 105; (1985) 276 E.G. 923... 11.16
Pratt (Valerie) v. Hill (George) (a firm) (1987) 38 Build.L.R. 25, C.A.... 10.05
Preston v. Torfaen Borough Council, [1993] E.G.C.S. 137; [1993] NPC
    111; The Times, July 21, 1993; The Independent, September 24, 1993,
    C.A.. 10.09
Price v. Cromack [1975] 1 W.L.R. 988; 119 S.J. 458; [1975] 2 All E.R.
    113, D.C... 2.48
Price's Patent Candle Co. v. London County Council [1908] 2 Ch. 526,
    C.A.. 2.05
Pride of Derby and Derbyshire Angling Association v. British Celanese
    [1953] Ch. 149; [1953] 2 W.L.R. 58; 117 J.P. 52; 97 S.J. 28; [1953]
    1 All E.R. 179; 51 L.G.R. 121, C.A.; affirming [1952] W.N. 227;
    [1952] 1 T.L.R. 1013; 96 S.J. 263; [1952] 1 All E.R. 1326; 50
    L.G.R. 488.. 2.40
Prior of Southwark case (1498) Y.B. 13 Hen. 7...................... 2.04
Proudce v. Department of Transport Ref/82/1989 R.V.R. Vol. 31, No. 3,
    p. 103... B–06
Proudfoot v. Hart (1890) 25 Q.B.D. 42; [1886–90] All E.R. 782; 59
    L.J.Q.B. 389; 63 L.T. 171; 55 J.P. 20; 38 W.R. 730; 6 T.L.R. 305,
    C.A.. 11.16
Puckett & Smith's Contract, Re [1902] 2 Ch. 258; 71 L.J.Ch. 666; 87
    L.T. 189; 50 W.R. 532, C.A................................. 11.06

Quick v. Taff Ely Borough Council [1986] Q.B. 809; [1985] 3 W.L.R.
    981; (1985) 129 S.J. 685; [1985] 3 All E.R. 321; (1985) 18 H.L.R.
    66; [1985] 2 E.G.L.R. 50; (1985) 276 E.G. 452; (1985) 135 New
    L.J. 848, C.A.. 11.16

R. v. Bata Industries et al (1992) 9 O.R. (3d) 329.................... 13.17
—— v. Blackbird Holdings (1991) 6 C.E.L.R. (N.S.) 138.............. 13.17
—— v. Erie Battery Inc. Taylor George Gordon and Joseph Ted
    D'Amico (April 1992) Unreported............................ 13.17
—— v. Chappell (1984) 128 S.J. 629; (1984) 80 Cr.App.R. 31; (1984) 6
    Cr.App.R. (S.) 342; [1984] Crim.L.R. 574, C.A................ 2.78

R. v. Epping (Waltham Abbey) JJ., ex parte Burlinson [1948] K.B. 79;
[1948] L.J.R. 298; 63 T.L.R. 628; 112 J.P. 3; 92 S.J. 27; [1947] 2
All E.R. 537; 46 L.G.R. 6. . . . . 2.70
—— v. Hallam [1957] 1 Q.B. 569; [1957] 2 W.L.R. 521; 121 J.P. 254;
101 S.J. 268; [1957] 1 All E.R. 665; 41 Cr.App.R. 111, C.A. 2.48
—— v. Inner London Crown Court, ex parte Sitki, (1993) 157 J.P. 523;
[1993] C.O.D. 249; The Times, October 26, 1993, C.A. 5.28
—— v. Khan; R. v. Crawley [1982] 1 W.L.R. 1405; (1982) 126 S.J. 657;
[1982] 3 All E.R. 969; (1983) 76 Cr.App.R. 29; (1982) 4 Cr.App.R.
(S.) 298; [1982] Crim.L.R. 752, C.A. 2.80
—— v. Metropolitan Stipendiary Magistrate, ex parte London Waste
Regulation Authority; Berkshire County Council v. Scott, The
Times, January 14, 1993; [1993] J.E.L. Vol. 2, No. 2, p. 281. . . 2.59, 5.20
—— v. North Hertfordshire District Council, ex parte Cobbold [1985] 3
All E.R. 486. . . . . 5.28
—— v. Oxford Crown Court, ex parte Smith (1990) 154 J.P. 422; [1990]
C.O.D. 211; (1990) 154 L.G.Rev. 458; (1990) 154 J.P.N. 333;
(1990) 2 Admin.L.R. 389. . . . . 2.76
—— v. Rechem International Newport Crown Court, September 10,
1993. . . . . 6.38
—— v. Secretary of State for Social Services, ex parte Association of
Metropolitan Authorities [1986] 1 W.L.R. 1; (1986) 130 S.J. 35;
[1986] 1 All E.R. 164; (1985) 83 L.G.R. 796; (1985) 17 H.L.R.
487; (1985) 82 L.S.Gaz. 3174. . . . . 6.15
—— v. Secretary of State for the Environment, ex parte Friends of the
Earth, The Times, April 4, 1994. . . . . 6.31
—— v. Seelig; R. v. Lord Spens [1992] 1 W.L.R. 149; [1991] 4 All E.R.
429; [1991] BCC 569; [1991] BCLC 869; (1992) 94 Cr.App.R. 17;
(1991) 141 New L.J. 638; The Independent, May 3, 1991; The Times,
May13, 1991, C.A. 3.09A
—— v. Shephard [1993] A.C. 380; [1993] 2 W.L.R. 102; [1993] 1 All
E.R. 225; (1993) 137 S.J. (LB) 12; (1993) 157 J.P. 145; (1993) 96
Cr.App.R. 345; [1993] Crim.L.R. 295; (1993) 143 New L.J. 127;
The Times, December 17, 1992, H.L. 3.09A
—— v. Shorrock [1993] 3 W.L.R. 698; [1993] 3 All E.R. 917; (1993) 143
New L.J. 511, The Times, March 11, 1993, C.A. 2.14
—— v. Staines Local Board (1888) 60 L.T. 261; 53 J.P. 358; 5 T.L.R. 25,
D.C. 2.48
—— v. Trimble (1877) 36 L.T. 508; 41 J.P. 454, D.C. 2.71
—— v. Varnicolor Chemical Severin Argenton and Tri-Colour of Mira
Inc—September 1992, unreported. 13.17
—— v. Westminister City Council, ex parte Monahan [1990] 1 Q.B. 87;
[1989] 3 W.L.R. 408; (1989) 133 S.J. 978; [1989] 2 All E.R. 74;
[1989] 1 PLR 36; (1989) 58 P. & C.R. 92; [1989] J.P.L. 107;
[1989] J.P.L. 107; [1989] C.O.D. 241, C.A.; affirming. 8.14
RHM Bakeries (Scotland) v. Strathclyde Regional Council 1985 S.L.T.
214. . . . . 2.12, 13.02
Rapid Results College v. Angell [1986] 1 E.G.L.R. 53; (1986) 277 E.G.
856, C.A.; affirming [1985] 2 E.G.L.R. 66; (1985) 275 E.G. 247. . . 11.16
Ratford and Hayward v. Northaven District Council [1987] Q.B. 357;
(1987) 85 L.G.R. 443; [1986] 3 W.L.R. 771; (1986) 150 J.P. 605;
[1986] 3 All E.R. 193; (1986) 130 S.J. 786; 1986 PCC 268; [1986]
R.A. 137; (1986) 83 L.S.Gaz. 3253, C.A. 12.10

Ravenseft Properties *v.* Davstone (Holdings) [1980] Q.B. 12; [1979] 2
    W.L.R. 898; (1978) 123 S.J. 320; [1979] 1 All E.R. 929; (1978) 249
    E.G. 51; (1978) 37 P. & C.R. 502, D.C........................ 11.16
Read *v.* Croydon Corporation [1938] 4 All E.R. 631; 108 L.J.K.B. 72;
    160 L.T. 176; 103 J.P. 25; 55 T.L.R. 212; 82 S.J. 991; 37 L.G.R. 53.. 6.27
—— *v.* Lyons (J.) & Co. [1947] A.C. 156; [1947] L.J.R. 39; 175 L.T.
    413; 62 T.L.R. 646; [1946] 2 All E.R. 471, H.L.; affirming [1945]
    K.B. 216... 2.07, 2.09, 2.11
Redland Bricks *v.* Morris [1970] A.C. 652; [1969] 2 W.L.R. 1437; 113
    S.J. 405; [1969] 2 All E.R. 576, H.L.; reversing *sub nom.* Morris *v.*
    Redland Bricks [1967] 1 W.L.R. 976; 111 S.J. 373; [1967] 3 All
    E.R. 1, C.A... 2.38
Regina Fur. Co. *v.* Bossom [1958] 2 Lloyd's Rep. 425, C.A.; affirming
    [1957] 2 Lloyd's Rep. 446; [1957] C.L.Y. 1760................. F–06
Rickards *v.* Lothian [1913] A.C. 263; [1911–13] All E.R. 71; 82 L.J.P.C.
    42; 108 L.T. 225; 29 T.L.R. 281; 57 S.J. 281, P.C................. 2.07
Rochford Rural Council *v.* Port of London Authority [1914] 2 K.B. 916;
    83 L.J.K.B. 1066; 111 L.T. 207; 78 J.P. 329; 12 L.G.R. 979, D.C.... 2.48
Rockwool Case 1991 Danish Weekley Law Report 1991 674 H.......... 13.27
Roe *v.* Minister of Health; Woolley *v.* Same [1954] 2 Q.B. 66; [1954] 2
    W.L.R. 915; 98 S.J. 319; [1954] 2 All E.R. 131, C.A.; affirming
    [1954] 1 W.L.R. 128; 98 S.J. 30............................... 2.26
Rookes *v.* Barnard [1964] A.C. 1129; [1964] 2 W.L.R. 269; 108 S.J. 93;
    [1964] 1 All E.R. 367; [1964] 1 Lloyd's Rep. 28, H.L.; reversing
    [1963] 1 A.B. 623; [1962] 3 W.L.R. 260; 106 S.J. 371; [1962] 2 All
    E.R. 579; [1962] C.L.Y. 3036, C.A.; restoring [1961] 3 W.L.R.
    438; 105 S.J. 530; [1961] 2 All E.R. 825; [1961] C.L.Y. 8432....... 2.37
Rosewell *v.* Prior (1701) 12 Mod. 635; Holt, K.B. 500; 2 Salk. 460... 2.18, 2.19
Rylands *v.* Fletcher (1868) L.R. 3 H.L. 330; [1861–73] All E.R. 1; 37
    L.J.Ex. 161; 19 L.T. 220; 33 J.P. 70, H.L.... 2.03, 2.04, 2.05, 2.06, 2.07,
        2.08, 2.09, 2.10, 2.11, 2.12, 2.22, 2.24, 2.25, 2.36, 2.37, 2.42, 6.06, 13.02

SADDELWORTH U.D.C. *v.* Aggregate and Sand (1970) 114 S.J. 931; 69
    L.G.R. 103, D.C... 2.68
St. Anne's Well Brewery Co. *v.* Roberst [1928] All E.R. 28; 140 L.T. 1;
    92 J.P. 180; 44 T.L.R. 703; 26 L.G.R. 638, C.A................. 2.19
St. Helens Smelting Co. *v.* Tipping (1865) 11 H.L.Cas. 642; [1861–73]
    All E.R. 1389; 35 L.J.Q.B. 66; 12 L.T. 776; 29 J.P. 579; 11
    Jur.N.S. 785; 13 W.R. 1083; 11 E.R. 1483, H.L................. 2.15
Salmond & Spraggon (Australia) Pty. *v.* Joint Cargo Services Pty.; New
    York Star, The. *See* Port Jackson Stevedoring *v.* Salmond and
    Spraggon (Australia) Pty.; New York Star, The.................. 10.11
Salvin *v.* North Brancepath Coal Co. (1874) 9 Ch. App. 705; 44 L.J.Ch.
    149; 31 L.T. 154; 22 W.R. 904............................ 2.26, 2.36
Sampson *v.* Hodson-Pressinger (1981) 125 S.J. 623; [1981] 3 All E.R.
    710; (1984) 12 H.L.R. 40; (1982) 261 E.G. 891, C.A.............. 2.19
Sandwell Metropolitan Borough Council *v.* Bujok [1990] 1 W.L.R. 1350;
    [1990] 3 All E.R. 385; (1990) 134 S.J. 1300; (1991) 23 H.L.R. 48;
    89 L.G.R. 77; (1991) L.G.Rev. 228; (1991) 3 Admin.L.R. 426;
    (1991) 155 J.P.N. 554, H.L.; affirming (1990) 22 H.L.R. 87; (1990)
    154 J.P. 608; 88 L.G.R. 521; [1990] C.O.D. 206; (1990) 154
    L.G.Rev. 611; (1990) 154 J.P.N. 528, D.C..................... 2.70
Schulmans Incorporated *v.* NRA (Queens Bench Division) unreported
    December 3, 1991; Summarised Water Law [1993] p. 25.......... 2.48

Scott-Whitehead v. National Coal Board (1987) 53 P. & C.R. 263; [1987]
   2 E.G.L.R. 227. . . . .   6.35
Scruttons v. Midland Silicones [1962] A.C. 446; [1962] 2 W.L.R. 186;
   106 S.J. 34; [1962] 1 All E.R. 1; *sub nom.* Midland Silicones v.
   Scruttons [1961] 2 Lloyd's Rep. 365, H.L.; affirming *sub nom.*
   Midland Silicones v. Scruttons [1961] 1 Q.B. 106; [1960] 3 W.L.R.
   372; 104 S.J. 603; [1960] 2 All E.R. 737; [1960] 1 Lloyd's Rep.
   571; [1960] C.L.Y. 2939, C.A.; affirming [1959] 2 Q.B. 171; [1959]
   2 W.L.R. 761; 103 S.J. 415; [1959] 2 All E.R. 289, [1959] 1 Lloyd's
   Rep. 289; [1959] C.L.Y. 3029. . . . . 10.11
Seaboard Offshore Ltd. v. Secretary of State for Transport ("The Safe
   Carrier") [1994] 2 All E.R. 99. . . . .   7.32
Sealand of the Pacific v. Robert. C. McHaffie (1974) 51 D.L.R. (3d)
   702. . . . . 10.07
Securities and Investment Board v. Danfell S.A. [1991] 4 All E.R. 883. . . 12.05
Sedleigh-Denfield v. O'Callaghan [1940] A.C. 880; [1940] 3 All E.R. 349;
   164 L.T. 72; 56 T.L.R. 887; 84 S.J. 657, 109 L.J.K.B. 893, H.L. . . . 2.18,
                                                                              2.36
Sefton v. Tophams (No. 2) [1967] 1 A.C. 50; [1966] 2 W.L.R. 814; 110
   S.J. 271; [1966] 1 All E.R. 1039, H.L.; reversing [1965] Ch. 1140;
   [1965] 3 W.L.R. 523; 109 S.J. 456; [1965] 3 All E.R. 1; [1965]
   C.L.Y. 3356, C.A.; affirming [1964] 1 W.L.R. 1408; 108 S.J. 880;
   [1964] 3 All E.R. 876; [1964] C.L.Y. 3125. . . . .   2.48
Shave v. Rosner [1954] 2 Q.B. 113; [1954] 2 W.L.R. 1057; 118 J.P. 364;
   98 S.J. 355; [1954] 2 All E.R. 280; 52 L.F.R. 337, D.C. 2.48
Simpson v. Weber [1925] All E.R. 248; 133 L.T. 46; 41 T.L.R. 302, D.C. . .   2.04
Sindall (William) plc v. Cambridgeshire County Council, *The Times,* June
   8, 1993. . . . . 11.07, 11.08
Smallman v. Smallman [1972] Fam. 25; [1971] 3 W.L.R. 588; 115 S.J.
   527; [1971] 3 All E.R. 717, C.A. 11.13
Smeaton v. Ilford Corporation [1954] Ch. 450; [1954] 2 W.L.R. 668; 118
   J.P. 290; 98 S.J. 251; [1954] 1 All E.R. 923; 52 L.G.R. 253. . . . 2.06, 2.18
Smedley v. Chumley and Hawkes (1981) 125 S.J. 33; (1982) 44 P. &
   C.R. 50; (1982) 261 E.G. 775, C.A. 11.16
Smith v. Bush (Eric S.); Harris v. Wyre Forest District Council [1990] 1
   A.C. 831; [1989] 2 W.L.R. 790; (1989) 133 S.J. 597; (1990) 9
   Tr.L.R. 1; 87 L.G.R. 685; (1989) 21 H.L.R. 424; [1989] 2 All E.R.
   514; [1989] 17 E.G. 68 and [1989] 18 E.G. 99; (1989) 139 New
   L.J. 576; (1989) 153 L.G.Rev. 984, H.L.; affirming. 10.06, 10.09
Smith v. Land and House Property Corporation [1884] 28 Ch.D. 7; 51
   L.T. 718; 49 J.P.182, C.A. 11.07
—— v. South Wales Switchgear [1978] 1 W.L.R. 165; (1977) 122 S.J.
   61; [1978] 1 All E.R. 18; (1977) 8 Build.L.R. 5, H.L. 12.07
Smithland & Improvement Corp. v. Celotex Corp. 851 F 2d 86 (3rd Cir.
   1988). 13.09
Societe Commerciale de Reassurance v. Evas International (formerly
   Evan (U.K.)) (Note); Evas Eil Actions, The [1992] 2 All E.R. 82;
   [1992] 1 Lloyd's Rep. 570, C.A. 2.42
Solloway v. Hampshire County Council (1981) 79 L.G.R. 449; (1981)
   258 E.G. 858, C.A. 2.23
Solomons v. Gertzenstein (R.) [1954] 2 Q.B. 243; [1954] 3 W.L.R. 317;
   98 S.J. 539; [1954] 2 All E.R. 625, C.A.; reversing [1954] 1 Q.B.
   565; [1954] 2 W.L.R. 823; 98 S.J. 270; [1954] 1 All E.R. 1008. . . . 11.20,
                                                                             12.10

Southern Water Authority *v.* Pegrum (1989) 153 J.P. 581; [1989]
    Crim.L.R. 442; (1989) 153 L.G.Rev. 672; (1989) 153 J.P.N. 578,
    D.C.. 2.48
Southport Corporation *v.* Esso Petroleum Co. *See* Esso Petroleum Co. *v.*
    Southport Corporation... 2.04
Speight, *Re* Speight *v.* Gaunt (1883) 22 Ch.D. 727; 52 L.J.Ch. 503; 48
    L.T. 279; 31 W.R. 401, C.A..................................... 12.10
Staat & Gemeente Ondekevk *v.* Shell Nederland Rajjinaderij BV & Shell
    Nederland Chemie BV, Court of Appeal, The Hague, November
    19, 1992.. 13.19
Standard Chartered Bank *v.* Walker [1982] 1 W.L.R. 1410; (1982) 126
    S.J. 479; [1982] 3 All E.R. 938; (1982) 264 E.G. 345; [1982]
    Com.L.R. 233; (1982) 79 L.S.Gaz. 1137, C.A..................... 11.20
Starrokate *v.* Burry (1983) 265 E.G. 871, C.A......................... 11.17
State *v.* Akzo Resins (Supreme Court, April 24, 1992)...... 13.19, 13.20, 13.21
—— *v.* Duphar (Philips) Court of Appeal, Amsterdam, December 1992 13.19
State of New York *v.* Shore Realty Corp. 759 F 2d 1032 (2nd Cir. 1985)
    affirmed 861 F 2d 15 (7th Cir. 1988)........................... 13.09
State *v.* Amersfoort (Dutch Supreme Court, February 21, 1990)... 13.19, 13.21
Stephens *v.* Cuckfield R.D.C. [1960] 2 Q.B. 373; [1960] 3 W.L.R. 248;
    124 J.P. 420; 104 S.J. 565; [1960] 2 All E.R. 716; 11 P. & C.R. 248;
    58 L.G.R. 213, C.A.; affirming[1959] 1 Q.B. 516; [1959] 2 W.L.R.
    480; 123 J.P. 262; 103 S.J. 294; [1959] 1 All E.R. 635; 57 L.G.R.
    147; 10 P. & C.R. 110; [1959] C.L.Y. 3243....................... 2.73
Sutton *v.* Temple (1843) 12 M & W 52; 13 L.J.Ex. 17; 2 L.T.O.S. 150; 7
    Jur. 1065; 152 E.R. 1108.. 11.18
Swale Borough Council *v.* Secretary of State for the Environment and
    Ward Construction (Medway) [1994] J.P.L. 263................... 8.12
Swan Fisheries *v.* Holberton, Queens Bench Division, December 14,
    1987, unreported.. 2.23
Swingcastle *v.* Alastair Gibson (A firm) [1991] 2 A.C. 223; [1991] 2
    W.L.R. 1091; [1991] 2 All E.R. 353; [1991] 17 E.G. 83; (1991) 135
    S.J. 542; [1991] CCLR 55; [1991] E.G.C.S. 46; (1991) 141 New
    L.J. 563; *The Times,* April 19, 1991; *Financial Times,* April 24, 1991;
    The Independent, may 16, 1991, H.L.; reversing [1990] 1 W.L.R.
    1223; [1990] 3 All E.R. 463; [1990] 34 E.G. 49; [1990] CCLR 127;
    (1990) 140 New L.J. 818, C.A.................................... B–03

TAI HIN COTTON MILL *v.* Liv Chong Hing Bank [1986] A.C. 80; [1985] 3
    W.L.R. 317; (1985) 129 S.J. 503; [1985] 2 All E.R. 947; [1986]
    FLR 14; [1985] 2 Lloyd's Rep. 313; (1985) 135 New L.J. 680;
    (1985) 82 L.S.Gaz. 2995, P.C................................... 10.08
Tate & Lyle Food and Distribution *v.* Greater London Council [1983] 2
    A.C. 509; [1983] 2 W.L.R. 649; [1983] 1 All E.R. 1159; [1983] 46
    P. & C.R. 243; (1983) 81 L.G.R. 4434; [1983] 2 Lloyd's Rep. 117,
    H.L.; reversing [1982] 1 W.L.R. 970; [1982] 2 All E.R. 854; (1982)
    80 L.G.R. 753, C.A.; reversing [1982] 1 W.L.R. 149; (1981) 125
    S.J. 865; [1981] 3 All E.R. 716................................. 2.16
Tenant *v.* Goldwin (1704) 1 Salk 21 360; Holt K.B. 500; 2 Ld Raym
    1089; 6 Mod Rep. 311; 91 E.R. 20 314........................... 2.04
Tennent *v.* Earl of Glasgow (1864) 2 M. (H.L.) 22; 2 Macph (Ct. of
    Sessions) (H.L.) 22; 36 Sc.Jur. 400............................ 13.02
Thake *v.* Maurice [1986] Q.B. 644; [1986] 2 W.L.R. 337; [1986] 1 All
    E.R. 479; (1986) 136 New L.J. 92; (1986) 83 L.S.Gaz. 123, C.A.;
    affirming [1985] 2 W.L.R. 215; (1985) 129 S.J. 86; [1984] 2 All
    E.R. 513; (1985) 82 L.S.Gaz. 871, D.C.......................... 10.07

Thames Water Authority v. Blue and White Launderettes [1980] 1
W.L.R. 700; (1979) 124 S.J. 100; (1979) 78 L.G.R. 237; [1980]
J.P.L. 402, C.A.. 6.38
Thanet District Council v. Kent County Council, [1993] C.O.D. 308; The
Times, March 15, 1993, D.C.............................. 5.21, 5.24
Thompson v. Gibson (1841) 7 M. & W. 456; [1835–42] All E.R. 623; 10
L.J.Ex. 330; 151 E.R. 845..................................... 2.19
—— v. Smith Ship Repairers (North Shields); Mitchell v. Vickers
[1984] Q.B. 405; [1984] 2 W.L.R. 522; [1984] 1 C.R. 236; [1984]
128 S.J. 225; [1984] 1 All E.R. 881; [1984] I.R.L.R. 93; (1984) 81
L.S.Gaz. 741.. 2.26
Tito v. Waddell (No. 2); Tito v. Att-Gen. [1977] Ch. 106; [1977] 2
W.L.R. 496; [1977] 3 All E.R. 129; Judgement on damages [1977]
3 W.L.R. 972 (N.)... 12.06
Tophams v. Sefton (Earl of). See Sefton (Earl of) v. Tophams........... 2.48
Tower Hamlets (London Borough of) v. London Docklands Development
Corporation (Knightsbridge Crown Ct. April 13, 1992)............. 2.48
Trevett v. Lee [1955] 1 W.L.R. 113; 99 S.J. 110; [1955] 1 All E.R. 406,
C.A.. 2.20
Turner v. Green [1895] 2 Ch. 205; 64 L.J.Ch. 539; 72 L.T. 763; 43 W.R.
537; 39 S.J. 484; 13 R. 551................................... 11.06
Tutton v. Walter (A.D.) [1986] Q.B. 61; [1985] 3 W.L.R. 797; (1985)
129 S.J. 739; [1985] 3 All E.R. 757; (1985) 82 L.S.Gaz. 3335....... 2.26

U.S. v. Dickerson 640 F. Supp. 448 (D Md. 1986).................... 13.09
—— v. Kayser-Roth Corp. 910 F 24 (1st Cir. 1990)................ 13.09
—— v. Mirabile 15 Envtl.L.Rep. 20, 994 (E.D. Pa. September 4, 1985) 13.09
—— v. Pacific Hide & Fur Depot Inc. 716 F. Supp. 1341 (D. Idaho
1989)... 13.09
—— v. Serajini 706 F. Supp. 346 (M.D. Pa 1988); 711 F. Supp. 197
(M.D. Pa 1988)... 13.09
—— v. Stringfellow 661 F. Supp. 1053 (C.D. Cal. 1987)............. 13.09
United States v. Fleet Factors Corp. 901 F. 2d 1550 (11th Cir. 1990).... 13.09
—— v. Maryland Bank & Trust Co. 632 F. Supp. 573 (O. Md. 1986).. 13.09
—— v. North Eastern Pharmaceutical & Chemical Co. Inc. 810 F 2d
726 (8th Cir. 1986).................................... 13.06, 13.09
—— v. Price 688 F 2d (3rd Cir. 1983)............................ 13.06

VAUGHAN v. Taff Vale Railway Co. (1880) S.H. & N. 679; [1843–60] All
E.R. 474; 29 L.J.Ex. 247; 2 L.T. 394; 24 J.P. 453; 6 Jur.N.S. 899; 8
W.R. 549; 157 E.R. 1351, Ex.Ch............................... 2.20
Victoria University of Manchester v. Wilson (1984) 2 Con.L.R. 45...... 10.07
Villenex Co. v. Courtney Hotel (1969) 20 P. & C.R. 575.............. 11.16

WALTERS v. Whessoe and Shell Refining Co. (1960) 6 Build.L.R. 23, C.A. 12.07
Warren v. Keen [1954] 1 Q.B. 15; [1953] 3 W.L.R. 702; 97 S.J. 742;
[1953] 2 All E.R. 1118, C.A.................................... 11.16
Waterville Industries, Inc. v. Finance Authority of Maine 984 F 2d 549
(1st Cir. 1993)... 13.09
Wates v. Rowland [1952] 2 Q.B. 12; [1952] 1 T.L.R. 488; [1952] 1 All
E.R. 470, C.A.. 11.16
Watney Combe Reid & Co. v. Westminster (City) London Borough
Council (1970) 68 L.G.R. 639, C.A............................. 2.71

Watts *v.* Marrow [1991] 1 W.L.R. 1421; [1991] 4 All E.R. 937; (1991) 23
    H.L.R. 608; 54 BLR 86; [1991] 2 E.G.L.R. 152; [1991] 43 E.G.
    121; 26 Con.L.R. 98; [1991] E.G.C.S. 88; (1991) 141 New L.J.
    1331; [1991] NPC 98; [1992] *Gazette,* January 8, 33; *The Independent,*
    August 20, 1991; The Guardian, September 4, 1991, C.A.; reversing
    [1991] 14 E.G. 111; [1991] 15 E.G. 113; 24 Con.L.R. 125......... B–03
West *v.* Bristol Tramway Company [1908] 2 K.B. 14; [1908–10] All E.R.
    215; 77 L.J.K.B. 684; 99 L.T. 264; 72 J.P. 243; 24 T.L.R. 478; 52
    S.J. 393; 6 L.G.R. 609, C.A..................................... 2.08
West Ham Central Charity Board *v.* East London Waterworks Co.
    [1900] 1 Ch. 624; [1900–3] All E.R. 1011; 69 L.J.Ch. 257; 82 L.T.
    85; 48 W.R. 284; 44 S.J. 243................................. 11.16
West (Richard) and Partners (Inverness) *v.* Dick [1969] 2 Ch. 424;
    [1969] 2 W.L.R. 1190; [1969] 1 All E.R. 943; 67 L.G.R. 293; 113
    S.J. 165, C.A.. 11.13
Westminster City Council *v.* Croyalgrange [1986] 1 W.L.R. 674; (1986)
    130 S.J. 409; (1986) 150 J.P. 449; [1986] 2 All E.R. 353; (1986) 83
    Cr.App.R. 155; (1986) 84 L.G.R. 801; [1986] Crim.L.R. 693;
    (1986) 136 New L.J. 491; (1986) 83 L.S.Gaz. 2089, H.L.; affirming
    (1985) 149 J.P. 161; [1985] 1 All E.R. E.R. 740; (1985) 84 L.G.R.
    68; (1985) 149 J.P.N. 149, D.C................................. 2.48
Westripp *v.* Baldock [1939] 1 All E.R. 279; 83 S.J. 192, C.A............ 2.04
Wettern Electric *v.* Welsh Development Agency [1983] Q.B. 796; [1983]
    2 W.L.R. 897; [1983] 2 All E.R. 629; (1984) 47 P. & C.R. 113.... 11.18
Wheat *v.* Lacon (E.) & Co. [1966] A.C. 552; [1966] 2 W.L.R. 581; 110
    S.J. 149; [1966] 1 All E.R. 582; [1966] R.V.R. 223; [1966] R.A.
    193, H.L.; affirming [1966] 1 Q.B. 335; [1965] 3 W.L.R. 142; 109
    S.J. 334; [1965] 2 All E.R. 700; [1963] C.L.Y. 2663, C.A.......... 2.32
Wilchick *v.* Marks and Silverstone [1934] 2 K.B. 56; [1934] All E.R. 73;
    103 L.J.K.B. 372; 151 L.T. 60; 50 T.L.R. 281; 78 S.J. 277......... 2.19
Wilden Pump Engineering Co. *v.* Fusfield [1985] F.S.R. 159, C.A.;
    reversing [1985] F.S.R. 581.................................... 3.09A
Wilkins *v.* Leighton [1932] 2 Ch. 106; [1932] All E.R. 55; 101 L.J.Ch.
    385; 147 L.T. 495; 76 S.J. 232................................. 2.18
Wilkinson *v.* Collyer (1884) 13 Q.B.D. 1; 53 L.J.Q.B. 278; 51 L.T. 299;
    48 J.P. 791; 32 W.R. 614, D.C................................. 11.16
Willment (John) (Ashford), *Re* [1980] 1 W.L.R. 73; (1978) 124 S.J. 99;
    [1979] 2 All E.R. 615; [1978] T.R. 483; [1979] S.T.C. 286......... 12.10
Wiltshire *v.* Essex Area Health Authority [1988] A.C. 1074.............. 2.34
Wimpey (George) & Co. *v.* New Forest District Council [1979] J.P.L.
    314; (1979) 250 E.G. 249...................................... 8.12
Wintle *v.* Conaust (Vic.) [1989] V.R. 951........................... 2.35
Wivenhoe Port *v.* Colchester Borough Council [1985] J.P.L. 396, C.A.;
    affirming [1985] J.P.L. 175............................. 2.66, 2.70
Woolmington *v.* D.P.P. [1935] A.C. 462; [1935] All E.R. 1; 104 L.J.K.B.
    433; 153 L.T. 232; 51 T.L.R. 446; 79 S.J. 401; 25 Cr.App.Rep. 72;
    30 Cox C.C. 234, H.L.. 3.09A
Wrothwell (F.J.H.) *v.* Yorkshire Water Authority [1984] Crim.L.R. 43,
    C.A... 2.48
Wychavon District Council *v.* National Rivers Authority [1993] 2 All
    E.R. 440; (1992) 136 S.J. (LB) 260; [1992] NPC 121; *The*
    Independent, September 9, 1992; *The Times,* September 17, 1992,
    D.C... 2.48

YNYS MÔN BOROUGH COUNCIL *v.* Secretary of State for Wales and Jones
    Borthers (Construction) Company [1993] J.P.L. 225.............. 6.15
Yorkshire West Riding Council *v.* Holmfirth Urban Sanitary Authority
    [1894] 2 Q.B. 842; 63 L.J.Q.B. 485; 71 L.T. 217; 59 J.P. 213; 9 R.
    462, C.A.. 2.48
Young *v.* Bankier Distillery [1893] A.C. 691; (1893) 20 R. (H.L.) 76; 1
    SLT 204... 2.21, 13.02

TABLE OF STATUTES

(All references are to paragraph numbers)

1875 Explosives Act (38 & 39
    Vict., c.17)........... 5.25
1897 Police (Property) Act (60
    & 61 Vict., c.30)...... 2.79
    Public Health (Scotland)
    Act (60 & 61 Vict.,
    c.38)—
    s.3................. 13.04
    s.16................ 13.04
    s.20–22 .... 13.04
    s.20............... 13.04
    s.146.............. 13.04
1923 Explosives Act (13 & 14
    Geo.5, c.17)......... 13.04
1925 Law of Property Act (15
    & 16 Geo.5, c.20).... 2.69,
                   11.20, 12.10
    s. 109 .... 12.10
1927 Landlord and Tenant
    Act (17 & 18 Geo.5,
    c.36)—
    s.18............... 11.17
1930 Third Parties (Rights
    against Insurers Act
    (20 & 21 Geo.5, c.25 A–07
1936 Public Health Act (26
    Geo.5 & 1 Edw.8,
    c.49)...... 2.63, 2.71, 2.76
    s.90(1) 6.39
    s.94(2) 2.78
    s.289.............. 2.76
1938 Leasehold Property
    (Repairs) Act (1 & 2
    Geo.6, c.34)......... 11.17
1945 Law Reform (Contribu-
    tory Negligence) Act
    (8 & 9 Geo.6, c.28)... 2.20
1947 Agriculture Act (10 & 11
    Geo.6, c.48).... 5.25, A–09,
                     A–11
1949 National Parks and
    Access to the
    Countryside Act (12,
    13 & 14 Goe.6, c.97).. 9.07

1954 Landlord and Tenant
    Act (2 & 3 Eliz.2,
    c.56)
    s.34................ 11.18
1957 Occupiers' Liability Act
    (5 & 6 Eliz.2, c.31)
    s.1(1) 2.33
     (3) 2.33
     (4) 2.33
     (5) 2.33
     (6) 2.33
    s.2(1) 2.32
     (4)(a) 2.32
1960 Radioactive Substances
    Act (8 & 9 Eliz.2,
    c.34).. 5.35, 5.36, 7.24, 8.10
1961 Factories Act (9 & 10
    Eliz.2, c.34)......... 12.10
1964 Scrap Metal Dealers Act
    (c.69).............. 3.03
    s.9(2) 3.03
1968 Medicines Act (c.67)..... 5.32
1972 Deposit of Poisonous
    Waste Act (c.21)..... 5.18,
          5.21, 5.22, 5.31, 5.32,
                    7.28A
    s.1................. 5.19
     (3) 5.19
     (7) 5.19
    s.2................. 2.31
    s.3................. 5.19
     (1) 5.20
     (4) 5.19
     (5) 5.19
     (7) 5.19
    s.4................. 5.19
     (5) 5.20
     (6) 5.20
    s.5................. 5.20
     (3) 5.19, 5.20
    s.6................. 5.20
    s.9................. 5.20
1972 Defective Premises Act
    (c.35).............. 11.06

1972 Local Government Act
(c.70)—
  s.100A(3) 3.18
  Sched. 12(A) 3.18
1973 Water Act (c.37)........ 6.27
Powers of Criminal
Courts Act (c.62)—
  s.35 .... 2.78
    (1A) 2.78
    (4) 2.78
    (4A) 2.78
  s.36(3) 2.78
  s.37 .... 2.78
  s.38 .... 2.78
  s.43 .... 2.78
    (2) 2.79
    (3) 2.79
  s.43A 2.79
1974 Health and Safety at
Work etc Act (c.37).. 1.09,
    7.19
Control of Pollution Act
(c.40)..... 5.08, 5.19, 5.23,
    5.29, 6.09, A–09
Pt. I .. 2.54, 5.11, 5.18, 5.54,
    6.11
Pt. II 6.41
  s.3 .... 2.59
    (1) 5.20
    (3) 5.26
    (c)(iii) 5.21
  s.4(4) 5.26
    (5) 5.20, 7.28A
  s.5 .... 5.20
    (3) 5.20, 5.22
    (4) 6.38
  s.6 .... 5.20
    (2) 5.20, 5.22
  s.9 .... 5.20
    (1) 5.22
  s.10 .... 5.20, 6.38
  s.11 .... 5.22
  s.16 .... 2.59
  s.17 .... 5.31
  s.18(2) 5.26
  s.30(1) 5.21
    (3) 5.21
    (5) 5.21, 5.32
  s.37(1) 5.28
    (2) 5.28

1974 Control of Pollution
Act—cont.
  s.46(4) 13.03
  s.88 .... 2.31
1975 Welsh Development
Agency Act (c.70)..... 9.08
1976 Insolvency Act (c.60)—
  s.14(1) 12.11
    (2) 12.11
1977 Unfair Contract Terms
Act (c.50)..... 10.06, 11.04
  s.11(3) 10.09
1978 Civil Liability (Contribution) Act (c.47)....... 2.40
1979 Sale of Goods Act
(c.54)—
  s.14 .... 6.27
1980 Industry Act (c.33)...... 9.08
Magistrates' Courts Act
(c.43)............... 2.78
Limitation Act (c.58).... 2.41
  s.2 .... 2.41
  s11 .... 2.41, 2.42
  s.14 .... 2.41
  s.14A 2.42
    (3) 2.42
    (6)(a) 2.42
    (b) 2.42
    (7) 2.42
    (8) 2.42
    (A)(10) 2.42
  s.14B 2.42
    (2) 2.42
  s.32(1)(b) 2.41
  s.33 .... 2.41
  s.36(1) 2.41
Local Government, Plan-
ning and Land Act
(c.65)............... 9.21
1982 Supply of Goods and Services Act (c.29)—
  s.13 .... 10.07
Derelict Land Act (c.42) 9.10,
    9.14
  s.1 .... 9.02
  s.2 .... 9.08
  s.3 .... 9.07
1984 Building Act (c.55)...... 8.16
Police and Criminal Evi-
dence Act (c.60)—
  s.67 .... 3.09A

1984	Police and Criminal Evidence Act—*cont.*	
	s.67(9)	3.09A
	s.69	3.09A
	Sched. 3, para. 8	3.09A
1985	Companies Act (c.6)	12.09
	s.4	2.09
	s.228(2)	12.09
	Local Government (Access to Information) Act (c.43)	3.12, 3.18
	Food and Environment Protection Act (c.48)	5.38, 6.11
1986	Latent Damage Act (c.37)	2.42
	Insolvency Act (c.45)—	
	s.14(5)	12.11
	s.33	12.10
	s.44(1)(a)	12.10
	s.143	12.12
	s.178–182	12.12
	Sched. 1	12.10
	Sched. 4	12.12
	Financial Services Act (c.60)—	
	s.47	12.05
	s.144	12.09
	s.146	12.09
	(2)	12.09
	s.163	12.09
	Public Order Act (c.64)—	
	s.38	6.33
1987	Consumer Protection Act (c.43)	6.27
1988	Welsh Development Agency Act (c.5)	9.08
	Environment and Safety Information Act (c.30)	3.12
	Criminal Justice Act (c.33)	2.78
	Pt. VI	2.80
	s.71(1)	2.80
	(2)(a)	2.80
	(b)(i)	2.80
	(ii)	2.80
	(3)(a)	2.80

1988	Criminal Justice Act —*cont.*	
	s.71(3)(b)(i)	2.80
	(ii)	2.80
	(4)	2.80
	(6)	2.80
	(7)	2.80
	(9)(c)	2.80
	s.102(i)	2.80
	s.105	2.78
	Sched. 4	2.80
	Local Government Finance Act (c.41)—	
1989	Control of Pollution (Amendment) Act (c.14)	5.30, 7.34
	Water Act (c.15)	6.03, 6.24, 6.41
	s.4(1)	6.04
	Companies Act (c.40)	12.09
1990	Town and Country Planning Act (c.8)	5.01, 6.11
	s.22(3)(b)	5.08
	s.31(2)	5.04
	(3)	5.04
	s.36(2)	5.04
	(3)	5.04
	s.38	5.09
	s.55	5.08
	(1)	8.02
	(3)	5.08
	(b)	5.08
	s.64	3.10
	(3)	3.10
	(5)	3.10
	s.69	3.10
	s.72	8.12
	s.73	6.17
	s.73A	6.17
	s.106	6.17, 8.13
	s.106A	6.17
	(4)	6.17
	s.123(A)	5.04
	s.188	3.10
	s.191	3.10
	s.192	3.10
	(6)	3.10
	s.215	2.73, 2.74, 2.75, 2.76, 2.77, 5.07

1990   Town and Country Plan-
     ning Act—*cont.*
     s.215(1) 2.73, 2.75
       (2) 2.73
       (3) 2.73
       (4) 2.73
     s.216(2) 2.74
       (3) 2.74
       (4) 2.74
       (5)(*b*) 2.74
       (6) 2.74
     s.217 . . . . 2.75
       (3) 2.75
       (4) 2.75
       (5) 2.75
     s.218 . . . . 2.75
     s.219(1) 2.76
       (2) 2.76
       (3) 2.76
         (*a*) 2.76
         (*b*) 2.76
         (*c*) 2.76
       (4) 2.76
       (5) 2.76
     s.285(3) 2.75
     s.294 . . . . 3.10
     s.336 . . . . 8.02
       (1) 2.74, 2.76
     Pt. III 2.75
   Planning   (Hazardous
   Substances) Act (c.10). . . .
          3.10, 6.11, A–10
     s.28 . . . . 3.10, 11.04
   Food Safety Act (c.16). . . 3.08,
                     6.31
   Environmental   Protec-
     tion Act (c.43). . 3.08, 5.09,
       5.18, 5.21, 5.23, 13.17,
         A–09, A–11, B–05
     Pt. I . . 1.06, 2.43, 3.10, 5.01,
               5.11, 5.15
     Pt. II   1.06, 2.54, 3.08, 5.01,
       5.10, 5.14, 5.21, 5.23,
                5.24
     Pt. III 2.66, 2.72, 13.04
     s.1(2) 5.11
       (3) 6.33
       (4) 2.43, 5.13
       (7) 5.12

1990   Environmental   Protec-
     tion Act—*cont.*
     s.1(8) 5.12
       (10)(*b*) 5.14
         (*c*) 5.14
       (11)(*a*)(iii) 5.14
       (12) 5.14
     s.2 . . . . 6.04
     s.3(4) 5.31
     s.4(3) 5.15
     s.6(1) 2.43, 5.11, 5.14
     s.7(1) 2.30
       (2) 5.13
         (*a*) 5.14
       (4) 2.43, 5.13, 5.14
       (7) 5.13
       (10) 5.13
       (11) 5.13
     s.13(1) 2.43, 5.14
       (2) 2.43
     s.14(1) 2.43, 5.14
       (2) 2.43
     s.17 . . . . 2.43, 3.09
       (8) 3.09A
     s.19(2) 3.09
     s.20 . . . . 3.10
       (2)–(4) 3.10
     s.23(1)(*a*) 2.43
       (2) 2.43
     s.24 . . . . 2.43
     s.26(1) 2.43
     s.27(1) 2.43
       (2) 2.43
     s.28(1) 5.14
     s.29(1) 2.58, 5.23, 5.29
       (3) 2.60
       (5) 2.58, 2.60
     s.30 . . . . 5.23
     s.32 . . . . 5.23
     s.33 . . . . 2.54, 2.59, 2.65
       (1) 2.31, 2.54, 2.57,
               2.58, 2.59
         (*b*) 5.23
         (*c*) 5.23, 5.28
       (6) 2.31, 2.54, 5.23
       (7) 2.54
       (8) 2.54
       (9) 5.23, 5.26
     s.34 . . . 2.65, 5.30, 7.31, 7.33

1990 Environmental Protection Act—*cont.*
s.34(1) 2.65, 7.31
(3) 7.32
(c)(i) 7.32
(4)(a) 7.32
(5) 7.33
(6) 2.65
s.35(3) 5.23
(12) 2.61
s.36(3) 5.23, 5.27
s.37(1) 5.28
(2) 5.28, 5.29
s.39 .... 5.23
(1) 5.29
(3) 5.29
(4) 3.09, 5.29
(5) 5.29
(6) 5.29
(7) 5.29
(9) 5.29
(10) 5.29
s.42 .... 3.09
s.43(1)(f) 5.29
s.50 .... 5.05, 5.09
s.51 .... 5.23
s.59 ...... 2.57, 2.58, 2.59
(2) 2.57
(3) 2.57
(4) 2.57
(3) 2.57
(6) 2.57
(7) 2.57, 2.59
(8) 2.58
s.61 .. 2.60, 2.61, 2.62, 3.08,
3.09, 11.16, 13.05,
A–11
(1) 2.61
(2) 2.60
(4) 2.61
(5) 2.62
(6) 2.61
(7) 2.62
(8) 2.63
(9) 2.63
(10) 2.63
(11) 2.64, 3.09A
s.63(2) 2.31, 5.26
s.64 .... 3.10

1990 Environmental Protection Act—*cont.*
s.64(3) 3.10
(6) 3.10
s.66 .... 2.02
s.69 .... 3.09
(8) 3.09A
s.69(A) 3.09A
s.71(2) 3.09
s.73(6) 2.31, 2.54
(7) 2.31
s.74 .... 5.23
(2) 5.27
(3) 5.27
(4) 5.27
(7) 5.27
s.75 .... 2.60, 3.03
(1) 2.60
(2) 2.56, 2.60, 5.24
(3) 5.24
(b) 2.60
(4) 5.24
s.79 .... 3.09
(1) 2.67
(4) 2.66
(7) 2.66, 2.67, 2.68,
2.71
s.80 .... s.71, 2.78
(1) 2.67
(3) 2.68
(4) 2.78
(5) 2.68
(6) 2.68
(7) 2.68
(8)(a) 2.68
s.81(1) 2.71
(3) 2.69, 2.71
(4) 2.69
(5) 2.69
s.81A 2.69, 2.70, A–11
(1) 2.69
(2) 2.69
(3) 2.69
(4) 2.69
(6) 2.69
(7) 2.69
(8) 2.69
(9) ... 2.63, 2.69, 2.70
s.81B A–11

1990 Environmental   Protec-
         tion Act—*cont.*
         s.81B(1) 2.69
                  (2) 2.69
                  (4) 2.69
                  (5) 2.69
         s.82 .... 2.70, 2.71
                  (2) 2.70
                  (6) 2.70
                  (8) 2.70
         s.83 .... 13.04
                  (1) 2.72
         s.143   1.05, 1.06, 3.01, 3.02,
                  3.03, 3.10, 3.13, 12.07,
                  A–19, A–20
                  (6) ... 3.02, 3.03, 3.08,
                  14.02
         Sched. 3,
            para. 2 2.67, 3.09, 3.09A
            para. 4 .... 2.67
         Sched. 15,
            para. 29 .... 6.04
1991 New Roads and Street
         Works Act (c.22)—
         s.219(1) 2.53
         Property Misdescriptions
            Act (c.29).......... 11.06
         Planning and Compensa-
            tion Act (c.34).. 3.10, 5.04,
            6.17
         Sched. 4,
            para. 17 .... 5.09
         Water   Industry   Act
            (c.56)..... 3.10, 5.01, 6.03,
            A–09
         Pt. II 6.27
         s.1(2) 6.05
         s.6(1) 6.37
                  (b) 6.05
                  (3) 6.27
         s.18 .... 6.31
         s.19(1)(b) 6.31
         s.37(1) 6.27
         s.38 .... 6.27
                  (2) 6.05
         s.49(3) 6.05
         ss.67–86 .... 6.31
         s.68(1) 6.27

1991 Water   Industry   Act—
         cont.
         s.69(2) 3.09
         s.71(1) 6.10
         s.72 .... 2.52, 6.33
                  (2) 2.52, 6.33
                  (3) 2.52, 6.33
                  (4) 2.52
                  (5) 2.52, 6.33
         ss.77–85 .... 6.27
         s.77 .... 3.09, 6.32
         s.80 .... 6.32
                  (7) 6.32
         s.81(2) 6.32
         ss.82–85 .... 6.32
         s.84 .... 3.09
         s.85 .... 6.36
         s.86(2) 3.09
                  (4) 3.09
         s.93(1) 6.27, 6.32
                  (2) 6.27
         s.94(1) 6.37
         s.95(2) 6.05
         s.106 .... 6.38
                  (2)(a)(i) 6.38
                  (b) 6.39
         s.111 .... 6.38, 6.39
                  (1)(b) 6.38
                  (c) 6.38
                  (2) 6.38
                  (3) 6.38
         s.113 .... 6.38
                  (6) 6.38
         s.118(1) 6.38
                  (2) 6.38
                  (3) 6.38
         s.119 .... 6.38
         s.120 638
         s.121 .... 6.38
                  (1) 6.38
         s.123 .... 6.38
         s.138 .... 6.38
         s.141(1) 6.38
                  (2) 6.38
         s.162(1) 2.53
                  (2) 2.53
                  (3) 2.53
                  (8) 2.53
         s.193(1) 6.05
         s.196 .... 3.10

1991	Water Industry Act—*cont.*		
	s.198	6.36	
	(1)	3.10	
	(2)	3.10	
	(5)	3.10	
	s.204(1)	6.38	
	(3)	6.38	
	s.209	2.30	
	s.218	6.33	
	s.219	6.39	
	Water Resources Act (c.57)	5.01, 6.03, 6.11, 6.33, 6.41, 8.11, 13.33, A–09	
	Pt. III	6.04	
	Pt. VI	6.04	
	s.1	6.04	
	(1)	6.04	
	(5)	6.04	
	s.16	6.10	
	s.19	6.04, 6.10	
	s.24	6.10	
	(1)	6.34	
	(2)	6.34	
	(4)	6.34	
	s.25(2)	6.34	
	s.27	6.34	
	s.29	6.34	
	s.30	6.10	
	s.35(3)	6.34	
	s.37(2)	6.35	
	s.38(3)(*a*)	6.35	
	s.39(2)	6.35	
	s.48(1)	6.34	
	(2)	6.34	
	(4)	6.34	
	ss.82–84	6.24	
	s.82	6.12	
	s.83	6.04, 6.10	
	(1)	6.12	
	s.84(1)	6.12	
	(2)	3.09	
	(*a*)	6.24	
	s.85	2.44, 2.46, 2.49, 2.50, 2.51	
	(1)	2.47	
	(3)	2.47	
	(6)	2.49	
	s.86	2.44	

1991	Water Resources Act—*cont.*		
	s.86(1)	2.44	
	(2)	2.44	
	s.87	6.10	
	(1A)	6.39	
	s.88	6.10	
	s.89(3)	2.46	
	s.92	5.38, 6.10, 6.14, 6.21	
	s.93	6.04, 6.10, 6.13	
	(2)	6.13	
	(4)	6.13	
	(5)	6.13	
	ss.94–96	5.38	
	s.94	6.10, 6.13	
	(2)	5.38	
	s.95	5.38	
	s.97	5.39	
	(2)	5.39	
	s.104	2.45	
	(4)	2.45	
	s.133	6.04	
	s.161	2.02, 2.50, 2.62, 6.04, 6.10, 11.16, 13.03, A–11	
	(1)	2.50	
	(*a*)	2.50	
	(*b*)	2.50	
	(3)	2.50	
	(4)	2.50	
	s.169	3.09	
	s.172	3.09	
	s.188	6.04	
	s.189	6.36	
	s.190	3.10, 6.04	
	(1)(*e*)	3.09	
	s.195	3.10, 6.36	
	s.198	6.36	
	s.199	6.10	
	s.202	3.09	
	(2)	6.36	
	(4)	6.36	
	s.203(1)	6.35	
	s.204	6.39	
	(2)(*k*)	6.36	
	s.209	3.09A	
	s.217(1)	2.49	
	s.221(1)	2.47	

1991 Water Resources Act—
      cont.
      Sched. 1,
          para. 4 . . . .   6.04
          para. 5 . . . .   6.04
      Sched. 20,
          para. 1 . . . .   3.09A

      Statutory Water Com-
          panies Act (c.58) 6.03,
                                        6.27

      Land   Drainage   Act
          (c.59). 6.03

      Water   Consolidation
          (Consequential Pro-
          visions) Act (c.60). . . .   6.03

1992 Local   Government
      Finance Act (c.14)—
      Sched. 13,
          para. 2 . . . .   13.04

1993 Radioactive Substances
      Act (c.12) 5.01, 5.35,
                              6.11, 7.30
      s.14 . . . .   7.30
      s.19 . . . .   7.30
      s.40(1) 5.32
      s.47 . . . .   7.30
      s.78 . . . .   5.25

1993 Leasehold Reform, Hous-
      ing   and   Urban
      Development   Act
      (c.28). 9.07
      s.158 . . . .   9.02
          (3) 9.02
      s.159(1) 9.02
          (3) 9.02
          (4) 9.02
      s.160 . . . .   9.03
          (1)(i) 9.04
      s.161 . . . .   9.03
      s.162 . . . .   9.03
      s.164(3) 9.04
          (5) 9.04
      s.167 . . . .   9.02
      s.171 . . . .   9.03
      s.177 . . . .   9.03

AUSTRALIA

1970 Environmental   Protec-
      tion Act (Vict.). 13.31
      s.31C 13.31
      s.45(1) 13.31
          (2) 13.31
      s.62A(1) 13.31
1986 Environmental   Protec-
      tion Act (W.A.). 13.32
1988 Environmentally   Haz-
      ardous Chemical Act
      (NSW). 13.29
      s.35(1) 13.29
1990 Contaminated Land Act   13.28
      Unhealthy   Building
      Land Act (NSW). . . .   13.29
1991 Contaminated Land Act
      (Qu.). 13.30

CANADA

1980 Ontario   Environmental
      Protection   Act
      (R.S.O., Ch. 141)—
      s.16 . . . .   13.17
      s.17 . . . .   13.17
      s.92 . . . .   13.17
1985 Fisheries   Act   (R.S.C.,
      Ch. F–14). 13.17
1988 Canadian Environmental
      Protection Act (S.C.
      Ch. 22). 13.17
      Pt. II 13.17
1990 Gasoline Handling Act
      (R.S.O., Ch. G.4). . . .   13.17
      Ontario Water Resourse
      Act   (R.S.O.,   Ch.
      E.19). 13.17
      s.30(2) 13.17

DENMARK

1990 Waste Deposits Act (Act
      No. 420 of June 13,
      1990). 13.27

GERMANY

1960 Waste Management Act   13.23
1972 Waste Disposal Act.....   13.23
1991 Environmental Liability
     Law...............   13.23
     s.6(I) 13.23

THE NETHERLANDS

1982 Soil Clean-up (Interim)
     Act..... 13.18, 13.21, 13.22
     s.2.................   13.18
     s.11 ....   13.18
       (2) 13.18
     s.12(1) 13.18
     s.17 ....   13.18
       (1) 13.18
     ss.18–20 ....   13.18
     s.21 .... 13.18, 13.19, 13.21
     s.33(1) 13.18
       (2) 13.18
1986 Soil Protection Act.....   13.21,
                                 13.22

UNITED STATES

1965 Solid Waste Disposal Act....
                                 13.06
1970 Resourse Recovery Act.. 13.06
1974 Safe Drinking Water
     Act......... 13.06, 13.08
1976 Resource Conservation
     and Recovery Act.... 13.06
     s.7003 ....   13.06
1977 New Jersey Spill Com-
     pensation and Control
     Act...............   13.14

1977 Toxic Substances Control
     Act—
     s.6(e) 13.16
1980 Comprehensive Environ-
     mental Response,
     Compensation, and
     Liability Act.. 13.06, 13.07,
                                 13.15
     s.101(20)(A) 13.09
       (24) 13.08
       (35)(A) 13.09
         (i) 13.09
         (B) 13.09
     s.103 ....   13.07
     s.104 ....   13.07
       (c)1 ....   13.08
     s.105(a)(8)(A) 13.07
     s.106 ....   13.09
     s.107 ... 13.07, 13.09, 13.10
       (b)(3) 13.09
       (f) 13.07
       (1) 13.09
     s.113(f) 13.10
       (2) 13.11
     s.121 ....   13.08
       (b) 13.08
     s.122 ....   13.11
     s.310 ....   13.10
1983 New Jersey Environmen-
     tal Clean-up Respon-
     sibility Act..........   13.14
1986 Superfund Amendments
     and Reauthorisation
     Act.......... 13.06, 13.09
1990 Oil Pollution Act.......   13.15
1993 Industrial Site Recovery
     Act...............   13.14
1994 Superfund Reform Act.. 13.13

TABLE OF STATUTORY INSTRUMENTS

(All references are to paragraph numbers)

1972 The Deposit of Poisonous
Waste (Notification of
Removal or Deposit)
Regulations (S.I. 1972
No. 1017)...... 5.19, 6.04

1980 The Control of Lead at
Work Regulations
(S.I. 1980 No. 1248).. 7.23
Control of Pollution
(Special Waste) Regu-
lations (S.I. 1980 No.
1709)..... 4.18, 5.01, 5.19,
7.33, A–09, A–10, A–11
reg. 2 .... 5.32
reg. 3(1) 5.33

1983 Asbestos (Licensing)
Regulations (S.I. 1983
No. 1649)........... 7.22

1984 Classification, Packaging
and Labelling Regu-
lations (S.I. 1984 No.
1244)......... 7.21, A–10

1985 Natural Mineral Waters
Regulations (S.I. 1985
No. 71)............. 6.11
Ionising Radiation Regu-
lations (S.I. 1985 No.
1333)............... 7.24

1986 Control of Pollution
(Supply and Use of
Injurious Substances)
Regulations (S.I. 1986
No. 902)............ 7.22
Control of Pesticides
Regulation (S.I. 1986
No. 1510)....... 5.01, 5.38

1987 Control of Asbestos at
Work Regulations
(S.I. 1987 No. 2155).. 7.22

1988 The Collection and Disposal of Waste Regu-
lations (S.I. 1988 No.
819).. 5.20, 5.21, 5.25, 5.38,
7.28, 7.28A, 7.28B

1988 Town and Planning
(Assessment of En-
vironmental Effects)
Regulations (S.I. 1988
No. 1199)........... 8.06
Control of Substances
Hazardous to Health
Regulations (S.I. 1988
No. 1657)...... 7.21, A–10
Control of Pollution
(Special Waste)
(Amendment) Regu-
lations (S.I. 1988 No.
1790)............... 5.31
Town and Country Plan-
ning General Develop-
ment Order (S.I. 1988
No. 1813).. 3.10, 5.02, 5.08,
6.15, 8.02, 8.03, 8.07, 8.11,
C–02
Art. 7 .... 3.10
Art. 27(4) 3.10
Art. 28 .... 3.10

1989 Water Supply (Water
Quality) Regulations
(S.I. 1989 No. 1147).. 3.09,
6.05, 6.31
Surface Waters (Classi-
fication) Regulations
(S.I. 1989 No. 1148).. 6.24
Trade Effluents (Pre-
scribed Processes and
Substances) Regu-
lations (S.I. 1989 No.
1156).......... 6.25, 6.38
Water Supply and
Sewerage Services
(Customer Service
Standards) Regu-
lations (S.I. 1989 No.
1159).............. 6.27
Sludge (Use in Agricul-
ture) Regulations (S.I.
1989 No. 1263).. 5.01, 5.38

1989 Surface Waters (Dangerous Substances) (Classification) Regulations (S.I. 1989 No. 2286)........... 6.24, 6.25

1990 Sludge (Use in Agriculture) (Amendment) Regulations (S.I. 1990 No. 880)............. 5.38

Nitrate Sensitive Areas (Designation) Order (S.I. 1990 No. 1013).. 5.38

Statutory Nuisance (Appeals) Regulations (S.I. 1990 No. 2276) 11.16
reg. 2 .... 2.68
    (2)(g) 2.71
    (h) 2.71
    (i) 2.71
    (6) 2.71
    (7) 2.71
    (a) 11.16
reg. 3(1) 2.68
    (2) 2.68

1991 Control of Pollution (Silage, Slurry and Agricultural Fuel Oil) Regulations (S.I. 1991 No. 324)... 5.01, 5.38, 6.10

Environmental Protection (Prescribed Processes and Substances) Regulations (S.I. 1991 No. 472)............... C–02

Environmental Protection (Applications, Appeals and Registers) Regulations (S.I. 1991 No. 507)........ 3.10

Environmental Protection (Prescribed Processes and Substances) Regulations (S.I. 1991 No. 614)........... 5.12, 5.14

Environmental Protection (Amendment of Regulations) Regulations (S.I. 1991 No. 836)............... 5.12

1991 Bathing Waters (Classification) Regulations (S.I. 1991 No. 1597).. 6.24

Controlled Waste (Registration of Carriers and Seizure of Vehicles) Regulations (S.I. 1991 No. 1624)...... 7.32, 7.34

Control of Substances Hazardous to Health (Amendment) Regulations (S.I. 1991 No. 2431).............. 7.21

Private Water Supplies Regulations (S.I. 1991 No. 2790)....... 3.09, 6.32

The Town and Country Planning (Development Plan) Regulations (S.I. 1991 No. 2794.......... 5.09, 6.11

The Town and Country Planning General Development (Amendment) (No. 3) Order (S.I. 1991 No. 2805).............. 6.15

Environmental Protection (Duty of Care) Regulations (S.I. 1991 No. 2839)............ 7.33

1992 Local Government (Publication of Information about unused and under-used Land) (England) Regulations (S.I. 1992 No. 73)................ 9.21

Controlled Waste Regulations (S.I. 1992 No. 588)....... 5.24, 5.38, 7.28

1992 Local Authorities (Calculation of Council Tax Base) Regulations (S.I. 1992 No. 612)............... 5.12

Planning (Hazardous Substances) Regulations (S.I. 1992 No. 656).............. 3.10
reg. 23 .... 3.10

1992 Town and Country Plan-
      ning General Regu-
      lations (S.I. 1992 No.
      1492)
      reg. 14(1)(c) 2.76
      reg. 16 .... 2.76

Town and Country Plan-
ning (Special Enforce-
ment   Notice)
Regulations (S.I. 1992
No. 1652)............ 3.10

Management of Health
& Safety at Work
Regulations (S.I. 1992
No. 2051)............ 7.20

Environmental Informa-
tion Regulations (S.I.
1992 No. 3240).. 3.12, 3.14,
                3.18, 11.04
reg. 1(1)(b) 3.12
reg. 2 .... 3.12
      (1)(b) 3.12
      (2)(a) 3.12
         (b) 3.12
         (c) 3.12
      (3) 3.12
      (4) 3.13
reg. 3 .... 3.12, 3.13
      (3) 3.13
      (4) 3.13
      (7) 3.12, 3.16
reg. 4 .... 3.12
      (1) 3.12
      (2)(a)–(e) 3.16
      (3) 3.12, 3.16
         (b) 3.17
         (c) 3.17

1992 The   Property   Mis-
      description (Specified
      Matters) Order (S.I.
      1992 No. 3834)...... 11.06
1993 Environmental Protection
      (Prescribed Processes
      and   Substances)
      (Amendment) (No. 2)
      Regulations (S.I. 1993
      No. 2405)........... 5.12
1994 Waste   Management
      Licencing Regulations
      (S.I. 1994 No. 1056).. 5.06,
      5.29, 5.38, 6.09, 7.28B, 7.34,
                        7.34A
      reg. 1(3) 5.24
      reg. 3 .... 5.27
      reg. 4 .... 5.27
      reg. 5 .... 5.27
      reg. 14 .... 5.28
      reg. 15 .... 5.28
      reg. 17(1) 5.25
         (2) 5.23
         (3) 5.23
      reg. 18 .... 5.25
      reg. 24(8) 5.24
      Sched. 1 .... 5.29
      Sched. 3 .... 5.25
      Sched. 4, para. 2–4 ... 5.05
            para. 2 ..... 5.09
            para. 3 .... 5.09,
                        5.23
            para. 4 ..... 5.23
               (2) .. 5.09
            para. 9(2) .. 5.24
               (3)–(5) ...
                        5.23
            para. 10(3) 5.24
      Pt. II 5.24

Preamble

Man's activities have always had the potential to contaminate the ground where they are carried out; instances may be found of potential problems arising from activities such as lead mining, pre-dating the Roman occupation of Britain.[1] However, compared with pollution of air and water, soil contamination may be less obvious and its consequences more long-lived. Perhaps this is partly the reason why less attention has been focused on the problem of contaminated land, in terms of legislative action within the UK and European Community, than the pollution of air and water. That position is changing; all countries, the UK included, are becoming more aware of the potential massive and serious problems resulting from soil contamination. This awareness may be partly a reflection of man's increasing technical ability to detect ever-lower levels of contamination. It may also be a consequence of the increasing need in many industrialised countries to reuse, and in some cases regenerate, land which has previously been used for industrial activity. It is also undoubtedly in some measure due to the public concern aroused by incidents such as Lekkerkerk in the Netherlands in 1975,[2] Love Canal in the United States in 1978,[3] and Loscoe in Derbyshire in 1986.[4] Such

---

[1] Examples of such potential problems from metal mining in Wales and lead mining in Derbyshire were given in Memoranda by the Welsh Office and by Amber Valley District Council to the House of Commons Environment Committee in its report into "Contaminated Land" (House of Commons Session 1989–90, first report, Vol. III, Apps. 2 and 3; 170–III). Other examples of truly historic contamination are residues of arsenic from mining and smelting activities in Cornwall and soil concentrations of cadmium from abandoned zinc mines in Somerset. Such contamination appears to have had few obvious health effects: see *The Observer*, March 8, 1992.

[2] In 1980 some 1,600 drums of illegally dumped toxic waste were discovered in the small town of Lekkerkerk. Between 1972 and 1975, 268 houses had been constructed on land which had been used for waste disposal and which had been reclaimed; the waste included chemicals from the dyestuffs industry and caused contamination of drinking water and underfloor voids. The area was evacuated and the waste removed at a cost of some £156,000,000 in 1981.

[3] Between 1947 and 1953, nearly 22,000 tonnes of chemical residues were dumped at Love Canal, New York State on an industrial waste disposal site. The site was capped and was sold to the Niagara Falls Board of Education for the sum of $1, with the caveat that the site should not be disturbed by building works. Nonetheless, a 16 acre development of school and houses was con-

1

incidents are considered by many to be the prime motivator for policy and legislation developments.

Whatever the cause, such concern is leading to significant changes in law and policy within the UK, European Community and various other countries. As a result, contaminated or potentially contaminated land is undoubtedly a growing concern for all those involved in land, whether as developers, planners, owners, occupiers and lenders, as well as their professional advisors. The object of this book is to provide an overview of the practical problems arising from soil contamination from the perspective of the legal system of England and Wales.

structed during the 1950s. Residents began to report illnesses and contaminated leachate in cellars in 1976, and in 1978 children and expectant mothers were evacuated, the site declared a national emergency and a state-sponsored remedial programme was put into action. More than 900 families were evacuated and hundreds of homes demolished. The site was officially declared habitable in September 1988. The cost of the clean-up (the subject of legal action against Hooker Corporation, which initially buried the waste) was estimated in 1989 as in excess of $250,000,000. Litigation followed in respect of alleged health effects, cancers, emotional effects, miscarriages and birth defects: *The Independent*, March 31, 1989.

At about 6.30 a.m. on March 24, 1986, Number 51 Clarke Avenue, Loscoe, Heanor, Derbyshire was destroyed by an explosion. Fortunately, the three occupants of the bungalow survived the incident, though all three of them were trapped in the rubble. The Tribunal appointed by Derbyshire County Council to report into the incident found that it was caused by an explosion of a mixture of landfill gas and air in the underfloor void of the property; this gas had migrated from a local landfill site containing substantial quantities of putrescible matter, and had been drawn into the underfloor void by an unusual and sudden drop in atmospheric pressure.

Discussion: What is Contaminated Land?

The Government's view

The House of Commons Environment Committee, under the chairmanship of Sir Hugh Rossi, considered the issue of contaminated land in its First Report, Session 1989–1990.[1] The Committee considered what was meant by the term "contaminated land" and made the fundamental point that the conventional distinction between pollution and contamination is not generally drawn in this context:[2]

> "The answer to the question, 'What is contaminated land?' is, however, by no means simple. At the outset of our inquiry Dr. Fisk, the Chief Scientist, Department of the Environment, reminded us that we use the word 'contaminated' rather loosely with respect to land. In other areas of pollution control, a scientific distinction exists between 'contamination'—the mere presence of a foreign substance, possibly harmless–and "pollution"—which poses or causes harm. But in this field the DoE itself and those involved in the subject appear to ignore this terminological nicety and use "contaminated land" as the conventional expression."

In its memorandum of evidence to the Commons Environment Committee, the Department of Environment suggested that contaminated land is difficult to define," . . . but may be regarded as land which represents an actual or potential hazard to public health or the environment as a result of current or previous use."[3] However, the DoE went on in its memorandum to link the issue of contamination with the actual or potential use of land:

> "The question of whether land can be considered contaminated depends critically on the actual or potential use of the land. For example a scrap yard contaminated by metal traces would constitute a hazard for subsequent agricultural use but the contamination would be of no account in construction of an office block."

[1] House of Commons, Session 1989–90, First Report; 170–I, II and III.
[2] *Ibid.*, Vol. I, para. 13.
[3] *Ibid.*, Vol. II, p. 2.

3

This approach was the subject of strong criticism by the Committee, both in questions to DoE officials[4] and also in the Committee's recommendations:[5]

> "We do not wish to be unnecessarily alarmist. Our concern is that by defining contaminated land narrowly and solely in relation to end-use the Department of the Environment may be underestimating a genuine environmental problem and misdirecting effort and resources. The DoE states that, at present, it is not possible to define contaminated land unambiguously. We accept that, at present, contamination should be regarded as a general concept rather than as something capable of exact definition and measurement. But there is land in the UK which is contaminated and which is a threat to health and the environment both on site and in the surrounding area. Where this threat is present, the current land use is irrelevant. The primary focus of central and local government activity must be upon land which is a hazard to health or the environment and not upon an administratively convenient sub-category . . . We recommend that the DoE concern itself with all land which has been so contaminated as to be a potential hazard to health or the environment regardless of the use to which it is to be put."

In its response to the Committee's report, the Government stated that the focus of its policies on contaminated land has always been to address threats to health and the environment by measures dealing with the problems as they arise through the various control systems: however, the Government expressed the view that the majority of such cases concern proposals for changes of use or redevelopment within the planning system.[6] It may or may not be correct that in 1990 when the response was published, issues of contaminated land tended to arise most frequently for consideration within the planning system; however, that in itself does not seem any reason why the use of land should be regarded as the litmus test for contamination. It is arguable that the insistence on identifying and appraising contamination only in the context of development has been a severe hindrance to the UK developing a clear policy for dealing with the problem.

---

[4] *Ibid.*, Vol. II, pp. 19–20.
[5] *Ibid.*, Vol. I, paras. 20–21.
[6] Department of the Environment, "Contaminated Land," Cm. 1161, July 1990.

4

The harm test

A more precise definition of contaminated land has been provided by the NATO Committee on Challenges to Modern Society ("CCMS")[7] as:

"Land that contains substances which, when present in sufficient quantities or concentrations, are likely to cause harm, directly or indirectly, to man, to the environment, or on occasion to other targets."

The crucial concept within this definition would appear to be the likelihood of harm (which as discussed below may take a variety of forms). In some cases, the current or proposed use of the land may have an important bearing on the likelihood of harm: which as far as people are concerned, may be much less when the land is put to a use such as a hard-surfaced car park, than when it is used for domestic gardens, where soil is left exposed to adults and children. On the other hand, in relation to the likelihood of some kinds of harm, a proposed use may be irrelevant. Land which is contaminated so as to represent a threat to groundwater will present such a threat regardless of whether or not any change of use is intended; similarly, where the land in question is producing methane or other explosive gases, the use of the actual land itself may be less relevant than uses to which adjoining or nearby land is put.

One commentator, discussing the CCMS definition, has put the point this way:[8]

"This definition is straightforward, but inevitably leads to the classification of large areas of land as 'contaminated' . . . This is not a reason to reject such a definition. It simply means that it should be qualified when necessary. For example, it might be decided that it is important to identify 'contaminated land that would be prejudicial to health were it to be developed for housing' or 'contaminated land likely to give rise to ground water contamination/pollution.' "

Derelict land and contaminated land

It is important to distinguish between contaminated land and derelict land. As the Department of Environment pointed out in its memoran-

---

[7] The NATO/CCMS study group began work in 1981, with Canada, Denmark, Germany, France, The Netherlands, the UK and the USA participating. The objective was to review current knowledge of remedial measures particularly in relation to their long-term performance.

[8] N.A. Smith, *Identification, Investigation and Assessment of Contaminated Land* (1991) Journal I.W.E.M. 5, December, p. 617.

dum to the House of Commons' Environmental Committee,[9] land which has been despoiled by previous development can be described in various ways, such as waste, derelict, contaminated, neglected, unused, under-used or vacant. Such categories are not mutually exclusive.

In contrast with contaminated land, the definition of which is discussed above, the Government defined derelict land as:[10]

> "Land so damaged by industrial or other development that it is incapable of beneficial use without treatment."

As the Government went on to say, land may be either derelict or contaminated, or both: a chemical waste tip might well be both derelict and contaminated, whereas a disused chalk quarry may be derelict but not contaminated, and the curtilage of an active chemical factory might be contaminated but not derelict.

The importance of derelict land is that this has, in the past, largely been the focus of Government in terms of grant aid.[11]

---

[9] Session 1989–90, First Report, Vol. II, p. 2.
[10] *Ibid.*
[11] See Chap. 9.

Chapter 1

INTRODUCTION

Causes of contaminated land

Contamination may arise from a wide variety of activities. One **1.01** category is the intentional deposit of material on land, whether as a means of disposing of that material, or in connection with development or construction activities. Examples are landfill sites, tips, lagoons for industrial effluent, deposits of dredgings, "made ground" and filled dock basins, and the deposit of sewage sludge on agricultural land.

Another category is contamination arising incidentally in the course of industrial activity, including spillages and leaks of materials from storage tanks and drums, escapes of materials such as dust and liquids in the course of the activity itself, and contamination resulting from deposition of airborne particulate matter. As well as contamination in the course of ordinary industrial activity, incidents such as floods, fires and explosions may give rise to significant contamination. Another possible cause of contamination are lax practices during the decommissioning and demolition of industrial facilities. Many pollutants are, by their nature, mobile and so capable of migration, whether in gaseous, liquid or particulate form; a site may therefore become contaminated without itself having been used for a contaminating purpose.

Various attempts have been made to compile lists of uses of land which are prone to cause contamination; this is discussed further in the chapter on identifying contaminated land. However, to give some initial indication of the types of use which may cause contamination, the House of Commons Environment Committee listed nineteen categories of use, which were said to represent the most common contaminating uses.[1]

The categories were as follows:

> waste disposal sites
> gas works
> oil refineries and petrol stations

---

[1] Session 1989–90, First Report, Vol. I, para.12.

power stations
iron and steel works
petroleum refineries
metal products, fabrication and finishing
chemical works
textile plants
leather tanning works
timber treatment works
non-ferrous metals processing
manufacture of integrated circuits and semi-conductors
sewage works
asbestos works
docks and railway land
paper and printing works
heavy engineering installations
processing radioactive materials

Consequences of contamination

1.02   As in modern industrial society the contamination of land is widespread, so too is the range of potentially harmful contaminants. These include toxic metals such as cadmium, lead, arsenic and mercury, which may present risks to human health. Other metals such as copper, nickel and zinc may prevent or inhibit plant growth. Contamination may involve combustible substances which may give rise to persistent underground fires. Putrescible wastes may degrade to produce flammable gases such as methane, which may then migrate and present the risk of explosion; toxic or asphyxiating gases may also be generated. Some contaminants, such as sulphates, chlorides and acids, may have an aggressive effect on building materials, concrete foundations, and services. Other substances, such as oils, tars, phenols and solvents, may present serious problems in terms of contamination of water supplies, either through groundwater or in some cases by causing deterioration of service mains. Fibrous or particulate contaminants may present dangers from inhalation—in particular asbestos.

Sources such as Guidance Note 59/83 of the Interdepartmental Committee on the Redevelopment of Contaminated Land (ICRCL)[2] identify various hazards or adverse effects which may need to be considered in connection with contaminated sites. These may be grouped as follows:

[2] (2nd Ed.), July 1987, p. 5.

(i) Ingestion and inhalation of toxic substances

Substances such as toxic metals may be ingested directly or indirectly. Direct ingestion can arise, for example, by young children playing on contaminated soil; some children suffer from the disorder of pica (compulsive eating of soil or other non-food materials),[3] though "ordinary" child's-play also may obviously result in ingestion in this way. Indirect ingestion may come about where food is contaminated, for example, where fruit or vegetables are contaminated by particles of soil or dust and are inadequately washed, or where water is contaminated and is used in food preparation.

(ii) Inhalation of toxic materials

Toxic substances, including metals and organic materials, may be inhaled in the form of dust or particles.

(iii) Direct skin or eye contact

Tars, oils, acids, corrosive and other chemical substances may cause problems on direct dermal contact, where workers or occupants of land are directly exposed to contaminated soil.

(iv) Uptake of contaminants by food plants

Where food plants and crops are grown in contaminated soil, elements such as cadmium, arsenic, copper, fluorine and lead may accumulate in the edible portions of the plant, making it unsafe to consume plants grown in such soil over a period of time. There may also be a risk to livestock grazing on herbage grown on contaminated soil.[4]

(v) Phytotoxicity

Phytotoxity is the prevention or inhibition of plant growth: it may be caused by, amongst other factors, contamination of soil by elements such

---

[3] Pica is often held out as a "worst case" in terms of risks from contamination. But it has been estimated by Martin Beckett of the Environmental Services Division, Mott McDonald Group, that the probability of a pica sufferer living in a place where contaminated soil is exposed is approximately 8.2 per 100 million (*i.e.* one in 12.2 million) for a population of 100,000. On a new development for 1000 people, the risk is one in 1.22 billion. Pica is not restricted to eating soil, and a child suffering from the disorder is just at much at risk inside their home as in the garden.

[4] Useful information is given at section 4 of the Ministry of Agricultures *Code of Good Agricultural Practice for the Protection of Soil* (Consultation draft, December 1992).

9

as boron, copper, nickel and zinc. Phytotoxic effects may become apparent long before concentrations of substances are such as to present a risk to human health; this is the case with zinc. Methane and similar gases may also have phytotoxic effects by depleting the oxygen content of soil.

(vi) Contamination of water

Contamination of water is increasingly becoming recognised as one of the most serious and intractable effects of soil contamination.[5] The degree of risk will depend upon the nature of the contaminating substances, in particular their mobility and persistence in soil, the nature of the soil and geological conditions, and the proximity of vulnerable water sources. Contaminated soil, as a form of land-based contamination, may have very significant effects on surface water quality, both of internal waters and of estuarial and coastal waters.[6] An even more difficult problem arises in relation to contamination of usable groundwater resources in the form of aquifers. Groundwater is a valuable resource, and many parts of the UK are dependent upon it as the principal source of potable water. Contamination of an aquifer may be an extremely difficult problem to eradicate and solutions, if possible at all, may be available only at extremely high cost.

(vii) Aggressive chemical effect on building materials and services

A variety of substances may have an aggressive effect on building foundations and on underground services. Sulphate may attack concrete; oils, tars, acids and other organic substances may attack plastic, rubber and other polymeric materials used in pipe work and service conduits or as jointing seals and protective coatings. Some substances have the ability to migrate through plastic pipes, without causing structural failure, but with serious contaminating effects on piped water supplies.

(viii) Fire

Some materials deposited on land may be of a more or less flammable nature: examples are coke particles, oils and tars, rubber, plastics and

---

[5] The issue is discussed in detail at Chap. 6.
[6] A striking example is given in the 16th Report of the Royal Commission on Environmental Pollution on Freshwater Quality (Cmnd. 1966, p. 87) where it is suggested that two former waste sites at Slacky Lane and Bentley Mill Lane, Walsall between them contribute about six tonnes a year of copper and 15 tonnes of nickel to the River Tame; this amounts to about one-sixth of the loads of these metals of the Tame at its confluence with the Trent. See also Chap. 6 generally.

many components of domestic waste. Underground combustion of such materials may come about, for example, by fires lit on the surface, by the general heating effect caused by microbial activity, or by contact with buried power cables. Once ignited, such underground fires may be extremely difficult to control and extinguish. As well as presenting a risk to structures on the surface, such fires may liberate extremely toxic gases and liquids in large quantities; examples are some of the serious fires which have occurred at major surface and underground tyre dumps.

(ix) Generation of toxic, flammable or explosive gases

Buried domestic and other putrescible wastes may decompose to form methane and other explosive and toxic gases. Such gases may migrate laterally and vertically for considerable distances following either natural geological features or service conduits. Such migration may be highly unpredictable and, if such gases accumulate in confined spaces beneath or within buildings, then significant risks are likely. In certain conditions, chemical reactions may produce highly toxic hydrogen sulphide ("bad eggs") gas.

(x) Aesthetic effects

The aesthetic effects of soil contamination are frequently overlooked, but may be difficult to eradicate and may have a serious effect on the value and marketability of property. Even relatively small quantities of oily or tarry substances may have a significant visual effect and may produce unpleasant and detectable odours. Such effects may be apparent at much lower concentrations than would be necessary to present a significant risk to health. Dyes and pigments may have a similar visual impact and substances such as phenols may have unpleasant effects on the taste of drinking water at low concentrations.

Contamination: interests and concerns

Contaminated land can be of concern to a wide variety of parties and **1.03** agencies. The following table attempts to summarise those concerns and to indicate where further discussion may be found later in this book.

Party	Main concerns	Further discussion
The general public	Protection of the environment generally; prevention of future contamination	*Chapter 5*
Owner of land	1. Liability	*Chapter 2*
	2. Costs of clean-up	*Chapter 7*
	3. Loss of value/and or unsaleability of site	*Chapter 11 Appendix B*
Occupier (owner or tenant)	1. Potential harm to health and safety of self, visitors, staff, etc.	*Chapter 2*
	2. Fitness for purpose/ inability to use property.	*Chapter 8*
	3. Liability to third parties or under lease terms.	*Chapters 2 and 11*
Lender/mortgagee	1. Protection of security.	*Chapter 11*
	2. Liability.	*Chapters 2 and 11*
Parties to corporate transactions	1. Liability.	*Chapters 2 and 12*
	2. Loss of value/ unsaleability.	*Chapter 11 and Appendix B*
	3. Fitness for purpose/ inability to utilise property or assets.	*Chapters 8 and 12*
	4. Clean-up costs.	*Chapter 7*
Developers	1. Liability.	*Chapter 2*
	2. Health and safety of site workers.	*Chapter 7*
	3. Effect on ability to develop; planning permission and building regulations approval.	*Chapter 8*
	4. Cost of remediation.	*Chapter 7*
	5. Ultimate saleability/ assurance of funders, purchasers, tenants	*Chapter 11*

Party	Main concerns	Further discussion
Local authorities	1. Potential harm to inhabitants of their area.	*Chapter 3*
	2. Nuisances.	*Chapter 2*
	3. Waste management.	*Chapter 7*
	4. Planning and building regulations approval.	*Chapter 8*
	5. Overcoming the effects of blight and its economic consequences; regeneration.	*Chapter 9*
	6. Liability - for example for failing to deal properly with enquiries.	*Chapter 3*
Urban development corporations and other regeneration agencies	1. Reclamation and regeneration.	*Chapter 9*
	2. Liability in the course of their activities.	*Chapter 2*
	3. Ensuring ultimate saleability of reclaimed land/assurance of funders, purchasers, tenants.	*Chapter 11 and Appendix B*
Water supply undertakers	1. Pollution of water resources.	*Chapter 6*
	2. Compliance with drinking water standards.	*Chapter 6*
	3. Cost of remedying contamination or its consequences.	*Chapters 6 and 7*
	4. Difficulty of pursuing polluters - public image, need for exemplary action.	*Chapters 2 and 6*
National Rivers Authority	1. Prevention of pollution of controlled waters; use of clean-up powers and prosecutions.	*Chapters 2 and 6*
	2. Consultee on planning applications and waste site applications.	*Chapters 6 and 8*

Party	Main concerns	Further discussion
National Rivers Authority—*cont.*	3. Safeguarding water sources through protection zone policies.	*Chapter 6*
	4. Achieving statutory water quality objectives.	*Chapter 6*
	5. Licensing discharges in the course of reclamation schemes.	*Chapters 2, 6 and 7*
Consultants and engineers	1. Identifying contamination.	*Chapter 3*
	2. Prioritising and advising on risks.	*Chapter 3*
	3. Advising on and implementing remedial/reclamation strategies.	*Chapter 7*
	4. Professional liability.	*Chapter 10*
Contractors	1. Health and safety of employees.	*Chapter 7*
	2. Liability for activities in the course of reclamation.	*Chapters 2 and 7*
Legal advisors	1. Protection of clients' interests generally.	*Chapters 3, 11 and 12*
	2. Advice on liabilities.	*Chapter 2*
	3. Adequate instructions to consultants.	*Chapter 10*
	4. Avoidance of personal liability.	*Chapters 3, 11 and 12*

How big a problem?

1.04　　As was pointed out by the House of Commons Environment Committee in its report, "Contaminated Land"[7] in contrast to a number of other western countries, the UK had, at that stage, never actively sought to identify contaminated sites and assess the amount of contaminated

---

[7] House of Commons, Session 1989–90, 1st Report, Vol. I, para. 22.

land comprehensively. The Welsh Office, in its memorandum submitted to the Committee,[8] referred to a survey suggesting that there were 746 contaminated land sites in Wales covering some 10,000 acres.[9] Work had also at that stage specifically been carried out by Her Majesty's Inspectorate of Pollution, in conjunction with local authorities, to identify and locate waste disposal landfill sites generating gas; this work had led to an estimate of 1,400 such sites potentially omitting gas in sufficient quantities to present hazards of fire and explosion. Apart from these two specific examples, the Committee were referred to no firm figures on contaminated land in Great Britain.

The Department of Environment in evidence to the Committee gave two different estimates.[10] One estimate, taken from sample cases, referred to at least 10,000 hectares of contaminated land in the UK; by the alternative method of extrapolating from most recent surveys of derelict land, the Department estimated a possible maximum total of 27,000 hectares of derelict land which should be classed as potentially contaminated in England (65 per cent. of the total amount of derelict land and 0.2 per cent. of the total land area). However, as numerous witnesses to the Committee pointed out, all DoE estimates excluded land which was both in use and contaminated.

Independent estimates of contaminated land offered to the Committee made an attempt to include land in current use: whilst equally imprecise, they were generally of much greater magnitude than the departmental figures. Some estimates were in the order of 50,000–100,000 potentially contaminated sites, affecting up to 50,000 hectares (150,000 acres) of land in the UK. Those consultancies putting forward such estimates did however acknowledge that only a small proportion of such land is likely to be in such a condition as to present an immediate threat to public health or to the environment.[11] Subsequent estimates have varied between 5,000 and 200,000 sites and up to 600,000 acres.[12] Any figure will inevitably be coloured by the use of different assumptions as to contaminative potential, extent and risk.[12a]

---

[8] *Ibid.*, Vol. III, App. II.

[9] Friends of the Earth in 1992 produced a further survey of the position in Wales referring to nearly 1000 sites in a condition such as to pose a threat to the environment or to health.

[10] *Ibid.*, Vol. I, para. 23.

[11] *Ibid.*, Vol. I, para. 24.

[12] Figures put forward at University of Cambridge Programme for Industry Seminar, "Contaminated Land. Science vs. Policy?" November 27, 1992. The CBI in its paper "Firm Foundations: CBI Proposals for Environmental Liability and Contaminated Land" (1993) suggested the area affected might be in the order of 200,000 hectares.

[12a] See the Government Consultation paper "Paying for Our Past" (March 1994), para. 2.10.

15

In the Department of Environment's 1993 study of the development capacity of the East Thames corridor it was estimated that of land listed in the report as having development potential, 19 per cent. had been put to uses involving the greatest hazards for redevelopment, such as gas and coke works, waste and scrap metal sites and petroleum and chemical manufacturing and refining plants.[13]

When the Government published its Environmental White Paper, "This Common Inheritance: Britain's Environmental Strategy"[14] in September 1990, the position was presented even more tentatively. In the brief section of the White Paper dealing with "derelict and contaminated sites," reference was made to the 1988 Derelict Land Survey which showed that, despite reclamation of 14,000 hectares since 1992, large areas of land required action. A total of about 40,000 hectares was derelict, three-quarters of which justified reclamation measures. In relation to contamination, as opposed to dereliction, all that the Government was able to say in the White Paper is:[15]

> "Contamination of land by chemicals and waste products is hard to define and measure exactly, but surveys suggest that over half of derelict land might be contaminated, and contamination is also found on other land. The nature of contamination and the possible risks to health and ground water supplies vary widely, and the Government needs better assessments of the scale of the problem."

The solution to this uncertainty at one stage proposed by the Government was the creation of registers of land subject to contaminative uses under section 143 of the Environmental Protection Act 1990; this proposal has however now been withdrawn.[16]

Examples of problems

1.05   The House of Commons Environment Committee Report[17] received evidence of a number of sites where serious problems had occurred as the result of contamination; other examples have subsequently been reported. The list given below is merely illustrative of the types of problems which can occur in practice.[17a]

---

[13] Llewelyn-Davies, "East Thames Corridor: A Study of Development Capacity and Potential" (HMSO, 1993) para. 4.52.
[14] Cm. 1200.
[15] *Ibid.*, para. 6.62.
[16] See Chap. 3.
[17] See n.7 above.
[17a] Another list is given in the report of the Parliamentary Office of Science and Technology, "Contaminated Land" (October 1993), p. 6, Box 2.1.

Chemical contamination	
Various sites within the area of Amber Valley, Derbyshire contaminated by lead, acid leachates, dioxins and gasworks residues.	Select Committee Report, Vol. I, para. 32.
Chemstar Site, Greater Manchester: contamination of former solvent recovery works where explosion and fire occurred in 1981: asbestos contamination removed at cost of £530,000; problems remaining of contamination of site and nearby gardens by solvents and up to 400 chemicals.	Select Committee Report, Vol. I. paras. 34–35.
Thamesmead, London Borough of Greenwich: housing estate built on filled quarry; contamination by toxic metals and "blue billy" gasworks waste. Remedial measures (partly funded by Derelict Land Grant) cost £250,000 at 1979 prices.	Select Committee Report, Vol. I, para. 36; see also *London Evening Standard*, March 29, 1993.
Hayle, Cambourne and other villages in Cornwall; garden soils with arsenic levels reportedly more than one part per hundred as a result of eighteenth and nineteenth century mining and smelting. No health effects apparent.	*The Observer*, March 8, 1992.
Shipham, Somerset; high soil concentrations of cadmium, resulting from abandoned zinc mines, found in gardens. No observed health effects.	*The Observer*, March 8, 1992.
Lumsden Road, Portsmouth; contamination of housing estate resulting from former "Glory Hole" site used for dumping wastes from naval yards between the wars; arsenic, asbestos, cadmium, and mercury among the substances. Residents evacuated.	*The Independent*, November 2, 1991; *Environment Business*, Supplement, February 1993.
Pembrey Country Park, Llanelli, Dyfed; possible contamination by explosives and other chemicals from former Royal Ordnance factory.	*The Observer*, June 14, 1992.
Bolsover, Derbyshire; alleged contamination of farmland by dioxins from Coalite Chemical works.	*The Independent*, March 26, 1992.

Chemical contamination—*cont.*	
St Mary's Island, River Medway; contamination from former Chatham naval dockyard. Clean-up completed by English Estates in 1993. In excess of 1.2m cubic metres of material contaminated by heavy metals and blue asbestos was removed.	*Environment Business,* Supplement, February 1993.
Neston Tank Cleaners, Queensferry, Clywd, Wales: contamination by oils, tars and solvents from tar distillery and tank farm. Area compulsorily purchased by local authority for remediation.	Environment Business, June 1993, p.4.
Winsor Park Estate, Beckton, East London: Estate owned by housing associations on former gasworks. Residents complaining of illnesses. 80 residents given legal aid to take action.	*The Times,* June 14, 1994.
Radioactive substances	
Former Laporte Works, Ilford: contamination of site of old gas-mantle factory by mildly radioactive thorium and radium. Programme of remedial works expected to cost in excess of £11m.	Select Committee Report, Vol. I, para. 37.
Great Cambridge Road, Enfield: retail site contaminated by materials including low-level radium 226 from former instrument-dial factory.	*Environment Business,* March 24, 1993.
Gases	
Explosion at Loscoe, Derbyshire from gas generated by putrescible matter in infilled quarry.	Report of non-statutory inquiry, Vols. I and II. 1987.
Ennerdale Road, Doncaster: council houses for the elderly built on former landfill site. "Pump and disperse" system used to reduce carbon dioxide and methane emissions to harmless levels.	*Environment Law Brief,* February 1993.
Boilly Lane, Killamarsh, Sheffield: migration of gas from former coal mines; five houses affected; remedial works by British Coal.	*The Surveyor,* February 6, 1992.
Kenilworth, Warwickshire: house built in 1981 on landfill site; high methane levels detected. Owners now suing builder and surveyor.	*The Times,* June 14, 1994.

Underground fires	
Callywhite Lane Industrial Site, Dronfield, Derbyshire: former tip developed in 1970s; signs of underground fire noticed in 1984. Subsequently affected safety of buildings. Local authority ordered to take remedial action under statutory nuisance provisions of Public Health Act 1936 at a cost of £600,000.	Select Committee Report, Vol. I, para. 33; *The Guardian*, February 1, 1990.
Underground fire at tyre dump, Powys, Wales; smouldered for 4 years; cost of extinguishing it by injection of liquid nitrogen followed by excavation, estimated at £4 million. Threat of water pollution; plans to divert local stream	*Sunday Telegraph*, January 16, 1994; *Surveyor*, January 27, 1994.
Asbestos	
Armley, Leeds; contamination of housing estate by asbestos dust from asbestos products factory; up to 258 houses (90 per cent. of the estate) affected. Early estimates of decontamination costs put at £6.3m (£7,500 per house)	*The Independent*, August 8, 1992.
Explosives	
Waltham Park, Waltham Abbey: proposal for 256 houses, business park and golf course on site of former Royal Ordnance explosives factory; opposed by local planning authority on safety grounds.	*The Times*, December 30, 1991.
Water pollution	
Sawston Mill, Cambridgeshire: pollution of statutory water company borehole by chlorinated solvents from tannery. Subsequent legal action by water company .	See para. 2.22.
Concern as to polluting effects of various old landfill sites on groundwater.	See para. 2.54.
Contamination of public supplies at Peterborough, Cambridgeshire by pesticide wastes from local disposal sites.	*The Independent*, February 13, 1992.

19

Water pollution—*cont.*	
Pollution of River Fal waterway system, Truro, Cornwall: metal contaminated water from Wheal Jane tin mine; serious effects on water quality, amenity and local economy.	*The Guardian*, February 14, 1992.

UK policy approaches

1.06   The House of Commons Select Committee suggested that any future policy on contaminated land should comprise the following elements:[18]

- improving holdings of information about contaminated land and raising awareness and technical proficiency among those involved in regulation and clean-up;
- preventing new generation of contaminated land;
- cleaning up contaminated land (removing contamination); and
- protecting people and the environment from the effects of contamination.

In relation to these policy areas, the key recommendations of the Committee included the following:

(1) the DoE should concern itself with all land that is contaminated so as to be a potential hazard to health or the environment, regardless of the use to which the land is to be put;

(2) a consistent approach should be taken to pollution of soil regardless of the initial cause of contamination;

(3) a range of quality objectives and standards should be derived and implemented for different classes of land use and for designated sensitive areas;

(4) a duty should be placed on local authorities to seek out and compile registers of contaminated land using a common methodology to be refined and published by the DoE;

(5) the Government should bring forward legislation to place upon vendors a duty to declare information in their possession about contamination present on site, however caused; and

(6) legislation should impose on operators (whether or not subject to other types of pollution control) a duty to carry out their activities in a way which avoids soil pollution.

These recommendations represent only a few of the 29 made by the Committee; they do, however, constitute the main recommendations as to the major thrust of policy.

[18] House of Commons, Session 1989–90, First Report, Vol. I, p. xi.

The Government, in its response to the Select Committee Report, identified three key issues for future action:[19]

(a) compilation of better public information on where land may be contaminated;

(b) development of a range of quality assessment criteria to which clean-up methods would be directed; and

(c) review of levels of central Government grand support to assist demonstration and clean-up programmes.

In relation to the issue of information, the Government's response referred to the work of an internal DoE working party, which had come to the view that there were genuine risks in terms of blight in carrying out enquiries on the extent of contaminated land, but that those problems could be reduced if information was compiled on previous or existing uses carrying a *potential* for contamination: such assessments could then provide a suitable basis for further sites and specific surveys as and when the need arose.[20] On that basis, the Government opted for registers of potentially, as opposed to actually, contaminated land, as embodied in section 143 of the Environmental Protection Act; the Government's justification for that option in terms of avoiding blight seems somewhat ironical in the light and subsequent history of the proposal for section 143 registers.[21]

In relation to the proposal of the Committee for reversal of the caveat emptor rule, the Government initially took the view that reversal of the rule would assist in early identification of contaminated land. However, the subsequent outcome of an inquiry by the Law Commission Standing Committee on Conveyancing into the principle of the caveat emptor rule came down in favour of retaining caveat emptor.[22] In the light of this report, the Government's final position was that heightened awareness of the problems of contamination, together with availability of registers identifying potentially contaminated land, would encourage purchasers and their solicitors to seek more information about contamination within conveyancing enquiry procedures and without the need for further legislative changes.[23]

On the issue of establishing quality objectives and standards, the Government expressed the view that the need for quality objectives for broad categories of end use was already met, to a significant extent, in

---

[19] Department of Environment, "Contaminated Land," Cm. 1161, July 1990, Introduction para. (ix).

[20] *Ibid.*, para. 2.3.

[21] See Chap. 3.

[22] See Chap. 11.

[23] Department of Environment, "Contaminated Land," Cm. 1161, July 1990, para. 2.11.

the current use of the advisory ICRCL "trigger concentrations."[24] The Government accepted that more weight needed to be given to the environmental implications of contamination, and suggested that consideration could be given to the need to amend trigger values in vulnerable areas, such as water protection zones. However, the Government suggested that this would be best done, on a case by case basis, in consultation with the National Rivers Authority and other interested parties.[25]

The recommendation of the Committee for a general statutory duty to avoid soil contamination was rejected. The Government took the view that the new proposals contained in Part I of the Environmental Protection Act for integrated pollution control, together with provisions in Part II of the Act—for example on the duty of care relating to waste and aftercare of waste disposal sites—rendered any such general provision unnecessary.[26] The Government, however, accepted the recommendation that a consistent approach should be taken to pollution of soil, regardless of the initial cause of the contamination—though the Government felt that the most heavily contaminated sites were likely to be those affected by site-specific activity, rather than by diffuse contamination.[27]

Therefore, development of a coherent policy on contaminated land in the UK remains at a relatively early stage, notwithstanding the considerable attention which has been given to the subject since the Commons Committee's Report. The most recent document to come from the Government, "Paying for Our Past"[27a] reveals that fundamental issues of policy on objectives, means, liability and information are still fluid. The proposal for registers of potentially contaminative uses has been an early casualty, having been dropped for fear of blight and uncertainty in the absence of any coherent general framework for dealing with land (and allocating financial responsibility) once identified as potentially contaminated.[28] Considerable progress also needs to be made on technical issues such as sampling strategies and a systematic framework for assessment and prioritisation of sites, as well as methodologies for arriving at soil quality standards and the selection of remedial technologies. The Department of Environment and the Construction Industry Research and Information Association (CIRIA) both have comprehensive programmes of research contracts and details of current research is given at Appendix E.

[24] *Ibid.*, para. 5.4.
[25] *Ibid.*, paras. 3.1 and 5.5.
[26] *Ibid.*, para. 5.13. See also Chap. 5.
[27] *Ibid.*, para. 5.3.
[27a] DOE/Welsh Office, March 1994.
[28] Department of Environment Press Notice 209, March 24, 1993; see also Chap. 3.

The funding of clean-up remains a major problematic issue in terms of the balance between public funding by way of grants or credit approvals for local authorities, as against application of the polluter pays principle by seeking to recover costs of clean-up from sources other than the public purse. Such matters involve considerable work in reviewing the whole issue of liability, and in seeking to arrive at both equitable and efficient financial provisions for action on priority sites.[29]

To a considerable extent, though not exclusively, policy on contamination is likely to be linked to more general policies on derelict land, with the overall aim of bringing such land back into constructive use. The Government admitted in its September 1990 White Paper that further measures would be required to prevent dereliction and to facilitate reclamation of derelict land.[30] Such measures, the Government indicated, could include:[31]

> "Extending local authorities' existing powers to tackle dereliction on privately owned sites, by making the reclamation works eligible for grant assistance, but providing clear powers for any costs reasonably incurred to be recoverable from the owner, either immediately or when the owner sells the land."

The issue was further considered by the Government's consultation paper, "Proposals to Prevent Land Becoming Derelict,"[32] where the options mooted were the extended use of restoration conditions in planning consents and the strengthening of local authority powers under planning legislation to require owners to remedy the condition of land. The paper concluded that given the scale of dereliction and the lack of demand in many parts of the country, grant régimes would be needed for some time; however, the Department felt that the proposals for placing greater responsibility on land owners would serve to make the holding of derelict land less attractive and market reclamation more attractive, thus, over time, lessening the flow of land into dereliction.

Naturally occurring contamination: radon

It is a mistake to assume that all problems of contamination stem from **1.07** human activity: harmful concentrations of metals, gases and other substances can occur naturally in the environment.[32a] Potentially haz-

---

[29] On the issue of liability, generally see Chap. 2. For an alternative approach, focussing on how to create the wealth to pay for clean-up, rather than who should pay, see R. Jackson, *Can we cut the Gordian Knot?* [1994] 9423 E.G. 114.

[30] "This Common Inheritance: Britain's Environmental Strategy," Cm. 1200, September 1900, para. 6.66.

[31] On this issue, see further, para. 2.76 below.

[32] DoE, February 1992.

[32a] See the discussion in "Contaminated Land" (Parliamentary Office of Science and Technology, October 1993), para. 2.23.

ardous gases such as methane and carbon monoxide can be found naturally in certain conditions, as can the radioactive gas radon which is produced naturally by the decay of heavy elements such as radium and uranium. It has been estimated that around 100,000 houses in the UK, mainly in Devon and Cornwall, are subject to levels of radon which present sufficient health risks to cause concern.[33]

These concerns began to be recognised during the 1980s and in January 1987 the then Minister of State for the Environment announced that the UK Government was in response to advice from the National Radiological Protection Board (NRPB),[34] implementing a programme on radon.[35] There followed the production of advice, "The Householders' Guide to Radon"[36] which provides guidance as to the problems and solutions. In January 1990 the Government announced[37] a reduction by 50 per cent. of the existing action level for radon, from 400 to 200 becquerels per cubic metre (Bq.m³). In November 1990 the NRPB formally designated Devon and Cornwall as Radon Affected Areas, the implication being that all homes in such on area should have radon measurements made.[38] A programme of surveys is indertaken principally by the DoE, acting through the NRPB: these are either "directed surveys" as part of a selective programme or "on demand" surveys carried out at the request of individual householders. Further work has been carried out by the Building Research Establishment (BRE)[39] and measures to avoid danger to health and safety from radon are required by the Building Regulations.[40]

The issue of radon was considered by the House of Commons Environment Committee in its 1991 Report, "Indoor Air Pollution"[41]— the conclusion being that the rate of progress in identifying homes affected by radon had in the past been too slow. The Government has recognised the need for urgency[42] and work has now been completed on

---

[33] Dr. S. Wozniak, "Ground for Concern," L.S.Gaz., No. 28, July 22, 1992, p. 19; M. Tyler and K. Mylrea, "Radon—A Rising Issue," Property Journal, October 1990, p. 6.

[34] "Exposure to Radon Dangers in Dwellings," ASP–10 (HMSO, 1987).

[35] Hansard, January 27, 1987, cols. 189–197.

[36] (3rd ed.) (1992).

[37] NRPB, "Human Exposure to Radon in Homes." Documents of the NRPB 1(1) (HMSO, 1990).

[38] NRPB, "Radon Affected Areas: Cornwall and Devon." Documents of the NRPB 1(4) (HMSO, 1990).

[39] BRE, "Radon: Guidance on Protective Measures for New Dwellings" (HMSO, 1991).

[40] See para. 8.16 generally.

[41] Session 1990–91, Sixth Report.

[42] Cm. 1633: "Government Response to the Sixth Report from the House of Commons Select Committee on the Environment."

assessing the extent of Radon Affected Areas in Derbyshire, North-amptonshire, and Somerset.[43]

Identifying contaminated land

The identification of potentially contaminated land is important for **1.08** many different purposes, for both public authorities and private individuals and companies. Complete certainty in this area is rarely if ever possible, but there are a variety of techniques which can be used to assess whether land may be subject to contamination, the nature of that contamination and the possible risks which it presents. These range from "desk studies" of available documentary sources of information on the site, through to full site investigations with sampling and analysis of soil and groundwater. The issue of identification and appraisal is dealt with in detail in Chapter 4 and information sources are discussed in Chapter 3.

Institutions dealing with contaminated land

The fragmented approach towards contaminated land problems taken **1.09** in the UK undoubtedly reflects, to some extent, the number of different institutions having responsibility for policy and action in this field. The main bodies currently having such responsibilities include the following:

(1) *Her Majesty's Inspectorate of Pollution* (in Scotland, HM Industrial Pollutions Inspectorate) in relation to contamination by processes subject to integrated pollution control, and in relation to contamination involving special waste.[44]

(2) *National River Authority* (River Purification Authorities in Scotland) in relation to contamination with implications for the pollution of controlled waters, and in relation to proposals which may give rise to such contamination.[45]

(3) *Local Waste Regulation Authorities* (County Councils or Metropolitan Waste Authorities) in relation to the deposit of controlled waste on land and in relation to development control functions involving the deposit of such waste.[46]

(4) *District Councils* in relation to other types of development control, control under the Building Regulations, and in relation to statutory nuisance.[47]

---

[43] NRPB, "Radon Affected Areas: Derbyshire, Northamptonshire and Somerset." Documents of the NRPB 3(4) (HMSO, 1992).
[44] As to special waste, see para. 5.31.
[45] See Chap. 6.
[46] See para. 5.18.
[47] See para. 2.65 and Chap. 8.

(5) *The Health and Safety Executive* in relation to hazards arising in or from the workplace, including some risks arising from remediation of contaminated land, and in relation to certain regulations made under the Health and Safety at Work, *etc.* Act 1974 which have a bearing on contamination, for example those relating to asbestos and lead.[48]

(6) *The Departments of State* (the Department of Environment, Scottish Office and Welsh Office), have responsibility in relation to the formation of policy on contaminated land, as well as carrying out a number of supervisory and appellate functions in relation to decision made by other authorities; they also administer the relevant systems of grant aid.[49]

(7) *Regeneration agencies.* (The Urban Regeneration Agency—known as English Partnerships—and the various urban development corporations) deal with the reclamation and regeneration of damaged or derelict land, with substantial powers of compulsory purchase.[50]

(8) *The Interdepartmental Committee on the Redevelopment of Contaminated Land* (ICRCL). When the Commons Environment Committee reported in 1989, they expressed the view that the ICRCL had been attempting to fulfil three functions, those of developing standards, providing advice and developing policy; the Committee felt that those tasks could best be performed by structures within the DoE and recommended that the ICRCL should be abolished. The Government did not accept that recommendation, and was satisfied that the ICRCL should continue to provide a useful focus for the development of technical guidance in the area; however, the Government announced that in future, the role of the ICRCL would be to ensure liaison and to facilitate input from other Government departments, rather than to oversee work on the development of contaminated land policy or research, including clean-up criteria.[51] The Government announced at the same time its intention to reconstitute its Contaminated Land Branch, within the Central Directorate of Environmental Pollution, to coordinate policy and to manage the programme for research within the area. It would fall to this branch to prepare guidance notes and to disseminate advice on contaminated land.

Greater coherence should result from the Government's proposals for creation of a unified environment agency, although there will remain the

[48] See Chap. 7.
[49] See Chap. 9.
[50] See Chap. 9.
[51] Department of Environment, "Contaminated Land" Cm. 1161, July 1990, para. 5.10.

dichotomy between policy-making and regulatory functions, and between control at central and local levels.

The European Community dimension

In all areas of environmental law, it is essential to pay close attention **1.10** to the underlying law and policy of the European Community. Contaminated land is no exception, although it should be stressed at the outset that Community policy on this issue is extremely rudimentary when compared with other environmental issues. Certain E.C. measures have a bearing on contaminated land, although they are not directly concerned with the subject; the main examples are the various Community measures on waste management[52] and the directive on protection of ground water.[53] It may also be that the general attention being given by the Community to issues of liability for environmental harm or impairment will have an important bearing on this area, although this seems likely to occur in the medium rather than the short term; these various measures and initiatives are considered in the text in conjunction with the relevant UK policy and law.[54]

Article 130R of the European Community Treaty, as amended by the Maastricht Treaty on European Union, requires that Community policy on the environment shall contribute to the pursuit of (*inter alia*) preserving, protecting and improving the quality of environment; and protecting human health. Paragraph 2 of the Article goes on to state that Community policy on the environment shall aim "at a high level of protection taking into account the diversity of situations in the various regions of the Community." It must be based on the following principles:

   (i) the precautionary principle;
  (ii) the principle that preventative action should be taken;
 (iii) the principle that environmental damage should as a priority be
       rectified as source; and
  (iv) the principle that the polluter should pay.

All of these principles may be seen as highly relevant to the development of a Community policy on contamination of land.

In March 1992, the European Commission adopted the fifth of its environmental action programmes designed to protect and enhance the quality of the environment in the Community.[55] This programme

---

[52] See para. 5.40.
[53] See para. 6.08.
[54] See para. 2.81.
[55] "Towards Sustainability: a European Community Programme of policy and action in relation to the environment and sustainable development" COM(29) 23 Final, Vols. I–III.

contains relatively little which deals directly with soil contamination, although such contamination is identified at section 5.5 as one of the problems relating to "the urban environment." To judge from the action programme, the main concern of the Community in relation to soil contamination would appear to be its effects of groundwater quality. Section 5.4, on the management of water resources, sets the following three objectives in relation to ground water:

> (i) to maintain the quality of uncontaminated ground water;
> (ii) to prevent further contamination of contaminated ground water; and
> (iii) to restore contaminated groundwater to a quality required for drinking water production purposes.

In relation to these objectives, a target is given running to the year 2000 to prevent all pollution of ground water from point sources and to reduce pollution from diffuse sources, according to best environmental practices and best available technology.

Community developments in relation to liability for the cost of repairing environmental damage may also have a bearing on UK policy in this area in due course.[56]

Comparative approaches

1.11 It is instructive to compare the approaches taken to the problem of contaminated land in other jurisdictions. Whilst there may be variations in legal systems, industrial history and soil and geological conditions, problems such as leaking oil tanks, spillages of solvent from drums and inadequately engineered waste facilities tend to be common throughout the developed world.

As already mentioned,[57] it is to countries such as the United States and The Netherlands that one turns to find examples of the most serious soil contamination incidents so far recorded in developed countries (excluding those of the former Eastern bloc); the fact that legislation is further advanced is probably symptomatic of the significant problems encountered there. This is not to say that solutions adopted in other countries are to be followed without question; comparisons can be equally as useful in terms of learning from mistakes as from successes. Certainly, the House of Commons Environment Committee in its Contaminated Land Report was in some respects critical of both the Dutch and the US approaches. In particular, in relation to The Netherlands, it was questioned whether the approach of multifunc-

---

[56] See para. 2.81.
[57] See Preamble, nn. 2 and 3.

28

tionality was a sensible use of resources: the object of this policy is to clean up contaminated sites in such a way that any end use is possible— as the Committee put it "in effect, to return contaminated land to a pristine condition in which it would be fit for agriculture, irrespective of the intended use of the site."[58] The Committee accepted that multifunctionality might well represent a worthwhile policy objective, if only as a counsel of perfection, given the unusual hydrogeology of The Netherlands: however, the Committee rejected the concept as a basis for future UK policy on the basis that cost would far outweigh the benefits and indeed that it was scientifically and technically impossible to clean many sites fully without merely shifting the problem elsewhere.[59] The Government, in its response to the Commons Committee's Report agreed with that view that the concept of multifunctionality should be rejected as a basis for cleaning up contaminated land.[60] This appears to be vindicated as a decision in that the Dutch are currently re-evaluating the multifunctionality approach.[61]

Similarly, the approach taken by the United States under the Comprehensive Environmental Response, Compensation and Liability Act 1980, and other "Superfund" legislation was subject to critical scrutiny by the Committee. The impression of the committee was that the Superfund programme was excessively bureaucratic, complex, costly and largely ineffectual—as the matter was put in a memorandum submitted to the Committee in evidence:[62]

> "The net effect is a lengthening queue of sites awaiting classification, a small number of clean-ups, and endless expensive litigation to determine who was responsible for depositing which wastes where and when—and, therefore, who should pay the remedial costs."

The Netherlands and United States are by no means the only countries which could be cited as examples of alternative approaches to the problem of contaminated land: considerable strides have been made in this respect in Germany, Canada and Australia. In order to include within this book some comparative material, a brief summary is given at Chapter 13 as to the policy approaches and legal position in various significant jurisdictions; it is hoped that this comparative material will be helpful by way of analogy or contrast with the UK position.

[58] House of Commons Environment Committee, Session 1989–90, First Report, "Contaminated Land," Vol. I, para. 61.
[59] *Ibid.*, para. 66 and conclusion 5(i).
[60] Department of Environment, "Contaminated Land," Cm. 1161, July 1990, para. 3.1.
[61] See Chap. 13.
[62] House of Commons Environment Committee Report, para. 70, referring to a written memorandum submitted by Mrs. Sonia Withers and Mr. Richard Hawkins.

Chapter 2

LIABILITY

Introduction

2.01   Issues of liability for contaminated land are a natural focus of attention for lawyers and source of concern to their clients. Such concern is concentrated by the awareness of aggressive liability regimes applying in other countries[1] and by actual or tentative proposals within the Council of Europe and European Community[2] which may ultimately require substantial changes to the UK approach.

One of the self-evident problems of any liability scheme for contaminated land is that land, of its nature, can change hands; concurrent estates and interests can also be created in it. A range of parties may therefore be potentially responsible, thus raising policy issues to be addressed and policy choices to be made.

Another important feature of contaminated land is its stability and permanence when compared with the other media of air and water; a contaminated site *may* become less of a problem over time but, unlike a slug of pollution in a watercourse, it will not go away. Indeed, the problems of uncontained and migrating contaminants may only become apparent after some years. There is thus the possibility for "long tail" liability many years after the actions which may have created the problem; with this there goes the prospect of retrospective liability, *i.e.*, liability for conduct which when undertaken was in breach of no legally binding requirements and which may indeed have been in accordance with current accepted best practice. If experience in the USA and other jurisdictions is any guide, it is this feature of retrospective liability which is likely to be the most controversial of all aspects.[3]

Finally, there is the relationship between contaminated land and land policy generally. Wider considerations may influence the policy adopted

---

[1] See Chaps 1 and 13.
[2] See paras. 2.80–2.82.
[3] See for example, Advisory Committee on Business and the Environment, "Report of the Financial Sector Working Group" (DTI and DoE, 1993) Part III.

on liability in order to achieve goals such as urban regeneration or the restoration of derelict land. For example, the issue was addressed briefly in the Government's white paper. "This Common Inheritance"[4] at paragraph 6.66, where it was suggested that further measures were needed to prevent dereliction and that amongst the options under consideration were the widening of powers to tackle dereliction (including contamination) on privately-owned sites: including powers of cost recovery from the owner either immediately or on disposal. The Government's review of the arrangements for controlling and remedying contaminated land includes issues of liability.[4a] No firm conclusions have yet been reached, but the Government has not ruled out the possibility of changes to the common law and suggests that the current mix of strict and fault-based approaches strikes a reasonable balance.[4b] Nor does the Government see it as inconsistent with the polluter pays principle to provide for the enforcement of regulatory obligations on others, especially the owner.[4c]

Nature of liability

Liability for contaminated land can arise in various forms of which **2.02** essentially there are three:

(1) Criminal liability

Various statutes may impose criminal liability, for example offences in relation to waste management, water pollution, statutory nuisance and health and safety matters.

(2) Civil liability

Where contaminated land causes harm to persons or property, or interference with recognised rights (such as the right of a water abstractor or riparian owner) civil liability may arise on ordinary principles.

(3) "Clean-up costs"

Whether or not an offence has been committed or civil liability has been incurred, a variety of statutory provisions may give rise to liability by allowing or requiring the relevant authority either—

[4] Cm. 1200, September 1990.
[4a] See Chap. 3.
[4b] "Paying for Our Past: the arrangements for controlling contaminated land and meeting the costs of remedying to the environment" (DoE/Welsh Office, March 1994).
[4c] *Ibid.*

(a) to serve notice requiring remedial measures to be taken, *e.g.* abatement notices for statutory nuisance; or

(b) to carry out remedial work itself and to recover the cost, *e.g.* powers under section 61 of the Environmental Protection Act 1990 or section 161 of the Water Resources Act 1991.

The law, both statutory and judge-made, has developed on a piece-meal basis and without any clear conceptual framework. Thus in terms of statutory provisions, liability may turn on the nature of the con-tamination (in particular, whether or not it is waste) and its effect (*e.g.* whether controlled waters are affected).

The general scheme of the chapter is to consider first the issues of civil liability and then to address together the statutory provisions as to criminal liability and clean-up costs.

CIVIL LIABILITY

Civil liability generally

2.03   Any attempt to extract clear principles from the common law relating to environmental problems is an exercise certain to lead to frustration. The basic ingredients of the law of tort are well known:

(a) nuisance;

(b) negligence;

(c) trespass; and

(d) the rule in *Rylands* v. *Fletcher*.

To these may be added, in appropriate cases:

(e) action for breach of statutory duty.

What is far from clear is how these various components inter-relate and to what extent their requirements differ. It can be argued, and has been, that nuisance is merely a subset of negligence; that *Rylands* v. *Fletcher* grew from, and is really part of, the law of nuisance; and that *Rylands* v. *Fletcher* has been substantially overtaken and emasculated by principles of negligence.

In many areas of fundamental importance the law remains uncertain, for example the extent to which negligence or foreseeability of harm are relevant to the tort of nuisance. It has been said of nuisance that it is ". . . both attacked and burdened because it has lost all sense of that for which it stands. It needs to rediscover its own principles before it can turn its attention to the protection of the world.[5]

[5] C. Gearty, "The Place of Private Nuisance in a Modern Law of Torts" [1989] C.L.J. 214, at 216; see also F.H. Newark, "The Boundaries of Nuisance" (1949) 65 L.Q.R. 480.

Such confusion is reflected in recent cases. Actions are usually brought relying on a number of different legal bases, and it may be unpredictable which issues will be fastened on the court. In the Irish case of *Hanrahan* v. *Merck Sharp & Dohme (Ireland) Ltd.*[6] an action against a pharmaceutical plant in respect of allegedly harmful emissions was based on negligence, nuisance and *Rylands* v. *Fletcher*; the Supreme Court concurred with the trial judge who treated the claim solely as one in nuisance.

In the case of *Cambridge Water Company* v. *Eastern Counties Leather plc*[7] a claim for pollution of a supply borehole by chlorinated solvents from two tanneries was brought in negligence, nuisance and *Rylands* v. *Fletcher*. The trial judge considered all three heads, devoting most attention to *Rylands* v. *Fletcher* and ultimately dismissing the claim on all three grounds. The Court of Appeal focussed instead on the nuisance aspect and held one of the two tanneries liable, making only brief (and obscure) reference to the main arguments put to them on the *Rylands* v. *Fletcher* issue.[8] On appeal to the House of Lords, *Rylands* v. *Fletcher* again became a dominant issue.[9]

It is beyond the scope of this chapter to provide a detailed summary of the various components of the law of tort, in respect of which reference should be made to the standard texts. However, the main strengths and weaknesses of each area in relation to typical contaminated land issues will be referred to, together with those areas where the law is still developing and remains inherently uncertain.

In practice there will be two main variables which need to be assimilated: how the contamination arose and the type of harm to which it gave rise. These may well affect the appropriate cause of action.

Cause of contamination:

    (a) deliberate deposit of waste materials;
    (b) "active" accidental spillages in the course of handling materials;
    (c) "passive" accidental spillages, *e.g.* from a leaking pipe or tank;
    (d) deposition of emitted airborne materials;
    (e) release of contaminants by excavating or otherwise disturbing already contaminated soil.

Nature of damage:

    (a) physical injury or harm to health;
    (b) physical damage to property;
    (c) interference with ordinary comfort and enjoyment of land;

[6] [1988] I.L.R.M. 629.
[7] [1992] Env.L.R. 116.
[8] [1994] 2 W.L.R. 53; [1993] Env.L.R. 287; [1994] J.E.L. Vol. 6, No. 1, p. 137. The case is referred to in detail in various paras. below.
[9] [1994] 2 W.L.R. 53.

(d) interference with the exercise of rights, *e.g.* riparian or abstraction rights;

(e) diminution in the value of property, *e.g.* by rendering it unsuitable for development without expenditure.

Direct or immediate damage: trespass

2.04   Trespass is of potential application to environmental actions, though in practice its use in contaminated land situations is likely to be limited. Such limitation stems from the historic roots of the tort: in its original form the tort was one for which the writ of trespass—"that fertile mother of actions"—would lie.[10] The writ was the remedy for all forcible and direct injuries, whether to persons or to property and in that sense was the antithesis of the action of trespass on the case (or simply "case") which dealt with injuries which were consequential as opposed to forcible and direct. The test was whether the injury followed so immediately upon the act of the defendant as to be a direct part of the act as opposed to a consequence of it.[11] In the *Prior of Southwark's Case*[12] the prior complained because the defendant, a glover, had made a lime pit for calf-skins so close to a stream as to pollute it (possibly one of the earliest reported cases on contaminated land). It was held that if the glover had dug the lime pit in the prior's soil the action ought to be in trespass; but if it was made in the glover's soil it should be an action on the case.

In practice this means that trespass will be of limited application to the typical contaminated land situation. As well as its more obvious manifestations, the tort includes the placing or projecting of any object or substance on to the plaintiff's land: this has been held in one Canadian case to include the accidental discharge of carbon monoxide gas from a vehicle exhaust into a dwelling.[13] Thus the placing of waste or some noxious substance on the plaintiff's land would be trespass,[14] as would placing it on the boundary so that it falls onto or comes into contact with the plaintiff's land.[15] In that respect trespass is not limited to incursions on the surface, and trespass may be committed to underlying strata.[16] Thus, for example, trespass might be committed

[10] Salmond and Heuston, *The Law of Torts* (20th ed., 1992) p. 5.
[11] *Ibid.*, p. 6.
[12] (1498) Y.B. 13 Hen. 7, f.26, pl.4; summarised by Denning L.J. in *Southport Corporation* v. *Esso Petroleum Co. Ltd.* [1954] 2 Q.B. 182, at 195.
[13] *McDonald* v. *Associated Fuels* [1954] 3 D.L.R. 775.
[14] Salmond and Heuston, *op. cit.*, p. 48.
[15] *Simpson* v. *Weber* (1925) 41 T.L.R. 302; *Westripp* v. *Baldock* [1939] 1 All E.R. 279.
[16] *Corbett* v. *Hill* (1870) L.R. 9 Eq. 671, 673.

where an occupier of land or contractor, in carrying out engineering works, breaches some form of containment which results in the immediate ingress of contaminated material on to the plaintiff's land.

More typically however, pollutants will leach or migrate over a period of months or years as the result of gravity, groundwater flow, or gas generation. Such incursions will be consequential rather than direct, and so arguably trespass will not be an appropriate remedy.[17] As was said in the Irish case of *Hanrahan* v. *Merck, Sharp & Dohme (Ireland) Ltd.*[18]:

> "the claim based on trespass has not been proceeded with, presumably because it could not readily be said that any of the loss or damage complied of was a direct or immediate result of the acts complained of. The loss or damage could more properly be said to be an consequential on the conduct complained of."

However, there is at least one decision which suggests that matter deposited on the plaintiff's land by the back washes and under currents of a tidal river constitutes a trespass.[19]

A further restriction is that trespass will be actionable only by the person in possession of the land, *e.g.* entitled to immediate and exclusive possession.[20]

However, if the difficulties of direct injury and title to sue can be surmounted, trespass is a powerful remedy since it is actionable irrespective of fault and without proof of actual damage.[21] Where damage is caused, the measure of damages will be the resulting loss to the plaintiff: whether this is the diminution in value of the land or the cost of reinstatement will depend on the circumstances.[22]

---

[17] *Tenant* v. *Goldwin* (1704) 2 Ld. Ray. 1089; *Price's Patent Candle Co.* v. *L.C.C.* [1908] 2 Ch. 526. The availability of trespass as a remedy has also been doubled where oil is discharged in navigable waters and is carried by the flow: see *Southport Corporation* v. *Esso Petroleum Co.* [1954] 2 Q.B. 182 at 195 and [1956] A.C. 218 at 242 and 244; but *c.f.* the same case at [1953] 3 W.L.R. 773 at 776 and [1954] 2 Q.B. 182 at 204.

[18] [1988] I.L.R.M. 629 at 632.

[19] *Jones* v. *Llanrwst Urban District Council* [1911] 1 Ch. 893. It appears from the report at (1911) 27 T.L.R. 133 that the deposit was not made directly on to the plaintiff's land; however the case might equally well have been decided on nuisance or *Rylands* v. *Fletcher*.

[20] See Clerk & Lindsell, *Torts* (16th ed., 1989) para. 23–08.

[21] *Ibid.*, para. 23–07. The distinction will of course be academic if actual damage has occurred: *Home Brewery plc* v. *William Davis & Co. (Loughborough) Ltd.* [1987] 1 All E.R. 637.

[22] The cost of reinstatement may, for example, exceed the diminution in value of the land—not an unlikely circumstance in some contamination cases: see *Nalder* v. *Ilford Corpn* [1951] 1 K.B. 822, 830, and para. 2.36.

Rylands *v.* Fletcher: liability for escapes

2.05   The classic formulation of the *Rylands* v. *Fletcher* doctrine is stated by Blackburn J. in the judgment of the Exchequer Chamber in that case[23]:

> "We think that the true rule of law is, that the person who for his own purposes brings onto his lands and collects and keeps there anything likely to do mischief if it escapes, must keep it in at his peril, and, if he does not do so, is prima facie answerable for all the damage which is the natural consequence of its escape . . . it seems but reasonable and just that the neighbour, who has brought something on his own property which was not naturally there, harmless to others so long as it is confined to his own property, but which he knows to be mischievous if it gets onto his neighbour's , should be obliged to make good the damage which ensues if he does not succeed in confining it to his own property. But for his act in bringing it there no mischief could have accrued, and it seems but just that he should at his peril keep it there so that no mischief may accrue, or answer for the natural and anticipated consequences. And upon authority, this we think is established to be the law whether the things so brought be beasts, or water, or filth, or stenches."

Thus the essential requirements for liability under the tort may be seen to be as follows:

(a) the defendant must bring, collect and keep something on his land for his own purposes;

(b) the thing must be not naturally there;

(c) the thing must be known to be likely to do harm if it escapes;

(d) the thing must escape; and then

(e) the defendant is liable for the natural and anticipated consequences. The House of Lords decision in *Cambridge Water Company* v. *Eastern Counties Leather plc* established that foreseeability of damage of the relevant type is a prerequisite for recovery.[24]

These various requirements are considered below. The rule in *Rylands* v. *Fletcher* has many attractions for the plaintiff. It is a rule of strict, though not absolute, liability with no requirement to show fault on the part of the defendant and no defence of due diligence or the equivalent. It does not appear to depend on the plaintiff having any interest in land

---

[23] *Rylands* v. *Fletcher* (1866) 1 Exch. 265 at 280: approved by Lord Cairns at (1868) 3 App. Cas. 330, 339.

[24] [1994] 2 W.L.R. 53; see para. 2.10.

or being an occupier of land. It may apply to cases where the damage complained of is not so repeated or continuous as to constitute a nuisance.[25]

Nonetheless, there have proved to be many difficulties in applying the rule to modern industrial society, and until the House of Lords decision in *Cambridge Water Company* v. *Eastern Counties Leather plc* one of the main difficulties lay in the requirement that the use of land in question be "non-natural."[26] It remains to be seen whether, after that decision, the rule will prove to be powerful tool in the context of environmental liability under modern law.

Rylands *v.* Fletcher: bringing and accumulation on land

In some contaminated land cases this aspect of the rule may present **2.06** no difficulty whatever: quite clearly a manufacturing company which purchases and stores solvent on its land is doing so for its own purposes; as is a waste management company which receives waste for deposit in one of its landfill sites.[27]

In some cases the potentially harmful material is not actually brought onto the land by the defendant but is in fact generated there—examples would be waste generated and stored within a chemical plant or methane gas generated by the decomposition of waste within a landfill site. It should make no difference to the issue of liability whether the defendant acquired the harmful material or generated it himself on site; indeed the formulation of the rule by Blackburn J. with its reference to "fumes and vapours" and "stenches" is clearly confirmatory of that position. Certainly the rule has been held in a Canadian case to apply to methane gas escaping from a municipal landfill site.[28]

However, this aspect of the rule will probably present difficulties in the case of subsequent owners or occupiers of land, who cannot be said to have accumulated on land noxious materials which were already in place when they acquired the property; nor could contaminants which have already been spilled or dispersed into soil by a previous occupier be said to be held for their own purposes. Any remedy in such circumstances would appear to lie in the tort of nuisance or possibly negligence.[29]

---

[25] *Hanrahan* v. *Merck, Sharp & Dohme (Ireland) Ltd.* [1988] I.L.R.M. 629 at 633.
[26] See para. 2.07.
[27] Though there remains some doubt as to the position of local authorities and statutory undertakers: *c.f. Smeaton* v. *Ilford Corporation* [1954] Ch. 450, at 469, 472 and *Dunne* v. *North Western Gas Board* [1964] 2 Q.B. 806.
[28] *Gertsen* v. *Municipality of Metropolitan Toronto* (1973) 41 D.L.R. (3d) 646.
[29] See para. 2.13 and 2.25.

Rylands *v*. Fletcher: things "not naturally there"

2.07   The original statement in the formulation of the *Rylands* v. *Fletcher* doctrine that it applies to things not naturally on the defendant's land has subsequently become equated to the issue of whether the defendant's use of land was natural or non-natural[30] as such the requirement has proved to be one of the most important and controversial limitations on the rule.[31]

Thus whether a use of land—be it the storage and use of solvents, the deposit of waste, or general manufacturing—is categorised as natural or non-natural will be decisive as to liability under *Rylands* v. *Fletcher*. In *Gertsen* v. *Municipality of Metropolitan Toronto*[32] the Ontario High Court held decisively that the filling of a small ravine in a highly populated area with putrescible refuse was a non-natural use; the court had regard to the unsuitable geology and geography, the known problems of gas-generation and that the primary purpose of filling the ravine was "selfish and self-seeking" rather than for the benefit of the immediate local community.

Similar arguments have fared much less well in the English courts. In *British Celanese Ltd.* v. *A.H. Hunt (Capacitors) Ltd.*[33] The manufacture of electrical and electronic components in 1964 on an industrial trading estate was held not to be a non-natural use:

> ". . . nor can the bringing and storage on the premises of metal foil be a special use in itself. The way the metal foil was stored may have been a negligent one; but the use of the premises for storing such foil did not, by itself, create special risks. The metal foil was there for use in the manufacture of goods of a common type which at all material times were needed for the general benefit of the community."[34]

Of even more relevance to typical contaminated land issues is the decision in *Cambridge Water Company* v. *Eastern Counties Leather plc*.[35] There Ian Kennedy J. at first instance had to consider whether the storage of

---

[30] [1868] 3 App Cas 330 at 339; *Rickards* v. *Lothian* [1913] A.C. 263; *Read* v. *Lyons & Co. Ltd.* [1947] A.C. 156.

[31] Newark, *Non-Natural user and Rylands* v. *Fletcher* (1961) 24 M.L.R. 557.

[32] (1973) 41 D.L.R. (3d) 646 at 666. See also *Chu* v. *District of North Vancouver* (1982) 139 D.L.R. (3rd) 201 (fill material used to extend garden at edge of ravine; material slumped after heavy rain, demolishing homes below it; held to be a non-natural use).

[33] [1969] 1 W.L.R. 959.

[34] *Ibid.*, p. 963 (Lawton J.)

[35] [1992] Env.L.R. 116.

organochlorine solvents in drums at a tannery in a village with various current and historical industrial uses was natural or non-natural. The brief passage from his judgment dealing with this decisive issue refers to two elements: (a) whether the storage created risks for adjacent occupiers; and (b) whether the activity was for the general benefit of the community. He regarded the magnitude of the storage and its geographical location as inevitable considerations and referred to the creation of employment as being clearly for the benefit of the local community. On that basis the storage was held to be a natural use of the land[36]:

> "In reaching this decision I reflect on the innumerable small works that one sees up and down the country with drums stored in their yards . . . Inevitably that storage presents some hazard, but in a manufacturing and outside a primitive and pastoral society such hazards are part of the life of every citizen."

However, the House of Lords[37] took a somewhat different approach to the question of natural use, having already decided that the rule in *Rylands* v. *Fletcher* was confined by the requirement of foreseeability of harm.[38] Lord Goff referred to the way in which the principle had become more complex since the simple notion of "natural use" was first introduced. He took at his starting point the formulation of Lord Moulton in *Richards* v. *Lothian*[39]:

> "It is not every use to which land is put that brings into play that principle. It must be some special use bringing with it increased danger to others, and must not merely be the ordinary use of the land or such a use as is proper for the general benefit of the community."

In particular, Lord Goff felt that if the closing words "such a use as is proper for the general benefit of the community" were interpreted widely, it was difficult to see how the exception could be kept within reasonable bounds. Lord Goff did not feel able to accept that the creation of employment as such, even in a small industrial complex, was sufficient to constitute a use as being a natural use; nor could the mere fact that solvents were commonly used in the tanning industry have that effect. He therefore held that the storage of substantial quantities of chemicals on industrial premises should be regarded as almost a classic case of non-natural use and found it difficult to see how the imposition of strict liability for their escape could be thought to be objectionable: this is potentially an extremely important finding in terms of future develop-

---

[36] [1992] Env.L.R. 116 at 139.
[37] The issue did not arise in the judgment of the Court of Appeal: see para. 2.03.
[38] [1994] 2 W.L.R. 53.
[39] [1913] A.C. 263, 280.

ment of the rule. Lord Goff expressed the view that following recognition that foreseeability of harm of the relevant type is a pre-requisite of liability under the rule, the courts might feel less pressured to extend the scope of the concept of natural use.

Rylands *v.* Fletcher: harmful propensities

2.08   The *Rylands* v. *Fletcher* doctrine applies only to things likely to do mischief if they escape. What is relevant here has been said to be not the knowledge of the defendant or any other particular witness, but "the common experience of mankind in general":[40] it must be doubtful, however, whether this can apply to complex chemicals, whose harmful properties may be a subject for the expert.

In the *Cambridge Water Company* case[41] at first instance it was held that the onus lies with the defendant to establish the harmless nature of the substances in question, and also that what is to be considered is the consequences of an escape of the entire quantity of the substance rather than the amount which actually did escape.[42]

It is possible to see how difficulties may arise in future with this aspect of the rule. Arguments may be raised as to how far the surrounding of the site are relevant: for example, methane gas generated from a landfill site in open countryside will vent harmlessly[43] into the atmosphere—but once a housing estate is constructed nearby the considerations are entirely different.

Rylands *v.* Fletcher: escape

2.09   There must be an escape from the defendant's land in order to establish liability under *Rylands* v. *Fletcher*.[44] More precisely, there must be an escape "from a place where the defendant has occupation or control over land to a place which is outside his occupation or control."[45] What is relevant is control or occupation as opposed to legal title.[46]

Therefore where harmful consequences such as a methane gas explosion occur within the defendant's own land the rule will have no application. It appears that the thing which escapes need not be the thing which was accumulated so as to give rise to application of the rule:

[40] *West* v. *Bristol Tramways Company* [1907] 2 K.B. 14, at 21.
[41] [1992] Env.L.R. 116.
[42] *Ibid.*, at 133.
[43] Leaving aside its possible effects as a greenhouse gas.
[44] *Read* v. *J. Lyons & Co. Ltd.* [1947] A.C. 156.
[45] *Ibid.*, at p. 168 (Lord Simon).
[46] *Benning* v. *Wong* (1969) 122 C.L.R. 249, at 294.

for example, if explosives accidentally cause rocks to be thrown from the land the rule will apply to damage caused by the rocks.[47] This will be important where, for example, refuse on land generates gas which escapes.

Where contaminated land is resulting in a continuing escape of contaminating substances, following the *Cambridge Water Company* case[48] it may be argued that there is no liability where the contaminants in question have passed out of the control of the defendant by becoming "irretrievably lost" in the ground. This difficult issue is considered below.[49]

Rylands *v.* Fletcher: liability for natural and anticipated consequences and the relevance of foreseeability

It was not clear until the House of Lords decision in *Cambridge Water* **2.10** *Company* v. *Eastern Counties Leather plc*[50] how far concepts of remoteness of damage based upon foreseeability are applicable to the strict liability principles of *Rylands* v. *Fletcher*. The House of Lords in that case held that, given the historical connection between the rule in *Rylands* v. *Fletcher* and the tort of nuisance, it would be logical to extend the rules on foreseeability which apply to nuisance to *Rylands* v. *Fletcher*[51] Thus not only must the thing which escapes be of such a nature as to be likely to cause harm if it does escape, but also the kind of harm which occurs must be reasonably foreseeable if damages are to be awarded; otherwise the damage will be too remote. The introduction of foreseeability in this sense does not affect the strict nature of liability under the rule; fault remains irrelevant.[52]

Rylands *v.* Fletcher: the future

As a principle of liability, *Rylands* v. *Fletcher* has been both diminished **2.11** and enhanced by the decision in *Cambridge Water Company* v. *Eastern Counties Leather plc*.[53] It has been diminished in the sense that it was regarded as essentially an application of the principles of nuisance to

---

[47] *Miles* v. *Forest Rock Granite Co.* (1918) 34 T.L.R. 500.
[48] [1994] 2 W.L.R. 53, H.L.
[49] See para. 2.24.
[50] [1994] 2 W.L.R. 53.
[51] As to foreseeability in nuisance, see para. 2.23.
[52] For further discussion of this point see para. 2.26.
[53] [1994] 2 W.L.R. 53.

isolated escapes and accordingly subject to the same requirement that the kind of harm which occurred was reasonably foreseeable. On the other hand, the element of uncertainty which hung over the rule following some obscure remarks by the Court of Appeal which might have confined it to passive escapes[54] has been removed. Also, the courts are less likely in future to come to strained conclusions as to what constitutes a natural use of land.[55] The rule therefore seems set to continue to fulfil a useful role in environmental cases; indeed the Lords' decision overall may well have enhanced that role.

However, the decision also places a brake on any attempts to develop *Rylands* v. *Fletcher* into a "general rule of strict liability for damage caused by ultra-hazardous operations", as in the USA.[56] The decision in *Read* v. *J. Lyons & Co. Ltd.*[57] was regarded as having foreclosed that particular development. Additionally, the House of Lords expressed the view that the imposition of strict liability in relation to operations of high risk was a matter for Parliament, rather than the courts, since statute could lay down more precisely than the common law the precise scope and criteria of such liability. The rapid development of international, EC and domestic law on the subject of environmental protection was seen as another reason why the courts should be reluctant to venture into the area.

Rylands *v.* Fletcher: Scotland

2.12   *Ryland* v. *Fletcher* is not part of Scots law and the suggestion that it may be "is a heresy which ought to be extirpated".[58] Nonetheless Scots law by a different route can arrive at a situation bearing a strong resemblance to strict liability for hazardous activities.[59]

NUISANCE

Generally

2.13   Nuisance is the traditional "environmental tort" and as such may be expected to play a large role in relation to problems emanating from contaminated land. However, the very breadth and flexibility of the tort

---

[54] [1994] 2 W.L.R. 53; [1993] Env.L.R. 287, 296.
[55] See para. 2.07.
[56] *Restatement of Torts* (2nd. ed., Vol. 3 1977), para. 519.
[57] [1947] A.C. 156.
[58] *R.H.M. Bakeries (Scotland) Ltd.* v. *Strathclyde Regional Council* 1985 S.L.T. 214, at 217 *per* Lord Fraser.
[59] See Chap. 13 (Scotland).

give rise to a number of uncertainties. Its essence lies in some *activity or condition* which unduly interferes with the use or enjoyment of land.[60] The fact that it can apply both to activities and to conditions is crucial to an understanding of its application. The operation of a landfill site may constitute a nuisance, but, equally, so can the condition of that site once completed.

It must also be appreciated that the interference which constitutes the tort of nuisance can take a multiplicity of forms, amongst them:

(i) physical harm to persons or to property, such as damage to crops from percolating gas, or migrating chemicals which have an aggressive effect on service conduits;

(ii) interference with the enjoyment of land, for example restrictions on growing crops or on allowing children to play in contaminated soil;

(iii) interference with an easement or other interest in land, or with a natural right such as the abstraction of water.

Finally, nuisance may be concerned with some on-going activity where the primary objective of the plaintiff is to secure an injunction to restrain its continuance; equally, however, it can take the form of a concluded interference in which case the action is for damages. The two situations may raise very different considerations in regard to the issue of foreseeability[61] and both situations may be relevant in the case of contaminated land.

Public nuisance

If contamination is such as to endanger the life, health or property of a **2.14** sufficient number of citizens, or to interfere with their reasonable comfort, then it may constitute a public nuisance.[62] As such it is a crime as well as a tort and any individual wishing to take action will need to show particular damage beyond that suffered by the general public.[63]

It is conceivable that a public nuisance could be constituted, for example, by land contaminated with harmful particulate matter which may be dispersed over a wide area, or by land generating methane gas in such quantities to threaten the safety of a large number of dwellings, or by contamination which affects a major aquifer so as to present a health risk to consumers of the water.[64] The words of Lindley L.J. in *Att.-Gen.* v. *Tod Heatley*[65] are relevant in this respect:

---

[60] See para. 2.03.
[61] See para. 2.23.
[62] See J.R. Spencer, "Public Nuisance—a Critical Examination" [1989] C.L.J. 55.
[63] Clerk & Lindsell, *Torts* (16th ed., 1989) para. 24–68.
[64] *Gibbons and others* v. *South West Water Services Ltd.* [1993] Env.L.R. 266 (C.A.).
[65] [1897] 1 Ch. 560, p. 566.

"Now is it, or is it not, a common law duty of the owner of a vacant piece of land to prevent that land from being a public nuisance? It appears to be that it is . . . If the owner of a piece of land does permit it to be in such a state, *e.g.* smothered or covered with filth, that is a public nuisance, he commits an indictable offence. It is no defence to say 'I did not put the filth on but somebody else did.' He must provide against this if he can. His business is to prevent his land from becoming a public nuisance."

It is not necessary to show that a landowner had actual knowledge of a public nuisance on their land but merely that he was responsible for a nuisance which he knew or ought to have known would be the consequences of activities carried out on his land.[66] Knowledge of risk, or the means of knowledge, may thus suffice.

Nature of nuisance: location

2.15   Where nuisance involves injury to property or interference with an easement the locality of the activity is not relevant.[67] Where interference with physical comfort is involved, locality will be relevant and whether the interference constitutes a nuisance is an issue of degree.[68]

In many cases the ingress of contaminants into the plaintiff's land will constitute physical injury rather than interference with comfort. However it is possible to envisage cases where the effect is manifested principally in non-physical damage, such as a diminution in the value of property: whether this falls within the category of "material injury to property" may be regarded as open to serious doubts.[69]

Nuisance—who can sue?

2.16   Private nuisance offers protection only to the owner or occupier of land or, in the case of interference with rights, the person entitled to the rights.[70] The requirement that the plaintiff must have an interest in land in order to sue for nuisance may present problems to spouses or minors who have no such interest.[71] However, it has been suggested that this

---

[66] *R.* v. *Shorrock* [1993] N.L.J. 511 (C.A., Criminal Division).

[67] *St Helen's Smelting Co.* v. *Tipping* (1865) 11 H.L.C. 642; *Halsey* v. *Esso Petroleum Co. Ltd.* [1961] 2 All E.R. 145; *Horton's Estate Ltd.* v. *James Beattie Ltd.* [1927] 1 Ch. 75.

[68] See Clerk & Lindsell, *Torts* (16th ed., 1989) paras. 24–03—24–07 and see *Gillingham Borough Council* v. *Medway (Chatham) Dock Co. Ltd.* [1992] J.P.L. 458.

[69] *Ibid.*, para. 24–04; also Winfield & Jolowicz, *Tort* (13th ed., 1989) p. 388; Salmond & Heuston, *Law of Torts* (20th ed., 1992) pp. 63–64.

[70] *Tate & Lyle Industries Ltd.* v. *Greater London Council* [1983] 2 A.C. 509.

[71] *Malone* v. *Laskey* [1907] 2 K.B. 141; *Cunard* v. *Antifyre Ltd.* [1933] 1 K.B. 551; *Nunn* v. *Parkes & Co.* (1924) 59 L.Jo 806.

may no longer be an insuperable problem in the light of statutory rights in the matrimonial home and on the basis of more recent authority.[72]

Where injury to land has been inflicted over successive ownerships, it will be possible to recover in respect of damage caused before the plaintiff became owner, provided that it is a loss which he as current owner has suffered.[73]

Nuisance: liability of originator

The person who created a nuisance will be liable for it, irrespective of **2.17** whether he is the occupier of land. In certain circumstances, there can be liability for nuisances created by an independent contractor: in particular where it is reasonably foreseeable that the works to be carried out are likely to result in a nuisance unless preventive means are employed.[74]

Thus the waste contractor who operates and fills a landfill site will be liable if that site results in a nuisance; and will continue to be liable irrespective of whether or not he ever held any right or interest in the site.[75] Similarly where a company, delivering oil, spills the cargo onto land in the course of unloading it, the company will be responsible for any ensuing nuisance. Whether a contractor who negligently installs a pipe which some time later fails, causing contamination, is liable for the nuisance is rather more debatable.

Nuisance: liability of owner or occupier

As explained above, nuisance may arise from either an activity or from **2.18** a condition. Contaminated land, by its state and condition, may constitute a nuisance. This leads to the disturbing conclusion that liability may attach to an owner or occupier of land for contamination which they did not create, either because a third party created it during their ownership, or because it already existed when they acquired the land.

There are cases which indicate that an owner of land may be liable for a nuisance created by a predecessor in title, provided that he knew, or ought to have known of its existence by the exercise of reasonable

---

[72] See Pugh and Easter [1993] N.L.J., September 17, p. 1301, citing *Motherwell* v. *Motherwell* (1976) 73 D.L.R. (3rd) 62; *Devon Lumber Co. Ltd.* v. *MacNeill* (1987) 45 D.L.R. (4th) and *Khorasandijian* v. *Bush, The Times,* February 19, 1993.

[73] *Masters* v. *Brent London Borough Council* [1978] Q.B. 841.

[74] *Bower* v. *Peate* (1876) 1 Q.B.D. 321.

[75] *Gertsen* v. *Metropolitan Municipality of Toronto* (1973) 41 D.L.R. (3rd) 647, pp. 669–671.

diligence[76]: failure to make proper investigations means that it was his fault "to contract for an interest in land in which there was a nuisance."[77] Knowledge for this purpose includes not only actual knowledge of the nuisance, but also cases where ignorance is due to failure to use reasonable care to ascertain the relevant facts.[78] What constitutes reasonable investigation in relation to possible contamination of land has undoubtedly changed over the years and will continue to do so. Whilst the position is not entirely clear, it seems likely that liability in such circumstances will only arise where the defendant not only was aware of the nuisance but was in a position to take steps to prevent it.[79]

The other main line of cases of relevance in this area deals with nuisances naturally occurring on land or resulting from the act of a trespasser. The position here is that the occupier will be liable if knowing of the nuisance (or where he should have known of it by the exercise of reasonable diligence) he fails to take prompt and effective steps to prevent it.[80] The authorities were reviewed at length in the decision of the Court of Appeal in *Leakey* v. *National Trust*[81] where in relation to a naturally-occurring nuisance it was held that failure to abate the nuisance may result in liability: however, the duty is limited in scope to doing what is reasonable in all the circumstances to prevent or minimise the known risk of damage or injury. This will involve consideration of issues of the likely extent of the damage, the practicability of action and its difficulty and cost, the resources of the defendant and the plaintiff's resources and ability to protect himself from damage.

What is not clear, but is of great importance, is to what extent these limiting factors, which apply in the case of naturally-occurring nuisances, would also apply where a nuisance has arisen artificially by the activities of a predecessor in title either by deliberate action in depositing waste on land or by negligence or accident in spilling materials on land. Both natural and artificial nuisances may be capable of discovery by the exericse of diligence and there would seem to be little basis in policy or logic for distinguishing between them: neither results directly from the fault of the defendant. In *Cambridge Water Company* v. *Eastern Counties Leather plc*[82] the House of Lords clearly thought that the principles of *Leakey* v. *National Trust* and similar cases might apply to land contaminated by previous spillages of chemical solvents; however the point

---

[76] *Broder* v. *Saillard* (1876) 3 Ch.D. 692; *Wilkins* v. *Leighton* [1932] 2 Ch. 106.
[77] *Rosewell* v. *Prior* (1701) 12 Mod. 635.
[78] *Brew Bros. Ltd.* v. *Snax (Ross) Ltd.* [1970] 1 Q.B. 612 at p. 636 *per* Sachs L.J.
[79] *Smeaton* v. *Ilford Corporation* [1954] Ch. 450 at 462.
[80] *Sedleigh-Denfield* v. *O'Callaghan* [1940] A.C. 880; *Goldman* v. *Hargrave* [1967] 1 A.C. 645.
[81] [1980] Q.B. 485.
[82] [1994] 2 W.L.R. 53.

remains to be fully tested. The position is further complicated by remarks of the House of Lords concerning the situation where contaminating substances have become "irretrievably lost"; these remarks are considered below.[83]

Nuisance: disposal of property

The originator of a nuisance cannot escape his liability by disposing of **2.19** property: he will remain liable even though he can no longer take steps to abate the nuisance.[84]

The position is different where the owner of property who did not create the nuisance sells it; here, though there is little authority, he will on principle cease to be liable.[85] The position may be different if the vendor has undertaken a continuing contractual responsibility to take remedial action.

Where property is disposed of by way of granting a lease, the position becomes more complex. If the owner knew, or ought to have known, of the nuisance before letting he will remain liabile irrespective of whether the tenant has covenanted to repair.[86] If the nuisance arises after the tenancy commenced, the landlord may still be liable if he has either the duty to repair the property (by covenant) or a power to do so (by right of entry).[87] It has been said that where the nuisance arises after the lease was granted, the test of an owner's duty to his neighbour depends on "the degree of control exercised by the owner in law or in fact for the purpose of repairs."[88] The cases establishing these propositions in general relate to the physical condition of the buildings or other structures on the demised premises and it may be open to argue that contaminated soil raises different issues. In any event, the position between the landlord and tenant will be governed by the terms of the lease and the landlord may well have a right of redress against the tenant.[89] The fact that the landlord may be liable for nuisance under

---

[83] See para. 2.24.

[84] *Thompson* v. *Gibson* (1841) 7 M. & W. 456; *Rosewell* v. *Prior* (1701) 12 Mod. 635.

[85] Clerk & Lindsell, *Torts* (13th ed., 1989) para. 24–34, p. 1383.

[86] *Brew Bros Ltd.* v. *Snax (Ross) Ltd.* [1970] 1 Q.B. 612; *Sampson* v. *Hodson-Pressinger* [1981] 3 All E.R. 710.

[87] Clerk & Lindsell, *op. cit.*, para. 24–34, p. 1382.

[88] See Brew Bros. Ltd. v. *Snax (Ross) Ltd.* [1970] 1 Q.B. 612 at 638 *per* Sachs L.J. citing *Mint* v. *Good* [1951] 1 K.B. 517 at 528. Compare, however, the suggestion by Phillimore L.J. at p. 644 that a lease with a full repairing covenant to a responsible tenant must represent "reasonable care" by the landlord.

[89] See Chap. 11 generally.

47

these principles will in no way relieve the tenant from liability, either as the originator of the nuisance or as the occupier of premises: nor will the fact that under the lease the landlord may have covenanted to repair relieve the tenant.[90]

Possible defences

2.20   The following arguments may be raised (though not necessarily successfully) by way of defence to a nuisance action:

(1) *Exercise of care and skill*   Since nuisance focuses on the effect on the plaintiff rather than the conduct of the defendant, negligence will not usually be an issue: liability is in this sense strict.[91] Whether the nuisance was inevitable notwithstanding the exercise of all due care and skill may, however, be an issue in the defence of statutory authority.[92]

(2) *Act of trespasser*   The defendant will not generally be liable for the acts of a trespasser unless, possibly, the defendant is regarded as having some positive duty to control them. There may, as explained above,[93] be a duty to take reasonable steps to abate the nuisance caused by the trespasser once the defendant is aware of it.

(3) *Coming to the nuisance*   It is not a defence that the plaintiff came to the nuisance. So, for example, development near a landfill site may result in a nuisance to the occupants of the houses and the fact that the landfill was there first will provide no defence. However, it may be that a defence based on contributory negligence could be raised if reasonable investigations prior to the development would have revealed the problem.[94]

(4) *Regulatory authority*   The activity has regulatory authority, *e.g.* planning permission.[94a]

Pollution of surface waters

2.21   Contaminated land may disperse pollutants into surface waters, either directly or through groundwater. Alteration to the natural quality of the

---

[90] *Wilchick* v. *Marks and Silverstone* [1934] 2 K.B. 56; *St Anne's Well Brewery Co.* v. *Roberts* (1929) 140 L.T. 1.

[91] *Cambridge Water Company* v. *Eastern Counties Leather plc* [1994] 2 W.L.R. 53 (House of Lords).

[92] *Vaughan* v. *Taff Vale Railway Co.* (1880) 5 H. & N. 679; *Manchester Corporation* v. *Farnworth* [1930] A.C. 171.

[93] Para. 2.18.

[94] The Law Reform (Contributory Negligence) Act 1945 applies to nuisance: *Caswell* v. *Powell Duffryn Associated Collieries Ltd.* [1940] A.C. 152; *Trevett* v. *Lee* [1955] 1 W.L.R. 113.

[94a] *Gillingham Borough Council* v. *Medway (Chatham) Dock Co. Ltd.* [1992] J.P.L. 458.

stream will be actionable as a nuisance by the riparian owner.[95] On general principles of nuisance as discussed above, liability may extend to the originator of the nuisance and to the occupier in respect of the condition of his land once he has actual or constructive notice of it.[96]

Interference with a legal profit à prendre of fishing (*e.g.*, by killing fish) will also be actionable, and indeed is actionable by analogy to trespass without proof of pecuniary loss.[97]

Pollution of groundwater

Unlike surface waters in a defined channel, no person has proprietary **2.22** rights in percolating underground waters.[98] However, subject to the statutory requirements as to abstraction licences or any statutory limitations on volume, every landowner has the right to abstract as much percolating water as they wish from the strata underlying their property: and, by pumping, to draw water from beneath the land of others.[99]

In *Cambridge Water Company* v. *Eastern Counties Leather plc*[1] the plaintiff's borehole was contaminated by chlorinated solvents spilt on the defendant's site. At first instance a claim based on nuisance failed because it was held that the type of harm which had occurred was not foreseeable.[2] However, the Court of Appeal came to a different conclusion based on interference with the right of an owner to have such of the water as he abstracts come to him in an uncontaminated condition. The Court of Appeal also relied upon the case of *Ballard* v. *Tomlinson*[3] in which the

---

[95] *Young* v. *Bankier Distillery* [1893] A.C. 691.

[96] Paras. 2.17 and 2.18.

[97] *Nicholls* v. *Ely Sugar Beet Factory Ltd.* [1936] 1 Ch. 343; *Fitzgerald* v. *Firbank* [1897] 2 Ch. 96; *Broderick* v. *Gale and Ainslie Ltd.* [1993] Water Law, Vol. 4, Issue 4, p. 127.

[98] *Bradford Corporation* v. *Ferrand* [1902] 2 Ch. 655.

[99] *Acton* v. *Blundell* (18430 12 M. & W. 324; *Chasemore* v. *Richards* (1859) H.L.C. 349.

[1] [1992] Env.L.R. 116; [1993] Env.L.R. 287 (C.A.); [1994] 2 W.L.R. 53 (H.L. and C.A.).

[2] See para. 2.23.

[3] (1885) 29 Ch.D. 115. See also *Hubbs* v. *Prince Edward County; Boyd and Boyd* v. *Prince Edward County and Preston* (1957) 8 D.L.R. (2nd) 394 (not cited) a case where the defendant, knowing of the presence of drinking wells on the plaintiff's land, placed a massive pile of sand mixed with calcium chloride and sodium chloride on bare limestone some 100–120 feet away. The defendants were liable for the ensuing contamination of the wells in nuisance and negligence. The report contains the evocative sentence: "Just before Christmas 1955 Mrs. Boyd noticed that the blooms dropped off her Christmas cactus, that cream curdled when placed in tea and that water from both wells has a most unpleasant and salty taste . . ."

defendant, by disposing of sewage and refuse into a disused well on his property, contaminated the nearby abstraction source of a brewery. It was held that this case was not distinguishable and that it was sufficient that the defendant's act, whether deliberate, negligent or non-negligent, caused the contamination:[4]

> "*Ballard* v. *Tomlinson* decided that where the nuisance is an interference with a natural right incident to ownership then the liability is a strict one. The actor acts at his peril in that if his actions result by the operation of ordinary natural processes in an interference with the right then he is liable to compensate for any damage suffered by the owner."

The House of Lords, however, did not regard *Ballard* v. *Tomlinson* as determinative. The main focus there was the argument that the plaintiff had no property in percolating water and therefore no cause of action for its pollution.[5] The concept of natural rights was held to equate to those rights which are protected by the law of tort.[6] However, whether liability attaches to any particular act depends on the relevant rules of tort (nuisance and *Rylands* v. *Fletcher*) and those rules include foreseeability of damage. Thus *Ballard* v. *Tomlinson* was essentially concerned with the plaintiff's title to sue rather than the criteria for a successful action, and does not confer any special status on the protection of groundwater abstraction rights.

Nuisance: the foreseeability issue

2.23   The Court of Appeal decision in the *Cambridge Water Company* case left the issue of foreseeability in relation to environmental harm (at least so far as interference with natural rights of abstraction is concerned) in a state of some doubt. Prior to that decision the tendency had been to assimilate nuisance with negligence to the extent that damages were only recoverable in respect of reasonably foreseeable harm.[7] Certainly that was the approach adopted Ian Kennedy J. at first instance.

[4] [1993] Env.L.R. 287 at p. 295.
[5] This is clearer from the fuller report at 54 L.J. Ch. 404.
[6] Megarry & Wade, *The Law of Real Property* (5th ed., 1984) p. 842; A.W.B. Simpson, *A History of the Land Law* (2nd ed., 1986) pp. 263–4.
[7] *Overseas Tankship (UK) Ltd.* v. *Miller Steamship Co. Pty (The Wagon Mound (No. 2))* [1967] 1 A.C. 617; *Solloway* v. *Hampshire County Council* (1981) 79 L.G.R. 449; *Home Brewery* v. *Davis (W) Ltd.* [1987] Q.B. 339; *Swan Fisheries* v. *Holberton* Queens Bench Division December 14, 1987, unreported (a case on riparian rights); *Anglian Water Services Ltd.* v. *H.G. Thurston & Co. Ltd.* [1993] E.G.C.S. 162 (C.A.—tipping of large quantities of spoil on land damaged sewage pipes beneath the surface; the existence of the sewer was not known and damage was not foreseeable).

The House of Lords, in a passage which was strictly *obiter*, considered the issue of foreseeability of damage in nuisance. The Lords emphasised that although liability for nuisances created by the defendant (or those for whom he was responsible) is strict, it does not follow that the defendant should be held liable for a type of damage which he could not reasonably foresee. It was seen as reasonable to equate the rules on remoteness in nuisance with those in negligence; this was supported by the Privy Council's decision in *The Wagon Mound (No. 2)*.[8]

Therefore in cases of nuisance caused by contaminated land it will be necessary to consider to what extent the damage caused was reasonably foreseeable. It is not necessary that the precise type of damage be foreseeable, but rather the kind of damage in general. Foreseeability of "harm" in the abstract is not sufficient: in the *Cambridge Water Company* case it was held that the reasonable supervisor of ECL's premises prior to 1976 would not have foreseen the groundwater pollution which resulted from repeated spillages of small amounts of solvent, although it could have been foreseen that if a significant quantity were spilled someone might be overcome by fumes.

It remains to be seen how the concept of foreseeability will be worked out in practice in the contaminated land context. Clearly there have been major advances in the awareness of effects on the environment by chemical substances since 1976, and in relation to spillages of solvent occurring during the 1990s it would not be difficult to demonstrate a general awareness in the industrial community of the risks of pollution. Clearly, also, the courts will be concerned not with what the defendant actually foresaw but what he could have been reasonably expected to have foreseen. The degree of foresight to be imputed to a back street garage may be different from that to be imputed to a major chemical company.[9] In an interesting sequel to the *Cambridge Water Case*, Anglian Water Services Limited has issued a writ against the US State Department, claiming substantial damages for pollution of the company's Beck Row Borehole in Cambridgeshire by tertiary butyl methyl ether emanating from a petrol station at RAF Mildenhall, operated by the US Air Force. The claim is based on negligence, nuisance and *Rylands* v. *Fletcher*, and so foreseeability can be expected to be an important issue.[9a]

The foreseeability issue will extend not only to the harmful characteristics of the substance in question but also to its properties and means of transport in the environment. Arguments may therefore arise as to whether the defendant ought reasonably to have been aware of the possible migration of contaminants off site by groundwater flow or other

[8] [1967] 1 A.C. 617.
[9] See also para. 2.26 below.
[9a] Action 1994–A–No. 1165, Queen's Bench, May 19, 1994.

means. On the other hand it would probably not be necessary that the defendant could have foreseen precisely where the substance would go; in the *Cambridge Water Company* case Lord Goff summarised the position of the "reasonable supervisor" at ECL as follows:

> "Even if he had foreseen that solvent might enter the aquifer, he would not have foreseen that such quantities would produce any sensible effect upon water down-catchment, or would otherwise be material or deserve the description of pollution."

The closing words of that extract impliedly introduce another dimension of foreseeability: that of the material effect of the contamination.[10] The real harm to Cambridge Water Company's interests was caused by the combination of small quantities of solvent in the aquifer and introduction (four years after the spillages ceased) of EC legislation prohibiting the presence of those quantities in water for human consumption.[10a] It is possible to see how such arguments might arise in future in relation to new or more stringent legislation on soil quality standards or the presence of certain substances in the environment. A defendant might foresee that spillages on his land could migrate to his neighbour's but without any material adverse effects; if however soil clean up legislation is introduced in future years which requires the neighbour to remove or neutralise those contaminants present on his land, the contamination will hence become material. One answer might be that the reasonable industrial undertaking operating now would be aware of the possibility of more stringent legislative developments in the area of soil contamination, and that the future materiality of the contamination was therefore foreseeable.

Nuisance: continuing pollution and foreseeability

2.24   Consequent upon the House of Lord's ruling on foreseeability in the *Cambridge Water Company* case, another issue arose. It was asserted during the course of argument that pools of neat solvent were still in existence at the base of the chalk aquifer beneath ECL's premises and that the escape of solvent was continuing; it was argued that since the adverse effects of that escape were now foreseeable, ECL were liable under nuisance and *Rylands* v. *Fletcher* for that continuing escape.

The House of Lords rejected that argument.[11] It was said that "long before the relevant (EC) legislation came into force, the PCE had

---

[10] See also para. 2.36.
[10a] This has been described as "a singular feature" of the case: see A. Ogus [1994] J.E.L. Vol. 6, No. 1, p. 151, at p. 155.
[11] [1994] 2 W.L.R. 53.

become irretrievably lost in the ground below"; it had "passed beyond the control of ECL". In such circumstances, it was held, ECL should not be under any greater liability that that imposed for negligence, or for naturally occurring nuisances under the line of cases including *Leakey* v. *National Trust.*[12]

What this appears to suggest is two possible stages of liability for the original pollution. The first stage is that of the spillage or other incident causing pollution. Here liability is strict, through the damage will be too remote if it was not reasonably foreseeable. This stage extends until such time as the contamination has passed beyond the control of the polluter by passing irretrievably into the relevant environmental medium. At the point there is a second stage of potential liability where liability is based on negligence, or at least on notions of reasonableness.

This leaves the question of at what point the transition occurs. Some forms of contamination, such as waste contained in a landfill site, may not be irretrievable in that they could be excavated and removed; the same goes for contaminants such as heavy metals which are fixed in soil. Even contaminated groundwater may not be totally beyond control, given modern remediation methods.[13]

If contaminants have passed beyond control, it must be questionable whether it can ever be correct to impose liability on the basis of negligence or under the principles of *Leakey* v. *National Trust* since these are based upon the reasonableness of measures which could be taken. Conceivably, contamination might be said to have passed beyond control at a certain date but at a later date—given improvements in remedial technologies perhaps combined with a worsening environmental impact—it might become reasonable to expect the polluter (or future owner) to do something about it.[13a]

NEGLIGENCE

Generally

The tort of negligence may of course be of relevance to environmental **2.25** litigation, but the case law has tended instead to focus attention on the torts of nuisance and *Rylands* v. *Fletcher*. The need to establish a duty of care owed to the plaintiff and failure to exercise the relevant standard of

---

[12] [1980] Q.B. 485; see para. 2.18.
[13] See Chap. 7 generally.
[13a] Indeed, the NRA has subsequently taken steps, with the cooperation of the defendant in the *Cambridge Water* case, to secure treatment of the contaminated groundwater: see para. 2.50.

care are major difficulties which do not have to be overcome in relation to the other environmental torts.

Detailed consideration of the rules of negligence is beyond the scope of this chapter, but the tort's potential application to issues of contaminated land can be appreciated from the following paragraphs.

Liability for spillages

2.26   Where damage arises from spillage of substances such as solvents the essential issue will be what damage was reasonably foreseeable at the time: failure to exercise proper care or good housekeeping is not sufficient of itself to ground liability.[14]

In the *Cambridge Water Company* case small spillages of solvent were found to have occurred over a period of years prior to 1976. Ian Kennedy J. emphasised the need for some relationship at least between that type of harm which could have been foreseen and that which actually occurred:[15] to say simply that "pollution" could have been foreseen and did in fact occur was too wide a category.[16] Some types of harm could have been foreseen from spillages (*e.g.* danger from fumes) but the type of harm which occurred was different; nor could it have been foreseen that small regular spills would have the same effect as one major spill. The reasonable plant manager would not have expected the spills to get into the aquifer or, if they did, to cause appreciable harm.[17]

Standards of awareness of course change over time, and it is submitted that it would be very difficult to argue that the relevant damage would not have been reasonably foreseeable had the spills occurred during the late 1980s or 1990s: the effect of industrial solvents on groundwater is now a matter of widespread concern. The exact point at which such awareness came to be accepted as a reasonable component of plant management is of course open to argument; one issue which may be relevant are the standards expected by regulatory authorities, though this may certainly not be the decisive issue. The existence of official advice or guidance will be a relevant factor,[18] though a distinction may need to be drawn between what was known in specialist circles and what was general knowledge in the relevant industry or sector.[19] In any event,

---

[14] *Cambridge Water Co.* v. *Eastern Counties Leather PLC* [1992] Env.L.R. 116 at pp. 139, 145.

[15] See *Hughes* v. *Lord Advocate* [1963] A.C. 837.

[16] [1992] Env.L.R. 116 at p. 142.

[17] *Salvin* v. *North Brancepath Coal Co.* (1874) 9 Ch. App. 705, at p. 708.

[18] See *Roe* v. *Minister of Health* [1954] 2 Q.B. 66; *Gunn* v. *Wallsend Slipway and Engineering Co. Ltd.*, *The Times*, January 23, 1989; *Tutton* v. *A.D. Walter Ltd.* [1986] 1 Q.B. 61.

[19] *Cartwright* v. *GKN Sankey Ltd.* (1973) 14 K.I.R. 349.

the courts are likely to be very wary of imputing foreseeability with the benefit of hindsight, however sympathetic they may be to the plaintiff.[20]

Liability for landfill gas

The most detailed reported judicial discussion of liability on negli- **2.27** gence for the escape of landfill gas occurs in the Canadian case of *Gertsen* v. *Municipality of Metropolitan Toronto*.[21] The defendants, the municipal waste disposal authority and the local borough authority were found to be negligent in respect of the disposal of household garbage mixed with earth into a ravine in a residential area. The landfill was carried out between 1958–59 under an agreement between the authorities on land owned by the borough.

In 1963 the gas generated by the site had caused a flash fire in a garage on nearby property, seriously injuring the owner. The plaintiff purchased the property in 1967 and in 1969 suffered serious injury when an explosion occurred in the same garage.

It was held that both defendants knew or ought to have known of the generation of methane gas as a potential danger. Even if unaware of it before 1965 they were certainly aware of it thereafter. Their negligence lay not only in burying the waste but in failing to take proper steps thereafter to prevent the migration of gas or disperse it safely, to inspect the effectiveness of such steps as had been taken, to warn adjoining owners of the dangers, and (in the case of the borough) in granting permits for the construction of garages and outbuildings on the adjoining land.

Natural methane

Liability for failure to foresee the possible presence of methane as a **2.28** natural phenomenon and to take appropriate measures to alleviate the risks from it was considered in the action following the disastrous explosion at the Abbeystead Pumping Station in Lancashire in 1984.[22] Factors which were regarded as relevant in that case included:

(i) the magnitude of the risk and the difficulty of the measures needed to eliminate it; the distinction between transient "stress methane" and long term "reservoir methane" was relevant in this context;

(ii) British Standards Association documents and general scientific literature current at the relevant time;

---

[20] *Thompson* v. *Smiths Ship Repairers (North Shields) Ltd.* [1984] Q.B. 405.
[21] (1973) 41 D.L.R. (3rd) 646.
[22] *Eckersley* v. *Binnie & Partners*, Court of Appeal, February 18, 1988 (unreported).

(iii) the professional man should command the corpus of knowledge which forms part of the professional equipment of the ordinary member of his profession. He should not lag behind other ordinarily assiduous and intelligent members of his profession in knowledge of new advances, discoveries and developments in his field; but "the law does not require of a professional man that he be a paragon, combining the qualities of polymath and prophet";

(iv) the first instance judge found the defendant engineers "to some slight degree negligent in not keeping abreast with, passing on to [their clients] and considering, in relation to design, developing knowledge about methane between handover and 1984". The Court of Appeal regarded this suggestion as placing "startlingly onerous responsibilities" upon professionals and suggested that if any such duty were to be imposed then its nature, scope and limits would need to be very carefully and cautiously defined.

Negligence: potential relevance

2.29   Despite the difficulties discussed above, negligence is a possible cause of action in relation to contaminated land and may be particularly apt in cases where:

(i) the defendant's conduct caused the contamination; or

(ii) the defendant, being aware of the dangers from contamination, failed to take steps to prevent or to warn;[23] or

(iii) the defendant's actions resulted in pre-existing contaminants being released.

BREACH OF STATUTORY DUTY

General principles[24]

2.30   As protection of the environment and human health becomes increasingly regulated by statute, so it is arguable that the role of the tort of breach of statutory duty should become correspondingly more signifi-

---

[23] Effectively this may impose liability for an omission; but such liability certainly seems capable of arising in a similar basis in nuisance. See para. 2.18.

[24] See Winfield & Jolowicz, *Tort* (13th ed., 1989); Salmond & Heuston, *Law of Torts* (20th ed., 1992); Clerk & Lindsell, *Torts* (16th ed., 1989).

cant. However, this does not appear to be the case in practice. In most instances statutes are silent on the issue of civil liability[25] and in recent years the courts have been wary of inferring that statutory requirements may give rise to a civil cause of action.

In particular, there will be the need in general to demonstrate either that the statutory obligation or prohibition was imposed for the benefit of a particular class of persons or (more obscurely) that the statute created a public right, interference with which caused the plaintiff to suffer special damage peculiar to himself.[26] Unlike the health and safety, consumer or factories legislation, which clearly have in mind a class of individuals (albeit very large) as the object of protection, environmental legislation is generally intended to protect society at large, or indeed the environment at large as opposed to persons. Indeed, the tendency in some recent environmental legislation is to provide explicit restrictions on that legislation being used to protect the health and safety of persons at work in its own rights.[27]

Therefore in the absence of any express provision giving a civil remedy for breach of statutory duty, the arguments for imposing such a duty in relation to environmental offences, whilst not impossible, would appear tenuous.[28]

Unlawful waste deposits

Section 73(6) of the Environmental Protection Act 1990 is one of the **2.31** few environmental provisions which does provide an express civil cause of action. Under the subsection where any damage is caused by waste which has been deposited on land so as to commit an offence under section 33(1) (controlled waste) or section 63(2) (other waste) then the person who deposited it, or who knowingly caused or knowingly permitted the deposit so as to commit an offence, is liable for the damage. This liability is subject to possible defences under subsection 73(6) and (7).

It should be noted that liability is not confined to cases where waste is deposited on land without a licence; it may also arise where waste is deposited on a licensed site in a manner likely to cause pollution of the environment or harm to human health.[29] However, the offence of breach of site licence conditions will not give rise to liability under this provision.[30]

[25] But see para. 2.31 below.
[26] *Lonhro Ltd.* v. *Shell Petroleum Co. Ltd. (No. 2)* [1982] A.C. 173.
[27] See Environmental Protection Act 1990, s.7(1).
[28] Compare the express provisions on liability of water undertakers for escapes of water: Water Industry Act 1991, s.209.
[29] S.33(1)(c).
[30] The offence here is under s.33(6), not s.33(1).

Similar provision for liability was made by the Deposit of Poisonous Waste Act 1972, s.2 and by the Control of Pollution Act 1974, s.88. The implications of these provisions for historical unlawful deposits remains to be tested.

OCCUPIERS' LIABILITY

Duty to visitors

2.32   An occupier of premises owes the same duty, the "common duty of care", to all his visitors, except in so far as he is free to and does extend, modify or exclude his duty by agreement or otherwise.[31] The duty is to take such care as in all the circumstances of the case is reasonable to see that the visitor will be reasonably safe in using the premises for the purpose for which he is invited or permitted by the occupier to be there.[32]

The duty will therefore be applicable if land is contaminated in such a way as to present risks to visitors in relation to the purposes for which they are on the premises. Since these statutory rules regulate the position in relation to dangers *due to the state of the premises* or to things done *or omitted* to be done on them[33] it will be irrelevant that the occupier was not responsible for creating the contamination; in that sense the Act may require the taking of positive remedial steps to ensure safety. The test of who is the "occupier" is based upon the degree of control over the premises rather than ownership or exclusive rights of occupation.[34]

In many cases the most practical way of discharging the duty may be by means of warning signs or notices; however, a warning will not be treated without more as absolving the occupier from liability, unless in all the circumstances it was enough to allow the visitor to be reasonably safe.[35]

Duty to trespassers

2.33   An occupier of premises owes a duty to persons other than his visitors in respect of any risk of their suffering injury on the premises by reason of any danger due to the state of the premises or to things done or omitted to be done on them.[36] The duty only comes into being if:

[31] Occupier's Liability Act 1957, s.2(1).
[32] *Ibid.*, s.2(2).
[33] *Ibid.*, s.1(1).
[34] *Wheat* v. *E. Lacon & Co. Ltd.* [1966] A.C. 552; see generally Winfield & Jolowicz, *Tort* (13th ed., 1989) pp. 209–210.
[35] S.2(4)(a).
[36] Occupier's liability Act 1984, s.1(1).

(a) the occupier is aware of the danger or has reasonable grounds to
believe that it exists;

(b) the occupier knows or has reasonable grounds to believe that
the other is in the vicinity of the danger concerned or that he
may come into its vicinity; and

(c) the risk is one against which, in all the circumstances of the
case, he may reasonably be expected to offer the other some
protection.[37]

Thus an occupier will not fall under the duty if he is not or has no
reason to be aware that the site is contaminated so as to present a
danger; nor if he could not reasonably anticipate the presence of
trespassers. However, many contaminated sites are of the very type to
attract trespassing children, scavenging adults, or gypsies, travellers or
other itinerants. Such circumstances can, in practical terms, present very
real difficulties for the occupier of the site, given that they may quite
naturally be reluctant to advertise to the whole world by warning signs
the fact that the site may be dangerously contaminated.

The occupier will first need to consider whether the risk is one in
respect of which he may reasonably be expected to offer protection: this
will depend principally on the nature of the risk, site conditions and on
the nature of the likely trespass. Obviously, more will be expected of the
occupier where small children are trespassing on bare toxic soil than
where adults are trespassing; since it may be anticipated that small
children are more likely to ingest soil. On the other hand in some cases
the risks to adults and children may be identical—for example the risk of
exposure to radioactive materials. Also, the risk that a trespasser may
disturb contaminants, for example by scavenging, should be considered.
Assuming it is reasonable to expect some steps to be taken the duty is to
take such care as is reasonable in all the circumstances.[38] In appropriate
cases the risk may be discharged by taking reasonable steps to give
warning of the danger or to discourage persons from incurring the risk;[39]
further, no duty is owed in respect of risks voluntarily accepted.[40] In
many cases the nature of contamination will not be such as to present an
obvious indication of risk: in practical terms the options will lie between
the use of warning signs or the construction of physical barriers.
However, a warning sign may not of itself be sufficient if trespass by
small children or even young adults may be anticipated and in such
cases the only safe solution may be steps physical to prevent access.[41] It

---

[37] *Ibid.*, s.1(3).
[38] *Ibid.*, s.1(4).
[39] *Ibid.*, s.1(5).
[40] *Ibid.*, s.1(6).
[41] Any barriers used will need to be properly maintained: see *Adams* v. *Southern Electricity Board, The Times*, October 21, 1993.

has not been settled whether the occupier's own financial resources are to be taken into account in determining what steps may be reasonably required[42] though this may be a very important practical issue in relation to a derelict and contaminated site.

GENERAL ISSUES

Causation and proof

2.34   One of the first general problems to be faced in any action involving soil contamination—the legal uncertainties apart—is that of proof. It may be extremely difficult to demonstrate a causal link between the acts or omissions of the defendant, or the state of the defendant's land, and the harm which is alleged to have resulted therefrom.[43] On normal principles it is for the plaintiff to prove (save where there are admissions) all the necessary ingredients of the tort; as such it is not necessary for the defendant to disprove anything.[44]

In some cases this burden may be capable of discharge reasonably easily: in particular where a given site is the only possible source of the particular contaminants in the relevant area of search. However in many cases there may be a number of possible sources of the problem or the contaminant in question, such as industrial triazines, may be ubiquitous. Discovery may of course assist the plaintiff,[45] as may the use of public sources of information and liaison with relevant public agencies. Public registers of waste disposal licences and prescribed process may be particularly useful, as may information held by public authorities which falls within the Environmental Information Regulations 1992:[46] this may include, for example, monitoring data held by the authorities.[47]

Expert evidence is likely to be crucial in such actions and may well involve a number of fields and disciplines depending on the nature of the case.[48] These may include: process engineering, hydrology, geo-

---

[42] Compare *British Railways Board* v. *Herrington* [1972] A.C. 877; see Winfield & Jolowicz, *Tort* (13th ed., 1989) p. 226.

[43] For a helpful practical discussion, see C. Pugh and M. Day, *Toxic Torts* (London 1992), Chap. 6.

[44] *McGhee* v. *National Coal Board* [1973] 1 W.L.R. 1; *Hotson* v. *East Berkshire Area Health Authority* [1987] A.C. 750; *Wiltshire* v. *Essex Area Health Authority* [1988] A.C. 1074.

[45] For example, it may reveal damaging surveys or consultants' reports commissioned by the defendant before litigation was in contemplation.

[46] S.I. 1992 No. 3240.

[47] *Ibid.*, reg. 2; information voluntarily supplied without any legal obligation to the authority is the subject of an exception by reg. 4. See further, Chap. 3.

[48] See C. Pugh and M. Day, *op. cit.*, Chap. p. 8.

logy, hydrogeology, chemistry, toxicology, ecology, biology, biochemistry, civil engineering, geotechnical engineering, materials science, waste management and even industrial archaeology. An expert witness should make it clear to the court when an issue or question falls outside his or her area of specialism or expertise.[49] The expert should also be wary of over-dramatising problems, as this may rebound on him seriously in the dispassionate atmosphere of the court.[50]

In the *Cambridge Water Company* case[51] detailed inquiries were carried out before any litigation to identify the source of the contaminants: these included the sinking of various boreholes by the Anglian Water Authority and further work by the British Geological Survey. This resulted in a considerable amount of data, calculations and deductions, none of which was admitted by the judge, who based his findings on the expert evidence before him. This evidence concerned both the general structure and behaviour of chalk aquifers and of the specific aquifer in question. It is notable that the trial judge generally preferred the evidence of a civil engineer who had subsequently specialised in hydrology and hydrogeology and that of a qualified geologist and hydrogeologist to that of an equally senior civil engineer who had practised in geotechnical engineering; his chosen specialism involved consideration of ground loadings and this required an understanding of groundwater influences, but his knowledge of the particular subject was "considerably less detailed".[52]

Concurrent causes

Problems can arise in that harm which is related to pollution may **2.35** have come about from one or more of a number of sources between which it may be impossible to allocate responsibility. Two situations must be distinguished. The first is where it is clear that one source has made a material contribution to the damage, but its extent is not clear. The inability to allocate contributions precisely will not be a bar to recovery,[53] though it may raise issues of joint and several liability.[54] The second situation is where it is clear that only one exposure among a

[49] *National Justice Compania Naviera S.A.* v. *Prudential Assurance Company Ltd. (Ikarian Reefer), The Times*, March 5, 1993.
[50] See *Foliejohn Establishment* v. *Gain S.A.*, July 7, 1993 (Chancery Division), para. 11.10 below.
[51] [1992] Env.L.R. 116 (first instance); [1993] Env.L.R. 287 (C.A.): [1994] 2 W.L.R. 53 (C.A. and H.L.).
[52] *Ibid.* at pp. 121–122. See also the helpful summary of Stuart-Smith L.J. as to evaluation of expert evidence in *Loveday* v. *Renton & Wellcome Foundation Ltd.* [1990] 1 Med.L.R. 117.
[53] *Bonnington Castings* v. *Wardlaw* [1956] A.C. 613.
[54] See para. 2.40 below.

number could have triggered the problem.[55] Various approaches have been taken to this second situation, principally in the field of product liability: these range from holding no-one liable because of lack of proof of causation through to holding all potentially responsible parties jointly and severally liable for the entire harm, leaving the potentially liable parties to have recourse against each other. The joint and several liability approach was adopted in The Netherlands in the landmark case of the *DES Daughters*.[56] based on Article 6:99 of the 1992 Dutch Civil Code. Other suggested bases of liability put forward in the *DES* case founded on market share were rejected as potentially adverse to the interests of the plaintiffs. It remains to be seen to what extent this approach may be adopted elsewhere in Europe and applied to environmental liability as opposed to product liability.

Remedies: damages

2.36   Two distinct questions arise in relation to the issue of damages: first, whether damage is a pre-requisite of actionability and, second, the type of damage which may be recovered. Contaminated land may cause physical damage to property, personal injury, or even death. In such cases, damages will be assessed on ordinary principles, and will be limited by the principle of foreseeability.[57] Where nuisance results in damage to personal property or personal injury to the plaintiff, such damages can be recovered as consequential.[58] On the other hand, nuisance may involve only interference with the use of land, for example by preventing the use of a garage or other outbuildings, or the use of a garden for young children to play in[59]: damages here will be based on diminution in the value of the property.

However, contamination of land or groundwater by migrating pollutants may be a gradual, even imperceptible, process, and thus the issue arises of the point at which material damage occurs. Some torts are actionable without proof of damage, such as trespass[60] and interference with easements or profits.[61] Others, such as negligence and *Rylands* v.

---

[55] *Wintle* v. *Conaust* [1989] V.R. 951 (F.C.).
[56] Supreme Court of The Netherlands, October 9, 1992, Case No. 14667 (RvdW 1992, No. 219) [1993] Env.Liab. C525; see also [1993] Env.Liab. 72 at p. 73, van Dunne, Bierboons and Van).
[57] See paras. 2.23 and 2 26.
[58] *Halsey* v. *Esso Petroleum Co. Ltd.* [1961] 1 All E.R. 145; subject to some doubts as to whether personal injury can be sued for in nuisance: see *Cunard* v. *Antifyre Ltd.* [1993] 1 K.B. 551.
[59] *Gertsen* v. *Municipality of Metropolitan Toronto* (1973) 41 D.L.R. (3rd) 646.
[60] Para. 2.04.
[61] Para. 2.21.

Fletcher, clearly require material damage in order to be actionable and unless there is such damage pure economic loss will be irrecoverable. With nuisance, the position appears to depend upon the type of nuisance in question: some nuisances involve an encroachment upon land and are actionable without proving actual financial or physical damage.[62] In other cases, where the nuisance involves physical damage to land, it is necessary here to show actual, as opposed to prospective, damage.[63] Where the nuisance is of the type involving interference with the use and enjoyment of land, no actual financial loss or interference with health need be proved.[64]

The problem lies in pigeon-holing a typical contaminated land situation within these categories: ingress of contaminants could constitute a physical encroachment, they could cause damage and they could interfere with the use of land. The real harm to the plaintiff may lie in the fact that the development potential of his land is affected— where the migration of chemical contamination means that development of a site cannot take place without costly decontamination works what is the true nature of the damage and is it recoverable?

It seems likely that, in such contamination cases, the court will require there to be some actual and substantial damage. The mere presence of detectable traces of contaminants will not of itself constitute such damage,[65] even if a more serious cumulative effect may be foreseen in the future. As the matter was put in a well-known passage from *Salvin* v. *North Brancepath Coal Co.*:[66]

> "It would have been wrong, as it seems to me, for this Court in the reign of Henry VI to have interfered with the further use of sea coal in London, because it had been ascertained to their satisfaction, or predicted to their satisfaction, that by the reign of Queen Victoria both white and red roses would have ceased to bloom in the Temple Garden."

The damage from contamination may only come about when it is discovered, or when increasingly strict regulatory standards apply,[67] or when a regulatory body takes action, or when proposals for development are adversely affected, or when a transaction is aborted. In this respect,

---

[62] *Fay* v. *Prentice* (1845) 1 C.B. 828; in one case, it has been reported that a substantial settlement has been reached for alleged contamination of farmland by dioxin, involving restrictions in sale of produce and consequent economic loss: see *"Coalite Dioxin Settlement"* [1993] E.L.R. December 5, 1993.

[63] *Sedleigh Denfield* v. *O'Callaghan* [1940] A.C. 880, 919.

[64] *Crump* v. *Lambert* (1867) L.R. 3 Eq. 409.

[65] *Cambridge Water Co.* v. *Eastern Counties Leather PLC* [1992] Env.L.R. 116. 144.

[66] (1874) 2 Ch. App. 705, 709.

[67] [1992] Env.L.R. 116, 144.

each case will depend on its own facts. Once such damage is shown, then in principle the quantum of damages will be the sum required to put the plaintiff back into the position he would have been in had the tort not been committed: in general, this may be either the cost of remedial measures or the diminution in the value of the land.[68]

The *Cambridge Water Company* case gives some indication of possible approaches to damages in aquifer pollution cases.[69] The plaintiffs in that case first tried pumping the contaminated water to waste. When it was apparent that this was not removing the contaminants, the course adopted was to move up-catchment and tap the aquifer above the source of pollution; this involved research, the acquisition of land, construction of a new pumping station and the laying of new mains. The possible alternative solutions of blending with uncontaminated water and constructing an air-stripping plant were both rejected. It was held contrary to the arguments of the defendants, that it was reasonable not to adopt the air-stripping solution, which could have given rise to other environmental problems. The quantum of damage was thus effectively the cost of the new source of supply, less any element of betterment to reflect over-design of the new pumping station. The defendants argued unsuccessfully that the correct approach was to take the value of the polluted borehole and treat that as redundant, applying an inflation correction.

The courts will be wary of awarding damages in lieu of an injunction in the case of a continuing nuisance, because there will be nothing to prevent the plaintiff pocketing the damages, selling his property, and leaving the defendant exposed to further actions by the purchaser.[70]

Remedies: exemplary damages

2.37   The case of *AB* v. *South West Water Services Ltd.*[71] raised, in a very stark way, the potential applicability of exemplary damages to pollution cases. The action arose from the contamination of public water supplies at Camelford, Cornwall by the accidental introduction of some 20 tonnes of aluminium sulphate. Consumers of the water brought actions for damages under negligence, nuisance, public nuisance, contact, breach of statutory duty and the rule in *Rylands* v. *Fletcher*. Those claims included aggravated and exemplary damages on the basis of alleged arrogant and high-handed responses to the problem by the water undertaker. Liability for breach of statutory duty was in fact admitted by the defendant, who had already been prosecuted for and convicted of public nuisance.

---

[68] Clerk & Lindsell, *Torts* (16th ed., 1989) para. 24–16.
[69] [1992] Env.L.R. 116, 147.
[70] *Bar-Gur* v. *Squire* [1993] E.G.C.S. 151.
[71] [1993] 1 All E.R. 609.

The Court of Appeal held following *Rookes* v. *Barnard*[72] that there was binding House of Lords authority that awards of exemplary damages should be restricted to torts recognised in 1964 as being capable of grounding such a claim. On that basis it does not appear, in the absence of further House of Lords authority to the contrary, that exemplary damages can be awarded for negligence or for breach of statutory duty (unless the statute itself expressly creates such a remedy). Nor, the Court of Appeal held, could exemplary damages be awarded for public nuisance.

On the other hand, there was (at least arguably) authority in favour of private nuisance as a cause of action for which exemplary damages could be awarded.[73] However, it appears from the decision that such awards "should be confined to those cases of private nuisance where there is deliberate and wilful interference with the plaintiff's rights of enjoyment of land and the defendant has calculated that the profit or benefit for him will exceed the damages he may have to pay."[74] The Court of Appeal held that the defendant's conduct did not fall within that description, nor was the privatised water company to be regarded as an agency of Government which might have brought it within the other category of cases where exemplary damages might be awarded.[75] Therefore the potential applicability of exemplary damages to contamination cases, whilst not to be ignored, is relatively limited.

Remedies: injunctive relief

Where ongoing activity is causing contamination of land which is **2.38** resulting in a nuisance (for example by contaminating an aquifer) an injunction restraining the continuation of that action may be an appropriate and effective remedy. In the *Cambridge Water Company* case at first instance Ian Kennedy J. had no doubt that if there were continuing spillages, there should be an injunction to restrain their continuance, indeed in appropriate circumstances a quia timet injunction.[76]

However, where the spillage or other contamination has already happened, any injunctive relief is likely to be essentially mandatory in

---

[72] [1964] A.C. 1129, read in conjunction with *Cassell & Co. Ltd.* v. *Broome* [1972] A.C. 1027.

[73] *Bell* v. *Midland Rly. Co.* (1861) 10 C.B.N.S. 287; *Guppys (Bridport) Ltd.* v. *Brookling* (1983) 14 H.L.R. 1.

[74] [1993] 1 All E.R. 609 at 621, *per* Stuart-Smith L.J.; *Rookes* v. *Barnard* [1964] A.C. 1129 at 1225 *per* Lord Devlin.

[75] [1964] A.C. 1129 at 1225 *per* Lord Devlin; [1993] 1 All E.R. 609 at 628 *per* Sir Thomas Bingham M.R.

[76] [1992] Env.L.R. 116 at 144. As to *quia timet* injunctions, see Clerk & Lindsell, *Torts* (16th ed., 1989) para. 7–07.

form, requiring the defendant to remove or neutralise contaminants, or at least to keep them within his own boundary. Any such remedy would be at the discretion of the court and would need to follow the principles laid down in *Morris* v. *Redland Bricks Ltd.*:[77]

(a) the jurisdiction should be used cautiously and only in cases where extreme or at least very serious damage would be likely to ensure were the injunction withheld;
(b) the damage which would follow refusal of the injunction must be such that any damages awarded in respect of it would be an inadequate remedy;
(c) the defendant must be able to comply legally;
(d) the cost to the defendant must be taken into account relative to the risk of damage; and
(e) the defendant must know exactly what he has to do to comply, so that he may give precise instructions to his contractors.

This last principle is particularly important and would preclude the grant of any injunction in general terms such as "to remove contaminants to safe levels" or "to take all necessary steps to ensure containment of contaminants within the defendant's land."

A mandatory injunction will be refused where the defendant has himself carried out sufficiently effective works.[78]

Remedies: abatement

2.39   Whilst in theory the self-help remedy of abatement may be available in contaminated land cases, it is one which will need to be considered and exercised with extreme caution. It has been said that a man may enter a neighbour's land "and remove an accumulation of filth and offal which interferes with the use and enjoyment of his own property."[79] Entry on a neighbour's land to carry out extensive remedial works in relation to contaminated land is, however, a different matter altogether, and not one to be undertaken lightly.[80] In particular, it will need to be a case where the plaintiff would be likely to be able to obtain a mandatory injunction;[81] as little damage as possible should be caused to the wrongdoer and other third parties; entry must be peaceable; and in most

---

[77] [1970] A.C. 652 at pp. 665–6.
[78] *Leakey* v. *National Trust* [1978] Q.B. 849, affirmed on other grounds at [1980] Q.B. 485.
[79] Clerk & Lindsell, *Torts* (16th ed., 1989) para. 8–18, citing *Jones* v. *Williams* (1843) 11 M. & W. 176.
[80] The principles are set out at Clerk & Lindsell, para. 8–18.
[81] See para. 2.38.

cases prior notice will need to be given. In practice therefore to avoid risks to the plaintiff, the nature of the works will need to be agreed in most significant details with the defendant: the remedy is unlikely to be employed in any but the most straightforward and urgent cases.

Works of abatement carried out on one's own land raise different considerations. Such action is not risk free. In *Midland Bank plc* v. *Bardgrove Property Services Ltd. and John Willmott (G.B.) Ltd.*[82] the plaintiffs carried out sheet piling work on their own land at a cost of £230,000 to counteract the probability of future subsidence resulting from excavations on adjoining land; no opportunity was given to the defendants to do the work themselves. It was held that no cause of action arose until there was actual physical damage; accordingly there was no right to recover money spent to prevent anticipated future instability.

Where contamination migrates by means of transport in water, whether surface groundwater, the decision in *Home Brewery Co. Ltd.* v. *William Davis & Co. (Leicester) Ltd.*[83] may be relevant. It was held in that case that:

(a) an occupier of land has no cause of action against the occupier of higher adjacent land for permitting the passage of natural, unchannelled water onto the lower land;

(b) however, nor is the lower occupier under any obligation to accept such water and as such is entitled to take steps consistent with his reasonable user of land to prevent it entering, even if that causes damage to the higher land;

(c) if those steps by the lower owner are unreasonable and the damage to the higher land is reasonably foreseeable, the occupier of the higher land will have an action in nuisance; and

(d) general works of construction or infilling which "squeeze out" water from the lower to the higher land resulting in reasonably foreseeable damage will also be actionable.

Joint and several liability

Contaminated land cases may raise issues of joint and several liability **2.40** in various ways. Two or more parties may be joint tortfeasors in the strict sense of having together committed a tort (as in the case of a landowner and a waste contractor who enter into a tipping licence which results in a tort); alternatively they may both be liable in respect of the same tort (for example the former landowner who is responsible for having caused a nuisance and his successor in title who is responsible in respect of its continuance).

[82] [1992] N.P.C. 83.
[83] [1987] 1 Q.B. 339.

Other than these cases, there are situations where two or more parties have contributed in some way to damage suffered by the plaintiff. This may be the case where the actions of the parties have created a single source of pollution, for example where a number or companies have independently disposed of wastes at the same site. Alternatively, the parties may have created separate sources of pollution, which have then contaminated the same property; as where a number of industrial companies all contribute to the contamination of an aquifer.

In such cases the essential, though often difficult, distinction to be drawn is between those cases where the actions of the defendants cause different damage to the plaintiff and those cases where they cause the plaintiff to suffer a single injury. In the first case the causes of action against each tortfeasor are distinct and the plaintiff may recover from each only that part of the damage for which they were responsible.[84] In the second case the plaintiff may recover the entirety of his loss against all or any of the tortfeasors, irrespective of the extent of their individual participation.[85] Statutory rights of contribution between the joint tortfeasors exist in these circumstances.[86]

The distinction outlined above may be difficult to draw, but by way of illustration, where a number of parties create a single source of pollution which then migrates onto the plaintiff's land their liability would appear to be joint and several; the same would seem to be the case where, from independent sources, the parties contaminate the plaintiff's land with the same or similar substances in such a way that the separate pollution cannot be distinguished. If by contrast one party had contaminated the plaintiff's land with migrating heavy metals and another with organic compounds, so that the two types of contamination could be distinguished, it would seem arguable that liability should not be joint and several, there being no reason why either party should be held liable for injury which they clearly did not cause.

The situation was considered in the *Cambridge Water Company* case[87] where there were two potential sources of the contaminant solvents affecting the plaintiff's borehole; both were tanneries. It was concluded that the vast majority of the contamination came from the premises of Eastern Counties Leather plc and that on the evidence it was not possible to find that the second defendants, Hutchings and Harding Ltd., had produced any measurable effect on the water of the borehole. Ian Kennedy J. said:[88]

[84] *Performance Cars Ltd.* v. *Abraham* [1962] 1 Q.B. 33.
[85] *Dougherty* v. *Chandler* (1946) 46 S.R. (N.S.W.) 370, 375. See also the discussion on concurrent causes at para. 2.35 above.
[86] Civil Liability (Contribution) Act 1978.
[87] [1992] Env.L.R. 116.
[88] *Ibid.*, at 146.

"I cannot think it right that a contributor whose addition is insignificant must be held liable because his mite is associated with a clear case of pollution by another. I suspect there can be no rule to meet every case and that each case must be seen on its own".

As such Hutchings and Harding Ltd. were not jointly liable, nor indeed liable at all. The position might well have been different had their contribution to the pollution been "sensible", albeit not as substantial as that of Eastern Counties Leather.[89]

Limitation of actions: the Limitation Act 1980

Under the Limitation Act 1980, s.2 an action founded on tort shall not **2.41** be brought after the expiration of six years from the date on which the cause of action accrued. This general provision does not apply to actions for negligence, nuisance or breach of duty where the damages claimed include damages in respect of personal injuries to the plaintiff or any other person: in such cases by section 11 the limitation period is three years from:

    (a) the date on which the cause of action accrued; or

    (b) the date of knowledge (if later) of the injured person.[90]

Limitation is potentially an extremely important and difficult issue in contaminated land cases, given the long time-scales which can be involved before harm occurs or before harm, having occurred, is detected. It may be very difficult to pinpoint the time at which any cause of action accrued.

In many cases involving contaminated land there may be a continuing wrong as contaminated groundwater or gas migrates over time onto the plaintiff's property: here it can be said that fresh causes of action continue to accrue and that action can be brought in respect of whatever portion of the continuing wrong lies within the limitation period.[91] This is easy to state but much more difficult to apply. Similarly, where groundwater is polluted, it is arguable that damage continues to occur for so long as the pollutants remain in the groundwater, regardless of how long it has been since the defendant's acts or omissions which caused the pollution.[92] Certainly, limitation appears not to have been a

---

[89] *Pride of Derby & Derbyshire Angling Association Ltd.* v. *British Celanese Ltd.* [1952] 1 All E.R. 1326 at 1342; [1953] 1 Ch. 149, pp. 152–153.

[90] See s.14; on the issue of knowledge see *Nash and Others* v. *Eli Lilly & Co.* [1993] 4 All E.R. 383.

[91] See Clerk & Lindsell, *Torts* (16th ed., 1989) para. 9–34.

[92] An analogy can be drawn with *Darley Main Colliery* v. *Mitchell* (1886) 11 H.L. Cas. 127 which holds that a fresh action or withdrawal of support for land will lie for each separate incident of subsidence, however long since the defendant ceased acting.

problem for the plaintiff in the *Cambridge Water Company* case, even though it was some seven years from the date when spillages were found to have ceased to the date when the plaintiff's well was closed down.

Where damage is an essential ingredient of the tort, the rule is that there is no cause of action and the limitation period does not begin to run until the damage occurs. In some cases involving contaminated land it may be obvious when the damage occurred (for example a methane explosion); in other cases it may be obscure (for example contamination of a water supply source or aggressive effect on foundations or services). The difficulty for a plaintiff is that in general the time runs from the date the damage occurred, not the date on which it was discovered or reasonably could have been discovered.[93] In claims involving personal injury the difficulty is alleviated by section 11 of the Limitation Act:[94] in other cases the only argument open to the plaintiff may be that some fact relevant to the plaintiff's right of action has been deliberately concealed from him by the defendant.[95]

It should be noted that the general time limit for actions based on tort does not apply to claims for injunctions or other equitable remedies, except in so far as the court may apply those time limits by analogy.[96]

Limitation of actions: latent damage

2.42   Sections 14A and 14B of the Limitation Act 1980, inserted by the Latent Damage Act 1986, deal with actions in respect of latent damage other than those involving personal injuries (to which section 11 applies). By subsection (4) the limitation period is either:

(a) six years from the date on which the cause of action accrued; or
(b) three years from the "starting date" if that period expires later than the six-year period mentioned at (a).

The "starting date" is the earliest date on which the plaintiff or any person in whom the cause of action was vested before him had both the knowledge required for bringing an action and a right to bring it.[97] Knowledge in this sense means knowledge of the material facts about the damage[98] and other facts such as causation and the identity of the defendant.[99] It includes knowledge which the plaintiff might reasonably

[93] *Pirelli General Cable Works Ltd.* v. *Oscar Faber and Partners* [1983] 2 A.C. 1.
[94] Also by the discretionary power of the court to disapply the time limits of s.11 and s.33.
[95] S.32(1)(*b*); though see also para. 2.42 below.
[96] S.36(1).
[97] S.14A(5).
[98] S.14A(6)(*a*) and (7).
[99] S.14A(6)(*b*) and (8).

have been expected to acquire from facts observable or ascertainable by him or from facts ascertainable with the help of appropriate expert advice which it is reasonable for him to seek.[1]

By section 14B an overriding time limit is applied to actions for negligence not involving personal injuries: this is a period of 15 years from the date (or, if more than one, the last of the dates) on which there occurred any act or omission:

(a) which is alleged to constitute negligence; and

(b) to which the damage in respect of which damages are claimed is alleged to be attributable (in whole or in part).

The effect of this "long-stop" provision is to bar any cause of action to which the section applies even if the cause of action has not yet accrued and even if the starting date for reckoning the period under section 14A has not yet occurred.[2]

The potential significance of these provisions in relation to contaminated land situations depends to a large extent on the meaning given to the term "negligence" in sections 14A and 14B. It appears that the word covers only the tort of negligence *per se* and not, for example, the tort of nuisance, at least where negligence is not involved.[3] If correct, this is be a potentially significant difference between negligence and the other torts, since it could frequently be argued in contaminated land cases that the ordinary six-year period should be extended in accordance with the provisions of section 14A to allow, for example, expert evidence to be taken to establish the source of groundwater contamination.

Conversely, the overriding time limit of section 14B could be important in the context of, say, a landfill site completed more than 15 years ago. If it is alleged that the site was operated or engineered negligently then the 15-year period would run from the completion of the site at the latest: though it might be argued that failure to monitor or to take remedial action constitute further acts or omissions so as to defer the commencement of the period. If it is correct that section 14B does not apply to nuisance or *Rylands* v. *Fletcher*, time in respect of those torts would run from the time the cause of action accrued, which might well allow an action to be brought after the expiry of the 15-year period under the section.

---

[1] S.14A(A)(10).

[2] S.14B(2).

[3] Clerk & Lindsell, *Torts* (16th ed., 1989) para. 9–55, p. 418. The term "negligence" has been construed as referring to the tort of negligence, and not to claims in contract: see *Société Commerciale de Réassurance* v. *ERAS (International) Ltd. Re ERAS EIL Appeals (Note)* [1992] 2 All E.R. 82 (C.A.); *Iron Trade Mutual Association Insurance Co. Ltd.* v. *J.K. Buckenham Ltd.* [1990] 1 All E.R. 808.

LIABILITY UNDER THE ENVIRONMENTAL PROTECTION ACT 1990, PART I

Generally

2.43   To the extent that contamination of land arises from the carrying on of a process prescribed for central or local control, the provisions of Part I of the Environmental Protection Act 1990 are relevant. Contamination of soil or groundwater by prescribed or other harmful substances as a result of a release from a Part A process prescribed for integrated pollution control may well involve breach either of a condition of the authorisation or of the general obligation of section 7(4) of the Act to use best available techniques not entailing excessive cost to prevent or curtail emissions. Similarly where such contamination occurs as a result of deposition of airborne matter there may be a breach of the Act's requirements for Part B processes prescribed for local authority air pollution control.

The legal consequences of such breaches are as follows:

(a) Carrying on the process otherwise than in accordance with the conditions of authorisation (express or implied) is an offence, as indeed is carrying on the process without any authorisation at all.[4] The offence is punishable by a fine not exceeding £20,000 on summary conviction or an unlimited fine and a term not exceeding two years' imprisonment on conviction on indictment.[5]

(b) If the enforcing authority is of the opinion that the operator is contravening any condition of the authorisation or is likely to do so, it may serve an enforcement notice.[6] This is therefore a course of action only open in cases of an ongoing infraction or one which it is anticipated will recur. In such cases the notice will specify the matters constituting the contravention and the steps required to remedy it;[7] thus the notice may be suitable for use where an ongoing release is causing contamination, but is not apt to achieve remediation of historic contamination or a single, non-recurrent, release.

(c) If the enforcing authority is of the opinion that continuation of the carrying on of the process, generally or in a particular manner, involves an imminent risk of serious pollution of the environment then a prohibition notice may be served.[8] This

[4] S.6(1), 23(1)(*a*).
[5] S.23(2).
[6] S.13(1).
[7] S.13(2).
[8] S.14(1).

notice will specify the steps to be taken to remove the risk and direct that the authorisation shall cease to have effect for the purpose of authorising the process until such time as the notice is withdrawn.[9] Whilst soil or groundwater contamination may present an imminent risk of serious pollution, in order to enable the procedure to be used that risk must be the result of that process being continued or being continued in a particular manner: therefore as with the enforcement notice, a prohibition notice will only be of real relevance in case of ongoing release.

(d) Where an enforcement notice or prohibition notice is served, failure to comply with the notice will constitute an offence, punishable by the same penalties as for breach of section 6, referred to at (a) above.[10]

(e) Where an enforcement or prohibition notice is served, and the enforcing authority is of the opinion that proceedings for an offence under (d) above would be an ineffectual remedy, the authority may take injunctive proceedings in the High Court (or in Scotland, any court of competent jurisdiction) for the purpose of securing compliance.[11]

(f) Where a person is convicted of an offence under (a) or (d) above in respect of any matters which appears to the court to be in his power to remedy, the court may order him to take specified steps for remedying those matters; this may be in addition to or instead of any punishment.[12] The scope of this power is not entirely clear: it could be argued that it may be used to secure general measures of a remedial nature, for example decontamination. However, strictly speaking, the "matters" to be remedied would appear to be those in respect of which the accused was convicted, *i.e.* the breach of condition or non-compliance with the notice. The marginal note to the section refers to the "cause of offence", but this does not appear to correspond with the actual wording of the provision.

(g) Where the commission of an offence under (a) or (d) above causes any harm which it is possible to remedy, the chief inspector (or, in Scotland, a river purification authority) may arrange for any reasonable steps to be taken towards remedying the harm and may recover the cost of taking those steps from any person convicted of the offence.[13] Wide powers of entry exist to facilitate such steps.[14] The provision therefore constitutes the

[9] S.14(2).
[10] S.23(2).
[11] S.24.
[12] S.26(1).
[13] S.27(1).
[14] S.17.

closest approximation to a general "clean up" power to be found in Part I of the Act; however, the power extends only to the remedying of actual "harm"[15] and not to anticipatory or preventive measures. It does not appear that the enforcing authority must wait for a conviction before exercising these powers, though no costs may be recovered until conviction. The written approval of the Secretary of State is necessary before the powers are exercised; also where steps are taken on or will affect land in the occupation of anyone other than the person on whose land the prescribed process is being carried on, the permission of that person is needed.[16]

WATER POLLUTION

Criminal liability for water pollution: principal offences

2.44   Section 85 of The Water Resources Act 1991 creates the principal offences in relation to pollution of controlled waters. Some of these may be of relevance in the case of surface waters or groundwater polluted by the ingress of substances from contaminated land:

(1) Causing or knowingly permitting any poisonous, noxious or polluting matter or any solid waste matter to enter controlled waters. Clearly, this offence may be applicable to a contaminated land situation.[17]

(2) Causing or knowingly permitting any matter, other than trade effluent or sewage effluent, to enter controlled waters by being discharged from a drain or sewer in contravention of a prohibition imposed under section 86 of the Act. This offence, being dependent on the matter in question being discharged through a drain or sewer, is perhaps unlikely to be relevant in the majority of contaminated land situations.

(3) Causing or knowingly permitting any trade effluent or sewage effluent to be discharged:
   (a) into any controlled waters; or
   (b) from land in England and Wales, through a pipe into the sea outside the seaward limits of controlled waters.

---

[15] See s.1(4) for the definition of "harm" which clearly could result from, or indeed constitute, soil contamination.
[16] S.27(2).
[17] See further para. 2.46 below.

The second limb of the offence is not relevant here, but, to the extent that the material which enters controlled waters from contaminated land is regarded as trade effluent or sewage effluent, the first limb may be of relevance.[18]

(4) Causing or knowingly permitting trade effluent or sewage effluent to be discharged, in contravention of a section 86 prohibition, from a building or from fixed plant:

    (a) on to or into any land; or

    (b) into waters of a lake or pond which are not inland freshwaters.

This offence is only committed if the discharge contravenes a prohibition imposed under section 86 by notice served by the NRA on the discharger or by virtue of regulations prescribing either substances or processes for this purpose.[19] The implication of this is that in the absence of such a prohibition, trade and sewage effluent may be discharged in the ways mentioned in the subsection without any discharge consent. For example, therefore, trade effluent may be discharged (subject to any requirement for a waste management licence) onto land or into a pit, or into a pond or lagoon, provided that it does not itself discharge into a river or watercourse or into another lake or pond which so discharges.

The provision only applies, and consequently an offence can only be committed, where the discharge is from a building or from fixed plant. Thus the removal of trade effluent from open land (e.g. leachate from a landfill site) by road tanker to a settlement lagoon would not be within the subsection, whereas conveyance of the same material by a system of pipework would.

(5) The entry of matter into land freshwaters so as to impede the flow, thereby aggravating pollution. Its relevance to most contaminated land situations would appear to be limited.

(6) The contravention of the conditions of any discharge consent. In practice most discharges from contaminated land are of their nature likely to be unconsented.[19a]

"Controlled waters"

The offences referred to above are in the main related to the pollution **2.45** of controlled waters. The definition of this term is provided by section 104 of the Water Resources Act and encompasses:

[18] See further para. 2.47 below.
[19] S.86(1) and (2); no such prescriptive regulations have as yet been made.
[19a] On the collateral challenge to consent conditions by way of defence to prosecution, see *R. v. Ettrick Trout Co. Ltd. and William Baxter* [1994] Env. L.R. 165.

(1) territorial waters extending seaward for three miles from the territorial sea baselines;

(2) coastal waters, *i.e.* those within the territorial sea baseline as far as the high tide level or fresh water limits and including any enclosed dock adjoining such waters;

(3) waters of relevant lakes or ponds, *i.e.* any lake or pond (whether natural or artificial or above or below ground) which discharges into a relevant river or watercourse (see below) or into another lake or pond which is itself a relevant lake or pond[20];

(4) Waters of relevant rivers or watercourses above the fresh water limit.[21] This term includes underground and artificial rivers or watercourses but excludes public sewers and sewers or drains which run into public sewers;

(5) Groundwaters, *i.e.*, "any waters contained in underground strata".[22]

Some of these provisions are subject to the power of the Secretary of State to make an order providing how waters are to be treated in terms of these definitions.[23]

The "poisonous, noxious or polluting matter" offence

2.46 As stated above, the offence relating to the entry of poisonous, noxious or polluting matter into controlled waters is of relevance to contaminated land. The Act provides no definition of the phrase "poisonous, noxious or polluting"; nor until recently was there any judicial authority on the point.

In *National Rivers Authority* v. *Egger UK Ltd.*[24] a ruling was given in the context of a submission relating to the meaning of the term "polluting" in section 85. The defence argued that the word can only be understood in the context of what the matter in question affects, harms or worsens; in other words that some form of demonstrable effect was a prerequisite. The prosecution argued that all that was necessary was that the matter discharged was, of its nature, capable of causing harm. The judge accepted the prosecution's argument and suggested that the correct test was to look at the nature of the discharge and ask:

---

[20] Together, relevant lakes or ponds and relevant rivers or watercourses are known as "island freshwaters."

[21] *Ibid.*

[22] On groundwater protection see further, Chap. 6.

[23] S.104(4).

[24] Newcastle upon Tyne Crown Court, June 15–17, 1992 (unreported).

"Is that discharge capable of causing harm to a river, in the sense of causing damage to uses to which a river might be put; damage to animal, vegetable or other—if there is such other life which might live in a river, or damaging that river aesthetically? . . . One looks at that test in relation, it seems to me, to a natural, unpolluted river, and if the discharge is capable of causing such harm, then the offence is made out; the material amounts to polluting matter. . . It is, in my view, wholly unnecessary to prove that damage was, in fact, caused."

The case is authority only in relation to the word "polluting" and did not consider "poisonous" and "noxious". However, while "polluting" is a wider term than "poisonous" or "noxious" the same problem occurs: is it necessary to show that the entry of the matter had a poisonous or noxious effect, or simply that it was of its nature poisonous or noxious? The terms would appear to relate principally to the characteristics of the substance.

The issue is a very important one since unlike incidents of surface water pollution (as in the *Egger* Case), water pollution resulting from contaminated land may take years to present any signs of harmful effects. Even then, the harm is unlikely to present itself in any obvious form such as dead fish; but may, rather, have aesthetic effects such as discolouration from leaching or may present a threat to public or private abstraction sources. If the argument is accepted that capability to cause harm is sufficient and that "harm" is determined by effect on legitimate uses of surface and groundwater, then the task of bringing prosecutions under section 85 for pollution from contaminated sites will be eased considerably. The suggestion in *Egger* that the test is to be applied in relation to "a natural, unpolluted river" will also make the prosecution's task easier by avoiding, for example, arguments by the defence that their contribution to the state of an already less than pristine aquifer or watercourse could not be regarded as "polluting".

By section 89(3) of the 1991 Act, a person will not be guilty of the offence by reason only of permitting water from an abandoned mine to enter controlled waters. The issue of the polluting effects of such mine water has given rise to much public controversy, particulary as former mines are closed in increasing numbers. In one case[24a] British Coal has successfully defended a private prosecution by the Anglers' Cooperative Association in relation to pollution of the River Rhymney, though it is

---

[24a] *R.* v. *British Coal Corporation*, Cardiff Crown Court, December 2, 1993—*Sweet & Maxwell Environmental Law Bulletin*, No. 1, January 1994 (the successful defence was on grounds of causation, rather than the specific statutory defence).

possible that an appeal and civil injunctive proceedings may follow.[25] A recent report of the National Rivers Authority highlights the lack of any effective means of redress against pollution from abandoned mines under current statutory provisions.[25a]

The "trade effluent" or "sewage effluent" offences

2.47 By section 85(3), the discharge of trade effluent or sewage effluent into any controlled waters may result in an offence. If trade or sewage effluent is discharged then it does not matter whether the material is poisonous, noxious or polluting: it is the origin of the effluent which is crucial, not its characteristics. "Sewage effluent" is defined by section 221(1) as including any effluent from the sewage disposal or sewage treatment works of a sewage undertaker. Whilst the intention behind the definition is probably the ordinary outflow from sewage treatment works, it is conceivable that the definition might also extend to effluent resulting from soil contamination works site.

"Trade effluent" includes, by section 221(1), any effluent which is discharged from premises used for carrying on any trade or industry, other than surface water or domestic sewage. The application of this definition to contaminated land situations is problematic, though it is certainly possible to envisage situations where the offence could be relevant. Leachate from a still operational landfill site (possibly one which has ceased to receive waste but is being actively managed) can be regarded as trade effluent; as can waste oils or solvents leaking from tanks or drums on an industrial site.

It should be noted, however, that the language of section 85(3) is materially different to that of section 85(1): whereas the latters refers to an *entry* of matter into controlled waters, section 85(3) refers to the *discharge* from premises used for trade or industry. It does not necessarily follow that every entry of matter from such premises into controlled waters can be aptly described as a "discharge".[25b]

---

[25] *Environment Business*, December 15, 1993, p. 1.

[25a] *Abandoned Mines and the Water Environment*, Water Quality Series No. 14, March 1994.

[25b] This argument appears to have been accepted by magistrates in the unsuccessful prosecution of Coal Products Limited by the NRA (Chesterfield Magistrates Court, 1994). The magistrates held that tar deposits from a closed coal carbonisation site which had seeped into the River Rother had not been "discharged", that term implying release via a pipe or similar connection. Accordingly there was no case to answer under s.85(3).

Causing and knowingly permitting

The offences in relation to controlled waters may be committed either **2.48**
by causing or by knowingly permitting. In the case of pollution from
contaminated land the offence of "causing" will be committed by the
person who initially caused the contamination. Causation in this respect
will be approached in an everyday commons sense way and does not
imply any requirement of intention or negligence.[26] Thus an accidental
spillage which has the consequence of contaminating land and subsequently surface water or groundwater may constitute the offence. The
storage or handling of material can be sufficient to establish causation in
that sense.[27]

However, a charge of causing will not appropriate where the defendant's role is a completely passive one,[28] for example where contaminated material leaches onto the defendant's property from another site
and thence into controlled waters or where the defendant's land is
contaminated by a spillage caused by a trespasser or equivalent third
party.[29] Here a charge of "knowingly permitting" may be the appropriate course: permitting is a looser and vaguer concept than causing[30] and
may have various shades of meaning ranging from giving permission, or
giving control, through to failing to prevent.

In cases of historic contamination, where the owner or occupier of
land was not the cause, criminal liability will turn on the issue of
"knowingly permitting", There are two elements to this offence: the
failure to prevent pollution, and knowledge on the part of the defendant.[31] Clearly, a landowner if he does not know that his land is

---

[26] *Alphacell Ltd.* v. *Woodward* [1972] A.C. 824 (H.L.); *Wrothwell Ltd.* v. *Yorkshire Water Authority* [1984] Crim.L.R. 43; *Southern Water Authority* v. *Pegrum and Pegrum* (1989) 153 J.P. 581; *National Rivers Authority* v. *Yorkshire Water Services Ltd., The Independent,* November 19, 1993; *The Times,* November 24, 1993; *National Rivers Authority* v. *Alfred McAlpine Homes East Ltd.; The Times,* February 3, 1994; *The Independent,* February 3, 1994.

[27] *Southern Water Authority* v. *Pegrum* (above).

[28] *Price* v. *Cromack* [1975] 1 W.L.R. 988; *Wychavon District Council* v. *National Rivers Authority,* [1993] 2 All E.R. 440; [1992] Water Law 169; *National Rivers Authority* v. *Welsh Development Agency, The Times,* December 29, 1992; [1993] Env. Liability, CS27. But compare the *Yorkshire Water* case at n. 26 above, where the sewage undertaker was liable for discharges of substances from their treatment works which had been introduced into the sewer by unknown persons and which the undertaker could not have prevented or been aware of.

[29] *Moses* v. *Midland Railway Co.* (1915) 113 L.T. 451; *Impress (Worcester) Ltd.* v. *Rees* [1971] 2 All E.R. 357: *National Rivers Authority* v. *Wright Engineering Ltd., The Independent,* November 19, 1993.

[30] *McLeod* v. *Buchanan* [1940] 2 All E.R. 179; *James & Son Ltd.* v. *Smee* [1955] 1 Q.B. 78.

[31] *Alphacell Ltd.* v. *Woodward* [1972] A.C. 824 *per* Lord Wilberforce.

contaminated and is polluting controlled waters cannot be guilty of the offence. However, the crucial question is exactly what knowledge is necessary for the offence and whether such knowledge may in any circumstances be inferred. There is authority to suggest that as well as knowledge that land is contaminated, there must also be knowledge that contaminants are entering controlled waters and that such contaminants are of their nature poisonous, noxious or polluting.[32] However, there is also authority to suggest that it may be possible to infer such knowledge in the absence of evidence from the defence that there was no knowledge; and also that deliberately shutting one's eyes to the obvious may constitute constructive knowledge.[33] As Lord Bridge stated in *Westminster City Council* v. *Croyalgrange Ltd.*[34]: ". . . it is always open to the tribunal of fact, when knowledge on the part of the defendant is to be proved, to base a finding of knowledge on evidence that the defendant has deliberately shut his eyes to the obvious or refrained from inquiring because he suspected the truth but did not want to have his suspicions confirmed."

However, once the landowner is aware of the situation, be becomes vulnerable to the argument that, by failing to prevent the continuation of the pollution, he is knowingly permitting it. In such cases the crucial question is likely to be what steps the defendant could have taken to prevent the pollution: a man cannot be taken to permit that which he cannot control.[35] In some statutory contexts the word "permit" connotes giving permission, leave or licence for some thing to be done.[36] However, it can also mean abstention from taking reasonable steps to prevent something, where it is within a man's power to prevent it.[37] The difficulty then may lie in what constitutes reasonable steps: this may not necessarily equate to any steps which may be scientifically demonstrated to

---

[32] *R.* v. *Hallam* [1957] 1 Q.B. 569, 573; *Schulmans Incorporated Ltd.* v. *NRA* (Queens Bench Division, unreported, December 3, 1991); summarised at *Water Law* [1993] p. 25 in an article by David Wilkinson.

[33] *Westminster City Council* v. *Croyalgrange Ltd.* [1986] 1 W.L.R. 674; *Schulmans Incorporated* case and article cited at n. 32 above.

[34] [1986] 1 W.L.R. 674, p. 684.

[35] "One cannot permit that which one does not control:" *Tophams Ltd.* v. *Earl of Sefton* [1967] A.C. 50, at 65 (Lord Hodson). See also, on different statutory wording, *R.* v. *Staines Local Board* (1888) 60 L.T. 261, at 264: "A man cannot be said to suffer another person to do a thing which he has no right to prevent."; *Yorkshire West Riding Council* v. *Holmfirth Urban Sanitary Authority* [1894] 2 Q.B. 842; *Rochford Rural Council* v. *Port of London Authority* [1914] 2 K.B. 916.

[36] *Lomas* v. *Peek* [1947] 2 All E.R. 574; *Shave* v. *Rosner* [1954] 2 Q.B. 113, *Kent County Council* v. *Beaney* [1993] Env.L.R. 225.

[37] *Berton* v. *Alliance Economic Investment Co.* [1922] 1 K.B. at p. 759; *Bromsgrove District Council* v. *Carthy* (1975) P. & C.R. 34; *Tophams Ltd.* v. *Earl of Sefton* [1967] A.C. 50 at p. 62, 64–5, 68, 75, 83, 85.

have a remedial or mitigating effect.[38] Such steps may include, for example, the exercise of contractual rights to exert legitimate pressure on another party to cease polluting activity.[39]

Penalties for water pollution offences

The offences under section 85 are subject to imprisonment for a term **2.49** not exceeding three months and/or to a fine not exceeding £20,000 on summary conviction. On conviction on indictment, imprisonment may be for a term up to two years and the fine is unlimited.[40]

There is the usual provision whereby criminal liability may be imposed on directors, managers, secretaries and similar officers where the company's offence was committed with the consent or connivance or was attributable to any neglect on their part.[41]

To date, only relatively few prosecutions have involved contamination of soil and surface waters. In November 1989, Mid-Sussex Water Company were fined £20,000 and ordered to pay £5,000 costs when 1000 gallons of diesel oil leaked from a corroded pipe into a borehole at Poverty Bottom, near Seaford, Sussex. In August 1992, knitwear manufacturer Pringle of Scotland was prosecuted successfully by the NRA for polluting an unconfined sandstone aquifer with chlorinated solvents discharged from a soakaway forming part of the company's effluent disposal system. A request by the NRA for the case to be referred to the Crown Court was refused and on a plea of guilty the company was fined £5,000 and ordered to pay costs of £21,908 (including the NRA's extensive investigations) and compensation of £1,890.[42]

Anti-pollution works and operations

Section 161 of the Water Resources Act 1991 contains powers to **2.50** prevent, remedy and mitigate pollution which may be of great significance in contaminated land situations. The power applies where it appears to the NRA that any poisonous, noxious or polluting matter[43] or any solid waste matter is:

(a) likely to enter any controlled waters; or

[38] See *Mayor and Corporation of High Wycombe* v. *The Conservators of the River Thames* (1898) 78 L.T. 463, at 465.
[39] *London Borough of Tower Hamlets* v. *London Docklands Development Corporation* (Knightsbridge Crown Court, April 13, 1992).
[40] S.85(6).
[41] S.217(1).
[42] ENDS Report No. 211 (August 1992) p. 37.
[43] As to the meaning of "poisonous, noxious or polluting" see para. 2.46.

(b) likely to be present in any controlled waters; or
(c) likely to have been present in any controlled water.[44]

In such cases the NRA is entitled to carry out works and operations to prevent the matter entering controlled waters[45]; in the contaminated land context this could include, for example, excavating and removing the matter or constructing some impervious barrier between it and the controlled waters. Where the matter has already reached the controlled waters then the works may include removing and disposing of the matter, remedying or mitigating any pollution which has been caused, and restoring the water and dependent flora and fauna to their previous condition.[46] In the case of polluted groundwater this may involve solutions such as pumping and treatment.

The sting of the section lies in subsection (3) which provides:

"Where the Authority carries out any such works or operations as are mentioned in subsection (1) above, it shall, subject to subsection (4) below,[47] be entitled to recover the expenses reasonably incurred in doing so from any person who as the case may be:

(a) caused or knowingly permitted the matter in question to be present at the place from which it was likely, in the opinion of the Authority, to enter any controlled waters; or
(b) caused or knowingly permitted the matter in question to be present in any controlled water."

The wording imposing liability here is similar to the offences relating to water pollution in section 85 of the Act in that they extend not only to the original polluter but also to a subsequent owner or occupier of land who knowingly permits the entry of polluting matter to continue.[48] It should also be noted that permitting potentially polluting matter to remain in place may also result in liability if in the Authority's opinion it may migrate into controlled waters in future.

These powers present a potentially heavy threat to the owner or occupier of contaminated land; liability is effectively strict and may operate retrospectively. However, in one sense the power is an unattractive one for the NRA in that potentially heavy costs must be incurred before steps can be taken to recover them, with no certain prospect of recovery. This is particularly the case where groundwater contamination

---

[44] As to "controlled waters," see Subs. (6) and para. 2.45; the definition includes surface water and groundwater.
[45] S.161(1)(a).
[46] S.161(1)(b).
[47] Subs. (4) provides that expenses are not recoverable in respect of works or operations relating to water from abandoned mines.
[48] See para. 2.48.

is widespread and involves many potential sources: for example the extensive contamination of the chalk aquifer at Luton and Dunstable by chlorinated solvents from industrial sources.[49] Section 161 provides no express power to recover costs of investigation and remediation, feasibility studies as opposed to the actual clean up operations themselves.

Arguments may also arise after the costs have been incurred as to whether the works or operations were reasonable. In practice, it may be that the powers of section 161 are most effective as a threat to compel landowners or polluters to cooperate "voluntarily" in clean-up schemes. It is understood, as an interesting postcript to the *Cambridge Water Company* case,[49a] that the NRA and Eastern Counties Leather plc have reached agreement on a treatment strategy to contain pollution and treat groundwater at the company's site. Water is to be pumped from July 1994 and treated at the company's treatment plant, subject to continuing monitoring by the NRA.

NRA: Enforcement Policy

A decision whether to prosecute or take other enforcement action in relation to contaminated land problems is, like all other similar decisions, a matter of policy for the agency concerned: informal field policies used by the NRA to provide guidance to investigating and legal staff will be relevant in this respect. **2.51**

Incidents may be categorised as *major, significant* or *minor*. A prosecution may be expected to follow major incidents: in the context of groundwater pollution which entailed closure of potable, industrial or agricultural abstraction sources would certainly be regarded as major, as would an incident making extensive remedial measures necessary. Where closure of such sources was not necessary but there was nonetheless an effect on water quality, the incident might be regarded as significant but not major; though harm to usable groundwater resources would no doubt be taken very seriously whether or not specific abstraction sources were affected. The decision whether to take action would turn on factors such as negligence, previous site history, standards of precautions and operational management and the extent of cooperation in remedial measures. Minor incidents are seen as those where there proves to have been no notable effect on water resources and will normally give rise to a warning rather than a prosecution. Soil contamination may also result in pollution of surface water, in which case issues such as effect on amenity, fish kill, harm to aquatic life and risk to abstraction sources will also be relevant.

[49] ENDS Report No. 213 (October 1992), p. 6.
[49a] See para. 2.03 *et seq.*

As a matter of practice, any enforcing agency will have regard to its likely prospects of securing a successful outcome before initiating a prosecution: this will be particularly relevant in contaminated land cases where issues of proof and causation may be extremely difficult—obvious recent spillages aside.

All of these factors, which are of general application, should be considered together with the NRA's published statements on groundwater protection published in 1992.[50] In the section on *Contaminated Land* policy D1 states:

> "The NRA will encourage the implementation of effective remedial measures to prevent pollution of groundwater by existing direct or indirect discharges from any contaminated site. Where pollution occurs the NRA will prosecute in appropriate cases under section 85 of the Water Resources Act 1991."

The explanatory note to policy D6 recognises the difficulties of pinpointing individual sites or incidents in some areas of historical groundwater pollution and the policy simply states:

> "In areas where historical industrial development is known to have caused widespread groundwater contamination, the NRA will review the merits and feasibility of groundwater clean-up depending upon local circumstances and available funding."

Contamination of water sources

2.52   By section 72 of the Water Industry Act 1991 a person commits an offence if he is guilty of any act or neglect whereby the water in any waterworks which is used or likely to be used:

(a) for human consumption or domestic purposes; or
(b) for manufacturing food or drink for human consumption,

is polluted or likely to be polluted.

"Waterworks" includes for the purposes of the section:

(a) any spring, well, adit, borehole, service, reservoir or tank; and
(b) any main or other pipe or conduit of a water undertaker.[51]

The offence may therefore involve either public or private water supplies. Two exclusions apply: one relating to the cultivation of land in accordance with the principles of good husbandry, the other to the reasonable use of oil or tar on public highways.[52]

---

[50] National Rivers Authority: *Policy and Practice for the Protection of Groundwater* (1992). See further Chap. 6.
[51] Subs. (5).
[52] Subss. (2) and (3). See further, Chap. 6.

The offence is punishable on summary conviction by a fine not exceeding £5,000 and, in the case of a continuing offence, to a further fine not exceeding £500 for each day the offence is continued; on indictment the penalty is an unlimited fine and/or up to two years' imprisonment.[53] It has been reported that Severn Trent Water is to bring a prosecution (presumably under this provision) against a Telford company which polluted the River Severn with industrial solvent, causing serious disruption to domestic supplies in the Worcester area.[53a]

Powers of water undertakers to deal with contamination

Section 162 of the Water Industry Act 1991 confers on water **2.53** undertakers certain powers to deal with contamination. By section 162(1) street works[54] may be carried out to secure that water in a relevant waterworks[55] is not polluted or contaminated; such works may include opening up the street, tunnelling or boring, opening up any sewer or drain and moving or removing earth and other materials. Perhaps more importantly, subsection (2) enables works to be carried out on any land other than a street for securing that water in any relevant waterworks is not polluted or otherwise contaminated.[56] By subsection (3) in relation to land which the undertaker owns or over which it has the necessary rights, the works may extend to the construction of "drains, sewers, watercourses, catchpits and other works" for the purpose of intercepting foul water or otherwise preventing the pollution of reservoirs and abstraction sources of strata.

Whilst these powers are undeniably useful, they include no statutory power to recoup the cost of such measures from any person.

---

[53] Subs. (4).

[53a] *The Times*, June 15, 1994.

[54] "Street" has the same meaning as in the New Roads and Street Works Act 1991; s.219(1).

[55] "Relevant waterworks" means any waterworks containing water which is or may be used by a water undertaker for providing a supply of water to any premises; "waterworks" includes water mains, resource mains, service pipes, discharge pipes, springs, wells, adits, boreholes, service reservoirs or tanks: subs. (8).

[56] The provisions of s.159 as to notice to the owner and occupier of the land apply to the exercise of this power: subs. (2).

Waste-Related Contamination

Generally

2.54   The deposit of waste on or in land can be a significant source of potential contamination and the disposal and management of waste is subject to a strict regime of control under Part II of the Environmental Protection Act 1990 and, before that, Part I of the Control of Pollution Act 1974.[57] The unlawful deposit of waste in or on land constitutes an offence, as does its keeping, treatment and other forms of disposal.[58] Where damage[59] is caused by waste deposited in or on land so as to constitute a criminal offence, by section 73(6) of the Environmental Protection Act any person who made the deposit, or knowingly caused or knowingly permitted it, is liable for that damage, except where the damage was duly wholly to the plaintiff's fault or where the plaintiff voluntarily accepted the risk.[60]

The problem of old landfills

2.55   Of particular current concern is the increasing number of old landfill sites which are being identified as the source of potential problems, principally gas generation or water pollution. Many such sites date from the 1940s and were completed in the 1970s and 1980s, if not earlier, when the prevalent policy approved by the Department of Environment was "dilute and disperse" or "attenuate and disperse" and before the problems of methane and other landfill gas generation came to be widely appreciated.[61]

---

[57] See Chap. 5 generally.
[58] Environmental Protection Act, s.33(1).
[59] "Damage" is defined at subs. (8) to include death and personal injury, including any disease and any impairment of mental condition.
[60] Subs. (6). By subs. (7) the statutory defences available in criminal prosecutions under s.33 may also be proved by way of a defence to a civil action under s.73(6).
[61] A number of sites under scrutiny have been referred to in ENDS Report, for example:
    (a) Ewelme Landfill, Oxfordshire (liquid and solid industrial and commercial wastes—suspected contamination of aquifer and local wells by chlorinated hydrocarbons) ENDS Report 203, p. 8.
    (b) Bentley Mill Lane, West Midlands (suspected major contamination of watercourses by copper and nickel) ENDS Report 189, p. 7.
    (c) Harwell Laboratory UK Atomic Energy Authority Landfill, Oxfordshire (pollution plume of organic solvents identified; suspected contamination of aquifer and abstraction boreholes) ENDS Report 186, p. 6.
    (d) Higher Kiln Landfill, Devon (various liquid wastes possibly including

Typically, such sites will have received either domestic putrescible wastes, or liquid industrial wastes, or both; as a practical matter industry and society at large enjoyed the benefits of low waste disposal costs at such sites. The price for such practices effectively arose later in terms of actual or potential pollution, in some cases putting at risk public or private potable water supplies, affecting surface water quality, and potentially infringing the EC groundwater directive 80/68/EEC.[62] In a number of cases such sites have attracted the attention of waste disposal authorities, district environmental health departments and the National Rivers Authority: however, current powers under water protection and statutory nuisance provisions are ill-adapted to deal with such complex and historical problems.[63]

The solution of the Government has been two-fold:

(a) to make it impossible for existing site licences to be surrendered without the concurrence of the authority and without the environmental problems being addressed[64]; and

(b) to introduce new duties and powers in relation to the investigation of potential problems at old sites and their remediation where necessary.[65]

"Waste" and "controlled waste"

The wide definition given to "waste" by section 75(2) of the Environmental Protection Act is referred to elsewhere, as has the meaning of the term "controlled waste".[66]   **2.56**

In the context of contaminated land these terms are capable of being applied widely. As well as the obvious example of domestic or industrial refuse disposed of by final deposit in a landfall site, the following situations also need to be considered:

(1) storage of waste materials, such as scrap metal or drums of chemicals, on the surface of land where contamination may result from leakage or leaching;

oil and chrome wastes from tanning; suspected contamination by organic compounds being List I substances under EC Groundwater Directives) ENDS Report 209, p. 11.
See also the report by Friends of the Earth: "Hit or Miss—Groundwater Contamination Associated with Landfill Sites in the East Anglia" (January 1994, available from 26–28 Underwood Street, London N1 7JQ).

[62] See para. 6.08.
[63] See paras. 2.50 and 2.71.
[64] See para. 5.29.
[65] See para. 2.60 *et seq.*
[66] See paras. 5.21 and 5.24.

(2) "made ground"—where usable ground has been created for industrial or other purposes by the deposit of materials such as rubble, slag, foundry sand or other potentially contaminative materials;

(3) general soil contamination from the handling of waste materials, for example the accumulation of particulate matter such as asbestos from demolition, ship-breaking or railway-carriage breaking;

(4) the deposition on soil of airborne particulate waste matter, such as lead, emitted from industrial premises or from vehicles;

(5) industrial slap heaps and effluent lagoons or ponds;

(6) deposits on land of water-borne waste matter, such as oil;

(7) contaminated dredgings from canals or docks; and

(8) general spillages of liquids or powders in the course of industrial activity—though the substance may originally have been product or raw material, it may become waste as a result of the spill, having become contaminated or otherwise unusable.

Removal of waste unlawfully deposited: section 59

2.57   Section 59 of the Environmental Protection Act contains powers of waste regulation authorities or waste collection authorities to require the removal of waste deposited on land in contravention of section 33(1). The power is exercisable by notice served on the occupier of the land requiring him to do either or both of the following:

(a) remove the waste from the land within a specified period not less than 21 days beginning with the service of the notice;

(b) take within such a period specified steps with a view to eliminating or reducing the consequences of the deposit of the waste.

The recipient of the notice may appeal against it within the 21-day period to the magistrates' court or to the sheriff in Scotland, who must quash the requirement of the notice if satisfied that:

(a) the appellant neither deposited the waste nor knowingly caused nor knowingly permitted its deposit; or

(b) there is a material defect in the notice.[67]

If the notice is not quashed, its requirements may be modified by the magistrates, for example by extending its period for compliance.[68] The notice is of no effect pending determination of the appeal.[69]

[67] Subss. (2) and (3).
[68] Subss(3) and (4).
[69] Subs. (4).

Failure to comply with the requirements of a section 59 notice without reasonable excuse is punishable by a fine on summary conviction of up to £5,000 and to a further fine of up to £500 for each day that the failure continues after conviction.[70] Additionally, the waste authority may itself do what was required by the notice and recover its expenses reasonably incurred from the defaulter.[71]

Section 59: summary power

A separate summary power is given to waste authorities by subsection **2.58** (7). This is a power to remove waste which appears to have been deposited on land in contravention of section 33(1) and to take other steps to eliminate or reduce the consequences of the deposit. It is exercisable where:

  (a) it is necessary to remove the waste forthwith or take other steps in order to remove or prevent pollution of land, water or air or harm to human health;[72] or
  (b) there is no occupier of the land; or
  (c) the occupier neither made nor knowingly permitted the deposit of the waste.

Where these powers are exercised the authority may recover its costs (including ultimate disposal of waste removed) from either[73]:

  (a) the occupier in a case falling within (a) above unless he proves his innocence in relation to the deposit; or
  (b) in any of cases (a)–(c) any person who deposited or knowingly caused or knowingly permitted the deposit of *any of*[74] the waste.

The occupier or other person may escape liability by demonstrating that costs were incurred unneccessarily.

Problems with section 59

As with so many other anti-pollution powers, section appears 59 **2.59** ostensibly very significant, but is perhaps less useful in practice. Certainly many waste authorities have encountered difficulties in using it precursor, section 16 of the Control of Pollution Act 1974. Some of the main problems would appear to be as follows:

[70] Subs. (5).
[71] Subs. (6).
[72] See definitions at subss. 29(1) and (5).
[73] Subs. 59(8).
[74] The italicised words are significant, effectively creating joint and several liability in the case of commixed deposits.

89

(1) The deposit of waste giving rise to the problems may have predated in whole or in part the controls exercised by section 33(1), or indeed control under section 3 of the Control of Pollution Act 1974;

(2) The occupier of the land may not have been involved with the deposit in which case he will have a complete defence to the requirements of any notice. In such a case the authority will have to rely on its summary powers under subs. (7) the cost of which will be irrecoverable if the original "depositor" cannot be traced or is no longer existence;

(3) The summary power under subs. (7) involves the authority in potentially heavy expenditure with no certain prospect of cost recovery;

(4) It may be extremely difficult to frame the requirements of the notice with sufficient precision in a case involving contamination of land as well as waste deposits, so as to avoid a successful challenge to the notice on appeal;[75]

(5) The burden of proving all the elements necessary to succeed in a prosecution for non-compliance with a notice under section 59 rests with the prosecution and is the high criminal burden;[76]

(6) The whole procedure rests on waste having been *deposited* on land in contravention of section 33: this refers to the initial putting down of the waste on land and not its retention there.[77]

Whilst there are features in section 59 which do lend themselves to contaminated land problems, overall the section appears better adapted to dealing with incidents such as fly-tipping and unlicensed temporary deposits of waste, such as at transfer stations.[78]

Harmful waste deposits: section 61

2.60   Section 61 of the Environmental Protection Act 1990, when in force, will confers new and potentially very significant powers upon waste regulation authorities.[79] The section is possibly misleadingly described in the marginal note as: "Duty of waste regulation authorities as respects closed landfills." This may well accord with the primary intention underlying the section of dealing with the increasingly recognised

---

[75] *Berridge Incinerators* v. *Nottinghamshire County Council* Nottingham Crown Court, June 12, 1992, unreported.

[76] *Ibid.*

[77] *Ibid.*

[78] See *R.* v. *Metropolitan Stipendiary Magistrate, ex parte London Waste Regulation Authority; Berkshire County Council* v. *Scott, The Times,* January 14, 1993.

[79] The section has not yet been brought into force; nor is it clear when it will be.

problems of harmful gas generation and leachate dispersal from landfill sites; however, the word "landfill" does not appear in the section itself.[80]

The express purpose of the section is to detect and deal with land which is in such a condition, by reason of "relevant matters", that it may cause pollution of the environment or harm to human health. Those "relevant matters" are: "the concentration or accumulation in, and emission or discharge from, the land of noxious gases or noxious liquids caused by deposits of controlled waste in the land." The logical progression contemplated by this wording is therefore:

(1) Are there deposits of controlled waste in the land?

"Controlled waste" bears the meaning given at section 75 of the Environmental Protection Act, namely household, industrial or commercial waste.[81] Though it appears somewhat obliquely, in the context of powers of entry and inspection, it seems that the term includes waste deposited before the term "controlled waste" passed into statutory currency.[82] It should be noted that the section refers to deposits *in* (not on) the land; the section therefore probably could not be used to deal with deposits of waste on the surface of the land only.

(2) Are the deposits causing noxious gases or noxious liquids to be concentrated or accumulated in the land and to be emitted or discharged from the land?

The wording of the provision in this respect is complex. The noxious gases or liquids in question may be generated by the waste (*e.g.* gas caused by microbial processes) or may result from the ingress of water which is contaminated by the waste to form leachate. The waste itself may of course be in liquid form and be noxious; for example where industrial liquid waste has been disposed of to landfill. It would appear that the word "noxious" refers to the inherent characteristics of the liquid or gas rather than any demonstrable harmful effect;[83] that aspect being dealt with by the separate reference to pollution of the environment or harm to human health.

The wording of subs. (2) also requires that there must be a concentration or accumulation in the land *and* a discharge or escape from the land. It is arguable therefore that the section only applies

---

[80] See also para. 2.56.
[81] See para. 5.24.
[82] Subs. (3)(*b*).
[83] See para. 2.46.

where there is or has been an actual escape, rather than a prospective one; this, however, sits rather uneasily with the references to the condition of the land having the potential to cause pollution or harm. It may be suggested, therefore, on reading subs. (2) together with subs. (1) (with which it is intimately linked) that the reference to "emission or discharge" contemplates a prospective, as well as an actual, discharge which may have the harmful results referred to in subs. (1). In any event it is clear that a concentration or accumulation of noxious substances in land is not of itself enough and that there must be either an actual emission or discharge, or at least a prospective one.

(3) Is the land in such a condition that it may cause pollution of the environment or harm to human health?

This requirement relates the condition of the land to the risk of harm. "Pollution of the environment" is defined by section 29(3) to mean pollution due to the release or escape into any environmental medium from. . .

"(c) the land in . . . which controlled waste is deposited. . ."

of substances or articles constituting or resulting from the waste and capable (by reason of the quantity or concentrations involved) of causing harm to man or any other living organisms supported by the environment.

"Harm" is given a wide definition by subsection 29(5) to include harm to health and interference with ecological systems; in the case of man it includes offence to his senses and harm to property.

These definitions interact in a rather complex way with the other requirements of section 61 as referred to above; effectively it means that the envisaged release or escape must involve concentrations or quantities of substances capable of causing harm. There would appear to be little difficulty where gas or leachate is migrating from a waste site onto other land; however, what of the situation where gas generation presents a risk to buildings constructed on the site where the waste was deposited and presents a danger to their occupants? Since "pollution of the environment" involves a release or escape from the land, such on-site risks may not be covered on a strict reading. However, as an alternative to "pollution of the environment" it may be that there is the risk of "harm to human health" in relation to the occupiers of the land—but, even in such cases, subsection (2) appears to require an "emission or discharge" from the land.

Section 61: Duty to inspect

Section 61(1) obliges waste regulation authorities to inspect land in **2.61** their area to determine its condition: the only land excluded is that where a waste site licence authorising the treatment, keeping or disposal of waste is in force.[84] The existence of a site licence would appear to be an absolute bar: thus if land is subject to problems from historic deposits of waste and there is now a licence for a waste treatment process unrelated to those historic deposits, section 61 would not apply.

Authorities have powers of entry and inspection under subsection (3): these apply to land where controlled waste has been deposited (whether under a C.O.P.A. or E.P.A. licence or not) and to any land where there may be concentrations or accumulations of noxious gases or liquids. Having identified land in the condition referred to in subs. (1) the authority must keep its condition under review for pollution or harm to health.[85]

Section 61: duty to avoid pollution or harm

Where, following inspection of land under its statutory duties, it **2.62** appears to the authority that the condition of the land is, by reason of the relevant matters affecting it, such that pollution of the environment or harm to human health is likely to be caused[86] then it is the duty of the authority[87]:

> "to do such works and take such other steps (whether on the land affected or on adjacent land) as appear to the authority to be reasonable to avoid such pollution or harm."

Unlike other provisions relating to clean-up, section 61 gives no detail as to the types of such measures: they may in practice include the physical removal of polluting matter, gas control measures, and the installation of impervious membranes or other barriers. The measures would appear to be essentially preventive in nature, as opposed to remedial: section 161 of the Water Resources Act may be usefully contrasted in that respect.[88] It is arguable, therefore, that measures purely of a remedial nature (for example treatment of contaminated groundwater or the restocking of affected rivers) are not within the subsection. The NRA must be consulted where pollution of water is likely to be caused.[89]

[84] S.35(12).
[85] Subss. (4) and (6).
[86] See para. 2.60 as to these matters.
[87] Subs. (7).
[88] See para. 2.50.
[89] Subs. (5); in Scotland, the relevant river purification authority.

Section 61: cost recovery

2.63   By subsection 61(8) where works or steps are taken in fulfilment of the duty to prevent pollution or harm, the authority is entitled to recover all or part of its costs from "the person who is for the time being the owner of the land". Cost recovery is subject to three important constraints:[90]

  (a) no costs can be recovered where the authority accepted surrender of the waste management licence which authorised the activities in the course of which the waste was deposited;

  (b) such part of the costs as the owner can show were incurred unreasonably cannot be recovered; and

  (c) in deciding whether to recover any costs and if so, how much, the authority must have regard to any hardship which the recovery may cause to the owner of the land.[91]

Inherent in the provision are two major uncertainties. First, there is the question of who constitutes the "owner for the time being". Clearly a freehold owner would fall within that description, but would the owner of a term of years as the owner of a legal estate? If so, is the length of the term relevant in that the owner of a 999-year ground lease would be treated differently to the tenant under a 25-year lease or a periodic tenancy? What of the owners of beneficial interests in the land, or the purchaser under an uncompleted contract of sale? Is a mortgagee in possession an owner? All of these, and more, are questions which in the absence of any statutory definition of owner, will have to await determination by the courts.

Earlier environmental legislation, such as the Public Health Act 1936, made matters clearer by defining owner by reference to the person receiving or entitled to receive the rack rent from the premises and it was also clear from decided cases that a wide range of persons holding interests in land could fall within the definition.[92] It must be questionable, however, how far this law is relevant in the absence of an equivalent definition in the E.P.A. A similar definition is provided by section 81A(9) of the E.P.A.,[93] but only for the purposes of that section.

The second major uncertainty relates to steps taken on "adjacent land" (*i.e.*, land other than that on which the waste was deposited). Can costs be recovered from the owner of that land? This depends on whether the words "the land" refer back to the words "in relation to waste on

---

[90] Subs. (9): see also para. 2.58 above on s.59.
[91] Subs. (10).
[92] For example mesne tenants, agents, ground lessees, banks, mortgagees. See cases cited at *The Environmental Protection Act 1990—Text and Commentary*, S.R. Tromans, p. 43–159 (Sweet & Maxwell, 1991, 2nd ed., 1993).
[93] See para. 2.69.

any land" at the start of subsection (8) or to the land on which the steps were taken.

Presumably if costs may be recovered from adjacent landowners, considerations of hardship as referred to in subsection (10) may be very important: though clearly hardship can also arise for a subsequent owner of the land where waste was deposited.

Section 61: guidance

By subsection 61(11) it is the duty of waste authorities to have regard **2.64** to any guidance issued by the Secretary of State as respects the discharge of their functions under the section.

Waste: the duty of care

The potentially broad nature of the statutory requirements concerning **2.65** waste has already been discussed.[94] One of the refinements introduced by the Environmental Protection Act 1990 was the duty of care as respects waste: this is discussed elsewhere in the context of preventing contamination.[95] The question arises as to the extent to which the requirements of the duty of care may bite upon the occupier of land contaminated by waste: if the duty does apply then failure to prevent escape of the waste from control (*e.g.* by dispersal into groundwater) may result in criminal liability unless all measures applicable to the occupier to prevent the escape have been taken. The sanction for such an offence is a fine of up to £5,000 on summary conviction and an unlimited fine on conviction on indictment.[96]

The operative words of the section in this respect would appear to be:[97]

". . . the duty of any person who . . . keeps . . . controlled waste . . ."

Is the occupier of land in which waste has been deposited a person who "keeps" the waste? Waste stored on a land in a readily recoverable form, in drums or some other container or repository, may be said to be "kept", and it could be asked whether that waste would cease to be "kept" if it were covered with a layer of topsoil. On the other hand, it seems much less apt to speak of waste being "kept" where it comprises material infilled or used to provide "made ground": still less apt where

---

[94] See para. 2.56.
[95] E.P.A. 1990, s.34; see Chap. 5.
[96] Subss. 34(1) and (6).
[97] Leaving aside cases where the defendant is the producer, carrier, treater or disposer of the waste.

liquid waste has been spilt or disposed of into land so as to be physically irrecoverable in its original form. "Keep" is not defined in the Act, but in ordinary usage would appear to involve retaining the waste with at least a limited degree of continuity.[98] It must be questionable, to say the least, that the occupier of a closed landfill site is "keeping" the waste in that sense: in the context of section 33 of the E.P.A. such an interpretation would have the curious result of requiring a waste management licence to be retained for the site in perpetuity.

Thus, whilst it cannot be said that section 34 can never apply to historically contaminated land, it appears that it is unlikely to be of widespread application.

STATUTORY NUISANCE

Relevant statutory nuisances

2.66 Section 79 of the Environmental Protection Act lists some eight matters which constitute statutory nuisances for the purposes of Part III of the Act. Of particular relevance to contaminated land are:

  (a) any premises in such a state as to be prejudicial to health or a nuisance[99]; and
  (b) any accumulation or deposit which is prejudicial to health or a nuisance.[1]

Category (c) refers to fumes or gases emitted from premises and so might appear to be relevant, but in fact only applies to private dwellings.[2]

Land which is contaminated by toxic, corrosive or otherwise harmful materials, or which is generating flammable, toxic or explosive gases may clearly be said to be "prejudicial to health": the phrase is defined by subsection (7) to mean "injurious", or likely to cause injury, to health. Even in the absence of a threat to health or safety of persons, it is arguable that contaminated land may constitute a "nuisance": in the context of statutory nuisance the word is equated either to interference with reasonable personal comfort[3] or with private or public nuisance at

[98] See *Blue* v. *Pearl Assurance Co.* [1940] 3 W.W.R. 13, at p. 19–20.
[99] "Premises" includes land: subs. (7).
[1] In *Coventry City Council* v. *Cartwright* [1975] 1 W.L.R. 845, this phrase was said to have the underlying conception of "an accumulation of something which produces a threat to health in the sense of a threat of disease, vermin or the like."
[2] Subs. (4).
[3] *Betts* v. *Penge Urban District Council* [1942] 2 K.B. 154; *Wivenhoe Port* v. *Colchester Borough Council* [1985] J.P.L. 175 (affirmed [1985] J.P.L. 396).

common law.[4] In the case of the nuisance limb, the situation must be such as to affect adjoining or neighbouring property and a "a nuisance cannot rise if what has taken place affects only the person or persons occupying the premises where the nuisance is said to have taken place."[5] No such restriction would appear to apply to cases where the situation is such as to fall within the "prejudicial to health" limb.

Duty to inspect and investigate

By section 79(1) every local authority[6] is under a duty to cause its area **2.67** to be inspected from time to time top detect statutory nuisances: so far as contaminated land can constitute a statutory nuisance this duty would appear to be honoured more in the breach than the observance; though, naturally it is the symptoms of contaminated land, rather than its mere existence, which constitute the nuisance.

Also, where complaint is made by a person living within its area, the authority must take such steps as are reasonably practicable to investigate the complaint.[7]

The requisite powers of entry, investigation, testing and sampling are to be found at Schedule 3, paragraph 2 of the E.P.A.

Summary proceedings

The main remedy for statutory nuisance lies in the duty upon local **2.68** authorities to serve an abatement notice where they are satisfied that a statutory nuisance exists or is likely to occur or recur.[8]

The notice may require abatement of the nuisance or the execution of works or the taking of other steps; it is the power to require the execution of works which is likely to be of most relevance in contaminated land cases. It must specify the time or times within which the requirements of the notice are to be complied with. Failure to comply with the notice, without reasonable excuse, is a summary offence.[9] It is generally a defence to prove that the best practicable means were used to prevent the nuisance, or counteract its effects.[10] However, the defence is only

[4] *National Coal Board* v. *Neath Borough Council* [1976] 2 All E.R. 478.
[5] *Ibid.*, at p. 482.
[6] Generally, London Borough councils and district councils: subs. (7).
[7] Sched. 3, para. 4 contains substantial powers for the Secretary of State in the event of default.
[8] S.80(1).
[9] Subss. (4)–(6). Lack of finance may not be "reasonable excuse:" see *Saddleworth Urban District Council* v. *Aggregate and Sand* (1970) 114 S.J. 931.
[10] Subs. (7).

available in relation to categories (a) and (e) (the most likely to be applicable to contaminated land if the nuisance arises on industrial, trade or business premises).[11]

It is possible to appeal against the notice to the magistrates' court within 21 days beginning with the date on which the appellant was served with the notice.[12] The various grounds of appeal are stated at regulation 2 of the Statutory Nuisance (Appeals) Regulations 1990[13] and include arguments as to the unreasonableness of the requirements of the notice. Where, *inter alia*, compliance with the notice would involve expenditure, the bringing of an appeal has the effect of suspending the notice.[14] The cases where the notice is not suspended are defined at regulation 3(2), but it seems likely that any notice involving remedial works for contaminated land would properly be suspended pending the outcome of the appeal.

Abatement by local authority and cost recovery

2.69   By section 81(3) where an abatement notice has not been complied with the local authority may, whether or not they take proceedings for an offence, abate the nuisance and do whatever may be necessary in the execution of the notice.

Under section 81(5), if the authority is of the opinion that proceedings for an offence would constitute an inadequate remedy, they may take High Court proceedings to secure abatement.

The expenses of the authority may be recovered from various persons, including the owner of the relevant land or premises.[15] The Noise and Statutory Nuisance Act 1993[16] has inserted new powers to make such expenses a charge on the premises. Under section 81A, as inserted, where any expenses are recoverable from a person who is owner of the premises, the authority may serve notice on him which has the effect of making the expenses carry interest at such reasonable rate as the authority may determine, and of making the expenses and accrued interest a statutory charge on the premises.[17] "Owner", for this purpose only, is defined as a person (other than a mortgagee in possession) who, whether in his own right or as trustee for any other person, is entitled to

---

[11] Subs. 8(*a*). This means premises used for any industrial, trade or business purposes: see subs. 79(7).
[12] Subs. (3).
[13] S.I. 1990 No. 2276.
[14] *Ibid.*, reg. 3(1).
[15] S.81(4).
[16] S.10.
[17] S.81A(1). The authority has the powers and remedies of a Law of Property Act 1925 mortgage by deed: subs. (8).

receive the rack rent of the premises or, where the premises are not let at a rack rent, would be so entitled if they were so let.[18]

The notice served by the authority must specify the amount claimed, the rate of interest, and the effect of the relevant provisions.[19] A copy must also be served on every person who to the knowledge of the authority, has an interest in the property capable of being affected by the charge.[20] Appeal lies against the notice to the county court, within 21 days of service, by every person served with a copy of the notice; on appeal the notice may be confirmed, modified as to amount, or quashed entirely.[21]

Where the expenses are charged on property under secton 81A, the local authority may by order declare the expenses to be payable with interest by instalments within a specified period.[22] Those instalments may be recovered from the owner or occupier for the time being.[23] The occupier is protected by a statutory right to deduct sums recovered from him in this way from the rent of the premises.[24] and by his liability being limited to the amount of rent due from him at the relevant time.[25]

Summary proceedings by persons aggrieved

Section 82 provides a summary procedure for any person "aggrieved" **2.70** by the existence of a statutory nuisance to make a complaint to the magistrates' court. Such a complaint can lead to an abatement order being made by the magistrates and to a fine.[26] The procedure may be particularly useful where the nuisance is caused or arises on land owned by the local authority itself.[27]

Applying the procedure to contaminated land, clearly a person whose health or safety or that of their family[28] was prejudicially affected by, for example, gas or harmful fibres escaping from contaminated land would be a "person aggrieved". The same might be the case if damage to their property[29] had occurred or was threatened or if their personal comfort or

---

[18] Subs. 81A(9).
[19] Subs. 81A(2).
[20] Subs. 81A(3). The charge takes effect 21 days from the date of service, subject to any appeal: Subs. (4).
[21] Subss. 81A(6) and (7).
[22] S.81B(1).
[23] S.81B(2).
[24] S.81B(4).
[25] S.81B(5).
[26] Subss. (2) and (8) "Owner" is now defined by s.81A(9) (see para. 2.69 above), but only for the purposes of s.81A.
[27] R. v. Epping (Waltham Abbey) Justices, ex p. Burlinson [1948] 1 K.B. 79.
[28] Sandwell Metropolitan Borough Council v. Bujok [1990] 3 All E.R. 385.
[29] But see Wivenhoe Port v. Colchester Borough Council [1985] J.P.L. 175, suggesting that harm to or diminution in value of property is not sufficient.

enjoyment of their property was interfered with. There must be some genuine grievance and it seems doubtful that an environmental pressure group (for example) could use the procedure.[30]

Action under section 82 must be preceded by notice in writing as required by subsection (6).

Who is liable?

2.71 An abatement notice under section 80 is to be served on the person responsible for the nuisance except:

(a) where the nuisance arises from any defect of a structural character, when it is to be served on the owner of the premises; and

(b) where the person responsible for the nuisance cannot be found or the nuisance has not yet occurred, in which case it may be served on the owner or occupier of the premises.

Thus in the case of contaminated land, where the person who caused the contamination can be found, he is the proper recipient of the notice; there is no power to serve the notice on the owner or occupier where the originator of the nuisance *can* be found but is insolvent, or now has no power to remedy the condition of the land.

"Owner" and "occupier" are not defined, thus giving rise to various possible problems.[31] This position contrasts with that under the Public Health Act 1936 where "owner" was defined by reference to the person receiving or entitled to receive, the rack rent from the premises. The absence of a definition appears to be a conscious decision on the part of the Government, giving flexibility to the authority.

On appeal against an abatement notice it can be argued that the notice should have been served on some person other than the appellant or alternatively that it might lawfully have been served on some other person instead of or in addition to the appellant and that it would have been equitable for it to be so served.[32] The court may make such order as it thinks fit as to the person by whom the work is to be executed, the contribution to the cost of the work to be made by any person, and the proportions in which expenses recoverable by the authority are to be

---

[30] *Att-Gen. (Gambia)* v. *N'Jie* [1961] 2 All E.R., 504 at 511.

[31] See para. 2.63. It has been held in a different contect that the term "occupier" is not limited to the owner or possessor of land and is a question of fact and degree depending on the nature of the rights or permission enjoyed: *O'Gorman* v. *Brent London Borough Council, The Times,* May 20, 1993.

[32] Statutory Nuisance (Appeals) Regulations 1990, reg. 2 paras. (2)(*g*), (*h*) and (*i*).

borne by the appellant and by any other person.[33] The court in this respect must be satisfied that the other person has received a copy of the notice of appeal as required by regulation 2, paragraph (4) and must have regard, as between an owner and occupier, (a) to the terms and conditions, express or statutory, of any tenancy, and (b) to the nature of the works required.[34] Whilst the terms of any lease are clearly relevant it appears that they are not conclusive and that it is not possible to exclude the power of apportionment by agreement.[35]

One point which should be considered in the context of liability is the definition of "person responsible": by section 79(7) this means "the person to whose act, default or sufferance the nuisance is attributable". It is possible to argue that this is a wider concept than simply the person who originally caused the nuisance, e.g. by contaminating the land. It may be that it can extend to a subsequent owner of land who fails to take reasonable steps to abate a nuisance of which he is aware.[36] This could widen the range of potentially liable parties beyond the actual originator and the current owner or occupier. Where more than one person is responsible, by section 81(1) action may be taken under section 80 against each of them even if the matters for which each is individually responsible would not be a nuisance in its own right: effectively a provision of joint and several liability.

Where a person transfers material to another for deposit on their land, and that deposit subsequent constitutes a nuisance then there will be difficulties in directing that person to abate the nuisance, which may involve entering land over which they have no rights or control;[37] it will be a question of fact however whether they can be to be the "person responsible" as mentioned above.

Where the authority takes action itself to abate a nuisance under section 81(3), it may recover expenses reasonably incurred from "the person by whose act or default the nuisance was caused".[38] If that person happens to have been the "owner" of the premises then costs may also

---

[33] *Ibid.*, para. (6).

[34] *Ibid.*, para. (7). On similar provisions in a different context see *Watney Combe Reid & Co.* v. *Westminster City Council* (1970) 214 E.G. 1631.

[35] See *Monk* v. *Arnold* [1902] 1 K.B. 761; *Monro* v. *Lord Burghclere* [1918] 1 K.B. 291; *Horner* v. *Franklin* [1905] 1 K.B. 479.

[36] On different wording in the Public Health Act 1936, see *Clayton* v. *Sale Urban District Council* [1926] 1 K.B. 415 (failure by owner to make good a breach in a flood bank resulting in flow of contaminated water onto adjoining land). The equivalent (but differently worded) provisions in Scotland have been held to apply to a subsequent purchaser: *Clydebank District Council* v. *Monaville Estates Ltd.* 1982 S.L.T. (Sh. Ct.) 2: see also Chap. 13 (Scotland).

[37] See *Mayor & Corporation of Scarborough* v. *The Rural Sanitary Authority of the Scarborough Poor Law Union* (1876) 34 L.T. 768; *R* v. *Trimble* (1877) 36 L.T. 508.

[38] S.79(7).

be recovered from "any person who is for the time being the owner thereof": again, there are potentially heavy difficulties over the meaning of the term "owner". The court may apportion the expenses between persons by whose acts or defaults the nuisance is caused in such manner as the court considers fair and reasonable. These provisions are also subject to the power referred to above to charge the expenses on the property and to order payment by instalments;[39] in this case the occupier has a statutory power to deduct expenses recovered from them from the rent payable.[40]

Similar provisions as to liability apply in the case of summary proceedings by aggrieved individuals under section 82; however, there is no express procedure for arguing that some other person should be responsible or for the apportionment of expenses as is the case with notices under section 80.

A person who is forced to spend money on abating a nuisance caused by some third party may have the right to recover the cost from the person responsible as a matter of unjust enrichment.[41] The expenditure must have been made under compulsion, but a statutory nuisance abatement notice would constitute such compulsion.[42]

Scotland

2.72   The provisions of Part III of the E.P.A. on statutory nuisances do not apply to Scotland.[43]

PLANNING POWERS

Section 215 notices

2.73   Under section 215 of the Town and Country Planning Act 1990, if it appears to a local planning authority[44] that the amenity of a part of their area, or of an adjoining area, is adversely affected by the condition of

---

[39] See para. 2.69 above.
[40] It seems doubtful whether this right of deduction can override the statutory power of appointment in such manner as is fair and reasonable.
[41] See Goff and Jones, *The Law of Restitution* (3rd ed., 1986) pp. 309–325, especially pp. 314–315.
[42] *Gebhardt* v. *Saunders* [1892] 2 Q.B.D. 452.
[43] S.83(1). See Chap. 13 (Scotland) for a summary of the position.
[44] The term includes metropolitan and non-metropolitan district councils, London boroughs, enterprise zone authorities, urban development corporations, housing action trusts, the Norfolk and Suffolk Broads authorities, and National Park county councils or planning boards.

land in their area, they may serve notice on the owner and occupier of the land. The notice shall require specified steps to be taken for remedying the condition of the land within such a period as may be specified;[45] the notice takes effect at the end of such period as is specified in the notice, which must be not less than 28 days after service of the notice.[46]

The power is phrased in wider terms than was the case under earlier legislation which was held not to apply to an operational breaker's yard, not being "open land" within the initial formulation of the section.[47] The present wording covers any land, whether operational, unused or derelict, and whether or not covered by structures. It is quite conceivable that contaminated land could, in appropriate circumstances, adversely affect the amenity of an area, though the term "amenity" is not defined in the Act: contamination could, for example, kill vegetation or wildlife, pollute water or have other adverse aesthetic effects.

Section 215 notices: sanctions

Notice under section 215 may be served on the owner[48] and on the **2.74** occupier of the land. Where the owner or occupier fails to comply with the notice he shall be guilty of an offence.[49] The offence lies not in having caused the condition affecting amenity, but in failing to comply with the notice to remedy it; therefore the section can affect a subsequent owner or occupier. Indeed, where the owner or occupier changes during the period specified in the notice for compliance, there is a procedure for having the subsequent owner or occupier brought before the court.[50] In such circumstances it may be possible for the original owner or occupier to avoid liability if he proves: (a) that failure to take the relevant steps was attributable to the default of the new owner or occupier; and (b) that he himself took all reasonable steps to ensure compliance with the notice.[51]

[45] S.215(2).
[46] S.215(3) and (4).
[47] *Stephens* v. *Cuckfield Rural District Council* [1960] 2 Q.B. 373.
[48] "Owner" is defined by s.336(1) as any person, other than a mortgagee in possession, who whether in his own right or as trustee for some other person, is entitled to receive the rack rent, or would be so entitled if the land were let at rack rent.
[49] S.216(2). The offence is triable only summarily and is punishable by a fine not exceeding level 3 (currently £1,000) with a further fine of £100 for each day following the first conviction on which the requirements of the notice remain unfulfilled (subs. (6)).
[50] S.216(3) and (4).
[51] S.216 (5)(*b*).

Section 215 notices: appeals

2.75 By section 217, a person on whom a section 215 notice is served, or any other person having an interest in land to which the notice relates, may, at any time within the period specified in the notice as the period at the end of which it is to take effect, appeal against the notice on specified grounds. Those grounds are:

   (a) the condition of the land does not in fact adversely affect amenity within section 215(1);

   (b) the condition of the land is attributable to, and is such as results in the ordinary course of events from the carrying on of operations or a use of land which is not in contravention of Part III of the Planning Act. This defence may be important where the contamination is the result of carrying on some pre-1947 or other lawful use or some operation or use with the benefit of planning permission or permitted development rights. However, the condition must be such as results in *the ordinary course of events* from those activities: contamination might be said to arise in the ordinary course of events from, say, use of land for landfill purposes, whereas spillage of oil might not necessarily arise in the ordinary course of events from operating an oil depot or vehicle maintenance workshop;

   (c) the requirements of the notice exceed what is necessary for preventing the condition of the land from adversely affecting amenity. Again this could be very important, given the wide range of remedial or clean-up options that might be available on a given site; it would probably in most cases deter a local authority from pursuing a full-scale decontamination or reclamation scheme; and

   (d) the period specified in the notice as the period within which any steps required by the notice are to be taken falls short of what should reasonably be allowed.

Any appeal under the section is made to the magistrates' court for the area where the land is situated; pending final determination or withdrawal of the appeal the notice is of no effect.[52] On appeal the magistrates may correct any immaterial informality, defect or error in the notice and may quash the notice or vary its terms in favour of the appellant.[53] There is a further right of appeal to the Crown Court from the magistrates' decision.[54]

[52] S.217(3).
[53] S.217(4) and (5).
[54] S.218.

By section 285(3) the validity of a notice may not be questioned in any other proceedings (including by way of defence to a prosecution) on grounds (a) or (b). Other arguments on *ultra vires* may be heard by the magistrates or Crown Court, or indeed at the stage of a prosecution for non-compliance; there is no need to go to the expense of separate judicial review proceedings for that purpose.[55]

Section 215 notices: execution of works and cost recovery

Section 219(1) allows the local planning authority, where steps **2.76** required by the notice have not been taken within the specified time:

(a) to enter the land and take those steps; and
(b) to recover from the person who is then owner of the land any expenses reasonably incurred in doing so.

The steps which may be taken are linked to those required by the original notice: there is no more general power to take preventative or remedial measures. Reasonably incurred expenses may be recovered from the owner of the land at the time the steps were taken: "owner" is defined by section 336(1) of the Act.[56] There is no power to recover costs from an occupier: however, it is provided that expenses incurred under this section by the owner (or by the owner or occupier in complying with a section 215 notice) shall be deemed to be incurred or paid for the use and at the request of the person who caused or permitted the land to come to be in the condition it was when the notice was served.[57] This somewhat unusual provision therefore gives a potential right of cost recovery on equitable principles from the occupier or from a former owner or occupier.

By subsections (3)–(5) regulations under the Act[58] may:

(a) apply provisions of the Public Health Act 1936 allowing the sale of materials removed in executing works,[59] giving power to require the occupier to permit the owner to execute works to the premises,[60] and limiting the liability of persons holding premises as agents or trustees in respect of recovery of expenses;[61]

---

[55] *R* v. *Oxford Crown Court, ex p. Smith, The Times,* December 27, 1989.
[56] See para. 2.75, n. 43.
[57] Subs. (2).
[58] See the Town and Country Planning General Regulations 1992 (S.I. 1992 No. 1492), reg. 16.
[59] Subs. (3)(a). The provision does not apply to refuse removed.
[60] Subs. (3)(b). Procedure is by complaint to the magistrates court.
[61] Subs. 3(c). Liability is limited to the total amount of money he has or has had in his hands.

(b) adopt section 289 of the Public Health Act 1936 so as to give the owner of land the right, as against all other persons interested in the land, to comply with the requirements of the notice;[62] and

(c) provide for the charging on land of any expenses recoverable by a local authority under section 219(1).[63]

Proposed extension of section 215 powers

2.77   The possible extended use of section 215 powers in the context of derelict land has been canvassed by the Government in its consultation paper, *Proposals to Prevent Land Becoming Derelict.*[64] The paper points out that section 215 powers are currently not widely used "because they do not provide for full scale reclamation, merely tidying up, and the landowner can claim as a defence that the condition of the land is attributable to its past development if that development itself was not in breach of planning control."[65] The paper proposes that the powers should be extended to enable planning authorities, after giving reasonable notice to the landowner, to reclaim derelict land to a minimum standard whatever the previous use.

However, the Government sees such proposals as powers of last resort to deal with problems of serious dereliction, for example where the land is causing a serious nuisance in health and safety terms or is a major environmental eyesore, or where dereliction is contraining the development of neighbouring land[66] It is also proposed that the power be used only where the owner-occupier had been given sufficient notice and had failed to produce a scheme of reclamation of his own which would be eligible for derelict land grant.[67] The cost of the works carried out by the local authority would then be supported by DLG funds. Consideration is also given to the possible extent of cost recovery by the authority, with three alternatives being put forward:

(i) recovery of the whole cost (as now);

(ii) treating the scheme as a non-local authority application for DLG by the owner, and requiring the owner to pay only that element not covered by the notional element of grant; or

---

[62] Subs. (4). As adapted, the right is against any person having an interest in premises other than the owner: Town and Country Planning General Regulations 1992, reg. 14(1)(*c*).

[63] Subs. (5). This provision has not been implemented, though the Government has invited views on whether such a power is needed: *Proposals to Prevent Land Becoming Derelict* (DoE, February 1992, para. 29).

[64] DoE, February 1992.

[65] Para. 22.

[66] Para. 23.

[67] Para. 24. On DLG generally, see Chap. 9.

(iii) recovery of only the increase in the value of the land due to the local authority's reclamation work.

The Government acknowledges that each of these alternatives have their potential drawbacks, but takes the view that reforms would give more confidence to local authorities and greater incentives (depending partly on the severity of the clawback provisions) for landowners to come forward with their own schemes.[68]

POWERS OF CRIMINAL COURTS

Compensation orders

Under section 35 of the Powers of Criminal Courts Act 1973 a court **2.78** by or before which a person is convicted of an offence instead of or in addition to dealing with him in any other way, may, on application or otherwise make a compensation order requiring him to pay compensation for any personal injury, loss or damage resulting from that offence or any other offence taken into consideration by the court in determining sentence; the court must give reasons if it does not make an order in cases where it is empowered to do so. Monetary limits are placed on the powers of magistrates' courts in this respect by section 40 of the Magistrates' Court Act 1980. Subject to these limits, compensation shall be of such amount as the court considers appropriate, having regard to any evidence and to any representations made on behalf of the accused or the prosecution.[69]

In determining whether to make a compensation order and its amount, the court is under a duty to have regard to the accused's means so far as known; including the possible proceeds of sale of any property to be confiscated.[70] Where the court considers that it would be appropriate to impose a fine and make a compensation order, but the offender has insufficient means to satisfy both, then preference shall be given to compensation.[71]

Appeal against compensation orders lies to the Court of Appeal, which may quash or vary the order irrespective of whether the conviction is quashed.[72] The order may also be reviewed by the magistrates' court on specific grounds, including where the loss, injury or damage in respect of

[68] Para. 27.
[69] Subs. (1A).
[70] Subs. (4).
[71] Subs. (4A).
[72] S.36(3).

which the order was made is held to be less in civil proceedings than was originally taken to be the case.[73] Section 38 of the Act, as substituted by the Criminal Justice Act 1988, section 105, deals with the relationship between compensation orders and damages in civil proceedings: the civil damages are assessed without regard to the order, but the plaintiff may only recover the amount by which civil damages exceed the compensation, together with a sum equal to any portion of the compensation which he fails to recover.[74]

The courts' powers under the section are dependant upon the accused having been convicted of an offence.[75] In theory therefore the various offences referred to above in relation to water, waste, statutory nuisance[76] and the like may give rise to a compensation order: the power is not confined to cases where there is civil liability.[77] However, the procedure is intended for cases where the issues are clear and simple and where generally no great amount is at stake[78]; it is preferable for substantial claims to be dealt with in civil proceedings and the absence of any civil remedy of damages is a factor to be taken into account by the court.[79] This will tend to restrict the use of compensation orders in the majority of contaminated land cases where the issues of civil liability will of their nature be legally, evidentially and technically complex.

Power to deprive offender of property

2.79   Section 43 of the Powers of Criminal Courts Act 1973 applies where a person is convicted of an offence and the court is satisfied (*inter alia*) that any property which was in his possession or under his control at the time when the summons was issued or when he was apprehended had been used or was intended to be used for the purpose of committing or facilitating the commission of any offence. The court may make an order which has the effect of depriving the offender of his rights, if any, in the property[80] the proceeds may be applied to compensate any person injured or who has suffered loss or damage.[81]

---

[73] S.37.

[74] Judgment in respect of the latter amount may be enforced only with leave of the court.

[75] *Herbert* v. *Lambeth London Borough Council, The Times,* November 27, 1991.

[76] *Ibid.* However, despite the comments of Woolf L.J. to the contrary, unlike the position under the Public Health Act 1936, s.94(2), no offence is committed under s.80 of the Environmental Protection Act 1990, until there is failure to comply with the abatement notice: s.80(4).

[77] *R* v. *Chappel* [1984] Crim.L.R. 574.

[78] *Stones' Justices Manual* (124th ed., 1992) para. 3–785, p. 869.

[79] *Herbert* v. *Lambeth London Borough Council* (n. 75 above).

[80] Subs. (3). The property shall be taken into the possession of the police and dealt with under the Police (Property) Act 1897.

[81] S.43A.

The power will in practice be of limited application to offences involving contaminated land: it has been held not to extend to real property[82] and in any event it would be highly artificial to speak of land being "used" for the commission of an offence in the context of the section. However, the section could certainly apply to a vehicle used (say) for illicit waste disposal. It should also be noted that the term "facilitating the commission of an offence" is given an extended definition to include the taking of any steps after the offence has been committed for the purpose of avoiding apprehension or detection[83] thus equipment used for the purpose of concealing an offence may be vulnerable to an order under the section.

Confiscation of proceeds of offence

Part VI of the Criminal Justice Act 1988 allows the Crown Court and **2.80** magistrates' courts to make confiscation orders against a convicted offender where certain criteria apply, namely:

(a) if found guilty in the Crown Court the offence must be one to which Part VI applies or if found guilty in a magistrate's court the offence must be one listed in Schedule 4 to the Act;[84]

(b) the court must be satisfied that the offender has benefitted from the offence;[85] and

(c) that benefit must be at least the "minimum amount".[86]

The sum to be paid under the order shall be such as the court thinks fit[87] but must be at least the minimum amount and must not exceed (i) the benefit in respect of which it is made; or (ii) the amount appearing to the court to be the amount that might be realised at the time the order is made, whichever is the less.[88]

The Act contains detailed provisions as to statements by the prosecution, enforcement of orders, restraint orders prohibiting the dealing with realisable property, charging orders, and bankruptcy, winding up and insolvency.

The power to make such orders is limited in the case of magistates' courts to specified offences in Schedule 4, which do not at present

---

[82] *R* v. *Khan* [1982] 1 W.L.R. 1405.

[83] Subs. 43(2).

[84] Subs. 71(2)(*a*), (3)(*a*) and (9)(*c*).

[85] S.71(2)(*b*)(i) and 3(*b*)(i); benefit is defined as obtaining property as s result of or in connection with the offence (s.71(4)) and "property" includes money (s.102(i)).

[86] S.71(2)(*b*)(ii) and (3)(*b*)(ii). The minimum amount is £10,000 or such other amount as may be specified by statutory instrument: s.71(7).

[87] S.71(1).

[88] S.71(6).

109

include environmental offences. However, the Crown court can make orders in request of any indictable offence, which would include most environmental offences as offences triable "either way". The use of confiscation orders therefore is possible in environmental cases and may indeed be highly appropriate in cases of cynical pollution designed to make significant profits.[89]

EC Proposals on liability for waste

2.81   The issue of civil liability at least for certain forms of environmental damage was addressed by the Commission of the EC in its proposal for a Directive on civil liability for damage caused by waste.[90] The proposal referred to the possible adverse effects of disparities among laws of Member States concerning such liability and to the principle established in Article 130R of the EC treaty that the polluter should pay; "the strict liability of the producer constitutes the best solution to the problem." In its amended form of June 1991, the proposed Directive provided that: "the producer of waste shall be liable under civil law for the damage and impairment of the environment caused by waste, irrespective of fault on his part.[91]

"Producer" was defined to include not only the actual producer of the waste but also: those carrying out pre-processing, mixing or other activities changing the nature or composition of the waste; importers of waste into the Community; the person having control of the waste when the incident giving rise to the damage or impairment of the environment occurred, if not able to identify the actual producer within a reasonable period; and the person responsible for the installation to which waste was lawfully transferred.[92] One notable feature of the proposal was the imposition of liability for not only personal injury and damage to property, but also "impairment of the environment", defined as any significant physical, chemical or biological deterioration.[93]

The only defences provided to liability were of a limited nature, *e.g.* malicious acts or omission of third parties and force majeure.[94] A limitation period of three years was proposed from the date on which the plaintiff became aware or should have become aware of the damage or impairment, with a long-stop period of 30 years from the date of the

[89] Michael Fordham, "The Profits of Pollution," [1993] N.L.J. 230.
[90] Com (91) 219 Final—Syn 217; O.J. No. C 192/6 23.7.91. See also the House of Lords Select Committee on the European Communities *Paying for Pollution*, Session 1989–90, 25th Report, HL Paper 84–1.
[91] Art. 3.1.
[92] Art. 2.1(*a*) and 2.2.
[93] Art. 2.1(*c*) and (*d*).
[94] Arts. 6 and 7.

relevant incident.[95] Whilst the proposal was not intended to apply retrospectively to damage or impairment arising from an incident which occurred before its implementation,[96] difficulties over deciding what was the "incident" could have rendered this comfort somewhat illusory. In any event, the proposal was ultimately withdrawn in favour of a more general scheme of environmental liability.[97]

EC Proposals on environmental liability

On March 17, 1993 the Commission adopted a communication on **2.82** repairing damage to the environment.[98] This so-called "green paper", issued as a consultative document, considers various issues relating to the different forms of liability and their shortcomings, how environmental damage is defined and the mechanisms by which such damage may be made good. The Commission's work reflects not only experience within member states, but also the Council of Europe's convention on civil liability.[99] Any system adopted by the Community is likely to lean conceptually on the principle that an individual should repair the damage he causes; this principle being closely linked to the fundamental tenets of preventive action and the "polluter pays principle". The Green Paper itself recognises however that civil liability has serious limitations so far as redressing what the Paper calls "damage from the past" is concerned.

Effectively, what appears to be envisaged is an integrated programme using no fault civil liability where damage may be linked to a particular party's actions and, where damage is not so attributable, using compensation systems to spread the cost of restoration action among economic sectors. A common issue which will probably need to be addressed in all member states is how to define and treat impairment of the environment which falls outside accepted categories of physical injury, damage to tangible property and interference with the party rights; in particular at what point impairment becomes sufficiently serious to impose liability.[1] The issue is essentially one of policy as to who decides what is an acceptable level of environmental damage: attitudes on this issue can vary geographically and on a cultural basis, and can change over time in the light of new scientific information or hypothesis.

Any proposal is also likely to have to address the extremely difficult issue of insurance coverage and whether any element of compulsory

[95] Arts. 9 and 10.
[96] Art. 13.
[97] See para. 2.82.
[98] Com (93) 47.
[99] See para. 2.83.
[1] See para. 2.36 on the position under English law in this respect.

111

insurance can be built into the scheme in the light of the current lack of any substantial market for such insurance products. The Green Paper has subsequently been the subject of a joint hearing of the European Parliament and Commission, and of a series of seminars funded by the Commission.[1a] The European Parliament and the Economic and Social Committee have delivered opinions supporting a no-fault liability régime at European level, though with serious reservations as to the applicability of such a régime to historic contamination.

Council of Europe Convention

2.83   The Council of Europe has produced, through its Committee of Experts on compensation for damage caused to the environment (CJ–EN) on a Convention on Civil Liability for Damage Resulting from Activities Dangerous to the Environment.[2] This work builds on earlier international efforts in relation to matters such as nuclear substances and the carriage of dangerous goods and takes the general stance that strict liability in this field is desirable, taking into account the "polluter pays" principle.

The general aim of the Convention is to ensure that "adequate compensation for damage resulting from activities dangerous to the environment and also provides for means of prevention and reinstatement."[3] "Dangerous activities" are defined by Article 2 to include the following, provided they are performed professionally or are conducted by public authorities:

(a) the production, handling, storage, use or discharge of one or more dangerous substances[4] or any operation of a similar nature dealing with such substances;

(b) the production, culturing, handling, storage, use, destruction, disposal, release or other operation dealing with genetically-modified organisms;

(c) the operation of an installation or site for the incineration, treatment, handling or recycling of waste,[5] provided that the quantities involved pose a significant risk to man, the environment or property; and

[1a] See the comments of the European Environmental Law Association Working Party at [1994] Env. Liability I.
[2] The approved text was released in March 1993 and the convention was finally concluded at Lugano on June 21, 1993. See [1994] Env. Liability II (M.J. Bowman) for a summary.
[3] Art. 1.
[4] Defined at Art. 2.2.
[5] Installations or sites are further specified at Annex II.

112

(d) the operation of a site for the permanent disposal of waste.

"Damage" is defined[6] so as to include not only loss of life or personal injury and damage to property but also impairment of the environment and the costs of preventive measures; damages for impairment (other than for loss of profit from such impairment) are limited to the costs of measures of reinstatement actually undertaken or to be undertaken.

The Convention also includes some relatively sophisticated provisions of a transitional nature dealing with retrospective liability and in particular with closed waste disposal sites.[7] Under article 5 the regime applies to incidents occurring after the entry into force of the Convention in respect of the relevant Contracting Party; where the incident consists of a continuous occurrence or series of occurrences having the same origin and part of those occurrences took place before the entry into force of the Convention, the provisions on liability apply only to damage caused by occurrences or part of a continuous occurrence taking place after the entry into force. "Incident' is defined by article 3(11) to mean any sudden occurrence or continuous occurrence or any series of occurrences having the same origin, which causes damage or creates a grave and imminent threat of causing damage. By article 5(2) in respect of damage caused by waste deposited at a site for the permanent deposit of waste, the provisions apply to damage which becomes known after the entry into force of the Convention. However, it does not apply:

(a) if the site was closed in accordance with the provisions of internal law before the entry into force of the Convention; or
(b) in cases where the site is operational after such entry into force, if the operator can prove that the damage was caused solely by waste deposited there before such entry into force.

Other provisions deal with causation, joint and several liability, limitation periods and jurisdiction.[8]

Article 12 requires Contracting Parties to ensure that, "where appropriate, taking due account of the risks of the activity and of the financial capability of the operator", operators participate in a financial security scheme or have or maintain a financial guarantee to cover liability under the Convention.

Articles 13–18 constitute a code on access to information on the environment held by public bodies and bodies with public responsibilities for the environment; also a person suffering damage is entitled to request the court to order an operator to provide him with specific

[6] Art. 2.7.
[7] Art. 5. See also Art. 7 in relation to liability in respect of sites for the permanent deposit of waste.
[8] Arts. 10, 11, 17 and 19.

information, in so far as is necessary to establish the existence of a claim for compensation under the Convention.

Article 18 contains potentially far-reaching provisions giving substantial rights of action to any associations or foundation "which according to its statutes aims at the protection of the environment": such rights include standing to seek an order for the operator to take preventive measures or measures of reinstatement.

The Convention is expressed not to limit or derogate from the rights of persons suffering damage under national law or to limit such provisions concerning protection or reinstatement of the environment.[9] Also, in their mutual relations parties who are members of the EC are to apply Community rules rather than the rules of the Convention save in so far as there is no Community rule governing the subject in question.[10]

The Convention enters into force following the expiry of three months from the date on which three states, including at least two members of the Council of Europe, ratify the Convention.[11]

---

[9] Art. 25.1.
[10] Art. 25.2.
[11] Art. 32.3. The Convention was immediately signed when opened for signature on June 21, 1993 by Cyprus, Finland, Greece, Italy, Liechtenstein, Luxembourg and The Netherlands.

Chapter 3

INFORMATION

Generally

This chapter deals with the various sources of information which are **3.01** relevant to assessing the possible contamination of land; this includes the responsibilities of public bodies to collate and make available such information. The process of site investigation is a related issue which is covered in Chapter 4. Other related issues dealt with in other chapters are information on water resources which may be affected by contamination[1] and enquiries of local and other authorities in the context of property transactions.[2]

Improving public access to environmental information was one of the key principles set out in the environmental white paper "This Common Inheritance"[3], not least because it will raise the standard of informed public debate. Public registers have been the traditional means of making available information on the environment,[4] and it was the register model which the Government adopted for its proposed system of information on land subject to contaminative uses.[5] This proposal was subsequently abandoned by the Government following consultation, but there is still potentially a considerable amount of information in the public domain which may assist in determining the nature and extent of contamination. Access to such information is assisted by the Environmental Information Regulations 1992[6] which implement Directive 90/313/EC on the freedom of access to information on the environment.[7] Information held by public bodies may fall into a number of categories:

(1) information obtained or collated by the Authority as a result of its own investigations or monitoring;

---

[1] See Chap. 6.
[2] See Chap. 11.
[3] Cm. 1200, September 1990; see paras. 1.20 and 17.21–28.
[4] See T.P. Burton, *Access to Environmental Information. The UK Experience of Water Registers* [1989] J.E.L. 192.
[5] Environmental Protection Act 1990, s.143; see para. 3.02.
[6] S.I. 1992 No. 3240; see para. 3.11 *et seq.*
[7] O.J. No. L158, 23.6.90, p. 56.

    (2) information supplied to the Authority in support of an application (for example for an authorisation or licence);

    (3) information obtained by the authority from a third party pursuant to a legally enforceable request;

    (4) information supplied to the Authority voluntarily by a third party; and

    (5) information as to actions taken by the Authority (for example, issue, refusal, revocation or variation of a licence, or enforcement action).

In each case what must be considered is:

    (a) whether the information is subject to inclusion on a public register; and if not

    (b) whether the information is subject to disclosure under the Environmental Information Regulations.

Information provided on possible contamination may reveal business opportunities, for example in the clean-up field, or the availability of land at a cheaper price than would otherwise be the case, in which event a commercial judgment can be made whether to make an offer on the basis that the present owner may have over-estimated clean-up costs. Attention has tended to centre however on the adverse effects of such information on land values and the uncertainties as to the possible magnitude of blighting effects.

PROPOSAL FOR REGISTERS OF CONTAMINATIVE USES

Section 143 registers: the statutory framework

3.02   The clause which became section 143 of the Environmental Protection Act 1990 was introduced by the Government at House of Lords' Committee stage. The House of Commons Environment Committee in its report on contaminated land had recommended the creation of registers of contaminated land compiled by local authorities and using common methodology and compatible computer hardware and software.[8] In making the announcement of the new proposal the Government indicated that their prime intention was to provide a means of alerting interested parties to the potential for contamination so that,

---

[8] Session 1989–90, First Report, 170 I—III, paras. 78–85; see also the Government's response (Cmnd. 1161).

where necessary, more detailed site surveys could be undertaken.[9] Public registers of contaminated land were in fact not particularly innovative. The Dutch Inventory extended to some 110,000 sites, the German equivalent to 100,000 or so and there were inventories or registers in Finland and Denmark. Perhaps the most common characteristic that those registers have was that the number of contaminated sites far exceeded preliminary estimates.

Section 143, which was to come into force on a date to be appointed, would have imposed a duty on local authorities,[10] as respects land in their area "subject to contamination", to maintain, in accordance with regulations, a register in the prescribed form and containing the prescribed particulars. The expression "subject to contamination" is somewhat misleading: as defined in section 143 it does not connote actual contamination, but rather land which is being or had been put to a "contaminative use", being such uses of land to be specified in regulations as may cause land to be contaminated with noxious substances.[11]

Section 143 registers: consultation and abandonment

It was initially evisaged that regulations implementing section 143 **3.03** would come into force on April 1, 1992. A consultation paper was issued in May 1991 which canvassed the relevant issues of policy and methodology and provided a draft schedule of contaminative uses grouped under the following categories and comprising some 42 sub groups, in some cases themselves comprising a number of separate activities.

Titles of main contaminative use profiles given in the May 1991 consultation paper were:

(1) Agriculture
(2) Extractive industry
(3) Energy industry
(4) Production of metals
(5) Production of non-metals and their products
(6) Glass making and ceramics
(7) Production and use of chemicals
(8) Engineering and manufacturing process
(9) Food processing industry

[9] DoE News Release No. 279.
[10] Defined by subs. 143(6) as District Councils, London Boroughs and Scottish Planning Authorities.
[11] Subs. 143(6).

117

(10) Paper pulp and printing industry
(11) Timber and timber products industry
(12) Textile industry
(13) Rubber industry
(14) Infrastructure
(15) Waste disposal
(16) Miscellaneous

The width of this proposal was subject to fierce criticism: it would have included, for example, the manufacture of metal goods, the storage of petroleum, the repair of electrical equipment, educational and research laboratories, and premises housing dry-cleaning operations.

After considerable criticism, revised proposals on the form and content of the registers were subsequently issued in July 1992, the principal concession by the Department of Environment being to reduce the list of contaminative uses of land from 42 to eight. However, it was accompanied by a suggestion that the list could be extended in future. The reduction in the list of contaminative uses was intended by the Department of Environment to offset criticism of the proposed registers. The concept was that the eight in the list concerned were uses where there was a very high probability that the land would be contaminated unless appropriately treated. The revised list found in Schedule 1 of the draft regulations comprised:

(1) Manufacture of gas, coke and bituminous material from coal;
(2) Manufacture of refining of lead or steel or an alloy of lead or steel;
(3) Manufacture of asbestos or asbestos products;
(4) Manufacture, refining or recovery of petroleum or its derivatives, other than extraction from petroleum-bearing ground;
(5) Manufacture, refining or recovery of other chemicals, excluding minerals;
(6) Final deposit of household, commercial or industrial waste, as defined in section 75 of the Environmental Protection Act, other than waste consisting of ash, slag, clinker, rock, wood, gypsum, railway ballast, peat, brick, tiles, concrete, glass, other materials or dredging spoil, or where waste is used as a fertiliser or in order to condition the land in some other beneficial manner;
(7) Treatment at a fixed installation of household, commercial or industrial waste by chemical or thermal means; and
(8) Use as a scrap metal store within the meaning of section 9(2) of the Scrap Metal Dealers Act 1964.

It was readily apparent however, looking at the list concerned, that there would be hard cases where it would be difficult to determine whether or not in a given instance the use was or was not within the list.

There were also a number of strange anomalies, for example the exclusion of processes involving metals other than lead and steel, and the exclusion of deposits of slag.[12]

Following further concerted criticism of the proposal, it was announced in March 1993 that the intention was not to proceed with the introduction of the registers, principally on the ground that entry on the register would have had a blighting effect, without any clear indication of how confidence in the site could be restored.[13] Instead, a "wide-ranging review" of existing powers and duties relating to identification, assessment, treatment and control of contaminated land was instituted.[14]

The proposed register: criticisms

In announcing the abandonment of the register proposal, the then **3.04** Secretary of State added that the principal criticisms of the registers were threefold:

(1) the register would not contain some sites which are not actually contaminated, "while missing other sites that are actually contaminated by other former uses not on the prescribed list";

(2) there was no way of removing sites from the register even if contamination had been dealt with satisfactorily; and

(3) when sites were found to be actually contaminated, it remained unclear "what action should be taken, what remediation measures should be carried out and by whom, which regulatory authority should be involved, and where the liability for the cost of remediation or compensation should fall."

These identified problems only serve to illustrate the difficulty at the outset in confusing the principle of a register of historic contaminative uses, on the one hand, and that of sites which were actually contaminated and therefore required remediation on the other. To that extent the proposed register was hybrid in that it was to include a Part B which would have included sites which had been the subject of investigation or remedial works.

As the proposal stood at the second consultation stage whenever an entry was proposed to be made, advance notification had to be given by the authority to those interested in the land affected. Authorities were required to take all reasonable steps to ensure that any person having an

---

[12] *See The Surveyor*, October 8, 1992, p. 8.

[13] DoE News Release No. 209 and Scottish Office News Release 0442/93 (March 24, 1993). The Scottish release is in fact somewhat more candid about the blight aspects, referring to "an already subdued property market."

[14] See para. 3.06 below.

interest in the land, which presumably included mortgagees and lessees, should be given two months' prior notice before the entry on the register was made. There was no right to make representations or objections to the proposed entry and thus no duty on the authority to take into account any representations or objections made; however the rules of natural justice would probably have ensured that they did take account of them. In particular there was no statutory right of appeal and a landowner dissatisfied with the decision to enter his property in the register was left to appeal by way of judicial review.

As indicated above, Part A of the registers would have included those sites where the authority was satisfied that there was a historic contaminative use; Part B would have included sites where there had been an investigation and/or treatment had been undertaken. Once a site had been treated it would remain in Part B but with a note to the effect that remediatory works had been carried out. However, that note could not necessarily be assumed to imply that the remediatory works carried out were satisfactory. Those who carried out the remediation could point to their instructions which may or may not have been adequate. In any event no liability would attach to an authority if the remedial works noted in the register subsequently turned out to be inadequate.

There were other criticisms and concerns, a summary of which is as follows:

(1) a site could be contaminated but not included in the register; it could have been put to a use falling outside the scope of the Regulations or its history might not have been fully appreciated.

(2) entry on the register could give rise to an immediate problem for landowners, putting them at least under an obligation to assess the nature of the contamination and what should be done about it, if for no other reason than to protect the value of the asset;

(3) entry on the register did not of itself imply any duty enforceable upon the landowner to remove the contamination concerned;

(4) possible failure by the local authority to enter details of the site at all, despite knowledge of a contaminative use in one of their departments, or of recording the contaminative use unsatisfactorily or in a misleading way, gave rise to problems of the liability of the authority in such circumstances;

(5) the possible entry on the register of a site for which there was no justification equally gave rise to liability problems; and

(6) the extent to which the authority, having collated information, was thereafter bound to reveal it to an enquirer with a sufficient interest in obtaining it, or indeed otherwise, gave rise to concern; the vendor of a site might hold a diametrically opposite view on this aspect from that of a purchaser for obvious reasons.

Alternative proposals

The Royal Institute of Chartered Surveyors first suggested an alterna- **3.05** tive proposal in its response to the May 1990 Consultation Paper. In essence the RICS advised against a retrospective register and suggested that a more practical solution would be to introduce a requirement for all future planning applications to be supported by a site appraisal report. In their view that report would deal with the actualities on the ground, namely whether or not there was contamination requiring treatment; the applicant would then be required to indicate the treatment proposed to render the site suitable for the use described in the application. The cost to the local authority of investigating such applications could be recoverable from the applicant through a general charging system.

The Council of Mortgage Lenders (CML), amongst others, considered the Royal Institute of Chartered Surveyors' proposals, as did the Local Authorities Associations, the Standing Local Authority Officers' Panel on Land Reclamation, the Law Society, the Law Society of Scotland and the Scottish Housebuilders Federation. Generally, it was agreed that the RICS proposals had a number of advantages including the following:

(1) the system could be introduced rapidly;
(2) the cost of the site analysis accompanying each planning application need not be high and would be borne by developers rather than the Government.
(3) there should be no blighting effects, since the site analysis would specify any remedial action. Future purchasers would be able to see that any necessary clean-up action had been taken; and
(4) registers of information kept with planning applications by Local Planning Authorities would be fully up to date.

It can be seen that the RICS proposals are distinct in principle from the former proposals of the Government for registers of contaminative uses of land, which were directed to the provision of information. The RICS proposals amount to a means by which sites, the subject of planning applications, would be cleaned up for the use proposed. Further, the Government's proposed registers contained historic information relevant to past uses and the information therein did not necessarily infer present contamination, let alone its level. Thus RICS proposals were directed to the realities on the ground.

The main argument against the RICS proposal is its linkage of investigation to the development or redevelopment of land. As a representative of the Institution of Environmental Health Officers put it in a letter to *The Times* of April 24, 1993: "This would leave many acres of land continuing to present a risk to health . . . Setting up registers of

121

land that may be contaminated was the first step towards a clear system of identification, investigation and remedial treatment."

Review of the register generally

3.06 As mentioned above, on March 24, 1993 Michael Howard, the then Secretary of State for the Environment, withdrew the proposals for statutory registers of contaminative uses of land and announced a review conducted by an inter-departmental group under the chairmanship of the Department of the Environment. The terms of reference of that review are important in the present context:

> "To review the powers and duties of public authorities which relate to the identification, assessment, and appropriate treatment or control of land that could cause pollution of the environment or harm to human health, having regard to the need to minimise the cost which existing and new regulatory burdens placed on the private sector; to consider the mechanism for recovering authorities' costs in controlling or remedying pollution of such land sufficient to ensure its safety and health for the environment, and its return to beneficial use where practicable; to consider the implications of these for the role of the Environment Agency; to report initially on any statutory changes needed in the short term and on the scope of any longer-term studies that should be put in hand; and to undertake and report on those studies."

The initial outcome of the review was the March 1994 consultation paper, "Paying for Our Past", which is considered below.

Aspects of the review

3.07 The review goes far wider than any re-consideration of replacing the registers with some other mechanism for recording and disseminating information concerning sites put to contaminative uses. There is reference not only to the identification of such sites, but also their assessment and the appropriate treatment or control of land that could cause pollution of the environment or harm to human health. The sting however is in the tail in that this is followed by the phrase: "Having regard to the need to minimise the cost with existing and new regulatory burdens placed on the private sector." It would appear to follow that if Government funding is not generally to be made available—and this would appear to be the case at a time of cut-backs of Government spending—then it is only in a situation where the land is to be put to a remunerative use, for example on sale or lease to a commercial concern, or to be redeveloped, that there is a realistic opportunity to require clean-up at the expense of those involved in the transaction or one of them. The concept of "the polluter pays" lies in the public domain and belongs to a quite separate approach to contamination, namely where the situation is such that an environmental agency of one sort or another ought to intervene on behalf of the general public and insist the site be cleaned up at the expense of those at fault. Bearing in mind that many sites have existed for years without causing major public concern, the opportunities of enforcing clean-up in this way may be limited.

However, the whole question of ensuring that sites which are contaminated are cleaned up in the public interest is a quite separate topic from the dissemination of information to those who may wish to know of a site's past in the context of a commercial transaction. The issue of the powers of public authorities turns in this context primarily upon whether or not they can go further than merely looking at their own and other available desk-top records and actively seek out possible contamination, for example by serving notice on a landowner that they intend (possibly at his expense) to carry out an investigative process. No doubt the review would carefully consider such proposals in serious cases where there is public concern. Whether this is phrased as a power or a duty is of course all important to the local authority concerned. Bearing in mind their present insurance position local authorities might well resist the suggestion that they had a duty to act in other than the most extreme cases; they might further require their liability to be excluded or limited in the legislation concerned.

There are several ways in which an authority might otherwise be liable in circumstances where a duty was cast upon them. One would be for inadequate instructions to an environmental consultant, in cases where one was used, or to an environmental contractor, and another would be where the report received after investigation was misunderstood or misinterpreted or inappropriate action taken. A landowner whose site was the subject of investigation might rightly resent an investigation being made public in circumstances where it was subsequently proved the site was not contaminated at all. Equally, a prospective purchaser would justifiably feel aggrieved if he was not informed that a site investigation was in process or proposed. The issue may also arise under any future scheme of liability, whether criminal or civil, as to what extent reliance on decisions taken by inspectors or other public officials may constitute due diligence.[14a] What will also need to be considered here are the powers and duties of public authorities in relation to other records such as the planning register and local land

---

[14a] See *Carrick District Council* v. *Taunton Vale Meat Traders Ltd.*, *The Times*, February 15, 1994 (a Food Safety Act case).

charges register, the subject of enquiries prior to contract. It may then be relevant to look at the issue of registration errors and compensation in respect of local land charges, which may be indicative of the way in which the matter will be approached by the review.

Further consultation—"Paying for Our Past"

3.07A   As part of the review of contaminated land and liabilities, in March 1994 the Government issued the further consultation paper, *Paying for our Past: the arrangements for controlling contaminated land and meeting the cost of remedying the damage to the environment.* The paper does not present any firm proposals, but rather sets out a number of "preliminary conclusions" and poses a series of questions for respondents, grouped under seven issues:

  A. What should the objectives be within policy?
  B. How should the statutory framework meet the objectives?
  C. What relationship should the statutory framework have with the common law?
  D. Should there be any extension of strict liability?
  E. Who should pay for putting right environmental damage?
  F. How should markets be provided with information?
  G. What other roles should public sector bodies have?

The Government's position (so far as it is apparent) in relation to each of these issues is as follows:

Issue A—policy objectives—the broad aims of Government policy are to prevent or minimise further land contamination and, where practicable, to remedy it where it has occurred. However, the Government feels that this policy "must also work with the grain of the market", which points to a need to specify more clearly the policy's objectives. The need is recognised to balance priorities for action against resource costs. The Government's preliminary conclusions on this issue are that the policy objectives could be:

  — to prevent or minimise new pollution where practicable and to place the onus on the polluter to remedy or to render harmless any pollution which does occur;
  — to act on existing contamination which poses unacceptable, actual or suspected risks to health or the environment;
  — to improve sites in line with the "suitable for use" approach as and when hazards are tackled when development is proposed or promoted;
  — to encourage development of, and an efficient market in, land which has been subject to actual or potential contamination or where such contamination has been tackled; and

124

— to minimise financial and regulatory burdens.

These possible objectives themselves contain a number of inherent uncertainties, in particular the linkage of prevention of new contamination to practicability, and the issue of when a risk reaches an unacceptable level.

Issue B—statutory framework—the preliminary conclusions start from the premise that there is a continuing need for a regulatory framework, including cost recovery by regulators in respect of preventive or remedial action. However, the various régimes governing such regulatory action are said to vary to an extent that may not be fully justified, so that there should be some harmonisation on the basis of the provisions of the Environmental Protection Act 1990. Voluntary action is said to be preferable to formal enforcement action, and regulators should do more to encourage it. On the issue of who should be liable under a statutory regime, the paper contemplates that there might be "indirect" responsibility allowing lenders, financial institutions, trustees and the like to be pursued for clean-up costs. However, the extent of liability should not be determined by the availability of resources (the "deepest pocket") and the possibility of limitations on liability is not ruled out—though these would need to be framed so as to avoid abuse, and would have to be weighed against the effect on public finances.

Issue C—relationship with common law—the common law is seen as having its own role and functions, which are distinct from any statutory regime but which may contribute to the relevant policy objectives. However, the existence of differences which are too great between common law and regulatory powers can create tensions and uncertainties and disrupt the efficient working of the market. Overall, a cautious approach is advocated to changes to the common law, but its amendment should not be ruled out.

Issue D—possible extension of strict liability—the Government is tentatively of the view that the current mix of strict and fault-based approaches to liability "strikes a reasonable balance" and that a strong case would be needed for the introduction of any defence that would weaken the ability of regulators to secure remediation, or which would pass costs to the taxpayer. Generally the approach towards any extension of defences (such as compliance with regulatory consents) and towards limitation periods is a conservative one, no doubt driven partly by the need to minimise burdens on the public purse.

Issue E—who should pay?—It is not regarded as inconsistent with the polluter pays principle to provide for the enforcement of regulatory obligations on others, especially "the owner". The Government sees it as important to make evasion of liability through corporate or contractual

125

devices as difficult as possible and to ensure that regulators have the freedom to act quickly on appropriate cases even where liability is unclear. The possible hardship to private householders is recognised, but the only suggestion for alleviating such liability is the general one that provision requiring financial hardship to be taken into account could be extended to all statutes.

Issue F—how should markets be provided with information?—The Government suggests that the private sector has shown itself capable of fulfilling some of the intended purposes of section 143 registers; also many authorities have collated information which is available to the public. However, it is acknowledged that informational inadequacies are still causing market problems and that the problem is particularly acute in the domestic conveyancing market and for small or medium sized enterprises, where the costs of investigation may be prohibitive, or a substantial disincentive.

The Government's preliminary conclusions are tentative. It intends to continue the research programme funded through the Department of Environment; it will continue discussions with Local Authority Associations and with the Law Society; it will also continue to discuss the land quality statement proposal with the RICS (though it acknowledges that the RICS proposal would result in many sites not being covered for many years). It also states that, "It appears that implementing section 143 . . . may not be necessary to ensure an efficient market in land and to ensure that contamination is put right". In reviewing the vendor's duties of disclosure of any knowledge of actual or potential contamination, the Government feels it important to distinguish the "major commercial transactions" from "those involving domestic and SME vendors". For the former category, the Government sees any change adding little to the existing balance of incentives to make disclosures; however, ". . . the particular difficulties in ensuring the generation and transmission of such information in the domestic and SME markets may shift the balance of advantage there". These remarks, delphic and opaque even by the best Government standards, may foreshadow a rethinking of the current caveat emptor rule,[14b] at least to some extent.

Issue G—other roles for public sector bodies—local planning authorities are to determine the priority to be given to contamination in the light of their particular circumstances and within the framework of Government policy guidance. English Partnerships and the Welsh Development Agency will also have their proper role to play: though the funds available "will always be finite". More significantly, the new Environmental Agency could be given a general responsibility to establish a framework of guidance "to improve understanding of risks".

[14b] See Chap. 11 generally.

126

Finally, and importantly, the future of section 61 of the Environmental Protection Act 1990[14c] is to be reviewed and its entry into force is to be deferred pending outcome of the current review and institutional charges consequent upon formation of the Agency. This represents a potentially serious setback to any attempt to tackle problems posed by closed landfill sites within the framework of Part II of the Environmental Protection Act.

Overview—"Paying for Our Past", even judged as a consultation paper, is inconclusive. It is however apparent that section 143 will not be implemented in the short to medium term and, more likely, will never be implemented in its current form. It is also clear that whatever the outcome of the review, it will be driven in no small measure by constraints on public expenditure and consequently the desire to see costs borne by the private sector. Within the context of transactional information, the main development is probably the oblique suggestion that the *caveat emptor* rule might be open for review.

OTHER FUNCTIONS RELATING TO INFORMATION

Powers to obtain information

In most cases those authorities with responsibility for environmental **3.08** protection are provided with statutory powers in support of their functions: such powers can include rights of entry on land, sampling, taking photographs, investigation of records, the power to demand information, and the like. Some of these powers may be of relevance to the investigation of possibly contaminated land, though there are as yet no powers of investigation explicitly and specifically for that purpose. In some cases the legislation goes further, and imposes duties as to investigation or monitoring. The following table sets out details of the main duties and powers:

[14c] See Chap. 2.

Duties to investigate/monitor

Statutory Provision	Authority	Nature of Duty
E.P.A. 1990, s.42	Waste regulation authority	Ensuring that waste management activities do not cause pollution, harm to health or serious detriment to amenity, and that conditions of waste management licence are compiled with.
E.P.A. 1990, s.39(4)	Waste regulation authority	Inspection of land following application to surrender waste management licence to determine likelihood of pollution or harm to health.
E.P.A. 1990, s.61	Waste regulation authority	Inspection of land where waste has been deposited, where no licence in force, to determine whether condition may cause pollution or harm to health.
E.P.A. 1990, s.79	District/London Borough Council	Inspection of area to detect statutory nuisances and investigation of complaints of statutory nuisance by residents of area.
Water Industry Act 1991. s.69(2) and Water Supply (Water Quality) Regulations 1989, (S.I. 1989 No. 1147).	Water supply undertaker	Monitoring sources of water supply for compliance with requirements on water quality.
Water Industry Act 1991, s.77	District/London Borough Council	Steps considered appropriate for keeping themselves informed about the wholesomeness and sufficiency of water supplies in their area.
Private Water Supplies Regulations 1991, (S.I. 1991 No. 2790).	District/London Borough Council	Monitoring of private supplies serving premises in their area.
Water Industry Act 1991, s.86(2)	Drinking Water Inspectorate	Investigations required by Secretary of State as to compliance with statutory drinking water quality obligations

Statutory Provision	Authority	Nature of Duty
Water Resources Act 1991, s.84(2)	National Rivers Authority	Monitoring extent of pollution in controlled waters.

Powers to investigate/monitor

Statutory Provision	Authority	Purpose/nature of power
E.P.A. 1990, s.17	HMIP/Local enforcing authority	Powers for exercise of enforcement functions on premises (a) on which a prescribed process is carried on or (b) has been carried on (whether or not the process was prescribed when it was carried on) and which is believed to give rise to a risk of serious pollution. Powers include: entry, examination, measurements, photographs, sampling, testing, requiring information from individuals, requiring production of computer and other records, requiring other necessary facilities and assistance.
E.P.A. 1990, s.19(2)	HMIP/Local enforcing authority or Secretary of State	Power by notice in writing to require any person to furnish such information as the authority reasonably considers it needs for the discharge of its functions under Part I.
E.P.A. 1990, s.69	Waste regulation authorities	Powers for discharging functions under Part II relating to control of waste; exercisable on land on or in which waste is or has been deposited, treated, kept or disposed of and land believed to be affected by the deposit, treatment, keeping or disposal of waste on other land. Powers include: entry, examination, measurements, photograph, samples, testing, requiring information from individuals, requiring production of computer and other records, requiring other necessary facilities and assistance.

Statutory Provision	Authority	Nature of Duty
E.P.A. 1990, s.71(2)	Waste regulation authorities or Secretary of State	Power by notice in writing to require any person to furnish such information as the authority reasonably considers it needs for the discharge of its functions under Part II.
E.P.A. 1990, Sched. 3, para. 2	District and London Borough Council	Powers for investigating and abating statutory nuisances: powers include entry, inspection, measurement, testing, sampling.
Water Industry Act 1991, s.84	District/London Borough Council	Powers to ascertain whether there has been contamination of water sources in breach of s.72 and to discharge their functions in relation to water supply.
Water Industry Act 1991, s.86(4)	Drinking Water Inspectorate	Powers of entry,inspection, measurements, tests, inspection of water undertakers' records.
Water Resources Act 1991, s.169	National Rivers Authority	Powers to investigate whether provisions on water pollution have been contravened: entry, inspection, measurement, testing, sampling of water, effluent or land.
Water Resources Act 1991, s.172	National Rivers Authority	Powers for purpose of ascertaining whether any statutory power or duty conferred on the NRA should be carried out: entry, inspection, measurement, testing, sampling of water, effluent or land.
Water Resources Act 1991, s.202	National Rivers Authority	Power to serve notice requiring the provision of information reasonably required for the purpose of carrying out functions relating to water pollution.

Limitations on investigative powers

3.09   In some cases the investigation of contamination may also involve the investigation of a possible criminal offence or offences: for example where contamination has resulted from a recent spillage which has entered

130

controlled waters or from unlawful deposits of controlled waste. In such cases the principles relating to criminal investigations may impose limitations or conditions on the powers to obtain information and the ways in which such information can be used.

(1) The general privilege against self-incrimination is capable of being over-ridden by clear statutory provisions which require information to be given in answer to the request of a statutory authority.[15] However in some cases where there is a statutory right to obtain such information, enforceable by criminal sanctions, it is provided that no answer given shall be admissible in any proceedings. Examples of such provisions are section 17(8) of the Environmental Protection Act 1990 and section 69(8) of the same Act.[16]

(2) In some cases there are specific conditions and restrictions on how the powers are to be exercised, for example requiring notice to be given (save in an emergency) before entering residential premises.[17]

(3) Specific evidential conditions apply to the results of analysis of samples of effluent or water if they are to be admissible in respect of legal proceedings, where the sample was taken on behalf of the NRA.[18]

(4) Some statues provide that the power to compel the production of documents does not extend to those covered by legal professional privilege, for example sections 17(10) and 69(11) of the Environmental Protection Act. This will cover communications between clients and legal professional advisers, whether external or "in-house", provided that the communication was confidential and was genuinely for the purpose of obtaining and communicating legal advice. It will not cover communications with other professional advisers, such as engineers or chemists,[19] nor communications with a lawyer for purposes other than legal advice. Nor will it cover a document communicating legal advice if that is copied to other persons within the client

---

[15] *Woolmington* v. *D.P.P.* [1935] A.C. 462, 481; see also C.H. Rolph [1993] N.L.J. 1206. On privilege against self-incrimination in civil proceedings see *A.T. & T. Istel Ltd.* v. *Tully, The Times,* July 24, 1992 (H.L.).

[16] The sections draw a distinction between England and Wales, where the answer is not admissible in any proceedings, and Scotland where it is not admissible in criminal proceedings.

[17] See Environmental Protection Act 1990, Sched. 3, para. 2; Water Resources Act 1991, Sched. 20, para. 1.

[18] Water Resources Act 1991, s.209; see *e.g. NRA* v. *Harcros Timber and Building Supplies Ltd., The Times,* April 2, 1992.

[19] *Wilden Pump Engineering Co.* v. *Fusfield* [1985] F.S.R. 159.

organisation for purposes other than disseminating that legal advice. Notes recording meetings for advice between legal advisers and clients are also covered.[20]

(5) The Code of Practice which applies to police officers under section 67 of the Police and Criminal Evidence Act 1984 does not apply directly to other enforcing agencies. However, section 67(9) of the 1984 Act states that: "persons other than police officers who are charged with the duty of investigating offences or charging offenders shall in the discharge of that duty have regard to any relevant provisions of such a Code." Whilst it is an issue for consideration in each case whether the person in question had the duty of investigating criminal offences,[21] it seems clear that the duties of NRA and HMIP inspectors and the officers of waste regulation authorities include such a duty. The problem is that not all investigations by such officers will be for investigating offences: they may be routine monitoring or inspections, in the course of which it becomes apparent that an offence may have been committed. Thus it seems possible that the obligations of the investigator could change during the course of the monitoring exercise.

(6) Computer records present particular evidential problems which may be of practical importance in pollution cases. By section 69 of the Police and Criminal Evidence Act 1984, a statement in a document produced by computer is not admissible as evidence if any fact stated therein unless it is shown:

(a) that there are no reasonable grounds for believing that the statement is inaccurate because of improper use of the computer;

(b) that at all material times the computer was operating properly or, if it was not, that any problem was not such as to affect the production of the document or the accuracy of its contents; and

(c) that any relevant provisions specified in rules of Court have been satisfied.

These requirements have been held to apply to all computer evidence, whether or not it constitutes hearsay.[22] Evidence as to operation may be tendered orally or by way of a certificate under Schedule 3, paragraph 8 of the Act: the person giving such a certificate will need to be in a position of responsibility

[20] *Balabel* v. *Air India* [1988] Ch. 317.
[21] *R.* v. *Seelig and Spens* (1992) 94 Cr.App.R. 17; *Joy* v. *Federation Against Copyright Theft Ltd.* (Q.B.D., January 14, 1993).
[22] *R.* v. *Shephard* [1993] A.C. 380.

and familiarity in relation to the computer, but not necessarily a computer expert.[23]

Information held on registers

Information may be obtained from local and other authorities in some **3.10** cases by way of a search of a public register, where such registers exist. The Government's proposals for registers of contaminative uses under section 143 of the Environmental Protection Act appear unlikely to be implemented, at least in their current form.[24] However there are other specific registers which may yield useful information.

(a) The Register of Planning Applications

Section 69 of the Town and Country Planning Act 1990[25] makes provision for a register of planning applications to be kept in the manner prescribed by the General Development Order. The register must be available for inspection by the public at all reasonable hours.[26] Under article 7 of the General Development Order 1988[27] the register is divided into two parts. Part I contains details of applications for planning permission, but it is Part II, which provides details of the final decision of the planning authority, which is the more important. It may thus be possible from the register to see whether land has at any stage had the benefit of planning permission relating to a potentially contaminative use: what the register cannot conform is whether that permission was implemented. However, the fact that many permissions may be granted in general terms, such as general industrial use, will frequently limit the usefulness of the register in this respect.

(b) Other Planning Matters

As well as the register of planning applications, useful information may possibly be obtained from other registers maintained under the Town and Country Planning Act 1990. These include:

(i) applications made under section 64 of the Act (now repealed) to determine whether planning permission is required;[28]

(ii) notices of proposed development submitted by Government departments under Circular 18/84 (Welsh Office 37/84)—these

---

[23] *Ibid.*
[24] See para. 3.02 ff.
[25] As amended by the Planning and Compensation Act 1991.
[26] S.64(5). General Development Order 1988, art. 27(4).
[27] S.I. 1988 No. 1813.
[28] S.64(3).

should be kept on a non-statutory addendum to the Planning Register and the existence of such entries noted on the statutory register;[29]

(iii) applications for established use certificates under section 191 of the Act (since replaced by certificates of lawful use);[30]

(iv) applications for certificates of lawfulness of existing use or development under section 191 and certificates of lawfulness of proposed use or development under section 192;[31]

(v) enforcement notices, stop notices and breach of condition notices[32] and special enforcement notices in relation to Crown land.[33] These registers may provide very useful information as to the existence of previous potentially contaminative uses in breach of planning control, such as the tipping of waste, car-breaking, scrap metal dealing and tyre storage.

(c) Hazardous Substance Consents

The presence on, over or under land of certain hazardous substances in specified quantities requires either actual or deemed consent under the Planning (Hazardous Substances) Act 1990. A register of applications and consents must be kept by the hazardous substances authority under section 28 of that Act.[34] The substances in question tend to be designated because of their potential to cause serious injury by inhalation or explosion, *e.g.* chlorine and LPG, but their storage in bulk may also be indicative of heavy industrial activity which could have caused contamination.

(d) Waste Licensing

Section 64 of the Environmental Protection Act 1990[35] requires waste regulation authorities to maintain registers containing specified particulars including current and recently current applications for waste management licences and current or recently current licences granted by the authority. "Recently current" licences means those in force within the last 12 months.[36] The registers are to be open to inspection at the

---

[29] Circular 18/84, para. 29.

[30] S.192(6).

[31] General Development Order 1988, art. 27(4).

[32] Section 188 and General Development Order 1988, art. 28.

[33] S.294 and Town and Country Planning (Special Enforcement Notice) Regulations 1992, (S.I. 1992 No. 1652).

[34] See also the Planning (Hazardous Substances) Regulations 1992, (S.I. 1992 No. 656), reg. 23 as to the form of the register.

[35] The section came into force on May 1, 1994.

[36] S.64(3).

principal offices of the waste disposal and waste collection authority at all reasonable hours and reasonable facilities must be made available, at a reasonable charge, for obtaining copies.[37] Information as to waste-related activities such as landfill, transfer and treatment will be extremely useful, both in relation to the land to be acquired, and adjacent or nearby land. The register will also contain details of matters such as statutory notices and conditions, which may be indicative of a problematic site, and of certificates of completion, which are crucial documents in terms of statutory liability.[38]

(e) IPC and local authority air pollution control

Statutory registers must also be kept in relation to prescribed processes under Part I of the Environmental Protection Act 1990.[39] Again, the register will provide potentially useful information as to the use of land (at least, relatively recent uses) which may have contaminative potential. Registers relating to IPC process (centrally controlled by HMIP and by HMIPI in Scotland) can be consulted at local authority level, and in Scotland also at the offices of river purification authorities.[40]

(f) Water Pollution Control Registers

Water discharge consents granted by the NRA are required to be kept on public registers under section 190 of the Water Resources Act 1991. Information as to such consents may not help greatly in assessing whether land is potentially contaminated, though some consents (e.g. discharge from break layers during reclamation schemes) may be indicative of a contamination issue. More pertinently, the register must contain details as to samples of water taken by the NRA in the exercise of its water pollution control functions, the results of analysis of such samples, information acquired by the NRA under arrangements with any other person for such purposes, and finally steps taken in consequence of any of this information.[41] Thus the register may contain relevant information as to the state of groundwater or adjacent surface water which may have a significant bearing on contaminated land.

(g) Trade effluent discharge registers

Registers of consents and agreements to discharge trade effluent to sewers must be kept by sewerage undertakers.[42] The nature of the

---

[37] S.64(6).
[38] See para. 5.29.
[39] S.20 and the Environmental Protection (Applications, Appeals and Registers) Regulations 1991, (S.I. 1991, No. 507).
[40] S.20(2)–(4).
[41] S.190(1)(e).
[42] Water Industry Act 1991, s.196.

135

consent and in particular the substances referred to in its conditions (together with a description of the nature of the effluent) may be indicative of the types of previous and current trade uses of premises.

(h) Waterworks and sewers

Under the Water Industry Act 1991 records must be kept by water undertakers of the location of water mains and other service pipes and underground works: these records must be kept for inspection, free of charge, at the undertaker's office.[43] Since water pipes may be vulnerable to attack from contaminants, their presence or proximity can be useful information. However, the records may not necessarily show pipes or works laid or completed before September 1989.[44] Section 199 of the Act requires the sewerage undertaker to keep records of the location and relevant particulars of public sewers and adopted drains. It may well be useful to know whether sewers run under contaminated land (and their route) since the ingress of contaminants into sewers can result ultimately in the pollution of controlled waters.

PUBLIC ACCESS TO INFORMATION

The European Directive

3.11   The European Directive on freedom of access to information on the environment[45] only applies to information held by "public authorities" (Article 1), which are defined to mean any public administration at national, regional or local level with responsibilities, and possessing information, relating to the environment;[46] excluded is any body acting in a judicial or legislative capacity. From the United Kingdom perspective, the exemption in respect of judicial or legislative bodies may prove problematic. Appeals against the decisions of Her Majesty's Inspectorate of Pollution, waste regulation authorities, the National Rivers Authority and other enforcement agencies are dealt with by the Department of the Environment who may be acting in a judicial capacity in dealing with the issue concerned. Further, it may be that reports prepared with a view to advising Government departments on the preparation of legislation cannot be disclosed.

---

[43] *Ibid*; s.198(1) and (2). See also the Water Resources Act 1991, s.195 for a corresponding obligation on the National Rivers Authority.

[44] S.198(5).

[45] 90/313/EC, O.J. No. L158, 23.6.90, p. 56.

[46] Art. 2.

The UK Government interprets the term "public authority" to include "central and local government and other bodies with regulatory responsibilities for the environment". A non-exhaustive list of the main bodies which the Government believes to be covered is given in Annex D to the Consultation Paper issued by the Government on their proposals for implementing the Directive[47] and amounts to over 200 such entries. Some are surprising, such as Development Corporations, Animal Procedures Committee and the Poisons Board. In practice there will need to be a register of sources or a central enquiry point if access to information from all sources is to be fully available.

The information which must be provided under the Directive is also widely drawn. It may be in any form, for example written, visual, aural or databased; it must be referable to the state of water, air, soil, fauna, flora, land and natural sites; and to activities or measures adversely affecting, or likely to affect these.[48] Further activities or measures designed to protect water, air, etc.—including administrative measures and environmental management programmes—are also included. Under Article 3 member states may provide as reasons to refuse requests for information, "public security", "international relations," and "national defence." Other exceptions include material which has attached to it some commercial and industrial confidentiality. The Consultation Paper issued in response to the Directive recognises that material supplied voluntarily by a third party should not be released as this would otherwise provide a significant disincentive for third parties to provide government departments with information which may be important to the department concerned but which the supplying party does not wish to have released elsewhere. Within government departments it is proposed, as far as the United Kingdom is concerned, that a statement will be published of the principal areas in which the department concerned holds unrestricted environmental information with details of a contact point for further enquiries.

The Directive does not require that the party seeking the information concerned has an "interest" in it. Under paragraph 1 of Article 3 of the Directive "any natural or legal person" must be provided with information "at his request and without his having to prove an interest". The "need to know" argument thus cannot be raised.

Under Article 5 of the Directive, member states are allowed to charge for supplying the information but a charge must not exceed a "reasonable cost". The UK consultation paper envisages an Authority requiring a reasonable fee to cover "the copying costs, including the element for

---

[47] The Government's proposals for the implementation in UK law of the EEC directive on the freedom of access to information on the environment, January 27, 1992.
[48] Art. 2.

137

associated staff and resource costs". The provision of accommodation within the building so that a personal inspection can be carried out is a more difficult matter.

Under Article 4 of the Directive, anyone who considers that he has been unreasonably refused or ignored may seek judicial administrative review of the decision in accordance with the relevant national legal system.

The Environmental Information Regulations 1992: scope

3.12 The public clearly has the right of access to information required to be kept on open registers: beyond this, however, there are general rights to certain types of information under the Environmental Information Regulations 1992.[49] These Regulations are intended to implement EC Directive 90/313/EEC on the freedom of access to information on the environment.[50] The Regulations cover the following information[51]:

(a) information which relates to the environment; and

(b) is held by a relevant person in an accessible form and otherwise than for the purposes of judicial or legislative functions; and

(c) is not covered by other statutory provisions[52] (such as those on public registers) which require information to be provided on request or made available for inspection by the public.

The concept of information which "relates to the environment" may be applicable to information on contaminated land in various respects: the statutory definition includes information relating to "the state of any soil or the state of any natural site or other land"[53]; it also refers to activities or administrative or other measures—for example soil sampling and clean-up—which are designed to protect environmental media.[54]

The information must be held by a "relevant person": this expression covers Ministers of the Crown, government departments, local authorities and other persons provided in each case they are carrying out public administrative functions at whatever level with responsibilities in relation to the environment, as well as other bodies with such responsibilities and under governmental control.[55] As well as the Department of

---

[49] S.I. 1992 No. 3240.
[50] See para. 3.11 above.
[51] Reg. 2(1).
[52] For example, the Environment and Safety Information Act 1988, or the Local Government (Access to Information) Act 1985.
[53] Reg. 2(2)(a).
[54] Reg. 2(2)(c).
[55] Reg. 2(3).

Environment and Transport, Ministry of Agriculture, Fisheries and Food, Scottish and Welsh Offices, local authorities, HMIP, HMIPI, NRA and river purification authorities, the Regulations may also apply to the Health and Safety Executive insofar as it can be said to have responsibilities for the environment.[56]

The Regulations require environmental information to be made available by the body holding it to any person who requests it: this requirement is subject to the ability to refuse requests that are manifestly unreasonable or too general, and the right to make a reasonable charge.[57] By regulation 3(7), restrictions or prohibitions contained in any rule of law or other statutes are disapplied: the only applicable exceptions to the general obligation of disclosure are therefore those provided by regulation 4. The exceptions to disclosure are:

(a) information not held "in accessible form" (reg. 2(1)(*b*));
(b) information held for the purposes of judicial or legislative functions (reg. 1(1)(*b*)); and
(c) information which is capable of being treated as confidential (reg. 4(1)).

This final category, of confidential information, is subject to a complex definition. Information is to be capable of being treated as confidential if, and only if, it is:[58]

(a) information relating to matters affecting international relations, national defence or public security;
(b) information relating to, or to anything which is or has been the subject matter of, any legal or other proceedings (including disciplinary proceedings and administrative inquiries and hearings) whether actual or prospective;
(c) information relating to the confidential deliberations of any relevant person or to the contents of any internal communications of a body corporate or other undertaking or organisation;
(d) information contained in a document or record which is still in the course of completion; or
(e) information relating to matters to which any commercial or industrial confidentiality attaches or affecting any intellectual property.

Information falling within one of these categories is capable of being confidential and as such may (not must) be withheld. If, as well as

---

[56] See para. 3.11 above.
[57] Reg. 3: the obligation to make information available is stated to be a duty owed to the person making the request — hence, presumably, an action for breach of statutory duty will lie if the request is improperly refused or (more controversially) if incorrect information is given.
[58] Reg. 4(3).

falling within one of these categories, the information falls within regulation 4(3) then it *must* be treated as confidential. For example, its disclosure must constitute breach of an agreement or a rule of law; or it must be personal information on an individual; or information supplied to the relevant person by someone who was not under, and could not have been put under, any legal obligation to disclose it.

It will be appreciated that these exceptions are strictly and narrowly defined and that, consequently, there is considerable scope for using the Regulations to obtain information held by the relevant authorities as to the condition of land. It could be argued that the wording of regulation 2(2)(*a*), in referring to "the state of any soil or the state of any natural site or other land" suggests that only information as to actual physical contamination (as opposed to the potential for contamination) is covered—however, regulation 2(2)(*b*) refers also to information on activities or measures which adversely affect the state of (*inter alia*) soil, or are likely to have that adverse effect: this covers squarely information as to past potentially contaminative uses.

The Environmental Information Regulations 1992: practical points

3.13   The Environmental Information Regulations were accompanied by Department for the Environment guidance on the freedom of access to information on the environment. The purpose of the Guidance is stated at paragraph 7 to be "to advise organisations on the implementation of the Regulations bearing in mind that only the courts can give authoritative decisions on their interpretation."

The Regulations define "information" to include "anything contained in any records"; it then defines "records" to include "registers, reports and returns, as well as computer records and other records kept otherwise than in a document". Thus any written record whether or not reduced to microfiche, in the housing, environmental services, planning, estates or other departments of a local authority are included in the term "records". Most correspondence in a local authority's files would be classed as a record for these purposes; even a marginal note, where for example it referred to a site inspection, would be a relevant record.

Under regulation 3, subject to the provisions of the Regulations, the authority who holds any information to which the Regulations apply "shall make that information available to every person who requests it".[59] In particular they have a duty to ensure that every request is responded to as soon as possible and in any event within two months

---

[59] Reg. 3(4).

after it is made. Where the response contains a refusal to make information available, the refusual must be in writing and specify the reason for refusal. The authority is protected to some extent by regulation 3(3) under which they may "refuse a request for information in cases where a request is manifestly unreasonable or is formulated in too general a manner". There are arrangements for the provisions of a charge for the information. No difficulty should be experienced in this regard bearing in mind that, for example, the archives department of county councils now usually charge £12 per hour for research of their records and there is no reason why a similar system should not be introduced here. It is customary to issue a notice that the search may take two to four weeks in view of the pressure of other work, or the extent of the enquiry.

Available information should be taken to mean any information held by a body whether or not it is obtained as a result of the body's environmental responsibilities.[60] Thus it includes information collected before the Regulations came into force on December 31, 1992, for example when collating material in preparation for the proposed registers under section 143 of the Environmental Protection Act 1990. It also includes information passed for safe keeping to the Public Record Office, because ownership still rests with the providing body until such time (normally 30 years) that it is released for general inspection. It includes information contained in documents such as maps and records and the term "record" includes registers, reports, returns, computer records (*e.g.* databases) and other non-documentary records.[61] What it does not include, according to the Guidance, is "non-existent information that could be created by manipulating existing information". Further it does not include information destroyed in accordance with established office procedures.[62]

The Guidance draws an important distinction between information collected by the body itself and that derived from a secondary source. In the latter case there is a further distinction to be made between that supplied to a body under some statutory power and that given voluntarily. These distinctions affect the conditions under which the information may be released to a third party.[63]

As we have seen, information relates to the environment if it relates to the "state" of any water or air, flora, fauna, soil, etc. "The state" should be taken to include "physical, chemical and biological conditions" at any moment in time, *i.e.* past, present or future.[64] Water[65] should be

---

[60] Para. 15, Guidance.
[61] Reg. 2(4).
[62] Para. 15, Guidance.
[63] Para. 16, Guidance.
[64] Para. 17, Guidance.
[65] *Ibid.*

taken to include underground and surface water, both natural and in man-made structures including inland waters, for example rivers, canals, and lakes as well as estuaries and seas. Air[66] extends not only to the limits of the atmosphere but also the air within buildings and other natural or man-made structures above or below ground. Fauna and flora[67] should be taken to include all land surfaces, building land covered by water and underground strata, and soil to include the in-situ upper layer in which plants grow.[68] The term "natural site"[69] includes sites of special scientific interest and areas of outstanding natural beauty.

It might be thought that the information with which the Regulations are concerned relate only to the United Kingdom. However, that is in fact not so. There is no territorial restriction in the Regulations. However, as the Guidance points out, the release of environmental information relating to overseas territories may be restricted for reasons of international relations, including matters covered by international law.[70] The environmental information the body concerned is required to produce concerns the state of water or air, flora or fauna, etc. in all its conditions—physical, chemical or biological; there is no direct reference to human health. However, the pollution or contamination concerned may be such that danger to human health arises and that fact may be recorded in the environmental information concerned; if it is, it should be made available to those who seek it.[71]

Reports on the environment may be commissioned by public bodies from outside organisations. In general, bodies should seek to ensure that the copyright of any such completed reports rests with them. If not, it should be made clear to the organisation concerned that under the terms of the Regulations, the body may be obliged to make copies of their report or parts of their report available to the public.

The question also arises to what extent solicitors, agents or private individuals may request information through correspondence or by personal inspection. The Regulations appear to draw a distinction between "information that is readily available", defined as "not requiring collating or editing", and other information; the former should be made available by a verbal or written response, or inspection by the caller concerned. Where collating and editing is required, however, and significant staff time may be involved, then there is no reason why the procedure adopted in respect of other records, for example by the archives department, should not be followed in these cases.[72]

[66] *Ibid.*
[67] *Ibid.*
[68] *Ibid.*
[69] *Ibid.*
[70] Para. 18, Guidance.
[71] Para. 19, Guidance.
[72] Para. 27, Guidance.

142

There is of course a problem with the accuracy of information the body in question holds. It could for example be based on opinion rather than fact, or inferred, dependent on forecasts, or derived from samples; it could have come from a source which was biased. It is not reasonably practicable, even if it could be afforded, for the body in question to validate the information concerned. The Guidance recommends that for these and other reasons, bodies would be well advised to protect themselves by issuing a disclaimer where appropriate about the accuracy of the information they release to the public and its source.[73] However, this would not protect the Authority in every circumstance. One proposal would be for the question of liability for negligent answers causing economic loss to be dealt with by Regulations rather than left to the common law.[74]

The Environmental Information Regulations 1992: internal communications and unfinished documents

The 1992 Regulations refer to information relating to the contents of **3.14** internal communications of a body corporate or other undertaking or organisation; these may be withheld. Included are ministerial and member correspondence, letters to and from members of the public, information passed between officials in the course of their duties, for example memoranda, internal minutes of meetings within a ministry or council, and submissions to ministers and members.[75]

Where a relevant body is in the course of carrying out a study which involves inspection, testing, evaluation, monitoring or research, and in the process collects data, the question arises whether it is necessary for that information to be released despite the fact that the report is uncompleted. The Guidance suggests[76] that access to that information should await completion of the study or report so that analysis and interpretation can proceed unhindered. This would not prevent the body in question granting premature access if it so wished, and if the study was aborted on cost or other grounds any interim reports or completed data sets[77] should be released as soon as reasonable.[78] In particular the Guidance states that data which are part of routine regular monitoring

---

[73] Para. 21, Guidance.
[74] As is the case with local land charges.
[75] Para. 52, Guidance.
[76] Para. 53, Guidance.
[77] Para. 54 of the Guidance deals with the problem of what constitutes a "completed data set."
[78] Para. 53, Guidance.

should not be regarded as part of an unfinished set but should normally be released as soon as practicable after it is collected, or according to a planned and published timetable.

Access to information: commercial confidentiality

3.15 Bodies will need to be careful when handling requests for what may be commercially confidential information to avoid the possibility of legal action through wrongful release. There is the real possibility of facing an action for damages and/or an injunction. The Guidance suggests[79] that where information in its entirety is deemed restricted on grounds of commercial confidentiality, it could be so annotated together with release date to avoid unproper disclosure. On the other hand where part only of the information concerned is deemed restricted, an edited version containing any non-sensitive information could be prepared and marked "public access copy".

Where the body in question has a discretion, it will not normally be appropriate to withhold information in response to a general claim that disclosure might damage the reputation of the supplier and hence his commercial competitiveness. Nether will it be reasonable to withhold information which could be obtained or inferred from other publicly accessible resources.[80] Where however it is agreed that information should be withheld, then this should be limited to the minimum time necessary to safeguard the commercial or industrial interest concerned. It is suggested that information retained in this way should be reviewed from time to time.

The Guidance suggests the method by which commercial confidentiality should be approached, namely that the provider of environmental information should be informed that it is subject to public release, and given the opportunity to claim commercial confidentiality by:

    (i) identifying the information to be protected;
    (ii) giving, if deemed necessary by the body, cogent evidence of the need for the protection of such information on the grounds of confidentiality; and
    (iii) justifying a period of time over which protection is sought.

Unlike provisions in the Environmental Protection Act 1990, Part I, dealing with the exclusion of information from public registers on the

---

[79] Para. 61, Guidance.
[80] Para. 58, Guidance.

ground of confidentiality,[81] the Regulations contain no reference to prejudicing commercial interests to an unreasonable extent: thus there is no statutory mandate for exercising discretion based on the likely harm flowing from release of the information.

Relationship to statutory restrictions

Some statutes contain restrictions on the disclosure of information obtained **3.16** under statutory powers: for example, by making it an offence to disclose it to third parties. Regulation 3(7) overrides such restrictions or prohibitions, subject to regulation 4(3). By regulation 4(3) information must be treated as confidential (there is no discretion) if it is capable of being so treated within one of the categories of regulation 4(2)(*a*)–(*e*) and its disclosure in response to the relevant request would contravene any statutory provision or rule of law or would involve the breach of any agreement.[82]

Personal information and volunteered information

Personal information on an individual who has not consented to its **3.17** disclosure must be treated as confidential under regulation 4(3)(*b*). Great care is required in handling such information, including addresses of individual properties so far as these relate to individual occupants; it may be possible to avoid these difficulties by excision or by the issue of information in summary form.[83]

Similarly, information which has been supplied voluntarily (i.e. where the person complying it was not under, and could not have been put under, any legal obligation to supply it) is to be treated as confidential, except where there is some overriding statutory provision or the person in question has consented to its disclosure.[84] Information is frequently supplied "voluntarily" in the course of making a licence or other application: usually however there will be legal rights to obtain such information if it is not forthcoming and so the confidentiality principal will not apply.[85] It is not in the spirit of the Directive to refuse to release all volunteered information on principle: suppliers should therefore be encouraged to waive the exemption and the information labelled appropriately for future reference once access permission is given.[86]

---

[81] S.22.
[82] Para. 63, Guidance.
[83] Para. 64, Guidance.
[84] Reg. 4(3)(*c*).
[85] Para. 68, Guidance.
[86] Para. 69, Guidance. Though the Guidance does not say so explicitly, the authority should presumably advise the supplier frankly of the possible consequences of consent when requesting the waiver.

Local Government meetings: information

3.18   Under the Local Government (Access to Information) Act 1985, the
public has rights of access to council, committee and sub-committee
meetings and to papers and background papers relating to these
meetings. Those background papers are often referred to in the agenda
item concerned. There is thus a correlation between rights of access to
information and rights of access to meetings. However, information
which is defined as "confidential" by section 100A(3) of the Local
Government Act 1972 (reinserted by the 1985 Act) cannot be released,
and that defined as "exempt" by Schedule 12A to the 1972 Act may be
released only at the discretion of the Local Authority if they resolve the
public should be excluded from the relevant part of the meeting. Under
the Environmental Information Regulations, however, the public appear
to have wider rights of access to any environmental information held by
the local authority.[87]

---

[87] Para. 51, Guidance.

Chapter 4

INVESTIGATION AND APPRAISAL

Investigation in context

Land may be investigated for possible contamination by various **4.01**
parties and for various reasons, among which are:

Local and other statutory authorities	In exercise of statutory functions, powers and duties,[1] in the context of proposals for development or otherwise.
Prospective purchasers or lenders	In order to assess actual or prospective liabilities, value, fitness for purpose; may be assessed against existing use or against development proposals.
Existing owners	In order to assess actual or prospective liabilities, as part of regular management or compliance audit process; or in the context of proposals for development; or as preparation for marketing the property.

Whilst all investigations will share common features, the nature of the
investigation process, and in particular the appraisal process, will be
coloured by the underlying purpose for which it is being undertaken.
This chapter aims to provide an outline of the main features of
investigation and the relevant sources of guidance. The remediation and
reclamation of land is dealt with elsewhere,[2] as is the appointment and
use of consultants and other professional advisers.[3]

The issue of terminology can be confusing in this area, as often terms
such as "environmental audit," "environmental assessment" and "Phase
I or Phase II audit" are used loosely.

---

[1] See Chap. 3 above.
[2] Chap. 7.
[3] Chap. 10.

Environment audit as a concept refers to the ongoing process of evaluating environmental performance of a facility or company against objective and systematic criteria. Its use will not generally be appropriate in the context of investigating potential site contamination; though an audit in that sense may be appropriate where a business is being acquired as a going concern.

Environmental assessment is generally used to describe the process of identifying and appraising the likely environmental impacts of proposed development; that is certainly the sense in which it is used in planning law. Again, it is not an appropriate term to describe the process of investigating contaminated land, though data from such investigations may be an important part of the environmental assessment process.

Probably the clearest and most accurate terms to apply to contaminated land are investigation and appraisal—these are the terms used in this chapter. The concepts of "Phase I" and "Phase II" audits again tend to be used loosely, but broadly Phase I refers to the initial process of investigation which will include a site reconnaissance visit (sometimes called a "walk-over" investigation) but will not include physical sampling and analysis. Phase II is often used to refer to further investigation, involving such sampling, which may or may not be advisable in the light of the preliminary investigation and appraisal.

Sources of guidance

4.02   The main general guidance for contaminated land investigations is currently provided by the British Standards Institution Draft for Development DD 175: 1988, "Code of Practice for the Identification of Potentially Contaminated Land and its Investigation" (commonly known as DD 175).

The publication was not issued as a British Standard because it was not possible to achieve sufficient consensus amongst experts as to what constituted "best practice": in a sense, therefore, the document represents the lowest common denominator on which those engaged in drafting it could agree. It was recommended that the Code of Practice should be applied on a provisional basis so that information and experience of its practical application could be obtained. Since its issue in 1988 no modifications have been made to the draft and it has not been replaced by a formal British Standard. It therefore still remains the main source of general guidance for contaminated site investigations, despite its limitations and shortcomings.

It is important from a legal point of view that the Code of Practice is readily understood as there may be clauses in a contractual obligation,[4]

---

[4] See Chap. 11.

or one imposed by a planning condition or planning obligation, that refer to it in whole or in part.

Apart from DD 175 reference may also be made to various guidance notes of the Interdepartmental Committee on the Redevelopment of Contaminated Land (ICRCL).[5] These include guidance of a general nature on assessment in the context of redevelopment (ICRCL Guidance Note 59/83) and guidance dealing with problems encountered on specific types of site.[6] The proposal for registers of potentially contaminated land also generated some useful guidance, in particular the Pilot Survey Methodology prepared for Cheshire by Environmental Resources Ltd.[7] and the DoE's own consultative proposals of May 1991.[8] At a more general level, the Confederation of British Industry has produced a useful publication, *Tackling Contamination: Guidelines for Business* which gives information on how to deal with contamination in terms of site investigation, risk assessment, use of consultants and similar matters.[8a]

Main Steps in investigation and appraisal

Whilst there is no universally accepted sequence of approach for site investigations (and indeed different sites and differing circumstances may require different approaches) it is important to adopt a systematic approach. The most logical sequence is: **4.03**

— identification
— investigation
— assessment
— remedial action
— monitoring

Both DD 175 and ICRCL 59/83 expand this approach into a series of broadly similar questions:[9]

(1) What is the history of the site? This provides a preliminary indication of the likelihood of finding contamination.
(2) What is the site's intended use, or where development is not proposed, its current use? This provides an initial check on the possible significance of contamination.

[5] For details of the role of ICRCL generally see Chap. 1.
[6] See para. 4.17 *et seq.* below.
[7] DoE, "Pilot Survey of Potentially Contaminated Land in Cheshire—A Methodology for Identifying Potentially Contaminated Sites" (July 1990).
[8] "Public Registers of Land which may be Contaminated—A Consultation Paper."
[8a] (1994). From CBI, Centre Point, 103 New Oxford Street, London WC1A 1DU.
[9] See DD 175, pp. 3–4; ICRCL 59/83, para. 23.

(3) What hazards might affect the suitability of the land for that use?

(4) Which contaminants could give rise to those hazards?

(5) What contaminants are present, at what concentrations and in what distribution?

(6) Based on the results of that investigation, are there hazards and if so, how could they be removed or reduced?

(7) On the basis of this information, how suitable is the site for the proposed or actual use?

(8) What remedial treatment is practicable, and what monitoring is needed to enable the site to be used for its intended purpose?

DD 175 is concerned primarily with steps 1, 4 and 5, and with 2 and 3 to a lesser extent. It is not concerned with steps 6–8 dealing with appraisal and remediation.[10]

It should also be noted that the Guidance in ICRCL 59/83 is essentially orientated towards investigation in the context of redevelopment and does not lay substantial emphasis on the investigation of off-site liabilities—for example, for the migration of contaminants off-site. To this extent the Guidance is unsatisfactory in that it does not provide for any appraisal of public liability issues or any consideration of the off-site element, which may in fact be crucial. Such appraisal involves the collation of further information, for example on:[11]

- geology and hydrogeology
- proximity of housing or other sensitive uses
- location of licensed or private water abstraction sources
- location of groundwater protection zones as defined by the NRA[12]
- attitudes of regulatory authorities
- other local potential sources of contamination
- surface watercourses and site drainage

Investigation is also increasingly carried out in the context of the transfer of sites which are already developed:[13] this is not the type of investigation envisaged by DD 175 and ICRCL 59/83, though of course the same basic methodology is applicable. Such investigations in the transactional context raise different practical issues to the investigation of undeveloped sites and these issues are considered elsewhere.[14]

---

[10] DD 175, p. 4.
[11] See para. 4.21 *et seq.* below on risk assessment.
[12] See Chap. 6.
[13] See generally Chap. 11 on property transactions.
[14] Para. 4.15.

Site history: problematic uses

As may be apparent from the history of the proposal for registers of **4.04**
contaminative uses, discussed at Chapter 3, it is probably impracticable
to construct a completely comprehensive and workable list of such uses.
Almost all categories of previously used land may show some signs of
contamination, but certain uses clearly have a more serious contaminative potential: indeed some uses may be almost certain indicators of the
existence of contamination. DD 175 provides the following list of uses
which are examples of sites particularly likely to have been contaminated
by their past or present uses[15]:

- asbestos works
- chemical works
- docks and railway land, especially large sidings and depots
- gasworks, other coal carbonization plants and ancillary by-
  products works
- landfills and other waste disposal sites;
- metal mines, smelters, foundries, iron and steel works, metal
  finishing
- munitions production and testing sites
- oil refineries, petroleum storage and distribution sites
- paper and printing works
- plants and heavy engineering installations, e.g. ship-building
  and shipbreaking
- installations involving the processing of radioactive materials
- scrap yards
- sewage works and farms
- tanneries
- industries making or using wood preservatives

The following table (Table 4 from DD 175) gives a further indication
of likely contaminants on the various types of site. Caution must be
exercised however (as the Table warns) in that other types of site may be
contaminated and other contaminants may be present; examples include
electronics and microelectronics manufacturing facilities, airfields and
research and development sites. Some ubiquitous contaminants may be
present on almost any site. These include: hydrocarbons, polychlorinated biphenyls (PCBs), asbestos, sulphates and many metals used in
paint pigments or coatings.

---

[15] See also Mary R. Harris in *Reclaiming Contaminated Land*, ed. T. Cairney,
(Blackie, 1987) pp. 32–38 which provides a useful summary of each type of
activity and its potential problems.

Industry	Examples of site/use	Likely contaminants
Chemicals	Acid/alkali works Dyeworks Fertilizers and pesticides Pharmaceuticals Paint works Wood treatment plants	Acids; alkalis, metals, solvents, (*e.g.*, toluene, benzene); phenols,specialized organic compounds
Petrochemicals	Oil Refineries Tank farms Fuel storage depots Tar distilleries	Hydrocarbons; phenols, acids; alkalis and asbestos
Metals	Iron and steel works Foundries, Smelters Electroplating, anodizing and galvanizing works Engineering works Shipbuilding/shipbreaking Scrap reduction plants	Metals, especially iron, copper, nickel, chromium, zinc, cadmium and lead; asbestos
Energy	Gasworks Power stations	Combustible substances (*e.g.*, coal and coke dust); phenols; cyanides; sulphur compounds; asbestos
Transport	Garages, vehicle builders and maintenance workshops Railway depots	Combustible substances; hydrocarbons; asbestos
Mineral Extraction Land Restoration (including waste disposal sites)	Mines and spoil heaps Pits and quarries Filled sites	Metals (*e.g.*, copper, zinc, lead); gases (*e.g.*, methane); leachates
Water supply and sewage treatment	Waterworks Sewage treatment plants	Metals (in sludges) Microorganisms
Miscellaneous	Docks, wharfs and quays Tanneries Rubber works Military land	Metals; organic compounds; methane; toxic, flammable or explosive substances; micro-organisms

Preliminary Investigation: methodology and relevant information

In a preliminary investigation there are two main stages, namely:[16] **4.05**

(1) the collection and examination of information on the site history from published maps, plans and photographs, and existing site records and enquiries. From such information it is often possible to deduce the types of contaminant that may be present and their distribution; and

(2) a site reconnaissance or inspection by visiting the site. An inspection should not be carried out before the available historical information about the site has been collected and examined, unless this is made necessary by the imminent demolition or clearance of the site.

The information relevant to a preliminary investigation is:[17]

(i) the history of the site, details of its owners, occupiers and users;

(ii) the processes used, including their locations, raw materials, products, waste residues and methods of disposal;

(iii) the layout of the site above and below ground at each stage of development, including roadways, storage areas and other hard cover areas;

(iv) the presence of waste disposal tips, made ground, abandoned pits and quarries, with or without standing water;

(v) mining history including shafts and roadways (worked seams);[17a]

(vi) information on geology and hydrogeology, including the presence of groundwater and surface water.

Investigation should not be confined solely to the boundaries of the site. It will be relevant to know the history of neighbouring land, both from the point of view of assessing whether contaminants from such land may affect the site and in considering what may be the likely impacts of any contamination on the site on such land.

Sources of information on site history

Helpful and detailed guidance on the available sources of information **4.06** is to be found:

[16] DD 175, para. 4.1.

[17] *Ibid.*, In the ordinary course of site appraisal for redevelopment a geotechnical investigation may also be required: see BS 5930.

[17a] See Minerals Planning Guidance MPG12: Treatment of Disused Mine Openings and Availability of Information on Mined Ground (1994) which reviews the problems and methods relating to disused mine openings, developing the more general guidance in Planning Policy Guidance Note PPG14: Development on Unstable Land.

(a) at Table 1 of DD 175[18]:

(b) at section 3.2 and Annex A (Evaluation of Data Sources) of the Cheshire Pilot Study; and

(c) at Annex F of the DoE Consultation Paper of May 1991.[19]

Broadly, the sources may be grouped as follows:

Source	Comments
Public registers	See Chapter 3. Cover matters such as licensed waste disposal sites, planning permissions.
Maps	1. O.S. series maps at various scales are available from the 1840s. Coverage will not necessarily be complete and some series (e.g., O.S. 1:1250) cover only urban areas. 2. 1:500 Town maps covering period 1863–93. 3. British Geological Survey series maps. 4. Soil Survey and Land Research Centre maps. 5. Archaeological and historical maps. 6. Tithe survey maps 1836–60 and enclosure plans. 7. Plans of statutory undertakers e.g., for railways, canals and gas works. 8. Insurance plans for certain major towns. 9. Specialised town plans e.g., public health maps.
Meteorological and hydrological records	Weather observations; groundwater level data; surface water run-off data
Photographs	1. Ground-based photographs of old buildings, industrial operations, etc. 2. Aerial photographs, vertical and oblique. Various collections give good coverage from 1946 onwards. Much of the UK has been photographed by the RAF and for commercial purposes.

[18] Reproduced at Appendix C.
[19] See para. 3.03.

Source	Comments
Photographs—*cont.*	3. More specialised forms of imagery such as thermal infra-red imagery, multispectral imagery, satellite imagery. Specialised skills are required in interpreting such material, but it can usefully reveal matters such as vegetation which is stressed by contaminants or patterns of landfill gas flow. These technologies may be expected to become more important as they are more widely understood and become more accessible.
Collated data sources	1. DoE 1973–74 survey of landfill sites.
	2. DoE Despoiled Land Survey: may identify tip sites but will not show "reclaimed" sites.
	3. Local authority and water company records, *e.g.*, of burial sites of livestock with suspected anthrax or notifiable diseases; sites used for sludge disposal. MAFF also holds records of buried diseased animal corpses.
	4. Survey of mineral workings between 1947–82 (updated 1982–88).
	5. Local authority records of premises regulated for environmental health purposes, scrapyards, and garages.
	6. Records of Alkali Inspectorate and Industrial Air Pollution Inspectorate.
	7. Archival material of British Coal (in particular, mines abandonment plans,) British Gas, British Rail, British Waterways Board, water companies, other individual companies.
	Note: rights of access to certain environmental information—see Chapter 3.
Local history	1. Trade directories—may cover smaller sites (*e.g.* hatters, tripe dressers, dyers, tin plate works) but locations may be imprecise.
	2. Local history collections, museums (*e.g.* the Halton Chemical Museum in Cheshire), history society materials.
	3. Street names can give useful indications of past uses, *e.g.* Leadmills, Gas Street, Foundry Lane.

Source	Comments
Local history—*cont.*	4. Natural history society records often contain geological and other useful information, *e.g.* county naturalist trusts.
Local knowledge	1. Local residents. 2. Local authority and other officers. 3. Current or former employees. Such knowledge is a potentially valuable but often neglected source of information.
Legal documents	1. Leases. 2. Planning agreements. 3. Licences *e.g.* tipping licences.

Commercial contaminative use searches

4.06A   In response to market demand for information on past potentially contaminative uses, a small number of commercial organisations are now offering such searches for a fixed fee, based on public records, maps and other data of the type mentioned above. Costs typically range from £250–£450 per search. Whilst such searches can never be fully conclusive, they can provide valuable information in assessing whether further investigation is merited. As has been suggested, such searches "can help to bridge the gap between the relative weakness of pre-contract enquiries and the expense of detailed site investigations."[19a] However, where it is immediately apparent that a site lies in an industrialised area, it may be preferable in practical terms to proceed straight to a Phase I investigation.

Companies currently offering this type of service are:

I.C.C. Legal Services Ltd,
 16–26 Banner Street,
 London, EC1Y 8QE
 Tel: 071 253 0063

Plansearch UK,
 21 North Crescent,
 Featherstone,
 South Staffs., WV10 7AY
 Tel: 0902 865961

Past Use Land Searches,
 2 Castle Road,
 Lavendon,
 Olney,
 Bucks., MK46 4JD,
 Tel: 0234 2413856

Site reconnaissance

4.07   The general procedure is set out in DD 175 and includes:[20]

[19a] See [1994] Gazette, April 13, p. 15.
[20] DD 175, para. 4.3.4.

156

(1) route selection for traversing the site on foot;

(2) any areas of discoloured soil, polluted water, blighted vegetation or significant odours should be noted;

(3) changes between the present conditions and information obtained from the site history should be noted *e.g.*, changes in the position of buildings and infrastructure;

(4) all structures above and below ground, including foundations, tanks and pits should be inspected and recorded, including fill material and made ground; materials such as slag, asbestos, scrap and industrial chemical waste should be noted and recorded as well as signs of subsidence and disturbed ground; the location of overhead power and telephone lines and underground services should also be noted;

(5) likelihood of adjacent premises being affected by further stages of the investigation or subsequent development of the site should be identified, together with any evidence of, or opportunity for, cross boundary contamination;

(6) areas suitable for temporary use during investigations for depots, offices, sample storage and mobile laboratories should be identified;

(7) a suitable water supply should be located;

(8) the location of the nearest telephone and emergency services should be noted;

(9) where relevant, the depth of any standing water, the presence of any perched water, the directional flow of rivers, streams, etc. should be noted, together with flood levels and any tidal fluctuations; and

(10) the location of covered shafts or sub-surface features.

Site reconnaissance may also include on-site sampling or testing, using portable instruments which may suffice to detect certain contaminants such as emissions of flammable or toxic gases or radioactivity. Care is needed, however, in the selection and use of such instruments and in interpreting the data they produce.[21] It will also often be useful to take photographs or video footage at this stage.

Interpretation of information from preliminary assessment

Interpretation and assessment of information from enquiries and site **4.08** reconnaissance requires experience, care and skill. The object is to form an overall view of the potential for contamination and the likely hazards

---

[21] *Ibid*, para. 4.3.5.

which it may present. It may be possible to obtain an idea of those areas of the site where contamination is likely to be concentrated ("hot spots"), or of the possible extent of different contaminants in different parts of the site.

To reiterate, it is important to adopt a systematic approach and to cross-check material in terms of consistency and verification. This may involve, for example, further enquiries on site history or consultation with statutory authorities following conclusion of the site reconnaissance and in the light of observations made then. In some cases this stage can elicit vital fresh information and it may even be appropriate to ask the relevant statutory authority to participate in a visit to the site.

For those appraising the work done on the preliminary assessment, it will be relevant to consider the following questions:

(1) Has the consultant made use of all relevant sources of information?

(2) Has any approach been made to the relevant regulatory authorities and to what extent have they expressed unequivocal views on the site?

(3) Has the site reconnaisance been adequate and does it corroborate or contradict what the consulted information sources might suggest?

(4) Has the assessment taken full account of the purpose for which it was commissioned, *i.e.*, pre-acquisition, assessment of liabilities, proposals for development, etc.?

Site sensitivity

4.09   For contaminants that could adversely affect human health or the growth of plants and animals, an approximate order of sensitivity of site uses is as follows:

Most sensitive   — Residential developments with gardens

— Agricultural land or allotments

— Amenity areas, recreational land, parks, landscaped gardens.

— Commercial and industrial buildings, *e.g.*, offices.

Least sensitive   — Hard surfaced areas, *e.g.* vehicle parks.

Where the hazards produced by the contaminants might affect the integrity of buildings or building services, the relative sensitivities are different. If, for example, the principal hazard of the site is the emission of flammable gases, the order of sensitivities may then be:

158

Most sensitive	— Uses involving the construction of buildings on site.
	— Uses requiring the growth of plants, especially deep-rooted varieties.
Least sensitive	— Other uses, *e.g.* amenity areas, parking spaces.

The value of "sensitivity scales" of the type shown above is that they can help to decide whether or not an investigation is needed. They can also suggest which contaminants should be included in the investigation.[22]

As well as these aspects of sensitivity discussed in DD 175, there is another aspect of sensitivity which in some cases may be far more important. This relates to the sensitivity of the site's setting, which is dependent on neighbouring user, geology and hydrogeology, surface water, nearby abstraction sources, etc. This is why the ICRCL triggers can never form an absolute basis for risk assessment: for example, organic contamination well below any of the specific ICRCL triggers for housing may be an issue of grave concern in relation to water pollution.

Sampling Programme

As DD 175 points out, there is no single recommended formula for **4.10** designing a sampling programme: sampling needs to be carefully designed to suit the particular needs of each site, taking into account the methods of analysis to be used.[23] In each case the objectives of sampling must be clear; for example, is it intended to identify mean or maximum concentrations or generic or specific contaminations? Decisions will need to be made on the following issues:

(1) Number of stages of sampling

Single stage, multi-stage with interim assessment of data, or repeated sampling to assess changes in site conditions. The crucial determining factor here will often be the time available.

(2) Number of sampling points

This decision will turn on various factors—principally, the size and topography of the site, practical and operational constraints, the likely distribution of contaminants as revealed by the preliminary assessment, the proposed use of the site, and the degree of confidence required.

---

[22] DD 175, p.4.
[23] Para. 5.4.1. See also C Fergusson and A. Abbachi, "Incorporating Expert Judgement into Statistical Sampling Designs for Contaminated Sites." Land Contamination and Reclamation [1993] Vol. 1, No. 3 p. 135.

DD 175 recommends that the minimum number of sampling points should be as follows:[24]

Area of Site (hectares)	Minimum number of sampling points
0.5	15
1.0	25
5.0	85

However, when surveys are undertaken at operational sites where significant areas are inaccessible due to the presence of buildings, buried services or production plant, it is often difficult to find suitable locations to achieve this sampling density.

Total assurance can never be obtained as without prohibitive cost it cannot be possible to guarantee that any sampling regime will locate every pocket of contamination. The overall aim should be to ensure that contamination subsequently discovered will not be such as to present major problems.

(3) Sampling patterns

Various possible sampling patterns are suggested: these include regular grid, stratified random and unequal. Stratified random sampling involves dividing the site into a number of cells of equal size, then taking an equal number of samples from each cell from locations chosen at random within the cells. Unequal sampling is suggested when an initial investigation has identified areas where the greatest contamination is likely to occur. A higher density of sampling in these areas may be appropriate to better define the nature and extent of this contamination. Zig-zag, X or W patterns are sometimes used for assessing agricultural land, and recent DoE research suggest that a herringbone form of pattern may be appropriate to some sites.

A minimum of three samples per sampling point is recommended: one sample to represent the surface and near surface layers, the second to represent the greatest depth of interest and the third at random intermediate depth. Geological investigations are shown to be essential as unless the strata are known the greatest depth of interest cannot be calculated.[25] The issue of depth is of critical importance and depends to some extent on the proposed use of a site: very shallow sampling may be sufficient for land which presents no off-site or water hazards, and which is to be hard surfaced as a car park; deeper sampling will be needed for areas to be landscaped or planted, and deeper still where foundations are to be sunk. Assessing possible threats to an aquifer will involve the deepest sampling of all. The cost of sampling at a range of depths across

[24] Para. 5.4.3.
[25] Para. 5.4.6.

the whole site—which is very considerable—can be reduced by a flexible and pragmatic approach. It is also crucial to decide whether samples at various depths are to be bulked or separately analysed.

(4) Sampling methods

Consideration must be given to the methods to be used for sampling solids, liquids and gases. Considerable practical guidance on this issue is given in DD 175.[26] In particular, it will need to be decided whether to sink boreholes or dig trial pits, or a combination of the two. Each method offers its own advantages and disadvantages: trial pits for example are cheaper than mechanically excavated boreholes and allow visual observation of soil conditions; however they are more disruptive and can be used only for stable soils up to a depth of 3–6m. It is also important to consider whether groundwater samples need to be taken.[27]

(5) Other sampling

Consideration is needed as to whether other forms of sampling are advisable, for example sampling of soil, microorganisms or plants, testing for radioactivity and testing of calorific values for potential combustibility.[28]

(6) On-site testing

In most investigations the samples collected from the site are sent to a laboratory for detailed examination. But there are three instances where DD 175 recommends on-site testing:[29]

(i) for the detection and initial analysis of contaminants (such as toxic gases) found during the reconnaissance visit made as part of the preliminary investigation, and which may present hazards for further work on site;

(ii) the determination of properties and contaminants that can change rapidly with time after the sample has been collected; examples could include pH, dissolved oxygen and turbidity of liquid samples;

(iii) the rapid analysis of soil or fill materials excavated during clearance or development of the site, in order to decide whether they should be disposed of or retained.

Another obvious example where on-site testing is important (not mentioned in DD 175) is the use of portable geiger-counters to detect the presence of radioactive materials.

[26] Para. 6.4.
[27] See Chap. 6 on water issues.
[28] Paras. 6.4.4–7.
[29] Para. 7.1.

(7) Off-site sampling

It should always be considered whether off-site sampling is necessary; for example sampling of an adjacent watercourse to detect possible leaching of contaminants off-site. Such sampling is often necessary and frequently desirable in order to understand fully the behaviour of contaminants on a site being investigated. In practice, off-site sampling is probably neglected in many cases where it should be carried out. Of course, such sampling raises difficulties in its own right, such as access and the potential problem of causing concern amongst neighbours.

(8) Background samples

It may be necessary to sample known "clean"areas on site or off-site to establish background concentrations, since in many urban locations water and soil quality are generally impaired, for example due to lead from motor vehicle emissions.

Sampling procedures

4.11   The following practical issues will need to be addressed in the planning and execution of the sampling programme:

(1) Health and safety

Risks to the investigators from toxic materials or other site hazards such as concealed underground structures; presence of any particular risks such as asbestos, toxic metals, tarry materials, radioactive or explosive materials.[30]

(2) Demolition and clearance

It may be necessary to remove parts of buildings or other site structures. Great care is needed to avoid spreading contaminants. BS 6187 on demolition should be followed where practicable, and specialist contractors may be needed. Care should be taken in disposing of any rubble or waste materials.[31]

(3) Avoidance of damage

Care needs to be taken to ensure that the process of investigation does not in fact create problems, for example by boring through concealed

---

[30] DD 175, para. 6.1. See also para. 7.18 *et seq.* below.
[31] DD 175, para. 5.3. See also para. 7.28 *et seq.* below.

cables or pipelines, or by puncturing or disturbing strata so as to liberate contaminants.

(4) Site security

The site must be kept safe and secure. This may involve the fencing or capping of boreholes and the backfilling and sealing of trial pits.[32]

(5) Confidentiality

Investigations may be extremely confidential, particularly in the case of those carried out in the context of a proposed transaction. Careful instructions on this aspect may need to be given to the investigators.

(6) Sample preservation

Precautions will be needed to prevent the deterioration of samples which are to be analysed off-site, e.g., temperature control and use of stabilising agents.[33] Care is needed in the use of appropriate and clean containers, and the avoidance of cross-contamination.[34]

(7) Visual observations

No sampling strategy can guarantee to detect every possible pocket of contamination. For this reason, visual observations during boring, digging, excavating and similar operations are a valuable additional safeguard. Ideally, qualified and experienced staff should be present during such operations, but if this is not possible at all times, any unusual observations should be reported by the contractor to the consultant; this should be dealt with contractually between the consultant and contractor.

Selection of contaminants for analysis

The selection of the suite of contaminants for analysis will be based on **4.12** the results of the preliminary investigation and on any observations made during sampling. For all sites the choice should be based on an assessment of the principal hazards against the proposed end use for the site, taking into account the site history.[35] The physical properties of the

---

[32] DD 175, para. 5.2. See also paras. 2.32 and 2.33 on occupiers' liability.
[33] DD 175, para. 7.5.
[34] British Standards Institution B5 6068: Guidance on the Presentation and Handling of Samples.
[35] DD 175, para. 8.1.

possible contaminants will also be relevant, for example their persistence and dispersion characteristics.

DD 175 suggests the following minimum analyses to be undertaken for particular end uses.

Minimum analyses to be included in investigations, depending on site history[36]		
WARNING. Consideration should be given to the inclusion of other contaminants if the site history has identified former uses likely to have introduced them.		
Hazard (see note 1)	Typical end uses where hazard may exist	Analyses

Direct ingestion of contaminated soil by children	Domestic gardens, recreational and amenity areas	total arsenic free cyanide
		total cadmium polynuclear
		total lead aromatic
		                        hydrocarbons
		                      phenols
		                      sulphate

Uptake of contaminants by crop plants (see note 2)	Domestic gardens, allotments and agricultural land	total cadmium (see note 3) total lead (see note 3)
Phytotoxicity (see notes 2 and 3)	Any uses where plants are to be grown	total copper total nickel total zinc

Attack on building materials and services (see note 2)	Housing developments, commercial and industrial buildings	sulphate oily and tarry
		sulphide substances
		chloride phenols
		                    mineral oils
		                    ammonium ion

Fire and explosion	Any uses involving the construction of buildings	methane sulphur potentially combustible materials (*e.g.* coal dust, oil, tar, pitch)
Contact with contaminants during demolition, clearance, and construction work	Hazard mainly short-term (to site workers and investigators)	polynuclear asbestos aromatic radioactive hydrocarbons materials phenols oil and tarry substances

[36] DD 175, Table 3.

Hazard (see note 1)	Typical end uses where hazard may exist	Analyses	
Contamination of ground and surface water (see note 2)	Any uses where possible pollution of water may occur	phenols cyanide sulphate	soluble metals
NOTE 1.	The hazards listed are not mutually exclusive. Combinations of several hazards may need consideration.		
NOTE 2.	The soil pH should be measured, as it affects the importance of these hazards.		
NOTE 3.	Uptake of harmful or phytotoxic metals by plants depends on which chemical forms of these elements are present in the soil. It may therefore be necessary to determine the particular forms, if the total concentrations present indicate that there exists a possible risk.		

For soil and water samples a phased approach to analysis is often most suitable as this can avoid unnecessary expenditure. The results of the initial analyses give an indication of the type and degree of contamination, which allows more selective analysis of the remaining samples. Use of screening methods can also be useful, particularly for organic compounds. For example, a total solvent extract will indicate where polyaromatic hydrocarbons (PAHs) are most likely to be present, or total organochlorine analysis will indicate whether any samples should be analysed for polychlorinated biphenyls, chlorinated pesticides or chlorinated solvents.

Analysis

The value of the most meticulous site investigation can be negated by **4.13** sub-standard analysis. There are various accreditation schemes for laboratories in relation to the analysis of specific components by specific methods.[37] These include NAMAS (National Measurement Accreditation Service), BS 5750 and GLP (Good Laboratory Practice, administered by the Department of Health) as well as various international standards such as EN 45001, ISO Guide 25 and ISO 9000, EN 29000. However, there is currently no official laboratory accreditation for the analysis of contaminated land as such though work is proceeding in this

---

[37] This section is based on a paper by J.A. Day, Environmental Services Division, "Laboratory of the Government Chemist" given at a seminar on Contaminated Land: The Planning Dilemma (London, April 20, 1993).

area through a working group of NAMAS on waste disposal and contaminated land. In particular, NAMAS accreditation is given for specific tests only and should not be taken as an indication of overall competence. Whether the laboratory is accredited or not, it should still be asked for a quality assurance statement under BS 5750 or some other relevant criteria. The laboratory of the Government Chemist is currently working to establish a scheme for proficiency testing in soils analysis, CONTEST.[38]

There are a wide variety of methodologies available for chemical analysis, and a wide variety of methods which may be used for pre-treating samples in preparation for analysis.[39] Pre-treatment methods include drying, sieving, and various extraction techniques such as water, salts, acids and solvents. Analytical techniques range from classical wet chemistry or colorimetric techniques through to highly specialised instrumental methods such as spectroscopy and spectrometry. Some laboratories make use of recognised methods such as those of the Standing Committee of Analysts "bluebook" or US Environmental Protection Agency Protocols. One very effective way of ensuring quality of analysis is by validation against certified reference materials, though the applicability of this method is limited by the number of such materials. Participation by a laboratory in recognised proficiency testing schemes is another indicator of reliability.

Ultimately, the whole procedure from custody and transport of the sample to treatment and analysis must be such as to give total confidence that the results are defensible in relation to each step. The use of blank or spiked samples, provided by the laboratory for transfer to site and subsequent analysis with the samples collected on site, is an effective way of guarding against sample deterioration, cross contamination, and other potential problems.

In practice it is often the case that the testing regime will be more rigorous than the sampling regime selected. Coverage of samples may be reduced to an extent which is inadequate, on cost grounds; yet those samples may then be subjected to testing of disproportionately high quality.

Reports on sampling and analysis: what to expect and how to judge their adequacy

4.14   The crucial point in any report is that it should present the data in a clear and understandable form appropriate to the intended readership.[40]

---

[38] See Dr. Ian Rix, "Industrial Waste Management," September 1993. Further details can be obtained from L.G.C., Queens Road, Teddington, Middlesex, TW11 0LY; Tel: 081 943 7494.

[39] See also DD 175, para. 8.3.

[40] See also Chap. 10 on the use of professional advisers.

166

A recommended scheme for the order and content of the report is given at DD 175 and is broadly as follows[41]:

(a) *Summary* A description of the work carried out, stating the aims and main findings together with their implications and a brief account of the conclusions and recommendations.

(b) *Introduction* Details of the location and history of the site including a brief description of its current status and conditions, as shown by the preliminary investigation. If possible, details of the proposed end use(s) should be given.

(c) *Sampling* An explanation of the sampling strategy adopted, including plans showing the positions of the sampling points and their relation to the site history should be given. Details of the materials encountered in trial pits in boreholes should also be given: photographs and data from the original record logs are usually best for this purpose. The methods used for collection and stabilisation of samples should be stated.

(d) *Analysis* The sub-sampling procedures should be described. It is not necessary for the analytical methods to be stated in full unless new or rarely used techniques and procedures were used. Information on the performance characteristics of the analytical method should be given where possible. It is often most convenient to present the detailed analytical data in an appendix, but a minimum of tabulated summaries of the results obtained should always be given in the main text.

(e) *Discussion of results and risk assessment.* Discussed below at paras. 4.16–4.25.

(f) *Conclusions and recommendations* The client or solicitor, faced with a report, will need to assess and examine critically its adequacy for the purpose in hand. Techniques for investigation used in the UK currently lack the scientific certainty which might be expected in other legal contexts such as forensic evidence. Nonetheless there are three basic questions which can usefully be asked:

    (1) **Has enough data been collected?** The sampling density achieved (in terms of sampling locations per hectare) can be compared with the guidance in DD 175. If land is intended for residential development, is there approximate correspondence between the number of sampling points and the number of proposed homes? Has the possible necessity for off-site sampling been addressed?[42]

    (2) **Has the right data been collected?** Are the data relevant to the questions which the investigation was designed to

---

[41] Para. 9.2; also 9.3 on presentation of analytical data.
[42] See para. 4.10.

answer? The data will be quite different if assessing the health risks on land intended for residential use than when considering the possible aggressive effect of contamination on buildings.[43]

(3) **Has the data been interpreted properly?** Has intelligent (as opposed to dogmatic) use been made of ICRCL or any other relevant guidelines? Have inappropriate guidelines (*e.g.* GLC guidelines) been used?

Developed sites

4.15   In some cases the site under investigation will already be developed: it may have been the subject of past investigation or remedial work. Such investigations will frequently take place in the context of a proposed transaction where the main concern may be potential future liabilities. This type of investigation raises its own practical considerations, among which are the following:

(1) What previous reports on the site exist?

(2) To what extent can legal reliance be placed on those reports?[44] Is their benefit assignable to the purchaser or can they be reissued to the purchaser or a collateral warranty given?

(3) To what extent can previous reports be relied on in the technical sense? For what purpose were they commissioned and are the nature of the original instructions together with any limitations apparent from the face of the report? How old are they? It may be unwise to rely on reports prepared some years ago in a different regulatory climate.

(4) Is there any further relevant information since those earlier reports, *e.g.* post remediation monitoring data?

(5) Were any remedial works carried out adequately and have any measures such as gas alarms[45] or venting trenches been properly maintained?

(6) It is often advisable to ask an independent consultant to verify the adequacy of earlier work and reports. Further sampling may be constrained by the form of the built development, which may also conceal the natural ground and any signs of contamination. Nonetheless a site visit by an experienced consultant may often flag up potential problems which might otherwise go unnoticed.

[43] See para. 4.09.
[44] See Chap. 10 generally.
[45] See British Standards Institution BS 6959: Code of Practice for the Selection, Installation, Use and Maintenance of Apparatus for the Detection and Measurement of Combustible Gases.

Assessment of findings: generally

Ultimately the findings of site investigations will need to be assessed. **4.16**
It is all too easy to lose sight of the fundamental issue of why the land is
being assessed in any given case when considering issues such as trigger
levels and action levels and techniques such as risk assessment. Broadly
speaking, there are four main purposes:

A. Assessment of current on-site risks, *i.e.* to present users, occupiers, buildings, services, plants, etc.	B. Assessment of current off-site risks, *i.e.* to neighbouring occupiers, ground and surface water and other off-site targets, from the site as it is.
C. Assessment of future on-site risks, *i.e.* eventual users, occupiers, buildings, services, plants, etc., in the light of proposals for development of the site.	D. Assessment of future off-risks, *i.e.* to neighbouring occupiers, ground and surface water and other off-site targets, from the site in the light of proposals for future development.

The distinction between purposes A/C and B/D is that A and C look
to the site itself and its fitness for a particular purpose, actual or
intended, whereas B and D are concerned with risks of liability resulting
from the effects of the site on its environment. On the other hand, the
distinction between A/B and C/D is between actual circumstances and
anticipated changes, which may affect the sensitivity to on-site risks or
which may lessen or increase the off-site risks to the environment. Those
anticipated changes also have an economic dimension in that they may
increase the range of options open to reduce the risk.[46]

The ICRCL guidelines for data interpretation referred to below[47] are
expressed to be for use only in situation C, *i.e.*, assessment of on-site risks
in the case of sites being considered for development. They do not apply
to sites already in use, not to those in the course of development, and
must certainly not be regarded or used as standards which all sites must
meet.[48] The reasons for this are expressed in economic terms:[49]

---

[46] *i.e.* by changing the end use, or the layout and design of development, or by
incorporating remedial or control features.
[47] See para. 4.17.
[48] ICRCL Guidance Note 59/87, para. 38; see also DD 175 which refers at para.
10.1 to protection of eventual users or occupiers when assessing the suitability
of a contaminated site for development.
[49] *Ibid.*

169

"Trigger concentrations have been set on the basis of an implied economic condition. The cost of taking remedial action, which normally increases development costs and extends the time required, has to be weighed against the likely risks. Where the risks are judged to be high, then remedial action will be necessary unless the original proposals are to be abandoned. The cost of abandoning a completed building which is already in use is likely to be judged high, and the practical constraints on designing and implementing remedial measures will certainly be much greater than before development started. The risks might, in these circumstances, have to be regarded as acceptable: in the case of a site still to be developed, this judgment might well be different."

The undesirable consequences of concentrating solely on development and end-use in judging the significance of contamination has already been noted.[50] Risk assessment as a technique is adaptable to all four situations.

Use of trigger concentrations: ICRCL Guidance

4.17 Concentration of contaminations found in samples may be compared with published reference values: the "threshold" and "action" trigger concentrations proposed by ICRCL were formulated for this purpose.[51]

The main limitation on use of these values—that they are intended to be applied only to sites where redevelopment is being considered—has already been mentioned.[52]

The way in which the ICRCL figures work is by defining three possible concentration zones for each contaminant. This can be shown diagramatically.[53]

---

[50] See Chap. 1 generally.
[51] ICRCL Guidance Note 59/83 (2nd ed., July 1987).
[52] See para. 4.16.
[53] Fig. 1 from ICRCL Guidance Note 59/83.

INTERPRETATION OF "TRIGGER CONCENTRATIONS"

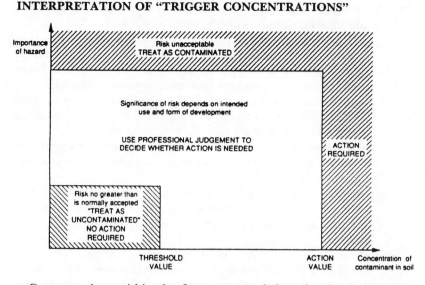

Concentrations within the first zone, *i.e.* below the threshold trigger level, present no significant risk and no remedial action should be needed, even though levels may be above normal background values. At the other extreme, in the third zone *i.e.* above the action trigger level, the risks are sufficiently high that the presence of the contaminant must be regarded as undesirable or even unacceptable, and some type of remedial action will be required. In the intermediate zone, *i.e.* between the threshold and action levels, there is a need to consider whether the risks are such that remedial action is required and here informed judgment is essential.

Tables provided in the Guidance give trigger concentrations for a number of organic and inorganic contaminants: these are reproduced at Appendix D. The ICRCL list defines tentative trigger concentrations for a number of soil contaminants based on differing levels of sensitivity of intended future use of the site, from domestic gardens and allotments through to buildings and hard cover. The list is divided into three types of contaminant, those which may pose hazards to health, those which are phytotoxic but not normally hazardous to health and those associated with former coal carbonisation sites. All contaminants listed are assigned a threshold trigger concentration but only those in the list of contaminants associated with coal carbonisation sites are assigned action levels. It is most important not to take these figures out of context and so the relevant text of the Guidance is also reproduced. The following limitations should be noted in addition to those already mentioned[54]:

---

[54] *Ibid.*, paras. 33–39.

(1) the figures are subject to a number of conditions and footnotes and have no validity without these;

(2) all values in the list apply to concentrations determined on spot samples based on adequate site investigation prior to redevelopment. They do not apply to averaged, bulked, or composite samples, nor to sites which have already been developed;

(3) some contaminants (*e.g.* radionuclides and asbestos) may present a hazard even in low concentrations, making their threshold concentration effectively zero;

(4) where there is no quantifiable "dose-effect" relationship it will be very difficult to specify a precise trigger value for the relevant contaminant;

(5) the figures apply only to a limited number of contaminants, and to a great extent the assessment of risk and the need for remedial action must depend on subjective or qualitative criteria; and

(6) the risks and consequences of contamination should be seen in the light of contamination or surrounding areas in similar use or equivalent areas elsewhere; this does not, however, mean that opportunities to clean the site or reduce the risks should not be taken when they arise.[55]

As a final word of caution, it should be reiterated that the figures in the ICRCL tables are open to misuse. They should not be viewed in the respect of providing acceptable or unacceptable boundaries. The present range of contaminants listed is restricted, yet the tables still include some values which are seldom needed to make decisions on assessment of hazards. An example quoted by Martin Beckett (Secretary of ICRCL from 1980–90) is the threshold trigger concentration for arsenic on land to be used for parks, playing fields and recreational uses. He says:[56]

"The best that can be said for this value is that it is unjustified and unnecessary: the worst may be that its retention can lead to the mistaken conclusion that remedial action is required."

The values should only be taken as guidance and used with caution. Most important of all:[57]

"Guideline information should aim to accommodate the exercise of professional judgment."

and[58]:

---

[55] *Ibid.*, para. 39.

[56] "Trigger Concentrations: More or Less?" Land Contamination & Reclamation [1993] Vol. 1, No. 2, p. 67 at p. 69.

[57] Mary R. Harris in "Reclaiming Contaminated Land," ed. T. Cairney, Blackie, 1987 p. 12.

[58] "Contaminated Land: Development of Contaminated Land—Professional Guidance," Institution of Environmental Health Officers, p. 29.

"In providing advice it should always be remembered that pragmatism and intelligent appraisal should generally take precedence over the dogmatic application of what are only intended as guidelines."

Other values and standards

The ICRCL values referred to above are not comprehensive in the **4.18** range of contaminants covered, and some consultants supplement these values by making use of the Dutch scheme of soil quality based on "A, B and C Guidelines" under the 1987 Soil Protection Act.[59]

The Dutch scheme, which is currently under review,[60] has three categories (A, B and C). Under this scheme, the A value is a background figure below which the soil can be considered to be uncontaminated and is also the target level to which contaminated sites should be cleared after remediation. The B value indicates that some contamination is present and that further investigation is necessary, and the C value is an action level where clean-up is required.

The Dutch system has been adopted by a number of other countries including Denmark, Germany, Norway and certain territories of Canada. However, they do not necessarily all attach the same conditions to the various standards or accept the concept of clean-up to a multi-functionality standard.

Use is sometimes also made of figures formulated by the Greater London Council's Scientific Branch in 1979 based on then current experiences in relation to the disposal of soils to landfill from contaminated land, particularly former gas works and sewage farms.[61] These cover a wider range of contaminants than ICRCL values and group concentrations into categories: uncontaminated, slight contamination, contaminated, heavy contamination and unusually heavy contaminations. These values are not, however, generally accepted by consultants and their use other than within Greater London and for the purpose for which designed needs to be treated with a great deal of caution. They were developed principally in the context of disposing of contaminated soil rather than assessing remedial options, as a forerunner to the Special Waste Regulations 1980, as the Department of Environment has stated on many occasions.[62]

[59] See the summary of Dutch law given at Chap. 13.
[60] The proposed changes involve replacing the A, B and C values with general criteria based on a target-value (the former A value) and an intervention value (the former C value); these would be subject to both site-specific and land-use based modifications.
[61] R.T Kelly, "Site Investigation and Material Problems" (1979), published in *Reclamation of Contaminated Land*, Society of Chemical Industry, 1980.
[62] M.A. Smith, "Identification, Investigation and Assessment of Contaminated Land" (1991) J. I.W.E.M., December, 617 at p. 620.

Specific substances

4.19   Other sources of guidance deal with investigation and assessment in relation to specific contaminants, *i.e.*:

(1) Sulphate

Guidelines relating to the quality of concrete required to resist sulphate attack for structures located in high sulphate soils has been issued by the Building Research Establishment.[63]

(2) Landfill gas

Comprehensive technical guidance on site investigation and monitoring for landfill gas is provided in Waste Management Paper No. 27.[64] It is suggested[65] that as a guide buildings should be evacuated where concentrations of flammable gas at or above 20 per cent. L.E.L. (lower explosive limit) or carbon dioxide in excess of 1.5 per cent. by volume are detected. The Building Research Establishment has published guidance on the measurement of gas emissions.[66]

(3) Petroleum

The Institute of Petroleum has published a comprehensive Code of Practice dealing with the investigation, monitoring and remediation of petroleum-based contamination.[67] This covers crude oil, gasolines, middle distillates (*e.g.*, diesel and kerosene), heavy fuel and lube oils, bitumen and petrochemicals.

(4) Asbestos

ICRCL Guidance Note 64/85[68] deals with asbestos on contaminated sites. This includes guidance on sites which may contain asbestos, survey techniques, and assessment of findings.

Guidance on specific types of site

4.20   The ICRCL has published specific guidance on the following types of site which should be consulted as appropriate.

---

[63] Concrete in Sulphate-Bearing Soils and Groundwaters, BRE Digest 2501.

[64] HMSO, 1991 (2nd ed.). The gas is typically 65 per cent. methane/35 per cent. carbon dioxide.

[65] *Ibid.*, para 7.14., as amended by the 2nd ed. (1991).

[66] *Measurement of Gas Emissions from Contaminated Land*, D. Crowhurst, DOE Building Research Establishment, 1987.

[67] *Code of Practice for the Investigation and Mitigation of Possible Petroleum-based Land Contamination.* Institute of Petroleum, London, 1993, 61 New Cavendish Street, London, W1M 8AR. Tel: 071-636 1004.

[68] (2nd ed.), October 1990.

ICRCL Guidance Note		Subject
17/78	(8th ed.), December 1990	Development and after-use of landfill sites
18/79	(5th ed.), April 1986	Redevelopment of gas works site
23/79	(2nd ed.), November 1983	Redevelopment of sewage works and farms
42/80	(2nd ed.), October 1983	Redevelopment of scrap yards and similar sites
		Sites presenting fire hazards
61/84	(2nd ed.), July 1986	Restoration and aftercare of
70/90	(1st ed.), February 1990	metalliferous mining sites for pasture and grazing

Risk assessment: generally[68a]

Essentially, risk assessment is a systematic approach allowing health **4.21** and environmental risks, either present or future, to be identified, evaluated, quantified and managed.

A risk assessment study comprises two parts:

(i) an estimation of the probability that a potential hazard is realised under site specific conditions;

(ii) an estimation of the adverse affects to health and the environment if the hazard is realised.

The aim of the assessment is to identify, evaluate and quantify the health and ecological risks posed by either an existing site or a proposed remediated site.

In a systematic risk assessment both the health risk and the environmental risk should be addressed. It is also important to understand the difference between the various types of human risk assessment, societal and individual: otherwise the comparison of results may be incorrect and misleading.[69] The risks of a contaminant to the general population cannot be evaluated if in reality the hazards presented by the contaminant target only one specific sector of the population. In most cases it will be individual rather than societal risk assessment which is relevant.

[68a] See the summary by Dr Marcus Ford and Dr Peter Rowley, *Liabilities for Contaminated Sites in Western Europe: The Development and Implementation of Remedial Standards* [1994] Env. Liability 42.

[69] See the helpful discussion of risk and tolerability of risk in the HSE document *The Tolerability of Risk from Nuclear Power Stations* (HMSO 1988, revised 1992) pp. 2–15.

In the context of any study, the health risk is the long-term impact on human health posed by residual contamination to future users of the site, neighbours and casual visitors. The environmental risk survey looks at the threat of ecological damage to sensitive neighbouring areas and ecosystems caused by migration of residual contamination from the site. Even when there is no dangerous or high contamination level it may be necessary to establish the aesthetic risk. Liability can emanate from aesthetic degradation, which will also heighten public perception of environmental damage. For example odours may present serious problems in some cases of contaminated land, regardless of whether any air quality or soil quality standards are being exceeded.

As a practical matter any risk assessment will also need to take account of the potential liabilities of a developer or current or future owner of land; this may in many cases be the decisive factor as to the level of remedial work required. The difficulty here lies in assessing not only the current state of the law and the potential liabilities it may create, but also the likely attitudes or regulatory authorities in practice, and how law and policy may change over the lifetime of a site.

Health and environmental risk assessment in themselves are of very little use to the owner, prospective purchaser, lender, developer, etc. What is ultimately necessary is a commercial risk assessment, discussed below.[70]

Health risk assessment

4.22 There are four main tasks to enable a health risk assessment to be concluded:

(1) Identification of the potentially problematic contaminants

The site assessment report will provide the data.

(2) Identification of the potential human exposure pathways

The study should trace the pathway from the source of the contaminated release, through the environment, to the hazards where humans are exposed to the consequences. Particular attention should be paid to:

- the mechanism of the release of the contaminant to the environment;
- any environmental transport medium for the released contaminant;
- the human point of contact with the contamination and transport medium (receptor group);

---

[70] See para. 4.24.

- the human exposure route from the transport medium to the receptor group *e.g.*, the ingestion of contaminants in food (plants) etc. The Table at the end of this section gives an overview of typical exposure routes and points.

(3) Identification of the receptor or "target" group

To identify possible exposure pathways, human activities near the site should be defined so that the most likely receptor groups can be evaluated. Exposure routes are not always restricted to dangers on site. Selection of the targets or "target envelope" can be an especially complex matter, given the lack of epidemiological or toxicological data for exposure to many contaminants. The characteristics of the contaminant need to be taken into consideration, especially in the case of environmental exposure: particularly relevant here are the persistence of the contaminant (*i.e.*, how long it remains in the environment), its mobility in soil and groundwater, the driving forces causing such mobility, and any tendency to bio-accumulation. The fact that the characteristics of contaminants may change with conditions such as pH, temperature and oxidation also needs to be kept in mind.

(4) The consequences to human health

The amount of exposure to the selected contaminant or contaminants is to be determined. The exposure is assessed and then converted into terms of contaminant intake, which is the amount of chemical substance taken into the body per unit of body weight over time. The following table shows typical values used in daily intake calculations.

Parameter	Standard Value
Average adult body weight	70 kg
Amount of water ingested daily, adult	2 litres
Amount of air breathed daily, adult	20m^3

The extent of human exposure to contaminants is highly dependent upon the exposure pathway, *e.g.* different types of soil. Exposure will vary significantly between children and adults, reflecting differences in age-related human activities, and will also vary markedly with the different types of land use.

The results of the exposure assessment should be combined with those of a toxicity assessment, which is a study of the toxicity of the selected contaminants as well as an assessment of the combined toxicity from exposure to them collectively.

177

The process of risk assessment is in some cases the key to evaluating the level of contamination that can be deemed acceptable at a site. The results should show estimated levels of human exposure to the contaminants and what is thought to be the Acceptable Daily Intake (ADI) for both short-term and long-term exposure to the hazards.

The overall aim of the risk assessment exercise is to identify and manage the risks attached to the particular site, and ultimately to reduce those risks for the future to an acceptable level; this inevitably involves considering the marginal cost of additional remediation measures against the further, and possibly small, diminution in risk which they would achieve.[71] The human risk assessment exercise is now a relatively familiar one; the focus is on the reduction of potential adverse health effects resulting from long term exposure to the levels of contamination remaining after remedial works have been carried out on site. The issue generally is therefore chronic toxocity resulting from exposure over a long period, as opposed to acute toxocity through direct contact, ingestion, etc. However, in some cases the nature of the contamination may be such that acute health risks in the short term have to be taken into account. Professionals working in the field will, in carrying out such risk assessment, make use of the various modelling techniques now available for quantitative risk assessment. Such techniques may be useful, for example, to assess the risk of contaminants being transported by groundwater flows.[72]

Typical exposure points and routes		
Transport/ Exposure Medium	**Typical Exposure Point (Receptor)**	**Major Exposure Route**
Air	• Nearest residence to source	Inhalation
	• Nearest population magnet (*e.g.* shopping centre, industrial park)	Inhalation
	• Other residence/population at point of highest concentration	Inhalation
Surface Water	• Abstraction point for potable use	Ingestion, dermal
	• Abstraction point for agricultural use	Ingestion (food) dermal
	• Abstraction point for other uses (*e.g.* industrial)	Dermal

[71] See also para. 4.24 on commercial risk assessment.
[72] See Chap. 6 on groundwater generally.

178

Transport/ Exposure Medium	Typical Exposure Point (Receptor)	Major Exposure Route
Surface water— *cont.*	• Nearest point for swimming/ contact sports	Ingestion, dermal
	• Nearest point for fishing	Ingestion (food)
Ground- water	• Aquifers and NRA groundwater pro- tection zones	Ingestion, dermal
	• Nearest surface water in hydraulic continuity with aquifer	As for surface water
	• Nearest public or private abstraction well	Ingestion (drinking and food)
	• Nearest agricultural well	Ingestion (food), dermal
	• Nearest well for other uses (*e.g.* industrial)	Dermal
Soil	• On-site	Dermal, ingestion
	• Immediately adjacent to site	Dermal, ingestion
	• Nearest cropland	Ingestion (food)

Environmental risk assessment

This encompasses the risk posed by the residual contaminant levels on **4.23** site to the ecological community of the site, *i.e.*, flora and fauna, and the impact of residual contaminant levels migrating to the surrounding environment. The process involved is very similar to the assessment of the health risk. Emphasis is placed on migration pathway delineation, *e.g.*, free phase product movement through soil, and a contaminant mobility assessment. These studies cannot normally be based solely upon preliminary site investigation data as further site specific investiga- tions may be needed.

Commercial risk assessment

So far as the solicitor and client are concerned, the use and application **4.24** of any health and environmental risk assessment must be as ingredients of an overall commercial risk assessment. Ultimately this will be an issue of commercial judgment rather than scientific certainty. Potential lia- bility issues will clearly be relevant. Also relevant will be the commercial context, which will have a bearing on the likelihood and consequences of

179

the risk. Such considerations will include whether or not the site is already owned or whether it is proposed to acquire it or some interest in it; whether it is proposed to develop the site; whether it is to be used for the owner's business; and whether it is proposed to hold it as a short or long-term asset.

Clearly, the commercial considerations may be very different where the site is being purchased as a short term investment, as opposed to a long-term holding, for example by pension fund trustees. Where the land is to be used as the site of the owner's business, the risks of certain types of contamination may be very high; for example involving the acquisition of other accommodation, major site works, disruption of business operations, etc. Where a site is imminently to be developed, any contaminative problems may need to be addressed sooner rather than later.

A logical framework of analysis is needed in each case, but there will be many imponderables, and often the personal circumstances of the client will be crucial: for example, can the client afford the suggested remedial works and what will be the risks of not undertaking them, deferring them, or opting for some cheaper solution? In practice there will often be great resistance to the outlay of considerable sums on what could transpire to be an open-ended exercise. It needs to be considered whether embarking on the exercise could indeed make the site more difficult to sell if remedial works are not entirely satisfactory or if continuing monitoring is an on-cost in respect of the site. Many of the companies involved in using or developing potentially contaminated sites may be operating on comparatively small profit margins: this will be another relevant factor to be taken into account and may colour the commercial risk assessment process dramatically.

Finally, the process may involve the consideration of the respective merits of a number of possible sites. Potentially contaminated land may be well located or available on advantageous terms, but against this will need to be set considerations such as potential delays, planning difficulties, clean-up costs, and the risks of doing nothing.

Summary of the investigation and appraisal process

4.25   In concluding it may be helpful to summarise briefly the overall procedure of investigation.

Stage One

A study that should establish the presence, nature and likely extent of contamination and define the sectors of a site which require more detailed investigation. A full history of the site should have been compiled along with a report detailing the site visit and enquiries. The implications of the results should be considered in respect of value, planning and legal liability.

Stage Two

If Stage One indicates the need for further research, then sampling and analytical surveys should be conducted to identify the precise constituents and distribution of the contamination. The report should include all the relevant data and an analysis equating the investigation results to the current or intended land use. Identified hazards should be the subject of appraisal and risk assessment. Feasibility studies should equate the cost of alternative remedial techniques with the client's business priorities and funding requirements.

Stage Three

The production of a detailed remedial programme (see Chapter 7) appropriate to the likely end use of the site.

In the context of the site being developed and where physical sampling is deemed necessary the procedure from start to finish can be represented as follows (see p. 182):

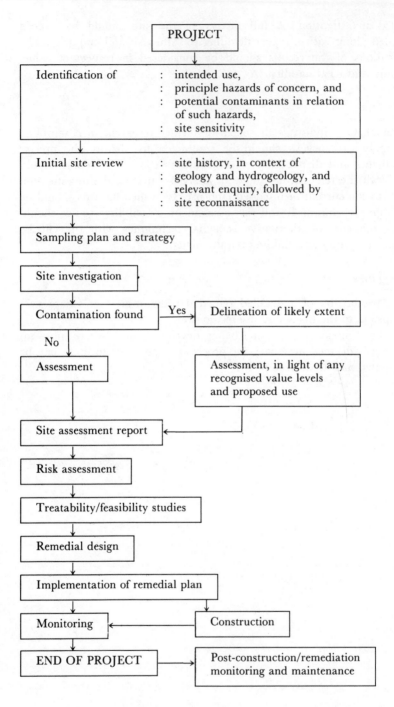

Chapter 5

PREVENTION

Generally

Whilst much of this book focusses upon the problems of rectifying the **5.01**
consequences of past contaminative activity, it is also of crucial importance that future soil contamination is, so far as possible, avoided. This
chapter considers the preventive mechanisms available in relation to soil
contamination. Broadly, these are currently as follows:

(1) the planning system;
(2) integrated pollution control;
(3) waste management law;
(4) rules relating to hazardous or "special" waste;
(5) regulation of the spreading of sludge on agricultural land and
    other agricultural activities;
(6) legislation on the prevention of water pollution (dealt with in
    Chapter 6).

In tabular form the respective roles of each system can be amplified as
follows:

Legislation	Type of control	Reference
Town and Country Planning Act 1990, as amended.	Land use in the sense of operational development or change of use.	5.02, *et seq.* See also Chapter 7 generally.
Environmental Protection Act 1990, Part I.	Control over operational aspects of prescribed processes; concerned (*inter alia*) with discharge of prescribed and other harmful substances to land.	5.11 *et seq.*

Legislation	Type of control	Reference
Environmental Protection Act 1990, Part II; replacing Control of Pollution Act 1974, Part I.	Control over deposit, disposal, keeping and treatment of controlled waste; duty of care imposed on waste producers and others in control of waste.	5.18 *et seq.*
Control of Pollution (Special Waste) Regulations 1980.	Control over "special waste" by means of consignment note system of documentation.	5.31 *et seq.*
Radioactive Substances Act 1993.	Control over keeping and use of radioactive material and accumulation and disposal of radioactive waste.	5.35 *et seq.*
Control of Pollution (Silage, Slurry and Agricultural Fuel Oil) Regulations 1991. Control of Pesticides Regulations 1986. Sludge (Use in Agriculture) Regulations 1989.	Controls over various potentially contaminative agricultural activities.	5.38 *et seq.*
Water Resources Act 1991 and Water Industry Act 1991.	Controls over entry of polluting substances to controlled waters (including groundwater); protection of water resources; controls over trade effluent and sewage disposal.	Chapter 6 generally; See also para. 2.44 *et seq.*

Town and Country Planning

Generally

5.02   The land use planning system is potentially a useful tool in preventing soil contamination. It can operate in one of two main ways:

(a) by exercising control over the siting of possibly contaminative developments, for example by preventing uses with a heavy contaminative potential being located over vulnerable ground-water resources on unsuitable strata; or

(b) by imposing obligations as to anti-contamination measures, whether by way of planning permission or under a planning agreement. These obligations may take the form either of ongoing measures during the operation of the permitted development, or measures by way of decommissioning, restoration or aftercare to ensure that when the use ceases the site is rehabilitated with no long term adverse effects.

The main problem with using the planning system in this way is that not all potentially contaminative development will require planning permission. The nature of an industrial operation may change so that potentially contaminative substances are stored or kept on land in much greater quantities than previously, or new substances may be introduced into a process: such changes may well not constitute a material change in the use of land, and unless they involve operational development such as the installation of new buildings, plant or equipment, planning permission may not be required. Similarly, it may be possible to enlarge existing facilities or introduce new plant and equipment whilst remaining within the tolerances permitted for industrial development under the General Development Order 1988, Schedule 2, Part 8.[1]

The second main problem is the issue of how far planning controls may be used so as to duplicate or overlap with other forms of statutory control. This is an issue which has given rise to considerable discussion,[2] and is considered subsequently below.[3]

Use of the planning system in protecting water resources

Increasing attention has focussed upon use of the planning system as a **5.03** means of protecting vulnerable surface and ground water resources, in particular with publication in 1992 of the National Rivers Authority's document "Policy and Practice for the Protection of Groundwater." This issue is considered in detail in its own right in Chapter 6 on the protection of water resources.

Development plan policies

Structure plans, local plans and unitary development plans must all **5.04** include policies in respect of conservation of the natural beauty and amenity of the land in the plan-making authority's area, and the

[1] S.I. 1988 No. 1813.
[2] S. Tromans, "Town and Country Planning and Environmental Protection," J.P.E.L. Occasional Paper No. 18 (1991) p. 6.
[3] Para. 5.05.

improvement of the physical environment.[4] Government policy is that environmental considerations should be taken into account in drawing up all development plan policies.[5] Local plans and Part II of unitary development plans may include detailed development control policies which, for example, control particular aspects of development to minimise pollution, or control development in particular parts of a plan area by reference to the physical or geological characteristics of the area.[6]

Planning authorities should also take account of the need to identify land for the location of those types of development which may have the potential to pollute, the need to separate potentially polluting and other land uses to reduce conflicts, and the possible impact of that potentially polluting developments on land use, including effects on health, the natural environment, or general amenity.[7]

Whilst development plan policies have traditionally been concerned with pollution issues such as dust, noise, fumes, etc., there are signs that some planning authorities are now extending the list of possible pollutants to include those which may give rise to contaminated land problems.[8] Examples are given elsewhere[9] of local plan and UDP policies relating to contaminated land, and one aspect of these policies is the prevention of further contamination by control over land use.

Government policy

5.05   The Government has stated that it attaches great importance to controlling and minimising pollution and that it will apply policies to prevent pollution at source, minimise risk to human health and the environment, encourage and apply the most advanced technical solutions,[10] and apply a "critical loads" approach to pollution in order to protect the most vulnerable environments. The Government's view is that its control systems should ensure that after any development or use of land has ceased, land (and water resources) should be left in such a condition as to be capable of the agreed after use; pollution control and planning regimes are seen as complementary means of reaching these

---

[4] Town and Country Planning Act 1990, ss.123(A), 31(2) and (3) and 36(2) and (3), in each case substituted by the Planning and Compensation Act 1991.
[5] PPG 12, "Development Plans," para. 5.9 and s.6.
[6] PPG 12, para 5.54.
[7] Draft PPG: "Planning and Pollution Control," (March 1993), para. 2.13.
[8] Department of Environment, "Planning, Pollution and Waste Management" (Environmental Resources Limited and Oxford Polytechnic School of Planning, HMSO, 1992) para. B7.7.
[9] See Chap. 8, Annex.
[10] Draft PPG: "Planning and Pollution Control," (March 1993) para. 1.10, citing the 1990 White Paper, "This Common Inheritance", Cm. 1200.

objectives.[11] The Government's approach is a precautionary one which applies particularly where there are good grounds for judging either that action taken promptly at comparatively low cost may avoid more costly damage later, or that irreversible effects may follow if action is delayed:[12] this approach may be particularly applicable in avoiding potentially serious problems of soil or groundwater contamination.

The Government sees the development control system as having an important role to play in determining the location of development which may give rise to pollution. The potential for pollution, where it affects the use of land, will be a material consideration to be taken into account in deciding whether to grant planning permission for it; similar considerations may arise in deciding whether to take enforcement action against existing unauthorised development.[13]

Whether the concerns about potential pollution are so serious as to make the development unacceptable in principle is a matter for the planning authority: despite concerns about potential releases, they may be satisfied that planning permission can be granted where it will fall to the pollution control authority to take potential releases into account in considering the application for any authorisation or licence. Alternatively, they may conclude that the wider impact of potential releases on the development and use of land is unacceptable in all circumstances, despite the grant or potential grant of a pollution control authorisation or licence.[14]

It is clear in principle that a planning authority must have regard to the controls to be exerted by other authorities over a polluting activity; pollution implications of proposed development should not be ignored but nor should the planning authority ignore the existing systems of control to deal with those possible impacts.[15] It may be that the decision maker is satisfied that residual difficulties or uncertainties apparent at the planning stage are capable of being overcome by other means of control, or at the other extreme evidence of problems may be so damning that any reasonable person would refuse planning permission: between those extremes is a spectrum of situations which call for the exercise of planning judgement.[15a]

Apart from policy, planning authorities (together with other "competent authorities") are placed under specific statutory duties in relation

[11] *Ibid.*, para. 1.11.
[12] *Ibid.*, para. 1.12.
[13] *Ibid.*, para. 1.30.
[14] *Ibid.*, para. 1.35.
[15] *Gateshead Metropolitan Borough Council* v. *Secretary of State for the Environment and Northumbria Water Group plc* [1994] J.P.L. 255 (upheld by the Court of Appeal, May 1994); see also T. Kitson and R. Harris [1994] J.P.L. 3.
[15a] *Ibid.*, p. 262.

(inter alia) to the determination of planning applications and appeals, to discharge their functions so far as they relate to the recovery or disposal of waste, with the following "relevant objectives":[15b]

    (a) ensuring that waste is disposed of without endangering human health and without using processes or methods which could harm the environment and in particular without:
        (i) risk to water, air, soil, plants or animals; or
        (ii) causing nuisance through noise or odours; or
        (iii) adversely affecting the countryside or places of special interest; and
    (b) implementing, so far as material, any plan made under the plan-making provisions (*i.e.* a waste plan under section 50 of the Environment Protection Act 1990[15c] or a development plan under the Town and Country Planning Act 1990).

These duties are intended to implement the requirements of the Directive 91/156/EEC (the waste framework directive).[15d] However, nothing in these duties requires a planning authority to deal with any matter which the relevant pollution control authority has power to deal with:[15e] thus leaving the relationship between planning and pollution control powers much as it was before.

Planning conditions and obligations

5.06   The imposition of planning conditions is one of the most controversial areas in terms of relationship between planning and pollution control; as the Government points out in its draft PPG on planning and pollution control, the increasing scope and the effectiveness of pollution control regulations is reducing the need to use planning conditions or obligations to control the polluting aspects of a development which is subject to statutory regulation by a pollution control authority.[16] Planning authorities should not seek to control through planning measures matters which are the proper concern of the pollution control authority, except where planning interests can be clearly distinguished.[17]

[15b] Waste Management Licensing Regulations S.I. 1994 No. 1056, Sched. 4, paras. 2–4.
[15c] See para. 5.09. Other more strategic objectives also apply, including an adequate network of installations for waste disposal, self sufficiency, proximity, waste reduction and waste recovery.
[15d] Para. 5.40 below.
[15e] 1994 Regulations, Sched. 4, para. 2(2).
[16] Para. 3.23.
[17] Para. 3.24. See also the explanation of "relevant duties" of planning authorities under the Waste Management Licensing Regulations 1994: para. 5.05 above.

However, it may not be clear in all cases that there are adequate pollution control mechanisms to prevent soil becoming contaminated, for example where the process in question is not subject to integrated pollution control or does not involve the deposit, keeping, treatment or disposal of controlled waste.[18] In such circumstances it may be appropriate for a planning authority to impose conditions as to precautionary works and preventive measures in order to avoid soil contamination occurring: it is certainly the case that a planning authority may make use of its longer term planning powers to ensure decontamination of soil or the removal of chemicals and, where appropriate, reinstatement of land to the standards required for the agreed after use.[19]

In its consultation paper of February 7, 1992, "Proposals to Prevent Land Becoming Derelict, the Government put forward a proposal for the extended use of restoration conditions in planning consents. The consultation paper points out that such conditions have been comprehensively applied in the minerals industry for 15 to 20 years and have been effective in preventing many worked out mineral sites from becoming derelict:[20] non-mineral developments have not been subject to such conditions because, unlike minerals, such developments have been regarded as "permanent" or it has been assumed the market would ensure the recycling of such land.[21] However, as the Derelict Land Survey demonstrates, this assumption has not always been justified in relation to industrial development, which has led to the need for reclamation by local authorities using derelict land grant resources.[22]

The Government suggested that one way to reduce this call on DLG resources would be to build on the current experience of the mineral planning system and to advise planning authorities to extend the use of restoration and conditions where new planning consents are granted: the benefits of such an approach would accrue only very gradually, and the standard of reclamation laid down in such conditions would need careful consideration.[23] In general, the Government's view was that land previously used for development should be reclaimed to a standard which enables it to be returned to a similar use, including the treatment of any contamination: however, the Government recognised that this could prove a considerable cost deterrent to industrial development and comments were invited as to the appropriate standard of reclamation.[24]

Comments were also invited as to targeting of the industries to which such restoration conditions should apply: the Government's view as

[18] See paras. 5.11 and 5.18.
[19] Para. 3.25.
[20] See MPG7, "The Reclamation of Mineral Workings."
[21] Para. 8.
[22] Para. 9.
[23] Paras. 10–13.8.
[24] Para. 14.9.

expressed in the consultation paper was that commercial development or light industry would not be an appropriate target for such conditions, which should be directed rather at purpose built major industrial developments such as refineries, chemical plants and heavy engineering plants.[25] The paper acknowledged that there could be problems with enforcement, particularly if the owner could not be identified or faced financial difficulties: bank guarantees, sinking funds or bonding arrangements were suggested as appropriate for discussion as a possible means of meeting these problems.[26]

Use of planning powers under section 215 of the Town and Country Planning Act 1990

5.07   In the same consultation paper referred to in the preceding paragraph, the use of extended powers under section 215 of the Town and Country Planning Act was suggested as a means of combating industrial dereliction. This issue is considered in the chapter on liability for contaminated land.[27]

Planning and waste disposal

5.08   Section 55(3) of the Town and Country Planning Act 1990 declares for the avoidance of doubt that for the purposes of the definition of "development" the deposit of refuse or waste material involves a material change of use, notwithstanding that the land is comprised in a site already used for that purpose, if:

(i) the superficial area of the deposit is extended, or
(ii) the height of the deposit is extended and exceeds the level of the land adjoining the site.

This wording has given rise to certain difficulties in interpretation, but it should be noted that the definition is expressed to be only for the purposes of section 55 and "for the avoidance of doubt". It is therefore relevant, for the avoidance of doubt, in considering whether "development" has taken place. Clearly, certain activities involving the deposit of waste could be categorized either as a material change in the use of land, or as engineering or other operational development. In *Bilboe* v. *Secretary*

---

[25] Para. 15.10.
[26] Para. 18. For an analysis of the effectiveness of such mechanisms, see Department of the Environment "Review of the Effectiveness of Restoration Conditions for Mineral Workings and the Need for Bonds" (HMSO, 1993).
[27] See para. 2.77.

of State for the Environment[28] the Court of Appeal made clear that in the context of waste the operational and change of use limbs are mutually exclusive and that section 55(3)(*b*) (then section 22(3)(*b*)) makes it clear that the deposit is waste if to be equated to a change of use rather than operations.[29]

Waste occurs as an expression in various contexts in the General Development Order 1988. For example, at Schedule 2, Part 6 of the General Development in the context of permitted development for agricultural operations, the GDO does not allow development involving the depositing of waste materials on agricultural land where the waste materials are brought onto the land from elsewhere (subject to certain specified exceptions). This condition was introduced to 1985 to overcome the problems being experienced in practice by many local planning authorities in relation to the deposit of waste on agricultural land. In interpreting this condition the question may arise as to whether the tipped materials are in fact waste: surplus excavated material may well be regarded as waste in the hands of the builder or other person from whom it originated, regardless of its potential agricultural value as material for raising land.[30]

The issue of the deposit of waste material also arises in Part 8 of Schedule 2 to The GPO. Class D of this Part permits:

> "The deposit of waste material resulting from an industrial process on any land comprised in the site which was used for that purpose on July 1, 1948 whether or not the superficial area or the height of the deposit is extended as a result."

Under both the Control of Pollution Act 1974[31] and the Environmental Protection Act 1990[32] the existence of planning permission, or at least the appropriate established or lawful use rights, is a fundamental prerequisite to the grant of a waste site licence; indeed, the effect of such permission or rights is to restrict the grounds upon which the waste licence can then be refused.[33]

---

[28] (1978) 39 P. & C.R. 495.
[29] Query, however, whether the wording of the subsection in fact justifies such a sweeping decision.
[30] See the planning appeal decisions at [1988] J.P.L. 663 and [1989] J.P.L. 379 and 878.
[31] See para. 5.20.
[32] See para. 5.23.
[33] The grounds of such rejection are however much wider under the Environmental Protection Act than under the Control of Pollution Act 1974: see para. 5.27.

191

Waste policies and development plans

5.09   Topics to be covered by structure plans will include major industrial developments and waste treatment and disposal facilities: they should include strategic waste policies to ensure that detailed waste local plans provide for facilities and arrangements to meet the estimated need over the plan period, reflecting the trend towards larger, higher standard sites able to fulfil a more strategic role and taking account of availability of areas for industrial use which may be suitable for waste incineration.[34] In particular, such plans may show broad areas of search for sites that are appropriate for waste disposal by landfill, having regard to existing provision and future needs, as well as to access, geology, hydrogeology and other relevant factors; they may also set out criteria for the acceptability of sites.[35]

Section 38 of the Town and Country Planning Act 1990 (as substituted by Schedule 4, paragraph 17 of the Planning and Compensation Act 1991) contains provisions relating to "waste policies". These are defined as detailed policies in respect of development which involves the depositing of refuse or waste materials other than mineral waste. Section 38(2) requires local planning authorities either to prepare a waste local plan for their area or to include their waste policies in the minerals local plan. "Waste local plan" means a plan which contains waste policies as defined above. The obligation does not apply to "excluded authorities": those which are an authority for a National Park or for an area where waste policies are not a county matter. By section 38(4) the local planning authority for a National Park must either prepare a waste local plan for its area or include waste policies in its minerals local plan or its general local plan for the National Park. In formulating waste policies, the local planning authority must have regard to any waste disposal plan for its area made under section 50 of the Environmental Protection Act 1990.[36]

Government advice suggests that waste plans and policies should provide the requisite development plan framework for deciding applications for development associated with the deposit, treatment, storage, processing and disposal of refuse or waste materials.[37] The waste disposal plan prepared under the Enironmental Protection Act and the waste policies of local planning authority are intended to be complementary: the waste disposal plan considers the types and quantities of waste arising in the area, the availability of disposal facilities and the need for

---

[34] Draft PPG: "Planning and Pollution," paras. 2.10 and 2.11.

[35] *Ibid.*, para. 2.11.

[36] The Town and Country Planning (Development Plans) Regulations 1991 No. 2794, reg. 9(2).

[37] PPG 12, para. 3.13: complete coverage is required within five years from 1992.

further provisions, whilst the waste local plan addresses the land use implications of waste policies, such as suitable locations and the planning criteria likely to apply.[38]

As well as taking account of the waste disposal plan and any strategic policies in regional guidance and structure plans, the local waste policies should also take account of:[39]

- the principle of regional self-sufficiency in waste disposal;
- the need to minimise the impact of transport requirements on the road system;
- any relevant policies of waste minimisation and recycling;
- opportunities afforded by waste incineration to reduce the land-take demands and transport requirements imposed by landfilling;
- opportunities afforded for energy recovery;
- the existence of relevant waste management and pollution control systems;
- the various treatment methods, including recycling, required prior to disposal.

There is also a statutory requirement to have as objectives the establishment of an adequate and integrated network of waste disposal installations, the promotion of Community and national self-sufficiency in waste disposal, the disposal of waste in one of the nearest appropriate installations (proximity), and encouraging the prevention or reduction of waste and waste recovery.[39a]

The plan should identify broad areas of search which are likely to contain sites for whatever method of recycling, treatment or disposal is required to meet demand in the plan period, as well as areas which are judged inappropriate for such sites, having regard to environmental, geological, hydrogeological and access constraints. Criteria should also be included against which applications for waste management developments will be considered, for example in terms of land suitability, impact on adjoining land use, aftercare and site restoration requirements.[40]

Planning conditions or obligations and waste disposal

The legitimate boundary between planning conditions and waste site licensing conditions remains difficult in practice.[41] **5.10**

---

[38] *Ibid.*, para. 3.14.
[39] Draft PPG: "Planning and Pollution," para. 2.20.
[39a] Waste Management Licensing Regulations 1994 (S.I. 1994 No. 1056), Sched. 4, paras. 2 and 4(2) and (3): seee also para. 5.05 above.
[40] *Ibid.*
[41] See para. 5.06.

The traditional approach is that planning conditions should not duplicate or conflict with other requirements, but can be used to provide control where licence conditions cannot, for example aftercare.[42] This approach is given expression in the draft PPG: "Planning and Pollution", where it is stated that where planning permission is given for landfill (including land raising) sites, local planning authorities may in particular wish to impose conditions or obligations, as appropriate, on matters including:[43]

- the area to be filled;
- the timescale of operation and any phasing for land use purposes;
- the general nature of the waste accepted or excluded (but not to the level of detail appropriate to the waste disposal licence);
- removal and preservation of topsoil and subsoil and their replacement at the restoration stage;
- standards for minimum depths of soil materials at restoration;
- a requirement to ensure that the final soil cover material is free of obstructions to cultivation and plant growth;
- specification of final contours and allowance for settlement;
- "aftercare" management of the land for a maximum of five years following restoration. This will cover matters such as drainage, monitoring groundwater quality, pre-planning cultivation, fertilizer application, sowing or planting and management of vegetation;
- the restoration of the site, where development has stopped before completion, or a licence has been revoked.

The legitimate scope of planning conditions for aftercare and restoration of sites may need some reconsideration, given the increased scope under Part II of the Environmental Protection Act 1990 for waste regulation authorities to deal with such matters under site licence conditions.[44] The draft PPG on "Planning and Pollution" points out that as a result of the introduction of such controls, there should be little need for planning permissions to make provision for monitoring and control of the site by the operator after landfill operations have ceased: however, until these new provisions are brought into force, it may be necessary for planning authorities to use planning conditions or obligations for such a purpose, where appropriate.[45]

Also, planning authorities should seek to ensure, as far as possible, that restoration and planning conditions do not affect or restrict the use

[42] Circ. 1/85, para. 19; Waste Management Paper 4, para. 3.7.
[43] Para. 5.7.
[44] See para. 5.23 *et seq.*
[45] Para. 5.9.

of pollution control measures that may be required on landfill sites, such as methane emission limitation measures: consultation between the relevant authorities will be necessary to ensure that such measures do not unnecessarily prevent the effective restoration of the site to its intended afteruse.[46]

Issues of soil and groundwater contamination often feature heavily in planning appeals concerning waste facilities, not only landfill sites but also incinerators and other forms of waste treatment facility.[47] A good example is provided by a planning appeal concerning the waste incineration plant operated by Berridges at Wigwam Lane, Hucknall, Nottinghamshire.[48]

On the appeal, detailed conditions were imposed by the inspector, and endorsed by the Secretary of State, including conditions as to drilling bore holes for the inspection of concrete floors, bunding, taking and analysis of soil samples to ascertain the presence of chemical contamination, the formulation of a detailed scheme for removal or treatment of any contamination, regrading of the site, the submission of a detailed scheme for the construction of impervious concrete surfaces, drainage channels, containment and discharge facilities (including a fail-safe drainage channel around the working area) to supplement the normal draining encatchment provisions, submission of a plan indicating the relevant operational and storage areas for approval by the planning authority, and restoration of the site in the event of cessation of the use.[49]

INTEGRATED POLLUTION CONTROL

IPC generally

Part I of the Environmental Protection Act 1990 introduced the **5.11** system of integrated pollution control. The objective of the system is the protection of the environment—defined as comprising air, water and land[50]—from harm caused by the release of substances. IPC can therefore be used to minimise the contamination of land and groundwater. It is not possible here to provide a detailed analysis of IPC and reference should be made to other works on this issue.[51]

---

[46] Para. 5.8.
[47] "Department of Environment, Planning, Pollution and Waste Management" (Environmental Resources Limited and Oxford Polytechnic School of Planning, HMSO, 1992) ss.C3 and C6.
[48] Appeal ref. APP/M3000/A/87/072007, June 29, 1989.
[49] These conditions were in addition to others designed to deal with emissions.
[50] Environmental Protection Act 1990, s.1(2).
[51] See S. Tromans, "Environmental Protection Act 1990: Text and Commentary" (Sweet & Maxwell, 2nd edn., 1993).

The need for authorisation

5.12   The mechanism through which IPC works is the requirement for an authorisation granted by the relevant enforcing authority in order to carry on a prescribed process.[52] The processes prescribed for control, a number of which have significant potential for soil contamination, are detailed in the Environmental Protection (Prescribed Processes and Substances) Regulations 1991 as amended.[53] Currently they are:

Chapter 1: Fuel Production Processes, Combustion Processes (including Power Generation)
  Section 1.1—Gasification and associated processes
  Section 1.2—Carbonisation and associated processes
  Section 1.3—Combustion processes
  Section 1.4—Petroleum processes

Chapter 2: Metal Production and Processing
  Section 2.1—Iron and Steel
  Section 2.2—Non-ferrous metals
  Section 2.3—Smelting processes

Chapter 3: Minerals Industry
  Section 3.1—Cement and lime manufacture and associated processes
  Section 3.2—Processes involving asbestos
  Section 3.3—Other mineral fibres
  Section 3.4—Other mineral processes
  Section 3.5—Glass manufacture and production
  Section 3.6—Ceramic production

Chapter 4: The Chemical Industry
  Section 4.1—Petrochemical processes
  Section 4.2—The manufacture and use of organic chemicals
  Section 4.3—Acid processes
  Section 4.4—Processes involving halogens
  Section 4.5—Inorganic chemical processes

---

[52] S.6(1). The relevant authority in England and Wales is HM Inspectorate of Pollution (s.1(7)) and, in Scotland, HM Industrial Pollutions Inspectorate or the river purification authority (s.1(8)).

[53] S.I. 1991 No. 614, as amended by S.I. 1991 No. 836; S.I. 1992 No. 614 and S.I. 1993 No. 2405. The Regulations also make provision as to the date from which IPC applies to new and existing processes (Sched. 3). A consultation paper on review of the categories of prescribed processes was published by the Department of Environment in March 1993 and further amendments reflecting the outcome of that consultation exercise have been made by S.I. 1994 Nos. 1271 and 1329.

Section 4.6—Chemical fertiliser production
Section 4.7—Pesticide production
Section 4.8—Pharmaceutical production
Section 4.9—The storage of chemicals in bulk

Chapter 5: Waste Disposal and Recycling
Section 5.1—Incineration
Section 5.2—Recovery processes
Section 5.3—The production of fuel from waste

Chapter 6: Other Industries
Section 6.1—Paper and pulp manufacturing processes
Section 6.2—Di-isocyanate processes
Section 6.3—Tar and bitumen processes
Section 6.4—Processes involving uranium
Section 6.5—Coating processes and printing
Section 6.6—The manufacture of dyestuffs, printing ink and coating materials
Section 6.7—Timber processes
Section 6.8—Processes involving rubber
Section 6.9—The treatment and processing of animal or vegetable matter

Objectives of authorisations

5.13 Authorisations for the carrying on of a prescribed process must contain such conditions as the enforcing authority considers appropriate for achieving a number of objectives specified at section 7(2) of the Act. These include:

(a) the use of best available techniques not entailing excessive cost (BATNEEC)[54] for preventing the release of substances prescribed for any environmental medium into that medium or, where that is not practicable by such means, for reducing the release of such substances to a minimum and for rendering harmless any such substances which are so released;

(b) the use of BATNEEC for rendering harmless any other substances which might cause harm if released to any environmental medium[55];

---

[54] As to the interpretation of BATNEEC, see subs. 7(10) and (11); "Integrated Pollution Control: A Practical Guide" (DoE and Welsh Office, 1993) s.7; and the various process Guidance Notes issued by the Chief Inspector as to the techniques and options available to be employed.

[55] "Harm" is defined by s.1(4) to mean harm to the health of living organisms or other interference with the ecological systems of which they form part and, in the case of man, is to include offence caused to any of his senses or harm to his property.

197

(c) compliance with any prescribed statutory limits, requirements, quality standards or quality objectives; and

(d) where the process is likely to involve the release of substances into more than one environmental medium, the use of BAT-NEEC for minimising the pollution which may be caused to the environment taken as a whole by the releases, having regard to the best practicable environmental option available in respect of the substances which may be realeased.[56]

In addition to such specific conditions, there is implied into every authorisation by virtue of section 7(4) a general condition requiring the use of BATNEEC:

(a) for preventing the release of prescribed substances to the relevant environmental medium or, where that is not practicable by such means, for reducing the release of such substances to a minimum and for rendering harmless any such substances which are so released; and

(b) for rendering harmless any other substances which might cause harm if released into any environmental medium.

The relationship of IPC to soil contamination

5.14   Since IPC is concerned with minimising pollution to the environment as a whole, it is certainly a relevant means of seeking to control and minimise the contamination of soil which may be caused by prescribed processes. What it cannot do is to regulate the final disposal of controlled waste by deposit in or on land,[57] which is dealt with by Part II of the Environmental Protection Act. Subject to that constraint, IPC will be concerned with releases to land or groundwater of any potentially harmful substances, and particularly with prescribed substances. In relation to land, "release" includes any deposit, keeping or disposal of the substance in or on land,[58] In relation to water, it includes any entry into water[59] and any release into groundwater is such a release.[60] "Groundwater" is defined widely to mean any waters contained in any underground strata or in a well, adit or borehole sunk into underground strata.[61]

The substances prescribed[62] for release to water are:

[56] S.7(7).
[57] S.28(1).
[58] S.1(10)(c).
[59] S.1(10)(b).
[60] S.1(11)(a)(iii).
[61] S.1(12).
[62] Environmental Protection (Prescribed Processes and Prescribed Substances) Regulations 1991 (S.I. 1991 No. 472), as amended, Sched. 5.

(1) mercury and its compounds;

(2) cadmium and its compounds;

(3) all isomers of hexachlorocyclohexane;

(4) all isomers of DDT;

(5) pentachlorophenol and its compounds;

(6) hexachlorobenzene;

(7) hexachlorobutadiene;

(8) aldrin;

(9) dieldrin;

(10) endrin;

(11) polychlorinated biphenyls;

(12) dichlorvos;

(13) 1, 2-dichloroethane;

(14) all isomers of trichlorobenzene;

(15) atrazine;

(16) simazine;

(17) tributyltin compounds;

(18) triphenyltin compounds;

(19) trifluralin;

(20) fenitrothion;

(21) azinphos-methyl;

(22) malalthion; and

(23) endosulfan.

The substances prescribed[63] for release into land are:

(1) organic solvents;

(2) azides;

(3) halogens and their covalent compounds;

(4) metal carbonyls;

(5) organo-metallic compounds;

(6) oxidising agents;

(7) polychlorinated dibenzofuran and any congener thereof;

(8) polychlorinated dibenzo-p-dioxin and any congener thereof;

(9) polyhalogenated biphenyls, terphenyls and naphthalenes;

(10) phosphorus;

(11) pesticides (defined as chemical substances or preparations used for various purposes related to pest control); and

(12) alkali metals and their oxides and alkaline earth metals and their oxides.

IPC will therefore be used to ensure that wastes for disposal to land are produced in such a form as to minimise the likely polluting effects. Further, the general concept of "good housekeeping" inherent in the use

---

[63] *Ibid.*, Sched. 6.

of BATNEEC means that steps should be taken to avoid and minimise the consequences of spills; a number of the Chief Inspector's process guidance notes refer to issues such as the loading and unloading of vehicles in designated areas, contingency plans, site design and validated emergency procedures to cover spillages or leakages on site.

A good example of the relevance of IPC to soil contamination is provided by the IPC authorisation granted to Rechem International Limited in respect of their high-temperature incinerator at Pontypool, Gwent.[64] Conditions on this authorisation include the following:

(1) By a given date (September 1, 1993) the operator shall have begun an ongoing environmental monitoring programme, acceptable to the Chief Inspector, for the assessment of the impact of the Company's operations on levels of PCBs, PCDDs/PCDFs and heavy metals in local soils and herbage;

(2) By a given date (October 1, 1993) the operator shall have produced a detailed report of PCBs and PCDDs/PCDFs contamination of all site soil areas, to include proposals acceptable to the Chief Inspector for the treatment of areas of the site to minimise migration of PCBs and PCDDs/PCDFs to air or to controlled waters;

(3) Operational requirements relating to bunding, impermeable site surfaces, drainage channels routed to a sump or holding tank, and treatment or incineration of contaminated surface water.

It should, however, be remembered that conditions on IPC authorisations are subject to two important limitations. First, they are concerned with preventing or rendering harmless emissions from the prescribed process: they cannot therefore be used to require clean-up of historic contamination caused by unrelated processes. Secondly, the conditions are linked to the "carrying on" of the process both in their imposition[65] and enforcement.[66] It will not therefore be possible to use IPC conditions as a means of imposing clean up requirements when a prescribed process has ceased to operate.

Air pollution control

5.15   It should be mentioned, for the sake of completeness, that Part I of the Environmental Protection Act 1990 creates a parallel system of air pollution control, administered by local authorities. The objective of this

[64] Ref. No. AG7946, July 16, 1993.
[65] Ss.7(2)(a) and 7(4).
[66] Ss.6(1), 13(1) and 14(1).

system is to prevent or minimise pollution of the environment due to the release of substances into the air (but not into any other environmental medium).[67] Whilst the applicability of the system to soil contamination is thereby limited, it is not completely ousted in that its functions are not limited to controlling pollution of the air: they could be used in relation to pollution of soil caused by the deposition of substances originally released into the air.

Chemical release inventory

The Government proposes to institute an annual inventory of releases **5.16** from industrial processes of polluting substances. A consultation paper on the proposal was issued in November 1992.[68] The consultation paper suggests that the US Environmental Protection Agency's Toxics Release Inventory shows that annual aggregation of releases of polluting substances from major sources can help regulatory bodies to identify and target environmental "blackspots" as well as providing industry and the general public with useful information.[69] The proposal would be linked to the IPC system and would be complementary to the public registers kept under that régime.[70] Thus one component would be the release of substances to land.

EC proposals for integrated pollution control

The Commission has presented a proposal for a directive on integ- **5.17** rated pollution prevention and control.[71] The proposal has many features which are familiar from the UK system of IPC; like that system the objective is to prevent where practicable emissions from prescribed installations or to minimise them, so as to achieve a high level of protection for the environment as a whole.[72] "Emission" is defined to include the deposit, disposal or storage of substances in or on land which may contribute to or cause pollution[73]; unlike IPC in the UK there appears to be no restriction on conditions dealing with the final disposal of waste by deposit on land. Furthermore, unlike IPC it is an express requirement that the permit shall contain conditions to the effect that,

[67] S.4(3).
[68] Department of Environment: "Proposed Chemical Release Inventory," November 26, 1992.
[69] Para. 9.
[70] Para. 12.
[71] O.J. C311/6, 17.11.93, Com (93) 423 final.
[72] Art. 1.
[73] Art. 2.

when the installation has permanently ceased operation, all measures shall be taken in order to ensure that no harm to the environment occurs:[74] as already explained, such conditions are not possible on IPC authorisations in the UK.[75] The present proposal lists the most important polluting substances and preparations;[76] these must be the subject of emission limit values.[77] For land, the proposed list simply refers to wastes identified as hazardous under Directive 91/689/EEC.[78]

WASTE MANAGEMENT LAW

Generally

5.18   Control over where waste is deposited, how and by whom, is a fundamental component of preventing the contamination of land with all its attendant problems. The issue of contaminated land formed part of the enquiry by the House of Commons Environment Committee which led to its report, "Toxic Waste":[79] the report scathingly condemned the minimalist and laissez-faire attitudes surrounding the issue of waste disposal in the UK and concluded with the recommendation that the Department of Environment should pay more attention to the problem of contaminated land, particularly with regard to environmental protection, public health and safety.[80] The report is by no means the only one to have been critical of waste disposal policy and practice over the past 20 years.[81]

It is not the intention of this chapter to provide a comprehensive analysis of waste disposal law—reference can be made to other works for

---

[74] Art. 8.4.
[75] See para. 5.14.
[76] Annex III.
[77] Art. 8.2.
[78] See para. 5.40.
[79] Session 1988–89, 2nd Report, H.C. 22–I, II and III.
[80] *Ibid.*, para. 273.
[81] See also: House of Lords Select Committee on Science and Technology, First Report, Session 1980–81, "Hazardous Waste Disposal," H.L. 273–I and II (July 1981); Royal Commission on Environmental Pollution, 11th Report, "Managing Waste: The Duty of Care" (Cmnd. 9675, December 1985); DoE, DoE (Northern Ireland), Welsh Office and Scottish Office, Hazardous Waste Inspectorate Reports 1–3—First Report, "Hazardous Waste Management: an Overview" (June 1985), Second Report, "Hazardous Waste Management: Ramshackle and Antediluvian?" (July 1986), 3rd Report (June 1988); House of Commons Environment Committee, Session 1990–91, Seventh Report, "The E.C. Draft Directive on the Landfill of Waste," H.C. 263 I and II (July 1991).

this.[82] However, an awareness of the way in which waste disposal law has evolved is essential to the understanding of contaminated land problems. Whilst there was some early local legislation which regulated waste disposal,[83] national legislation truly began with the Deposit of Poisonous Waste Act 1972. The legislative history since then falls into three stages:

(1) the Deposit of Poisonous Waste Act 1972;
(2) the more comprehensive system of waste disposal licensing introduced by Part I of the Control of Pollution Act 1974; and
(3) the system of waste management licensing under the Environmental Protection Act 1990, Part II.

For the purpose of investigating and assessing historically contaminated land it is important to be aware of that history.

The Deposit of Poisonous Waste Act 1972

Prior to the enactment of this legislation, there was no general control **5.19** over the deposit of poisonous, noxious or potentially polluting waste. Control over new sites could be achieved through the planning system to an extent, though many sites enjoyed the benefit of lawful or established use rights. The question of what wastes were suitable for disposal on a site, whether they should be segregated from other wastes, and what (if any) special precautions should be taken in their disposal were matters for the best judgment of the site operator. The result of such lack of control was the existence of open dumps, such as the notorious Malkins Bank in Cheshire, used from the 19th century until 1932 as a salt and chemical works, and after that date for the indiscriminate tipping of toxic waste from a variety of industries covering some 15 hectares up to depths of 15 metres.[84]

However, what caught the attention of the public was the well-publicised discovery of cyanide waste dumped on open land in Nuneaton so as to present a gross and obvious threat to local children. Within a matter of months, the Deposit of Poisonous Waste Act 1972 received Royal Assent on March 30, 1972. The Act was of an emergency nature, never intended to be more than a stop-gap, and was replaced by the Control of Pollution Act 1974 and the Special Waste Regulations 1980 made under that Act.

---

[82] See J.H. Bates, *UK Waste Law* (1993); S.R. Tromans, *The Environmental Protection Act 1990: Text and Commentary* (2nd edn., 1993).

[83] The Essex County Council (Canvey Island Approaches, etc.) Act 1967 contained the requirement (s.46) for prior written consent to be obtained from the county council and the local authority before refuse was deposited.

[84] The site is graphically described by Professor Kenneth Mellanby in *Waste and Pollution: The Problem for Britain* (1992), pp. 56–7.

Section 1 of the Act, which came into force on March 30, 1972, made it an offence to deposit waste on land, or to cause or permit waste to be deposited, where the waste was "of a kind which is poisonous, noxious or polluting and its presence on land is liable to give rise to an environmental hazard." By subsection (3):

"The presence of waste on any land is to be treated as giving rise to an environmental hazard if the waste has been deposited in such a manner, or in such quantity (whether that quantity by itself or cumulatively with other deposits of the same or different substances) as to subject persons or animals to material risk of death, injury or impairment of health, or as to threaten the pollution or contamination (whether on the surface or underground) of any water supply; and where waste is deposited in containers, this shall not of itself be taken to exclude any risk which might be expected to arise if the waste were not in containers."

The degree of risk relevant for this purpose was to be assessed with particular regard to the measures, if any, taken by the depositor of the waste, or by the owner or occupier of the land, or by others for minimising the risk; and the likelihood of the waste or its container being tampered with by children or others.

By subsection (7) nothing done in accordance with the terms of any consent, licence or approval granted under an enactment was to be taken to be a breach of section 1; but planning permission was expressedly stated not to be sufficient authority for this purpose.

Section 3, which came into force on August 3, 1972, instituted a system of notification, requiring notices specifying various particulars to be given to the relevant authorities[85] before waste was removed from any premises with a view to being deposited elsewhere or before waste was deposited on land. The requirement applied to waste of any description (the word was not defined) whether solid, semi-solid or liquid, other than that specified in regulations by the Secretary of State as not being so poisonous, noxious or polluting that it need not be subject to the section.[86] The Deposit of Poisonous Waste (Notification of Removal or Deposit) Regulations 1972[87] provided two categories of exemption from the notification requirements: an unqualified exemption for certain specified types of waste[88] and a qualified exemption for waste of a prescribed description and deposited pursuant to certain types of statutory authority.[89] This "exclusive list" approach was criticised by the

[85] The local authority and river authority or river purification board: ss.3(5) and 7.
[86] Subs. 3(4).
[87] S.I. 1972 No. 1017.
[88] Ibid., reg. 3 and Sched.
[89] Ibid., reg. 4.

204

House of Lords Select Committee on Science and Technology in its 1981 Report on hazardous waste disposal as "being too wide ranging and sometimes imprecise."[90]

This policy of providing authorities with information as to the nature, quantities and location of hazardous waste deposits was continued by section 4 of the Act, which applied to the commercial operators of refuse tips and required the provision of information as to the location of the tip, the nature and chemical composition of the waste, the quantity deposited, and the name of the person who brought the waste to the tip and of their employer. Local authorities operating tips themselves were required to give notice of similar particulars to the river authority or river purification board.[91]

Whilst the Act was a considerable step forward, its scope was limited: its approach in recognising the significance of environmental hazards— especially groundwater pollution—as well as harm to human health was basically sound, but the definitional provisions were imprecise and were interpreted inconsistently by different authorities.[92]

The Control of Pollution Act 1974

Part I of the Control of Pollution Act 1974 replaced the Deposit of **5.20** Poisonous Waste Act 1972 by providing a more comprehensive system of controls over the disposal of "controlled waste."[93] In particular, it was made an offence to deposit controlled waste on land, or to use any plant or equipment for the purpose of disposing of controlled waste or of dealing in a prescribed manner[94] with controlled waste, unless the relevant land was occupied by the holder of a waste disposal licence and the deposit or use was in accordance with the licence conditions.[95] The key term "deposit" was not defined in the Act and has given rise to difficulties of interpretation, in particular as to whether temporary deposits of waste on land are within the term.[96] Greater penalties applied

[90] Session 1980–81, First Report, H.L. 273–I, para. 13.
[91] S.5(3).
[92] H.L. 273–I, n. 6 above, para. 10.
[93] See para. 5.21.
[94] See the Collection and Disposal of Waste Regulations 1988 (S.I. 1988 No. 819), reg. 8 and Sched. 5.
[95] S.3(1).
[96] See *Leigh Land Reclamation Ltd. and others* v. *Walsall Metropolitan Borough Council* [1992] 1 Env.L.R. 16; [1991] J.E.L. Vol. 3, No. 2, P. 281 which suggested that waste was "to be regarded as deposited when it is dumped on the site with no realistic prospect of further examination or inspection to reject goods of which deposit is not allowed under the licence." The decision presented obvious difficulties to waste disposal authorities in seeking to enforce the Act: see D.

to the deposit of waste which was poisonous, noxious and polluting, the presence of which on land was likely to give rise to an environmental hazard.[97]

Section 5 of the Act provided for the grant of waste disposal licences: in particular, where an application was received for a disposal licence for a use of land, plant or equipment for which planning permission was in force, the waste disposal authority was under a duty not to reject the application unless the authority was satisfied that its rejection was necessary "for the purpose of preventing pollution of water or danger to public health."[98]

By section 6 the licence could include such conditions as the authority thought fit to specify:[99] these could relate to such matters as:

(a) duration of the licence;
(b) supervision of activities by the licence-holder;
(c) the kinds and quantities of the waste allowed, the methods of dealing with them and the recording of information relating to them;
(d) the precautions to be taken on land to which the licence relates;
(e) the steps to be taken with a view to facilitating compliance with the conditions of the relevant planning permission;
(f) hours; and

Laurence "Wastes Management," May 1992, p. 13; S. Tromans [1991] J.E.L. Vol. 3, No. 2, p. 289. That view of "deposit" has since been disapproved by another decision of the Divisional Court, *R.* v. *Metropolitan Stipendiary Magistrate, ex p. London Waste Regulation Authority: Berkshire County Council* v. *Scott* [1993] J.E.L. Vol. 5, No. 2, p. 281. In this later case it was held that deposits of a temporary nature were within the ambit of section 3(1), which was not concerned only with final deposits or disposals: to hold otherwise would be an "unnecessary erosion of the efficacy of the Act."

[97] Ss.4(5) and 4(6); the definition being in the same terms as that of the Deposit of Poisonous Waste Act 1972, see para. 5.19 above.
[98] S.5(3); see *Berridge Incinerators* v. *Nottinghamshire County Council* (High Court, 1987; unreported but cited at para. 2.7 of Circ. 13/88).
[99] In appeals against conditions under s.10 of the Act, the Secretary of State has frequently expressed the view that, whilst high standards with regard to waste handling and disposal are a desirable objective, conditions should be reasonable in that: (a) they should reflect the nature and scale of operations on, and the circumstances of, the particular site; (b) they should afford adequate protection to local amenities from operations on the site; and (c) they should not impose an unreasonable burden on the operator. Waste Management Paper No. 4 on "The Licensing of Waste Facilities," HMIP, (revised 1988) contained general guidance on licence conditions and gives illustrative examples. Waste Management Paper 4 was re-issued in April 1994 to coincide with the entry into force of the new waste management licensing system under Part II of the Environmental Protection Act 1990.

(g) the works to be carried out, in connection with the land, plant or equipment, before the activities authorised were begun or while they were continuing.

By section 9, the authority was under a duty to take the steps needed:

(a) for the purpose of ensuring that the activities to which the licence relates do not cause pollution of water or damage to the public health or become seriously detrimental to the amenities of the locality affected by the activities; and

(b) for the purposes of ensuring that the conditions specified in the licence are complied with.

During the 20 years or so following enactment of the Control of Pollution Act, the risks presented by landfill without strict control of gas and leachate have become more fully perceived. This is reflected in the increased comprehensiveness and complexity of licence conditions. In 1977, for example, a licence relating to a landfill site for putrescible waste might typically have run to three or four pages with perhaps 25 conditions the majority of which would have been intended primarily to address local short-term problems of amenity,[1] such as mud on roads, the cover of obnoxious materials, prohibitions on burning, and control of vermin. The licence for a corresponding site in the 1990s will often exceed 70 pages in length with hundreds of conditions and sub-conditions, and with detailed requirements as to a working plan, monitoring leachate and gas, leachate and gas control measures, water balance records, and containment. The requirements as to containment will frequently be highly technical, dealing with phasing, cell construction, the use of clays and synthetic liners, capping, and materials testing (both before and after emplacement).

Definition of "controlled waste" and exemptions

5.21 The Control of Pollution Act 1974, unlike the Deposit of Poisonous Waste Act 1972, provided a definition of waste, as follows:[2]
"Waste" includes:

(a) any substance which constitutes a scrap material or an effluent or other unwanted substance arising from the application of any process; and

[1] In *Attorney General's Reference (No. 2 of 1988)* [1990] Q.B. 77, it was held that a condition prohibiting the creation of public nuisances of all kinds could not lawfully be imposed under s.6(2).
[2] S.30(1).

(b) any substance or article which requires to be disposed of as being broken, worn out, contaminated or otherwise spoiled,

... and for the purposes of this Part of this Act any thing which is discarded or otherwise dealt with as if it were waste shall be presumed to be waste unless the contrary is proved."

The courts gave a broad interpretation to this definition (which was repeated in the Environmental Protection Act 1990) so as to cover materials which may have a useful purpose or economic value but which the holder, for whatever reason, wishes to dispose of.[3]

"Controlled waste" was defined to mean "household, industrial or commercial waste or any such waste"[4]: these three categories being defined by section 30(3). It has been held that the words "or any such waste" do not have the effect of widening the concept of controlled waste beyond those three strict categories.[5] The main types of waste not covered by the definition are:

(a) radioactive waste;[6]
(b) explosives;[7]
(c) waste from any mine of quarry;[8] and
(d) waste from premises used for agriculture.[9]

The definitions were "fine-tuned" by the Collection and Disposal of Waste Regulations 1988[10] which specified types of waste to be treated as industrial and commercial waste.[11]

Also, Schedule 6 of the Regulations provided a number of exemptions, where waste could be deposited or disposed of without a licence.[12] These exemptions have now been replaced by new regulations to coincide with implementation of Part II of the Environmental Protection Act 1990.[13]

---

[3] See *Long* v. *Brooke* (1980) Crim.L.R. 109: *Berridge Incinerators* v. *Nottinghamshire County Council* (High Court, 1987, unreported but cited at DoE Cir. 13/88, para. 2.7); *Kent County Council* v. *Queenborough Rolling Mill Company* [1990] 2 L.M.E.L.R. 28. Compare the more recent guidance of the Government issued in 1994: see para. 5.24.

[4] S.30(1).

[5] *Thanet District Council* v. *Kent County Council*, Divisional Court, February 26, 1993, (seaweed held not to be controlled waste).

[6] S.30(5).

[7] S.30(1).

[8] S.30(3)(c)(ii).

[9] *Ibid.*

[10] S.I. 1988 No. 819.

[11] Reg. 6 and 7 and Scheds. 3 and 4; see also para. 5.24.

[12] Reg. 9 and Sched. 6; see also para. 5.25.

[13] See paras. 5.23 and 5.24.

Shortcomings of the Control of Pollution Act 1974

The system of waste licensing instituted by the Control of Pollution **5.22** Act suffered from a number of problems in preventing land becoming contaminated.[14] Chief among these were the following:

(a) the inability to exercise long term control over aftercare and monitoring, in that a licence could be surrendered unilaterally by the operator and conditions could not relate to activities after the deposit of waste had ceased.[15] This problem could only partially be overcome by the practice of seeking to impose planning conditions or planning agreements as to long term precautions;[16]

(b) case law established that there were difficulties in enforcing breaches of condition which were not related directly to a deposit of waste;[17]

(c) the controls and powers centred around the protection of public health, amenity and the protection of water resources,[18] rather than the protection of the environment generally or the prevention of contaminated land; and

(d) most seriously of all, waste disposal authorities were able to operate their own sites under a special procedure provided by section 11 by which the authority specified the conditions in a resolution, which it then monitored and "policed" itself. Whilst the strict terms of section 11 provided broadly equivalent controls to sites in private hands, in practice double standards applied in many cases, with lax procedures and controls being applied at many local authority sites: some of which were to present great problems in future years.

These problems were coupled with a prevalent philosophy during the 1970s and much of the 1980s that "dilute and disperse" or "attenuate and disperse" was an acceptable means of utilising the environment's putative capacity to degrade and disperse waste. The result has been, in some cases, serious problems of contaminated soil and ground-

---

[14] See Nicola Atkinson [1991] J.E.L. Vol. 3, No. 2, p. 256.
[15] See s.6(2).
[16] See *e.g.*, Waste Management Paper No. 4, "The Licensing of Waste Facilities," paras. 3.7, 3.8, 3.10.
[17] *Leigh Land Reclamation Ltd. and others* v. *Walsall Metropolitan Borough Council* [1991] 1 Env.L.R. 16; [1991] J.E.L. Vol. 3, No. 2, p. 281. s.6(3), which provides a power to specify conditions the breach of which would be of itself an offence, was never used by the Government for that purpose.
[18] S.5(3), 9(1).

water, uncontrolled leachate, and persistent problems of gas generation. These problems are frequently of a long term nature, arising only after closure of sites: the House of Lords Select Committee on Science and Technology in its 1981 Report on hazardous waste disposal referred to landfill as follows:[19]

> "Well-executed landfill is acceptable. But it is a low technology process which relies on natural degradation and attenuation, and the only way of proving its safety, or rather proving that the level of risk is tolerable since there can be no absolute guarantee of safety, is by constant vigilance, to check that no pollution has happened. At the same time the scope for abuse is considerable, whether through ignorance, negligence, wilful short-cuts or accidents."

More directly, the Report concluded:[20]

> ". . . the waste disposal industry has sometimes been skating on thin ice."

Having said that, it still probably remains the case that the really grave cases of landfill pollution generally concern deposits which predate the Deposit of Poisonous Waste Act 1972.[21] Nor does the more recent trend towards containment landfills on the continental model with impermeable clay and synthetic liners necessary avoid all problems for the future: containment brings with it potential attendant problems of leachate build-up, and there are serious doubts about the long term integrity of synthetic liners.[22]

The Environmental Protection Act 1990, Part II

5.23   The Environmental Protection Act introduced a new scheme of waste management licensing intended to remedy some of the perceived deficiencies of the site licensing system under the Control of Pollution Act. Part II of the 1990 Act[23] creates a system of waste management licensing: as with the C.O.P.A. system this refers to the concept of "controlled waste", but has introduced the concept of "directive waste" with important changes to the approach to defining waste.[23] Also there are important differences in detail as to the scope of the two systems:

---

[19] Session 1980–81, First Report, H.L. 273–I, para. 129.
[20] *Ibid.*, para. 185.8.
[21] *Ibid.*, para. 122.
[22] See *e.g.*, "Doubts over Containment Cloud the Future for Landfill," *The Surveyor*, May 27, 1993, p. 4.
[23] See para. 5.24.
[23] See para. 5.24.

(1) the 1990 Act applies not only to the deposit and disposal of controlled waste, but also to its treatment and keeping;[24]

(2) the 1990 Act contains an important additional restriction on treating, keeping or disposing of controlled waste in a manner likely to cause pollution of the environment or harm to human health[25]—this applies irrespective of whether a site licence is in force;

(3) the old distinction between controlled waste and controlled waste liable to give rise to an environmental hazard is discontinued, though offences relating to special waste carry a higher tariff of penalties;[26]

(4) waste disposal authorities are replaced by waste regulation authorities and waste disposal authorities, each with different responsibilities;[27] thus ending the "poacher and gamekeeper" problem—waste disposal authorities may in any event no longer operate active disposal sites themselves but must do so either by way of contract with a private sector contractor or through the medium of an arm's length company;[28]

(5) the criteria for site licensing are widened to include the prevention of pollution of the environment and harm to human health;[29]

(6) conditions on this licence may extend to activities to be carried out after the deposit of waste or other authorised activities have ceased;[30]

(7) such conditions are capable of enforcement *per se*, it being a separate offence to contravene a condition;[31]

(8) a new requirement is imposed that the holder of the licence be a "fit and proper person";[32] and

(9) more stringent requirements are imposed as to the surrender of licences.[33]

---

[24] S.33(1)(b). As a result of amendments made by the Waste Management Licensing Regulations 1994, it now also covers those operations listed in Parts III and IV of Schedule 4 to the Regulations (Sched. 4, paras. 9(3)–(5). These are waste disposal operations and waste recovery operations as listed in Annexes IIA and IIB of the waste framework directive 91/156/EEC.

[25] S.33(1)(c): the concepts of harm to the environment and to health are extremely widely defined at s.29(1).

[26] S.33(9).

[27] Ss.30, 51.

[28] Ss. 32 and 51, Sched. 2.

[29] S.35(3).

[30] S.35(3).

[31] S.33(6).

[32] Ss.36(3) and 74: see para. 5.27.

[33] S.39: see para. 5.29.

To what extent these innovations will result in greater control and improved standards depends upon the resourcing of inspection and enforcement agencies and on the nature of the Government advice as to how the various powers and discretions are to be exercised.

The implementation of Part II of the 1990 Act has been dogged by delay and frustration on the part of both regulatory authorities and the waste industry. Originally scheduled to take effect on April 1, 1993, implementation was subject to first a short delay, then indefinite postponement apparently on the basis of the need to achieve consistency with EC law. The provisions were ultimately implemented on May 1, 1994, subject to certain transitional exceptions.[33a]

Controlled waste and "Directive waste"

5.24   As with the Control of Pollution Act, the regulatory scheme of the 1990 Act applies to "controlled waste": defined at section 75(4) to mean household, industrial or commercial waste, or any such waste.

The fundamental problem is what is meant by "waste" to begin with. By section 75(2) waste includes:

(a) any substance which constitutes a scrap material or an effluent or other unwanted surplus substance arising from the application of any process; and

(b) any substance or article which requires to be disposed of as being broken, worn out, contaminated or otherwise spoiled,

and by section 75(3) any thing which is discarded or otherwise dealt with as if it were waste shall be presumed to be waste unless the contrary is proved. The courts have consistently held that the correct approach is to view material by reference to the person disposing or wishing to dispose of it; this has resulted in materials which may have economic value or usefulness to the recipient or some other person being regarded as waste.[34] This approach has led to difficulties and anomalies for industry, particularly following the introduction of waste carrier licensing.[35] Many would regard a more sensible definition as relating to material which has no useful purpose, or is not suitable for any such purpose, and is therefore being finally disposed of: at least this is the gist of the numerous representations made to the Government's Deregulation Task Forces established in 1993.

[33a] The Environmental Protection Act 1990 (Commencement No. 15) Order 1994 No. 1096.

[34] See *Long* v. *Brooke* [1980] Crim.L.R. 109; *Berridge Incinerators* v. *Nottinghamshire County Council* (1987, unreported); *Kent County Council* v. *Queenborough Rolling Mill Company* [1990] L.M.E.L.R. 28; DoE Cir. 15/88, para. 2.7.

[35] See Chap. 7.

The response to those concerns has been the assimilation, under the Waste Management Licensing Regulations 1994,[36] of the concept of waste embodied in the waste framework directive 91/156/EEC.[36a] Pending primary legislation to repeal the existing definition of waste in section 75(2) of the 1990 Act, this assimilation has been achieved by including "directive waste" within the term "waste"as used in the Control of Pollution Act 1974, Part I and the Environmental Protection Act, 1990, Part II.[36b] Directive waste is defined[36c] to mean any substance or article in the categories set out in Part II of Schedule 4 to the 1994 Regulations which the producer or person in possession of it discards or intends or is required to discard, but with the exception of anything excluded from the scope of the waste framework directive by article 2 of the directive: the categories in Part II of Schedule 4 (substances or articles which are waste when discarded) correspond to categories Q1–Q16 of the directive.[36d] Whilst the definition of waste includes directive waste, for the purposes of Part II of the 1990 Act, waste which is not directive waste shall not be treated as household, industrial or commercial waste;[36e] hence it will not be controlled waste, the statutory definition of controlled waste being household, industrial or commercial waste "or any such waste".[36f]

In conjunction with these statutory changes, the Department of Environment has issued new guidance on the meaning of waste which supersedes that provided in Circulars 13/88 and 14/92.[36g] The guidance makes no reference to the cases decided under the previous law since "these do not necessarily determine what is waste for the purposes of the Directive".[36h] The guidance is complex and voluminous, but takes as its central theme the view that the purpose of the Directive is to treat as waste "those substances or objects which fall out the commercial cycle or out of the chain of utility".[36i] The issue of whether a substance or object has been "discarded" so as to make it waste is considered by the

---

[36] S.I. 1994 No. 1056.
[36a] See para. 5.40.
[36b] Waste Management Licensing Regulations 1994, Sched. 4, para. 9(2) and 10(3).
[36c] *Ibid.*, reg. 1(3).
[36d] See para. 5.40.
[36e] 1994 Regulations, reg. 24(8), inserting new reg. 7A into the Controlled Waste Regulations 1992 (S.I. 1992 No. 588).
[36f] The words "or any such waste" have been held not to have the effect or enlarging the definition of controlled waste, but rather covering the situation where waste comprises a mixture of household industrial or commercial waste: *Thanet District Council* v. *Kent County Council*, Queen's Bench Division, February 26, 1993 (seaweed held not to be controlled waste).
[36g] Circ. 11/94 (W.O. 26/94, S.O. 10/94), Annex 2.
[36h] *Ibid.* para. 2.8.
[36i] *Ibid.* para. 2.14.

Government within this context. Another suggested new concept is whether or not the substance or article can be used in its present form or as a raw material without being subjected to a "specialised recovery operation".[36j] An example of the approach taken by the Government is that of by-products from food and drink processing industries which are sold or given away for further processing into food and drink products or for use as animal feed; these are being put to immediate use by an operation which is not specialised waste recovery and accordingly are not seen as being discarded.[37]

Ultimately the issue of whether a substance or object is directive waste will be a matter for the courts, or for the European Court of Justice on a reference. The Government's guidance is an attempt to reconcile the perceived intention of Directive 91/156/EEC with the demands of deregulation; it remains to be seen whether it will be sufficiently robust to survive judicial scrutiny. In the meantime, the Department's advice is that it is the responsibility of the holder to decide whether the substance or object in his possession is waste, taking advice is necessary.[38]

Exceptions to controlled waste and exemptions from licensing

5.25   Four categories of waste are explicitly placed outwith the definition of controlled waste. These are:

(1) radioactive waste within the Radioactive Substances Act 1993[39];
(2) substances which are explosives within the meaning of the Explosive Act 1875[40];
(3) waste from any mine or quarry[41]; and
(4) waste from premises used for agriculture within the meaning of the Agriculture Act 1947.[42]

Concern has focussed on the consistency between EC and UK law in relation to the last two of these categories of waste. The Government takes the view that it is possible for these categories to be excluded from the types of waste subject to control as "already covered by other

---

[36j] *Ibid.* paras. 2.28–2.30.
[37] *Ibid.* para. 2.33(*b*)(i).
[38] *Ibid.* para. 2.51.
[39] S. 78.
[40] Subs. 75(2). "Decommissioned explosives" are excluded from the scope of the waste framework directive 91/156/EEC by Art. 2. The Government understands the term "decommissioned" in this context to cover all waste explosives: Circ. 11/94, para. 1.17(*e*).
[41] Subs. 75(7)(*c*).
[42] *Ibid.*

legislation".[43] However, the exclusions under the waste framework directive are significantly narrower than those in the 1990 Act, in that they do not apply to non-natural agricultural wastes or non-mineral mining and quarrying waste. The Government's intention is, following consultation, to extend waste management controls in respect of such wastes and to consider what scope if any exists for exemptions.[43a]

In addition to these excluded categories, it is also possible for the Secretary of State to provide that the requirements of waste management licensing do not apply in prescribed cases.[44] Exemptions to waste disposal licensing under the Control of Pollution Act 1974 were granted by the Collection and Disposal of Waste Regulations 1988.[45] The exemptions have now been revised and are contained in Schedule 3 of the Waste Management Licensing Regulations 1994.[46] The Regulations provide exemptions extending to some 43 paragraphs: some of these relate to activities involving waste which are subject to other forms of control. Others are very specific, covering activities such as sewage from sanitary conveniences on trains, peatworking and dredging wastes, and spent railway ballast; the exemptions also include a number of categories designed to facilitate beneficial activities such as the reuse, recycling and recovery of waste. Some exemptions are of a more general nature, for example the keeping or deposit of waste at the place where it is produced pending its treatment or disposal elsewhere, or the treatment or disposal of waste as an integral part of the process which produces it. A number of the exceptions are of relevance to the reclamation or clean-up of contaminated land and are discussed in that context in Chapter 7.

Care is needed in interpreting these complex exemptions. They extend only to section 33(1)(a) and (b) of the Act (licensing requirements) but not to section 33(1)(c) (dealing with waste in a potentially harmful manner).[47] Some of them only apply if the activity is carried on with the consent of the occupier; most do not apply to special waste.[47a] Even where an exemption applies, it is an offence to carry on the relevant activity (if an establishment or undertaking) without being registered.[47b]

---

[43] Directive 91/156/EEC, art. 2.

[43a] Circ. 11/94, paras. 25–28 and Annex 1, para. 1–17.

[44] Subs. 33(3).

[45] S.I. 1988 No. 819, reg. 9 and Sched. 6.

[46] S.I. 1994 No. 1056. They are explained at Annex 5 of Circ. 11/94: Environmental Protection Act 1990, Part II; Waste Management Licensing: The Framework Directive on Waste.

[47] Reg. 17(1).

[47a] Reg. 17(2) and (3). See para. 5–33 as to special waste.

[47b] Reg. 18.

Waste other than controlled waste

5.26   Various waste streams are excluded from the definition of controlled waste[48] some of which may have significant potential to cause pollution. A statutory means of controlling the deposit of such waste was provided by section 18(2) of the Control of Pollution Act 1974. This subsection provided that a person was guilty of an offence if they deposited waste other than controlled waste on land[49] (or caused or knowingly permitted such deposit) in a case where, if the waste were controlled waste and any disposal licence were not in force, an offence would be committed under section 3(3) of the Act. The effect of the provision was to prohibit the deposit of non-controlled waste which satisfied the criteria of section 3(3) of the Act, *i.e.* it was poisonous, noxious or polluting, and its presence was likely to give rise to an environmental hazard and it was deposited in such circumstances that it may reasonably be assumed to have been abandoned or disposed of as waste. No offence was committed if the act was done in pursuance of and in accordance with the terms of any consent, licence, approval or authority granted under any enactment, excluding planning permission.[50]

Thus the effect of section 18(2) was quite intelligible: unfortunately the same cannot be said of its successor, section 63(2) of the Environmental Protection Act 1990, which suffers from clumsy and inept draftsmanship. Section 63(2) creates an offence of depositing on land waste other than controlled waste (or knowingly causing or knowingly permitting such deposit) in a case where if the waste were special waste and any waste management licence were not in force an offence would be committed under section 33. The problem stems from the fact that the old wording of section 3(3) of C.O.P.A. which referred to the nature of the waste (poisonous, noxious or polluting) and the manner of its deposit (so as to create an environmental hazard) was a test which could equally well be applied to non-controlled as to controlled waste. Section 3(3) has been replaced in the E.P.A. by section 33(9) which creates enhanced penalties for offences which relate to special waste. By definition, waste which is not controlled waste cannot be special waste:[51] the assumption required by section 63(2) cannot therefore logically follow. If what is intended is that section 63(2) applies to non-controlled waste which exhibits the requisite characteristics to make it special waste if it were controlled, then the wording of the section seems inapt: furthermore, it would represent a significant narrowing of control when compared with the wording of sections 18(2) and 3(3) of C.O.P.A. read in conjunction.

[48] See paras. 5.21 and 5.25.
[49] "Land" for this purpose included water covering land above the low water mark which is not water in a stream: subs. 18(2) and 4(4).
[50] See s.62(1).
[51] See para. 5.32.

In any event, where waste other than controlled waste is to be treated, kept, or disposed of at a licensed site (*e.g.*, a site receiving agricultural waste as well as household waste) then conditons may relate to the non-controlled waste as well as the controlled waste.[52]

Relevance of "fit and proper person"

Section 36(3) of the 1990 Act states that, subject to the requirements **5.27** of the planning status of the site being satisfied, a waste regulation authority to whom an application for a licence has been duly made shall not refuse that application save on specified grounds, if it is satisfied that the applicant is a fit and proper person. The requirement of "fit and proper person" is to be determined by reference to the carrying on by him of the activities to be authorised by the licence and the requirements of the licence.[53] A person is to be treated as not being fit and proper if it appears to the authority:[54]

(a) that he or another relevant person[55] has been convicted of a relevant offence;[56]

(b) that the management of the activities to be authorised by the licence are not or will not be in the hands of a technically competent person;[57] or

(c) that that person who holds or is to hold the licence has not made and either has no intention of making or is in no position to make financial provision adequate to discharge the obligations arising from the licence.

Whilst the first two criteria are relevant to good waste management and so should help to avoid future occurrences of waste-related contamination, it is the third issue of adequate financial provision which is perhaps the most relevant to ensuring the long term aftercare and monitoring of sites post-closure; thus addressing one of the fundamental problems of landfill as a disposal option. Detailed guidance on the application of the fit and proper person test is given in Chapter 3 of Waste Management Paper No. 4: The Licensing of Waste Management Facilities.[57a]

---

[52] S.35(5).

[53] S.74(2).

[54] S.74(3).

[55] See s.74(7) and Waste Management Licensing Regulations 1994, reg. 3.

[56] An offence can be overlooked by the authority for this purpose, if it considers it proper to do so: s.74(4).

[57] See the Waste Management Licensing Regulations 1994, regs. 4 and 5.

[57a] April, 1994. The guidance considers various forms of financial assurance for the post-closure phase, such as bonds, escrow accounts, trust funds, in-house funds or mutual arrangements.

Licence conditions

5.28   The key to ongoing control of waste disposal activities is through the imposition and enforcement of conditions. A waste management licence shall be granted on such terms and conditions as appear to the waste regulation authority to be appropriate and the conditions may relate not only to the activities which the licence authorises but also to precautions to be taken and works to be carried out in relation to those activities:[58] *e.g.*, the installation of gas venting, impervious caps and liners, etc. Requirements imposed by way of condition can relate to preparatory precautions or works before waste disposal commences, or to such matters after waste disposal ceases.[59] Such conditions must be related to the general purpose of waste management licensing which is to prevent harm to human health, pollution of the environment, or serious detriment to local amenity;[60] these grounds are significantly wider than those stated in the Control of Pollution Act 1974.[61] Licence conditions may be modified during the term of the licence by notice served on the holder to any extent which in the opinion of the authority is desirable and is unlikely to require unreasonable expense on the part of the licence holder.[62] Additionally, the authority is under a duty to modify licence conditions to the extent necessary to ensure that the activities authorised do not cause pollution of the environment, harm to human health or become seriously detrimental to the amenities of the locality.[63]

Under the Waste Management Licencing Regulations 1994[64] conditions must be specifically imposed to deal with waste oils and groundwater protection as required by EC legislation.[65] Guidance as to the licensing of waste facilities is provided in Waste Management Paper No. 4; the current edition was issued in April 1994 to coincide with the implementation of Part II of the 1990 Act. The guidance covers a wide range of facilities and places emphasis on the importance of long term controls; in relation to landfill sites a distinction is made between those sites which are designed to contain leachate and gas so that there should

---

[58] S.35(3).
[59] *Ibid.*
[60] See s.36(3).
[61] See *Att.-Gen.'s Reference (No. 2 of 1988)* [1989] 3 W.L.R. 397 (conditions against creation of public nuisances of all kinds was invalid). As to the effect of an invalid condition on the licence see *R.* v. *North Hertfordshire District Council, ex p. Cobbold* [1985] 3 All E.R. 487; *R.* v. *Inner London Crown Court, ex p. Sitki, The Times,* October 26, 1993.
[62] S.37(1).
[63] S.37(2).
[64] S.I. 1994 No. 1056.
[65] Regs. 14 and 15. See generally Chap. 6 on groundwater protection and also Circ. 11/94, Annex 7.

be no significant releases, and sites which require no specific measures for landfill gas or leachate management since they are limited to the acceptance of wastes which pose no significant pollution threat to the environment. Appendix A to the Paper contains a useful checklist of the key matters to be covered by conditions, though not all may be appropriate to every site. These include issues of site infrastructure, site preparation, waste reception and site operations, as well as general considerations. Of particular reference to avoiding soil contamination are issues such as bunding, containment system design, installation, supervision and testing, liner protection, leachate and gas control, provision of monitoring facilities, and surface water control and drainage.

It should also be remembered that general control can be exerted over both licensed and unlicensed sites where waste is kept, treated, or disposed of, by way of the prohibition in section 33(1)(c) of the Environmental Protection Act if these activities where carried out in a manner likely to cause pollution of the environment or harm to human health.[66]

Surrender of licences

Under section 37(2) of the 1990 Act, the waste regulation authority **5.29** must modify the conditions of existing licences to the extent required to ensure the authorised activities do not cause pollution of the environment, harm to human health, or serious detriment to the amenities of the locality. This duty of variation allows both for problems to be addressed as they come to light, and also, to an extent, for licence conditions to keep pace with changing standards of environmental protection.[67]

A major problem with licences under the Control of Pollution Act 1974 was the ease with which they could be cancelled by the holder when no longer required.[68] This is no longer the case under the 1990 Act. A site licence may be surrendered only if the authority accepts the surrender.[69] The application to surrender must be accompanied by prescribed information and evidence,[70] the authority must inspect the

[66] See [1993] "Wastes Management," p. 12 (J. Miekle).
[67] This flows from the extremely wide and flexible definitions given to "harm to the environment" and "harm to human health" by s.29(1).
[68] S.8(4) simply required the holder to deliver the licence to the issuing authority and to give notice he longer required it.
[69] S.39(1).
[70] S.39(3); the information required is prescribed in the Waste Management Licensing Regulations 1994, Sched. 1 and includes details of engineering works carried out in the case of landfills or lagoons, the presence of contaminants and geological, hydrological and hydrogeological information.

219

land,[71] and must determine whether it is likely or unlikely that the condition of the land, so far as that condition is the result of the use of the land for the treatment, keeping or disposal of waste (whether or not in pursuance of the licence) will cause pollution of the environment or harm to human health.[72] If satisfied that the condition of the land is unlikely to have those effects, the authority shall accept the surrender,[73] but only after referring the proposal to the National Rivers Authority.[74] Surrender is effected by the waste regulation authority issuing a certificate of completion, on which the licence shall cease to have effect.[75] If the authority is not satisfied that the condition of the land is unlikely to have the specified adverse effects it shall refuse to accept the surrender.[76]

The effect of these provisions is therefore that the holder of a site licence will remain responsible for the aftercare of the site until surrender is accepted: conditions can be tightened up as mentioned above, and can relate to post-closure activities and precautions.[77]

The same applies to licences granted under the Control of Pollution Act in existence on the relevant appointed day, which are then treated as site licences granted under the new provisions.[78] The impending stringency of the new provisions undoubtedly led to a number of licence holders taking steps to surrender licences unilaterally while this was still possible under COPA:[79] whether this avoids liability entirely however remains to be seen on an individual and site specific basis.[80]

The Government's initial intention was that section 39 would be complemented by the provisions on "closed landfills" at section 61. The effect of the two provisions read together would have been that the waste

---

[71] S.39(4).

[72] S.39(5).

[73] S.39(6).

[74] S.39(7); if the NRA requests that surrender be not accepted then either the NRA or WRA may refer the matter to the Secretary of State and the surrender shall not be accepted except in accordance with his decision.

[75] S.39(9).

[76] S.39(6). Appeal lies to the Secretary of State against refusal or deemed refusal (s.39(10)) under s.43(1)(*f*)). Guidance to operators and waste authorities is to be provided in Waste Management Paper 26A, "Landfill Completion" (April 1994) which includes guidance on assessing completion, relevant criteria as to leachate and gas, and the completion report.

[77] S.35(3) see para. 5.28.

[78] S.77(2).

[79] A survey by Friends of the Earth published in May 1993 revealed that one in four of the landfill site licences extant in England at the beginning of 1993 had since been surrendered: see ENDS Report 220, May 1993, p. 9. These include the licence for at least one site (Helpston, Peterborough) which presents a significant threat to underlying aquifer resources: see *The Independent,* June 17, 1933. See also para. 2.55.

[80] See Chap. 2 on liability generally.

regulation authority would be under a duty to take steps to remediate closed sites presenting a risk of harm to the environment or to human health by virtue of noxious gases or liquids: but, if the authority had previously granted a certificate of completion in respect of the land there would be no ability to recover its costs from the owner for the time being. Thus, acceptance of surrender would effectively shift the risk in relation to future problems from the owner to the authority.[81] The Government's decision not to implement section 61 with the rest of Part II of the 1990 Act[81a] could be said to have unbalanced the whole scheme by removing one important component, whilst leaving the long-term liability position unclear.

The duty of care and waste carrier registration

Two important practical components of the legislative structure for **5.30** ensuring the safe and responsible disposal of controlled waste are the statutory "duty of care" imposed on waste producers and others having control of waste[82] and, secondly, the provisions as to registration of waste carriers.[83] Both issues are discussed below in the context of the reclamation and remediation of contaminated sites.[84]

SPECIAL WASTE

Generally

Both the Control of Pollution Act 1974[85] and the Environmental **5.31** Protection Act 1990[86] allow special provision to be made by regulations for controlled waste which is, or may be, particularly dangerous or difficult to dispose of. The regulations currently dealing with such waste are the Control of Pollution (Special Waste) Regulations 1980.[87] The regulations constitute the means by which EC Directive 78/319/EEC on

---

[81] The shift may not be absolute given the other possible grounds of liability apart from s.61: see Chap. 2.
[81a] See para. 3.07A.
[82] Environmental Protection Act 1990, s.34.
[83] Control of Pollution (Amendment) Act 1989.
[84] See Chap. 7.
[85] S.17.
[86] S.62.
[87] S.I. 1980 No. 1709, as amended by S.I. 1988 No. 1790. The Regulations came into force on March 16, 1981, replacing the Deposit of Poisonous Waste Act 1972, which was repealed from the same date.

toxic and dangerous waste[88] was implemented. However, EC law in this area is currently in the course of reform,[89] and consequent changes to the UK legislation can be anticipated.[90]

The problem of defining waste which requires special control is a very real one.[91] Terms employed have included "special waste", "toxic waste", "hazardous waste" and "difficult wastes". All of these have their limitations, principally because so much depends on the way in which substances are encountered and handled as to whether they are hazardous or not.[92] The House of Commons Environment Committee regarded "difficult waste" as the best concept, but stressed the need for a systematic, comprehensive and comprehensible set of definitions, taking into account concentration and exposure, while supporting the fundamental principle of a two-tier system of classification.[93]

The definition of "Special waste"

5.32   Currently the term "special waste"[94] applies to any controlled waste[95] which *either*

> (a) consists of or contains any of a number of substances listed at
> Schedule I of the Regulations, namely:
>> (1) acids and alkalis;
>> (2) antimony and antimony compounds;
>> (3) arsenic compounds;
>> (4) asbestos (all chemical forms);
>> (5) barium compounds;

---

[88] O.J. L84, March 31, 1978.

[89] Implementation of Directive 91/689/EEC (O.J. L.337/20, 31.12.91) on hazardous waste was in September 1993 delayed from January 1, 1994 for a period of 12 months, as a result of difficulties in agreeing a list of hazardous wastes as required by Art. 4 of the Directive. It was found to be impossible to define hazardous waste in a definitive way, since hazards depend on the concentrations of various constituents within the waste and the circumstances in which it is encountered. Directive 78/319/EEC will remain in force in the interim period.

[90] See the DoE/Welsh Office Consultation Paper, "Special Waste and the Control of its Disposal" (February 1990).

[91] House of Commons Environment Committee, "Toxic Waste" Session 1988–9, 2nd Report, H.C. 22–I, para. 30.

[92] *Ibid.*, para. 30. See also Royal Commission on Environmental Pollution, 11th Report, Cmnd. 9675 (1985) paras. 2.8, 2.18; also House of Lords Select Committee on Science and Technology, "Hazardous Waste Disposal" (Session 1980–81, First Report, H.C. 273–I, para. 8).

[93] *Ibid.*, paras. 35 and 36.

[94] Special Waste Regulations 1980, reg. 2.

[95] See para. 5.24.

(6) beryllium and beryllium compounds;

(7) biocides and phytopharmaceutical substances;

(8) boron compounds;

(9) cadmium and cadmium compounds;

(10) copper compounds;

(11) heterocyclic organic compounds containing oxygen, nitrogen or sulphur;

(12) hexavalent chromium compounds;

(13) hydrocarbons and their oxygen, nitrogen and sulphur compounds;

(14) inorganic cyanides;

(15) inorganic halogen-containing compounds;

(16) inorganic sulphur-containing compounds;

(17) laboratory chemicals;

(18) lead compounds;

(19) mercury compounds;

(20) nickel and nickel compounds;

(21) organic halogen compounds, excluding inert polymeric materials;

(22) peroxides, chlorates, perchlorates and azides;

(23) pharmaceutical and veterinary products;

(24) phosphorous and its compounds;

(25) selenium and selenium compounds;

(26) silver compounds;

(27) tarry materials from refining and tar residues from distilling;

(28) tellurium and tellurium compounds;

(29) thallium and thallium compounds;

(30) vanadium compounds;

(31) zinc compounds.

and by reason of the presence of such substance,

(i) is "dangerous to life" as defined by Part II of Schedule 1, *i.e.*, a single dose of not more than five cubic centimetres[96] would be likely to cause death or serious damage to tissue if ingested[97] by a child of 20 kg. body weight, or exposure to it for fifteen minutes or less would be likely to cause serious damage to human tissue by inhalation, skin contact or eye contact; or

[96] A sample of five cubic centimetres taken from any part of a consignment of mixed waste can result in the consignment being classified as special waste: Sched. 1, Part II, Para. 4.

[97] Where waste is in such a form that the ingestion of five cubic centimetres is not possible, or there is no risk that a toxic amount could be assimilated if the waste were to be ingested, then it is not to be regarded as "dangerous to life".

(ii) has a flash point of 21°c or less.

or

(b) is a medicinal product, as defined in section 130 of the Medicines Act 1965 (*i.e.*, substances or articles manufactured for treatment of human beings or animals) which is available only in accordance with a prescription given by an appropriate practitioner as defined in section 58(1) of the Medicines Act (doctors, dentists and veterinary surgeons).

Whilst radioactive waste is generally excluded from the definition of controlled waste,[98] the regulations on special waste may apply to radioactive waste.[99] However, for the purposes of the Special Waste Regulations, *e.g.* in deciding whether the waste is "dangerous to life" no account is to be taken of its radioactive properties.[1]

This approach adopted by the Regulations of an inclusive list replaces that used in the Deposit of Poisonous Waste Act 1972 of an exclusive list; that is to say a list of known wastes presenting no significant hazards and defining as hazardous any wastes not so listed. The exclusive list approach was too wide ranging and was prone to give rise to serious uncertainty.[2]

Regulation of special waste

5.33   The term "special waste" may be used in site licences, for example by excluding the deposit of such waste from disposal at a site completely, or restricting its disposal to certain parts of a site, or by imposing special conditions as to its disposal.

The Special Waste Regulations themselves impose a means of control based upon documentary tracking of special waste from the point of removal from the premises at which it was produced to the point of ultimate disposal: the system is known as "the consignment note system." It works as follows:

(1) The producer of special waste must, before the waste is removed from the premises at which it is produced, prepare six copies of a standard form consignment note. One copy must be furnished

---

[98] See para. 5.25.
[99] Reg. 3(1).
[1] Radioactive Substances Act 1993, s.40(1) and Sched. 1, Pt. I, para. 4B and Pt. II, para. 17A, inserted by Sched. 5, para. 11 on a transitional basis until the repeal of s.30(5) of the Control of Pollution Act 1974.
[2] House of Lords Committee on Science and Technology, "Hazardous Waste Disposal," Session 1980–81, First Report, H.L. 273–I, paras. 91 and 153.

to the disposal authority for the area in which it is to be disposed of, not more than one month and not less than three clear days before the removal of the waste.[3]

(2) On collection of the waste, both producer and carrier must complete further portions of the consignment notes. The producer retains one copy and sends another to the waste disposal authority for his own area (where the waste is to be disposed of outside that area).[4] The other copies are given to the carrier.[5]

(3) The carrier transmits the copies to the person disposing of the waste, who completes a further part of the form.[6] The carrier retains one copy himself.[7]

(4) The disposer retains one copy and furnishes another to the disposal authority in whose area the waste was produced.[8]

In the case of regular consignments, it is possible for the producer's waste authority to waive the requirement for transmission of individual consignment notes by directing the producer to furnish copies at intervals not exceeding 12 months.[9]

Also, the consignment note requirements do not apply so as to require records to be kept of waste disposed of by pipeline or within the curtilage of a factory or other premises at which it has been produced.[10]

Registers and site records

Producers, carriers and disposers of special waste are required to keep **5.34** registers of their copies of consignment notes: the producer and carrier for a period of two years, the disposer until his site licence is surrendered or revoked (at which stage the register is to be furnished to the disposal authority for the site).[11]

Any person making a deposit of special waste on land must record the location of each such deposit, and keep such records until his disposal licence is surrendered or revoked—at which time the records must be sent to the disposal authority for retention.[12] These records must be kept on the basis of a site plan, either with a grid or with translucent overlays

---

[3] Reg. 4(1)–(4).
[4] Reg. 4(5) and (6).
[5] Reg. 4(7).
[6] Reg. 5(1) and 6(1)(*a*).
[7] Reg. 6(1)(*c*) and 5(1).
[8] Reg. 6(1)(*b*) and (*c*).
[9] Reg. 9.
[10] Reg. 8.
[11] Reg. 13.
[12] Reg. 14(1).

showing deposits in relation to the contours of the site.[13] The deposits must also be described by reference to the register of consignment notes.[14] The exceptions to this latter requirement are waste disposed of by pipeline, or within the curtilage of a factory or other premises at which it is produced, or waste disposed of by a disposal authority at a site within their own area—in which case the deposits must be described by reference to the composition of the waste and its date of disposal.

In the case of liquid wastes discharged without containers into underground strata or disused workings the record shall comprise only a written record of the quantity and composition of the waste so discharged.[15]

RADIOACTIVE SUBSTANCES

Generally

5.35   Control over radioactive materials and wastes is provided by the Radioactive Substances Act 1993 which consolidates the Radioactive Substances Act 1960 and subsequent amendments.[16] Broadly, no person may keep or use radioactive materials[17] on premises used for the purposes of an undertaking carried on by him unless he is registered under the Act or can claim the benefit of an exemption.[18] Further, sections 13 and 14 of the Act require an authorisation to be obtained for, respectively, (a) the disposal of radioactive waste[19] on or from premises used for the purposes of an undertaking carried on by him; and (b) the accumulation of radioactive waste on such premises with a view to its subsequent disposal. These requirements are backed up by criminal offences and penalties.

---

[13] Reg. 14(2).
[14] Reg. 14(3).
[15] Reg. 14(4).
[16] The legislation is explained in the Departmental publication, "Radioactive Substances Act 1960: A Guide to the Administration of the Act" (HMSO, 1982).
[17] Defined by s.1.
[18] S.6(1). Various exempting orders have been made for items such as luminous articles, geological specimens, lead, phosphatic substances, testing instruments and smoke detectors.
[19] Defined by 2(4). The definition covers waste material which has been contaminated by contact with or proximity to radioactive waste: it may therefore include, for example, irradiated soil.

Application of control

A number of the most serious instances of soil contamination in the **5.36**
UK to date have involved radioactive materials from premises used for
purposes such as instrument dial manufacture.[20] Hopefully, the system of
control now applied both to radioactive substances and radioactive
wastes should reduce the risk of such contamination for the future. In
practice, a considerable amount of low-level liquid radioactive waste is
authorised for disposal by discharge to sewer; however, there are also
solid wastes which require other disposal routes and higher level wastes
which require more sophisticated disposal methods.

One of the basic objectives of UK radioactive waste management is
that of radiological protection of individuals and the general public:[21]
however consideration must be given not only to the radiological
exposure of man but also that of other living environmental resources.[22]
The Government's policy is that where it can be done safely, it is
desirable to use conventional methods of disposal, such as disposal on
local authority refuse tips, taking into account factors such as the nature
of the tip and the amount of non-radioactive material available to cover
the waste. Each case is considered on its metits on an individual basis.[23]
Small amounts of low level solid waste are authorised for disposal with
ordinary refuse ("dustbin disposal") which are regarded as presenting
no hazard either to the refuse collectors or at the disposal site.[24] Within
certain limits and subject to special precautions being observed, solid
wastes which are too radioactive for dustbin disposal may be disposed of
at suitable landfill sites: immediate cover by at least 1.5 metres of
inactive refuse is generally required.[25] Waste unsuitable for such "special
precautions" landfill disposal is sent for disposal at the Drigg Site,
Cumbria, operated under authorised by British Nuclear Fuels Ltd.

Site records

By section 20 of the 1993 Act the chief inspector may by notice impose **5.37**
requirements in relation to site and disposal records. These requirements
may deal with the retention of copies of records for a specified period
after the authorised activities have ceased and the provision of copies to

---

[20] See Chap. 1.
[21] "Radioactive Substances Act 1960: A Guide to the Administration of the Act"
(HMSO, 1982), para. 46.
[22] *Ibid.*, para. 49.
[23] *Ibid.*, para. 50.
[24] *Ibid.*, para. 54.
[25] *Ibid.*, para. 56.

the chief inspector if registration is cancelled, authorisation revoked, or the relevant activities cease.[26] Such disposal records, in particular, may be useful in identifying the location of recently disposed of radioactive wastes. Such records do not appear to be expressly covered by section 39 which deals with public access to certain records under the Act, but in any event access may be ensured by the general regulations on public access to environmental information.[27]

AGRICULTURE

Generally

5.38   Agricultural activity has the potential to give rise to soil or groundwater contamination, both through escapes of stored substances such as fuel oil, and through the intentional application to land of pesticides, nitrates and sewage sludge. The following constitute the main legal means by which such pollution is controlled:

(1) Storage installations and stores

The Control of Pollution (Silage, Slurry and Agricultural Fuel Oil) Regulations 1991[28] made under section 92 of the Water Resources Act 1991 contain detailed requirements relating to specified types of agricultural storage installations. These relate to siting, construction, capacity and integrity of containment and pre-notification of the NRA before the installation is used.

(2) Pesticides

The sale, supply, use and application of pesticides are controlled under the Food and Environment Protection Act 1985, Part III and by the Control of Pesticides Regulations 1986.[29] Pesticides with inorganic elements with the potential to cause long-term soil contamination problems are not generally authorised or applied now. Most modern pesticides are organic compounds with relatively short degradation lives, and their rate of application is controlled. The Regulations are supplemented by two codes of practice,[30] which give advice on means of

---

[26] S.20(2).
[27] See Chap. 3 generally.
[28] S.I. 1991 No. 324.
[29] S.I. 1986 No. 1510.
[30] *The Code of Practice for the Suppliers of Pesticides to Agriculture, Horticulture and Forestry* (MAFF, 1990) and *The Storage of Approved Pesticides: Guidance for Farmers and Other Professional Users*, Guidance Note CS 19, HSE, 1988.

preventing and minimising the consequences of accidents involving pesticides, *e.g.*, the bunding of stores. Government policy is to limit the amounts used to the minimum necessary for the effective control of pests compatible with the protection of human health and the environment.[31] EC law now provides for a system of registration and mutual recognition of plant protection products, subject to Uniform Principles for granting authorisation.[32]

(3) Nitrates

Section 94–96 of the Water Resources Act 1991 provide for the designation of nitrate sensitive areas (NSAs) by Ministerial Order. The object of such orders is the prevention or control of the entry of nitrate into controlled waters as the result of, or of anything done in connection with, the use for agricultural purposes of any land.[33] Such orders may prohibit or restrict the carrying on of activities, or may require positive preventive measures: they may also provide for the payment of compensation. The measures required may be on a voluntary basis by agreement,[34] or may be mandatory. The procedures for designation vary depending on whether the scheme is to be voluntary or mandatory.[35] The Nitrate Sensitive Areas (Designation) Order 1990[36] has designated ten NSAs, to operate on a voluntary basis. Since the Order was enacted, EC legislation has been approved dealing with the protection of waters against nitrate pollution[37] and requiring, *inter alia*, the designation of "vulnerable zones" which drain into waters which are or could be affected by such pollution.[38] Action programmes must be established in respect of such designated vulnerable zones.[39]

(4) Sewage sludge

About 50 per cent. of sewage sludge produced in the UK is disposed of to agricultural land. The application of sewage sludge (or indeed other waste) onto agricultural land, for the purpose of beneficially conditioning

---

[31] Cm. 1200, para. 13.20.
[32] Dir. 91/414/EEC concerning the placing of plant protection products on the market (O.J. No. L230, 19.8.91).
[33] S.94(2).
[34] S.95.
[35] See Sched. 12.
[36] S.I. 1990 No. 1013.
[37] Dir. 91/676/EEC concerning the protection of waters against pollution caused by nitrates from agricultural sources (O.J. L375/1, 31.21.91).
[38] Art. 3(2).
[39] Art. 5. Details of the 72 zones intended for designation in England and Wales have now been published for consultation: DoE News Release No. 307, May 18, 1994.

the land, has benefited from an exemption from disposal licensing under the Collection and Disposal of Waste Regulations 1988, subject to certain particulars being furnished to the disposal authority. The supply and use of sewage slude in agriculture, provided it is within the terms of the Sludge (Use in Agriculture) Regulations 1989 (see below) is entirely exempted from the controlled waste regime.[39a] Exemptions are provided by the Waste Management Licensing Regulations 1994 for sludge spread on certain premises other than agricultural land, for spreading of materials other than sludge (*e.g.* waste food) on agricultural land and for the storage of sludge prior to spreading.[39b] These exemptions are subject to complex qualifications and to the general requirement, derived from EC law, that the activity results in benefit to agriculture or ecological improvement.

The disposal of sludge to agricultural land is regulated by Directive 86/278/EEC,[40] implemented in the UK by the Sludge (Use in Agriculture) Regulations 1989.[41] The Regulations prohibit the supply and use of sewage sludge for application to agricultural land unless various requirements are fulfilled. These include the regular testing of the sludge for pH, chromium, zinc, copper, nickel, cadmium, lead and mercury, the testing of the soil for similar parameters, limits on the rate of application, and that no fruit or vegetable crops (other than fruit trees) are growing or being harvested at the time.[42] Various precautions are specified after sludge or septic tank sludge has been used on agricultural land, e.g., restricting the grazing of animals or the harvesting of forage crops for a period of three weeks.[43] Information must be supplied by the occupiers of the agricultural land to the sludge producer, who must maintain a register giving specified particulars including the address and area of each agricultural unit on which the sludge was used.[44]

The Department of Environment has issued a Code of Practice for the agricultural use of sewage sludge, which complements the Regulations.[45] This document discusses both the benefits and the constraints of the use of sludge: examples are given of the various effective sludge treatment processes. Of particular concern is how sludge quality may be affected by trade effluent inputs to sewer—for example effluent from abattoirs and animal processing plants are likely to be significant sources of pathogens.[46] More detailed guidance is given on monitoring sludge and

[39a] Controlled Waste Regulations 1992, reg. 7(1) (*b*) and (*c*).
[39b] Annex 2, paras. 7 and 8.
[40] O.J. L181, 4.7.86.
[41] S.I. 1989 No. 1263 as amended by S.I. 1990 No. 880.
[42] Reg. 3.
[43] Reg. 4.
[44] Reg. 6.
[45] HMSO, 1989.
[46] Para. 3.1.

soil and in particular the importance of soil pH is stressed; crop damage from phytotoxic elements is more likely to occur on acid soils, and where the pH value for a representative soil sample is less than 5.2, the sludge producer should seek specialist expert advice.

In practice the main burden of complying with the Regulations in terms of monitoring falls upon the privatised sewerage plcs who are the producers of the sludge. It may be that the practice of spreading sludge on agricultural land will become increasingly controversial. A recent technical report on soil fertility agents, commissioned by the Ministry of Agriculture and the Department of the Environment, emphasises the importance of the precautionary principle and its relevance to the problems of heavy metal pollution. The report in particular recommends reduced limits for zinc. Another report on food safety and animal health was conducted by the Steering Group on Chemical Aspects of Food Surveillance. The Report concludes that in relation to food safety the hazards associated with lead, cadmium and copper on sewage sludge are the most relevant. Nonetheless, it considers there is no justification for proposing changes to current limits for lead and cadmium in soil. In relation to animal health, ingestion of lead, cadmium, copper and fluoride are seen as of greatest concern, and further research is recommended. The need for continued efforts to reduce the input of metals into sewage slude and thence to agricultural land is emphasised.

Codes of practice

Under section 97 of the Water Resources Act 1991 Ministers may **5.39** approve codes of practice giving practical guidance to persons engaged in agriculture as to activities that may affect controlled waters and providing what appear to be desirable practices for avoiding or minimising the pollution of such waters. Contravention of an approved code of practice does not of itself give rise to criminal or civil liability, but will be taken into account by the NRA for certain purposes in determining whether legislative requirements have been contravened.[47] Ministers have issued codes of good agricultural practice for the protection of water[48] and of air.[49] The code for water gives detailed guidance on matters such as storage of silage, sludge and fuel oil, disposal of milk and dairy products, vegetable and animal processing wastes, animal carcases, nitrates, pesticides and sheep dip.

In December 1992 the Ministry of Agriculture, Fisheries and Food and the Welsh Office Agriculture Department published a draft "Code

[47] S.97(2).
[48] S.I. 1991 No. 2285.
[49] 1992.

of Good Agriculture Practice for the Protection of Soil." The draft code described the main risks of damage to soil and provides guidance on its protection. The Code advises, for example, the avoidance of excessive application of phosphorus in fertilisers and manures, which can cause eutrophication of waters. Section 4 of the draft Code deals with contamination, including the risks of take-up of contaminants by crops and ingestion by livestock: useful and relatively detailed guidance is given for individual substances. Caution is urged as to the acceptance of wastes for beneficially conditioning land: it is pointed out that this should be regarded as a long-term physical improvement and that a temporary increase in water content through the moisture in dilute wastes should not be regarded as beneficial conditioning.

EC Waste Legislation

"The Framework Directives"

5.40   EC directives on waste are becoming increasingly important in shaping the direction of UK waste legislation.

The cornerstone is Directive 91/156/EEC amending Directive 75/442/EEC on waste (the Waste Framework Directive).[50] This Directive defines waste as any object or substance in the categories set out in Annex I which the holder discards or intends or is required to discard: this concept has now been incorporated expressly into UK law.[50a] "Holder" means the producer of the waste or the person in possession of it. The key concept is that of "discard", which is not defined, though case law suggests that the definition of waste does not exclude substances or objects capable of economic re-utilisation or intended for such re-utilisation.[51] That being the case, the categories of waste set out at Annex I of the Directive are extremely wide, not least because of Category Q16, which refers to "Any materials, substances or products which are not contained in the above categories."

Certain types of waste are excluded from the scope of the Directive[52] but these do not correspond exactly to the exclusions which apply in UK legislation.[53] For example, only certain types of agricultural wastes are excluded.

---

[50] O.J. L78/32, 26.3.91.
[50a] See para. 5.24.
[51] *Vessoso and Zanetti*: (Cases C–206 and 207/88 and C–359/88) [1990] 2 L.M.E.L.R. 133.
[52] Art. 2.
[53] See para. 5.25.

In particular, Member States are required to take the necessary measures to ensure that waste is recovered or disposed of without endangering human health or harming the environment and in particular (*inter alia*) without risk to water, air, soil and plants and animals.[54] With limited exceptions, specified at Article 11, any establishment carrying out the wastes disposal operations listed at Annex IIA must obtain a permit.[55]

Directive 91/689/EEC deals with hazardous waste.[56] It contains additional requirements, such as the recording and identification of every site where tipping or discharge of hazardous waste takes place. Different categories of hazardous waste must not be mixed, nor must hazardous waste be mixed with non-hazardous waste.[57] The Directive attempts to create a definition of hazardous waste by reference to a complex scheme involving the description and constituents of the waste and various properties which render waste hazardous.[58] The task of providing an exhaustive and definitive list has proved more difficult than was anticipated; in particular because the hazard will vary according to circumstances. Implementation of the Directive has therefore been postponed by 12 months to December 31, 1994.

The proposed Landfill Directive

Of particular relevance to the UK waste industry is the proposed **5.41** Directive on the Landfill of Waste.[59] The direct antecedents of this proposal go back to 1987, when the European Parliament passed a resolution on the waste disposal industry and "old waste dumps".[60] The proposed Directive proceeds on the basis that technical standards for landfill should be harmonised at a high level of environmental protection. Its main features are:

    (1) the classification of landfill sites into those for:
        (a) hazardous wastes;
        (b) municipal and non-hazardous wastes and for other compatible wastes; and
        (c) inert waste;[61]

---

[54] Art. 4.
[55] Art. 10. As to the relevance of exemptions in UK law, see para. 5.25 above.
[56] O.J. L377/20, 31.12.91.
[57] Art. 2.
[58] Annexes I, II, and III.
[59] Com (91) 102 Final, April 27, 1992.
[60] O.J. No. C190, July 20, 1987, p. 154; see also the Resolution of the Council of Ministers calling for improvements in waste disposal practice—O.J. No. C122, May 18, 1990, p. 2.
[61] Art. 4.

(2) all landfills must comply with requirements set out at Annexes I, III and IV in order to avoid environmental damage.[62] These cover general requirements such as location, access, waste control and leachate management, stability, gas control and the protection of soil and groundwater. A landfill "must meet the necessary conditions, naturally or artificially achieved, to prevent pollution of the soil or groundwater";[63] these include detailed criteria as to permeability. Annex III provides detailed rules for waste acceptance in the various classes of landfill, based on the characteristics of the eluate and the compatibility of the different waste types. "Joint disposal" of wastes may take place only under strictly defined circumstances and certain wastes may not be jointly disposed.[64] Annex IV provides equally exacting control procedures to be applied in the operational and aftercare phases;

(3) applications for permits must fulfil at least the requirements of Annex II with regard to information to be provided;

(4) the competent authority shall not issue a permit unless the project complies with the requirements laid down in the Directive;[65]

(5) certain wastes must not be accepted in a landfill, including most significantly, wastes in a liquid state unless compatible with the type of wastes acceptable and with site operating procedures and, secondly, any other type of waste which does not fulfil Annex III criteria (unless assigned to a mono-landfill);[66]

(6) wastes are to be asssigned only to the appropriate type of landfill,[67] primary responsibility for acceptance resting with the site operators who must provide written justification for each delivery accepted;[68]

(7) the control programme specified in Annex IV must be carried out during the operational and aftercare phases;[69]

(8) a procedure is provided for closure of sites—following "definitive closure" the operator shall be in charge of its maintenance, monitoring and control for a period of 10 years or a shorter period if the competent authority authorises it;[70]

---

[62] Art. 5.
[63] Annex I, para. 8.1.
[64] Art. 6.
[65] Art. 7.
[66] Art. 9; "mono-landfill" is defined at Art. 3(f) as a site where only one defined type of waste is deposited, being comparable with respect to origins, composition and leachate characteristics.
[67] Art. 10.
[68] Art. 11.
[69] Art. 12.
[70] Art. 13.

(9) the operator shall be liable under civil law for the damage and impairment of the environment caused by the landfilled waste, irrespective of fault on his part;[71]

(10) existing sites shall not continue to operate unless the future operation of the remaining part of the site meets the conditions laid down in the Directive;[72]

(11) at the time of receiving the permit, the operator must provide a financial guarantee or other equivalent, to cover the estimated costs of closure procedures and aftercare operations;[73] and

(12) Member States shall ensure the establishment of one or more "landfill aftercare funds" to cover aftercare costs and rectification of environmental damage where these cannot be recouped from the operator.[74]

The proposal was considered by the House of Commons Environment Committee,[75] which noted, "seeping through the text", an apparent antipathy towards landfill as a means of waste disposal.[76] Whilst the proposed Directive, the Committee felt, had some merits, it failed to recognise the good aspects of well engineered landfill practice and should allow more flexibility for Member States to attain common standards commensurate with their own "cultural patrimony."[77] The Committee also expressed itself to be "appalled" at the poor standard and patchy coverage of the statistics on landfill presented to the inquiry and recommended that the Government should allocate sufficient resources to develop a national database on sites, compiled in conjunction with users such as the NRA, HMIP and waste regulation authorities and including information on site location, age, size, type, throughput, ownership and management and monitoring regimes.[78]

The UK Government stated its approach to landfill in general and co-disposal in particular in its reply to the Second Report of the House of Common Environment Committee, "Toxic Waste."[79] It was suggested there that around 90 per cent. of household and commercial waste is landfilled, generally at separate facilities to those receiving industrial waste. However, where the two types were disposed of together, co-disposal was, the Government suggested, "particularly well-suited to the

---

[71] Art. 14.

[72] Art. 15; a period of grace of five years to achieve a permit is given by Art. 15.4, after which the site must be closed.

[73] Art. 17.

[74] Art. 18.

[75] Session 1990–91, 7th Report, H.C. 236—I, July 17, 1991.

[76] Para. 40. See also R.G.P. Hawkins [1992] J.E.L. Vol. 4, No. 2, p. 307.

[77] Para. 42.

[78] Para. 14.

[79] Cm. 679, April 1989, paras. 1.10–1.14.

geology of certain parts of the UK" and "a safe long-term disposal method for a wide range of wastes." The allegedly happy experience in the UK was contrasted with the "indiscriminate dumping of industrial waste without thought or record" which had led to grave pollution problems in other countries and had turned public opinion against even properly engineered landfill.

The Government has subsequently published a document[80] setting out the case for properly controlled co-disposal—defined as "the calculated and monitored treatment of industrial and commercial, liquid and solid wastes by interaction with biodegradable wastes in a controlled landfill site." The brochure attempts to clarify some of the terminological confusion which has arisen and to make the case for the perceived environmental benefits of co-disposal; "a vital form of landfill waste disposal in the UK".[81]

---

[80] "UK Landfill Practice: Co-disposal—Using Nature's Techniques to Treat Difficult Wastes" (DoE, September 1993).
[81] The brochure refers to some 300 sites licensed for co-disposal.

Chapter 6

WATER

INTRODUCTION

Contaminated land and water pollution

The Royal Commission on Environmental Pollution considered the **6.01** issue of water quality in its comprehensive report, "Freshwater Quality."[1] This report stressed the importance of freshwater as a vital resource for human survival and consequently the need to adopt a sustainable approach towards it.[2] Processes giving rise to cumulative long-term deterioration of freshwater, the report advocated, must be brought under firmer control.[3] Among those processes is water pollution from contaminated land.[4]

Contaminated land, the report emphasised, can present problems both to groundwater and surface water quality. Groundwater may be threatened by deliberate discharge of pollutants into aquifers, or by percolation through the overlying ground, the latter being the more widespread threat.[5] Examples were given of contamination of public and private water supplies, sometimes leading to illness, by leaking sewers, cesspits and septic tanks, and by the commercial use of common chlorinated solvents.[6] Contaminated land was seen as a significant problem, the Royal Commission's views being based on a number of reports specially commissioned from the Water Research Centre:[7] those reports referred to industrially contaminated land, landfill sites, mines and quarries as sources of concern.[8]

[1] Cmnd. 1966, June 1992.
[2] Para. 1.18.
[3] Para. 1.22.
[4] Para. 1.19.
[5] Paras. 5.9–5.10.
[6] Paras. 5.10, 5.14.
[7] Para. 7.56.
[8] See also John Mather, *The Impact of Contaminated Land on Groundwater: a United Kingdom Appraisal*, Land Contamination and Reclamation, Vol. 1, No. 4, p. 187 (1993); The National Rivers Authority report, *Contaminated Land and the Water Environment* (Water Quality Series, No. 15, March 1994) also gives a number of examples, based on actual investigations by the NRA.

In some cases individual contaminated sites may present major problems for surface water quality. The example was given of the River Tame which rises in the Black Country and flows through the Birmingham conurbation.[9] Two former waste sites at Slackey Lane and Bentley Mill Lane near Walsall contribute between them about six tonnes per year of copper and 15 tonnes of nickel to the river—amounting in average conditions to about one-sixth of both the copper and nickel loads of the Tame at its confluence with the Trent. Cleaning up the sites may be necessary to meet the UK's obligation to reduce List II substances discharged to the North Sea by 50 per cent.

Other problems which have assumed recent prominence are the increasing usage by industry of chlorinated organic solvents[10] (dense non-aqueous phase liquids or DNAPLS, introduced between 1920–1950 and with sharply increased post-war usage peaking in the 1970s) and the threat presented by leaking underground liquid storage and distribution systems for raw and waste chemicals and hydrocarbons.[11]

The properties of DNAPLS are particularly conducive to groundwater contamination problems: small surface spills may permente the unsaturated zone and remain in pore spaces from which they may gradually be dissolved by infiltrating surface precipitation and so reach the groundwater. Larger spills with a sufficient "driving head" may penetrate directly into the groundwater system; being denser than water, the DNAPL may then "pool" when it reaches an impervious layer and migrate downslope by gravity, in some cases in the opposite direction to groundwater flow. It is possible for one litre of certain solvents to contaminate as much as 50 million litres of groundwater to levels unacceptable for drinking water.

The discharge of functions in relation to water generally

6.02   The bodies concerned with supply and protection of water are essentially the water undertakers and statutory water companies, the sewerage undertakers and the National Rivers Authority. Their functions are set out below. In respect of contaminated land, it is the National Rivers Authority which is charged with the prevention of pollution of water resources. However, the sewerage undertakers are concerned to ensure that a risk of pollution does not arise from the discharge of their functions, for example, that sewage does not enter

---

[9] Para. 7.20 and Box 7.4.
[10] See Mather, n. 8 above.
[11] R. Harris, *Groundwater Pollution Risks from Underground Storage Tanks*, Land Contamination and Reclamation, Vol. 1, No. 4, p. 197 (1993).

groundwater by leakage, or overflow from sewage treatment facilities, from the disposal of sewage sludge, or indeed from the main sewerage system itself. Equally, the water undertakers, as the suppliers of water to the ultimate consumer, are concerned that the National Rivers Authority should prevent pollution entering water resources to which they may have recourse in the disharge of their functions. Also, the water undertakers are themselves responsible for the treatment of water before it reaches the ultimate consumer and so have a vested interest in the protection of their own resources, whether in surface water boreholes or reservoirs.[12]

Function	Body	Powers and Duties
The treatment and supply of water to the consumer; clean water	Statutory water undertakers and water companies	see para. 6.27 *et seq.*
Sewage treatment and disposal; dirty water	Statutory sewage undertakers	See para. 6.37 *et seq.*
The prevention of pollution to water resources	The National Rivers Authority and (in relation to prescribed processes for integrated pollution control) Her Majesty's Inspectorate of Pollution (HMIP)	See para. 6.10 *et seq.*

Relevant domestic and EC legislation

The Water Act 1989 provided for privatisation of the former regional **6.03** water authorities and the creation of the National Rivers Authority. Subsequently, the relevant provisions have been split between two main Acts. The Water Resources Act 1991 is concerned with the role of the National Rivers Authority and the protection of water resources by way of abstraction, licensing and pollution control. The Water Industry Act 1991 deals with both water supply and sewerage services. Other relevant statutes are the Statutory Water Companies Act 1991, the Land Drainage Act 1991 and the Water Consolidation (Consequential Provisions) Act 1991.

The relationship between UK law and EC directives is important in the field of water law and reference is made to the various relevant

---

[12] See paras. 6.33.

measures throughout this chapter. However, the main measures are listed below. As with all directives, under article 189 of the Treaty of Rome, the measure is binding as to the result to be achieved, but leaves to member states the choice of form and method.

Directive	Subject	Date of Compliance
75/440/EEC O.J. L194, 25.7.75	Quality of surface water intended for the abstraction of drinking water; see para. 6.29	October 11, 1981
76/160/EEC O.J. L131, 5.2.76	Quality of bathing water	December 10, 1985 (unless derogations given)
76/464/EEC O.J. L129, 18.5.76	Pollution caused by certain dangerous substances discharged into the acquatic environment. Various "daughter directives" deal with specific dangerous substances; see para. 6.25	No date given in directive
78/659/EEC O.J. L222 14.8.78	Quality of fresh waters needing protection or improvement in order to support fish life	July 20, 1980; standards to be met by July 19, 1985
79/923/EEC O.J. L281, 3.11.76	Quality required for shellfish waters	November 5, 1981; standards to be met by November 5, 1987
80/68/EEC O.J. L20, 26.1.80	The protection of groundwater against pollution caused by various dangerous substances; see para. 6.08	December 19, 1981; existing discharges to be controlled by December 19, 1985
80/778/EEC O.J. L229, 30.08.80	Quality of water intended for human consumption ("the drinking water directive"); see para. 6.30	July 17, 1985 (subject to any derogations or delays granted)
91/271/EEC O.J. L135, 30.5.91	Urban waste water treatment	July 30, 1993— compliance required in accordance with timetable thereafter

Directive	Subject	Date of Compliance
91/676/EEC O.J. L375, 31.12.91	The protection of waters against pollution caused by nitrates from agricultural sources	December 19, 1993— compliance required in accordance with timetable thereafter

The functions of the National Rivers Authority

The NRA was established under section 1 of the Water Act 1989 and **6.04** is continued in existence by section 1 of the Water Resources Act 1991; its duty is to provide integrated management of the water environment in England and Wales. It is a corporate body[13] and is not to be regarded as the servant or agent of the Crown or enjoying any of the Crown's immunities or privileges.[14] It may, much in the same way as a local authority has powers so to do,[15] delegate its powers to a committee or sub-committee or employee who has been properly authorised to exercise them[16]: additionally delegation can extend to an individual member. There must therefore be the appropriate delegation agreement, which will be relevant where the question of any authorisation arises, for example, to enter into an agreement or to prosecute.

The NRA is organised into eight regional units. It has specific charging powers for the exercise of its functions, such as the issue of abstraction or impoundment licences.[17] It also has the power to issue levies under section 74 of the Local Government Finance Act 1988 for the purpose of its flood defence functions.[18]

The functions carried out by the former Regional Water Authorities in relation to the management of the water environment were transferred to the NRA on September 1, 1989 by section 4(1) of the Water Act 1989. Generally the NRA may carry out research into the demand for water and the availability of resources to meet that demand in England and Wales.[19] It is required to take the necessary action with regard to the conservation and redistribution of water resources[20] and is responsible,

---

[13] Water Resources Act 1991, s.1(1).
[14] Water Resources Act 1991, s.1(5).
[15] Sched. 1, para. 4, Water Resources Act 1991. The exception relates to flood defence functions.
[16] Sched. 1, para. 5, Water Resources Act 1991. In the case of local authorities delegation to a member (described as a "committee of one") is not lawful, as opposed to delegation to an officer.
[17] Water Resources Act 1991, Pt VI.
[18] Water Resources Act 1991, s.133.
[19] Water Resources Act 1991, s.188.
[20] Water Resources Act 1991, s.19.

subject to the approval of the Secretary of State, for setting minimum acceptable flows for particular inland waters, for licensing for abstraction or impoundment of water under the Act and for certain measures to cope with drought. The management of reservoirs will usually fall to the water undertakers whose supply emanates from them, but where a reservoir fulfills a river flow-regulating role it will be controlled under an operating agreement made between the relevant water undertaker and the NRA.

Control of water quality is maintained by ensuring that water quality objectives established by the Secretary of State under section 83 of the Water Resources Act 1991 are maintained for all relevant controlled waters. The NRA uses its powers to grant consents for discharges under Chapter II, Part III of the Act for this purpose so as to limit the entry of polluting matter into water. Under section 190 of the Act it records details of the consents granted and analyses samples of discharges made under those consents, entering them in the pollution register.

The NRA may make byelaws to prevent the pollution of controlled waters and will administer the operation of water protection zones established by Regulations made under section 93 of the Act. It has power to prosecute offences, and, where pollution has occurred or is likely to occur, it may conduct anti-pollution operations to remedy the situation.[21] However the NRA is not solely responsible in this matter. The Environment Protection Act 1990 introduced a system of integrated pollution control for processes prescribed under section 2 of the Act as being regulated by Her Majesty's Inspectorate of Pollution.[22] Processes are prescribed for this purpose by Part A of Schedule 1 of the Environmental Protection (Prescribed Processes and Substances) Regulations 1991.[23] Discharges into the sea, inland waters or groundwaters from such processes will be authorised by the Inspectorate and fall outside the pollution control regime of Part III of the 1991 Act.[24] In relation to these functions, a Memorandum of Understanding has been agreed between the NRA and Her Majesty's Inspectorate of Pollution to provide working arrangements for the discharge of their separate responsibilities.[25] The Government's intention is ultimately to create a unified Environmental Agency incorporating both the NRA and HMIP, paving legislation for this purpose being expected in 1994.

Currently it is not part of the NRA's functions to monitor land for contamination; their role is limited to the monitoring of pollution from such land by testing water quality on a regular basis or by responding to complaints or reports as to water pollution incidents.

---

[21] S.161. See further para. 2.50.
[22] See further para. 5.11.
[23] S.I. 1991 No. 472 as amended; see further para. 5.12.
[24] Environmental Protection Act 1990, Sched. 15, para. 29.
[25] *Integrated Pollution Control: A Practical Guide* (HMSO, 1993).

The provision of water and sewerage services

The Water Industry Act 1991 sets out the manner in which the **6.05** Secretary of State exercises control and supervision for the provision of both water and sewerage services. The initial appointments of companies as water or sewerage undertakers, or both, were made by him, although he may authorise the Director General of Water Services to make new ones.[26] These appointments are subject to conditions initially imposed by the Secretary of State. The standards of performance in connection with the provision of water or sewerage services are to be set out in regulations, the first of which were made by the Secretary of State alone.[27] The Director General of Water Services is not a member of the Department of the Environment;[28] nevertheless his appointment is by the Secretary of State, who may to some extent direct the exercise of his functions or may require him to obtain prior authorisation for certain actions.[29] In the event of a dispute between the customer and the undertaker it will be the Secretary of State who appoints an arbitrator in default of agreement.[30]

The quality of water supplied for domestic purposes will be the Secretary of State's particular concern; the relevant standards are prescribed under the Water Supply (Water Quality) Regulations 1989.[31] Further, in exercising his functions concerning the appointment and regulation of water and sewerage undertakers, or setting standards of performance in connection with the water supply, sewerage services or the carrying out of works on private land, the Secretary of State must act in a way that he considers best calculated to secure the general objectives of the Act. Thus, the relationship between the Secretary, the Director General of Water Services and the water and sewerage undertakers reflects a separation of functions and responsibilities.

Liability issues

Liability in relation to contaminated land is discussed at Chapter 2. **6.06** Nonetheless it may be helpful to summarise here the main heads of liability which may be of relevance in the context of water pollution.

---

[26] S.6(1)(*b*).
[27] Ss.38(2) and 95(2).
[28] S.1(2).
[29] S.193(1).
[30] S.49(3).
[31] S.I. 1989 No. 147; see further para. 6.31 below.

Nature of Liability	Cross reference
Nuisance	2.13 *et seq.*
Negligence	2.25 *et seq.*
Rylands v. *Fletcher*	2.05 *et seq.*
Interference with riparian rights	2.21
Interference with natural rights in groundwater	2.22
Trespass	2.04
Causing or knowingly permitting pollution of controlled water	2.44 *et seq.*
Liability to pay for anti-pollution works	2.50
Waste causing water pollution	2.31 and 2.57
Statutory nuisance	2.66 *et seq.*

GROUNDWATER

Introduction

6.07   Almost all types of rock in the Earth's upper crust contain openings called pores or voids.[32] This property is known as porosity: rocks containing a high proportion of such void space are known as "porous" or "highly porous." To a greater or lesser extent these pores may be filled with water. The situation where all the pores are entirely filled with water is known as saturation: it is the complete filling with water which distinguished the "saturated zone" from the "unsaturated zone"—where part only of the void space contains water. Where a well or borehole is sunk, this will fill with water until the water reaches a constant level, known as the "water table": this will generally correspond to the upper level of the saturated zone. The depth of the water table will vary from the surface level to 100 metres or more. All water which occurs naturally below the earth's surface is called sub-surface water, whether it occurs in the saturated or unsaturated zone; water in the saturated zone is called groundwater.

The extent to which groundwater is useable varies, depending on factors such as depth, salinity and quality. The other crucial factor as to the exploitability of groundwater resources is the ease with which water can flow through the relevant strata, known as permeability. Layers of rock which are sufficiently porous to store water *and* permeable enough to allow water to flow through them in economic quantities are known as

[32] See generally M. Price, *Introducing Groundwater* (London 1985).

aquifers. An aquifer may be "confined" in the sense of being surrounded above and below by impervious strata through which water cannot readily pass, *e.g.* clays or shales. In such circumstances the water in the aquifer will be under pressure so that the water will naturally rise if a borehole is sunk. The final factor which is crucial to the amount of groundwater available is the degree of replenishment from rainfall or from adjacent aquifers: this involves consideration of the water balance of the area.

The UK has a varied and interesting geology.[33] Much of Scotland, Wales and Northern Ireland is formed of older rocks with low permeabilities, so that these areas have little in the way of useful aquifers. The main aquifers in England and Wales consist of consolidated sedimentary rocks—principally chalk and sandstones: these are found generally in the south-eastern part of the British Isles. The porosity of the chalk will vary and in fact much of the groundwater movement within the chalk occurs in cracks or fissures. In the sandstone aquifers permeability is more dependent upon pore size and whether the sandstone is of a fine or coarse-grained nature.

It has been estimated that about one third of water abstracted in England and Wales for public supply comes from groundwater resources.[34] As many as 15 million people rely on groundwater for their drinking water, mostly in the Anglian, Severn-Trent, Southern and Thames Regions. A study commissioned by the Department of Environment and published in 1988[35] suggested that the general quality of most groundwater resources was good, but highlighted the vulnerability of such water to contamination from industrial and agricultural practices and the need for protective action. Another more recent issue which has been identified is the rising level of groundwater which is occurring within many conurbations, in some cases due to significant recharge from leaking underground water services combined with lower rates of industrial abstraction. This may in future years have pollution implications in causing the existing pollution load present in soil or groundwater to rise closer to the surface.

EC Policy on Groundwater

The EC legislation currently dealing with groundwater is the Council **6.08** Directive of December 17, 1979 on the protection of groundwater against

[33] *Ibid.*, p. 79.
[34] DoE News Release No. 680, December 2, 1988. The NRA Policy Document on the protection of Groundwater published in 1992 (see para 6.10) gives the figure as 35 per cent.
[35] Sir William Halcrow and Partners Ltd., *Assessment of Groundwater in England and Wales* (HMSO, 1988).

245

pollution caused by certain dangerous substances.[36] The preamble to the Directive refers to the urgent need for action to protect the
groundwater of the Community from pollution, particularly that caused
by certain toxic, persistent and bioaccumulable substances. The scheme
of the Directive is to place families and groups of certain substances into
two lists, I and II; List II being those substances which could have a
harmful effect on groundwaters and List I being those substances which
are considered to present more serious risks. Both Lists contain some
very broad generic categories. For example, List I refers to "substances
which possess carcinogenic, mutagenic or teratogenic properties in or via
the aquatic environment" whilst List II includes "substances which
have a deleterious effect on the taste and/or odour of groundwater and
compounds liable to cause the formation of such substances in such
water as to render it unfit for human consumption."

Member States are required to prevent the introduction of List I
substances into groundwater by prohibiting all direct discharges and by
subjecting to prior investigation any disposal or tipping for the purpose
of disposal of those substances which might lead to indirect discharge.
Such tipping must either be prohibited or authorised on the proviso that
all the technical precautions necessary to prevent indirect discharge are
observed.[37] Appropriate measures must also be taken to prevent any
indirect discharge of List I substances due to activities other than
tipping or disposal. The main exception to these requirements is where
investigations reveal that the groundwater in question is "permanently
unsuitable for other uses, especially domestic or agricultural": here the
discharge may be authorised provided the presence of List I substance
does not impede exploitation of ground resources (*e.g.* minerals) and if
all technical precautions have been taken to ensure that the substances
cannot reach other aquatic systems or harm other ecosystems.[38]

In relation to List II substances Member States must limit their
introduction into groundwater so as to avoid pollution: this requires
direct discharges and tipping for disposal which might lead to indirect
discharges to be subject to investigation.[39] In the light of that investigation, authorisation may be granted, provided that all the technical
precautions for preventing groundwater pollution are observed. Further,
Member States shall take the appropriate measures they deem necessary
to limit all indirect discharges of List II substances due to other
activities in or on the ground.[40]

The state of European groundwater was considered by EC Ministers
at a seminar at The Hague on November 26–27, 1991. A Report was

[36] 80/68/EEC. O.J. L20, p. 43.
[37] Arts. 3(*a*) and 4.1.
[38] Art. 4.2.
[39] Art. 5.1.
[40] Art. 5.2.

prepared for that seminar by the Dutch National Institute for Public Health and Environmental Protection (RIVM) and the National Institute for Inland Water Management and Waste Water Treatment (RIZA).[41] The Report painted a serious picture of practices which were leading to non-sustainable use of groundwater system: the most serious problems identified were pollution from pesticides and nitrates, pollution from industrial and urban areas, over-exploitation and intensified drainage, and point-source pollution from "illegal or improper dumping of municipal, industrial, mining and hazardous waste". For example, it was estimated that waste disposal could lead, if no remedial actions were taken, to a potential polluted area of groundwater systems of 20,000–60,000 km^2 within 50 years; some 2–4 per cent. of the land surface of the Community. The Report urged the adoption of a uniform and integrated approach to protection and sustainable use of groundwaters incorporating surface water, environment and physical planning.

This theme was restated in the EC Council resolution of February 25, 1992 on future Community Policy,[42] which took account of the final declaration of The Hague Ministerial Seminar. The Resolution calls on the Commission:

(a) to submit, if possible by mid-1993,[43] a detailed action programme; and
(b) to draft a proposal for revising the groundwater directive by incorporating it into a general freshwaters management policy, including freshwater protection.

UK Implementation of EC Groundwater Policy

The Government in its formal compliance letter to the European **6.09** Commission relating to the groundwater directive referred to the waste licensing and waste pollution provisions of the Control of Pollution Act 1974 as the means of implementation—despite the fact that not all of the relevant provisions were by then in force.[44]

The directive was explained in DoE Circular 4/82, issued on March 1, 1982.[45] This Circular put forward a somewhat relaxed interpretation of the

---

[41] *Sustainable Use of Groundwater: Problems and Threats in the European Communities,* Report No. 600025001, November 1991.
[42] 92/C 59/02, O.J. C59/2, 6.3.92.
[43] At the time or writing, no such Programme has been published.
[44] See N. Haigh, *Manual of Environmental Policy: The EC and Britain* (Longman, 1992), p. 4.7–5.
[45] Welsh Office 7/82.

directive, relating it essentially to whether the discharge in question would "force a change in the use of the aquifer or would make necessary a significant difference in the treatment of its water before use".[46] Also, the Circular suggested that pollution of groundwater occurring as the result of historical activities should not require action under the terms of the directive once those activities had ceased, unless it constituted a breach of continuing and enforceable conditions on the original consent.[47]

Misfortune befell the UK Government when a complaint was made to the Commission concerning a "dilute and disperse" landfill at Pakefield in Suffolk, from which pesticide residues were said to be leaching into groundwater. Infringement proceedings resulted in the issue of Circular 20/90[48] which contained firmer advice. It indicated the Government's agreement with the Commission that the three pesticides in question (bromoxynil, bromoxynil octanoate and chlorpyrifos) were to be regarded as List I substances, suggested that waste disposal authorities should seek the advice of the NRA at sites involving the disposal of List I substances, and that site licences should be reviewed where discharges were liable to affect groundwater adversely, other than that which was permanently unuseable.

Advice on the protection of groundwater in the context of waste disposal is now provided at Annex 7 of Circ. 11/94 on The Waste Management Licensing Regulations 1994. Waste Regulation Authorities are expected to consider whether the conditions imposed at existing operational waste sites achieve the level of protection required by the Directive and, if not, take whatever steps are necessary. This may involve variation of licence conditions to secure adequate monitoring of groundwater, containment of wastes disposed of in new phases of site construction, prohibition of deposit of wastes containing List I substances where that would lead to a discharge of those substances into groundwater; and prohibition of wastes where their composition or expected degradation products are such that this would lead to pollution of the groundwater by List II substances.[48a]

Groundwater protection responsibilities: the NRA

6.10   The general duties of the NRA under the Water Resources Act 1991 have been noted; they include the monitoring and protection of the quality of groundwater,[49] the conservation of water resources[50] and,

---

[46] Para. 8.
[47] Para. 14.
[48] Welsh Office 34/90.
[48a] Circ. 11/94, Sched. 4, para. 7.21. See also Chap. 5 on waste site licence conditions.
[49] S.87.
[50] S.19.

where appropriate, the enhanced conservation of the surface water environment which in many cases is dependent on the proper management of groundwater.[51] This chapter is only concerned with that part of the NRA's policy which is directed to problems of contaminated land.

The NRA's general policy on groundwater protection is set out in its 1992 document, *Policy and Practice for the Protection of Groundwater*.[52] This document places great stress on the NRA's duties referred to above, and on the implementation of EC policy on sustainable groundwater management.[53] This is regarded as a highly complex and difficult task, involving many interactive factors, and in which the NRA will seek to influence the decisions and policies of others whose actions can affect the protection of groundwater.

The document sets out how the NRA will meet its statutory responsibilities, and in particular aims to:

(a) ensure that all risks to groundwater resources, point source and diffuse, are dealt with in a common framework;
(b) provide a common basis for decisions affecting groundwater resources within and between its regions; and
(c) encourage compatibility of approach between the NRA and other bodies with statutory responsibilities for the protection of groundwater.

It contains the following useful summary of groundwater protection legislation directly implemented by the NRA.

Origin	Legislation	NRA Role
European	EC Groundwater Directive (80/68/EEC)	Competent authority in association with Waste Regulation Authorities and Mineral Planning Authorities.
	Directive on Diffuse Pollution by Nitrates (80/68/EEC)	Direction to monitor, identification of vulnerable zones.

---

[51] S.16.
[52] Referred to hereafter as NRA Policy and Practice.
[53] See para. 6.08 above.

Origin	Legislation	NRA Role
U.K.	Water Industry Act 1991, s.71(1)	Powers to control waste of water resources by artesian overflow.
	Water Resources Act 1991, s.24	Powers to control by licence most types of abstraction.
	Water Resources Act 1991, s.30	Power to protect groundwater resources during dewatering.
	Water Resources Act 1991, s.83	Provides for definition of Water Quality Objectives for controlled waters.
	Water Resources Act 1991, s.88	Powers to control discharges to controlled water.
	Water Resources Act 1991, s.92	Powers under regulations to require pollution prevention measures to be taken.
	Water Resources Act 1991, s.93	Provision for statutory water protection zones.
	Water Resources Act 1991, s.94	Provision for Nitrate Sensitive Areas (which may be used to implement the EC Nitrates Directive).
	Water Resources Act 1991, s.161	Powers to take remedial action to prevent pollution occurring or continuing.
	Water Resources Act 1991, s.199	Powers to preserve and protect groundwater during mineral exploration.
	Control of Pollution (Silage, Slurry & Agricultural Fuel Oil) Regulations	Powers to ensure high standards on all new and enlarged installations for silage, slurry and fuel oil to minimise the risk of pollution.

Groundwater protection—NRA and other relevant bodies

6.11   Whilst groundwater protection is a particularly significant part of the NRA's responsibilities, other bodies also exercise relevant powers. NRA Policy and Practice summarises these bodies and the arrangements for liaison with the NRA as follows:

Agency	Area of Responsibility	Relevant Legislation	Locus of NRA
Dept of the Environment	Sponsoring ministry of NRA	Water Resources Act 1991	Direct liaison
	Making of regulations and directions under the Water Resources Act 1991	Water Resources Act 1991	Direct liaison
	Determinations of appeals on licences to abstract from, and consents to discharge to, groundwater	Water Resources Act 1991	Regulating body
	Determination of appeals on waste management licences	Control of Pollution Act Part I/ Environmental Protection Act 1990	Statutory consultee
	Determination of planning appeals	Town & Country Planning Acts	Consultee
	EC Groundwater directive	80/68/EEC	Competent authority with others
	EC Nitrate Directive	91/676/EEC	Competent Authority
	Mineral Extraction policy, Land Use Planning Policies and Legislation	Town & Country Planning Acts & related Regulations	Consultee
	Contaminated Land Policy		Direct liaison
	Waste Management Policy		Direct liaison
Her Majesty's Inspectorate of Pollution	Discharge to groundwater from prescribed processes	Environmental Protection Act 1990	Direct liaison
	Prevention of land contamination from certain substances	Environmental Protection Act 1990	No formal contact

Agency	Area of Responsibility	Relevant Legislation	Locus of NRA
	Discharge of radioactive substances to groundwater	Radioactive Substances Act 1993	No formal contact
Ministry of Agriculture	Nitrate Sensitive Areas	Water Resources Act 1991	Direct liaison
	Control of Pesticide Regulations	Food and Environmental Protection Act 1985, S.I. 1986 No. 1510	Consultee
	Code of Good Agricultural Practice	Water Resources Act 1991	Consulteee
	Natural Mineral Water Regulations	S.I. 1985 No. 71	No formal contact
English County Councils Metropolitan Borough Councils	Waste Disposal Regulation, Waste Disposal Plans	Control of Pollution Act 1974, Town & Country Planning Acts, Environmental Protection Act 1990	Statutory consultee
Welsh District Councils	Competent Authority for waste to and redevelopment of contaminated land	EC Groundwater Directive (80/68/EEC)	None
County Councils, Metropolitan Borough Councils, National Parks Authorities	Development control over mineral extraction	Town & Country Planning Act 1990	Statutory consultee
District Councils & Unitary Authorities	Development planning	Town & Country Planning Act 1990	Statutory consultee

Agency	Area of Responsibility	Relevant Legislation	Locus of NRA
District Councils & Unitary Authorities— *cont.*	Storage of Hazardous Substances	Planning (Hazardous Substances) Act 1990	Statutory consultee for new consents
	Competent Authority for drawing up Registers of Contaminated Land	Environmental Protection Act 1990	Direct contact
	Competent Authority	EC Mineral Water Directive (80/777)	No formal contact
	Private water supply register/monitoring	Private Water Supply Regulations	Advisory contact
Local and Regional Planning Authorities	Forward Planning Policies, Local Structure and Subject Plans (Minerals/ Waste Disposal)	Town & Country Planning Acts	Statutory consultee
National Park Authorities	Development control; Local and Structure Plans	Town & Country Planning Acts, National Park Acts	Statutory consultee
English Nature and Countryside for Wales	Consultee on issue of licences to abstract and consents to discharge with conservation implications	Water Resources Act 1991	Direct contact

Statutory water quality objectives

The Water Resources Act 1991 sets out a framework for establishing **6.12** water quality objectives for the purpose of maintaining and improving the quality of controlled waters.[54] The Secretary of State may make regulations prescribing a system of classifying the quality of such waters (including groundwater)[55] and may establish water quality objectives for any description of waters by notice served on the NRA.[56]

[54] S.83(1). See also para. 6.23.
[55] S.82.
[56] S.83(1).

253

The Secretary of State and NRA are under a duty to exercise the powers conferred upon them to ensure, so far as practicable by the exercise of those powers, that these water quality objectives are achieved at all times.[57]

It is intended that statutory water quality objectives for groundwater should be established after those for rivers;[58] in setting those objectives due account will need to be taken of SWQOs for surface water, the use to be made of the groundwater, natural groundwater quality and cases where historical long term pollution from numerous sources has led to deterioration in quality.[59]

Statutory water protection zones

6.13   Section 93 of the Water Resources Act 1991 allows the Secretary of State to make provision by order designating any area as a water protection zone and prohibiting or restricting the carrying on in the designated area of such activities as may be specified or described. The procedure for making such orders is set out in Schedule 11 of the Act and can be initiated only by the NRA making an application to the Secretary of State.[60] The precondition for making the order is that the Secretary of State must be satisfied that it is appropriate, with a view to controlling the entry of any poisonous, noxious or polluting matter[61] into controlled waters, to prohibit or restrict the carrying on of activities which the Secretary of State considers are likely to result in the pollution of such waters.[62]

The order may confer power on the NRA to determine the activities affected and the circumstances in which they are prohibited or restricted; the consent of the NRA, which may be subject to conditions, can also be required.[63] The NRA has published a consultation document indicating its intention to make application to the Secretary of State for designation of the freshwater River Dee catchment as a water protection zone.[64] The main features of the proposed designation order are the requirement for the NRA's consent before the storage or use of particular chemical substances within certain, broadly industrial, sites; and the demonstration of a satisfactory risk assessment for both the operation and the storage. A transitional period is proposed during which deemed consents

---

[57] S.84(1).
[58] NRA Policy and Practice, p. 6.
[59] *Ibid.*
[60] Subs. 93(5).
[61] Except for agricultural nitrates; see below.
[62] Subs. 93(2).
[63] Subs. 93(4).
[64] River Dee Water Protection Zone (NRA Welsh Region, December 1993).

would be given to allow the risk assessment process to take place. The NRA is engaged in a project to formulate the relevant risk assessment methodologies, including computer software known as PRAIRIE (Pollution Risk from Accidental Influxes into Rivers and Estuaries).

Separate provisions apply to the designation of nitrate sensitive areas[65] and these are discussed elsewhere.[66]

Basis of classifying groundwater: vulnerability and risk

The NRA's approach to vulnerability is that wherever groundwater is **6.14** present there is the potential for it to be adversely affected by human activity: no soil or rock is completely impermeable, no pollutant completely immobile.[67] Nonetheless, the concept of vulnerability recognises that risks of pollution from a given activity are greater in certain hydrological, geological and soil situations than others.

Groundwater vulnerability is classified on the basis of four key variables which determine vulnerability.[68] They are:

(i) nature of overlying soil cover;
(ii) presence and nature of drift;
(iii) nature of strata; and
(iv) depth of water table (the unsaturated zone).

The risk of pollution by activities such as the spreading of sludge and manures, and from many other types of diffuse pollution, depend upon the attenuating characteristics of the soil. For this purpose the soil is taken to be the weathered zone affected by living organisms and undergoing seasonal change in moisture, temperature and gaseous composition. In the United Kingdom it may be up to as much as two metres in depth. Soils which have little ability to attenuate a variety of source pollutants are classified as soils of high leaching potential; soils with a moderate or high ability to prevent penetration are classified as soil of intermediate leaching potential, "I", and soil of low leaching potential, "L", accordingly.

In many areas drift deposits overlay the solid geology; they vary in thickness and lithology both vertically and horizontally, but where the drift is of substantial thickness and low permeability it can provide an effective barrier to surface pollutant migration. It is therefore relevant to vulnerability.

---

[65] S.94.
[66] See para. 5.38.
[67] NRA, Policy and Practice, p. 14.
[68] *Ibid.*, p. 14.

The way in which geological strata may contain groundwater has already been explained: where groundwater is present in exploitable quantities the strata are known as aquifers. However, even in relation to non-aquifers, groundwater flow does take place, although imperceptibly, and needs to be taken into account. Aquifers are categorised as:

(a) **major aquifers**—highly permeable formations which may be very productive and able to support large supply abstractions; and

(b) **minor aquifers**—fractured rocks without high primary permeability, but which are important for local suppliers and in providing base flow for rivers.

The depth of the unsaturated zone is important; this can play a significant role in attenuating the concentration of pollutants through physical, chemical and biochemical processes, and by acting as a delay mechanism in terms of travel times of pollutants.

The proximity of an industrial or commercial activity to a groundwater abstraction is one of the most important factors in assessing the risk to an existing groundwater source.[69] All sources, including springs, wells and boreholes are liable to contamination and need to be protected. With this in mind three groundwater protection zones are recognised;

(i) Zone I (inner source protection)

Zone I is designed to protect groundwater against the effects of human activity which might have an immediate effect upon the source. The area is defined by a 50-day travel time from any point below the water table to the source and has a minimum of 50 metres radius from the source. The 50-day travel time zone is based on the time it takes for biological contaminants to decay.

(ii) Zone II (Outer source protection)

Zone II is an area, larger than Zone I, defined by a 400-day travel time from any point below the water table to the source. The travel time is based upon that required to provide delay and attenuation of slowly degrading pollutants.

(iii) Zone III (Source catchment)

Zone III covers the complete catchment area of a groundwater source. The area will largely depend on the volume extracted and effective rainfall. It may vary from tens to a few thousands of hectares.

---

[69] *Ibid*, p. 19.

The NRA Ground Water Vulnerability Map of England and Wales scaled at 1:1,000,000 (1992) shows a number of highly vulnerable areas, in the south of England for example, in a line stretching from Marlborough north east through Luton and Cambridge to Thetford and up to Hunstanton; another around Salisbury and Winchester, and another in a westerly arc from Guildford to Brighton. This scale of map can however give only the broadest of indications and sub-regional maps at a scale of 1:100,000 are to be published. Ultimately, however, decisions will be taken based on site specific data rather than maps. The NRA has developed a methodology for defining Source Protection Zones, but acknowledges that any method is limited by the sufficiency of data available and is willing to subject the Zones to reappraisal in the light of changed circumstances or new knowledge.[70]

The way in which the NRA operate this system is that they would, for example, object to large graveyards or animal burial sites being established within Zone I; restrictions may also be likely within Zone II subject to evaluation and assessment.[71]

Similarly, new sewage works with their potential for contamination would be opposed within Zones I and II, and the laying of new mains sewers within Zone I.[72] New underground storage tanks for hydrocarbons would be opposed within Zone I and discouraged within Zones II and III; in any event the intention is ultimately to create restrictions on industrial oil storage under section 92 of the Water Resources Act 1991.[73]

The following paragraphs deal more specifically with the NRA's policy as it relates to contaminated land.

National Rivers Authority policy: consultation by local planning authorities

It is imperative that groundwater quality interests are taken into **6.15** account as material considerations where redevelopment is proposed, though at the same time the NRA's views will not be totally conclusive since other material considerations must also be taken into account.[74]

Policy D2 of the NRA's Policy and Practice reads:

> "The National Rivers Authority will seek to be consulted by local planning authorities about any application for development or other works on sites likely to be contaminated."

[70] *Ibid*, p. 20.
[71] *Ibid*, p. 47.
[72] *Ibid*.
[73] *Ibid*.
[74] See *Ynys Mon Borough Council* v. *Secretary of State for Wales and Jones Brothers (Construction) Company Ltd.* [1993] J.P.L. 225.

The written justification of Policy D2 reads:

"To ensure that groundwater quality interests are covered on sites where redevelopment is proposed, it is essential that consultation takes place between the developer and the NRA as early as possible before any site investigations commence. The possibility of contamination should be clearly indicated by the local planning authority or the applicant".

(a) The responsibilities of the local planning authority in respect of contamination

Although not a statutory requirement, the local planning authority should address the question of contamination and pollution on the form to be completed by the application for planning permission; most application forms devised by local planning authorities contain a question or questions relating to this aspect. Further, local planning authorities, whether or not they have compiled information preparatory to the now abortive section 143 registers or otherwise, may have at their disposal information which would suggest a possibility of contamination in respect of a given site; where this is the case, as a matter of good practice that information should be passed to the NRA.

(b) Responsibilities of the applicant

The applicant's responsibilities include correctly completing the application form for planning permission so as to disclose any contamination problem there may be in respect of a given site; and, further, to hold discussions with the NRA before any site investigations are carried out. This is a most important aspect in practice. Those carrying out site investigations depend entirely upon the quality of their instructions for the purposes of their report. If there are groundwater aspects in respect of contamination they should be instructed to consider these, probably in consultation with the NRA.[75]

(c) Consultation by the local planning authority

The local planning authority are required to consult certain statutory consultees; further, under the auspices of a non-statutory Code of Practice, there is general agreement that local planning authorities should consult certain other bodies in appropriate cases. Generally the essentials of consultation are (a) that the consultee is given a reasonable time in which to consider the application in question; and (b) that the

[75] See Chap. 4 generally on site investigations.

consultee be given sufficient information, including where appropraite background papers, to appreciate fully the planning consequences of the application.[76]

Under Article 18 of the Town and Country Planning (General Development) Order 1988[77] before granting planning permission a local planning authority is under a duty to consult certain parties depending upon the description of the development concerned. The table which follows the Article sets out those consultation requirements and includes:

(j) Development involving or including mining operations	The National Rivers Authority
(o) Development including the carrying out of works or operations in the bed of or on the banks of a river or stream	The National Rivers Authority
(p) Development for the purposes of refining or storing mineral oils and their derivatives	The National Rivers Authority
(q) Development involving the use of land for the deposit of refuse or waste	The National Rivers Authority
(r) Development relating to the retention, treatment or disposal of sewage, trade waste, slurry or sludge (other than the laying of sewers, the construction of pump houses in a line of sewers, the construction of septic tanks and cess pools serving single dwelling houses or single caravans or single buildings in which not more than 10 people normally reside, work or congregate, and works ancillary thereto).	The National Rivers Authority
(s) Development relating to use of land as a cemetery	The National Rivers Authority
(x) Development for the purposes of fish farming	The National Rivers Authority

Further, Appendix C of Circular 22/88[78] contains a number of other non-statutory consultation requirements:

[76] *R* v. *Secretary of State for Social Services, ex parte Association of Metropolitan Authorities* (1986) 1 W.L.R. 1; see generally Tromans and Turrall-Clarke, *Planning Law, Practice and Precedents* (Sweet & Maxwell), para. 3.40.
[77] S.I. 1988 No. 1813, as amended by S.I. 1991 No. 2805.
[78] *General Development Order Consultation.*

Proposals which could lead to an increased industrial discharge into a river or estuary (Circular 118/72)	The National Rivers Authority
Proposals which could lead to increased drainage problems in areas notified as having high water tables (Circular 17/82)	The National Rivers Authority

Also Circular 30/92 on *Development and Flood Risk* points out the need for consultation with the NRA in relation to run-off from new development and the risks of dispersal of contaminants which can arise from the flooding of contaminated land.[79]

It can be seen from the above mentioned consultation requirements that in respect of many of them a judgment is required whether or not groundwater is likely to be affected by the proposal, and that judgment in necessarily one which involves considerable expertise. Not all applicants have the requisite knowledge in-house, or the financial means to acquire it, and in those circumstances it is important that the NRA themselves monitor the register of planning applications.[80] It is understood that the NRA has now appointed town and country planning liasion officers in each of its regional offices.

National Rivers Authority policy: planning permission and the high risk of contamination

6.16   On sites where contamination of the land concerned is highly likely and consequently groundwater pollution is a concern, the local planning authority should require that the applicant carry out a thorough investigation of the site through a reputable specialist consultant so that the extent of the problem can be identified and effective measures for the protection of ground and surface quality identified. Policy D3 of the National Rivers Authority is to this effect:

> "The NRA will recommend to the local planning authority that it refuse planning permission for the redevelopment of contaminated sites where water resources could be adversely affected unless it is satisfied that the proposals include effective measures for the protection of groundwater and surface water quality. It will advise

[79] Paras. 17–21 (WO 68/92).

[80] This appears to be the practice in a number of regions, *e.g.* South West, where all applications are considered and those of concern are logged on retrieval systems: see Gray and Connell (1990) *Water Law*, p. 21.

local planning authorities where insufficient or technically weak information has been provided so that they can require the applicant to supplement the details provided".

The investigation report should accompany the planning application; if it does not, the local planning authority would be justified in refusing to deal with the application in its absence. In practice, if the applicant wants planning permission he is going to have to negotiate with the NRA so that they are reasonably satisfied on the adequacy of his proposals from their point of view.

The question of site investigations for certain purposes has already been dealt with.[81] However for the purposes of satisfying the NRA as to the protection of groundwater, investigations should include assessment of the leaching characteristics of contaminants in the ground[82] and of the geology/hydrogeology of the site, including existing groundwater quality. The report should include a strategy for dealing with the contamination concerned and minimising water pollution. If the groundwater pollution is likely to be significant, those details should include the remedial action proposed.

There can be little doubt that on any planning appeal the Secretary of State or his inspector would be likely to take the risks of ground-water pollution very seriously indeed. For example, such risks were the main reason for refusal in November 1991 of the appeal by Leigh Environmental Limited against refusal of their application for a regional waste treatment centre at Kirk Sandall Industrial Estate, Doncaster.[83] The proposed site lay on a strategic and unprotected aquifer, presenting an unacceptable risk of chemical pollution even with the most sophisticated multiple containment measures.

National Rivers Authority policy: conditions and agreements to protect water resources

Policy D4 reads as follows: **6.17**

"The NRA will seek to ensure that planning permissions contain conditions designed to protect water resources. The NRA will strongly encourage the local planning authority to enter into planning obligations with developers under section 106 of the Town and Country Planning Act 1990 to control and monitor ground-

---

[81] See Chap. 4.
[82] The NRA has been reported to be working to validate a leachability test developed by WRC for recommended use on contaminated land: see *Industrial Waste Management* (May 1993) and *Environment Business*, May 19, 1993.
[83] Ref. APP/F4410/A/89/126733, November 11, 1991.

water and groundwater contamination during and after redevelopment".

A proper consideration of sections 73 and 73A of the Town and Country Planning Act 1990 is important in this context.[84] Section 73 envisages an application for permission to develop land without compliance with the conditions previously attached to the permission in question. Where development has already taken place, the appropriate course is for the applicant to rely on section 73A under which permission can be obtained to retain buildings or works or continue the use of land without complying with a condition.

From the NRA's point of view, the possibility that conditions may be challenged in this way, and the limited recourse that may be had to breach of condition as a matter of enforcement in practice, has led them to prefer agreements under section 106 of the Act. Such an agreement runs with the land and is enforceable by injunctive proceedings. Modification and discharge of planning obligations is now dealt with under section 106A of the Act as introduced by section 12 of the Planning and Compensation Act 1991; however discharge can generally only be sought at the expiration of the relevant period, which is, in the absence of a prescribed period, five years beginning with the date on which the obligation was entered into.[85]

Circular 16/91[86] suggests that if there is a choice between imposing a condition or a planning obligation it would be preferable to use the condition, which the developer can appeal; certainly conditions should not be duplicated in obligations. However, there may be circumstances where both a condition and an obligation are justified, for example, if in unilateral obligations a planning condition is imposed that the development should not be commenced until the necessary works have been carried out.[87] In respect of a large site, most or all of which is contaminated, it may be necessary to agree the cleaning up of contamination in phases so that the building works may proceed, and the property be occupied, as each phase is cleared. For obvious reasons the design of the phases is one which will require specialist advice and is unlikely to turn on pure planning principles.

The explanatory material to Policy D4 suggests that planning obligations should require a remediation plan statement to be submitted for the approval of the local planning authority in consultation with the NRA. This statement should include details of further site investigations,

[84] See, for example, Tromans and Turrall-Clarke, *Planning Law, Practice and Precedents* (Sweet & Maxwell) para. 3.85.
[85] S.106A(4).
[86] Para. B6.
[87] See para. 8.12 below.

chemical analysis, criteria and standards for removal or treatment for contaminated soil and final restoration. Details of foundations, cover material, drainage and groundwater quality monitoring programmes should also be included. This requirement as reflected in the policy explanation for Policy D4 is, however, inadequate on its own. There should be a time limit within which the statement has to be submitted and the obligation should indicate what will happen if the statement is inadequate. What is important is that any remedial works required should be identifiable under the terms of the obligation, which should be rigorous in this respect, and the remedial works should be stated in such a way that they are related to the proposed development in terms of timing. Any other arrangement might lead to those working on site, or occupying buildings resulting from the development, being exposed to risk.

National Rivers Authority policy: development plans

The policies contained in the contaminated land section of the NRA **6.18** Policy and Practice do not refer explicitly to development plans as such. However the NRA have adopted model policies for protecting and improving the water environment generally; these were first published in 1990 and local planning authorities are encouraged to adopt such policies in their local and district plans, and indeed in unitary development plans.[87a] The policies in question are grouped under three headings:

(i) flood protection;
(ii) conservation and enhancement of the water environment, including recreation, navigation and fishing; and
(iii) water quality and water resources.

It is heading (iii) above which is most referable to the contaminated land situation. The policies in question are:

(a) There will be a presumption against development, including changes in land-use, which in the opinion of the local planning authority after consultation with the NRA pose an unacceptable risk to the quality of ground or surface water;
(b) New development will only be permitted in locations where main foul sewers, sewage treatment and surface water drainage of adequate capacity and design are available or can

---

[87a] See the NRA document, "Guidance Notes for Local Planning Authorities on the Methods of Protecting the Water Environment through Development Plans" (NRA, March 1994).

263

be provided in time to serve the development. Infill development where septic tanks are proposed will only be permitted where the ground conditions are satisfactory and the plot is of adequate size to provide an adequate subsoil drainage system;

(c) Development will not be permitted in areas around potable groundwater source or over vulnerable areas of aquifers which, in the opinion of the local planning authority after consultation with the NRA, pose an unacceptable risk to the quality of the underlying groundwater;

(d) The protection of water resources will be co-ordinated with the development plan to prevent any detrimental impact on existing users, nature conservation and recreation;

(e) New mineral workings or waste disposal sites will not be permitted where, after consultation with the NRA, it is considered there would be adverse effects on the water resources of rivers and other waters.[88]

As mentioned elsewhere[89] not every local planning authority incorporates reference to policies of this sort in their development plans. Where they are found, the policy will often take a form as follows:

"The Council will have regard to the National Rivers Authority (NRA) model policies (as set out in Appendix . . .) when considering applications for development. The council will consult the NRA in all appropriate cases".

National Rivers Authority policy: clean up operations

6.19   The removal of contamination for development purposes is dealt with elsewhere[90] However is it clear from Policy D5 that the removal or suitable treatment of material with a perceived water pollution potential is an NRA requirement:

"The NRA will wish to ensure that any discharge, seepage or drainage resulting from the redevelopment of a contaminated site will be of a quality and quantity that will not pollute groundwater".

The policy explanation suggests that the target concentration for key contaminants should be specified. These should relate to the leached concentration, not total concentration as specified in guidance issued by the Inter-Departmental Committee on the Reclamation of Contaminated

---

[88] See further Chap. 8.
[89] See Chap. 5 generally.
[90] See Chap. 8.

Land (ICRCL). Further, an estimate of the quantity and quality of any continuing discharge from the developed site should be made. The monitoring of continuing discharges should be dealt in any planning obligation.

The NRA's position on clean-up has been further explained in its March 1994 report, *Contaminated Land and the Water Environment*.[90a] The report emphasises the importance of estimating the scale of the problem and the nature of the problem with respect to the potential effect of contaminated land on the aquatic environment; this is a necessary precondition to prioritising those sites which may need to be remedied. It is suggested that where relevant concentration standards are being breached, the role played by contaminated land must be considered alongside point source inputs through the catchment management process, together with an economic assessment of necessary remediation. With regard to the totality of inputs, the report suggests that it will be necessary to wait for the NRA's current exercise on quantifying inputs of Red List and other substances into coastal waters; then to investigate further those catchments which make a significant (greater than 1 per cent.) contribution and examine them to see if contaminated land sites are a contributory factor. The NRA suggests that notwithstanding such information, any site known to be a source of PCB input of more than trace amounts a day should in view of the general evidence against this compound, be noted and prioritised for future study and action. The NRA acknowledges that with groundwater the problem is less easily defined and the relevant considerations must include assessment of the relative importance of groundwater resources for abstraction or augmentation of other supplies, the extent to which loss would affect water management options in the relevant area, the extent to which a lasting remedy could be effected, the time it will take, the cost, and the overall benefits in a water management context.

In view of this, the report suggests that it should be necessary for the proposed Environment Agency to consider contaminated land with respect to those sites within a catchment which could be shown to be:

(a) polluting, or with the potential to pollute, existing groundwater sources and/or render the water contained in a significant part of a usable aquifer to be unfit for potable use; or

(b) a cause of breaching a surface water quality standard; or

(c) in conjunction with the "Red List reduction" exercise—a significant (greater than 1 per cent.) contribution to the annual input of Red List substances in coastal waters; or a source of more than trace quantities of PCBs to surface waters.

Other sites identified as problematic in the course of drawing up catchment management plans will be characterised with regard to the

[90a] Water Quality Series, No. 15.

perceived level of risk which they present of contaminating water, or of preventing national or international targets from being achieved; they would therefore be considered alongside other risks to water quality within a given catchment.

The report states that having identified and prioritised land, questions naturally arise as to how and by whom the problem should be tackled. At present the NRA acknowledges that prosecution may follow if pollution is actually being caused, in cases where the owner of contaminated land is unwilling to undertake a plan of remedial action. However, one of the principal reasons for carrying out a prosecution, the report suggests, is the desire to change the behaviour of the offender, particularly where the discharge is being actively managed. Where there is an ongoing pollution problem as a result of a passive input, a successful prosecution may have little effect, and indeed the scale of remedial action may greatly exceed the owner's ability to carry it out. Consideration then needs to be given to the availability of grant aid funding for remediation and what may be done by the NRA (or subsequently the Environment Agency) under existing powers. Where a situation needs to be remedied by a scheme which would involve capital expenditure followed by a subsequent management maintenance programme, the NRA does not intend to take on an operational commitment. The NRA would be present only consider using its own resources (whether or not these might be recoverable from the polluter) in order to carry out *short term* remedial work involving capital monies and/or *time-limited operational* activities. Such remedial work will only be undertaken if, in the case of surface waters, it had been identified via the catchment management plan process or, in the case of groundwaters, a cost benefit analysis study indicates that it is in the wider interests of the NRA resource management role to do so. The NRA would, in any case, need to obtain the approval of the Department of Environment for any expenditure in excess of £0.5 million under its Scheme of Delegation; in effect, therefore, the Government would be the final adjudicator over the extent to which the NRA committed itself to long-term remedial action.

National Rivers Authority policy: industrial areas of widespread contamination

6.20   Policy D6 reads:

> "In areas where historical industrial development is known to have caused widespread groundwater contamination, the NRA will review the merits and feasibility of groundwater clean-up depending upon local circumstances and available funding".

There are a number of historical industrial areas, located on aquifer outcrops, where groundwater pollution is inevitable. Where groundwater pollution has resulted from a number of sources it is difficult to pinpoint individual sites or incidents. An example is the contamination of the aquifer at Luton by chemical solvents, where the individual effect of specific polluters cannot be identified and generally the aquifer cannot be recovered. Policy D6 envisages that in these circumstances the benefits and feasibility of a groundwater clean up operation have to be carefully considered; in many cases it may be best if efforts are directed towards the removal of any remaining sources of pollution and the monitoring of groundwater quality to ensure that any redevelopment does not cause further deterioration. Containment of polluted groundwater by engineering methods or by sacrificial pumping may also be appropriate. What is important is that fresh initiatives resulting in a planning application should not unnecessarily be held up on broad considerations relating to a much wider area than the application site, particularly in circumstances where the applicant is content to deal with any pollution problems arising from the prospect of redevelopment of the site with which he is concerned. Provided that the redevelopment proposed will not exacerbate an existing wider problem, nor inhibit a clean up of the wider groundwater contamination, then the proposal ought to be allowed to proceed on the basis that any contamination problem in respect of the site itself will be dealt with in the usual way in accordance with policy D4.

National Rivers Authority policy: industrial discharges

Policy D7 reads: **6.21**

> "The National Rivers Authority will encourage the manufacturing industry and others to improve operational practices to eliminate unauthorised discharges to land. Where contamination of groundwater or of surface water through contaminated groundwater flow in apparent the National Rivers Authority will require remedial measures to be undertaken to prevent further pollution".

Where the NRA suspect or anticipate pollution entering groundwater from existing industrial sites, their policy is to discuss those aspects with local management in order to improve operational practices and encourage remedial measures, where necessary, on a progressive basis. Particular reference is made to prevention of pollution at source from oil storage facilities. Section 92 of the Water Resources Act 1991 permits regulations to be made for these purposes.

There are a number of aspects involved here. Accidental spillage and leakage often arise from poor management practices and what is really required is a management handbook or code of practice indicating both bad and good practice.

National Rivers Authority policy: preferred locations

6.22   Policy B8 reads:

> "The National Rivers Authority will, by liaison with planning authorities and industry, seek to influence the preferential location of new industrial development in areas which are not vulnerable to groundwater pollution. The National Rivers Authority will also, by liaison with HMIP and other regulatory bodies, seek to ensure that authorisations granted to industry prevent further contamination of land and groundwater."

Where new industries are to be located on greenfield sites or indeed where urban sites are subject to proposals for a new use, it is important to ensure that the proposal is consistent with the protection of groundwater. The NRA is a consultee on draft development plans, and in that exercise will indicate areas vulnerable to groundwater pollution. This risk of contamination to vulnerable groundwater will be a material consideration; the availability of less vulnerable sites elsewhere will also be relevant. Thus where a proposal involves a significant use, storage or manufacture of List I or II chemicals[91] whether in raw or waste form, it should be located on non-aquifers. The proposals for the siting of such activities within Source Protection Zones[92] or on major aquifer areas would only meet with approval subject to adequate measures to prevent the migration of pollutants to groundwater. Such measures would include:

(a) minimum of underground storage of List I substances (prohibited within Zone I);

(b) no open storage for List I substances;

(c) secure bulk storage of potentially polluting substances within impermeable bunding;

(d) adequate containment and safe disposal for spillages;

(e) above ground pipework in positions not vulnerable to accidental damage.

---

[91] See para. 6.25 as to Lists I and II.
[92] See para. 6.14 as to Source Protection Zones.

Surface Water Quality

Generally

Contaminated land can have serious implications for surface water **6.23** quality, as well as for groundwater.[93] It is not the intention here to provide a detailed exposition of water law,[94] but simply to outline the main relevant areas in assessing the potential significance of contaminated land to controlled waters which may be affected. Liability issues relating to water pollution are discussed elsewhere.[95]

Classification of surface waters and quality objectives

An environmental quality objective (EQO) is a statement of the **6.24** quality to be aimed at for a particular aspect of the environment. For example, for a given stretch of water the objective might be to ensure that the water quality will allow healthy populations of coarse fish to be maintained. Environmental quality standards (EQSs) are by contrast generally more specific and quantitative; for example specifying the maximum allowable concentration of a given contaminant. The basic approach in the UK has been to relate quality criteria for water to actual or intended uses, such as suitability for potable supply, with or without advanced treatment; water suitable for game or coarse fisheries; water suitable for agricultural or industrial abstraction, and so on.[96]

However it was not until 1989 that the Water Act of that year placed EQOs for water on a statutory basis; the relevant provisions are now sections 82–84 of the Water Resources Act 1991. By section 82 the Secretary of State may make regulations prescribing a system of classifying the quality of any description of controlled waters according to specified criteria. Such regulations provide the basis for the establishment of statutory water quality objectives. Regulations have been made in relation to the quality of surface waters used for drinking water abstraction,[97] the presence in surface waters of dangerous substances,[98]

---

[93] See para. 6.01.
[94] See *e.g.*, John H. Bates, *Water and Drainage Law* (Sweet & Maxwell).
[95] See Chap. 2.
[96] See the report of the National Water Council, *"River Water Quality—The Next Stage"* (1978); DoE Circular 7/89, *"Water and the Environment,"* para. 10.
[97] See S.I. 1989 No. 1148 (in Scotland, S.I. 1990 No. 121).
[98] S.I. 1989 No. 2286 and 1992 No. 337 (in Scotland S.I. 1990 No. 1026).

bathing waters[99] and river eco-systems.[99a]Regulations are proposed for the classification of fisheries ecosystem waters.[1]

Under section 83 the Secretary of State may, in relation to classifications prescribed by regulations under section 82, serve notice on the NRA establishing water quality objectives. It is then the duty of the Secretary of State and the NRA to exercise their powers under the water pollution provisions of the Act,[2] to ensure, so far as is practicable, that such water quality objectives are met at all times. The NRA, for the purpose of carrying out its functions, is under a duty to monitor the extent of pollution in controlled waters.[3]

Where contaminated land is in proximity to controlled waters, the status of those waters and the existence of any scheme of classification or statutory water quality objectives will therefore be a very important consideration in terms of risk appraisal.[3a]

Dangerous substances

6.25   EC Directive 76/464/EEC[4] on pollution caused by certain substances discharged into the aquatic environment of the Community instituted an approach to pollution control based on the identification of dangerous substances and created a framework for the elimination or reduction of such pollution.[5] Directive 76/464/EEC itself provides only the framework, the detailed control being provided by the various "daughter directives" made under it.[6] The chemical substances in question are selected on the basis of their toxicity, persistence and bioaccumulation, and are divided into two categories. List I (the black list) comprises those substances which are considered to be most harmful and in relation to which pollution is to be eliminated. List II are those

---

[99] S.I. 1991 No. 1597.

[99a] S.I. 1994 No. 1057.

[1] The Surface Waters (Fisheries Ecosystem) (Classification) Regulations 1993 (DoE/Welsh Office Consultation Paper, October 1993). On the NRA's and Government's approach to classification, see also para. 6.26 below).

[2] See para. 6.02 *et seq.*

[3] S.84(2)(a).

[3a] See also the NRA report referred to at para. 6.19 above.

[4] O.J. L129/23, 18.5.76, as amended by 91/692/EEC (O.J. L377/48, 31.12.91).

[5] See generally, *Dangerous Substances in Water—A Practical Guide* (Environmental Data Services, 1st ed., 1992).

[6] See 82/176/EEC (O.J. L81, 27.3.82) on mercury; 83/513/EEC (O.J. L291, 24.10.83) on cadmium; 84/156/EEC (0.J. L74, 17.3.84) on limit values and quality objectives for mercury; 84/491/EEC (O.J. L274, 17.10.84) on HCH; 86/280/EEC (O.J. L181, 4.7.86) on DDT, carbon tetrachloride and PCB; 88/347/EEC (O.J. L158, 25.6.88) on "the drins", HCB, HCBD, and chloroform; 90/415/EEC (O.J. L219, 14.8.90) on EDC, TRI, PER and TCB.

substances which are regarded as less harmful, pollution by which is to be reduced (the grey list). The substances are listed on a non-specific basis (with the exception of mercury and cadmium which are List I substances). Categories include organohalogen, organophosphorus and organotin compounds, those possessing carcinogenic properties, persistent mineral oils and hydrocarbons and persistent synthetic substances (all List I). Substances belonging to various family groups (*e.g.*, zinc, copper, nickel, chromium, lead, arsenic, and silver) fall within List II. Contaminated land may well therefore present the threat of List I or List II substances entering the aquatic environment (which includes inland surface water, territorial and inland coastal waters and groundwater).

In view of the very slow progress towards agreeing daughter directives, an attempt was made by Directive 86/280/EEC[7] to speed up the process: this directive provides limit values, quality objectives, compliance periods and monitoring procedures which then apply to subsequent daughter directives. Directive 86/280/EEC does not however apply to groundwater.[8]

The UK's approach to compliance with Directive 76/464/EEC has been to formulate its own "Red List" which includes List I substances plus a number of others. These are prescribed for control by the Trade Effluent (Prescribed Processes and Substances) Regulations 1989, as amended.[9] In this way the Secretary of State exerts control over the discharge of Red List substances to sewers as a component of trade effluent. Such substances now also form part of the system for classifying inland and coastal waters for the purpose of setting statutory water quality objectives:[10] the relevant regulations specify an annual mean concentration in microgrammes per litre for each relevant substance and powers to control water pollution must be exercised in such a way as to achieve compliance with the objectives based upon that system of classification.[11] The approach to implementation of the dangerous substances directives is explained in Circular 7/89, Water and the *Environment.*[12] The Circular contains general guidance to the approach to List I and II Substances and on the specific substances covered by the daughter directives. In particular, the Circular points out that Member States are required to draw up specific programmes for the elimination of discharges of certain List I substances from diffuse, multiple or small

[7] O.J. L181/16, 4.7.86.
[8] *Ibid.*
[9] S.I. 1989 No. 1156 (as amended by S.I. 1990 No. 1629). See para. 6.38.
[10] See The Surface Waters (Dangerous Substances) (Classification) Regulations 1989 No. 2286 and 1992 No. 337; para. 6.24 above.
[11] See para. 6.24 above.
[12] W.O. 16/89.

271

point sources.[13] Competent authorities are asked to supply any information which may be helpful in formulating such programmes, to monitor waters which are likely to be affected by such sources, and to notify the Government where such sources contribute significantly to any instances of a quality standard being exceeded.[14] The potential of contaminated land to leach Red List substances or other dangerous substances such as PCBs into surface waters is an important consideration for the NRA in deciding its strategy in relation to a given site.[14a]

NRA policy

6.26   The NRA has been developing its own policy on the formulation of water quality objectives. A consultation document, *Proposals for Statutory Water Quality Objectives* was published in December 1991.[15] In the light of responses to that paper, the NRA published recommendations[16] for a scheme of water quality classification suggesting an approach based on six use classes relating to the actual or potential use of the relevant controlled waters: these being fisheries ecosystem, abstraction for potable supply, abstraction for industrial or commercial use, water sports, commercial harvesting of fish or shellfish, and special ecosystems. A general quality assessment scheme was also proposed for progress reporting purposes, based on chemical, biological, nutrient status and aesthetic factors. These suggestions were used as the basis of the Government's subsequent proposals on *River Quality*,[17] which also took account of the views of the Royal Commission on Environmental Pollution.[18]

The NRA in August 1993 published the first in a series of documents intended to set out its strategic aims and the methods by which they are to be achieved.[19] This document indicates the NRA's approach to securing an overall improvement in the quality of rivers, estuaries and coastal waters in England and Wales. A key element of that approach is that of catchment management planning, under which the major uses within a catchment are investigated and a catchment management plan is devised in consultation with interested bodies and the public. Individ-

---

[13] Para. 26.

[14] Para. 29.

[14a] See the NRA report, Water Quality Series, No. 15, referred to at para. 6.19 above.

[15] Water Quality Series No. 5.

[16] October 2, 1993.

[17] "River Quality, The Government's Proposals," DoE/Welsh Office, December 3, 1992.

[18] 16th Report, *Freshwater Quality*, Cm. 1966; see para. 6.01.

[19] "NRA Water Quality Strategy" (NRA, August 1993).

ual catchment needs are in this way intended to be balanced and reconciled with wider national water quality objectives. The various strands of NRA policy on point sources of pollution, diffuse sources of pollution and development control are also summarised.

CLEAN WATER SUPPLY AND ABSTRACTION

Water undertakers generally

The supply of clean water, that is water that has been treated for the **6.27** purposes of supply to the ultimate consumer, is the responsibility of water undertakers appointed by the Secretary of State or by the Director General of Water Services under section 6 of the Water Industry Act 1991. The instrument of appointment describes the area within which the undertaker concerned may exercise its functions.[20] The general powers of companies incorporated by statute and holding appointments are set out in the Statutory Water Companies Act 1991.

Formerly water was supplied to premises by statutory water companies or by local authorities under the provisions of the relevant local act. In 1989, 28 statutory companies remained; others, with local authorities, having been amalgamated into water boards such as the Metropolitan Water Board. The Water Act 1973 transferred the powers of local authorities to supply water to the new Regional Water Authorities, leaving 28 statutory companies with similar responsibilities. Under the new arrangements, with one or two exceptions, a local authority has no power to supply water in their area.

Riparian occupiers have the right to use waters flowing past their land, and farmers often do so where piped water supply is not available to distant fields. Further, some landowners have the advantage of a lake or spring on their property, to which they have sole right. Water used in this way is a private supply for the purposes of the Water Industry Act 1991[21] and thus the rules concerning the quality of such supplies as laid down in sections 77 to 85 of the Act will apply to it, whether or not the water is supplied to other premises or kept solely for personal use.[22]

The general duty cast on water undertakers is in most general terms:[23]

> "It shall be the duty of every water undertaker to develop and maintain an efficient and economical system of water supply within its area and to ensure that all such arrangements have been made:

[20] Subs. 6(3).
[21] Subs. 93(1).
[22] Subs. 93(2).
[23] Subs. 37(1).

(a) for providing supplies of water to premises in that area and for making such supplies available to persons who demand them; and

(b) for maintaining, improving and extending the water undertaker's water mains and other pipes,

as necessary for securing that the undertaker is and continues to be able to meet its obligations under this Part" (Part II of the Water Industry Act 1991).

This duty is enforceable by the Secretary of State or, in accordance with a general authorisation, by the Director General of Water Services.[24]

Standards of performance for these obligations may be set in Regulations made under section 38 of the Act; chief among these is the Water Supply and Sewerage Services (Customer Service Standards) Regulations 1989 as amended.[25] These are generally referred to as customer service standards.

The duty to supply water is statutory; there is no contract between a water undertaker and domestic consumer.[26] Thus, the warranties of implied quality and fitness for the purpose implied by section 14 of the Sale of Goods Act 1979 only apply to water supplied by a private supplier or to water supplied in pursuance of an agreement to an industrial or other user. However, the domestic consumer may well have a remedy in respect of injury or damage suffered from the supply of contaminated water, either under the common law of negligence,[27] or for breach of the statutory duty to supply wholesome water under section 68(1) of the Water Industry Act,[28] or under Part I of the Consumer Protection Act 1987, or for public nuisance.[29]

Water quality: generally

6.28   Water can be contaminated whilst it is in the source from which it is being or is to be abstracted. The pollution of raw water in rivers, groundwaters and lakes is a matter principally for the National Rivers Authority.[30] However, once the water enters the distribution system it can further be contaminated by corroded pipes, the materials used in the

---

[24] See paras. 6.02 and 6.05.
[25] S.I. 1989 Nos. 1159 and 1383.
[26] *Read* v. *Croydon Corporation* [1938] 4 All E.R. 631.
[27] *Ibid.*
[28] *Ibid.* See also John Bates, *Water and Drainage Law* (Sweet & Maxwell) para. 7.71.
[29] *A–B* v. *South West Water Services Ltd.* [1993] 1 All E.R. 609; see para. 2.37 above.
[30] See para. 6.04.

manufacture of the pipes, or by substances entering the system through cracks in the network. Once water has been abstracted for drinking, it is treated with coagulants to remove suspended matter and with chlorine or ozone for disinfection. Taste or odour problems are dealt with by powder-activated carbon. Water contaminated by nitrates can be dealt with by ion exchange or biological denitrification; storage of water to allow settlement or blending of different constituted waters can dilute the contamination and assist in purification. These are examples of the types of process in common use, but there are many others.

Water undertakers are placed under various statutory duties in relation to water quantity: these are explained below.[31] EC law is of critical importance in this context, as in some cases the relevant UK legislation was enacted to meet the relevant EC requirements.[32]

The surface water for drinking directive

European Community provisions address both surface water, in the **6.29** Surface Water Directive[33] and drinking water, in the Drinking Water Directive.[34] The former Directive applies only to surface waters and not to groundwater. Of the samples taken to assess parameters for which mandatory standards are set, 95 per cent. must meet those standards; for other parameters the figure is 90 per cent.

The purpose of the Directive is to ensure that surface water abstracted for use as drinking water reaches certain standards and receives adequate treatment before supply to the public. Various parameters are listed, in some cases with numerical values, against which water is to be classified as A1, A2, or A3. It is this classification that determines the form of treatment required, and water of lower quality than A3 cannot be used for the abstraction of drinking water save in defined exceptional circumstances.[35] Sampling is required at the points at which the water is abstracted before being sent for purification or treatment; in practice this will usually be taken to mean the point of abstraction from the reservoir. Directive 79/869/EEC[36] provides reference methods of measurement and frequencies of sampling and analysis, the latter depending on the quality of the water and the size of the population served by the source.

---

[31] Para. 6.31.
[32] Para. 6.30.
[33] 75/440/EEC, O.J. L194, 25.5.75.
[34] See para. 6.30.
[35] Art. 4.
[36] O.J. L271, 29.10.93.

The drinking water directives

6.30   The Drinking Water Directive[37] of July 15, 1980 relates to the quality
of water intended for human consumption, laying down quality standards with which water intended for human consumption must comply.
Article 7 of the Directive provides that Member States must fix
standards of drinking water for the parameters as set out in Annex I;
that Annex deals with concentrations of certain substances, such as
nitrates, sulphates, toxic substances such as cyanide, and micro-biological coliforms. Tables A and E in Annex I of the Directive set out two
types of standard, namely a maximum admissible concentration (MAC)
which must not be exceeded by the standards fixed by the Member
States and also guide level values which the Member States must use as
a basis for fixing their own standards.

A number of these parameters relate to substances which can present
difficulties in the case of contaminated land—for example metals such as
iron, copper, zinc, mercury, cadmium, nickel and lead, pesticides and
related products, hydrocarbons and mineral oils, phenols, polycyclic
aromatic hydrocarbons, and other organochlorine compounds. The
potential significance of these parameters in this context is starkly
illustrated by the litigation between Cambridge Water Company Limited and Eastern Counties Leather plc.[38]

The Directive applies to water intended for human consumption—
defined to include water used in food processing undertakings and
affecting the wholesomeness of the foodstuff in its finished form.[39] By
articles 9 and 10, Member States may make provision for derogations
from the Directive in certain circumstances: these include derogations to
take account of situations arising from the nature and structure of the
ground in the area from which the supply in question emanates.[40] It is
open to argument whether this wording can cover situations arising from
historic contamination of land and it has been suggested that such a
derogation can only be made to take account of something naturally in
the ground, not of a substance that has entered the area as the result of
human activity.[41]

Member States are required to take all necessary steps to ensure
regular monitoring of the quality of water intended for human consumption, the monitoring to be at the point where it is made available to the
consumer.[42]

[37] 80/778/EEC, O.J. L229/11, 30.8.80.
[38] See Chap. 2 generally.
[39] Art. 2.
[40] Appropriate 9.1(*a*).
[41] J. H. Bates, *Water and Drainage Law* (Sweet & Maxwell) para. 7.16.
[42] Art. 12.2.

The Directive has been controversial in that a number of the parameters are arguably not based on sound science and toxicology; compliance imposes very considerable costs on water undertakers in respect of treatment to meet the relevant requirements. This has led to proposals from the European water industry for changes to the Directive,[43] and to an EC sponsored seminar held in October 1993. It may be that proposals for review of the Directive will be forthcoming in due course.

The means by which the Directive is implemented in the UK are described below,[44] but particular difficulties have been experienced in relation to lead and nitrates. The UK government was found to be in breach of the Directive by the European Court of Justice in a ruling on November 25, 1992.[45] The case related to late implementation of the Directive for water used in food production and generally in Scotland and Northern Ireland; it was also found that the MAC for nitrates had been exceeded in some 28 supply zones, though the Commission's claim against the UK in relation to exceedances for lead failed.

Drinking water quality—public supplies

In relation to public water supplies the Drinking Water Directive is **6.31** implemented, and to a degree extended, by sections 67–86 of the Water Industry Act 1991 and the Water Supply (Water Quality) Regulations 1989[46] as amended.[47] Enforcement is by the Secretary of State and his Drinking Water Inspectorate. Amendments were made in 1991 to the Regulations and the Food Safety Act 1990 to ensure that water used in food production complies with the appropriate standards.

A general duty is placed on water undertakers when supplying water to any premises for domestic or food production purposes to supply only water which is wholesome at the time of supply;[48] whether water is or is not wholesome is to be judged in accordance with the Water Supply (Water Quality) Regulations.[49] The Regulations, which are highly detailed and complex, replicate and in some cases enhance the require-

---

[43] EUREAU, "Directive of July 15, 1980: Remarks on Its Application" (1984); and EUREAU, "Drinking Water Directive 80/778/EEC, Proposals for Modification—Views of EUREAU" 1991).
[44] Para. 6.31.
[45] Case C–337/89. See further, N. Haigh, *Manual of Environmental Policy: The EC and Britain*, pp. 4.4–8 and 4.4–9; and *Financial Times* European Court Report, December 1, 1992.
[46] S.I. 1989 No. 1147.
[47] S.I.s 1991 No. 1837 and 2790.
[48] S.68(1).
[49] S.67.

ments of the Drinking Water Directive parameters. They also make provision for the programmes of sampling and analysis which are carried out on a zonal basis.

Remedial action in respect of water that has become unwholesome is first and foremost enforcement action by the Secretary of State under section 18 of the Water Industry Act 1991. However, neither the Secretary of State nor the Director of Water Services are required to make an enforcement order if they are satisfied that the contravention is of a trivial nature or that the company has given and is complying with an undertaking to take all such steps as it appears to him to be necessary for the time being for the purposes of securing or facilitating compliance with a condition or requirement in a provisional enforcement order.[50]

Under section 70 of the Water Industry Act it is an offence, where a water undertaker supplies water by means of pipes to any premises, to supply water which is unfit for human consumption. The defence to proceedings under section 70 is for the undertaker to show that it:

  (a) had no reasonable grounds for suspecting that the water would be used for human consumption; or
  (b) took all reasonable steps and exercised all due diligence for securing that the water was fit for human consumption.

As matters stand, proceedings for an offence under this section are instituted either by the Secretary of State or the Director of Public Prosecutions.

The question of whether water is or is not fit for human consumption will be one of fact; it must be more than unwholesome, but there is no necessity that it shall be shown to be injurious or dangerous to health.[51] The leading example of the prosecution of a public supplier of water is the "Camelford Incident" where the South West Water Authority was successfully prosecuted in respect of water containing excessive aluminium sulphate resulting from an accidental discharge into their water treatment works from a tanker.[52] Litigation is also in progress against Yorkshire Water in respect of personal injuries allegedly suffered by consumers of water from the Barmby Water Treatment Works, North

---

[50] S.19(1)(*b*). As to the exercise of the Secretary of State's enforcement duties and the relationship to undertakings from the water supply company, see *R.* v. *Secretary of State for the Environment, ex p. Friends of the Earth Ltd., The Times*, April 4, 1994.

[51] Grieg (David) v. *Goldfinch* (1961) 105 Sol. J 367; *Guild* v. *Gateway Food Markets Limited* 1991 S.L.T. 578.

[52] The Authority was found guilty after a jury trial at Exeter Crown Court of causing a public nuisance and were fined £10,000 with a contribution of £25,000 towards the prosecution's costs. In relation to civil proceedings from the same incident, see *A–B* v. *South West Water Services Ltd.* [1993] 1 All E.R. 609; para. 2.37 above.

Yorkshire between December 1989 and May 1990 (the disease cryptosporidiosis).[53]

Local authorities also have responsibilities in relation to domestic water quality: these extend both to public and private supplies. In particular it is the duty of every local authority (district or metropolitan borough councils) to take all such steps as they consider appropriate for keeping themselves informed about the wholesomeness and sufficiency of water supplies provided to any premises in their area.[54]

Local authorities also have a duty to notify a water undertaker of anything that appears to it to suggest that supplies of water for domestic or food production purposes has been or is likely to become unwholesome; if the appropriate remedial action it not taken, the local authority can inform the Secretary of State.[55]

Drinking water quality: private supplies

Private supplies of domestic water presented particular problems for **6.32** the UK in implementing the Drinking Water Directive. They did not fall within the existing statutory framework at the time the Directive was agreed and, whilst comprising only one per cent of water supplied in the UK, their number (more than 100,000) posed significant administrative and resource difficulties. However it appears from a European Count judgment covering private supplies in Belgium that supplies serving single properties and used solely for domestic purposes are outwith the scope of the Directive.[56]

A private supply, for the purposes of the Water Industry Act, means any supply of water provided otherwise than by a water undertaker.[57] The general duty of local authorities to keep themselves informed as to the wholesomeness and sufficiency of supplies within their area referred to above[58] applies equally to private supplies.[59] Additionally, where a local authority are satisfied in relation to any premises in their area which are supplied with water for domestic or food production purposes by means of a private supply that the water has not been, is not or may not be wholesome, then the authority may serve a private supply notice requiring remedial action.[60]

---

[53] See the Practice Note in relation to interlocutory proceedings in the litigation, *Practice Note: Yorkshire Water Litigation, The Times,* May 13, 1993.
[54] S.77(1).
[55] S.78(1) and (2).
[56] Case C–42/89, July 1990.
[57] S.93(1).
[58] See para. 6.31.
[59] S.77.
[60] S.80.

The notice may be served on the owners or occupiers of the premises where the source of supply is situated and on any other person who exercises powers of management or control in relation to that source.[61] The notice must specify those steps which are, in the opinion of the authority, required to be taken for ensuring there is a wholesome supply. A period of at least 28 days must be given for representations or objections, and where objections are made and are not withdrawn, the notice must be confirmed by the Secretary of State before it takes effect.[62] Powers of enforcement, entry and information gathering are conferred by sections 82–85.

The Private Water Supplies Regulations 1991[63] provide the criteria for determining whether water supplied to premises for domestic purposes from a private supply is wholesome. The water must not contain any element, organism or substance (other than those for which an express parameter is given) at a concentration which would be detrimental to public health; for certain parameters, prescribed concentrations or values are given, which are not to be exceeded.[64] The Regulations also deal with the frequency of monitoring required to be undertaken by the local authority: this depends upon the number of persons supplied from the source and the average daily volume of water supplied, together with the type of premises supplied and the use to which the water is put.[65] The classification of all private supplies must be reviewed at least once a year.[66] Part V sets out the procedures to be followed in collection and analysis of samples. Charges may be levied on the owner or occupier of the relevant premises or the person managing or controlling the source in relation to costs reasonably incurred by the authority, subject to prescribed limits.[67]

The Regulations are explained in DoE Circular 23/91, "Private Water Supplies."[68] The Circular suggests that local authorities have scope to tailor their actions to the particular circumstances of individual supplies and that they should in all cases consult their medical advisors or the district health authority's Director of Public Health.[69] Local authorities are required by Direction to make themselves aware of the terms of any existing licence or agreement relating to private supply and to have regard to those terms in the exercise of their power to serve notices.[70]

[61] Subs. 80(7).
[62] Subs. 81(2).
[63] S.I. 1991 No. 2790.
[64] Reg. 3 and Sched. 2.
[65] Part IV and Sched. 3.
[66] Reg. 12.
[67] Reg. 20 and Sched. 5.
[68] W.O. 68/91.
[69] Paras. 1.5 and 1.8.
[70] Para. 1.5 and App. 1.

Contamination of water sources

The Public Order Act 1986 contains a number of offences[71] which **6.33** could apply to persons who contaminate or interfere with water or make it appear that water has been contaminated or interfered with, with the intention of causing public alarm or anxiety or causing injury to members of the public or economic loss to the water undertaker or supplier. Under section 72 of the Water Industry Act 1991, as amended, contamination of water sources is an offence. The section reads:

> "Subject to subsections (2) and (3) below, a person is guilty of an offence under this section if he is guilty of any act or neglect whereby the water in any waterworks which is used or likely to be used:
> (a) for human consumption or domestic purposes; or
> (b) for manufacturing food or drink for human consumption, is polluted or likely to be polluted".

Subsection (2) emphasises that there is no restriction or prohibition on any method of the cultivation of land which is in accordance with the principles of good husbandry; subsection (3) deals with the use of oil or tar on any highway maintainable at public expense so long as the highway authority take all reasonable steps for preventing pollution of the water in any waterworks.

For the purposes of this section, "waterworks" has an extended meaning.[72] It includes:

(a) any spring, well, adit or borehole, service reservoir or tank; and
(b) any main or other pipe or conduit of a water undertaker.

It is not clear to what degree this definition might extend to rivers, streams, or other surface water which constitute a source of supply. "Domestic purposes" is defined in section 218 of the Act and covers drinking, washing, cooking, central heating and sanitary purposes.

From the point of view of suppliers of clean water, this section is pivotal because it seeks to protect water sources from pollution. The water undertakers may not be content simply to rely upon the powers vested in the NRA under the Water Resources Act to protect their own commercial interests in sources of supply. Liability is strict under the section in the sense that the offence is committed once the act or neglect pollutes or is likely to pollute the water concerned. A defence that the perpetrator did not know or have reasonable grounds to believe that pollution would or was likely to take place would not appear to be

---

[71] S.38.
[72] Subs. 72(5).

available. It has been reported[72a] that Severn Trent plc is to prosecute a small business based in Telford, Vitalscheme, in respect of a chemical spillage in April 1994 which led to contamination of drinking water in the Worcester area and required Severn Trent to pay out almost £1 million, or £25 for every household affected.

A key question here is the meaning of the term "polluted." The way in which the term is normally used, and the way in which it is used elsewhere in environmental legislation,[73] would indicate that the introduction of a foreign substance is not of itself pollution; that substance must be likely to cause harm. Difficulty then arises in cases where substances are introduced in quantities or concentrations which exceed the relevant legislative parameters for drinking water, yet not in sufficient quantities or concentrations as to be shown to be likely to cause harm.[74]

Historically, many water undertakers protected their interests by substantial land purchases of areas around sources of supply to prevent contamination; that practice is now less prevalent, and undertakers are more dependent on the use of land use planning controls in relation to the gathering grounds of their sources of supply. The creation of statutory water protection zones may be a helpful step for them in this respect.[75]

Abstraction of water

6.34   With certain very limited exceptions, it is not possible for a riparian owner or other landowner lawfully to abstract water from surface or underground waters without an abstraction licence granted by the National Rivers Authority and in accordance with the provisions of that licence.[76] The restriction extends to the construction of boreholes or other means by which water is abstracted from underground strata, or the extension or installation of additional apparatus in relation or existing boreholes.[77] Contravention of these restrictions is an offence, as is non-compliance with the provisions of the abstraction licence.[78] Exemption

---

[72a] *The Times*, June 15, 1994.
[73] Environmental Protection Act 1990, s.1(3).
[74] See para. 2.36.
[75] See para. 6.13.
[76] Water Resources Act 1991, s.24(1). Where there is a single hydrological system with interconnected sources of supply and a single means of abstraction, the abstraction will be treated as taking place at the immediate source of supply and not at any other, more remote source: *British Waterways Board* v. *National River Authority, The Times*, August 4, 1992 C.A. (". . . no man could abstract the same water from two different places at the same time.").
[77] Subs. 24(2).
[78] Subs. 24(4).

from the requirement for a licence applies to the abstraction of small quantities of water for use on holdings contiguous with the relevant waters, or for domestic and agricultural purposes (other than spray irrigation).[79] Abstraction may also be carried out in the course of land drainage operations, or resulting from such operations, without an abstraction licence.[80]

Application for an abstraction licence may only be made by the occupier of land contiguous to the relevant inland waters or having a right of access to such land.[81] In the case of abstraction from underground strata the applicant must be the occupier of land consisting of or comprising the underground strata, or a right of access to an excavation into underground strata, into which water passes from those strata.[82]

The effect of an abstraction licence is that the holder is to be taken to have a right to abstract water to the extent authorised by the licence and in accordance with the provisions contained in it.[83] In any action brought against a person in respect of the abstraction of water from a source of supply it is a defence to prove that the water was abstracted in pursuance of an abstraction licence and that the provisions of the licence were complied with[84]: however, this does not exonerate the abstractor from any action in negligence or breach of contract.[85]

Abstraction licences and pollution

The interaction between water abstraction and pollution from contami- **6.35** nated land can be complex: in some cases a new source of abstraction may create new patterns of groundwater flow which may have the effect of mobilising contaminants or increasing their rate of migration.

In granting a licence for such abstraction, the NRA is under no express duty to have regard to the quality of the water to be abstracted, though there are obligations to have regard to the interests of other existing abstractors.[86] On the basis of the decision in *Scott Whitehead* v. *National Coal Board*[87] it is arguable that the NRA may owe a limited duty to abstractors to warn them of serious levels of contamination: whether the NRA is under a duty to exercise its powers to licence and control polluting discharges so as to protect existing abstractors is another

[79] S.27.
[80] S.29.
[81] Subs. 25(2).
[82] Subs. 35(3).
[83] Subs. 48(1).
[84] Subs. 48(2).
[85] Subs. 48(4).
[86] Water Resources Act 1991, subs. 39(2).
[87] (1987) 53 P. & C.R. 263.

283

issue.[88] The position of water undertakers is somewhat stronger in this respect than other abstractors in that section 203(1) of the Water Resources Act places a duty on the NRA to provide a water undertaker with information in its possession about the quality of controlled waters or other waters or pollution incidents. However, the duty extends only to such information as is in the possession of the NRA and applies only to such information as is reasonably requested by the undertaker for purposes connected with the carrying out of its functions.

Where it appears that a new or increased abstraction would have adverse effects in terms of pollution (for example, by mobilising existing soil contamination) this is a consideration which the NRA should take into account, in accordance with its general environmental duties, in determining the licence application.[89] Applications will be publicised locally[90] and it would be open to the owner of contaminated land who felt the proposed abstraction might have adverse consequences to make representations to the NRA.[91]

Information on abstraction sources

6.36   The location of existing and proposed abstraction sources is crucial information and commercial issues presented by contaminated land. The issue of information is discussed fully elsewhere, but it may be helpful here to list the available sources of information on abstraction.[92]

Type of Information	Statutory Provisions	Comments
Register of abstraction and impounding licences	W.R.A. 1991, s.189; Water Resources Licences Regulations 1965 (S.I. 1965 No. 574)	Kept by NRA. Covers applications for licences granted.
Maps of waterworks (resource mains, discharge pipes and other underground works) vested in the NRA	W.R.A. 1991, s.195	Kept by NRA in map form. Need not cover works before September 1, 1989 unless shown on existing statutory map.

[88] See S. Tromans [1987] Conv. 368.
[89] See J.H. Bates, *Water and Drainage Law* (Sweet & Maxwell) para. 4.32, citing decision letter WS/3474/521/6. December 30, 1971.
[90] Subs. 37(2).
[91] Subs. 38(3)(a).
[92] See generally, Chap. 3.

Type of Information	Statutory Provisions	Comments
Information about works for the purpose of searching for or abstracting water	W.R.A. 1991, s.198	Journal supplied by person sinking boreholes and kept by National Environment Regional Council. No requirement that it be made available to the public. Confidentiality in relation to matters other than water resources and supplies can be requested by the person supplying the information under section 205.
Maps of waterworks (resource and water mains, discharge pipes and other underground works) vested in a water undertaker	W.R.A. 1991, s.198	Kept by undertaker in map form. Not required to keep records of works completed before September 1, 1989 unless shown on existing statutory map.
Information on private sources	None. But note powers to require information (see below)	There is no provision for a register or other record of private wells or other sources of supply which do not need an abstraction licence. However, both the NRA and the relevant local authority may hold information on known private sources, and the provisions on public access to environmental information may well apply.

The statutory provisions for the obtaining of information should also be noted in this context. For the purposes of their functions in relation to water quality,[93] local authorities may serve notice on any person requiring the provision of information[94]: this power may be used for example to obtain information on the existence of private sources of supply. Similarly the NRA may give directions to any person abstracting water from a source of supply (not necessarily a licensable source) to give information as to the abstraction.[95]

A more general power applies to the NRA and the relevant Ministers to serve notice requiring information required for carrying out their functions in relation to water pollution.[96] Failure to comply with the notice without reasonable excuse is an offence.[97]

There is no specific statutory requirement that such information be made publicly available; indeed there are restrictions on the disclosure of certain information under section 204 of the Water Resources Act. However, consideration must also be given to the EC and domestic requirements on freedom of access to environmental information,[98] which may override such restrictions in some cases.[99]

Foul Sewage

Prevention of contamination by foul water

6.37   Foul water sewerage can be a source of contaminated land, for example from sewage treatment works or old sewage farms, from the disposal of sewage sludge effluent, or from the leakage of sewage from mains sewers or drains into underground strata. A brief overview of the law relating to foul sewage disposal is therefore given in the following paragraphs.

Under the EC's Urban Waste Water Treatment Directive[1] standards are established for the provision of sewerage systems, the treatment of sewage, the discharge of trade effluent to sewers, and the discharge of effluent from treatment works, as well as the disposal of sludge. Member

---

[93] See paras. 6.31 and 6.32.
[94] Water Industry Act 1991, s.85.
[95] Water Resources Act 1991, s.201.
[96] *Ibid.*, s.202(2).
[97] *Ibid.*, s.202(4).
[98] See generally Chap. 3.
[99] S.204(2)(*k*) makes express reference to the overriding effect of Community obligations.
[1] 91/271/EEC, O.J. No. L135/40, 30.5.91.

States must enact legislation, or take other measures, to enable them to comply with the Waste Water Directive by June 30, 1993. The Waste Water Directive defines "urban waste water" in Article 2.1 as domestic waste water or the mixture of domestic waste water with industrial waste water and/or run off rain water.

The principal sewerage undertaker for a locality will be the company appointed by the Secretary of State or the Director General of Water Services to fill that position for the area concerned.[2] As with clean water, the exercise of functions for a defined area is set out in the instrument of appointment. The duty cast on a sewerage undertaker is to provide, improve and extend the public sewer system either inside or outside its area and to cleanse and maintain it so that the area is, and continues to be, effectively drained. It must also make provision for the emptying of sewers and for dealing with their contents, including trade effluent.[3] This duty is enforceable under section 18 of the 1991 Act by the Secretary of State, or the Director General of Water Services.

Discharges into sewers

Under section 106 of the Water Industry Act 1991, the owner or **6.38** occupier of any premises has the statutory right to discharge foul or surface water from the premises into a public sewer through connecting drains or private sewers. This general right is however subject to restrictions concerning domestic sewage and the discharge of trade effluent.

By section 111 of the Water Industry Act no person may discharge or allow the discharge into the public sewer (or a drain or private sewer connecting with it) any matter likely to injure the sewer or drain or that might obstruct the flow of effluent through it or that might prejudicially affect the treatment and disposal of its contents. This means in effect that the matter discharged shall neither damage the sewer nor the sewage treatment works, nor so affect sewage sludge or effluent that is cannot be disposed of lawfully after treatment. Further, by sections 111(1)(*b*) and 111(2), chemical, refuse, waste steam or liquid at a temperature of more than 110 degrees fahrenheit may not be discharged into a sewer if it, either alone or in combination with other substances in the sewer, would be dangerous, a nuisance or prejudicial to health. Additionally, by section 111(1)(*c*) it is forbidden to allow petroleum spirit or carbide of calcium to pass into a sewer. Contravention of these prohibitions is an offence.[4]

---

[2] Water Industry Act 1991, s.6(1).
[3] S.94(1).
[4] S.111(3).

Section 106 itself contains reference to liquid or other matter that is prohibited under the Act or in any Act from being discharged into a sewer as trade effluent. Discharge from trade premises is dealt with in Article 11 of the Urban Waste Water Directive which requires discharge of industrial waste water to sewage systems or treatment plants to be subject to prior regulation and to specific authorisation by a competent authority or appropriate body. The right to discharge matter into a sewer under section 106 of the Water Industry Act does not extend to any liquid from a factory other than domestic sewage or surface or storm water or to any liquid from a manufacturing process.[5] In effect, the owner or occupier of trade premises (defined as any premises used or intended to be used for the carrying on of any trade or industry, which includes agricultural and research uses)[6] must have the consent of the sewerage undertaker to discharge any trade effluent from those premises into the public sewer system:[7] discharges from trade premises may not be made in any other way.[8]

The procedure is that the owner or occupier of the trade or industrial premises seeking to discharge trade effluent into a public sewer must make a written application known as a trade effluent notice to the relevant sewerage undertaker for consent to do so. The notice should state the nature and composition of the effluent, the maximum quantity that it is proposing to discharge on any given day and the highest rate at which it will be discharged.[9] It has been held, in a ruling on a Crown Court prosecution, that if a discharger knows that he will discharge traces of substances then the onus is on him to ask for permisson for those substances; however, if those substances are discharged because they were present in the process water used by the premises rather than produced by the trade process, then they will not be "trade effluent" and no consent will be needed.[10] The undertaker may require the applicant to provide information relating to and indeed plans of any sewer or drain to which effluent is to be discharged to the public sewer.[11] It is an offence to fail to provide such information as the applicant might reasonably be expected to supply.[12]

---

[5] S.106(2)(a)(i).
[6] S.141(1) and (2).
[7] S.118(1) and (3). Trade effluent has been held to include effluent from a launderette; it would not include, however, effluent from lavatories and washing facilities at trade premises—see *Thames Water Authority* v. *Blue and White Launderettes Ltd.* (1979) 78 L.G.R. 237.
[8] S.118(2).
[9] S.119.
[10] Ruling of His Honour Judge J. Crowther Q.C. in *R* v. *Rechem International Ltd.* (Newport Crown Court, September 10, 1993; CAO ref. 9305622, official transcript).
[11] S.204(1).
[12] S.204(3).

An undertaker may give its consent to a discharge that is applied for either conditionally or unconditionally or may refuse the application.[13] If consent is granted, then it will enure for the benefit of the premises so that if the undertaker substituted a new series of drains under section 113 of the Water Industry Act, the consent will remain effective in respect of discharges to the new sewers.[14] Effluent from separate and new premises cannot take advantage of an existing consent so as to enable it to discharge into the drains of any established premises which are adjacent. The conditions which an undertaker may impose on a consent are set out in section 121 of the Water Industry Act 1991.

Where the discharge is "special category effluent," then a special consent is required under certain sections of the Water Industry Act 1991.[15] In these cases the discharge contains either prescribed substances or more than the prescribed quantity of such substances, or the discharge derives from a prescribed process or the process involves the use of more than a prescribed amount of a prescribed substance. The substances or processes involved here will be prescribed either to meet the requirements of Article 3.2 of the Dangerous Substances Directive[16] or because the substance concerned is on the "Red List." Red List substances are those that are considered especially harmful and so should be controlled on an integrated basis by HM Inspectorate of Pollution (HMIP); they are specified in Schedule 1 to the Trade Effluents (Prescribed Processes and Substances) Regulations 1989.[17] Prescribed processes are listed in Schedule 2 to the Regulations, being those whose effluents contain chloroform or asbestos.

The NRA has no direct control over discharges to sewer. In one case[18] involving a chemical waste treatment facility and transfer station the NRA attempted to achieve such control by persuading the waste disposal authority to impose a waste site licence condition prohibiting any discharge of trade effluent or contaminated surface water to the foul sewer, or overflow to surface water sewer, watercourse or soakaway. On appeal, the Secretary of State held that the NRA in so doing were not exercising an appropriate means of control; responsibility for discharges to sewer rested with the sewage undertaker.

---

[13] S.121(1).
[14] S.113(6).
[15] Ss.120, 123, 127, 130 to 134 and 138.
[16] Directive 76/464/EEC; see para. 6.25 above.
[17] S.I. 1989 No. 1156 as amended by S.I. 1990 No. 1629.
[18] Site at Crompton Road, Ilkeston; reference by Derbshire County Council and appeal by Kenal Services Limited under ss.5(4) and 10 of the Control of Pollution Act 1974 (Ref. LEQ/5/4/110, July 30, 1993).

Discharge of surface or sub-surface water into sewers

6.39   The right of owners and occupiers of premises, other than trade or industrial premises, to discharge foul or surface water into a public sewer is not absolute; what matters is the character of the water discharged. There is no right to discharge foul water into a surface water sewer, nor, unless with the approval of the undertaker, to discharge surface water into a foul sewer.[19]

The sewerage undertaker will be concerned if surface water from contaminated land is to be discharged to sewer, in that the water may contain levels of contaminants which would present difficulties of treatment for the undertaker or could jeopardise the undertaker's ability to meet its own discharge consent. Where the discharge to sewer is consented, the undertaker will be deemed to have caused the ultimate discharge of the polluting matter to controlled waters,[20] and even if not consented, the undertaker may not have a defence to a charge of causing polluting matter to enter controlled waters.[21] If the surface water includes contaminants from the land which are prescribed substances and the effluent is to be regarded as trade effluent[22] then the special procedures requiring consent of the Secretary of State to the discharge to sewer will apply.[23]

Problems of the discharge of contaminated surface water can arise in the context of reclamation schemes for contaminated land, which may produce increased quantities of contaminated water running off the site. Excavated soil may need to be de-watered before it is acceptable for disposal to landfill, and this may produce substantial quantities of contaminated water. The sewerage undertaker may not be willing for such contaminated water to pass into the surface water collection system and may require a connection to be made with the foul sewer. In some cases pre-treatment may be required.

Another practical problem which can arise is the leakage of subsurface contaminated water into sewers which are cracked or damaged. The

---

[19] S.106(2)(b) Water Industry Act 1991. Foul water has been defined under the Public Health Act 1875, s.17 (now repealed) as "water containing excrement or other noxious matter" and surface water has been defined by s.90(1) of the Public Health Act 1936 as "rain water running off the surface of land or the roofs of buildings." S.219 of the Water Industry Act 1991 defines surface water to include water from roofs.

[20] Water Resources Act 1991, s.87(1A).

[21] See *NRA* v. *Yorkshire Water Services*, *The Independent* November 19, 1993, *The Times*, November 24, 1993, para. 2.48 above.

[22] If the effluent can be said to be produced in the course of a trade or industry at trade premises then this may be the case: arguably reclamation activities could be regarded as a trade and the site as trade premises.

[23] See para. 6.38.

prohibition in section 111 of the Water Industry Act[24] extends to any person who suffers or permits the relevant harmful matter as defined in that section to pass into a public sewer, or a communicating drain or private sewer: thus the provision could potentially extend to the occupier of land who allows such leakage to continue. Sewerage undertakers will sometimes insist upon steps being taken to protect public sewers during reclamation schemes; for example the replacement of contaminated soil with a layer or blanket of clean material.

Sewage treatment

Before sewage is discharged from treatment works it will have to meet **6.40** specific standards which are referred to in the European Community Urban Waste Treatment Water Directive.[25] These standards vary depending upon the classification of the water concerned; more stringent requirements are associated with sensitive areas designated under the provisions of Article 5 and Annex IIA of the Directive. Three types of sensitivity are prescribed:

(a) waters which are or which are likely to become eutrophic;
(b) surface freshwater from which drinking water will be extracted in which concentrations of nitrates are liable to exceed the 50 mg per litre limit;
(c) waters where more stringent treatment is needed to ensure the requirements of other EC Directives are met.[26]

The main reason for designating sensitive areas is eutrophication.[26a] This is defined in Article 2(11) as the enrichment of water by nutrients, particularly nitrogen and/or phosphorous, both of which can cause an accelerated growth of algae affecting in turn the balance or organisms present in water and the quality of the water concerned. There is also a procedure for the designation of "less sensitive areas" set out in Article 6 and Annex IIB. These refer to the marine areas, *i.e.* not fresh water ones. Thus open bays, estuaries and other coastal waters can be designated as less sensitive if the discharge of effluent into them does not adversely affect the environment, taking into account the quality and characteristics of the receiving waters and their vulnerability to eutrophication.[26b]

---

[24] See para. 6.38.
[25] 91/271/EEC, O.J. No. L135/40, 30.5.91. See para. 6.37 above.
[26] This would include water designated under the Bathing Waters Directive or the Fresh Water Fisheries Directive.
[26a] Some 22 sensitive areas (eutrophic) have been identified by the Government, with a further 20 areas designated for further monitoring and consideration: DoE News Release No. 303, May 18, 1994.
[26b] The Government has announced the identification of some 58 high natural disperson (less sensitive) areas: DoE News Release No. 304, May 18, 1994.

In sensitive areas more extensive treatment will be required.[27] The standards are set out in Table 2 of Annex I to the Directive. In less sensitive areas the treatment may be less stringent than that required by Article 4.[28] However, the works must provide primary treatment and research should show that the resulting discharge will not adversely effect the environment.

The residual sludge (whether treated or untreated) from sewage treatment works should be re-used, for example in agriculture, wherever possible; any disposal route, however, must minimise adverse environmental effects.[29] By December 31, 1998 the Government must have in place a scheme under which registration or authorisation is required to ensure that sewage sludge disposal is subject to general rules or registration or authorisation; by that date the Government must also ensure that no sludge is disposed of to surface waters, inland or coastal, by dumping from ships, discharged through pipelines or any other means.[30] In the meantime, Member States are obliged to ensure that the total amount of toxic, persistent or bioaccumulative materials in sludge disposed of to surface waters is licensed and progressively reduced.[31]

Contamination, beaches and bathing

6.41 The word "foreshore" is synonymous with "seashore";[32] the landward limit at the foreshore is the highest ordinary tide or the sea.[33] The concept of the seaward boundary is laid down in statute, but inconsistently. Some statutes specify the "low water mark of ordinary spring tides"; others merely refer to an undefined "low water mark."

The protection of beaches and bathing water has two aspects. On the one hand certain discharges into coastal waters are unlawful; secondly in 1976 the European Community approved a directive concerning the quality of bathing waters[34] which refers to areas designated as beaches used by a large number of bathers. The waters thus designated as bathing areas must meet the standards set out in the Annex to the Directive. The main objective of the Directive is to control sewage bacteria (coliforms) in the water by requiring that in 100 millilitres of

---

[27] Art. 5.3.
[28] Art. 6.2.
[29] Art. 14.1.
[30] Art. 14.2 and 3.
[31] Art. 14.4.
[32] *Mellor* v. *Walmesley* (1905) 74 L.J. Ch. 475 and *Government of State of Penang* v. *Beng Hong Oon* [1972] A.C. 425; see J.H. Bates, *Water and Drainage Law*, para. 104 *et seq.*
[33] *Blundell* v. *Caterall* (1821) 5 B. & A. 268.
[34] 76/160/EEC, (O.J. L31, 5.2.76).

water there should be no more than 10,000 coliforms in all in 95 per cent. of the samples taken;[35] a higher target is also set as an objective which Member States must endeavour to meet.[36] Other values are set for such parameters as pH, phenols and mineral oils. There are no set parameters for ammonia, heavy metals, cyanides, or pesticides at the present time. However, there is nothing to prevent Member States fixing values for themselves; alternatively, they can wait until they are set by the Community.[37]

The approach in England and Wales of the Government in implementing the Directive is to set limits on discharge consents granted under Chapter II, Part III of the Water Resources Act 1991.

As we have seen[38] there is a defence to prosecution for the discharge of polluting matter under section 85 provided under section 88 of the Water Resources Act 1991, namely a consent given under Chapter II. Section 88(2) and Schedule 10 refer to the process under which consent is obtained. In practice most consents already exist having been granted by virtue of Part II of the Control of Pollution Act 1974 (which still applies in Scotland).[39] Further, there are a number of consents which are "deemed" under the previous section 40(4) and section 32(3) of the Control of Pollution act 1974; they remain effective until applications in respect of them are finally determined. Such deemed consents issued under the previous provisions should have been replaced by individually determined consents by October 1992. It should be noted that there are powers of review, including revocation of consents and alteration and imposition of conditions under Schedule 10, para. 6 of the Water Resources Act 1991; however this duty to review and the powers in respect of previously granted consents are relevant only to those given under paragraphs 2 and 5 of Schedule 10. In practice therefore, a considerable number of discharges are likely to continue and the public interest is best served by concentration upon the Bathing Water Directive and its implementation; the Directive has undoubtedly led to the commitment of substantially greater expenditure on sewage treatment and disposal then would otherwise have been achieved in the UK.[40]

---

[35] Art. 5.1 and Annex.
[36] 500 total coliforms in 80 per cent. of samples.
[37] Art. 3.1.
[38] See para. 2.44.
[39] S.190(3), Water Act 1989. Sched. 27, Pt. I only repeals the provisions of that Act in relation to England and Wales.
[40] See N. Haigh, *Manual of Environmental Policy: The EC and Britain* (Longman) p. 4.5–7.

Chapter 7

Clean-Up

Clean-Up Methodologies

Introduction

7.01   Whilst the clean-up of contaminated land is by no means inevitably linked to its re-development, the prevalent approach adopted in the UK in the past has been to address problems of soil contamination in the context of proposals for the development and future use of land. It was this narrow approach which was criticised by the House of Commons Environment Committee in its 1990 Report on "Contaminated Land."[1] In its response to that Report the Department of Environment indicated that the focus of Government policies on contaminated land had always been to deal with threats to health in the environment; however, the response went on to say that the majority of cases concerned proposals for changes of use and development within the planning system— including derelict sites put forward for reclamation within grant-aided programmes.[2]

The main, and considerable, advantage of addressing contaminated land problems in this context lies in the possibility of land values changing, or being manipulated, so as to provide the funding to deal with what may be a possibly long-term and intransigent problem. At the same time, however, it seems increasingly likely that in future public opinion may require the clean-up of sites which are perceived as presenting an unacceptable risk to human health or the environment, regardless of whether or not proposals for development of that land are feasible or imminent. In any event, whether clean-up takes place in the context of a scheme of development or not, there are a number of legal problems which are likely to arise, and it is those problems which this chapter seeks to address.

[1] House of Commons, Session 1989–90, First Report, 170–I.
[2] Cm. 1161, para. 5.2.

It is widely accepted that clean-up operations and physical development of contaminated land can be problematic in that they may affect the concentrations of contaminated material and may increase the mobility of contaminants, either by physical dispersion or by altering ground conditions. It is therefore important to be aware of the general environmental controls which apply to such works, and similarly to the waste management and other legislation dealing with removal of contaminated material off-site.

Perhaps the most important point to recognise is that clean-up may be undertaken for a variety of purposes, as summarised below, and that the objectives and approach may vary widely depending on the underlying purpose:

Purpose	Matters arising
Transactional: in preparation for or in context of a sale, disposition or other transaction	• Risk of future liability • Fitness for purpose
Development: in the context of a proposal for the development or change of use of land	• Fitness for purpose • Satisfaction of regulatory bodies *e.g.*, planning, building control • Management of associated potential liabilities • Satisfaction of purchaser, tenant, funder, etc.
Regulatory: as a result of concerns by regulatory bodies, *e.g.*, NRA	• Reduction of environmental risk to acceptable level • Rectification of consequences of non-compliance, *e.g.*, a past spill
Liability: in the context of a dispute in nuisance, negligence etc., such as clean-up of a contaminated aquifer	• Rectification of damage • Possibly satisfaction of regulatory authorities
Internal audit: as part of review by owner of potential liabilities or responsibilities	• Fitness for purpose • Asset value • Risk management • "Good corporate citizenship"

Purpose	Matters arising
Insurance: as part of a proposal for writing environmental impairment liability insurance	• Risk management • Avoidance of future liabilities • Possibly, satisfying regulatory authorities

Forms of remedial action: generally

7.02   The issue of investigation and assessment of sites has already been discussed:[3] in the light of that investigation and assessment, a decision will need to be taken as to the form of any necessary remedial action. Broadly, those forms of remedial action which are currently in use are summarised in ICRCL Guidance Note 59/83, *Guidance on the Assessment and Redevelopment of Contaminated Land*:[4]

> (1) changes in the form or layout of development, for example in the relationship of foundations, services, landscape areas, etc. to the identified areas of contamination—such a change may often be easiest and most cost effective solution;
>
> (2) excavation of contaminated soil for disposal elsewhere, followed where necessary by replacement with clean material;
>
> (3) isolation of contaminated soil by covering it with a suitable thickness of clean inert fill or hard cover;
>
> (4) chemical, biological or physical treatment to destroy or immobilise the contamination; and
>
> (5) mixing the contaminated material with clean soil or sub-soil in order to reduce the maximum concentrations of contaminants to below the appropriate threshold trigger values.

These techniques are not necessarily mutually exclusive. They will often be used in conjunction; for example in the context of a footprint-specific reclamation scheme.

All of the options have their respective advantages and disadvantages, which are considered in the following paragraphs. ICRCL Guidance Note 59/83, for example, regarded off-site disposal as being "the option of last resort" in the sense that it does not solve the problem but merely transfers it to another site; however, it is a technique which continues to be widely used. In practice, the preferred method has usually been that of isolation of the contaminated soil by providing permanent hard cover. The most serious objection to this technique is that, whilst it isolates

---

[3] See Chap. 4.
[4] ICRCL Guidance Note 59/83 (2nd ed.), July 1987, para. 40.

the contamination from future contact with those using the site, it leaves the contaminated material in place with possible future adverse environmental effects, such as contamination of groundwater. Whether this option is acceptable will therefore depend upon the nature of the contaminants and the location of the site. Whether the option of diluting the contamination by mixing with clean or cleaner material is feasible will depend upon the factors such as the size of the site and the availability of suitable inert material. The solution of chemical, biological or physical treatment to destroy or immobilise contamination is obviously attractive, but can be expensive and is at present only proven in relation to a relatively limited range of contaminants.

It is perhaps not surprising that the House of Commons Environment Committee expressed concern that the remedial techniques customarily employed to clean-up contaminated land in the UK did not necessarily represent the best practicable environmental option; the Committee urged the Department of the Environment, through appropriate research, improved guidance and better targeted grants, to create a climate in which methods of destroying contaminants could develop. The Government's response to this suggestion was to refer to research then being funded at the Warren Spring Laboratory and internationally and to indicate an intention to improve the published guidance of redevelopment of contaminated land, including information and advice on remedial technologies.[5] The Government felt that the provisions in the Environmental Protection Act 1990, which would have the effect of raising landfill costs, might well encourage developers towards other forms of treatment: nevertheless, under current circumstances, the best practicable method for dealing with certain types of contamination would, the Government felt, remain removal to landfill, mixing with clean soil and burial beneath a suitable thickness of appropriate covering material.

Available remediation measures

There is a great variety of possible clean-up measures which may be **7.03** applicable either in-situ or ex-situ. Broadly, if the contaminated soil or fill is excavated it can be:[6]

(a) removed from the site and deposited elsewhere in a controlled manner;

(b) re-deposited on-site in a controlled manner; or

(c) treated (either on-site or elsewhere) to remove or destroy the contaminants or reduce their mobility or availability to the environment.

---

[5] Cm. 1161, para. 5.2.6.
[6] See para. 7.28 et seq. for controls over excavation.

If the soil is left in place it may be:

(a) contained or encapsulated; or

(b) treated to remove or destroy the contaminants or reduce their mobility or availability to the environment.

The treatment options referred to above may be categorised as:

- chemical
- physical
- thermal
- microbial
- solidification/stabilisation

The various possible options are more specifically listed in the following table.[7]

Disposal	Removal	excavate to on-site landfill area; excavate to off-site landfall
Engineering Solutions	Physical Methods	dilution and dispersal; capping/ cover; vertical barriers; horizontal barriers
	Hydraulic Methods	separation by pumping; hydraulic gradient management; plume containment
Clean-up Solutions	Ex-situ Treatment	incineration; vitrification/ solidification; soil washing; particle separation; dechlorification and chemical oxidation; solvent extraction; biological treatment; physical-chemical immobilisation; stripping (steam, solvent, air); solvent vapour extraction
	In-situ Treatment	vitrification/solidification; physical-chemical immobilisation; biological treatment; chemical oxidation; electro-kinetic stripping (steam, solvent, air) oxygenation (of waste water/ leachates); soil vapour extraction

Off-site disposal

7.04   Currently a common procedure for dealing with contaminated sites is to excavate contaminated material for disposal at a licensed landfill site,

[7] The options given are illustrative rather than comprehensive. For more detailed discussion, See M.A. Smith, *Available Reclamation Methods in Reclaiming Contaminated Land* (ed. T. Cairney, Blackie, 1987).

followed by replacement by imported clean material where necessary. This can be a fast and effective method of dealing with isolated pockets of highly contaminated soils. The main disadvantage of this method is that the contamination is merely transferred from one place to another, but also the process can be highly disruptive on-site and in relation to the traffic movements generated.

Increasing costs of landfill due to increasing environmental and regulatory controls, and from an increasing shortage of landfill capacity, particularly in the South-East, is likely to make this option less attractive in the future, encouraging the adoption of alternative methods of site remediation.

Also, excavation is not always as simple a solution as might be expected. Its feasibility will be determined by the availability of sites licensed to take the material, and which are willing to take it in the necessary quantities. This may well involve approval by the waste regulation authority for the landfill site, who may require considerable detail to be provided as to the nature and extent of the contamination and the steps taken to appraise it. For major schemes, it may be necessary to transport material to a number of sites, which is a complex logistical exercise. The exact limits of the contaminated material may be uncertain, as may the severity of the contamination, until excavation is in process. The removal and transport may itself present sensitive environmnetal problems such as dust, noise or traffic generation. Special precautions may be necessary for example to assure the safety of the public from lorry movements and to avoid and deal with the fall of contaminated material from vehicles. Excavation may have undesirable consequences in terms of stability and hydrogeology. Complications will also arise where contamination has spread off-site, or under buildings, or where work will be required to prevent contaminants from re-entering the site. Such factors mean that excavation and disposal need to be appraised carefully and will not always be the right solution, even on grounds of cost.

Isolation or encapsulation

Where areas of contamination are extensive it may be possible to **7.05** isolate the contamination by covering it with a suitable thickness of clean inert fill or hard cover. This is not really a remediation technique because no attempt is made to remove or reduce contaminants, merely to isolate them from the surrounding environment. It has to be accepted that no containment system can be 100 per cent. effective.

The covering of soil may be made up of several materials. Commonly, the contaminated area is first covered with a clay cap followed by a layer of gravel or similar material to prevent the upward capillary movement of contaminated liquid. Top soil may be placed above this if required. In addition to its function as a barrier the cover material may be used for the installation of buried services to prevent chemical attack by the contaminated material. Close attention will need to be paid to any plans for development as excavation below the level of the barrier may be required for foundations or major services, such as sewers.

Cover is a relatively cheap form of isolation, but apart from reducing water ingress will not prevent lateral or downward migration of contaminants. Isolation methods used to achieve these objectives include the injection of grout barriers, the installation of impervious liners, sheet steel piling or slurry walls, and the construction of venting trenches for gas. As an alternative to a physical barrier, chemical barriers may be feasible as a means for controlling groundwater contamination. These are generally classified as either precipitation or sorption barriers. Performance is dependent upon the site-specific characteristics of the groundwater.

Soil vapour extraction

7.06   Soil vapour extraction is used to remove volatile organic compounds (VOCs) from the layer of soil nearest the surface and above the water table, which is known as the unsaturated or vadose zone. The process uses vacuum pumps or air blowers to induce air flow through the soil. The volatile contaminants are carried along with the air stream to a series of extraction wells or trenches where the air is collected and passed to a treatment plant where the contaminants are removed, allowing cleaned air to be vented to the atmosphere. A number of treatment processes can be used to remove the VOCs from the air stream including activated carbon adsorption and catalytic oxidation.

One advantage of this method is that remediation can be undertaken to soils in situ and therefore excavation is unnecessary, which can be beneficial in operational sites, or where there are existing buried services which cannot be disturbed. However it is not suitable for heavier contaminants such as metals and heavy hydrocarbons; nonetheless the flow of air through the soil may be beneficial in enhancing the natural degradation of contaminants and may speed up other techniques such as bioremediation.

Bioremediation

7.07   Bioremediation processes utilise naturally occurring microorganisms present in the soil to degrade contaminants, principally organic. Bacteria remove contaminants from the soil by converting the chemical pollutants into cell biomass, carbon dioxide and water. Bacterial action has also been used successfully in some cases in relation to groundwater.

There are two bioremediation techniques, biostimulation and bioaugmentation. Biostimulation involves the addition of nutrients to stimulate naturally occurring bacteria in the soil so the natural degradation processes are enhanced. Bioaugmentation relies on the addition of specifically formulated biocultures to assist the bacteria naturally. Bioremediation techniques can be employed both in-situ as well as ex-situ; this can be useful where excavation is difficult, but treatment periods tend to be prolonged. Ex-situ treatment in shallow, lined treatment beds gives better control of the degradation process, but tends to be more expensive.

Although bioremediation offers certain potential advantages over other treatment methods, treatment times are generally measured in months rather than weeks, which can result in an unacceptable delay in the development of contaminated sites.

Another form of bioremediation uses plants to adsorb contaminants selectively. Certain plants have the ability to immobilise and detoxify heavy metals in their roots, whilst others serve to concentrate contaminants in their leaves, permitting safe disposal. In some cases, this approach can involve little more than encouraging the natural vegetation of the site.

Soil washing

Soil washing is based on the principle of solid-liquid extraction. It is a **7.08** volume reduction method in which contaminants are concentrated into small residual portions of the original contaminated soil volume, using chemical and physical methods. Soil contamination, especially by base materials, is often concentrated on the smaller soil particles or in the organic matter (humus). By separating the soil on the basis of particle size, contaminants become concentrated, leaving the bulk of the excavated material in a relatively clean state which can be returned to the site. The smaller volume of soil containing elevated concentrations of contaminants can be removed from the site for disposal. Contaminant groups which can be dealt with include: petroleum hydrocarbons, polyaromatic hydrocarbons (PAHs), polychlorinated biphenyls (PCBs), pesticides, cyanides and heavy metals. Soil is first excavated and screened to remove large rocks and other debris. The soil is then brought into intimate contact with a solvent in a reaction vessel, where the mixture is stirred to allow the contaminants to migrate into the solvent. After extraction, the treated soil is separated from the solvent allowing the solvent, to be recovered and re-used after treatment.

Both aqueous and organic solvents have been used. Additives such as surfactant, acids, bases, reducing agents and chelating agents have been used to improve the efficiency of the process by assisting in the mobilisation of the contaminants from the soils. Soil washing appears to be most effective in the remediation of sandy soils with a moderate to high permeability.

Soil washing plants can be built in modular form to facilitate transport and enable the treatment process to be undertaken on-site.

Electro-kinetic techniques

7.09   Electro-kinetic remediation involves passing an electric current through the soil by means of an array of suitable electrodes. Charged contaminants migrate through the soil and are concentrated in zones around the anodes or cathodes. The concentrated matrix of contaminants can be removed periodically by excavation for treatment or disposal. Alternatively, a solvent can be circulated around the electrode system which dissolves the contaminants and prevents excessive concentrations occurring at the electrode interface. However, this effluent may require pre-treatment to reduce concentrations of contaminants before disposal to foul sewer. The circulating solution can also be used to control the pH and redox potential at the electrode. The technique requires careful control of operating conditions to prevent excessive soil temperatures being generated and evolution of undesirable offgases at the electrodes due to excessive potentials. The method can be applied to heavy metal, cyanide, phosphate, nitrate and PCB contamination. Electro-kinetic methods also have potential for the containment of polluted groundwater plumes from contaminated sites by arranging the electrode array in the form of a picket fence across the direction of groundwater movement.

In-situ vitrification

7.10   Vitrification is a thermal treatment process which converts contaminated soil into a chemically inert, stable glass and crystalline material. An electrical current is passed through the soil between an array of electrodes. Sufficient temperatures are achieved to melt the soil which solidifies on cooling. Although the process produces an inert end product which can be safely disposed, high energy requirements and the possible generation of hazardous by-products are likely to limit the application of this technique.

Thermal methods

7.11   Heat can be used to remove organic contaminants from soils either by thermal desorption or by incineration. Volatile and semi-volatile contaminants can be removed by thermal desorption where they are driven-off by heating the excavated soil at a few hundred degrees and treating the gas evolved in a secondary combustion chamber or by adsorption to destroy or remove the contaminants. Other contaminants including hazardous substances can be removed by incineration at higher temperatures. Rotary kilns are commonly used which are provided with extensive fuel gas treatment controls. In some cases mobile plant may be used for on-site incineration. Incineration is a rapid clean-up technique, but the high cost and likelihood of air emission treatment being needed may make it unsuitable for some cases: for example, treatment of soils contaminated with chlorinated hydrocarbons can give rise to the formation of toxic chlorinated dibenzodins.

Stabilisation and solidification

Stabilisation and solidification treatment processes aim to reduce the **7.12** solubility, mobility and toxicity of contaminated soil. The processes also assist in improving handling characteristics and limit the potential for migration by reducing the surface area.

Stabilisation is the conversion of the contamination to a more chemically stable form, whilst solidification is the conversion to a more solid form. There are a number of proprietary processes which are commercially available, often based on the addition of cement lime, flyash or thermoplastics. The main limitations of such processes is that the contaminants are not removed and may remain a source of hazard if the treatment should fail in the long term.

Treatment of contaminated groundwater

Clean-up of contaminated groundwater presents its own specific **7.13** problems. Attempts may be made to isolate or affect the flow of the contaminated groundwater. One method which is not available for contaminated soil is that of "pump and treat", the nature of the treatment depending on the nature of the contaminant. Mobilization methods may be necessary to allow the contaminants to be separated.

One problem is that it may be difficult in advance to predict the cost and length of time involved in treating the contamination effectively: it may be necessary to construct a pilot scale treatment plant to carry out feasibility studies. The whole process may take several years to complete. Careful consideration will need to be given to the effect of pumping on local hydrogeology and groundwater flows.

Pump and treat also raises legal complications in that the abstraction of groundwater in substantial quantities, even if contaminated, will require an abstraction licence from the NRA. Similarly the treated

303

groundwater will either have to be reinjected into the aquifer, or otherwise disposed of, and this may entail the necessity of a discharge consent from the NRA, who are likely to have concerns about the quality of the treated water.

Selection of remedial techniques

7.14   The selection and adoption of remedial actions can only be done once there has been a thorough site investigation and assessment, not only of contamination, but also of the hydrogeology, geology, and ground engineering characteristics of the site. For example, engineering requirements may influence the choice of remedial measures. It is also essential to have clear objectives in assessing the various options.[8] Such objectives may be generated internally—for example the objective of developing the site for a certain purpose. Aternatively, they may be imposed externally—for example requirements of the Building Regulations, or legally binding standards such as those for drinking water, or consent conditions relating to discharges which have to be met. It must also be considered whether the objective is to achieve a long-term solution or simply deal with an immediate problem by way of partial solution.

Site specific criteria may be developed following a process of risk assessment. Performance requirements may also be relevant, for example based on specific design lives for building or other site structures, or measures sufficient to cope with once-in-hundred year floods or similar climatic events. Whilst selection of the appropriate remedial measures will be a mater for expert advice, it may be helpful to list those factors which commonly fall to be considered:[9]

(a) present and intended topography and the relation of site levels to surrounding areas, roads, etc.;

(b) adjacent land areas (*e.g.*, proximity of buildings and current and future uses);

(c) surface draining, adjacent water courses, groundwater levels and movement, underlying aquifers;

(d) propensity of site for flooding;

(e) location of existing services;

(f) maximum depth of excavation required for services or foundations (major services, especially sewers, usually have to be installed at considerable depths and this almost inevitably means digging into the contaminated materials even if all the

[8] See M. Smith, *Dealing with Contaminated Ground Conditions*, Land Contamination and Reclamation (1993) Vol. 1, No. 1, p. 22, at p. 25.
[9] *Ibid.*, at p. 27.

other work can be kept within any clean cover material laid over the site);

(g) the consequences of settlement within any imported clean soil cover and settlement of the underlying ground due to imposed loads from cover or buildings or for other reasons;

(h) the safety of workers and neighbours during site works;

(i) the environmental impact of site works;

(j) public acceptability must be considered, *e.g.*, the noise, visual aesthetics;

(k) institutional factors such as environmental standards, approvals required, potential liabilities;

(l) the significance of a future pollution incident on the site (*e.g.*, acid spill);

(m) the effect of building works (*e.g.*, foundations and services) on any completed reclamation works;

(n) the significance of any future site works (*e.g.*, extensions to buildings, repairs to services);

(o) possible future changes of land use;

(p) safety of workers engaged in future site works;

(q) need for long-term monitoring;

(r) need for long-term maintenance; and

(s) who is to be responsible in the long-term for monitoring, maintenance and enforcement of any controls of what may be done on the site.

How clean is clean?

Any owner or developer considering options for clean-up of contami- **7.15** nated land will inevitably be faced with the imponderable question of standards and criteria. The lack of any binding standards in the UK has already been noted,[10] and the more demanding approach adopted in the Netherlands of multifunctionability[11] appears increasingly untenable on economic grounds.[12]

Criteria therefore must be set on a site specific basis, utilising standards such as those of ICRCL or the Dutch "A,B,C" values, where these can be seen to be appropriate. Since each site will vary according to its current and intended use, setting, and other criteria, it may be questioned whether any approach other than a site specific one will ever be viable. Nonetheless, there must always be the possibility that

---

[10] See Chap. 4 generally.

[11] The process of restoring soil to a condition in which it can be used for any purpose. See Chap. 1.

[12] See Chaps. 1 and 13.

standards will change in the medium to long term in such a way as to impose restrictions or liabilities in respect of levels of soil or groundwater contamination which are presently unobjectionable. That is a commercial risk which has to be factored into the decision making process: it may loom large or small depending on individual circumstances. It is a risk (in the sense of changing legislation) which may also fall to be allocated between the parties to commercial transactions.[13]

Ultimately, no one can claim to be able to foresee the future, but any scheme of clean-up ought at least to be *durable* in the sense that it will continue to achieve the desired result for its desired life and *robust* in the sense that sufficient tolerance is built in to cope with human error and foreseeable natural or human events, *e.g.*, storms, drought, tree growth, etc. Particular risks to landowners are, however, imposed by legislation which in future (as in the USA) might require clean-up to achieve the objectives of other legal standards which are not necessarily health or risk-related, or which might require the application of technologies to achieve "permanent" solutions, or which might make unreasonable assumptions as to site uses.

Validation and monitoring

7.16   One vital area which appears to be consistently overlooked in practice is that of validation and post-remediation monitoring. Having carried out remedial treatment, it is important that it can be demonstrated that the treatment has been carried out properly and that it has been effective in achieving the initial objectives and performance criteria. Such assurance may be needed for various purposes: for production to a planning or other regulatory authority, or for future purchasers, funders, tenants, etc. who may be interested in the site.

There are two main aspects to the issue of validation. First there is the quality assurance aspect that the works have been carried out properly and to specification. Secondly, there is validation in the sense of testing to see that the required objectives have been achieved—for example that levels of contamination in soil or groundwater have been reduced to below any relevant target level or that the specified thickness of clean cover has in fact been provided over the full extent of the site. All too often in practice, a purchaser investigating a developed site is presented with a previous report of site appraisal, investigation and recommendations, but no evidence that those recommendations have been properly implemented, and no ongoing monitoring data. Such data may be particularly vital where groundwater treatment has been carried out, or where the problem concerns a gassing site.

---

[13] See Chaps. 11 and 12.

The solution to these issues is for the client to ensure that the remedial works are properly supervised by a qualified engineer or other consultant; and that they are subject to quality assurance in the sense of an audit trail to demonstrate and document that the works have been thoroughly and competently undertaken. The consultant can then be asked to certify that the works were carried out to specification, and the underlying documentary materials can be preserved for production to a future purchaser if necessary. Unfortunately, this ideal situation is still by no means the norm.

Post-remediation monitoring may be necessary, particularly where groundwater or gas are concerned. The prime objective is to ensure that there is advance warning of possible failure. Such monitoring needs to be planned as an integral part of the clean-up scheme, and provision made for monitoring wells, gas detection equipment, and similar facilities.

Relevant forms of monitoring include:[14]

(a) periodic site inspections;
(b) periodic water quality analyses;
(c) periodic groundwater quality monitoring;
(d) site temperature recording (*e.g.*, where combustible materials are involved);
(e) gas monitoring;
(f) site drainage efficiency monitoring;
(g) soil cover monitoring (to ensure that contaminants are not leaching upwards); and
(h) monitoring for specific contaminants (*e.g.*, by buried specific electrodes).

The scale and duration of the monitoring necessary will depend on the nature of the site, the type of clean-up and the degree of certainty which is required. Risk assessment will clearly pay an important role here. For some sites, such as those reclaimed for amenity purposes, it may suffice simply to check that the remedial action has been carried out satisfactorily. In others, such as those where there is a need to check the safety of a building or to protect human health, more thorough monitoring may be necessary. The duration of monitoring will also be determined by the nature of the contaminants: some contaminants are degradable and their effects will become less serious with time—*e.g.*, gas and some forms of phenolic contamination. The sensitivity of the site's future use is also an important factor. It is important to remember that the appropriate regulatory bodies may well require access to information such as the original treatment objectives, and all the monitoring results. Indeed it

[14] T. Cairney, *Long-term Monitoring of Contaminated Sites* in *Reclaiming Contaminated Land* (ed. T. Cairney, Blackie, 1987).

has been suggested that prime responsibility of such monitoring should fall to public bodies.[15]

Remediation and construction

7.17   If redevelopment has been proposed for a contaminated site the issue of future construction should be addressed at every stage of the investigation and remediation.

In the draft British Standard DD 175: 1988[16] the possibility of conducting site investigations for contaminants and geotechnical tests according to BS 5930 is mentioned. This British Standard "Code of Practice for Site Investigation" (BS 5930: 1981) deals with the investigation of sites for the purpose of assessing their suitability for civil engineering and building works. The aim of investigations performed in accordance with the standard is only to acquire knowledge of the characteristics of the site that affect the design and construction of the works and the security of neighbouring land and property. The standard assumes that due regard has been paid to the wider environmental and economic considerations affecting the community generally. The standard therefore has only limited application in respect of investigations undertaken to assess the nature and extent of soil contamination. However it may provide useful background information concerning the planning, method and reporting of investigations.

The advantages of combining geotechnical and contamination investigation and appraisal are obvious, but may in practice arise only rarely. The extent to which site remediation and construction are separate activities will depend on the strategy adopted to deal with the contamination. Before remediation is instigated, consultation with the developers and contractors is needed:

(i) the possibility of adapting the development to the site's contaminated conditions needs to be explored;

(ii) remedial options will be influenced by proposed construction, *e.g.*, if clean cover material is laid over the site, will excavation into the contaminated material be necessary to install major services/foundations?;

(iii) the remedial option chosen may involve the treatment of building materials to prevent chemical attack, or the protection of services by sub-surface barriers;

(iv) the demolition and clearance of existing structures and plant will need to be controlled. Uncontrolled site clearance and

---

[15] *Ibid.*, p. 179.
[16] See also Chap. 4 generally.

demolition can lead to the spreading of serious contamination over parts of sites that were relatively clean before the process started, adding to the hazards encountered at later states and to the cost of redevelopment.

In some cases, the reclamation and subsequent construction will be carried out by the same organisation (*e.g.*, the developer). This will enable a coordinated approach to be taken.

HEALTH AND SAFETY LAW RELATING TO DEVELOPMENT OF CONTAMINATED LAND

General requirements

Construction and reclamation works on contaminated land may **7.18** present risks to those working on the site. The Health and Safety Executive has produced guidance on the subject, *Protection of Workers and the General Public during the Development of Contaminated Land.*[17] This guidance summarises the types of risk which may be assocated with contaminated land, including the following[18]:

(a) *Skin absorption* of a range of materials may have general effects if the material is absorbed into the bloodstream, or may have localised effects causing skin irritation, dermatitis or skin cancer. Substances such as arsenic dust, tars, oils and corrosive substances are referred to in the guidance; contaminated groundwater can lead to skin irritation and possibly longer term skin sensitisation and dermatitis. There may be exposure to carcinogens such as napthylamines and benzo-pyrenes, and to cyanides which may cause rashes.

(b) *Skin penetration.* Materials may enter the body as a result of puncture wounds to the skin, for example micro-biological hazards such as leptospirosis (Weil's disease) or tetanus (lock jaw).

(c) *Ingestion.* Toxic materials may enter the mouth, for example by contact with the fingers if smoking and eating are allowed on site. The handling of contaminated clothing off-site may also present problems in this respect, for example where overalls are permitted to be taken home.

(d) *Inhalation.* Hazardous materials may be breathed in as of dust, vapours, gases, fumes or mist. Such substances can range from

---

[17] HS(G) 66, HMSO, 1991.
[18] Paras. 23–28.

mildly irritant to the highly poisonous. Examples given in the guidance are coal tars, heavy metals, toxic gases from chemical reactions between mixed wastes (for example, acid waste and complex cyanides in the mixture known as "Blue Billy"). Pitch residue dusts are known to have caused lung cancers in gas works staff, vapours generated from wastes such as phenols and volatile aromatics may cause problems, and asbestos dust and lead fumes and dusts are well known and recognised inhalation hazards.

(e) *Asphyxiation/Gassing.* Oxygen deficiency or gassing from hydrogen sulphide or sulphur dioxide, or other toxic gases, may occur during excavation work in trenches or manholes; entry into closed spaces such as basements or tanks also presents a significant risk in this respect.

(f) *Fire/Explosion.* Flammable gases such as methane or hydrogen sulphide may ignite where they exist in confined spaces. Similarly, underground fires from materials such as coke or tar residues or tarry wastes, may give rise to the generation of toxic gases.

The Guidance suggests that in all cases before work begins developers should always consider the possibility of the ground and associated buildings being contaminated and should assess the risks to health and the precautions required:[19]

"All derelict land, whether or not previously used for the industrial processes already described, may be regarded as potentially suspect. A full site investigation including analysis of soil and water samples and a geotechnical survey should be carried out. Initially the responsibility lies with the client for carrying out such works. However, the main contractor must ensure that this has been done."

General statutory duties

7.19 The general statutory duties contained in the Health and Safety at Work, etc. Act 1974 are the principal means by which the safety of site works is ensured. It is not the intention of this Chapter to duplicate the comments on those duties made in the standard works on health and safety law, but the duties can be summarised as follows:

(1) **Section 2** of the 1974 Act provides that it shall be the duty of every employer to ensure, so far as is reasonably practicable, the

---

[19] Para. 29.

310

health, safety and welfare at work of all his employees. By subsection (2) that duty extends, without prejudice to its generality, to the provision and maintenance of safe plant and systems of work, safety in respect of the use, handling, storage and transport of articles and substances, the provision of information, instruction, training and supervision, the maintenance of any place of work under the employer's control in a safe condition without risks to health, and the provision and maintenance of a safe working environment without risks to health.

(2) **Section 3** of the 1974 Act impose a duty on every employer to conduct his undertaking in such a way as to ensure, so far as is reasonably practicable, that persons not in his employment who may be affected thereby are not exposed to risks to their health and safety. By subsection (2) this duty extends to self-employed persons in respect of their own safety and that of other persons not being their employees.

(3) **Section 4** of the 1974 Act imposes duties on persons having control of premises in connection with the carrying on of a trade, business or other undertaking in relation to those who are not their employees but who use non-domestic premises made available to them as a place of work or as a place where they may use plant or substances provided for their use there. The duty is to take such measures as it is reasonable for a person in that position to take to ensure, so far as is reasonably practicable, that the premises, together with means of access and any plant or equipment in the premises, are safe and without risks to health. The duty under the section is of an absolute nature, subject to the limited qualification "so far as is reasonable practicable"; it does not require the occupier to take precautions against unknown and unexpected events.[20]

In a number of cases the basic duties are amplified by way of specific regulations dealing with problems such as asbestos and lead. Any approved codes of practice issued by the Health and Safety Commission will also be relevant and failure to comply with such codes of practice will be admissible evidence in criminal proceedings for contravention of the relevant duty.[21]

Failure to discharge the duties referred to above is an offence under section 73(1) of the 1974 Act subject to a fine exceeding £20,000 on summary conviction and an unlimited fine on conviction on indictment.[22]

[20] *Mailer* v. *Austin Rover Group Ltd.* [1989] 2 All E.R. 1087, HL.
[21] 1974 Act, s.17(2).
[22] 1974 Act, s.33(1A).

311

In any proceedings alleging failure to comply with a duty involving a requirement to do something so far as is practicable or reasonably practicable (as is the case with the duties mentioned above) it is for the accused to prove that it was practicable or reasonably practicable to do more than was in fact done to satisfy the duty; effectively therefore, the onus of proof rests with the defendant as regards the impracticability of further precautions than those actually taken.[23]

Risk assessment

7.20   The general duties referred to above are supplemented by additional requirements contained in the Management of Health and Safety at Work Regulations 1992.[24] Under these Regulations every employer must make a suitable and sufficient assessment of:

(a) the risks to the health and safety of his employees to which they are exposed while they are at work; and

(b) the risks to the health and safety of persons not in his employment arising out of or in connection with the conduct by him of his undertaking,

for the purpose of identifying the measures he needs to take to comply with the requirements or prohibitions imposed on him by or under the relevant statutory provisions.[25] Similar requirements apply to self-employed persons.[26]

The Regulations impose general requirements as to arrangements for the effective planning, organisation, control, monitoring and review of protection and preventive measures;[27] also there is an obligation to provide appropriate health surveillance of employees, having regard to the risks identified in the risk assessment.[28]

Regulation 7 may be important in the context of contaminated land—this requires an employer to ensure that none of his employees has access to any area occupied by him to which it is necessary to restrict access on grounds of health and safety unless the employee concerned has received adequate health and safety instruction.[29]

---

[23] 1974 Act, s.40.
[24] S.I. 1992 No. 2051.
[25] Reg. 3(1).
[26] Reg. 3(2).
[27] Reg. 4.
[28] Reg. 5.
[29] Reg. 7(1)(c).

Control of substances hazardous to health

Work carried out on a contaminated site is likely to involve potential **7.21** exposure to substances which may be hazardous to health and consequently the Control of Substances Hazardous to Health Regulations 1988[30] are of fundamental importance.

By regulation 6 of the Regulations, an employer shall not carry on any work which is liable to expose any employees to any substance hazardous to health unless he has made "a suitable and sufficient assessment of the risk created by that work to the health of the employees" and of the steps that need to be taken to meet the requirements of the 1988 Regulations; such assessments must be reviewed where there is reason to suspect that they are no longer valid or where there has been a significant change in the work to which the assessment relates.

By regulation 7, every employer is under a duty to ensure that the exposure of his employees to substances hazardous to health is either prevented or, where is not reasonably practicable, adequately controlled; so far as is reasonable practicable, this duty is to be fulfilled by measures other than the provision of personal protective equipment. Special provisions apply in relation to exposure to substances for which a maximum exposure limit has been specified in Schedule 1 of the Regulations or in respect of which an occupational exposure standard has been approved.[31]

Other provisions of the Regulations relate to the application of control measures, the monitoring of exposure, health surveillance, information, instruction and training.

The Regulations define "substance hazardous to health" as meaning any substance (natural or artificial and whether in solid, liquid, gaseous or vapour form, and including micro-organisms) which is[32]:

(a) a substance listed in Part 1A of the approved list as dangerous for supply within the meaning of the Classification, Packaging and Labelling Regulations 1984[33] and for which the general indication of nature of risk is specified as very toxic, toxic, harmful, corrosive or irritant;

---

[30] S.I. 1988 No. 1657, as amended by S.I. 1991 No. 2431; see also the approved Code of Practice on Control of Substances Hazardous to Health (1988) and the HSE Guidance published by HMSO *COSHH Assessment: A Step by Step Guide to Assessment and the Skills Needed for it* and *Health Surveillance under COSHH—Guidance for Employers*. The HSE publishes a complete list of HSC/E publication on COSHH, copies of which are available from the HSE Information Centre, Broad Lane, Sheffield, S3 7HO, tel: (0742) 892345.

[31] Reg. 7(4) and (5).

[32] Reg. 2.

[33] S.I. 1984 No. 1244, as amended.

(b) a substance which a maximum exposure limit is specified in Schedule 1 of the 1988 Regulations or for which the Health and Safety Commission has approved an occupational exposure standard;

(c) a micro-organism which creates a hazard to the health of any person;

(d) dust of any kind, when present at a substantial concentration in air; and

(e) a substance, not being a substance mentioned in any of the preceding sub-paragraphs, which creates hazards to the health of any person which is comparable with the hazards created by the substances mentioned in those sub-paragraphs.

The HSE Guidance on the protection of workers during the development of contaminated land states that in order to comply with the requirements of these Regulations the client and person in control of the site should ensure that sufficient information is provided on the nature, extent and level of the contamination so that the firms involved can then assess the risks to which they or their employees are likely to be exposed; however, each contractor must decide what precautions are necessary and take steps to ensure that these precautions are taken.[34] Those in control of sites should satisfy themselves that the various contractors have carried out an assessment which is sufficient and suitable and that the specified control measures are provided and are in fact used; in most cases this assessment should be in writing.

Asbestos

7.22 Asbestos contamination may be found on many sites. In some cases it may be found below ground, for example on former waste disposal sites where asbestos containing materials such as asbestos, cement or woven cloth may have been buried as a convenient means of disposal. At other sites it may be found above ground, for instance where it has been used for heat insulation, fire control or in the construction of roofs. The risk presented by disturbance of the asbestos is that of the release of fibres or dust into the atmosphere; the risk will be dependent upon the nature of the asbestos and its concentrations, and ambient conditions such as whether the site is wet. The relevant regulations are the Control of Asbestos at Work Regulations 1987,[35] which impose the following duties upon employers:

(a) not to carry out work which exposes or is liable to expose any employees to asbestos unless either the type of asbestos has been

[34] Para. 3.
[35] S.I. 1987 No. 2155.

identified by analysis or otherwise or the employer has assumed that the asbestos is crocidolite or amosite (the most difficult types of asbestos) and for the purposes of the Regulations has treated it accordingly;[36]

(b) not to carry out any work which exposes or is liable to expose any employee to asbestos unless the employer has made an adequate assessment of that exposure;[37]

(c) not to carry out work without previously notifying the enforcing authority of specified particulars set out at Schedule 1 unless either the work is not liable to expose an employee to asbestos at levels exceeding the action level or where the employer is licensed under the Asbestos (Licensing) Regulations 1983 to carry out the work and is doing so in accordance with the terms and conditions of the licence;[38]

(d) the provision of adequate information, instruction and training to employees liable to be exposed to asbestos;[39]

(e) the prevention of exposure of employees to asbestos or, where it is not reasonably practicable to prevent such exposure, reduction of exposure to the lowest level reasonably practicable;[40]

(f) ensuring the proper use and application of control measures and personal protective equipment, together with proper maintenance;[41]

(g) the provision of adequate and suitable protective clothing;[42]

(h) the prevention of the spread of asbestos from any place where the work is carried out or, where this is not reasonably practical, reduction of the spread to the lowest level reasonably practical;[43]

(i) ensuring that premises and plant are kept in a clean state and that where the work with asbestos has been completed, the premises are thoroughly cleaned;[44]

(j) the designation of asbestos areas and respirator zones;[45]

(k) adequate steps to monitor exposure of employees to asbestos where such monitoring is appropriate for protection of the health of their employees, together with the keeping of records;[46]

[36] Reg. 4.
[37] Reg. 5.
[38] Reg. 6.
[39] Reg. 7.
[40] Reg. 8.
[41] Regs. 9 and 10.
[42] Reg. 11.
[43] Reg. 12.
[44] Reg. 13.
[45] Reg. 14.
[46] Reg. 15.

(l) the maintenance of health records and the provision of adequate medical surveillance to employees exposed to asbestos;[47]

(m) the provision of adequate and suitable washing and changing facilities and the storage of protective clothing;[48] and

(n) ensuring that raw asbestos or waste containing asbestos is not stored, received or despatched unless in a suitable and sealed container properly marked and labelled in accordance with the relevant statutory requirements.[49]

Practical guidance on compliance with these duties is contained in the HSE Approved Code of Practice on Control of Asbestos at Work, which takes the form of annotations to the relevant Regulations; in particular, these provide guidance on the assessment of action levels in respect of single types of fibre and in respect of mixed exposure.

The HSE Guidance on protection of workers indicates that the precautions to be taken will depend on the extent and type of asbestos, the condition of the site and the work to be carried out; in this respect the precautions should match the risk.[50] For all asbestos contaminated materials the main aim should be to prevent its spread, and where work involves large scale excavation and removal, then additional precautions may be required such as segregation of areas and dust suppression.

PCBs

7.22A Polychlorinated biphenyls (PCBs) have been commercially available since the 1930s and were manufactured in the UK from 1954 until 1976. They were put to a wide range of industrial applications and were incorporated in manufactured products for both commercial and domestic use. Environmentally, the problems presented by dioxins are that they are persistent and can accumulate in soils, plants and the fatty tissues of living organisms; also, they can act as precursors for the formation under certain conditions of highly toxic dibenzofurans and dibenzodioxins. For these reasons the use of PCBs has been progressively restricted since the early 1970s: their use in new plant and equipment was banned in the UK in 1986.[50a] PCB contamination can arise from various sources, including leakage from equipment containing PCBs in the course of that equipment being used, maintained or disposed of; fires involving PCB-containing equipment can also result in significant releases.

[47] Reg. 16.
[48] Reg. 17.
[49] Reg. 18.
[50] Para. 10.
[50a] The Control of Pollution (Supply and Use of Injurious Substances) Regulations 1986 (S.I. 1986 No. 902) as amended by S.I. 1992 No. 31.

PCBs are the subject of Community legislation, Directive 76/403/EEC on the disposal of PCBs and PCTs.[50b] A draft directive on the disposal of PCBs has been issued, which includes proposals for the treatment of all significant PCB holdings and tighter regulation of PCB treatment and storage facilities.[50c]

At the third International Ministerial Conference on the Protection of the North Sea in 1990, the UK agreed with the other participating states to phase out and destroy the remaining PCBs in use by 1999. A consultation paper on an action plan for achieving this objective was issued in November 1993.[50d] The paper estimates that a maximum of 8,000 tonnes of PCBs remain in the UK for disposal—the most likely sources of PCB wastes being electrical and heat transfer equipment (*e.g.* transformers and capacitors) and underground mining equipment, where PCBs were used as hydraulic fluid. It is proposed to extend the ban on PCBs to include (*inter alia*) all objects (*e.g.* redundant transformer tanks and internal windings) which are so contaminated with PCBs that physical or chemical interaction with other objects would produce contamination above a 50ppm level: the Government acknowledges that this might even have to apply to fragmentised scrap metal. It is also proposed to extend the ban to the keeping and storage of PCBs and PCB containing equipment except for material registered with a company licensed to destroy PCBs.

The Paper also urges targeted monitoring of PCBs by the regulatory authorities, particularly to ensure that they are not discharged to rivers and groundwaters. The proposed action plan would also apply to other types of substances with similar properties to PCBs and which were used in similar applications: these are polychlorinated terphenyls (PCTs), polychlorinated napthalenes (PCNs) and polybrominated biphenyls (PBBs).

Waste Management Paper No. 6 deals with the disposal of PCBs: a new version of the paper was issued for consultation in November 1993 and is intended to replace the original version of 1976. PCB wastes arising mainly from the electrical equipment market are generally disposed of by high-temperature incineration; recycling of PCBs is now regarded as unacceptable. PCB wastes can also arise from the practice of retrofilling transformers, *i.e.* draining out the PCB liquid and replacing it with an alternative.

For the purposes of the advice in draft WMP No. 6, PCB wastes are taken to be those in which the PCB concentration is a material

[50b] O.J. No. L 108, 26.4.76.
[50c] Amended proposal for a Council Directive on the disposal of polychlorinated biphenyls and polychlorinated terphenyls 91/C299/05 Com (91) 373 Final, O.J. No. C299/9, 20.11.91.
[50d] UK Action Plan for the Phasing Out and Destruction of Polychlorinated Biphenyls and dangerous PCB Substitutes.

317

consideration in the selection and availability of a disposal route. A general threshold of PCB concentration at 50ppm is used for electrical equipment (whether containing PCBs or retrofilled), metal casings or equipment parts, PCB liquids drained from equipment and any other liquid wastes. For sludges, tarry liquids, soils or other loose wastes the suggested threshold PCB concentration is 10ppm. However, a note to the Paper makes it clear that this figure does not constitute a standard or guideline value for soil which remains on site: here appropriate values will depend on particular site-specific circumstances. Paragraph 4.33 of the draft deals with PCB-contaminated soils and suggests a common problem is contamination of transformer compounds due to spillages during maintenance activities or minor leaks from gaskets and seals which have accumulated over the years. Since PCBs are strongly absorbed by soils, the contamination is usually highly localised. However, migration must be anticipated in permeable ground, with the possibility of surface or groundwater contamination.

Chapter 7 of the draft paper is of particular importance, dealing with storage, handling and transport of PCB wastes which, as explained above, may include excavated PCB-contaminated soil.

Careful precautions are required in storage, including bunding, segregation from flammable materials and labelling. Only authorised personnel, with appropriate protection, should be allowed to enter the "working area". Disposal is dealt with in Chapter 8 and, essentially, disposal must employ treatment technologies capable of breaking down the PCB molecule: this involves a large input of energy, which at present in the UK means either high temperature incineration or chemical dechlorination. Various other options, not yet available or not considered appropriate in the UK are also discussed. Landfill as a diposal route should be prohibited "without exception" for lage quantities of materials such as soil and demolition waste significantly contaminated with PCBs, items such as large capacitors or transformers over 1kg gross weight and routine industrial arisings of PCB-contaminated waste. However, the occasional landfill site of "one-off" waste arisings only lightly contaminated with PCB "may be considered at suitable licensed sites": for example, soil from a contaminated transformer compound, if supported by documentary evidence of the PCB content. There is also however a very heavy "health warning" that landfilled PCBs "may cause a long term problem due to the continuous release of significant quantities of these compounds". In any event, quantities disposed of to landfill must be strictly limited so as to control overall concentrations, and there must be strict segregation from organic solvents and oils that might encourage migration. PCB disposal to landfill should not, the draft paper concludes, become routine on a widespread basis.

Lead

The Control of Lead at Work Regulations 1980[51] apply to work which **7.23** exposes both employees and other persons to lead as defined in regulation 2(1) (including lead alloys, any compounds of lead and lead as a constituent of any substance or material) which is liable to be inhaled, ingested or otherwise absorbed by persons. Thus, the regulations may apply to sites contaminated by lead in dust or any other form in which it may be inhaled, ingested or absorbed. The employer's duties extend by regulation 3 not only to employees but to any other person at work on the premises where the work with lead is being carried on and who is, or is liable to be, exposed to lead from that work. The main requirements of the Regulations are as follows:

(a) assessment of the work which may expose persons to lead to determine the nature and degree of exposure;[52]

(b) provision of adequate information, instruction and training to employees liable to be exposed to lead;[53]

(c) the provision, so far as is reasonably practicable, of such control measures for materials, plant and processes as will adequately control the exposure of employees to lead otherwise by the use of respiratory protective equipment or protective clothing;[54]

(d) provision of employees liable to be exposed to airborne lead with respiratory protective equipment of a type approved by the Health and Safety Executive as will adequately protect the employee against the airborne lead, unless other control measures provide adequate protection;[55]

(e) provision of adequate protective clothing unless the likely exposure to lead is not significant;[56]

(f) provision of adequate washing facilities, changing facilities and facilities for the storage of protective clothing;[57]

(g) steps to ensure that employees do not eat, drink or smoke in any place liable to be contaminated by lead (there is a corresponding duty on the employees in this respect);[58]

(h) adequate steps to secure cleanliness of workplace, premises, plant, respiratory protective equipment and protective clothing;[59]

[51] S.I. 1980 No. 1248; see also HSC Approved Code of Practice amplifying these duties.
[52] Reg. 4.
[53] Reg. 5.
[54] Reg. 6.
[55] Reg. 7.
[56] Reg. 8.
[57] Reg. 9.
[58] Reg. 10.
[59] Reg. 11.

(i) prevention, so far as is reasonably practicable, of the spread of contamination by lead from the place where the work is being carried out;[60]

(j) steps to ensure, so far as is reasonably practicable, that any control measures, respiratory protective equipment, protective clothing or other similar items are properly used or applied and maintained in an efficient state, efficient working order and good repair;[61]

(k) adequate monitoring procedures to measure concentrations of lead in air to which employees are exposed unless the exposure is not significant;[62] and

(l) medical surveillance of employees employed on work which exposes them to lead and appropriate biological tests as a part of that surveillance.[63]

The HSE Guidance on Protection of Workers suggests that although work with lead may be transitory there may still be instances where exposure to very high levels of lead can occur; nor does the fact that work is carried out in the open air necessarily indicate low-level exposures only.[64]

Radioactive contamination

7.24   Sites subject to radioactive contamination require special attention and are subject to the requirements of the Radioactive Substances Act 1993, and the Ionising Radiation Regulations 1985, and its accompanying Approved Code of Practice.[65] Before any development of the site begins, proposals for protecting site personnel and containing and safely removing the radioactive material should be agreed with the Health and Safety Executive and with HM Inspectorate of Pollution; it will almost certainly be necessary to use specialist contractors for this work, to carry out regular monitoring as required, and to enclose the area where the radioactive material is being dealt with.[66]

Buried explosives

7.25   Buried explosives present their own particular risks, in that disturbance may have immediate and sudden consequences both on site and off site; efforts should be made to prevent such events occurring, the first

[60] Reg. 12.
[61] Regs. 13 and 14.
[62] Reg. 15.
[63] Reg. 16.
[64] Para. 18.
[65] S.I. 1985 No. 1333 and Approved Code of Practice (HMSO, 1985), Pts. I and II.
[66] HSE Guidance on Protection of Workers, para. 13.

step being to obtain information on the site and the materials involved. The HSE Code of Practice for the Protection of Workers suggests that for the most part, sites where explosives might be present fall into two groups: the first comprises the discrete premises of former explosives factories and magazines; the second group consists of the more ill-defined areas used for war-time activities or which suffered from enemy action.[67] Information on both groups should be sought in the locality and detailed information may be available from the appropriate licensing authorities or from within the explosives industry. Any excavation work at such sites should proceed with great caution and discolouration of soil or the unearthing of unusual objects should be regarded as indicating the presence of explosives; work should then stop until the substances or articles can be identified. The contractor may choose to call in the Explosives Ordnance Disposal Unit from the Armed Services, or to consult the explosives industry.[68] Sites subject to wartime activity and areas affected by enemy action are more likely to involve items such as bombs and shells; well-established procedures exist for dealing with unexploded munitions, and any work should cease immediately and the police contacted.[69]

Anthrax

Anthrax spores may be found on any tannery or fellmonger site where **7.26** the premises have been used for a number of years; such organisms have also been found in premises previously used for the production of gelatin from crushed bone and in old wool sorting stations.[70] A common problem in such cases is that it may be impossible to identify with certainty those areas within a site which are high risk; in such a case the whole premises need to be regarded as a risk area. In the case of agricultural sites, the possibility exists of anthrax contaminated carcasses having been buried, in which case enquiries should be made of the Ministry of Agriculture, Fisheries and Food, and possibly local authority environmental health departments.[71] Where anthrax contamination is suspected, it is important to minimise possible skin contact with spores: good personal hygiene precautions and adequate protective clothing are therefore necessary. Workers should be made aware of the risk and, for example, all cuts and scratches on the skin should be covered. If the risk is thought to be low, and provided these precautions are rigidly followed, a full programme of

[67] *Ibid.*, para. 15.
[68] *Ibid.*, para. 16.
[69] *Ibid.*, para. 17.
[70] *Ibid.*, para. 19.
[71] *Ibid.*, para. 21.

immunisation is not recommended, though individual workers should be made aware that immunisation is an additional precaution they may wish to take: all persons who may possibly be exposed should be advised of the necessary precautions and provided with a copy of the relevant HSE pocket card on Anthrax.[72]

A recently reported planning decision[72a] refers to some of the difficulties of developing land contaminated by anthrax. The contamination in question consisted of the burial, in 1964, of a small number of cattle carcasses infected by anthrax. The exact location of the burial site was unknown. The view of the Assessor was that any surviving anthrax spores would be few in number and that, even if disturbed, would pose only insignificant risks to public health if correct precautions were undertaken. On this basis, the appeal was allowed and permission granted, subject to the following conditions:

(5) Development shall not begin until a scheme to deal with contamination of the site has been submitted to and approved by the local planning authority;

(6) The scheme referred to above shall include an investigation and assessment to identify the location of the animal burial pit within the site, the degree of contamination by anthrax and the measures to be taken to avoid risk to public health when the site is developed;

(7) Development shall not begin until the measures approved in the scheme to be carried out prior to the commencement of development have been implemented;

(8) Development shall not begin until a detailed assessment has been submitted to and approved by the local planning authority identifying any back-filled ground, zones of weakness, disused mine shafts and other signs of former mining activity. The details which form part of the reserved matters shall incorporate measures shown in the assessment to be necessary.

It may be noted that conditions (5) and (7) are framed as *Grampian*-style conditions,[72b] restraining commencement of development until approval and implementation of this scheme; the Secretary of State regarded these as equally effective as a planning agreement to secure remediation. Whilst removal of contaminated earth would be controlled by licence under the Animal Health Act 1981 under the direction of the District Veterinary Officer, the Secretary of State was not satisfied that this would be a comprehensive safeguard against possible health risks.

---

[72] *Ibid.*, para. 22.
[72a] [1994] J.P.L. 555.
[72b] See para. 8.12 below.

Contractual matters and design and management

It is important to address the health risks to all workers in the **7.27** contractual material relating to development of the site. The HSE Guidance on the Protection of Workers suggests that, where possible, details of the contamination and an outline of precautions to be taken should be included within tender documentation, as this can be a valuable basis on which contractors can make their assessments of risks to health and the precautions required.[73] This is particularly important for those undertaking ground works, and will also be helpful as general guidance in the case of the main contractor. In some cases, tender documentation has not only included details of contamination and appropriate precautions, but it is also required that a sum be set aside for dealing with those precautions as a separate part of the tenders: this is a procedure to be recommended since it will allow the developer to assess estimates of the cost of work, confident that control measures have been included. An occupational hygienist should be approved to provide general guidance and a report giving details of the precautions to be followed.[74]

The provision of such details at an early stage can greatly help in the design of the project, for example by avoiding the need for deep excavated trenches, such as for underground services, in contaminated ground.[75]

The proposed Construction (Design and Management) Regulations and Approved Code of Practice, which will implement the EC directive on minimum health and safety requirements at construction sites,[76] will have an important bearing on the respective responsibilities of site owner, contractor and design professionals. Draft regulations and a draft code of practice were issued for consultation in 1992, but were withdrawn for re-drafting to take effect by October 1, 1994.

Broadly, the proposed regulations aim to establish clear responsibilities for the general supervision and coordination of the design/planning/preparation stage and the construction phase of projects, and to ensure that during the construction phase particularly there is no doubt who leads the health and safety effort. The draft regulations proposed the appointment by the client of a "planning supervisor" to take responsibility in relation to the preparation stage and a "principal contractor" to take responsibility as to the execution stage. The planning

---

[73] HSE Code of Protection for Workers, para. 31.
[74] *Ibid.*
[75] *Ibid.*, para. 32.
[76] 95/57/EC, O.J. No. L245/6, 26.8.92.

supervisor would initiate a health and safety plan, sufficiently detailed to form part of the tendering process. The client would be responsible for ensuring that the planning supervisor is provided with all information about the state of the land or premises that the supervisor can reasonably be expected to take into account when deciding what measures should be taken; this might obviously extend to potential contamination or previous contaminative uses.

WASTE DISPOSAL

Licensing: the definition of waste

7.28   The concepts of "controlled waste" and "directive waste" have been discussed elsewhere.[77] It needs to be considered whether excavated soil or other material missing from groundworks is or is not waste falling within these concepts: this is a quite separate question from whether any of the exemptions from waste management licensing apply.[78] If the material in question is directive waste then it will be regarded as industrial waste, and hence controlled waste—the category of industrial waste includes:

(a) waste arising from works of construction or demolition, including waste arising from work preparatory thereto;

(b) waste arising from tunneling any other excavation; and

(c) waste removed from land on which it had previously been deposited and any soil with which such waste had been in contact.[79]

The crucial issue is therefore whether the material is directive waste, *i.e.* any substance or object set out within the categories as Part II of Schedule 4 to the 1994 Regulations which the producer or the person in possession of it discards or intends or is required to discard.

The relevant categories include "Contaminated materials, substances or products resulting from remedial action with respect to land" (Category 16). However, this does not necessarily mean that the material is waste: the question is whether the relevant person discards it or intends to discard it.

Within the context of a reclamation scheme it may in some cases be clear that excavated material is being discarded, or disposed of as waste.

---

[77] See para. 5.24.
[78] See paras. 5.28A and 5.28B.
[79] See the Collection and Disposal of Waste Regulations 1988, S.I. 1988 No. 819, reg. 6 and Sched. 3, paras. 6, 7 and 12; The Controlled Waste Regulations 1992, S.I. 1992 No. 588, reg. 5(1) and (2)(a) and Sched. 3, paras. 6 and 11.

For example, those materials which are so contaminated as to present a substantial hazard to man or the environment will often be placed within a specially engineered repository on site. This activity will normally be licensed in much the same way as a containment landfill, with conditions as to impermeability of linings and bunds. Frequently, conditions will restrict the material deposited to that arising on site, or will prohibit the emplacement of imported materials. It seems clear that such material is being treated as waste. It is not part of the commercial cycle or claim of utility[80] and is not being put to a beneficial use; the object is simply to isolate and dispose of it safely on-site.

On the other hand there are general site works whereby the less contaminated earth is moved around the site by way of spreading, mixing, grading, covering, contouring and landscaping. In the light of the Government's guidance on the meaning of directive waste at Annex 2 to Circular 11/94, there are strong arguments to be made that excavated material which is used in this way is not waste. In particular it may be said that its holder intends at all times that it shall be put to beneficial use; the only counter argument might be that the "beneficial use" is really only incidental to the main object of disposing of the material.[81] The guidance suggests that in such cases it may be helpful to ask whether the purpose of the "beneficial" use is wholly or mainly to relieve the producer of the burden of otherwise disposing of the material, and secondly whether the producer would be likely to seek a substitute for the material if it were not available to him.

Further complications may arise where highly contaminated soil is mixed with mildly contaminated or uncontaminated soil in order to allow its use on site by reducing contamination levels. The highly contaminated soil could not be put to immediate use without such mixing; this would seem to indicate that the material is waste until such time as mixing has resulted in the hazard being reduced to such a level that it can be put to beneficial use.[82] If correct, then the mixing process (and prior storage) would require a waste management licence in the absence of an applicable exemption, but the final emplacement of the material (no longer being waste) would not. An additional complication—which in this case seems unhelpful—is the Department's suggested distinction between specialised and non-specialised recovery operations and into which category the mixing of soil would fall.[83]

Another potential problem is that the excavated material may itself have been discarded as waste when it was originally placed on the site, for example in the case of "made ground" where the object may have

[80] Circ. 11/94, Sched. 2, para. 2.20.
[81] *Ibid.*, 2.40–2.41.
[82] *Ibid.*, para. 2.47.
[83] *Ibid.*, para. 2.33.

325

been essentially to dispose of materials such as slag, foundry sand or general refuse. The question is then when this material ceases to be waste. If it is immediately capable of beneficial use at the time of excavation without mixing or any other treatment, then there is an argument to be made that it has ceased to be waste;[84] otherwise, as explained above, it may cease to be waste after such treatment.

Exemptions from licensing: the position under COPA 1974

7.28A   The Collection and Disposal of Waste Regulations 1988 contained a number of potentially applicable exemptions from licensing, *i.e.*:[85]

(a) the deposit on land of material arising from certain types of excavation and of ash, slag or clinker, provided that the deposit is made for the purpose of construction currently being undertaken on the land on which the waste is deposited; and

(b) the deposit of the same types of waste on land for the purposes of future construction on that land, provided the deposit does not exceed three months in duration.

However, these exemptions did not apply where the waste was special waste or where its presence was likely to give rise to an environmental hazard within the meaning of section 4(5) of C.O.P.A. The definition of environmental hazard, which derived from the Deposit of Poisonous Waste Act 1972,[86] referred to risk to persons and animals and pollution of surface and groundwater: it also provided that the measures to be taken by the depositor of the waste for minimising the risks were to be relevant in assessing the risks. Thus some authorities took the view, having consulted the NRA, that provided material which was relatively mildly contaminated[87] was palced well above the water table and is covered by clean material, there was no environmental hazard and no licence was required. In other cases, however, authorities took the position that the degree of risk was such that a full disposal licence was required.

---

[84] *Ibid.*, paras. 2.47–2.50.
[85] Reg. 9 and Sched. 6, para. 5(1) and (2).
[86] See para. 5.19
[87] Sometimes thresholds derived from ICRCL levels or Dutch 'A', 'B' and 'C' levels were used for this purpose.

Exemptions from licensing: the current position

The Waste Management Licensing Regulations 1994[88] confer a num- **7.28B** ber of exemptions from the requirement for a waste management licence.[89] Some of these exemptions are of potential relevance to land reclamation and remediation activities and are summarised in the table below. However, a number of points should be noted in relation to such exemptions:

(1) exemption is only in relation to the need for a waste management licence: the prohibition on disposing of waste in an environmentally harmful manner under section 33(1)(c) still applies;

(2) certain of the exemptions only apply if the exempt activity is carried on by or with the consent of the occupier of the relevant land or where the person carrying on the activity is otherwise entitled to do so on the land;

(3) in general the exemptions do no apply insofar as the activity involves special waste; and

(4) in order to comply with the requirements of Directive 91/156/ EEC, where waste is disposed of or recovered by an establishment or undertaking, the exemptions only apply if the type and quantity of waste, and the method of disposal and recovery, are consistent with the need to attain the objectives of Schedule 4 of the Regulations: not to endanger human health, and without using processes or methods which could harm the environment, and in particular without risk to water, air, soil, plants or animals, causing nuisance through noise or odours, or adversely affecting the countryside or places of special interest.

---

[88] S.I. 1994 No. 1056.
[89] Reg. 17 and Sched. 3. The exemptions are explained at Circ. 11/94, Annex 5.

327

Nature of exemption	Reference	Qualifications
Spreading of waste consisting of soil, rock, ash or sludge, or waste arising from dredging inland waters or from construction or demolition work on any land in connection with the reclamation or improvement of that land if: (a) by reason of industrial or other development the land is incapable of beneficial use without treatment; (b) spreading is carried out in accordance with a planning permission for the reclamation or improvement of the land and results in benefit to agriculture or ecological improvement; and (c) no more than 20,000 cubic metres per hectare of such waste is spread.	Sched. 3, para. 9(1)	(a) Does not apply to special waste. (b) Occupier's consent required. (c) Does not apply to the disposal of waste at a site designed or adapted for the final disposal of waste by landfill.
The storage, at the place where it is to be spread, of any such waste which is intended to be spread in reliance upon the previous exemption.	Sched. 3, para. 9(2)	(a) Does not apply to special waste. (b) Occupier's consent required.
The treatment of waste soil or rock which, when treated, is to be spread on land under the exemption at para 9(1) if: (a) it is carried out at the place where the waste is produced or the treated product is to be spread; and (b) the total amount treated at that place in any does not exceed 100 tonnes.	Sched. 3, para. 13(3)	(a) Does not apply to special waste. (b) Occupier's consent required.

Nature of exemption	Reference	Qualifications
The storage of waste which is to be submitted to treatment under the previous exemption if: (a) the waste is stored at the place where the activity is to be carried on; and (b) the total quantity stored at the place does not exceed 20,000 tonnes.	Sched. 3, para. 13(4)	(a) Does not apply to special waste. (b) Occupier's consent needed.
The storage on a site of waste which arises from demolition or construction work or tunnelling or other excavations or which consists of ash, slag, clinker, rock, wood or gypsum if: (a) the waste is suitable for use for the purposes of "relevant work" which will be carried out at the site, i.e. construction work, including the deposit of waste on land in connection with provision of recreation facilities or the construction, maintenance or improvement of a building, highway, railway, airport, dock or other transport facility, but *not including* the deposit of waste in any other circumstances or any work involving land reclamation; and	Sched. 3, para. 19(1)	(a) Does not apply to special waste. (b) Occupier's consent needed.

Nature of exemption	Reference	Qualifications
(b) in the case of waste which is not produced on the side, it is not stored there for longer than 3 months before the relevant work starts.		
The use of waste of a kind mentioned in the previous exemption for the purposes of "relevant work" if the waste is suitable for those purposes.	Sched. 3, para. 19(2)	(a) Does not apply to special waste. (b) Occupier's consent needed.
The deposit of waste arising from dredging inland waters, or from clearing plant matter from inland waters, if either: (a) the waste is deposited along the bank or towpath of the waters where the dredging or clearing takes place; or (b) the waste is deposited along the bank of any inland waters so as to result in benefit to agriculture or ecological improvement. The total amount deposited must not exceed 50 tonnes for each metre of the bank to towpath along which it is deposited. Also (a) above only applies to an establishment or undertaking where the waste deposited is the establishment or undertaking's own waste.	Sched. 3, para. 25(1)	(a) Does not apply to special waste. (b) Occupier's consent needed. (c) Does not apply to waste deposited in a container or lagoon.

Nature of exemption	Reference	Qualifications
The temporary storage of waste, pending its collection, on the site where it is produced. Can apply to special waste if: (a) it is stored on the site for no more than 12 months; (b) in the case of liquid waste it is stored in a secure container[89a] and the total volume of the waste does not exceed 23,000 litres at any time; and (c) in the case of any other kind of waste it is stored in a secure container or in a secure place[89a] and the total volume does not in either case exceed 80 cubic metres or 50 cubic metres respectively.	Sched. 2, para. 41	(a) Occupier's consent needed.

Whereas under the previous relevant exemption which applied under the Collection and Disposal of Waste Regulations 1988 the critical questions were whether the waste was special waste and whether its presence was likely to give risk to an environmental hazard,[89b] under the 1994 Regulations the reference is simply to whether the waste is or is not special waste. However, where the waste is not special waste, but where the activity is carried out by an establishment or undertaking, the effect of regulation 17(4) is that the licensing authority will still have to consider whether the type and quantity of the waste, and the method of disposal or recovery, are consistent with attainment of the objectives of paragraph 4(1)(a) of Schedule 4, Part I to the Regulations. Since these objectives include avoiding danger to human health, harm to the environment and risk to soil and water, in practical terms the position may well be much the same as under the Collection and Disposal of Waste Regulations, described above.

Where one of the exemptions mentioned above applies, it is an offence for an establishment or undertaking to carry on, after December 31,

[89a] "secure container" and "secure place" are defined at reg. 17(5).
[89b] See para. 7.28A.

331

1994, an exempt activity involving the recovery or dispoal of waste without being registered with the appropriate registration authority.[89c] The requirements of registration are set out in regulation 18 of the 1994 Regulations: the information required is the name and address of the establishment or undertaking, the activity which constitutes the exempt activity and the place where the activity is carried on.

Thus, to summarise, the issues which need to be addressed in relation to schemes of reclamation and remediation are, so far as waste licensing is concerned:

(1) Does the activity involve the keeping, treatment, deposit or disposal of material which is waste?

(2) If so, are any of the exemptions from waste management licensing applicable, bearing in mind the types and quantities of the waste, the method of dealing with it and the environmental risks thereby created?

(3) If an exemption is applicable, and the activity is carried out by an establishment or undertaking, then registration with the waste regulation authority for the area will be required.

Special waste

7.29   Waste excavated in the course of reclaiming or remediating contaminated land may be of such a potentially hazardous nature as to constitute "special waste".[89d] If so, then the statutory requirements as to consignment note documentation must be observed if the waste is removed for off-site disposal.[89e] If the waste is disposed of on-site (for example, in a specially engineered repository) then records and site plans showing the composition of the waste and the date and location of its disposal will need to be kept.[89f]

Radioactive waste

7.30   Some contaminated sites may contain or comprise radioactive waste, or soil or other material which has been irradiated by contact with such waste, so as to be classified as radioactive waste itself.[90] In that case, the requirements of the Radioactive Substancs Act 1993 will need to be observed in relation both to the disposal of waste from the premises[91] and

---

[89c] Reg. 18(1).
[89d] See para. 5.32.
[89e] See para. 5.33.
[89f] See para. 5.34.
[90] See para. 5.35.
[91] S.13. See para. 5.36.

its accumulation with a view to subsequent disposal.[92] The requirement for authorisation for these activities applies to the person using "any premises for the purposes of an undertaking carried on by him." The term "premises" includes any land, whether covered by buildings or not, and "undertaking" is defined as including:[93]

". . . any trade, business or profession and, in relation to a public or local authority, includes any of the powers or duties of that authority, and, in relation to any other body or persons, whether corporate or unincorporate, includes any of the activities of that body."

These requirements could therefore potentially apply to consultants, contractors and sub-contractors on site, as well as the developer. The person to whom authorisation is granted must arrange for copies of the certificate to be posted on the premises concerned where they can conveniently be read by persons having duties on the premises which might be affected by the matters set out in the certificate.[94]

Policy as to on-site or off-site disposal is stated in the Government's Guide to the Administration of the Radioactive Substances Act:[95]

"Demolition wastes and other high volume wastes having a radioactive content of less than 4 Bq/g . . . should normally be authorised for removal to a tip and burial at a depth of at least 1.5 m. Wastes of less than 0.4 Bq/g . . . may be left on the site and, if significant economic savings can be made, this limit may be raised to 1 Bq/g . . . Burial of wastes with higher specific activity on the site at which they arise should only be authorised in special circumstances."

The duty of care: generally

Work on a contaminated site may well involve the production, **7.31** treatment, handling or disposal of controlled waste. Whether such waste is disposed of on-site, or is removed for disposal elsewhere, the duty of care created by section 34 of the Environmental Protection Act 1990 will be relevant.

With one exception,[96] the duty applies to any person who imports, produces, carries, keeps, treats or disposes of controlled waste or who, as

---

[92] S.14. See para. 5.37.
[93] S.47.
[94] S.19.
[95] HMSO, 1982, para. 58.
[96] Relating to an occupier of domestic property as respects the household waste produced on the property: s.34(2).

333

a broker, has control of such waste.[97] No definition of "producer" is provided by the Act, but the view of the relevant Government Department is that in the case of contracting, the producer of waste may be regarded as the person undertaking the works which give rise to the waste, not the person who issues instructions or lets contracts which give rise to the waste.[98] Where there are several contractors or sub-contractors on site, the Government suggests, the producer of a particular waste is the particular contractor or sub-contractor who (or whose employees) takes an action which creates waste, or who begins to treat something as if it were waste.[99] However, the client or contractor who makes arrangements for the carriage or disposal of waste, for example by letting a disposal sub-contract to a haulier, may thereby assume responsibility as a "broker".[1]

Nature of the duty of care

7.32   The duty imposed by section 34 requires the person under the duty to take all such measures applicable to him in the relevant capacity (producer, importer, carrier, etc.) as are reasonable in the circumstances:[1a]

(a) to prevent any contravention by any other person of section 33 (prohibition on unauthorised or harmful deposit, treatment or disposal, etc. of waste);

(b) to prevent the escape of the waste from his control or that of any other person; and

(c) on transfer of the waste, to secure:

(i) that the transfer is only to an authorised person or to a person for authorised transport purposes; and

(ii) that there is transferred with the waste such a written description of the waste as will enable other persons to avoid a contravention of section 33 and to comply with their own duty under section 34 as respects preventing escape of the waste.

[97] Subs. (1).
[98] Circular 19/91 (Welsh Office 63/91, Scottish Office 25/91), para. 17.
[99] *Ibid.*
[1] *Ibid.* See also para. 7.34A on registration of brokers.
[1a] It appears from the decision of the House of Lords in *Seaboard Offshore Ltd.* v. *Secretary of State for Transport ("The Safe Carrier")* [1994] 2 All E.R. 99 that in order to be liable the producer, *etc.* of waste must fail personally in the duty in order to be criminally liable, and that where the producer has taken all reasonable steps they will not be liable for the acts or omissions of subordinate employees.

Subsection 34(3) lists the persons who are authorised persons for the purpose of requirement (c)(i) above: in most cases where waste is being removed as part of a reclamation scheme the relevant categories of authorised person will be the holder of a waste disposal or waste management licence, or a registered carrier. However, it should also be noted that waste may be carried for "authorised transport purposes" between different places within the same premises:[2] a registered carrier therefore is not necessary in order to move waste around within the reclamation site. Various persons are exempted from the requirement to register as a carrier:[3] in particular the producer of the waste in question "except where it is building or demolition waste."[4] Some (but not necessarily all) waste arising from site reclamation or remediation works may be regarded as resulting from building or demolition works and thus the producer[5] of the waste cannot lawfully carry it off-site without being registered.

Section 34 makes provision for a code of practice providing practical guidance on how to discharge the duty of care:[6] such a code has been issued[7] and is admissible in evidence or any proceedings as to breach of the duty.[8]

In practical terms, therefore, all those involved with site reclamation activities will need to consider the applicability of the duty of care to their activities: this is so whether waste is disposed of on-site or whether it is removed for disposal. This will involve assessing the problems presented by the waste[9] and may often require expert assistance by way of analysis and advice on handling methods.[10]

The duty of care—transfer documentation

By subsection 34(5) the Secretary of State may make regulations **7.33** imposing requirements on any person who is subject to the duty of care as respects the making and retention of documents and the furnishing of documents or copies of documents. The Environmental Protection (Duty of Care) Regulations 1991[11] have been made under this subsection. The

[2] S.34(4)(a).
[3] The Controlled Waste (Registration of Carriers and Seizure of Vehicles) Regulations 1991 No. 1624, reg. 2.
[4] Ibid., reg. 2(1)(b).
[5] See para. 7.31 above on the meaning of "producer."
[6] Subs. (7).
[7] Department of Environment, Scottish Office, Welsh Office: Waste Management, The Duty of Care—a Code of Practice (HMSO, December 1991).
[8] Subs. (10).
[9] Code of Practice, paras. 1.5–1.8.
[10] Ibid., paras. 6.1 and 6.2.
[11] S.I. 1991 No. 2839.

Regulations require the transferor and transferee of waste, at the same time as the waste is transferred, to ensure that a "transfer note" is completed and signed on their behalf.[12] The transfer note must identify the waste and give details of its quality, form of containment (if any) and the time and place of its transfer.[13] It must also give details of the transferor and transferee, each of whom must keep the written description and transfer note for a period of two years.[14] It is not necessary, according to Departmental guidance[15] for each individual transfer to be documented, and multiple consignments, where the nature of the waste and the parties remain the same, may be covered by a single note for a period of up to a year. This procedure may be particularly suitable where large quantities of excavated contaminated soil are being removed in lorry loads for disposal to landfill, where it would be impracticable or onerous for a separate note to be completed for each trip.[15a]

Where the waste in question is special waste[16] compliance with the duty of care does not discharge the need for compliance with the Control of Pollution (Special Waste) Regulations 1980.[17]

Waste carrier registration

7.34   The Control of Pollution (Amendment) Act 1989 instituted a new system for the registration of waste carriers. By section 1 of the Act, it is an offence for any person who is not a registered carrier, in the course of any business of his or otherwise with a view to profit, to transport any controlled waste to or from any place in Great Britain. Exemptions to this requirement are provided by section 1(2), including the transport of waste within the same premises between different places in those premises; other exemptions are given by regulations,[18] including waste

---

[12] Reg. 2(1).

[13] Reg. 2(2). The transfer note can also be used to comply with the duty at s.34(1)(c)(ii) to provide an adequate written description of the waste: see Circ. 19/91 (Welsh Office 63/91, Scottish Office 25/91), para. 20.

[14] Reg. 3.

[15] Circ. 19/91, para. 21.

[15a] At the time of writing, cl. 20 of the Deregulation and Contracting Out Bill proposes an amendment to s.34 to make it clear that a transfer of waste in stages in treated as taking place when the first stage of the transfer takes place and that a series of transfers between the same parties of waste of the same description shall be treated as a single transfer taking place when the first in the series of transfers takes place.

[16] See para. 7.29.

[17] Circ. 19/91, para. 26.

[18] The Controlled Waste (Registration of Carriers and Seizure of Vehicles) Regulations 1991 No. 1624, reg. 3.

carried by the person who produces it, except if it is building or demolition waste.[19] Three statutory defences are given, namely:[20]

(a) transport in an emergency to avoid or reduce serious danger to the public or serious risk of damage to the environment, notice being given as soon as practicable thereafter to the regulation authority; or

(b) that the person neither knew nor had reasonable grounds for suspecting that what was being transported was controlled waste and took all such steps as it was reasonable to take for ascertaining whether it was such waste; or

(c) that the person acted under instructions from his employer.

Provision is made by regulation[21] as to applications for registration, certificates of registration, the keeping of registers, duration and revocation of registration, and appeals. Of particular importance is the power to refuse registration or to revoke registration where the applicant or holder, or another "relevant person",[22] has been convicted of a prescribed offence[23] and in the opinion of the authority it is undesirable that they be authorised to transport controlled waste.[24]

Also important are the powers provided by the Act and the regulations to seize and dispose of vehicles used for illegal waste disposal—effectively a means of inducing those with knowledge as to the identity of the person using the vehicle to come forward in order to reclaim the vehicle.[25]

Registration of waste brokers and dealers

The Waste Management Licensing Regulations 1994[25a] make provision **7.34A** for registration of waste brokers and dealers: it is an offence for an establishment or undertaking after December 31, 1994 to arrange (as dealer or broker) for the recovery of controlled waste on behalf of another person unless it is a registered broker of controlled waste.[25b] The requirement to register as a broker does not apply to persons who are to carry out disposal or recovery of the waste in question and who are duly licensed or otherwise authorised to do so, or who are to transport the

---

[19] Reg. 2(1)(*b*); see para. 7.31.
[20] S.1(4) and (6).
[21] S.I. 1991 No. 1624.
[22] As to "relevant person" see s.2(5).
[23] The offences are prescribed by S.I. 1991 No. 1624, reg. 1(2) and Sched. 1.
[24] S.3(1) and (2); reg. 5(1) and 10(1).
[25] S.6 and regs. 20–25.
[25a] S.I. 1994 No. 1056.
[25b] Reg. 20.

controlled waste as part of the arrangement and who are registered as waste carriers.[25c]

As mentioned above in the context of the duty of care,[25d] there is some doubt as to who is a "broker". Circular 11/94, Annex 8, suggests that an establishment or undertaking which acts as a broker has control of waste in the sense that it arranges for the disposal or recovery on behalf of another and is outside the chain of people who handle waste (*i.e.* the producer, holder, carrier, recovery operator, or disposal operator).[25e] An environmental consultant who contracts to arrange for the disposal of a producer's waste is instanced as an example of a broker.[25f] However, the guidance distinguishes those who on a building site (such as a main contractor, architect or engineer) arrange for disposal of controlled waste to an appropriate facility: it is suggested that they are acting as holders of the waste rather than brokers.[25g] Similarly, managing agents, janitors and development companies providing common services (including waste management) will not normally be acting as brokers, becuase they are producers of the waste concerned.[25h] Despite this advice, which in some respects is debatable, the final decision as to whether an establishment or undertaking is acting as a broker will be a matter for the courts: it would therefore be prudent to consult the relevant waste regulation authority as to their views on the need to register and, if in doubt, to do so.

Schedule 5 of the 1994 Regulations contains detailed provisions on registration, including the form for applications for registration and renewal. Registration or renewal may be refused (or registration revoked) where the applicant, or registered broker, or other "relevant person" has been convicted of a relevant offence and in the view of the authority it is undesirable that the applicant be authorised to arrange (as dealer or broker) for the disposal or recovery of controlled waste on behalf of other persons.[25i]

BUILDING CONTRACT ASPECTS

Generally[26]

7.35 Development may be commenced on a site under many types of contract structure, but the two that are probably the most widely used standard forms in the industry are the Joint Contracts Tribunal Stand-

[25c] See para. 7.34.
[25d] See para. 7.31.
[25e] Annex 8, para. 84.
[25f] *Ibid.*, para. 8.5
[25g] *Ibid.*
[25h] *Ibid.*
[25i] Sched. 5, paras. 3(13) and 5(1).
[26] See also para. 7.27 above.

ard Form of Building Contract 1980 Edition and the Joint Contracts Tribunal Standard Form of Contract With Contractor's Design 1981 Edition, known respectively as JCT '80 and JCT '81.

When looking at the two contract structures it is important to bear in mind that the contractor is only one part of the team who will carry out the development. He will assume different degrees of responsibility depending on the type of contract form under which he is engaged. Liability for site investigation work and for design may rest with other parties if the contract structure so dictates. It is important that all those involved in the development should have their responsibilities defined at the outset if at all possible: this is particularly so in circumstances where the development is on a contaminated or potentially contaminated site, where the potential for financially ruinous errors is great.

Development under JCT '80

When a development takes place under this form, the contractor is **7.36** responsible for the actual construction of the development, but site investigation work and design will be carried out by engineers and architects directly engaged by the developer. Such consultants will carry the primary responsibility for any problems arising as a result of inadequate site investigations or design if the standard JCT '80 is used unamended: however in practice it *may* be difficult to pin liability on to them.

The architect

The Standard Form of Architect's Appointment published by the **7.37** Royal Institute of British Architects sets out the services required from the architect. The obligations are set out in fairly general terms containing, for example, a requirement to visit the site and carry out an intitial appraisal and subsequently advise on the need for other consultants' services and on their scope. These are obligations which may be relevant to contaminated land development, but there is no specific requirement on the architect to consider the question of contamination, nor is there any specific obligation to ensure that any design takes into account the existence of any contamination.

It is, of course, true to say that if the architect is aware of contamination or a potential contamination problem, then he would undoubtedly be negligent not to make sufficient enquiries to enable him to design adequately so as to deal with the problem. However, from the point of view of a developer trying to complete a development, it is obviously more satisfactory if an obligation to take into account the contamination

339

in carrying out all of the services is actually included in the appointment. A specific reference to the need to consider contamination is more likely to result in a satisfactory design than the knowledge that there is a possibility of a negligence action in the future.

The engineer

7.38   Where a site is known or suspected by the developer to be contaminated, then either the developer or his architect would normally ensure that an initial site investigation is carried out by a competent engineer or environmental consultant. If this is to be provided as a preliminary service, then a full formal appointment will sometimes not be entered into. If this is the case, then to protect a developer, the engineer carrying out the exploratory work may be required to use the guidelines in the draft Code of Practice DD 175: 1988.[27] To the extent that an engineer employed to carry out site investigations is required to comply with this draft Code of Practice and fails to do so, this may be prima facia evidence of negligence on his part if any failure to identify the extent of contamination discovered subsequently can be shown to have resulted from non-compliance with these guidelines.[28] The engineer may however be able to show that any techniques actually employed by him were an acceptable alternative to those recommended by the draft British Standard, which is of course still only a draft and not a formal standard.[29]

If the employer does not obtain a preliminary site investigation, or if the engineer is not required to deal with the possible or actual existence of contamination, then the use of an unamended Standard Form Building Contract gives rise to enormous potential for disaster in the development.

The contractor's obligation under JCT '80

7.39   Clause 2 of JCT '80 obliges the contractor "to carry out and complete the works in accordance with the contract documents, using materials and workmanship of the quality and standards therein specified provided that where and to the extent that the approval of quality of materials and standards of workmanship is a matter for the architect, such quality and standards shall be to the reasonable satisfaction of the architect." The "Contract Documents" include the Contract Drawings,

[27] See Chap. 4 generally.
[28] See Chap. 10.
[29] See Chap. 4.

Bills of Quantities, Articles, Conditions and the Appendix to the Standard Form. Clause 8 of the Contract requires the materials, goods and workmanship to be of the standard described in the Bills of Quantities (or suitable alternatives).

Provided the contractor carries out the construction in accordance with the information provided to him by the designers, namely the architect and the engineer, he will be free of any responsibility for any inadequacies in the development resulting from contamination. If the design is inadequate, but the contractor nevertheless builds in accordance with it, he will have no liability for the ultimate suitability of the development. Further, if the architect and/or engineer have not specifically been required to direct their minds to the question of potential contamination, then there will be no action against them for breach of contract for failing to design properly to suit the site conditions, and the developer would at the end of the day have to look at the possibility of any liability in negligence.

Variations and the effect on payment

Assuming that part way into the project contamination is discovered **7.40** or more extensive contamination than originally was thought to exist is discovered, then under Clause 13 of the JCT '80 Form, variations can be ordered. The contractor is not obliged to carry out works insofar as they are outside the original contract documents; having tendered to carry out these works on a lump sum price, there is no reason why he should. The variations clause is intended as a protection for the developer so that, should extensive alterations to the design need to be carried out, the contractor can be instructed to carry them out (subject to rights of reasonable objection), and is obliged to do so, subject to those variations being valued for payment. The net effect is that if the contract documents do not provide a suitable method for development of the contaminated land and, alterations have to take place after commencement of the contract, then variations must be ordered for which the developer will ultimately have to pay. The contractor will be entitled to extensions of time to the extent that the variations ordered cause him delay, and will in these circumstances normally be entitled to claim his loss and expense arising as a result of this. This puts the employer in a position where he has to pay for the additional work as well as bearing all the costs of delay. While he may be able to recover these from the engineer or architect in a negligence action, this is not a certainty since the circumstances may be such that nothing amounting to negligence has occurred; alternatively, he may be able to recover a proportion of these increased costs but not the whole of them.

341

JCT '81—"design & build" contracts

7.41 Under this contract structure, the contractor takes on all of the obligations himself, that is, for designing and constructing the development. The contractor's obligation under Clause 2 of the Contract is to carry out and complete the works referred to in the Employer's Requirements, the Contractor's Proposals, Articles, Conditions and Appendices, "and for that purpose to complete the design for the works including the selection of any specifications for any kinds and standards of the materials, goods and workmanship to be used in the construction of the works so far as not described or stated in the Employer's Requirements or Contractor's Proposals."

There are two ways in which initial stages of the development can be dealt with:

(a) the employer retains an architect and engineer at a very early stage to carry out site investigation and initial design, and these appointments can subsequently be taken over by the appointed contractor; or

(b) the employer simply engages the contractor at the outset and the contractor takes all the responsibility for retaining the architect, engineer, and any other professional advice he needs.

The first situation can be dangerous for the employer where novation of the appointment of the contractor does not include a clause that says that the contractor takes over responsibility for work carried out by the architect/engineer beforehand.

The Employer's Requirements will set out in varying degrees of detail what the employer expects from the development. In a situation where a site is potentially contaminated, it is probably best from the employer's point of view if these requirements are kept to a minimum and require only an end result rather than specifying the means of obtaining it. This leaves the contractor responsible for ensuring that whatever design of construction he comes up with ultimately complies with the requirements and provides the employer with the end product that he has specified. Clause 2.5.1 imposes on the contractor a design liability to the employer equivalent to that which an architect or other appropriate professional designer would have. Ordinarily, someone responsible for both designing and constructing an item would have an obligation that the item be made fit for its purpose. This exclusion of the common law liability in this standard form of contract is frequently criticised, since it means that where a design fails, the employer must prove negligence on the part of the contractor rather than simply saying that the contractor has a strict liability to make the design suitable for the purpose for which the development is intended. Thus the provision is something that a developer of a contaminated site might well wish to amend; although it is as well to bear in mind that the imposition of a fitness for purpose obligation will inevitably carry cost consequences in that the contractor's price will increase to take account of the increased risk to him.

It should also be noted that clause 2.5.3. of the JCT '81 form of contract contains an exclusion of liability for loss of use, loss of profit and other consequential loss where the work is on a commercial property, rather than a residential one. This is actually a limitation on the contractor's liability and is something to which careful consideration needs to be given when using this form of contract for a development on contaminated land.

Finally, it should be noted that by clause 2 the design prepared by the contractor is deemed to include any design which he has caused to be prepared by others. This is an area where problems can arise where a design has been prepared before the contractor arrives on the scene and the designer's appointment is subsequently novated to the contractor, but without the contractor accepting liability for previous work carried out. To the extent that the design is not a design prepared by the contractor himself or a design which he has actually caused to be prepared by the professional designers, he does not have liability for it. It is vital, therefore from the employer's point of view, if original appointments are novated to the consultant, that this clause be extended to ensure that the contractor takes complete responsibility for the design.

Variations and cost effects

So far as cost increases are concerned, much the same problem arises **7.42** under the JCT '81 form as under JCT '80 referred to above. Clause 12 provides for changes in the Employer's Requirements after commencement of the Works. The definition of a "change" is anything "which makes necessary the alteration or modification of the design, quality or quantity of the Works as described by or referred to in the Employer's Requirements or the Contractor's Proposals including the addition, omission or substitution of any works. . . ."

The clause goes on at 12.4 and 12.5 to provide for valuation of this "changed" work. The more detail that is contained in the Employer's Requirements, the more opportunity the contractor will have to take advantage of this clause.

Some proposed solutions

The following points represent possible solutions from the employer's **7.43** point of view to some of the potential problems outlined above which may arise under the unamended standard JCT forms.

JCT '80

1. Amend the contract to include an obligation on the contractor to visit the site and conduct investigations to satisfy himself as to the suitability of the site for the development proposed. Disclaim responsibility on the part of the employer for any information provided to the contractor (*.e.g.*, site investigation reports) at the tendering stage.
2. Further, amend the payment provisions to disallow increased costs arising as a result of the contractor's failure to carry out adequate investigations.
3. Amend the Standard Form Architect's Appointment to oblige him to consider and investigate the possibility of contamination at the site.
4. Impose at least an obligation on any engineer to comply with DD 175 or equivalent specific requirements for site investigation.

JCT '81

1. Draft the Employer's Requirements so that they set out performance or end product requirements rather than specifying the means by which these are to be achieved.
2. Oblige the contractor to take responsibility for any designs which have been prepared or investigations carried out by previously appointed architects or engineers, either by obliging him to take responsibility for all professionals he engages, whether by novation of their appointments or otherwise; or alteratively by stating in the contract that the contractor is not entitled to rely on any information provided to him by the employer, whether by way of previously commissioned site investigation reports or initial designs.
3. Provide that where changes in the works are required as a result of the contractor failing to carry out adequate site investigations of his own, the contractor will not be entitled to additional payment for them.

Contracts and insurance

7.44   As has been discussed elsewhere,[30] there remains a great deal of uncertainty surrounding the potential liability of parties to a development in relation to contamination of neighbouring land or water. The insurance position is therefore extremely important, particularly since

[30] See Chap. 2.

344

the process of development may result in the risks of such contamination being increased.[31] With clean-up costs for contamination inevitably being high, litigation may well ensue between the parties to the development, and any affected neighbouring landowner. The developer may seek to pass on any claims to the contractor, engineer or architect as the parties responsible, in the knowledge that they are—or should be—insured. The end result of such claims could well be an unwary insurer paying the price of the neighbouring landowner's clean-up by virtue of a combination of contractual indemnities and broadly worded insurance policies, if those policies do not contain appropriate pollution exclusions.

Under the JCT 1981 Standard Form of Contract with Contractor's Design, Clause 20.2 provides that the Contractor shall be liable for and shall indemnify the employer against:

> "any expense, liability, loss, claim or proceedings in respect of any injury or damage whatsoever to any property real or personal insofar as such injury or damage arises out of or in the course of or by reason of the carrying out of the Works to the extent that the same is due to any negligence, breach of statutory duty, omission or default of the contractor, his servants or agents or of any person employed or engaged upon or in connection with the Works or any part thereof."

Clause 21 requires the contractor to insure against this risk.

Typical contractors' liability policies will provide cover for the contractor up to a specified amount for all sums which he becomes legally liable to pay as damages, including the claimant's costs and expenses, in respect of accidental loss of or damage to material or tangible property arising in connection with the contractor's business and occurring during the policy period. Cover is also available in respect of damages arising from nuisance claims, which do not require actual physical damage to tangible or material property.

Where a claim is brought by the developer against the contractor under clause 20 of the contract for an indemnity against any liability that the developer have to the neighbouring landowner, the contractor will undoubtedly notify his insurers. The wording of the typical policy is likely to give rise to some debate as to the meaning of "damage to property" in the context of contamination and clean-up costs. By its nature, a claim for remedial costs for clean-up work to neighbouring land or to groundwater is likely to be far higher than an average liability claim. Claims such as these may well not have been envisaged by the

---

[31] For example, by contaminants being disturbed or mobilised. On the other hand, development may by providing increased hard cover, lessen the risks of such mobilisation long-term.

insurance market at the time when standard liability policy wordings were drafted and were generally not envisaged when premiums were rated.

As referred to below, already substantial exclusions are already being written into recent general liability policies.[32] A series of claims in respect of clean-up costs succeeding against public liability policies written before such exclusions became common can only lead to a hardening of the market and an increase in premiums for liability insurance, as well as pollution exclusions being written into policies.

A similar problem exists in relation to the engineer's or architect's professional indemnity policy. Such policies will generally indemnify an insured for any sums which he becomes "legally liable" to pay arising from any claim or claims against him during the policy period resulting from a negligent act, error or omission. If the contractor is pursued by the developer for enforcement of his contractual indemnity, there is little doubt that the contractor might seek in turn to pass on the liability to the architect or engineer, who will in turn notify his insurers. Mindful of these risks, insurers of professional indemnity policies have also begun to exclude pollution risks.[33] Whilst the success of all these claims against insurance policies is ultimately dependent upon fault of the insured party being proved, it is nevertheless understandable that there is great disquiet amongst insurers at the degree of their potential exposure, which may be entirely disproportionate to the premium ratings.

Many policies now contain a pollution exclusion based on wording recommended by the Association of British Insurers, which excludes all liability in respect of pollution or contamination other than that caused by sudden identifiable, unintended and unexpected incidents taking place in their entirety at a specific time and place during the period of insurance.[34] This undoubtedly improves the position of insurers and will serve to keep premiums at a reasonable level. However, it leaves a dangerous gap in the cover available to those engaged to carry out work on developments on contaminated land and ultimately to those who may wish to sue them. Partly as a result of the US experience of environmental claims, there is reluctance to provide cover in this high risk, high cost area. Policies are, however, becoming available—inevitably at a price—specifically designed to provide cover for developers and contractors of derelict or contaminated land. Cover is subject to a stringent underwriting process and full environmental investigation. The current recession affecting the construction industry means that the availability of this cover has not yet made an impact, but the insurance market attributes

[32] See also Appendix F.
[33] See para. 10.12.
[34] See further, Appendix F on insurance.

346

this to the lack of major developments rather than a lack of interest in such insurance products. It is likely that coming years will see an increase in the availability of this type of policy.

The situation is not, then, entirely bleak. The insurance market is taking positive, if tentative, steps towards dealing with the pollution problem faced by developers of historically contaminated sites, and those whom they employ to carry out the works. Such insurance cover will not, of course, be available at low premiums. However, in view of the level of risk and uncertainty in the parties' positions, costly premiums may be more commercially attractive than a potentially enormous uninsured liability.

Chapter 8

Development

Introduction

8.01   This chapter deals with the town and country planning and building control aspects of developing contaminated land. The issue of remedial or clean-up work is covered in Chapter 7 and that of grants and funding in Chapter 9.

Town and Country Planning Controls

The need for planning permission

8.02   Many schemes for the clean-up of contaminated land arise within the framework of wider proposals for the the physical development and possibly the change of use of a site. In such cases, the issue of contaminated land is likely to be addressed as part of the application for that ultimate development and the planning permission for the new development will include the preparatory clean-up works. However, even where clean-up operations are undertaken on land with no immediate view to further development, for example in order to reduce the risk of liability or under compulsion or pressure from a regulatory authority, those operations may well of themselves constitute development requiring planning permission.

Development is defined by section 55(1) of the Town and Country Planning Act 1990 to mean "the carrying out of building, engineering, mining or other operations in, on, over on under or the making of any material change in the use of any buildings or other land." Whilst a reclamation scheme of itself may not involve building operations, which are defined by section 336 of the 1990 Act to include "rebuilding operations, structural operations of or additions to buildings, and other operations normally undertaken by a person carrying on business as a builder," it may well fall within the category of "engineering operations." Such operations are not exhaustively defined in section 336 of the 1990 Act and in view of the statutory definition of "building operations" it is perhaps a reasonable presumption that they are operations normally undertaken by a person carrying on business as an engineer. As such, they could well include the earth moving operations which will inevitably form part of most clean-up schemes. Such an approach would be consistent with the decision of Deputy Judge David Widdicombe Q.C. in *Fayrewood Fishfarms Limited* v. *Secretary of State for the Environment and Hampshire County Council*.[1] In that case, the Deputy Judge referred to engineering operations as being those of a type usually undertaken by, or calling for the skills of an engineer. It was not necessary that the engineer should actually be engaged on the project, not that any specific branch of the engineering profession (such as civil engineering) should be involved; nor was it necessary for there to be detailed plans of the proposed works, though the existence of such plans might constitute important evidence.

Section 336 of the 1990 Act defines engineering operations as including "the formation or laying out of means of access to highways," and therefore might apply to a reclamation scheme which has in mind the creation of such an access; it has already been mentioned that the more highly contaminated areas of the site are often used for hard covered areas, including access roads.

In any event, it will need to be considered in each case whether the operations in question are such as to benefit from any of the categories of permitted development under the Town and Country Planning General Development Order 1988, as amended.[2] Likewise, special considerations will apply in relation to schemes within enterprise zones and simplified planning zones; reference should be made to standard works on planning law for the position here.

Policy guidance on the development of contaminated land

The Government's approach to the development of contaminated **8.03** land is currently set out in Circular 21/87 (Welsh Office 22/87) at paragraph 1:

> "The Government wishes to encourage full and effective use of land in urban areas and re-use of sites which have previously been developed . . . Recycling of land helps to revitalize urban areas and reducing the need to use new sites outside built-up areas, thus

[1] [1984] J.P.L. 267.
[2] S.I. 1988 No. 1813.

assisting the protection of the greenbelt and safeguarding of the countryside. The re-use of contaminated land can contribute towards these objectives."[3]

The Circular goes on to point out the need to strike a balance between the risks and liabilities which may be the result of hazards from contamination and, on the other hand, the need to bring the land in question into beneficial use.[4] Contamination, or the potential for it, is a material planning consideration which needs to be taken into account at various stages of the planning process, including the preparation of development plans and the determination of planning applications; the best way of minimising the risks is to ensure that potential contaminated sites are identified at the earliest stage of the planning process.[5]

The Annex to the Circular contains more detailed guidance, covering issues such as the general approach to be followed, relevant powers and responsibilities, town and country planning, building control and financial assistance. The following points emerge from this guidance as relevant to development control:[6]

(1) Very few sites are so badly contaminated that they cannot be re-used at all, but the choice of new use may be restricted by contamination as well as by other planning considerations and the usual financial implications.

(2) Each site must be considered on its merits and treated with caution where appropriate.

(3) Where the previous history of the site suggests that contamination may have occurred, an investigation to assess the condition of the site and identify any particular problems or hazards will normally need to be undertaken by the prospective developer before deciding the most appropriate use. (This, however, begs the question of how the most appropriate use is to be determined; the most appropriate use from the point of view of contamination may not be the preferred or allocated use in the development plan).

(4) The findings of the investigation should enable the most suitable use to selected and the development should then be designed to

---

[3] See also the draft Planning Policy Guidance Note on Planning and Pollution Control (issued June 1992), para. 3.24. The draft guidance is apparently to be issued as PPG 23: *Planning and Pollution Control* (see Circ. 11/94 on Waste Management Licensing, para. 20).

[4] Circ. 21/87, para. 5.

[5] Circ. 21/87, para. 5; see also draft PPG on Planning and Pollution Control, n. 3 above, para. 3.25.

[6] Circ. 21/87, Annex, para. 2–3 and 12–17. Very similar guidance is contained in the draft PPG on Planning and Pollution Control, n. 3 above, paras 3.28–3.30 and Annex 6, paras. 3–11.

minimise the risks; the specific precautions needed will depend on the degree of risk and the sensitivity of the potential target or targets to the hazards.

(5) The responsibility for assessing whether or not the land is suitable for a particular purpose, including whether it is contaminated, rests primarily with the developer.

(6) When determining a planning application for land which it has reason to believe might be contaminated, it will be necessary for the local planning authority to consider whether the proposal takes proper account of contamination.

(7) Even before any planning application is made, informal discussions between the potential developer and the local planning authority can be very helpful; and in particular, the local planning authority may take the opportunity to bring potential problems of contamination to the attention of the developer. Applications need not, however, be delayed pending an investigation to establish the nature and the extent of contamination unless there is good reason to suppose that the land in question is actually contaminated.

(8) In districts which contain a significant number of potentially contaminated sites, the local planning authority may find it useful to include a question on contamination on its standard application form, together with a note to applicants on the subject.

(9) If an application is received without prior discussion and the authority suspects that the site may be contaminated, then the authority should advise the applicant that the land may be contaminated and of the factors which will be taken into account in determining the application.

(10) When it is known or strongly suspected that a site is contaminated to an extent that would adversely affect the proposed development, then investigation by the developer to identify any remedial measures required to deal with the hazards will normally be required before the application can be determined. If the information provided by the applicant is insufficient to enable the Authority to determine the application, the applicant may need to be asked to provide further information by way of direction under the General Development Order.

(11) Should the degree of contamination be such that remedial action is required to safeguard future users or occupiers of the site or neighbouring land, or protect any buildings or services from hazards, then planning permission may be granted subject to conditions specifying the measures carried out.

(12) Where there is only a suspicion that the site might be contaminated or where the evidence suggests that there is potentially

only slight contamination, planning permission may be granted; however, conditions should be attached to make it clear that the development will not be permitted to start until site investigation and assessment has been carried out and that the development itself will need to incorporate all the measures shown to be necessary in the assessment.

(13) The planning authority may grant planning permission without conditions relating to contamination, provided that it is satisfied on reasonable grounds that in the circumstances they are not now required.

(14) The assessment of the significance of contamination and associated risks requires careful professional judgment and the planning authority should obtain advice from experts in their own departments (such as environmental health, waste disposal, building control, land reclamation, surveying and engineering) as well as consulting with the National Rivers Authority and Health and Safety Executive (and where appropriate, English Nature and relevant service undertakers).

(15) Where planning permission is granted, a separate letter should be issued informing the applicant that the responsibility for safe development of the site rests with the developer and warning that the planning authority in determining the application on the basis of the information available to it, makes no representation that the land is free from contamination.

A subsequent (non-public) draft of the PPG on Planning and Pollution Control (dated March 1993) contained a number of additional points, in particular stating that the investigations into a site should be appropriate to the proposed end use and the likely impact of development on surrounding land and on the environment. It was also pointed out that planning authorities will need to distinguish between those precautions that can be taken under planning powers and those that are the responsibility of other agencies, including the Health and Safety Executive.

Development plan policies

8.04   In preparing their development plans local planning authorities need to take into account the environmental consequences of contaminated land: to that extent development plans provide an opportunity to set out policies for the reclamation and use of such land.[7] Local plans and Part 2

---

[7] Circ. 21/87, Annex, para. 9; see also draft PPG on Planning and Pollution Control, Annex 6, para. 1 and Department of Environment, *Development Plans: A Good Practice Guide* (1993), para. 3.101 *et seq.*

of unitary development plans should include detailed criteria to be applied in determining planning applications for development on land which is known to be, or which may be, contaminated: they may also set out any site-specific proposals for land use, so that they may be readily identifiable by landowners and prospective purchasers or developers.[8] Whereas the wording in Circular 21/87 was permissive as to the inclusion of such "detailed criteria" the wording proposed in the draft PPG on planning and pollution control is mandatory in that respect.

The strengthening of the content of the development plans as regards policies on contaminated land is consistent with the Government's general approach towards environmental considerations in development plans: in particular, proposed development plan policies should be the subject of appraisal as to their environmental consequences, and development plans should be drawn up in such a way as to take environmental considerations comprehensively and consistently into account.[9] Paragraph 6.18 of PPG 12 "Development Plans and Regional Planning Guidance"[10] reminds planning authorities that development plans are required by statute to include land-use policies and proposals for the improvement of the physical environment: such policies and proposals should not only aim to protect and enhance high quality environments, but to improve poor environments, for example by reclaiming contaminated and derelict land so that it can be brought back into use more quickly and reduce pressure on green-field sites. The increased attention which should be paid to the protection of ground-water resources as part of the development planning process[11] should also have an impact on policies relating to reclamation and development of contaminated land.

Examples of policies

It appears that as a matter of practice more authorities are inserting **8.05** specific policies relating to contaminated or potentially contaminated land in local and unitary development plans. A number of examples are set out at the end of this chapter which may be helpful. The examples given are found in consultation draft or deposit plans and may have been modified in some cases in the process leading to adoption.

These policies indicate the variety of approaches being taken in practice; they also reveal the reliance being placed in some cases on the

[8] Circ. 21/87, Annex, para. 10; proposed PPG, Annex 6, para. 2.
[9] See generally Cmnd. 1200, *This Common Inheritance—Britain's Environmental Stategy*; more specifically see PPG 12, para. 6.1 and 6.2.
[10] February 1992.
[11] PPG 12, para. 6.19; see also Chap. 6 generally.

Government's withdrawn proposals for section 143 registers or contaminative uses. Other policies of local plans and UDPs may also be relevant: for example those on vacant and under-used land, reclamation, community forests, etc.

Environmental assessment

8.06   The policies referred to above will apply to all types of planning application where there are indications that the site may be subject to contamination. Certain types of development will be subject to environmental assessment under the Town and Planning (Assessment of Environmental Effects) Regulations 1988,[12] implementing the EC Council Directive of June 27, 1985 on the assessment of the effects of certain public and private projects on the environment.[13] Detailed consideration of the scope and effect of those regulations are beyond the ambit of this work, and reference should be made to standard texts on planning law, as well as to DoE Circular 15/88 (Welsh Office 23/88) and the Department of the Environment and Welsh Office guide to environmental assessment procedures.[14] Where it appears that the type of development falls within Schedule 1 to those Regulations, or where it falls within Schedule 2 and it appears that the development would be likely to have significant effects on the environment by virtue of factors such as its nature, size or location, then the developer will need to prepare a environmental statement in support of the planning application, and the procedures of the Regulations as to publicity and consultation that will need to be followed. Many of the projects within the Directive and Regulations are of a traditional heavy industrial nature, and as such are very likely to be carried out on land with a history of industrial uses; similarly, other categories of project within the Regulations, such as urban development projects, industrial estate development projects, and even yacht marinas, may well be proposed for land with a history of potentially contaminative uses.

In a case where the environmental assessment procedures are applicable, then the environmental statement will need to provide the information referred to in Schedule 3 of the Regulations (Annex III of the Directive) for the purpose of assessing the likely impact upon the environment of the development. Schedule 3 refers to this information as including a description of likely significant effects, direct and indirect, on the environment of the development, explained by reference to its possible impact on:

[12] S.I. 1988 No. 1199.
[13] 85/337/EEC, O.J. No. L175/40, July 5, 1985.
[14] HMSO, 1989.

human beings;
flora;
fauna;
soil;
water;
air;
climate;
the landscape;
the interaction between any of the foregoing;
material assets; and
the cultural heritage.

To the extent that significant adverse effects are identified with respect to any of the foregoing, the statement must also include a description of the measures envisaged in order to avoid, reduce or remedy those effects; a summary in non-technical language of this information must also be included.[15] Whilst the development will not have itself caused the pre-existing contamination, the ground works or construction of the development may well affect the way in which that pre-existing contamination impacts upon the environment, for example by disturbing or dispersing contaminants. To that extent at least, it seems clear the environmental statement will need to address the issue of contamination. The development may also have an impact in another sense, that is by bringing residents, employees or other users of the development into possible contact wth the pre-existing contamination: whilst the wording of the Directive and Regulations are not exactly apt to cover that type of impact, it does not seem to stretch the wording unduly to regard such effect as an indirect one, not by altering the level of contamination, but by bringing human beings into possible new contact with its effects, and thereby creating a possible impact upon them.

In practice, it may well be sensible to use the environmental statement as a means of presenting to the Planning Authority information (which would be required in any event) to satisfy them that the contamination risks have been properly investigated and addressed.[16] The possible adverse result of this course is that information on site conditions, which may be of a sensitive nature, would be included within a document which must be made available to the public on request.[17]

---

[15] S.I. 1988 No. 1199, Sched. 3, para. 2.
[16] The House of Commons Environment Committee in its Report on "Contaminated Land" regarded environmental assessment procedures as a desirable model for information on contaminated sites.
[17] Environmental Assessment Regulations, reg. 18.

Landfill gas

8.07   ICRCL Guidance Note 59/83 on the assessment and redevelopment of contaminated land states at paragraph 43 that some hazards are such that sites where they occur should preferably not be built upon or utilised, but if they have to be then special precautions may be necessary. The first example given of such sites are those known or suspected to emit flammable gases; the guidance states that redevelopment while gas is still being emitted should take place only when either: (a) the proposed use would not be at risk from the emissions, which is unlikely; or (b) a system for collecting and extracting the gases safely can be provided.

This guidance is particularly relevant in relation to sites where putrescible waste may have been deposited in the past, both in relation to development on such land, and in relation to development on adjacent land which may be affected by gas generated from such sites. There are various sources of guidance on this issue. These include Circular 17/89 on "Landfill Sites: Development Control"; Waste Management Paper No. 27 on "The Control of Landfill Gas" (2nd ed., 1991); and ICRCL Guidance Note 17/78, (8th ed.). Paragraph 24 of the ICRCL guidance states that if it is absolutely essential and unavoidable to develop sites which are emitting landfill gas while emissions are still occurring, thorough investigation by or on behalf of the prospective developer is essential before seeking planning approval.

Other Government guidance follows this line of suggestions that ideally such sites should not be developed until wastes are biologically stabilised and that agriculture or public open space are the preferable uses for such sites. However, it is recognised that there will be pressures for other forms of development and that these are not precluded where expert advice has been taken and proper caution has been exercised.

Waste Management Paper No. 27 provides guidance in relation to development on and around "landfill sites." One general problem is what is meant by a "landfill site" in this context: the glossary to WMP27 states that landfill is "the engineered deposit of waste into or onto land in such a way that pollution or harm to the environment is minimised or prevented and, through restoration to provide land which may be used for another purpose." Clearly many gassing sites which have been filled in an uncontrolled manner may not meet this description, but nonetheless the advice of the Waste Management Paper ought still to hold good.

(1) Pre-stablisation use

After-use of landfill sites should normally be restricted to agriculture or similar uses at least until the site has stabilised[18]; where control

[18] Waste Management Paper No. 27, para. 9.2.

systems permit, the land may be used for open space, conservation or recreation.[19]

(2) Commercial uses

However, it is recognised that there will be pressure for other forms of development and in particular, older landfills in urban areas can be developed for non-housing uses such as supermarkets, light industrial units, warehouses and block of flats.[20] Many such sites have become prime sites as development has encroached upon them. Such developments require expert investigation, advice and the incorporation of precautionary measures into the design and construction phases; there are examples of developments which have run into difficulty through failing to take such factors into account.[21]

(3) Housing

It is difficult to ensure that protective measures are maintained to private housing, since such measures may be defeated by actions of individual occupiers outside the control of the developer or the authorities.[22] Such risks are naturally reduced where the development is of flats or other residential units with no private gardens. Domestic housing should not therefore be built on landfills which are gassing or have the capacity to produce significant quantities of gas.[23] It is also recommended that no housing should be built within 50 metres of any landfill site with gas concentrations in excess of certain levels; gardens of houses should not extend to within 10 metres of any such site.[24] Suggested levels given in this respect are 1 per cent. of flammable gas by volume and 1.5 per cent. of carbon dioxide by volume, measured in any monitoring point within the wastes over a 24 month period taken on at least our separate occasions, including two occasions when the atmosphere pressure was falling or was below 1,000 millibars.[25]

---

[19] *Ibid.*, paras. 1.31 and 9.2.
[20] *Ibid.*, paras. 1.31 and 9.3.
[21] *Ibid.*, para. 9.3.
[22] *Ibid.*, para. 9.3.
[23] *Ibid.*, para. 9.3.
[24] *Ibid.*, paras. 1.31 and 9.7.
[25] *Ibid.*, para. 7.9.

(4) Development near landfill sites

Great care should be taken with any development within 250 metres of "infilled wastes."[26] This is so whether the site is operational, awaiting restoration or restored.[27] The geology and topography of the area must be investigated, together with possible pathways for gas migration.[28]

(5) Highways

Various risks are associated with roads running over or adjacent to gassing sites, in particular where gas may accumulate in underground services or underpasses, or where there are potential sources in ignition such as street lighting.[29]

Under the General Development Order 1988, article 18, the waste disposal authority must be consulted on any application for development within 250 metres of land which is or has, at any time in the 30 years before the relevant application, been used for the deposit of refuse or waste and has been notified by the waste disposal authority to the planning authority for the purpose of the provision.

Therefore any developer wishing to seek planning permission on a former landfill site which is still generating gas, or within a radius of at least 250 metres of such a site, would be well advised to consider extremely carefully the form of the proposed development in the light of this policy and technical guidance, and to take expert advice as to monitoring regimes and management systems. It will be advisable for such systems to have a large degree of tolerance built into them to cope with any changes in the characteristics of the site due to site works.

A good example of a scheme successfully promoted in this way is the application by William Morrison Supermarkets plc for planning permission for the erection of a retail food store, associated car parking and landscaping.[30] An appeal against deemed refusal of permission by Wakefield Metropolitan District Council was the subject of a public inquiry in December 1990. The Inspector regarded the appeal site as an example of a landfill site within an urban area which had become a prime location for development; the site had a long history of mineral extraction, starting with coal mining and continuing up to the extraction of brick earth. The geological survey of the site indicated that permeability of rock was low, with no major faults known to exist within the

---

[26] Ibid., para. 1.31.
[27] Ibid., para. 9.4.
[28] Ibid., para. 9.6.
[29] Ibid., para. 9.8.
[30] [1991] J.P.L. 985. See also the decision at (1992) 8 P.A.D. 13 (Leicester City Council v. Barratt (East Midlands) Ltd.), para. 8.10 below, Table, item (8).

area. A variety of site investigations were carried out and it was agreed that there was no evidence of migration of gas off the site and that there was limited migration within the site; it appeared to the Inspector that the main source of potential risk was from explosive mixtures being formed beneath the proposed building or within it and from the build up of carbon dioxide within the building. Whilst the site had not been tipped extensively by bio-degradable matter, there were significant pocket of such waste which gave cause for concern; flammable gas concentrations were not found to be consistently high, but it was agreed that it was appropriate to regard the site as a whole rather than a collection of separate gassing areas.

It was recognised that the construction of the car park and store could give rise to problems with regard to gas generation, and the scheme involved the construction of a mechanically vented under floor area and the use of latest techniques of the design and construction of impermeable membranes, with pipes and venting trenches used throughout the area of the car park to channel gas and to discharge it to the air. The proposed system was designed to high tolerances, with in-built back-up systems, and based upon worst case assumptions. A regular and thorough system of inspection and maintenance, with an automatic gas alarm system was proposed. On this basis, the Inspector considered that persons inside the building would not be subject to unacceptable risk because of the presence of landfill gas and that the high-profile nature of the development would assist in encouraging the operator to maintain the systems to a high standard.

With this decision should be contrasted a planning appeal concerning residential development with vehicular access and landscaped open space at Erith Quarry, Bexley.[31] In that case, the site was a large and deep one which had been back-filled, and no serious attempt had been made to assess gas emission rates. There could be no assurance on the information available to the inquiry that the problems of gas migration from the deepest parts of the site to the zones allocated for building would be avoided. The inspector, whose recommendation the Secretary of State accepted, stated that it was difficult to exaggerate the seriousness of this absence of information in deciding whether it was safe for humdreds of people to live on the site. Such long term remedial measures as had been put forward by the appellants were, in the inspector's view, inevitably diminished in their effect by the fact that they addressed an illustrative proposal for flats "submitted with the barest of details" and that they were "made in the context of ignorance of the actual gas situation in the deeper parts of the site." In particular, the Inspector referred to the significant difference between the high-

[31] [1991] J.P.L. 992.

profile type of development such as a superstore or motorway service area and the type of development proposed in this case, where there was the likelihood of the land changing hands a number of times during the period of active gas production, the possibility of human error or inattention being greater on a low profile housing development, and the large number of ultimate individual occupiers who might make alterations to their dwellings or within their curtilage.

Sites containing combustible materials

8.08 Sites containing combustible materials are referred to in ICRCL Guidance Note 59/83 in the same way as sites known or suspected to emit flammable gases: that is to say that ideally sites where they occur should preferably not be built upon, but if they have to be then special precautions are necessary. In particular, such sites may ignite and smoulder underground, thereby putting buildings or other structures at risk; such underground fires may be extremely difficult to treat satisfactorily and measures taken may indeed increase the rate of combustion in certain circumstances.

The problem relating to this type of site are addressed in ICRCL Guidance Note 61/84 on the fire hazards of contaminated land.

Other specialist advice

8.09 The Inter-Departmental Committee on the Redevelopment of Contaminated Land (ICRCL) has produced a number of notes giving guidance on specific types of site or specific hazards. Such guidance will clearly be a material consideration in considering a proposal for development of a type to which the guidance relates. Reference has already been made to the guidance notes on the redevelopment of landfill sites and the fire hazards of contaminated land, and the full list of current ICRCL notes is as follows:

> ICRCL 17/78: Notes on the redevelopment of landfill sites;
> ICRCL 18/79: Notes on the redevelopment of gas work sites;
> ICRCL 23/79: Notes on the redevelopment of sewage works and farms;
> ICRCL 42/40: Notes on the redevelopment of scrap yards and similar sites;
> ICRCL 59/83: Guidance on the assessment and redevelopment of contaminated land;
> ICRCL 61/84: Notes on the fire hazards of contaminated land;
> ICRCL 64/85: Asbestos on contaminated sites;
> ICRCL 70/90: Notes on the restorating and aftercare of metalliferous; mining sites for pasture or grazing.

Copies of guidance notes may be obtained from:

> Department of the Environment,
> Publication Sales Unit,
> Building 1,
> Victoria Road,
> South Ruislip,
> Middlesex, HA4 0NZ

General advice on the problems of contaminated sites is also available from:

For Sites in England	*For Sites in Wales*
The Secretary,	The Scientific Adviser
ICRCL,	Environmental Protection
Department of the Environment	Branch
Room A342	Welsh Office
Romney House	New Crown Building
43 Marsham Street	Cathays Park
London SW1P 3PY	Cardiff CF1 3NQ

In relation to professional advice, a list of consultants had been compiled by The Royal Society of Chemistry drawing upon their own membership together with information from other professional institutions.[32]

Relevant appeal decisions

8.10 The following relevant appeal decisions illustrate the types and variety of issues which can arise in relation to proposals for the development of contaminated sites and the envolving approach of the Secretary of State and his inspectors.

---

[32] See also Chap. 10.

Decision	Comments
(1) Ref T/APP/Q1825/C/85/P6&F 1800/A86/49432/P6 of March 6, 1987: enforcement notice and planning appeal relating to use of land at Blaze Lane, Hunt End, Redditch, site of former sewage works and partial use as refuse tip. Appellant sought permission for five-year tipping and reclamation operation.	Site land been used for tipping of municipal wastes and the deposit of treated sewage sludge. Works decommissioned in 1977. Proposal for tipping and restoration of land for agricultural use. Main part of site generally suitable for this use, but chemically and physically undesirable material remained in former sediment tanks, filter and sludge beds. On consultation, MAFF advised as to the need for soil cover and Severn Trent Water Authority advised no need to remove sludge but suggested impermeable bund to be maintained to protect watercourses. Assessor's advice was that sewage sludge was main problem; it could spread to clean areas, ignite, or become fluid with poor load-bearing capacity. It would be practicable to disperse the sludge into soil and waste already on site. Inspector concluded that remedial measures were desirable, but the degree of contamination was not such as to justify an operation on the scale proposed. No evidence that site in present condition was presenting significant off-site problems or that it would be so if left undisturbed. Main problem was physical safety of site to visitors or trespassers, but the appellant had acquired the site knowing of those problems, on the basis of his commercial judgment. Appeal dismissed.
(2) Ref APP/W5780/A/85/026016 and APP/Z5060/A/026017 of October 28, 1986: appeals against refusal of outline permission for residential development of former Laporte Chemical Works, Ilford.	One reason for refusal given by local planning authority was that before permission could be given, detailed information would be required as to the exact nature and extent of contamination and what

Decision	Comments
	measures would be taken to overcome these problems.
	Inspector recommended that site could be decontaminated to levels acceptable for residential or commercial use at a cost; the cost was not a planning issue but a matter for commercial judgment.
	Recommended appeal to be allowed subject to conditions on decontamination.
	Secretary of State was satisfied that there was reasonable prospect of agreement being reached with British Rail for removal of contaminated material by rail via disused sidings. Appeal allowed subject to conditions requiring carrying out and submission of satisfactory soil survey, preparation and submission of scheme for decontamination, disposal of any radioactive waste in accordance with Radioactive Substances Act 1960 before commencement of development; and agreement with BR as to re-opening of rail siding for removal of chemically contaminated and radioactive waste.
(3) Ref P56/970 of December 24, 1991: appeal against refusal of permission for residential development of low cost housing at Coal Depot, Mwyndy Llantrisant.	Appellant placed reliance on policies in Mid-Glamorgan Structure Plan as to re-use of derelict land. Appellant's technical evidence was that levels of harmful substances (except for acidity) were below accepted ICRCL Guidelines for domestic gardens, landscaping and buildings: authority was somewhat critical but had no substantive evidence to challenge contention that site could be developed without adverse effects on amenity of future residents. The appeal was, however, dismissed on the basis of the proximity of nearby industrial activity (fuel briquette manufacture).

Decision	Comments
(4) Ref APP/N0220/A/91/1888868 of April 24, 1992: against refusal of permission for retail store on land at Luton Road, Dunstable.	Site largely occupied by vacant industrial buildings. Permission granted subject to conditions prohibiting commencement of development until investigation carried out to determine possible ground or soil contamination and the measures necessary for removal, neutralisation or isolation. Measures to be submitted to local planning authority for approval in writing; development to proceed solely in accordance with measures as approved save with prior written agreement of authority. Any ground found to be contaminated to be removed for disposal at suitably licensed site.
(5) Ref T/APP/R3705/A/113308/P3 of June 3, 1991: appeal against refusal of outline planning permission for housing and leisure scheme on land at Shuttington, Warwickshire, adjacent to Coventry canal.	Site of former colliery; eastern end of site occupied formerly by birckworks; clay-pit back filled with colliery waste which was subsequently excavated for motorway construction and replaced with industrial and domestic wastes, also some fly-tipping. One ground for refusal was lack of information on ground conditions and landfill history. Evidence of methane and carbon-dioxide above maximum safe thresholds. Technical report submitted at inquiry recommending removal of coal and enclosure of refuse within low permeability seal. Council argued that site was high-risk, that insufficient knowledge of gas generation and chemical contamination existed; and that there were significant risks of water pollution inherent in the proposed remedial scheme.

Decision	Comments
	Inspector concluded that further site investigation and consideration of remedial measures was essential before development. The imposition of suitable planning conditions depends on full information being available. Such issues were "a fundamental and material consideration" but ultimately the decisive factor in dismissing the appeal was conflict with planning policies.
(6) Ref P/PPA/LB/103 of August 11, 1988; appeal against refusal outline permission for residential development of former gas works site at Balcarres road, Musselburgh.	Production of gas at the site ceased in 1966. Applicants argued that planning permission should not be refused because of risk of contaminant by residues of former carbonisation process; could be dealt with by condition that decontamination to be carried out to the satisfaction of Regional Analyst. Regional Council warned that expensive rehabilitation might be required; district council argued that costs might render of negative value, effectively sterilising the site.
	Reporter heard that contamination of site remained unknown factor; if extent was directly related to period of use as gasworks, then costmight be greater burden that applicants anticipated. Concern expressed that costs might lead to attempt to increase density of development, which could be undesirable on a prominent site. Permission granted for limited residential redevelopment subject to condition that all underground structures and contaminants associated with the former gasworks to be removed to the satisfaction of the Regional Analyst prior to implementation of the permission.

Decision	Comments
(7) Ref T/APP/V1505/A/90/173829/ P3 of October 9, 1991: appeal against non-determination of application for residential development and open space on former sewage works, Billericay. (1992) 7 P.A.D.	Appeal allowed subject to condition that contamination survey to be submitted to local planning authority and scheme of remedial works to be submitted to local planning authority and approved before commencement of development.
(8) Ref APP/U2425/A/91/181881 of September 8, 1992: appeal against refusal of applications for starter homes and appartments plus shops on land at Barkby Thorpe Road, Leicester. (1992) 8 P.A.D. 13	Site used as tip for industrial waste, predominantly from a foundry. Main issue was adequacy of gas controls. Test is whether measures are effective in reducing risk: planning authority must accept that risk cannot be eliminated entirely. Though not flats, the housing would be based on communal open spaces so avoiding the difficulties inherent in private gardens. Consideration given to adequacy of proposals for gas barrier and to detailed monitoring results.

Water protection issues

8.11   Reference is made elsewhere[33] to the policy of the National Rivers Authority in relation to the protection of groundwater in the context of preventing pollution. However, the NRA's "Policy and Practice for the Protection of Groundwater"[34] also refers to the development of potentially contaminated sites. Policy D2 states that the NRA will seek to be consulted[35] by local planning authorities about any application for development or other works on sites likely to be contaminated to ensure that groundwater quality interests are properly covered. Rather more controversially, policy D3 states:

> "The NRA will recommend to the local planning authority that it refuse planning permission for the redevelopment of contaminated sites where water resources could be adversely affected unless it is satisfied that the proposals include effective measures for the

[33] See Chap. 6.
[34] 1992; discussed fully at Chap. 6.
[35] There is no specific right in the General Development Order 1988 for the NRA to the consulted on applications involving contaminated land.

protection of groundwater and surface water quality. It will advise local planning authorities where insufficient or technically weak information has been provided so that they can require the applicant to supplement the details provided."

In that implementation of planning permission may present or increase a threat to groundwater (for example, by disturbing contaminants) this policy seems unobjectionable. However, the supporting material to the policy suggests that on sites where contamination of the ground and pollution of the groundwater in highly likely there should be a thorough site investigation, including general geology/hydrogeology and existing groundwater quality: "where the site investigation reveals significant groundwater pollution the development proposals should include details of the proposed remedial action."

This approach is controversial in that it could be read as suggesting that any planning application relating to a contaminated site should include groundwater clean-up proposals. But where the proposed development will not worsen existing groundwater pollution nor increase the risk of it, any such requirement is arguably *ultra vires* as a non-material consideration to the development in question; any investigations or clean-up requirements are the subject of other and more specific provisions under the Water Resources Act 1991. Any demand by the planning authority for expenditure over and above that necessitated by the effects of the development itself so as to achieve improvements in groundwater quality could be regarded as akin to seeking injustifiable planning gain.[36]

Planning conditions

As mentioned above, a local planning authority will wish to be **8.12** satisfied that a prospective developer has adequately addressed the potential problems arising from the development of a contaminated site, and that measures will be applied to reduce any attendant risk to an acceptable level. In some cases what may be required is a single scheme of decontamination or other remediation; in other cases, such as landfill gas, monitoring may be required after the implementation of the planning permission for some considerable period.

A common problem is that, at the stage when the decision whether to grant permission is made, further works of monitoring may be required, or the detail of any scheme of remediation may remain to be finalised. The answer to this problem may lie, in many cases, in the imposition of an appropriately worded planning condition. Such a condition may, for

[36] See generally Circ. 16/91, Annex B.

example, require further monitoring work to be carried out to the satisfaction of the planning authority and that the results be provided to the authority; conditions may also require the preparation and submission to the planning authority for approval of a detailed scheme for remediation, decontamination or other measures such as gas control.

Any such condition must comply with the normal criteria applied as to validity as reflected in case law and in the six-fold test provided by Circular 1/85. On that basis, the condition must be:

(a) necessary;
(b) relevant to planning;
(c) relevant to the development to be permitted;
(d) enforceable;
(e) precise; and
(f) reasonable in all other respects.[37]

An example of conditions imposed by the Secretary of State in allowing an appeal against refusal for development of a retail store on land previously in industrial use and potentially subject to contamination is as follows:[38]

". . 4 . No development shall commence on site until an investigation and assessment has been carried out to identify possible ground or soil contamination and to determine measures necessary to remove, neutralise and isolate such contamination and the details of such investigation, assessment and measures proposed have been submitted to and approved in writing by the local planning authority. The development shall thereafter proceed solely in accordance with the measures as approved by the local planning authority and there shall be no variation or departure from the approved measures without the prior written agreement of that authority, excepting that such agreement shall not be unreasonably withheld or delayed.

. . 5 . In view of the previous use of the site, any ground found to be contaminated shall be recovered for disposal at a suitable licensed site."

Of particular relevance will be those types of conditions often called "*Grampian* conditions" which have the negative effect of prohibiting either the commencement of development or the occupation of buildings until certain conditions have been fulfilled.[39] In imposing such a condi-

---

[37] See also *Newbury District Council* v. *Secretary of State for the Environment; Same* v. *International Synthetic Rubber Co.* [1981] A.C. 578; [1980] J.P.L. 325.

[38] Ref. APP/N0220/A/91/188868, April 24, 1992. See para. 8.10 above. It is arguable that conditions 4 and 5 are inconsistent in that 5 would appear to prejudice the generality of 4.

[39] *Grampian Regional Council* v. *City of Aberdeen District Council* (1984) 47 P. & C.R. 633; [1984] J.P.L. 590; see also Circ. 1/85, Annes, para. 34.

tion, fulfilment of which may be outside the control of the applicant in that it may depend on the cooperation or consent of other landowners or authorities, the question of the prospects of the condition being fulfilled may arise. The perceived lack of reasonable prospects of fulfilling the condition does not preclude the grant of permission subject to the condition,[40] though difficulties of implementation may be a relevant factor to take into account in the case of competing sites.

A good example of the application of such a condition is the Dewsbury Road, Wakefield Appeal referred to above.[41] In that case, the planning authority did not consider it appropriate to embark upon negotiations for a planning agreement relating to gas control, because they considered that the site did not meet the criteria for allowing any development of gassing sites. Evidence before the inspector in terms of the design of the building and the draft operator's manual for the control systems indicated that it would be possible to control and monitor gas without putting the public at risk; a *"Grampian* condition" was put before the inquiry requiring details of the control and monitoring scheme to be agreed with the council. On this evidence, the inspector was satisfied that an acceptable scheme could be devised and that it would therefore be appropriate to impose a condition along the lines suggested. The final condition imposed by the inspector was:

> "The development hereby permitted shall not be commenced until details of measures to control and monitor landfill gas and a comprehensive management plan for gas control and monitoring have been submitted to and approved by the local planning authority; and the building shall not be occupied or open to the general public until those measures have been carried out in accordance with the approved details."

One problem which can arise in practice is that monitoring and gas control measures may involve works or operations being carried out on land outside the boundary of the planning application. Under section 72 of the Town and Country Planning Act 1990, conditions may be imposed on the grant of planning permission for regulating the development or use of any land under control of the applicant, whether or not it

---

[40] *British Railways Board* v. *Secretary of State for the Environment* [1994] J.P.L. 32; overruling *Jones* v. *Secretary of State for Wales and Ogwr District Council* (1990) 61 P. & C.R. 238. See also *Swale Borough Council* v. *Secretary of State for the Environment and Wards Construction (Medway) Ltd.* [1994] J.P.L. 236, which followed the *Jones* case.

[41] See para. 8.07. See also the planning appeal decision at [1994] J.P.L. 555, para. 7.27 above, where a *Grampian*-style condition was imposed in relation to an anthrax-contaminated site and was regarded as equally effective as a planning agreement.

is land in respect of which the application was made, or requiring the carrying out of works on any such land, so far as appears to the local planning authority to be expedient for the purposes of or in connection with the development authorised by the permission. For the purposes of the section, "control" is a question of fact and degree as to whether the applicant has control sufficient to satisfy the planning authority that he is in a position to comply with the condition concerned.[42] One problem in relation to contaminated land is that control may not simply be a matter or carrying out a single operation, such as the construction of an access road, but may also involve continued monitoring and intervention. This may involve the planning authority looking very carefully at whether there is such control; however, where there is no such control, a negatively worded "*Grampian* condition" may provide the answer, even if there is apparently little prospect of such a condition being fulfilled.[43]

In view of the decision in *Medina Borough Council* v. *Proberum Limited*[44] planning authorities will need to exercise considerable care in relation to applications for outline permission involving contaminated land. In that case a condition was imposed on outline planning permission requiring the approval of the authority as to details of access. It was held that there was an assumption in the case of outline permissions that all reserved matters can potentially be satisfied within the site which is the subject of the application; any authority granting outline permission for the development of contaminated land may therefore be in difficulties if it transpires that works outside the site may be required to achieve a satisfactory result. Again the answer may lie in the imposition of a *Grampian*-type condition.[45]

Planning obligations

8.13   It may be possible to avoid some of the difficulties referred to above in relation to conditions by use of planning obligations under section 106 of the Town and Country Planning Act 1990. Such obligations may be created by agreement or otherwise by any person interested in land and may:

(a) restrict the development or use of land in any specified way;

---

[42] *Wimpey (George) & Co. Limited* v. *New Forest District Council* [1979] J.P.L. 314; *Atkinson* v. *Secretary of State for the Environment and Leeds City Council* [1983] J.P.L. 599; *Pedgrift* v. *Oxfordshire District Council* [1991] E.G.C.S. 89.

[43] See n. 39 above.

[44] [1991] J.P.L. 159.

[45] It was held in the *Proberun* Case that the condition was not worded in such a way as to constitute a valid *Grampian* condition and even if it was, on the state of the law as it then was (since overruled), it was void as having no reasonable prospect of being fulfilled.

(b) require specified operations or activities to be carried out in, on, under or over the land;

(c) required the land to be used in any specified way; or

(d) require a sum or sums to be paid to the authority on a specified date or dates, or periodically.

The obligations may be negative in nature, for example restraining the commencement of development or the occupation of buildings until problems of contamination have been dealt with; on the other hand they may be positive in nature, actually requiring specified remedial works. Given that they may be entered into "by agreement or otherwise" such an obligation put forward unilaterally may be a useful alternative to the proffering of a draft *Grampian* condition on a planning appeal, as in the Dewsbury Road, Wakefield case mentioned above.

However, planning obligations may be of limited value in the context of off-site works because insofar as planning obligations relate to operations or activities to be carried out on land, they can affect only the land which is the subject matter of the obligation, and in which the person entering into the obligation holds an interest. Section 106 therefore does not allow an obligation to be entered into in relation to off-site works, except where the owner of the relevant land enters into the agreement or gives the undertaking. The solution in such cases is either a negative planning obligation akin to a *Grampian* condition and affecting the land which is the subject matter of the application; or alternatively an obligation as to payment of a sum or sums of money to fund the relevant off-site works. Whilst this latter solution may be acceptable in the case of off-site works such as highway improvements, it may be a less satisfactory solution in the case of possibly contentious and long-term off-site monitoring or remedial works in the case of contaminated land.

Further consideration as to the law relating to planning obligations is beyond the scope of this work, and readers are referred to the standard texts on planning law, and to Department of Environment Circular 16/91, "Planning Obligations" (Welsh Office 53/91).

"Overall advantage" issues

As mentioned earlier, Government policy favours the bringing of derelict **8.14** land back into beneficial use, both as a means of improving the local environment and as a way of reducing pressure for development in the green belt, urban fringe and rural areas. This is the case, for example, with the current proposals for the development of redundant and cleared Thames-side sites in central London and along the East Thames corridor.[46]

---

[46] See Department of Environment, "East Thames Corridor: A Study of Development Capacity and Potential" (HMSO, 1993) and DoE News Release No. 426, June, 1993.

The development of land may well provide the funds which would otherwise be lacking for problems of contamination on the site to be thoroughly addressed. It is therefore possible to envisage circumstances where an argument could be put forward in favour of granting planning permission for a more intensive or high value use of land than might otherwise be the case, if that is the only means by which the money can be made available for the site to be cleaned up and where clean-up is a necessary pre-condition of the site being brought back into beneficial use.

It seems clear from the case law, in particular *R* v. *Westminster City Council, ex p. Monahan*[47] that such financial consideratons may legitimately be taken into account as material by the planning authority. The Court of Appeal held in that case that it was legitimate for a planning authority to balance against the objections to the proposed inclusion of high value office elements within a scheme of development, that the provision of such offices, by way of departure from the development plan, was necessary to fund and achieve much-needed improvements to The Royal Opera House, Covent Garden. In that case, Kerr L.J. stated that:[48]

> "financial constraints on the economic viability of a desirable planning development are unavoidable facts of life in an imperfect world. It would be unreal and contrary to common sense to insist that they must be excluded from the range of considerations which may probably be regarded as material in determining planning applications . . . virtually all planning decisions involve some kind of balancing exercise."

Nicholls L.J. in his judgment amplified this point with a specific reference to contamination problems:[49]

> "For example, take a run-down site, littered with derelict buildings. The soil is contaminated from previous industrial use. Preparation of the site for development will be expensive. The planning authority is anxious that such an eyesore shall be removed, and housing is the preferred use. An application is submitted for development with high-density housing. In my view it is clear that in considering this application the planning authority is entitled to take into account, first, that a lower density of housing will not be commercially viable, having regard to the heavy cost of site clearance, so that, secondly, the probable consequence of refusing to permit the development south will be the absence of any development for the foreseeable future, in which event the eyesore will remain."

In practice, the crucial question will be whether the benefits to be achieved from remedial works are such as to overcome planning

[47] [1989] 3 W.L.R. 408, C.A.; [1989] J.P.L. 107.
[48] *Ibid.*, p. 425; see also pp. 434 and 435.
[49] *Ibid.*, p. 433.

objections to the development or additional density and whether the authority or inspector is satisfied that development in the form proposed is the only likely means of serving those benefits. Thus the issue will depend to a large extent on how serious the consequences would be of failing to remedy the contamination. The proposed scheme may be out of scale to the risks posed by the site in its current condition and thus may go further than is necessary to address any perceived problem.[50] On the other hand where those risks are severe, for example buried chemicals contaminating groundwater with toxic and persistent compounds, the benefits of reclamation may be sufficiently great to overcome even fundamental greenbelt policy objections.[51]

The problems of clean-up

As pointed our in the previous paragraph, it is possible to stress the **8.15** benefits to be gained from developing—and in the process cleaning-up—contaminated land. It should also be remembered however that some derelict and contaminated sites are important habitats for wildlife and many contribute to the richness and diversity of flora and fauna in urban areas.[52] Uncommon species such as herbs and acidic grassland may find such sites congenial: often they will be adjacent to wharves, canals or railways, which are well-organised as areas of potential wildlife importance.[53] A dramatic and unusual example which has been cited of unexpected natural benefits occurring on industrially damaged sites is the colonisation of highly alkaline spoil heaps of Leblanc process wastes in Cheshire and Lancashire by rare orchids and orchid hybrids.[54]

The issue of preservation of such areas in an urban setting (sometimes called "urban commons") has featured in public inquiries—for example the Dageham hospital site, East London where the inspector at the UDP inquiry found in favour of the development of the site in accordance with

---

[50] See para. 8.10. Table, appeal no. 1.

[51] See Appeal Ref: PNW/5143–219–6, April 10, 1989; Waverton, Cheshire, reported at *Chartered Surveyor Weekly*, May 4, 1989, p. 74; also Ref: LRP 219/R5510/10 [1993] J.P.L. 268 (corporate headquarters and business park at Harmondsworth for British Airways plc; benefits included removal of potential health risk from methane and leachate).

[52] See London Ecology Unit, *A Nature Conservation Strategy for London*, (Ecology Handbook No. 4).

[53] John G. Kelcey, *Industrial Development and Wildlife Conservation*, Environmental Conservation, Vol. 2, No. 2, Summer 1975; John G. Kelcey, *Industrial Development and the Conservation of Vascular Plants*, Environmental Conservation, Vol. 11, No. 3 Autumn 1984.

[54] See Kenneth Mellanby, *Waste and Pollution: the Problem for Britain* (Harper Collins, 1992), p. 64; see also Arnold Darlington, *Ecology of Refuse Tips*, (Heinemann, 1969).

Circular 12/91, there being other examples of urban commons within the borough. The concept of "urban common" is in any event ephemeral, in that colonisation of this type is likely to recur whenever a site becomes derelict. Leaving apart the unusual examples such as the Cheshire alkali sites, urban commons are in fact creatures of transition; as one site is cleaned up, so another may appear elsewhere.

BUILDING CONTROL

The Building Regulations 1991

8.16   Section 1 of the Building Act 1984 gives the Secretary of State power to make regulations with respect to the design and construction of buildings and the provisions of services, fittings and equipment. Contravention of building requirements is an offence under section 35 of the Building Act and, in addition, the local authority may itself take steps to remedy the defect and recover the cost from the person contravening the Building Regulations; alternatively, notice may be served requiring the owner or occupier to take the relevant action. Building Regulations may require plans to be deposited with the local authority for approval. These should be passed unless they are defective or show that the proposed work would contravene the Building Regulations.[55] Breach of a duty imposed by Building Regulations will give rise to a civil action if damage results.[56]

The current Building Regulations under the 1984 Act are the Building Regulations 1991.[57] The Regulations impose requirements with respect to the carrying out of "building work" which will include the erection of extension of a building.[58] Building work must be carried out so that it complies with the relevant requirements contained in Schedule 1 of the Regulations.[59] Part C of Schedule 1 to the Regulations contains the requirements relating to *Site Preparation and Resistance to Moisture*. Of particular relevance in relation to site contamination are requirements C1 and C2 which read as follows:

> **"C1.   Preparation of Site**
> The ground to be covered by the building shall be reasonably free from vegetable matter.

---

[55] S.16.
[56] S.38.
[57] S.I. 1991 No. 2768.
[58] Reg. 3(*a*).
[59] Reg. 4(*a*).

"C2. Dangerous and Offensive Substances

Precautions shall be taken to avoid danger to health and safety caused by substances on or in the ground to be covered by the building."

The Regulations themselves contain no technical detail, which is to be found in the relevant Approved Documents. Approved Document C, *Site Preparation and Resistance to Moisture* (Revised 1992) deals with contamination at section 3. The document states that if any signs of possible contaminants are present the Environmental Health Officer should be told at once. Confirmation of presence of the contaminants listed in the table below will require the relevant specified action (assuming the ground to be covered by the building, including foundations, will have at least 100 mm of in situ concrete laid over it.[60]

Signs of possible contaminants	Possible contaminant	Relevant Action
Vegetation (absence, poor or unnatural growth)	Metals Metal compounds*	None
	Organic compounds Gases	Removal
	Metals Metal compounds*	None
	Oily and tarry wastes	Removal, filling or sealing
	Asbestos (loose)	Filling or sealing
Surface materials (unusual colours and contours may indicate wastes and residues)	Other mineral fibres	None
	Organic compounds including phenols	Removal or filling

[60] Table 2, Section C2 of Approved Document C.

Signs of possible contaminants	Possible contaminant	Relevant Action
	Combustible material including coal and coke dust	Removal or filling
	Refuse and waste	Total removal, or see Guidance
Fumes and odours (may indicate organic chemicals at very low concentrations)	Flammable, explosive and asphyxiating gases, including methane and carbon dioxide	Removal
	Corrosive liquids	Removal, filling or sealing
	Faecal animal and vegetable matter (biologically active)	Removal or filling
Drums and Containers (whether full or empty)	Various	Removal with all contaminated ground

Note Liquid and gaseous contaminants are mobile and the ground covered by the building can be affected by such contaminants from elsewhere. Some guidance on landfill gas and radon is given in this document, other liquids and gases should be referred to a specialist.

* Special cement may be needed with sulphates.
  Actions assume that ground will be covered with at least 100 mm in situ concrete.

The Approved Document contains the following definition of the terms "removal", "filling" and "sealing" as used in the table[61]:

— **Removal** means that the contaminant itself and any contaminated ground to be covered by the building should be taken out to a depth of 1m (or less if the local authority or approved inspector agrees) below the level of the lowest floor and taken away.

— **Filling** means that the ground to be covered by the building is to be covered to a depth of 1m (or less if the local authority or

[61] Para. 2.4, S.C2.

approved inspector agrees) with a material which will not react adversely with any contaminant remaining and will be suitable for making up levels. The type of filling and the design of the ground floor should be considered together. Combustible material should be adequately compacted to avoid combustion.

— **Sealing** means that a suitable imperforated barrier is laid between the contaminant and the building and sealed at the joints, around the edges and at the service entries. Polyethylene may not be suitable if the contamination is a liquid such as a tarry waste or organic solvent.

Paragraph 2.5 of the approved document, entitled "Alternative Approach" suggests that in most hazardous conditions only the total removal of contaminants from the ground to be covered by the building can provide a complete remedy. In other cases, remedial measures can reduce the risk to acceptable levels; but these measures should only be undertaken with the benefit of expert advice.

The Approved document also contains specific reference to the problems of gaseous contaminants; landfill gas and methane and radon.[62] On landfill gas, the Approved document refers to the standard distance of 250 metres from a landfill site[63] as an area requiring investigation; it goes on to point out, however, that all cases where there is reason to suspect that the proposed building will be within the likely sphere of influence of a gassing site will require further investigation. Reference is made to BRE guidance on the construction of buildings near, but not on, landfill sites; the following threshold levels are suggested for dwellings as "broad guidelines":

| Methane | Level in ground unlikely to exceed 10 per cent. volume | No further protection needed provided ground floor is of suspended concrete and ventilated as recommended by BRE |
| Carbon Dioxide | Level in ground in excess of 1.5 per cent. by volume

Level in ground in excess of 5 per cent. by volume | Need to consider possible measures to prevent ingress

Specific design measures required |

The Approved Document acknowledges that in the case of houses, for management reasons, passive venting and protection is generelly the only viable solution and is effective only where gas concentrations in the ground are low or likely to remain so.[64]

[62] As to radon, see Chap. 1.
[63] See para. 8.07 above.
[64] See para. 8.07 above.

For non-domestic buildings, expert advice should be sought. The source of gas and its pressure relative to the atmosphere will need to be considered: the design of protection measures should be incorporated into the overall design of the building and satisfactory arrangements should be made for maintenance and monitoring.[65]

---

[65] Para. 2.11.

Annex

EXAMPLES OF DEVELOPMENT PLAN POLICIES

NORTH WARWICKSHIRE BOROUGH COUNCIL LOCAL PLAN 1993: POLICY E12

Contaminated land

The development of contaminated or potentially contaminated land will not be permitted unless it is demonstrated with a reasonable degree of certainty that practicable meauress can be taken to treat, contain or control the contamination so as not to:

(1) expose the occupiers of the development, including in the case of housing the normal use and enjoyment of gardens, to significant risk;

(2) threaten the structural integrity of buildings existing or erected on the site;

(3) lead to the contamination of any watercourse of aquifer

(4) cause the contamination of adjoining land, or allow such contamination to continue;

(5) cause unacceptable environmental conditions for the occupiers of nearby properties while the remedial measures themselves are being carried out; or

(6) expose site operatives to unacceptable risk to their health.

Contamination should normally be treated on site. However, where development is in accord with the development plan and the retention of contaminated material on the site is demonstrated to be inappropriate, removal and disposal to a licensed site will be permitted.

Explanation

Contaminated land is land which contains substances which are present in sufficient quantities or concentrations that they are potentially

379

capable of causing harm directly or indirectly to people, to the environment, or to building structures. Contamination is a material planning consideration which needs to be taken into account in planning decisions (Circular 21/87). The responsibility for assessing whether or not land is suitable for a particular purpose, including possible contamination, rests with the developer.

District Councils will be required to maintain a register of potentially contaminative land by the Environmental Protection Act 1990. Where a development is proposed on land known or suspected to be contaminated, investigations will need to be carried out by the developer, and a report supplied with the planning application, setting out the findings and indicating the action it is porposed to take to deal with the contamination.

Unless the contaminated material is already causing a problem by leaching into a watercourse or in some other manner, contamination should normally be dealt with on site. Removal merely moves the problem elsewhere, and can itself be a source of environmental harm through the disturbance and handling of the material.

The policy identifies the main issues to be addressed in developing proposals for the treatment of contamination on site. There is a particular problem where domestic waste is involved, since it may be producing landfill gas, which can migrate to adjoining land and properties with consequential risk of explosion. Structure Plan Policy E12 says that development will be prohibited in areas likely to be affected by landfill gas and leachate with gas producing potential.

NEWCASTLE UPON TYNE DEPOSIT DRAFT UDP 1993, POLICIES 6 AND 7

Contaminated land

Section 143 of the Environmental Protection Act 1990 will place a duty on local authorities to compile local registers of potentially contaminated land. This is land which because of its past use for certain specified industrial or waste disposal purposes, may now represent a possible hazard to health or the environment. The Government are currently consulting all interested bodies and regulations will be introduced to bring section 143 into force during the Plan period. Until then, the City Council will continue to encourage the reuse of contaminated land following reclamation.

Pol 6

INVESTIGATION AND RECLAMATION OF KNOWN OR POTENTIALLY CONTAMINATED LAND WILL BE ENCOURAGED, PARTICULARLY WHERE THE CONTAMINATION IS A CONSTRAINT TO DEVELOPMENT OR CAUSES A KNOWN OR POTENTIAL RISK TO HEALTH.

The re-use of contaminated land can contribute towards urban regeneration and reduce the need to use new sites outside the built-up area. The City Council will encourage the treatment of contaminated land, including the use of derelict land grant, to enable it to be re-used or permanently landscaped.

Pol 7

DEVELOPERS WILL BE REQUIRED TO UNDERTAKE A THOROUGH SITE INVESTIGATION WHERE A SITE IS, OR MAY BE CONTAMINATED. THE INVESTIGATION MUST IDENTIFY THE NATURE OF CONTAMINATION TOGETHER WITH THE REMEDIAL MEASURES REQUIRED TO TREAT OR REMOVE IT IN ACCORDANCE WITH THE BEST PRACTICABLE ENVIRONMENTAL OPTION APPROPRIATE TO THE PROPOSED DEVELOPMENT AND THE NATURE OF THE SITE. DEVELOPMENT WILL NOT NORMALLY BE ALLOWED TO COMMENCE UNTIL THESE MEASURES HAVE BEEN COMPLETED, UNLESS THEY ARE EFFECTED AS PART OF THE ACTUAL DEVELOPMENT PROCESS.

Developers will be required to investigate the site conditions of land which is known, or suspected to be seriously contaminated prior to planning permission being granted. On land where there is only slight or potential contamination, conditions may be imposed requiring site investigations before development begins on site.

In all cases any contamination must be treated or removed prior to development. Chemical and organic pollution should be treated, so as is possible, on site and leachate prevented from migrating from polluted sites prior to its treatment.

It is the responsibility of the developer to ensure the safe development and secure occupancy of the site.

BASILDON DISTRICT COUNCIL LOCAL PLAN (DEPOSIT) DRAFT 1993, POLICY C12

Hazardous substances

WHERE DEVELOPMENT IS PROPOSED FOR RESIDENTIAL OR OTHER ENVIRONMENTALLY SENSITIVE PURPOSES ON, OR ADJOINING, LAND WHICH IS THOUGHT TO BE CONTAMINATED BY HAZARDOUS SUBSTANCES ARISING OUT OF PREVIOUS LAND USES, THE COUNCIL MUST BE SATISFIED THAT ALL APPROPRIATE MEASURES TO DEAL WITH CONTAMINATION OF THE DEVELOPMENT SITE ARE UNDERTAKEN. SURVEYS WILL BE REQUIRED TO ENSURE THAT THE LAND IS CAPABLE OF BEING DECONTAMINATED AND RECLAIMED TO THE SATISFACTION OF THE COUNCIL.

When a proposal for residential development or indeed any other sensitive use is being considered on land or adjoining land, which has or may have been contaminated by a previous use, the District Council will need to be satisfied that any danger to prospective occupiers arising from possible pollutants in the soil etc, has been or is capable of being satisfactorily removed before planning permission is granted.

BARKING AND DAGENHAM UDP DEPOSIT DRAFT 1992, POLICY G27

Contaminated land

Policy G27

THE COUNCIL WILL AVOID THE CONTAMINATION OF LAND AND WILL:

  (i) IDENTIFY POTENTIALLY CONTAMINATED LAND AND, IF CONTAMINATION HAS OCCURRED, SEEK THE NECESSARY TREATMENT IN ORDER TO RECLAIM SUCH LAND FOR BENEFICIAL FUTURE USES;
 (ii) REFUSE DEVELOPMENT IN OR WITHIN 250 METRES OF ACTIVE GASSING LANDFILL SITES;
(iii) REFUSE APPLICATIONS FROM OPERATIONS WHICH MAY RESULT IN THE CONTAMINATION OF LAND.

Justification

Contaminated land poses a health hazard to the local community and the environment and therefore the Council will avoid and prevent the contamination of land within the borough.

There are a number of contaminated sites within the borough, which, in accordance with the new Environmental Protection Act 1990, the Council will identify, so as to ensure that appropriate measures can be taken to protect the local community. Therefore, the Council will refuse development on or within 250 metres of active gassing landfill sites and will not permit development on other contaminated sites unless the land is treated in order to reclaim it for suitable beneficial future uses.

As a result, the Council will require that developers of contaminated land undertake a detailed investigation of sites, in order to establish which pollutants are present and may use its powers to require that remedial work is undertaken to the satisfaction of the Council's Environmental Health and Building Control inspectors and other statutory bodies. In order to ensure that the development can proceed safely and efficiently, the Council will require that full details of satisfactory treatment are submitted before a planning application is considered.

SHEFFIELD DRAFT UDP DEPOSIT DRAFT 1993, POLICY GE25

Contaminated and unstable land

DEVELOPMENT WILL NOT BE PERMITTED ON, OR NEXT TO, CONTAMINATED OR UNSTABLE LAND OR CLOSED LANDFILL SITES UNLESS THEY ARE SHOWN TO BE SAFE.

Reasons for the Policy

Contaminated land and closed landfill sites may contain toxic chemicals and dangerous gases (*e.g.*, methane). These can be a hazard to the occupiers of new buildings, either on or adjacent to the site.

Toxic chemicals and poisonous gases can contaminate ground and surface waters and damage plants.

The Government's national planning guidance states that land contamination and instability need to be taken into account in the preparation of development plans and in deciding planning applications. It advises that in order to minimise associated risks, potentially contaminated or unstable sites should be identified at the earliest stage of planning.

383

Bringing derelict land back into productive use can help with the regeneration of the older areas of the city and helps to reduce pressures for development on greenfield sites.

How it will be put into practice

By:

- Carrying our a city-wide survey to identify all potentially contaminated land and closed landfill sites;
- Maintaining a register of such sites for reference in deciding planning applications;
- Monitoring all known closed landfill sites for potential hazards;
- Controlling immediate hazards identified on privately-owned sites through enforcement action;
- Taking remedial action to control immediate hazards identified on city council-owned sites;
- Requiring a land contamination survey, which is to the satisfaction of the city council, before any development is allowed on a contaminated site;
- Deciding planning applications;
- Use of conditions in granting waste disposal licences and other legislation relating to control of landfill site hazards.

Waltham Forest Draft UDP Deposit Draft 1992, Policy ENV6

WHEN CONSIDERING APPLICATIONS FOR DEVELOPMENT ON SITES WHICH ARE POSSIBLY CONTAMINATED, THE COUNCIL WILL NEED TO BE SATISFIED THAT THE DEVELOPMENT CAN SAFELY BE CONSTRUCTED AND USED.

When developments are proposed on any land which may have been contaminated by previous uses, or which has been used as a landfill site, careful consideration will be given to the suitability of the proposed uses.

There are a few sites in the borough which the Council consider are likely to be contaminated, and for these, developers will be required to carry out detailed site investigations in order to identify any pollutants present. They will need to decontaminate the land and provide full technical evidence at the time of any planning application to show that the development can safely proceed.

The Council will take account of Government advice contained in Circular 21/87 on the measures required to conduct a survey of sites subject to landfill to assess its suitability for development. The Council will also consult the Waste Regulation Authority on all such applications.

Chapter 9

FUNDING

Generally

Reclamation of contaminated land necessarily involves considerable **9.01** expenditure in the form of site clearance, consultants' and analysts' fees, removal or treatment of contaminated soil or groundwater, and gas control or other remedial measures. The high cost of such work will often act as a considerable barrier to investment in those areas which need it most: hence the various schemes which exist for financial assistance.

A variety of financial instruments currently exist which may be relevant to the reclamation and development of contaminated land. As a broad generalisation these fall into three categories:

1. the various programmes concerned with the reclamation of derelict land and the regeneration of urban areas. These include derelict land grant, city grant and various initiatives begun under the Government's "Action for Cities" programme;
2. those schemes designed to assist and promote the development of new technologies; and
3. aid available from the European Community.

The principal agencies currently concerned with land reclamation funding are the Department of Environment, local authorities, urban development corporations and in Wales, the Welsh Development Agency.

The Leasehold Reform, Housing and Urban Development Act 1993, created a new agency, the Urban Regeneration Agency (known as "English Partnerships")with specific responsibilities for the regeneration of vacant, unused, under-used, contaminated, derelict, neglected or unsightly land. The Agency's functions include the provisions of financial assistance and the Agency will subsume the derelict land grant and city grant Programmes previously operated by the Department of Environment; currently the relevant Departmental regional offices operate and administer the grant schemes as agents for the Agency.

It may be helpful to illustrate at the outset how the various sources of funding may potentially apply to various types of reclamation project.

385

Scheme	Source of funding
Private sector scheme outside Urban Programme Areas for reclaiming land which meets criteria of "derelict". Return on investment secondary.	Derelict land grant; DoE and in due course URA
Private sector funded scheme for major project in Urban Programme Area which will contribute directly to economic/physical regeneration. Risk and return with private sector.	City grant; DoE and in due course URA
Other private sector schemes in Urban Programme Areas.	Derelict land grant; DoE and in due course URA
Local authority scheme inside or outside Urban Programme Area	Derelict land grant; DoE and in due course URA
Local authority works on contaminated land/landfill gas not associated with reclamation scheme but which meet DoE criteria.	Supplementary credit approvals under DoE scheme
Scheme in area of Urban Development Corporation which meets objectives of regeneration, encouraging industry, providing housing/social facilities	UDC funding; city grant/DLG may also be involved
Scheme in Wales to assist regeneration/improve environment	WDA funding; DLG also relevant—administered by WDA on behalf of Welsh Office
Small private sector schemes in Urban Programme Areas not large enough to qualify for city grant but which contribute to economic development	Grants under Urban Programme administered by local authority
Private sector projects in City Challenge areas; authorities selected by competition with Action Plan. Authority may take risk-bearing share of up to 20%.	City Challenge funding used with modified city grant
Projects involving demonstration of innovative technology.	Environmental Technology Information Scheme (ETIS); Department of Trade and Industry
Major public sector projects at regional level	EC European Regional Development Fund; may be used as "package" with D.L.G.

The Urban Regeneration Agency: generally

The Urban Regeneration Agency (known as "English Partnerships") **9.02** was constituted by section 158 of the Leasehold Reform, Housing and Urban Development Act 1993. The Agency is a body corporate and is not a servant or agent of the Crown.[1] The main object of the Agency is to secure the regeneration of land in England which falls within one or more of a number of specified categories and which the Agency determines to be suitable for regeneration.[2] The relevant categories are:

(a) land which is vacant or unused;
(b) land which is situated in an urban area and which is under-used or ineffectively used;
(c) land which is contaminated, derelict, neglected or unsightly; and
(d) land which is likely to become derelict, neglected or unsightly by reason of actual or apprehended collapse of the surface as a result of the carrying out of relevant operations[3] which have ceased to be carried out.

In determining which land is suitable for regeneration, the Agency must have regard to any guidance or directions issued by the Secretary of State.[4] Additionally, the Authority has the object of securing the development of land in England which the Agency, with the consent of the Secretary of State and in accordance with any guidance or directions, determines to be suitable for development.[5]

The objects of the Agency are to be achieved in particular by the following means (or by such of them as seem to the Agency to be appropriate in any particular case), namely:[6]

(a) by securing that land and buildings are brought into effective use;
(b) by developing, or encouraging the development of, existing and new industry and commerce;
(c) by creating an attractive and safe environment; and
(d) by facilitating the provision of housing and providing, or facilitating the provision of, social and recreational facilities.

---

[1] Subs. 158(3). See also Scheds. 17 and 18.
[2] Subs. 159(1).
[3] "Relevant operations" has the same meaning as in s.1 of the Derelict Land Act 1982.
[4] Ss.159(1) and 167.
[5] Subs. 159(3).
[6] Subs. 159(4).

The Urban Regeneration Agency: powers

9.03   For the purpose of achieving its objects, the Agency may:[7]

    (a) acquire, hold, manage, reclaim, improve and dispose of land, plant, machinery, equipment and other property;

    (b) carry out the development or redevelopment of land, including the conversion or demolition of existing buildings;

    (c) carry out building and other operations;

    (d) provide means of access, services or other facilities for land;

    (e) seek to ensure the provision of water, electricity, gas, sewerage and other services;

    (f) carry on any business or undertaking for the purposes of its objects;

    (g) with the consent of the Secretary of State, form, or acquire interests in, bodies corporate;

    (h) act with other persons, whether in partnership or otherwise;

    (i) give financial assistance to other persons;

    (j) act as agent for other persons;

    (k) provide advisory or other services and facilities; and

    (l) generally do anything necessary or expedient for the purposes of its objects or for purposes incidental to those purposes.

These powers therefore include the reclamation and remediation of contaminated land; whilst the investigation and appraisal of land for possible contamination is not expressly mentioned, section 163 gives powers to enter and survey land for the purpose of ascertaining the nature of the subsoil.

Land which is vested in a local authority, statutory undertaker or other public body may be vested in the Agency by way of Ministerial Order.[8] The Agency may also acquire land by agreement or, on being authorised to do so by the Secretary of State, compulsorily.[9]

The Secretary of State may also make orders making the Agency the local planning authority in relation to the whole or any part of a designated area, for such functions and in relation to such kinds of development as may be specified.[10]

With the consent of the Secretary of State, the Agency may appoint an urban development corporation to act as its agent on such terms as may be agreed, for any of its functions except those of giving financial assistance.[11]

[7] S.160.
[8] S.161.
[9] S.162.
[10] S.171.
[11] S.177.

The Urban Regeneration Agency: financial assistance

One of the Agency's powers is the provision of financial assistance to **9.04** other persons.[12] The consent of the Secretary of State is required for the exercise of that power,[13] which may only be given in respect of qualifying expenditure, defined as:

(a) the acquisition of land;

(b) the reclamation, improvement or refurbishment of land;

(c) the development or redevelopment of land, including the conversion or demolition of existing buildings;

(d) the equipment or fitting out of land;

(e) the provision of means of access, services or other facilities for land; and

(f) environmental improvements.

The assistance may be given on such terms and conditions as the Agency, with the consent of the Secretary of State, considers appropriate; the terms may include provision as to repayment and recovery of proceeds of sale.[14]

Assistance may be given in any form except that the Agency may not purchase loan or share capital in a company; in particular it may take the form of:[15]

(a) grants;

(b) loans;

(c) guarantees; or

(d) incurring expenditure for the benefit of the person assisted.

As indicated below,[16] one of the first functions to be undertaken by the Agency is the assumption of responsibility for administering the grant regimes previously dealt with by the Department of Environment. It is not possible to say how those forms of grant may change, but certanly a degree of rationalisation is to be anticipated, possibly leading to a unified regime. Certainly it appears that the Agency will integrate derelict land grant into their unified system of financial support.[16a]

The Role of the Agency—generally

The role and likely structure of the Urban Regeneration Agency are **9.05** gradually emerging and it is now clear that the Agency will:

[12] S.160(1)(i).
[13] S.164; consent may only be given with Treasury approval.
[14] Subs. 164(5).
[15] Subs. 164(3).
[16] Para. 9.05.
[16a] See Action For Cities News Release No. 247, April 5, 1994.

(a) take over the functions of English Estates;[17] and

(b) subsume the derelict land grant and city grant Programmes previously operated by the Department of Environment and described below. Funding for these programmes stands at £177 million in 1993–94.[18]

It should be noted that the Agency's role will not be confined to urban areas and that it will also be responsible for reclaiming land in rural areas.

The Agency, it appears, will work alongside Urban Development Corporations as they run down, and will take over some of their work, some of which will also be transferred to local authorities.[19] It also seems likely that the Agency will be structured with regional teams having delegated powers.[20]

Urban Development Corporations

9.06 The Government has established a number of Urban Development Corporations, beginning with the London Docklands Development Corporation and Merseyside Development Corporation in 1981. The most recent UDCs to be created are Birmingham Heartlands (1992) and Plymouth (1993). A full list of current UDCs is as follows:

UDC	Date Est.	Area (ha)	Initial nature of area	Initial pop.	1991–92 expend. grant-in-aid (£m)	Total grant rec'vd so far (£m)	Private sector investm't sold to 1992 (£m)
Merseyside	March 1981	960*	Derelict dockland, polluted waterfront— complete dereliction	7000*	30	258	200
London Docklands	July 1981	2,226	Derelict docks and associated industry— 45% of area derelict	40,000	240	1,350	9,100

[17] English Estates currently administers programmes of some £90 million (1993–94) aimed at promoting the provision of industrial and commercial space, mainly in Assisted Areas.

[18] Action for Cities News Release 425, June 24, 1993.

[19] *Estates Gazette* (1993) Issue 9325, p. 38.

[20] *Ibid.*

UDC	Date Est.	Area (ha)	Initial nature of area	Initial pop.	1991–92 expend. grant-in-aid (£m)	Total grant rec'vd so far (£m)	Private sector investm't sold to 1992 (£m)
Trafford Park	Feb 1987	1,267	Mature industrial estate—one third derelict or under-used	40	28.1	92	556
Black Country	May 1987	2,600	Derelict metal-working and other industrial sites, with population interspersed	35,000	46.2	142	85.7
Teeside	May 1987	4,565	Former steel and chemical industry sites—more than half derelict or unused	950	56.2	161	580
Tyne & Wear	May 1987	2,375	Ship building and riverside industry, one-third derelict	3,700	31.4	126	450
Cardiff Bay	April 1987	1,100	Old docklands, 25% derelict or under-used	5,600	32.6	124	115
Central Manchester	June 1988	187	Heavily built-up mixed-use centre area, 40% derelict or under-used	250	16	43.5	186.6
Leeds	June 1988	540	Mixed industrial sites, including former power station, 20% derelict or under-used	2,600	13.6	39	116
Sheffield	June 1988	900	Former Steel sites, 40% derelict or unused	300	13.3	50	484

391

UDC	Date Est.	Area (ha)	Initial nature of area	Initial pop.	1991–92 expend. grant-in-aid (£m)	Total grant rec'vd so far (£m)	Private sector investm't sold to 1992 (£m)
Bristol	Jan 1989	360	Mixed industrial area, 20% derelict or under-used	1,500	16.5	35	44
Birmingham Heartlands	April 1992	1,000	Run-down industrial area, including former gas and electricity sites, 25% derelict or under-used	12,000	na	na	na
Plymouth	April 1993	na	Former naval victualising yard, former RAF base and adjoining land	na	na	na	na

Note: * Total following extension of areas in 1988
na–Not available
Source: *Financial Times*, September 18, 1992.

Each UDC has the objective of re-generating its designated area, in furtherance of which the UDC seeks:

(1) to bring land and buildings into effective use;
(2) to encourage the development of industry and commerce; and
(3) to ensure housing and social facilities are available to encourage people to live and work in its area.

UDC's have powers of compulsory purchase and are able to offer practical assistance and in some case financial assistance to private sector developers. Each UDC is the development control authority for its area. Particular emphasis is placed upon reclaiming and servicing land, renovating and re-using buildings, and providing adequate infrastructure; the overall objective is to encourage the development of land by the private sector, joint venture arrangements being actively encouraged. They enjoy considerable discretion as to how funds are allocated: government is by a small board appointed by the Secretary of State, typically including representatives of local authorities in the area and local property, industrial and business interests.

392

Local authorities

The general powers of local authorities to carry out reclamation works **9.07** derive from section 89(2) of the National Parks and Access to the Countryside Act 1949, as substituted by section 3 of the Derelict Land Act 1982. Under the sub-section, where it appears to local authorities that any land in their area:

(a) is derelict, neglected or unsightly; or
(b) is not derelict, neglected or unsightly but is likely to become so by reason of actual or apprehended collapse of the surface as the result of the carrying out of underground mining operations (other than for coal) which have ceased to be carried out,

the authority may carry out, for the purpose of reclaiming or improving that land or of enabling it to be brought into use, such works on that land or any other land as appear to them expedient.

The Welsh Development Agency

The Welsh Development Agency (WDA) was set up by the Welsh **9.08** Development Agency Act 1985.[21] It is administered though seven Welsh regional offices and its overall function is to assist in the regeneration of the Welsh economy and the improvement of the environment of Wales, *i.e.*:[22]

(a) to further the economic development of Wales or any part of Wales and in the connection to provide, maintain or safeguard employment;
(b) to promote industrial efficiency and international competitiveness in Wales; and
(c) to further the improvement of the environment in Wales, having regard to existing amenity.

The Welsh Development Agency has similar powers of reclamation, together with power to pay grants to any person and to acquire land compulsorily by agreement under section 16 of the Welsh Development Agency Act 1975, as substituted by section 2 of the Derelict Land Act 1982.

Its functions include the provision of finance to industry or prospective industry, the provision and management of industrial sites, and the restoration or improvement of derelict land.[23] Since the WDA's activities

---

[21] As amended by the Industry Act 1980 and Welsh Development Agency Acts 1988 and 1991.
[22] S.1(2).
[23] See s.16.

include the building of factories and industrial estates, land reclamation and the provision of investment capital, it plays a very significant role in the remediation of contaminated land. Its funding comes from Treasury funds through the Welsh Office; the most important source of funding for reclamation projects is grant-in-aid. The WDA also maintains a rolling programme of approved local authority reclamation projects.

The "Action for Cities" Initiative

9.09   The Government's "Action for Cities" initiative was launched in March 1988. Its various aspects are usefully summarised in the Department of Environment's Guide to *Grants in Urban Areas*.[24] This guide states the aim of the programme as:

"to bring new hope and a better quality of life to our inner cities."

The initiative covers a range of programmes administered by different Government departments, but the main urban regeneration grant regimes and programmes are currently under the aegis of the Department of Environment pending the Urban Regeneration Agency becoming operational. Programmes under the Action for Cities initiative are co-ordinated by the Action for Cities Co-ordination Unit (ACCU) at the Department of Environment, 2 Marsham Street, London SW1P 3EB (telephone 071–276–44427). A number of the instruments within the initiative are of a general nature, for example the enterprise zone experiment and registers of unused and under-used land. Those with the most obvious potential relevance to contaminated land reclamation are:

1. derelict land grant (not confined to urban areas and pre-dating the Action for Cities Initiative);
2. city grant;
3. urban development corporations;
4. city action teams;
5. urban programme; and
6. city challenge.

In terms of hard cash, the significant measures are derelict land grant and city grant, both of which will be administered by the Urban Regeneration Agency. Even the urban development corporations, who have wide ranging powers to allocate their financial resources as they see fit, are required by their guidance to endeavour to operate analogues of the DLG and city grant regimes when providing grant assistance to the private sector.[25]

[24] Department of Environment, October 1991.
[25] Mark White: "Contaminated Land, Can Grants be the Answer?," Estates Gazette (1993), Issue 9318, p. 100.

394

In relation to both forms of grant it should be noted that there is no statutory "right" to the grant and that in both cases there are budgetary constraints on the amount available in each year.

Derelict Land Grant: legal basis

The basis of derelict land grant is the Derelict Land Act 1982. Section **9.10** 1 of this Act empowers the Secretary of State to make grants in respect of "relevant expenditure" where it appears in relation to land to which the section applies that steps should be taken for the purpose of:

1. reclaiming or improving the land; or
2. enabling the land to be brought into use.

The power applies to:

(a) land which is derelict, neglected or unsightly; and
(b) in relation to a local authority in whose area it is situated, land which is not derelict, neglected or unsightly but is likely to become so by reason of actual or apprehended collapse of the surface as the result of the carrying out of underground coal mining operations.

"Relevant expenditure" is defined as meaning any expenditure which is incurred, with the approval of the Secretary of State, in or in connection with:

(i) the carrying out of the purposes of reclaiming or improving the land or enabling it to be brought into use, of any works on the land or any other land;
(ii) the carrying out of a survey of such land for determining whether any works for such purposes should be undertaken (whether or not such works are carried out ultimately); and
(iii) in relation to a local authority in whose area the land is situated, the acquisition for such purposes, of that land or any other land.

DLG is available in two forms:

(a) local authority—available in all areas; and
(b) non-local authority—available generally outside the 57 Urban Programme Areas (see below) and within those areas for schemes which are not eligible for City Grant.

The aim of DLG is to reclaim derelict land to a state in which it is capable of development, or has amenity value or contributes to nature or historic conservation. The basis of calculation is quite different from city grant, in that DLG is paid to offset all or part of the net loss on a project—the difference between the cost of the works and the increment in value of the reclaimed land.

The most recent research report on the subject concludes that DLG has been effective and has provided good value for money; most of the sites reclaimed to hard end-use standards have gone on to attract development projects and where development has occurred it has been achieved at over twice the speed for other vacant urban land.[25a]

Derelict Land Grant Policy

9.11   Derelict land grant policy is contained in Department of Environment Derelict Land Grant Advice Note 1:[26] the note sets out changes to the priorities and objectives of the derelict land grant programme and the changes and enhancements in its operation. Paragraph 1 of DLGA 1 states that:

> "The Government attaches high priority to the reclamation of derelict land. The legacy of dereliction arising from past industrial and extractive activity represents a significant waste of a vital national resource. Current policies are designed to encourage the return of derelict land to a beneficial use as soon as possible."

Paragraph 11 of DLGA 1 refers to the previous policy of directing DLG towards inner cities and the priority given to hard end use reclamation schemes; however, the Government's intention is now to allow a greater degree of flexibility in project selection, enabling the worst dereliction to be treated first wherever it is found and the land to be reclaimed for the most appropriate end use.[27] Paragraph 13 specifically refers to sites contaminated by industrial development and accepts that there is a need to make faster progress in dealing with contamination, subject to the constraints of resources available to the DLG programme as a whole.

The following operational objectives are stated to apply to the use of DLG, within the context of the planning policies and reclamation strategies of local authorities:[28]

>   (a)   Local authorities should, wherever possible, develop a strategic approach to reclamation involving both private and voluntary sectors;[29]

[25a] "Assessment of the Effectiveness of Derelict Land Grant in Reclaiming Land for Development" (1994).

[26] May 1991, replacing Circ. 38/85.

[27] See, for example the scheme for reclaiming a 31 acre chemical tip at Leeds Road, Huddersfield, mainly for public open space with the aid of a £511,880 grant: Action for Cities News Release YH/375/89, December 4, 1989. See also para. 9.12 on the relationship between DLG and site clean-up.

[28] DLGA 1, para. 17.

[29] See *The Strategic Approach To Derelict Land Reclamation*, HMSO (Johnson, Martin, Pierce and Simmons) 1992.

(b) In urban and urban fringe areas reclamation strategies should place emphasis on both economic regeneration and environmental improvements. Priority should be given to schemes intended to recycle land for development where this will reduce pressure on green-field sites and where there is a clear demonstration of sufficient demand for development either at present or in the forseeable future; reclamation for amenity use or environmental improvement can also be supported where such a use is designed to enhance the attractiveness of an area for residents, employees and investors;

(c) In rural areas emphasis should be placed on reclamation in areas of particularly high scenic quality, on nature conservation value, and on schemes to foster development;

(d) In carrying out reclamation schemes, emphasis should be placed on the need to secure maximum effectiveness, efficiency and economy; to deal effectively with any contamination present and where appropriate demonstrate new clean-up methods; to guarantee the maintenance of land after reclamation; and secure the early realisation of the intended end use.

The Government still adheres to its classic definition of derelict land for DLG operational purposes as:[30]

"Land so damaged by industrial or other development that it is incapable of beneficial use without treatment."

The guidance also refers to local authority reclamation strategies and rolling programmes and to the changes made in relation to the rules for DLG assistance to private sector land owners and for the voluntary sector.

Paragraphs 26–29 of the guidance address the relationship of derelict land grant with City Grant. It is pointed out that since the introduction of City Grant in 1988, DLG has generally not been available to bodies other than local authorities for reclamation schemes in the 57 Urban Programme areas.[31] The Government is aware that there are some schemes which would have previously qualified for DLG but, for a number of reasons, are not eligible to receive assistance under City Grant; non-local authority DLG has therefore been re-introduced into the Urban Programme as from May 1991, subject to the proviso that applications will not be entertained where the reclamation is part of a private sector project including a planned end use development falling within the eligibility criteria for City Grant. Such schemes must first be

---

[30] See DLGA 3: *The Operation of the Derelict Land Grant Scheme* (2nd ed.), July 1993, para. 6.
[31] See para. 9.16 below.

397

appraised under the City Grant procedures and DLG support will be available in exceptional circumstances only. Local authority DLG continues to be available in the Urban Programme areas.

The guidance also clarifies the relationship between DLG and Urban Programme Grant: DLG is the only local authority grant employed to assist the reclamation of sites designated as derelict. Urban Programme Grant can be made available for additional works such as landscaping and environmental improvements on already reclaimed derelict land; UPG also remains available for improvement works on vacant sites not defined as derelict for the purposes of DLG.

Finally, the Annex to the guidance provides useful clarification of the attitude of the DoE towards works eligible for grant: those works are such as the Department is satisfied are required for the purpose of reclamation, depending on the particular circumstances and nature of the scheme. As a general guide, this will include the works necessary to bring the site to the equivalent of a green-field state; for grant purposes the definition of green-field state for schemes with a "hard" after-use is:

> "A site which either has the bearing capacity of surrounding non-derelict land or a bearing capacity of 80 kN per square metre whichever is the lesser. 80 kN is equivalent to three quarter ton per square foot and is sufficient for warehousing and light industrial development. For environmental schemes a lower load bearing capacity may well be acceptable."

Derelict Land Grant and Contaminated Land

9.12   DLG has always been used for rectifying common forms of contamination: the most extensive areas of derelict land revealed by the DoE Survey of April 1988 included many with contaminative potential such as disused spoil heaps, iron and steel works, chemical plants, abandoned railways and military installations.[32] However, recent years have seen an increased emphasis on rectifying contamination, and the regional reports forming part of the Department of Environment's five year report on the DLG system 1988–92[33] give an interesting indication of the types of schemes where clean-up has been funded by DLG.

---

[32] *Survey of Derelict Land in England* 1988 (HMSO).
[33] *Derelict Land Grant: Development and Achievement Report 1988–92*, DoE (HMSO, 1993).

Region	Scheme	Details
North West	Chemstar Site, Tameside	Former chemical solvent recovery plant destroyed by fire and explosion in 1981. Contamination by solvents, benzene, PCBs which were found to be migrating from site. £0.75 million spent on surveys and appraisal; £1.3 million on removal/incineration of PCBs, removal of other chemicals, installation of barriers to migration.
South West	Various	Typically involve reclamation of sites contaminated with mine spoil and high concentrations of metals, *e.g.* arsenic, copper.
South East	Winchester	Grant of around £0.1 million to Bryant Homes/Portman Houses Ltd. to reclaim former landfill with high levels of methane for community centre and playing fields.
Eastern	Kelvedon, Essex	Small grant to help with removal of underground infrastructure and contamination on former gasworks site; intended for car showroom.
Merseyside	Vine Chemical Works, Halton	£3 million scheme for disused works and chemical waste heap; eight hectare site prepared for major retail extension to town centre.
Merseyside	Foundry Land, Widnes	County Council scheme to reclaim 21 hectares of land contaminated with chemical waste; laboratories and offices costing £2.5 million constructed on part of site.
West Midlands	Burbury Brickworks, Birmingham	Grant of £0.43 million for eight hectare site containing marl hole filled to depth of 20 metres with methane-generating domestic and industrial waste. Methane barrier and gas dispersion system. Site reclaimed for industry and public open space.
West Midlands	Snailbeach Lead Mine, Shropshire	Mine in area of outstanding natural beauty, worked for lead from early 1800s to 1911. Problems included contaminated by heavy metals, dominated by huge spoil heap,

Region	Scheme	Details
West Midlands—*cont*		known as the "White Tip" containing 250,000 cm. metres of material including lead, zinc, calcite and barytes. Intended to create pasture land/open space with conservation of listed buildings. £0.3 million approved for surveys/ feasibility study.
West Midlands	Burton Road, Dudley	30 hectare site; largest scheme in West Midlands. In course of reclamation by Dudley Metropolitan Borough Council for residential, public open space, playing fields. Includes filled and contaminated land as well as shallow coal workings, mine shafts and derelict building. Overall estimated cost of £6.5 million; DoE to receive "substantial payment" of aftervalue.
East Midlands	Corby Steelworks	Significant areas of heavily contaminated land to be reclaimed mainly for recreational amenity afteruses.
Yorkshire & Humberside	Thornton Road Gasworks, Bradford	One hectare site reclaimed at cost of £0.63 million for industrial use; mix of chemical, biological and engineering techniques.
Yorkshire & Humberside	Hickson & Welch site, Wakefield	Small clearance schemes by Wakefield Groundwork Trust; clearance of derelict railway line with disused gas installations.

Advice note DLGA 3[34] provides guidance on the costs eligible for grant, *e.g.* treatment of mineshaft and adits, canals, mills and industrial chimneys. The following specific guidance is offered on contaminated land and closed landfill sites:[35]

(1) Grant may be paid on the costs of treating contaminated land where such treatment forms part of a scheme for the reclamation of a derelict site and no one has an enforceable responsibility for dealing with the contamination. Typical works may include the "in situ" or otherwise on-site treatment of contaminated soils, liquids or semi-liquids, or their removal; the import-

[34] (2nd ed.), July 1993; See Annex A.
[35] *Ibid.*, paras. 27–30, replacing paras. 35 and 36 of DGLA 1.

400

ation and spreading of suitable capping materials; and the installation of vents and sealing, and special drains and membranes. Special foundations to resist the effects of contaminants, and work necessary to extinguish spoil tip fires caused by spontaneous combustion are also eligible for grant.

(2) The cost of works to deal with the effects of landfill gas arising from closed landfill sites is also eligible for grant on the same basis. In both cases consideration will be given to grant-aiding, as part of the reclamation scheme, works carried out on adjacent land which are necessary to prevent leachate or gas migrating from the reclaimed site. It is not necessary for the adjacent land to be in a derelict condition.

(3) Works to treat contaminated land and to deal with landfill gas which are not associated with a reclamation scheme will not be accepted for DLG, but local authorities may be eligibile for supplementary credit approvals (SCAs) to fund investigation and treatment under a special programme operated by the Department. These SCAs are available for works on sites formerly subject to a contaminative use which were redeveloped or abandoned before the problems of contamination could reasonably have been foreseen, or where the contamination results from a contaminative activity elsewhere. Sites which are still in contaminative use will not be eligible. Nor will works which form part of a commercial development, or a project which has been approved for DLG.

(4) Priority will be given to sites where preliminary sampling or site investigation indicates a significant risk to human health or the environment. Applications must show that the works proposed will ensure that the site will be made safe for its current use and that any threats to health or the environment are effectively dealt with. The SCA programme is intended primarily for local authority-owned sites but applications for sites which an authority considers it has a legal obligation to treat will also be considered.

Most importantly, it should be noted that the DoE applies the "polluter pays principle" when considering grant applications. There will therefore be a general presumption against paying grant to the person responsible for creating the dereliction.[36]

---

[36] *Ibid.*, para. 50.

Derelict Land Grant: availability and restrictions

9.13 The availability of DLG depends on the applicant, the general position being summarised as follows[37]:

(a) Local authorities may receive grant on the full range of eligible reclamation activities;

(b) Non local authority bodies may receive grant on a similar range of activities but with certain exceptions. For example they cannot receive grant for the treatment of land liable to subsidence; nor on some costs such as land acquisition;

(c) Voluntary bodies, unlike other non-local authority bodies, may receive grant towards costs of reclamation work carried out on private land. They may also receive grant for small clearance schemes on neglected or unsightly land whether or not they own the land.

Some types of reclamation work fall outside the scope of DLG and are not normally eligible for grant. The following are typical examples given in DLG Advice Note 3:[38]

(i) reclamation of marshland, moorland, mud flats, degenerate farmland or woodlands, or other under-utilised land which has never previously been developed;

(ii) reclamation of naturally unstable land, for example land subject to landslides;

(iii) reclamation of land in active and permanent use unless it is required in connection with a grant-aided reclamation scheme;

(iv) reclamation work which is part of a redevelopment scheme on non-derelict land;

(v) reclamation of mineral workings, waste tips, or landfill sites which are covered by enforceable restoration conditions or other arrangements providing for rehabilitation; and

(vi) reclamation schemes where the applicant intends to use waste products produced by his own industrial process.

There are also a number of general principles applied by the Department which may have the effect of restricting availability of grant. The "polluter pays principle" mentioned above[39] is one such, but others are:[40]

(1) Grant will not be paid where there is an existing enforceable responsibility for the land's reinstatement or rehabilitation, for

---

[37] DLGA 3, para. 13.
[38] *Ibid.*, para. 14.
[39] See para. 9.12 above.
[40] DGLA 3, paras. 51–56.

example where restoration was made a condition of the planning permission for the development which led to the dereliction; or where the land is subject to a formal reclamation agreement;

(2) In other cases the Department will wish to establish that the derelictor is willing to contribute towards the reclamation of the land by direct action by cash contribution, or by transferring the land at no cost to the grant applicant;

(3) If the Department is satisfied that the owner has no enforceable duty to restore the land, and that all practicable steps have been taken to identify the derelictor and make him contribute towards reclamation, grant may be approved subject to value for money being achieved. The Department may in exceptional cases agree to pay grant to a derelictor, but only where the reclamation would bring benefits of the kind described at point (5) below;

(4) Grant is not payable on profitable reclamation schemes, that is where the cost of reclaiming the land is estimated to be less than the increase in the value of the reclaimed site prior to the development (this does not include potentially profitable local authority schemes with a private development end use). The Department will carry out a full appraisal of non-local authority schemes to satisfy itself that reclamation would not proceed in the absence of grant: planning permission at least in outline form must have been given for such schemes. The land values used to assess the grant payable (if any) will be based on the open market values of the land to be reclaimed, before and after reclamation. The value of the land before reclamation will be assessed on the basis that grant is not payable. No account will be taken of any higher price which the applicant may have paid for the derelict land;

(5) Grant is not payable to non-local authority applicants where reclamation would have no wider economic, environmental or public safety benefit. To be acceptable for grant, proposals must involve the provision of new land for industry, commerce or housing, or the improvement of the amenity of an area, either by the provision of recreational land or other open space, or by the removal of dangers to the public;

(6) Grant is not normally payable for reclamation work on land which the applicant does not own. The applicant must hold the freehold or a long least (at least 30 years to run in the case of local authorities; 7 years for other applicants). However local authorities and voluntary bodies may in some cases receive grant for work carried out on private land, as described below.

403

Derelict Land Grant: amount

9.14 The expenditure which may be recompensed under derelict land grant is that for the carrying out of reclamation and improvement works, carrying out surveys for determining whether work should be undertaken and, in the case of local authorities, the cost of acquiring the land. The Government's information note on DLG for applicants other than local authorities refers to the following types of expenditure which may be approved:

(a) the cost of reclamation works necessary to bring the site to a greenfield state;

(b) approved costs incurred in carrying out a survey of derelict land;

(c) consultants' fees and legal expenses incurred in carrying out the works;

(d) administrative expenditure incurred in designing and carrying out reclamation schemes; and

(e) costs incurred in ensuring that vegetation planted in the reclaimed land becomes properly established.

The information note states that grant is payable on the net loss incurred by the freeholder or leaseholder (with at least seven years left to run) in carrying out reclamation works approved in advance by the Department. The net loss is determined by off-setting the approved total expenditure by the increased value of the land attributable to reclamation. An example is as follows:

(A) cost of reclamation works £500,000;

(B) value of site before reclamation £650,000;

(C) value of site after reclamation but before development £800,000;

(D) increased value of site (C–B) £150,000;

(E) eligibility of grant (A–D) £350,000;

(F) grant payable (50 per cent. of E) £175,000.

The percentage of expenditure recoverable under the grant varies depending upon the nature of the applicant and the location of the derelict land.[41]

In Assisted Areas and Derelict Land Clearance Areas grant is paid to local authorities and the English Industrial Estates Corporation at a rate of 100 per cent., and to bodies other than local authorities at 80 per cent. Outside these areas the grant rate is 50 per cent. for both local authorities and others, except that in national parks and areas of outstanding natural beauty local authorities may receive 75 per cent. grants.[42]

[41] Derelict Land Grant Act 1982, s.1(5).
[42] DGLA 1, Annex, para. 3.

Derelict Land Grant: mechanics of application

Application for derelict land grant is currently made to the appropriate **9.15**
regional office of the Department of Environment in whose area the site is
situated as listed below. General information on the procedure, and
information notes providing guidance for applicants, may be obtained from:
Department of the Environment
Minerals and Land Reclamation Division
Room C16/06
2 Marsham Street
London SW1P 3EB
Telephone: 071–276–04597

Regional Offices

NORTHERN REGIONAL OFFICE
Wellbar House, Gallowgate, Newcastle-Upon-Tyne NE1 4TX
Tel: 091–232–7545 Ext 2563

NORTH WEST REGIONAL OFFICE
Sunley Tower, Piccadilly Plaza, Manchester M1 4BE
Tel: 061–832–9111
  Lancashire: Ext 2431,
  Cheshire: Ext 2433,
  Cumbria: Ext 2436,
  Greater Manchester: Ext 2428

MERSEYSIDE TASK FORCE (inc. Ellesmere Port and
Neston Borough Council and Halton Borough Council)
Graeme House, Derby Square, Liverpool L2 7SU
Tel: 051–227–4111 Ext 2320

YORKSHIRE & HUMBERSIDE REGIONAL OFFICE
City House, New Station Street, Leeds LS1 4JD
Tel: 0532–438232
  South Yorkshire: Ext 2299,
  North and West Yorkshire, and Humberside: Ext 2301

WEST MIDLANDS REGIONAL OFFICE
Five Ways Tower, Frederick Road, Birmingham B15 1ST
Tel: 921–626–2000 Ext 2576

EAST MIDLANDS REGIONAL OFFICE
Cranbrook House, Cranbrook Street, Nottingham NG1 1FB
Tel: 0602–476121 Ext 304

SOUTH WEST REGIONAL OFFICE
Tollgate House, Houlton Street, Bristol BS2 9DJ
Tel: 0272–218171 or 218172

EASTERN REGIONAL OFFICE
Heron House, 49–51 Goldington Road, Bedford MK40 3LL
Tel: 0602–350062

SOUTH EAST REGIONAL OFFICE
Charles House, 375 Kensington High Street, London W14 8QH
Tel: (071) 605–9000

LONDON REGIONAL OFFICE
Millbank Tower, 21/24 Millbank, London
SW1P 4QU
Tel: (071) 217–4568

It is particularly important to discuss proposals for DLG schemes with the relevant regional office before starting work; this can also help to expedite the application when made.[43]

Application forms are available for, respectively, local authority applicants, applicants other than local authorities, and for small clearance schemes for neglected or unsightly land. Information will be required about the nature of the scheme and the scheme location, including whether the site presents any particular problems such as spoil heaps, industrial or chemical waste tips or military land. Supporting plans, specifications, bills of quantities, planning reports, site survey reports and valuations.[44] The effects of the site in its present condition, such as risk of toxicity to animals, contamination of adjacent land, and depression of surrounding land values, etc., will need to be categorised as low, medium or high. The benefits and objectives of the scheme will also need to be categorised in this way. Applications are considered having regard to local needs, and consultation with the relevant local authority. For private sector schemes the position regarding site ownership and planning permission (detailed or outline) will need to have been resolved before submitting an application.

It is normal practice to require reclamation works to be carried out after competitive tendering, with at least three tenders being required; the Department will also monitor the schemes in progress, including preliminary, interim and final site inspections and examination of final contract accounts.[45] The grant is normally paid only after the scheme has been completed to the satisfaction of the Department, on submission of a claim for payment together with an auditor's certificate of expenditure. It may be possible, in exceptional cases, to agree the payment of periodic grant during the reclamation scheme, at the discretion of the Department. Grant is not affected by subsequent disposal of the reclaimed land, though the Department makes it a specific condition of approval that where land is being reclaimed by an applicant who intends to develop it for freehold or leasehold disposal then, if it is not disposed of or used within three years, grant will be repayable in full.

[43] DGLA 3, para. 108.
[44] *Ibid.*, para. 109.
[45] *Ibid.*, para. 112.

City Grant

The general intention behind City Grant (which was introduced in **9.16**
May 1988) was to replace Urban Development Grants and Urban
Regeneration Grants in the areas of the 57 local authorities within the
Urban Programme, namely:

1. Barnsley
2. Birmingham
3. Blackburn
4. Bolton
5. Bradford
6. Brent
7. Bristol
8. Burnley
9. Coventry
10. Derby
11. Doncaster
12. Dudley
13. Gateshead
14. Greenwich
15. Hackney
16. Halton
17. Hammersmith and Fulham
18. Harringay
19. Hartlepool
20. Islington
21. Kensington and Chelsea
22. Kingston upon Hull
23. Kirklees
24. Knowsley
25. Lambeth
26. Lainbaurgh
27. Leeds
28. Leicester
29. Lewisham
30. Liverpool
31. Manchester
32. Middlesborough
33. Newcastle
34. Newham
35. North Tyneside
36. Nottingham
37. Oldham
38. Plymouth
39. Preston
40. Rochdale
41. Rotherham
42. St. Helens
43. Salford
44. Sandwell
45. Sefton
46. Sheffield
47. South Tyneside
48. Southwark
49. Stockton-on-Tees
50. Sunderland
51. Tower Hamlets
52. Walsall
53. Wandsworth
54. Wigan
55. Wirral
56. Wolverhampton
57. Wrekin

In theory, City Grant is available throughout England, but in practice
it is confined to:

(a) City Challenge areas (see below); and
(b) the 57 areas named above.

The general purpose is to support private sector capital projects which
benefit run-down urban areas in the city areas and which because of
their inner city site or location, cannot proceed without assistance. It

aims to bridge the gap between estimated costs and values of a project while allowing a developer to make a reasonable profit. It is confined to England and different arrangements apply in Scotland and Wales.

The general enabling power to pay City Grant is provided by Part III of the Housing and Planning Act 1986, and grant is payable at the discretion of the Secretary of State. General guidance as to policies and priorities in considering applications for assistance is contained in the Department of Environment *City Grant Guidance Notes*;[46] these notes however offer only general introductory advice; and specific advice on particular proposals should be obtained from the Department of Environment Regional·Offices, the Urban Programme Authorities, or (where applicable) the relevant Urban Development Corporation.

City Grant is limited to projects undertaken by the private sector, by which the Department means those funded by the private sector and in respect of which the private sector bears the risk; the grant is intended to encourage genuine new private sector investment rather than to provide an alternative source of funds for public sector projects. It is available to support capital investment in developing land and buildings and is normally confined to large schemes with a capital value on completion of over £500,000.[47] Priority is given to applications from within core urban areas to which the Urban Programme relates well; if outside the core area, the project must be shown to contribute directly to the economic and physical regeneration of the inner city. It is also available for projects in Urban Development Corporation areas, in which case application is made direct to the UDC rather than the Department of the Environment.

The scheme must be one which is unable to proceed without a grant, because costs (including reasonable profit) exceed values resulting from inner city locations. The intention is to bridge the gap between development costs and end value: *i.e.* sale value, capitalised rent, or value of the project to the business in the case of some types of business development. The project must also generate new private investment which would not otherwise occur in the area and should be capable of making a significant impact on the area without displacing existing investment; for example by providing jobs or private sector housing. Most projects will use derelict or long-vacant land or empty buildings.

The procedure begins by informal discussions with the regional office of the Department, or with the UDC, followed by formal application on a standard form. Projects are appraised in terms of their practical feasibility, the amount of grant needed, the benefits of the grant, and

[46] (3rd ed.), January 1992.
[47] Those with lower values may be eligible for support from the Urban Programme; see para. 9.19 below.

what abnormal costs or locational disadvantages make the grant necessary. Into this final category fall matters such as abnormal physical factors affecting the site, which may include dealing with contamination. The appraisal process, in addition to quantifiable benefits such as providing jobs and housing, also gives substantial weight to the environmental benefits of City Grant projects; these may include the removal of environmental nuisances and hazards, especially when these have impacts beyond the site boundary. Such benefits may often compensate for poor gearing or high costs per job or dwelling, and as such may help to justify the offer of grant.

Grant will be paid under a legal agreement between the Secretary of State, the developer and possibly a guarantor; a model legal agreement is annexed to the City Grant Guidance Notes. The relationship between City Grant and Derelict Land Grand is considered above.[48]

General details of the City Grant Scheme may be obtained from the Department of Environment, Inner Cities Directorate, Room P2/127, 2 Marsham Street, London SW1P 3EB; telephone: 071–276–4507. Details of schemes in receipt of City Grant may be obtained from the DoE press notices which are published in each case giving the identity of the developer, a brief description of the development and the amount of City Grant involved. For example, News Release 822 of December 8, 1992 announced a £35.5 million grant for Manchester's Victoria Olympic Arena, the largest grant so far made and estimated as likely to generate nearly £200 million private sector investment.

City Grant and Derelict Land Grant compared

As mentioned above,[49] it may well be that in due course DLG and City **9.17** Grant are assimilated within a single scheme to be administered by the Urban Regeneration Agency. Whereas DLG is available generally, City Grant is in practice currently available only in the 57 designated areas and is limited to large projects with private sector investment. DLG is available for large and small projects by the public, private or voluntary sector, but within the 57 designated areas will not generally be available for private sector projects which could qualify for City Grant.[50]

From a commercial perspective, the schemes as they currently stand can be contrasted as follows:[51]

1. Unless there is some legal obligation to rectify contamination, DLG is not a viable option to a developer seeking a financial

---

[48] See para. 9.11 above.
[49] See para. 9.09.
[50] See para. 9.16.
[51] "Contaminated Land: Can Grants be the Answer?" Mark White [1993] *Estates Gazette*, Issue 9318, p. 100.

return on assets. It may be appropriate when governing factors are not related to maximisation of profits;

2. If an end use can be identified which meets the relevant criteria, City Grant offers far better opportunities for a return or investment. However, the magnitude of the risk is also greater and a very careful feasibility analysis is required;

3. Substantial access to private funding is required to take advantage of City Grant.

City Action Teams

9.18   The government has created nine City Action Teams ("CATs") which bring together Government departments, local authorities, business people, community groups and voluntary organisations working in inner city areas. Such teams have been established for:

1. London
2. Nottingham/Leicester
3. Derby
4. Liverpool
5. Manchester
6. Birmingham
7. Newcastle-upon-Tyne
8. Leeds/Bradford
9. Cleveland

They are co-ordinated by the action for Cities Co-ordination Unit at the Department of Environment (ACCU). Further information may be obtained from ACCU at:

> Action for Cities Co-ordination Unit
> Department of Environment
> Room P2/101
> 2 Marsham Street
> London SW1P 3EB
> Tel: 071–276–3053

CATs have a small budget to help support local projects and may support by direct funding schemes which safeguard or create jobs, improve the environment, provide training places or encourage enterprise and the growth of business. There are no strict criteria for eligibility, with each proposal being judged on its merits.

Urban Programme

9.19   The Urban Programme is designed to help tackle the economic, environmental and social problems of urban areas by supporting a range of projects submitted by eligible local authorities.[52] In particular, its

---

[52] See list at para. 9.16.

funding may enable local authorities to make assistance available for private sector projects which contribute to the economic development of inner city areas. These can include grants for environmental improvements such as landscaping, the conversion of existing industrial or commercial buildings, and site preparation. As mentioned above,[53] this form of support may be useful for projects of an insufficiently large scale to qualify for City Grant.

Applications for assistance under the Urban Programme are made to the relevant local authority, which assesses the application and pays the grant.

City Challenge

City Challenge is a relatively new initiative introduced in 1991, which **9.20** aims to concentrate resources on key neighbourhoods over several years. In the pilot launch of the initiative in May 1991, the Secretary of State for the Environment selected eleven "pacemaker" areas to work up detailed plans for regeneration. The relevant authorities are:

1. Bradford
2. Dearne Valley (Barnsley, Doncaster and Rotherham)
3. Lewisham
4. Liverpool
5. Manchester
6. Middlesborough
7. Newcastle-upon-Tyne
8. Nottingham
9. Tower Hamlets
10. Wirral
11. Wolverhampton

Some £82.5 million a year is available over five years in respect of those authorities, which were selected after competition.[54] Each authority, working with the relevant DoE City Action Team, must prepare detailed projects and targets which, when agreed, will result in an implementation agreement with each authority setting out what must be achieved each year.

A new round of City Challenge is intended to be launched for 1993–94, which will be open to all 57 authorities falling within the Urban Programme.[55]

---

[53] See para. 9.16.
[54] Action for Cities News Releases No. 335 (May 23, 1991) and 474 (July 31, 1991).
[55] See para. 9.16 above.

411

City Grant is available to support private sector development projects in City Challenge areas: there are a number of variations to the normal city grant procedures in such cases.[56] In particular, in City Challenge areas local authorities may take a risk-bearing share (not exceeding 20 per cent.) in the developer, using money, guarantees or land as their stake. Additionally, where the City Challenge initiative is being implemented by a private sector led partnership (with any public sector impact being limited to the above local authority share) the partnership may itself be an applicant for city grant. If a City Challenge partnership wishes to support a private sector project, then this will normally need to be included within the Action Plan; in some cases the project may be too big or too uncertain in its timing for accurate estimation of the grant and in such cases the project should still be included in the action plan for consideration as a candidate for additional support from the Department of Environment's main city grant programme.

Information on unused and under-used land

9.21   Prior to 1989, the Department of Environment maintained a central register of unused and under-used land ruled by local authorities.[57] Circular 18/89 expressed the Government's view that maintaining such information and rendering it available to the public was more properly the reponsibility of local authorities. The Circular issued a Code of Practice[58] under the Secretary of State's powers under section 2(2) of the Local Government Planning and Land Act 1980: it applies to local authorities at all levels and applies to unused or under-used land of at least 0.1 hectare (0.25 acre) in area in which an authority or a subsidiary of an authority holds a freehold interest or a leasehold interest with seven years or more to run.

The code requires each authority to maintain a register of all land in its ownership to which, at March 31 in each year, the code applies; information must also be made available each year to regional offices of the Department and a plan of the land concerned must be made available to any member of the public on request. Statutory force has now been given to these obligations by the Local Government (Publication of Information About Unused and Under-used Land) (England) Regulations 1992).[59]

A parallel Code of Practice to that applying to local authorities has been issued to provide guidance to certain other public bodies, Govern-

---

[56] Annex D to City Grant Guidance Note, 1992 Edition (December 1991).
[57] Under s.95 of the Local Government, Planning and Land Act 1980.
[58] Circ. 18/89, Annex.
[59] S.I. 1992 No. 73.

ment department and other public holders of crown land.[60] These include development and urban development corporations, the Commission for the New Towns, the Housing Corporation, the Civil Aviation Authority, British Coal Corporation, the BBC, the Independent Broadcasting Agency, the Post Office, British Waterways Board, British Rail, London Regional Transport, Passenger Transport Executives and the National Rivers Authority.

Financial Assistance: New Technologies

The Department of Trade and Industry's Environment Unit offers a **9.22** wide range of assistance for businesses in effecting environmental improvements. The address of the Unit is:

> Environment Unit
> Department of Trade and Industry
> 151 Buckingham Palace Road
> London SW1W 9SS.

The unit offers an Environmental Helpline based at Warren Spring Laboratory which may be contacted on (0800) 585794. Alternatively the relevant DTI regional office, Scottish Office or Welsh Office are able to offer advice.

Three environmental technology schemes currently operate which may have relevance to contaminated land issues;

> (1) The Environmental Technology Innovation Scheme (ETIS);
> (2) Eureka Euroenviron; and
> (3) The DTI Environmental Management Option Scheme (Demos).

Environmental Technology Innovation Scheme

ETIS is a scheme set up by the Department of Trade and Industry **9.23** and the Department of the Environment to promote technological advances in the environmental field by encouraging innovation, improving environmental standards and assisting users or suppliers of environmental technology to become more competitive. The scheme in general aims to support collaborative research projects although in some cases support is available for single companies. It covers research into techniques, processes, materials or equipment in the areas of cleaner technologies, re-cycling, waste or effluent treatment and disposal and environmental monitoring: all projects must involve research of an

[60] Circ. 18/89, para. 5.

innovative nature. There are also a number of closely defined "priority areas" where the Government foresees a particular need for higher regulatory standards and where technology to meet those standards is not yet available at an acceptable cost; projects falling within such areas may be classified as "standards related". The significance of this designation is that single companies may in certain circumstances be eligible for funding where the project is standards related: in other cases the project must bc consortium based to qualify for funding. Companies wishing to collaborate but without any potential collaborators may make a first stage application and, if a project is found to be suitable, the ETIS office will assist in finding appropriate partners through its network of contacts. Eligible organisations are any UK firms, foreign owned firms with established research and manufacturing operations in the UK, UK research and technology organisations, UK higher educational institutions and research council laboratories. Public sector bodies such as local authorities and nationalised industries may participate but will not normally qualify for support.

Assessment of applications is carried out according to the following criteria:

    (1) whether the project could go ahead without assistance or if it did, whether it would be significantly delayed or reduced in scale;

    (2) the feasibility of the proposed research; the extent to which the project is innovative;

    (3) how the project will prove the concept of the innovative technology; and

    (4) the extent to which the project offers value for money.

Amongst the "priority areas" currently designated within the scheme is "treatment of organic contaminants in soil".[61] The DTI brochure describing the scheme refers to the currently limited range of treatment methods available and the need for permanent solutions which detoxify harmful contaminants, preferably without requiring large scale transport of material for treatment: ETIS aims to fund basic industrial research up to proof of concept stage, into any innovative methods of treating persistent organic contaminants in soils and associated groundwater, in situ or otherwise on site.

Eureka

9.24 Eureka is a pan-European initiative to foster collaborative technology projects; it is industry led and concentrates on projects which companies feel are ripe for international exploitation. The scheme involves all the

---

[61] DoE News Release 528 (July 29, 1993) refers to a grant made under ETIS to assist research into a novel in situ treatment process for contaminated soils.

western European nations, including Iceland and Turkey. An important aspect of the programme is the promotion of European collaboration in environmental research through the Euroenviron Secretariat in Denmark;

> Aboulevard 13
> DK–1635
> Copenhagen V
> Tel: 010 4531394344

Information may also be obtained from the appointed consultants in the UK:

> Environmental Resources Limited
> Eaton House
> Wallbrook Court
> North Hinksey Lane
> Oxford
> OX2 0QS
> Tel: (0865) 793004

A number of the projects proposed include those relating to soil clean-up. For example in 1991 the Government helped to fund research in the IPDOCS project (in pulp detoxification of contaminated soils) through the Euroenviron Programme as a means of moving toxins such as lead, mercury and cyanide and also organic contaminants like oil and solvents.[62]

Demos

The Demos Scheme provides support for two types of project: **9.25**

   (1) collaborative projects proving the feasibility of adapted or new techniques; and

   (2) projects illustrating best practice based upon proven techniques.

Organisations eligible for support include any UK companies, foreign owned companies with established technological capability and manufacturing facilities in the UK, research and technology organisations, government research establishment and higher educational institutions. The types of funding which may be offered relate to project costs such as consultancies and equipment purchased (up to 50 per cent.) and, secondly, reasonable out of pocket expenses incurrerd in demonstrating the equipment, process or technique to parties of visitors.

Normally projects will require a consortium of three or more organisations, though in some circumstances two partners are acceptable. Where

---

[62] DTI Press Release P/91/224, April 16, 1991.

currently available technology is involved, applications may be considered from single companies who must be user rather than suppliers of the technology.

The scheme is administered by the Environment Unit of the DTI; information on this scheme may be obtained from the Unit, and initial queries may also be directed to DTI regional offices and the relevant departments in Scotland, Wales and Northern Ireland.

EUROPEAN COMMUNITY INITIATIVES

LIFE Programme

9.26   Council Regulation EEC No. 1973/92[63] establishes a financial instrument for the environment (LIFE).

The general objective of LIFE is to contribute to the development and implementation of Community environmental policy and legislation by financing priority environmental actions in the Community. The fields of action eligible for Community financial assistance are defined in the Annex to the Regulation and include "actions to establish and develop techniques for locating and restoring sites contaminated by hazardous waste and/or hazardous substances."[64]

Within these fields, Community financial assistance may be provided for actions which are of Community interest, contribute significantly to the implementation of Community environmental policy and meet the conditions for implementing the "polluter pays" principle; the assistance will cover, in particular, preparatory measures, demonstration schemes, awareness campaigns and actions providing incentives or technical assistance.[65] In general, the rate of Community assistance is subject to the following ceilings:[66]

- 30 per cent. of the cost in the case of actions involving the financing of income generating investments (the operator's contribution to financing being at least as much as the Community assistance);
- 100 per cent. of the cost of measures designed to provide the information necessary for the execution of an action and techni-

---

[63] O.J. No. L206/1, July 22, 1992.
[64] This follows the wording used in Council Regulation EEC No. 2242/87 on action by the Community relating to the environment (O.J. No. L207/8, July 29, 1987).
[65] Art. 2.
[66] Art. 8.

416

cal assistance measures implemented on the Commission's initiative;

- 50 per cent. of the cost of other actions.

Proposals for action to be financed are to be submitted to the Comission by the Member States, though the Commission may ask any legal or natural persons established in the Community to submit their own applications for assistance in respect of measures of particular interest to the Community by way of notice published in the Official Journal.[67]

Commission communication 92/C331/06[68] gives the priority actions for 1993 under the LIFE Programme in relation to contaminated sites as being:

"Demonstration projects for the rehabilitation of sites which have been contaminated by waste and/or hazardous substances."

All UK applications or transnational applications with a UK lead partner are to be submitted on an official DoE form available from:

Room A130
Romney House
43 Marsham Street
London SW1P 3PY
Telephone: 071 276 8114

Structural Funds

The Community currently operates three main structural funds offer- **9.27** ing financial assistance at regional level:

(1) the European Regional Development Fund (ERDF);
(2) the European Social Fund (ESF); and
(3) the European Agricultural Guidance and Guarantee Fund (EAGGF).

---

[67] Art. 9. An invitation to submit proposals relating to new clean technologies was issued under this provision in December 1992: Commission communication 92/C336/12, O.J. No. C336/12, December 19, 1992.
[68] O.J. No. C331/11, December 16, 1992.

417

Detailed consideration of the complex issue of structural funding is beyond the scope of this work;[69] at the present time the funds are in any event the subject of considerable discussion within the Community.[70]

Of the funds, the most immediately relevant to land reclamation schemes is probably the ERDF.[71] In particular the ERDF contributes towards the objectives specified in Regulation 2052/88[72]: amongst these is the "conversion of regions seriously affected by industrial decline." Between 1989–91 some 1510 million ECU was allocated to the UK under this objective.[73] The ERDF operates by way of regional development plans prepared by member states and covering a period of 3–5 years; these programmes describe the region in question and its envisaged development, indicating where Community support will be requested. This leads to Community Support Frameworks which set the general priorities for funding: these frameworks will have amongst their objectives the improvement of the environment. Assistance may take a variety of forms including Community programmes, national programmes of Community interest, and projects. Programmes and operations are determined on a case-by-case basis; the majority of initiatives take the form of multi-annual operational programmes.

Whilst these programmes may be an extremely important source of funding for land reclamation and decontamination schemes, the main purpose of intervention is angled towards the general economic development of regions.[74] There must be a clear and demonstrable link between the project and the industrial and economic development of the area concerned: assistance is available only to public authorities in the assisted areas designated by the Government. Nonetheless, such assistance may be of vital importance in securing clean up of contaminated industrial sites: in 1992 British Coal was reported to be seeking assistance from the fund in respect of land contaminated by former mining activities.[75] Little information is sent to the Commission on

[69] For further information see the EC's guide, *Grants and Loans from the European Community* and L. Kramer, *Focus on European Environmental Law* (1992) p. 91 ff.

[70] Recent developments include the proposed creation of the cohension fund to assist Spain, Greece, Portugal and Ireland in major transport infrastructure and environmental projects: Com (92) 339 O.J. No. C248/14, September 25, 1992—subsequently approved. Consideration is now also under way of the basic principles established by the 1988 reforms of the structural funds; in particular it may be anticipated that environmental inprovements and conservation should be given greater prominence in regional policy.

[71] Reg. No. 1787/84 O.J. No. L169/1, June 28, 1984; No. 4254/88 O.J. No. L374/15, December 31, 1988.

[72] O.J. No. L185/9, July 15, 1988.

[73] O.J. No. C159/80; see Kramer, *op. cit.*, p. 93.

[74] Kramer, *op. cit.*, p. 97.

[75] *Waste Environ. Today (News J.)* Vol. 5, No. 7, July 1992, p. 7.

individual projects within these programmes and the emphasis of providing information relates to financial checks rather than evaluation of environmental benefits.

New arrangements for the joint funding of reclamation schemes by DLG and ERDF funding came into effect from the beginning of the year 1993–94. They involve creating "funding packages" for new schemes and recycling the DLG paid on existing schemes which is displayed by ERDF money.[76] Responsibility for preparing such packages rests with local authorities in consultation with the Department of Environment and DLG Advice Note 3 contains illustrative examples of the composition of such packages.[77]

Other Mechanisms

Apart from the structural funds, other aspects of EC funding which **9.28** require brief mention are:

(1) Envireg

Under Regulation 4253/88[78] The Commission may suggest to member states that they should ask for financial assistance for actions of particular interest to the Community but not covered by regional development plans. The Commission, on this basis, decided on May 2, 1990 to establish a Community initiative contributing to protection of the environment and promoting economic development known as Envireg.[79] The scheme, which involves Community assistance in the form of loans and grants is provided for specified measures and in specified areas; the UK is not at present among those areas; nor is the clean-up of contaminated land amongst the current specified measures.[80]

(2) The European Investment Bank

The Bank (EIB) was established pursuant to Article 130 of the EC Treaty.[81] Its task is to contribute to the balanced development of the Community by granting medium or long-term loans for investment projects. Projects, including their environmental aspects, are thoroughly investigated.

[76] DGLA 3.
[77] *Ibid.*, Annex D.
[78] O.J. No. L374/1, December 31, 1988, art. 11.
[79] Notice 90/C115/03; O.J. No. C115/3, May 9, 1990.
[80] These are: water infrastructure, waste treatment, agricultural use of sewage compost and sludge and installations for ships' waste.
[81] See L. Kramer, *Focus on European Environmental Law* (1992) p. 102.

(3) The European Investment Fund

Proposals have been approved for the creation of a European Investment Fund (EIF) to be managed by the European Investment Bank; these proposals arose from the conclusions of the December 1992 Edinburgh Summit. The present intention is that the fund should be used in relation to infrastructure projects, *e.g.*, road and rail networks telecommunication and energy, and to guarantee loans to small and medium-sized firms.

The proposal will involve amending the statutes of the EIB and as such will require not only adoption by the Council, but also satisfaction by Member States.

Chapter 10

CONSULTANTS

Introduction

Professional advice from consultants in various fields of expertise may **10.01** be required in the context of contaminated land. Such services may be required as part of a transaction such as a purchase or company acquisition, or in the context of a scheme for clean-up or redevelopment. Many different specialist types of expertise may be relevant but the main areas are:

> geology
> geo-chemistry
> engineering
> chemical engineering
> hydrogeology
> groundwater hydrology
> soil science
> toxicology

Added to these areas, various specialisms may be relevant in certain cases, *e.g.*:

ecology	asbestos contracting
mining engineering	radiochemistry
industrial archaeology	explosives and ordnance
meteorology	gas control
landfill engineering	land reclamation
landscape engineering	

This chapter gives guidance as to the issues which can arise when commissioning consultants and other experts to carry out contaminated land investigations and appraisals.

Selection of consultant

There are hundreds of companies, firms and individuals which offer **10.02** "environmental consultancy" services of one type or another. Many factors will be relevant to the choice of consultant apart from the obvious

question of price. In some cases it may be clear that a particular
specialist expertise is required, for example in dealing with a site
contaminated by radioactive material or asbestos. In other cases the
following factors may be relevant:

1. the consultant's experience in the particular kind of work
   involved. Some consultants may be able to characterise problems but not advise on clean-up methodologies; others may have
   a particularly strong track record in dealing with certain types
   of site, such as landfill;
2. the consultant's expertise—whether the relevant technical areas
   are adequately represented;
3. interpersonal skills—in some cases the ability of a particular
   person will be crucial, for example the ability to communicate
   technical issues clearly, or to negotiate with regulatory
   authorities;
4. capability and resources—the ability to field a large team where
   multi-site transactions are involved and there is a tight timescale for completion of investigations;
5. national or international reputation—whilst there are some
   excellent sole practitioner or small consultancies available, it
   may be that market perception or confidence in the outcome is
   so crucial as to require the emplopment of a "big name";
6. analytical support—some consultancies have in-house analytical
   facilities, but the majority make use of outside laboratories.
   Sound analysis is essential and support by an accredited
   laboratory is important;[1]
7. terms of engagement—these vary and some may be materially
   more disadvantageous to the client than others. The issue is
   discussed generally below[2]; and
8. professional indemnity and public liability insurance—it is
   important that these are adequate.[3]

Generally, when comparing consultants it is important to be sure that
like is being compared with like. It will therefore be helpful when
inviting consultants to submit their proposals for work to indicate clearly
their brief, the level of insurance regarded as acceptable, any conditions
of engagement which will not be acceptable, the timescale for the work,
and so forth. Caution needs to be employed when comparing prices, as
some fees quoted may be exclusive of matters such as hire of plant and
equipment, and analysis charges (which can be as expensive as the
investigation fees, if not more so).

[1] See paras. 10.06 and 10.11 below.
[2] See para. 10.06.
[3] See para. 10.12.

Sources of information on consultants

The profession of "environmental consultant" is an immature one **10.03**
compared with traditional disciplines such as engineering and therefore
the relevant trade and professional organisations are still at an early
stage of evolution. However, there are a number of sources of information as to consultants and their various strengths:

Institute of Environmental Assessment, Fen Road, East Kirkby, Lincolnshire, PE23 4DB, 0790 763613	Detailed database of consultants; free search service offered
Association of Environmental Consultancies (AEC) 2 Manchuria Road, London, SW11 6AE 071 978 4347	Free listing of members provided grouped under various specialisms, including contaminated land
Environmental Data Services (ENDS) Unit 24, Finsbury Business Centre, 40 Bowling Green Lane, London, EC1 0NE 071 278 7624	Produces authoritative and detailed directory of environmental consultants. Given details such as specialisms, site, geographical experience, accreditations etc. A customised database search can also be carried out for a small fee.
Association of Consulting Engineers, Alliance House, 12 Caxton Street, Westminister, London, SW1H 0Ql 071 222 6557	Holds data base of consulting engineer members of various specialisms, including contaminated land.
Institution of Civil Engineers, Great George Street, Westminister, London, SW1P 3AA 071 222 7722	
Institution of Chemical Engineers, Davis Building, 165–171 Railway Terrace, Rugby, Warwickshire, CV21 3HO 0788 78214	Jointly produce a publication listing organisations which offer consultancy services.

Royal Society of Chemistry, Burlington House, Piccadilly, London, W1V 0BN 071 437 8656	
Institution of Water and Environmental Management, 15 John Street, London, WC1N 2EB 071 831 3110	Many environmental consultants will be members of the Institution.
Association of Geotechnical Specialists, PO Box 70, Wokingham, Berks, RG11 4NL	Geotechnical scientists, though geotechnical capability is not necessarily an indicator of expertise in contamination issues.
Geological Society, Burlington House, Piccadilly, London, W1V 0BN 071 434 9944	Geologists and earth scientists; specialist groups in geology and ecology.
Geologists' Association, Burlington House, Piccadilly, London, W1V 9AG 071 434 9298	Geologists.
British Hydrologicial Society, Maclean Buildings, Crowmarch Gifford, Wellingford, Oxfordshire, OX10 8BB 0491 38800	Hydrologists.
Institution of Mining Engineers, Danum House, South Parade, Doncaster, South Yorkshire, DN1 2DY 0302 320486	Mining Engineers.
National Measurement Accreditation Service (NAMAS), National Physical Laboratory, Queens Road, Teddington, Middlesex, TW11 0LW 081 977 3222	Accreditation of analytical laboratory services.

The consultant's brief

Many problems arise in practice through failure to agree a clear and **10.04** adequate brief for the consultant's investigations and report. Prior to commencing work, the consultant should be asked to set out in writing the scope of his inquiry, the components of that work, and the end product to be expected by way of reports. Any divergence from that agreed scope of work should then be agreed only in writing. The purpose of the exercise is to protect the position of both client and consultant, to expedite the production of a final report (by avoiding disputes as to scope when the work is part-completed), to enable competitive tenders from consultants to be adequately compared, and to give certainty to the issue of the services included within any agreed fee or "not to exceed" estimate. Also, if the report is to be produced to a subsequent purchaser, tenant or lender they will, if properly advised, wish to see a copy of the initial letter of appointment which led to the work.

Ensuring that the scope of work is clear and adequate is an exercise requiring a degree of care and skill. Reference may be made to earlier material on what a typical site investigation will comprise in this respect.[4] It will be helpful for the client's initial letter to the consultant to give a clear indication of what is expected and within what timescale, together with any special considerations such as restrictions on site access, details of previous work and reports, etc.[5] From this the consultant can prepare a detailed draft scope of work for the client's consideration. Reference can usefully be made to any relevant published sources of guidance on investigation, in particular DD 175: 1988 or technical guidance on investigating matters such as landfill gas or spillages of petroleum, where these problems are known or suspected.[6]

The solicitor's role

A solicitor may well become involved, at the client's request, in **10.05** appointing a consultant and agreeing his brief and terms of work. The same may be true of other professions, particularly architects and surveyors. A measure of caution is advisable here. The solicitor, architect or surveyor will owe a duty to exercise proper care and skill in advising on or appointing a consultant[7] and also no doubt as to whether

[4] See Chap. 4.
[5] See para. 10.06.
[6] See Chap. 4.
[7] Clerk & Lindsell, *Torts*, para. 11.36; *Collard* v. *Saunders* [1971] C.L.Y. 116. An architect can also be liable for failure to make proper enquiries before advising on contractors: *Pratt* v. *George J. Hill Associates* (*a firm*) (1987) 38 B.L.R. 25.

the consultant's terms of engagement are acceptable from the client's point of view. The solicitor, architect or surveyor in question may or may not be experienced enough to discharge that duty adequately; if they are not competent to advise then they should tell the client so.[8]

Involvement in agreeing the detailed scope of work may be even more dangerous, especially given the standard exclusions in professional indemnity insurance cover which now apply to environmentally related claims.[9] If the agreed scope of work was inadequate, so that a purchaser suffers loss or damage, the consultant who undertook the work in accordance with the defective scope (or their insurers) will no doubt repudiate liability, leaving the purchaser with a potential claim against the solicitor or other advisor who agreed the scope on the client's behalf. For this reason, the solicitor should ensure either that the client themselves agrees the scope with the consultant, or at least that the client approves the scope before it is finalised.

The client's prime concern will often be to keep costs to the minimum in terms of numbers of sampling points, etc.; the solicitor should be wary (unless very sure of their ground indeed) to be seen to suggest that what will inevitably be a compromise between economy and confidence is going to protect the client to any greater degree than will actually be the case.[9a] Obviously the consultant should be asked to confirm expressly that the agreed scope is in their professional opinion adequate, but many may be understandably reluctant to do this where the scope has been subject to client-imposed cost constraints. An example is given below[10] of an initial letter from the client to the consultant, giving the client's essential requirements and requesting the consultant to prepare a detailed proposal.

Terms of contract

10.06 Most consultants have standard conditions of engagement or terms of work. These will vary from consultants to consultant and in some cases it will be necessary to negotiate variations to those standard terms in order to protect the client's interests. The following points will need to be considered.

---

[8] *Buckland* v. *Mackesy* (1968) 208 E.G. 969; *Neushul* v. *Mellish & Harkavy* (1967) 111 S.J. 399; *of Carradine Properties Ltd.* v. *D.J. Freeman & Co.* (1982) 126 S.J. 157 which suggests that the client's own experience and sophistication will also be relevant.

[9] See para. 10.12 below.

[9a] Where work is "designed down" to a low price, the same quality as for a higher price cannot be expected, but there will still be a minimum standard to be expected in terms of care and skill: *Brown* v. *Gilbert-Scott and Payne* (1993, Official Referees' Business, unreported).

[10] See App. A.

(1) Exclusion or limitation of liability

Some standard terms may seek to limit the consultant's liability to a given sum (or in some cases the amount of the fees or a multiple thereof) in respect of any one incident or series of incidents arising out of the same event. A total exclusion of liability for consequential loss or damage will not be acceptable; nor will a limitation to the amount of the consultant's fees. An exclusion cause will be subject to the Unfair Contract Terms Act 1977; amongst the factors to be taken into account in considering whether the exclusion was reasonable will be the bargaining power of the parties, whether it would have been practicable to obtain the advice elsewhere, the difficulty of the professional task being undertaken, and the practical consequences of upholding or striking down the exclusion.[11] This last consideration will bring in the issues of insurance and relative hardship. Exclusion of negligence will not automatically be unreasonable—as was said in one case:[12]

> "Sometimes breathtaking sums of money may turn on professional advice against which it would be impossible for the adviser to obtain adequate insurance cover. . . . In these circumstances it may indeed be reasonable to give the advice on a basis of no liability or possibly of liability limited to the extent of the adviser's insurance cover."

Given the difficult current state of the insurance market in respect of environmental risk,[13] this may be an extremely important point.

(2) Sub-contractors

The issue of sub-contractors and their potential liability is discussed below.[14] It should be clear to what extent the agreed work, or any aspect of it (*e.g.*, analytical testing) may be subcontracted. Some standard terms seek to restrict the client's ability to make claims against sub-contractors: generally this will not be acceptable.

(3) Indemnity

Site investigations can cause damage, for example by cutting into services or by mobilizing contaminants. A high proportion of consultant's standard terms seek to place such risks on the client, providing that the client shall indemnify the consultant against any losses,

---

[11] *Smith* v. *Eric S. Bush* [1990] 1 A.C. 831, at p. 858 *per* Lord Griffiths.
[12] *Ibid.*, p. 859,
[13] See para. 10.12 and App. F.
[14] See para. 10.11.

damages or claims arising.[14a] Again, such a provision will generally not be acceptable, save where the problem arises from the client's own negligence.

(4) Site conditions and safety

It will be reasonable for the consultant to require the client to notify any special site conditions, such as cables and drains, and any necessary safe operating procedures.

(5) Confidentiality

The consultant should undertake not to divulge or disclose to any third party any information of a confidential nature in connection with the project. Often this obligation will be restricted to any information which is expressly designated as confidential by the client.

(6) Third parties

As mentioned below it may be critical that third parties such as a purchaser or tenant can rely on the consultant's report.[15] If this is the case then the issue should be addressed at the outset: otherwise any such extension will need to be negotiated after the work is completed, for which the consultant may require an additional fee. It should be made clear exactly to whom the report should be extended, and how this should be done—whether by reissuing the report in their name, by written agreement, or by formal collateral warranty under seal.[16] It should also be clarified whether, or on what terms, the client can assign the benefit of the contract.[17]

(7) Insurance

Insurance is becoming an immensely difficult issue in relation to contaminated land and is considered separately below.[18] The agreement with the consultant should make clear which types of insurance the

---

[14a] Even if a client is aware of the risks of damage if work is not done properly, he will be entitled to assume that a competent consultant has taken all precautions necessary to assume that damage will not occur, and this may provide a defence to a negligence action against the client: see *Anglian Water Services Ltd.* v. *H.G. Thurston & Co. Ltd.* [1993] E.G.C.S. 162 (tipping of spoil to raise surface caused sewer fracture).

[15] Para. 10.09.

[16] Para. 10.10.

[17] See the comments on the case of *Linden Gardens Trust Ltd.* v. *Lenesta Sludge Disposals Ltd.* [1993] 3 All E.R. 417 at para. 10.08 below.

[18] See para. 10.12.

consultant should hold (third party, public liability and professional indemnity), the amount of cover required and the period for which that cover is to be maintained.

Standard of care and implied terms

The consultant will not normally be guaranteeing a given result and **10.07** his or her obligation will be limited to the exercise of reasonable professional care and skill. Failure to achieve the desired result (for example missing a pocket of contamination, or the failure of a particular method of clean-up) will not normally of itself be evidence of negligence.[19] There are at present no reported cases dealing with the standard of care to be expected of environmental consultants as such.[20] However, cases concerning architects, engineers, surveyors, and other property professionals can provide some guidance.[21]

(1) Site investigation

Care will need to be taken in advising on the appropriate method of site investigation: for example, trial pits may be useless for investigating certain forms of contamination or ground conditions, and boreholes may be the only reliable method.[22]

(2) Codes of practice

Departure from accepted codes of practice may involve a considerable risk of being found negligent in the absence of sound reasons for doing so.[23] Documents such as DD 175 may therefore be very important,[24] though it must be kept in mind that this document is not a formal British Standard, but only a draft—and many consultants will argue

---

[19] *Greaves & Co.* v. *Baynham Meikle* [1975] 1 W.L.R. 1095; *Thake* v. *Maurice* [1986] Q.B. 644; see also Clerk & Lindsell, para. 11–02.

[20] See however the case of *Eckersley* v. *Binnie & Partners*, Court of Appeal, February 18, 1986, para. 2–28 above (a case of professional negligence involving naturally occurring methane gas).

[21] See *e.g.* A.M. Dugdale & K.M. Stanton, *Professional Negligence* (2nd ed.), 1988, pp. 271 *ff*; Digby C. Jess, *The Insurance of Professional Negligence Risks* (2nd ed.), 1989, pp. 32 *et seq.*

[22] See *Investors in Industry Ltd.* v. *South Bedfordshire District Council* [1986] 1 All E.R. 787, p. 808.

[23] *John Maryon International Ltd.* v. *New Brunswick Telephone Co. Ltd.* (1982) 141 D.L.R. (3d) 193; *London Borough of Newham* v. *Taylor Woodrow (Anglian) Ltd.* (1980) 19 B.L.R. 99; *Bevan Investments Ltd.* v. *Blackhall & Struthers (No. 2)* [1973] 2 N.Z.L.R. 45; Dugdale & Stanton, *op.cit.* para. 16.11.

[24] See para. 4.02 above.

cogently that there may be circumstances where it should not be followed.

(3) Legal issues

Whilst a consultant will not be expected to be a legal expert, he will be expected to have a working knowledge or familiarity with the law so far as it is relevant to his work. The consultant who liaises with the relevant regulatory authorities can probably in most cases assume that they are acting legally and correctly, even where he has some doubts about the attitude they are taking.[25]

(4) Specialist advice

The consultant must be aware of his own limitations and where necessary advise the client to retain specialist advice, either from within his own firm or externally.[26] Given the multiplicity of disciplines which can be relevant to contaminated land, this can be a very real issue: an obvious example is the geotechnical expert who may not be qualified to advise no chemical contamination. Where the consultant participates in the selection of such specialist advisers, he will be under a duty to exercise reasonable care and skill in so doing.[27] Once the specialist has been appointed, the consultant's duties are likely to be confined to directing and co-ordinating the specialist's work; through the consultant cannot rely blindly on the specialist and may well be under a duty to warn the client of any danger or problem which arises of which a consultant of ordinary competence ought to be aware.[28]

(5) Design

Consultants may become involved in the design of remedial works, such as the installation of barriers, venting equipment or earthworks. The consultant's duty of care will not be discharged simply by relying on the views of others, for example planning or other regulatory authorities,[29] or manufacturers in relation to the suitability of materials or equipment.[30] The issue will be different where certain aspects of design are properly delegated to a specialist.[31] Special care will be needed when

[25] *B.L. Holdings* v. *Robert J. Wood & Partners* (1979) 12 B.L.R. 1.
[26] See n.8 above.
[27] See n.7 above.
[28] *Investors in Industry Ltd.* v. *South Bedfordshire District Council* [1986] 1 All E.R. 787, p. 808.
[29] *B.L. Holdings Ltd.* v. *Robert J. Wood & Partners* (1978) 10 B.L.R. 48; *Eames London Estates* v. *North Hertfordshire District Council* (1980) 259 E.G. 491.
[30] *Sealand of The Pacific Ltd.* v. *Robert C. McHaffie Ltd.* (1974) 51 D.L.R. (3d) 702.
[31] See n.28 above.

applying novel or relatively untried remedial techniques to think through and anticipate potential problems, such as specific site conditions.[32] The client should also be warned of the uncertainties inherent in new techniques.[33]

(6) Estimating cost

An important function of the consultant will often be to estimate the likely costs of remediation for an identified problem. Not surprisingly, many consultants are reluctant to commit themselves on this issue; often with good reason, since cost can vary enormously between different remedial techniques and problems of contamination can often be seen as greater when remediation is commenced than they might at first sight have appeared. Absolute accuracy is not required of a professional exercising such judgment, but certainly a serious under-estimate could give rise to liability.[34] The consultant may also be under a duty to monitor continuing costs and to warn if these appear to be getting out of hand.[35]

It will also be relevant to consider the implied terms of care and skill under the Supply of Goods and Services Act 1982, in particular the implied term of section 13 that the supplier of the service will carry out the service with reasonable care and skill.

Reliance on report: client

The consultant's potential liability lies in contract and tort vis-a-vis **10.08** the appointing party. However, in the light of the decision of the Privy Council in *Tai Hing Cotton Mill Ltd.* v. *Liu Chong Hing Bank Ltd.*[36] the contractual duties will be the relevant ones:[37] "Their Lordships do not believe that there is anything to the advantage of the law's development in searching for a liability in tort where the parties are in a contractual relationship. This is particularly so in a commercial relationship."

On ordinary principles of contract, the client who suffers loss or damage as a result of the consultant's breach will be able to recover as damages all losses (whether physical or purely financial), subject to any valid limitation of liability, so long as they arise naturally, according to the usual course of things, from the breach of contract or alternatively were in the contemplation of the parties when the contract was made.[38] If

---

[32] *IBA* v. *EMI and BICC* (1980) 14 B.L.R. 1.
[33] *Victoria University of Manchester* v. *Wilson* (1984) 2 Con. L.R. 45.
[34] *Columbus Co.* v. *Clowes* [1903] 1 K.B. 244.
[35] *J. & J.C. Abrams Ltd.* v. *Ancliffe* [1978] 2 N.Z.L.R. 420.
[36] [1986] 1 A.C. 80.
[37] *Ibid.*, at p. 107 *per* Lord Scarman.
[38] *Hadley* v. *Baxendale* (1854) 9 Exch. 341.

the client makes it clear to the consultant that one objective of the investigation is to guard against the inadvertent assumption of liabilities flowing from the condition of the site, then such liabilities may well be recoverable losses. Where the liability is of a criminal nature, for example a prosecution for pollution of controlled waters or in respect of statutory nuisance, it will be relevant to remember than as a general rule of public policy fines should be paid by the convicted party. However, it may still be possible to recover the fine as damages, at least where it was the advice of the consultant which led to the client committing the offence.[39]

It is conceivable, indeed in many cases likely, that the client may at some future stage dispose of the property which was the subject of the investigation or remedial work. Various questions can then arise, in particular whether the client can validly assign his contractual rights to the purchaser and whether the client, having disposed of the property, can still assert contractual rights against the consultant. These issues were considered in detail in the context of construction contracts by the House of Lords in *Linden Gardens Trust Ltd.* v. *Lenesta Sludge Disposals Ltd.* and another appeal.[40] The decision is not fully conclusive but suggests the following:

1. The assignment of the benefit of a contract may be prohibited by the terms of the contract. The wording of Clause 17(1) of the JCT form, which provides that "the Employer shall not without the written consent of the Contractor assign this Contract", was held, though "unhappily drafted" to have that effect;
2. Likewise, the assignment of benefits arising under a contract, *e.g.*, to enforce accrued rights of action, may be prohibited. Clause 17(1) was held to have this effect;
3. Such restrictions on assignment are not void as contrary to public policy;
4. A purported assignment in breach of such prohibitions will not be effective to vest the benefit of the contract or the cause of action in the assignee;
5. Where the client sells the property with an obligation to indemnify the purchaser against defects, loss flowing from that obligation may well be too remote to be reasonable under the criteria in *Hadley* v. *Baxendale*;
6. In general, lack of a proprietary interest by the plaintiff in the property at the date of the breach will preclude any claim for substantial damages[41];

[39] *Osman* v. *J. Ralph Moss Ltd.* [1970] 1 Lloyd's Rep. 313, C.A.
[40] [1993] 3 All E.R. 417.
[41] *The Albazero* [1977] A.C. 774; *cf* the more liberal approach of Lord Griffiths at [1993] 3 All E.R. 417 at pp. 421–2.

432

7. However, there are exceptions to this general rule which may avoid the situation where "the claim to damages would disappear . . . into some legal black hole, so that the wrongdoer escaped scot-free";[42]

8. Amongst those exceptions[43] is the case where to the knowledge of both parties the property is going to be occupied, and possibly purchased, by third parties and where it could be foreseen that damage caused by breach would cause loss to a later owned and not merely to the original contracting party. In such a case it appears proper to treat the parties as having entered into the contract on the footing that the client would be entitled to enforce contractual rights for the benefit of those who suffered from defective performance but who under the terms of the contract could not acquire any rights.

9. If the ultimate purchaser is given a direct cause of action against the contractor (for example by a collateral warranty)[44] then the exception referred to above has no application and the original client will not be entitled to recover damages for loss suffered by others who can themselves sue for such loss.

The implications of this important decision remain to be worked out in subsequent cases. However, consultants will need to consider carefully to what extent their terms of engagement are capable of protecting them against such liability.

Reliance on report: third party

A consultant's report may be produced to third parties such as a **10.09** purchaser, tenant and mortgagee, who may in some cases act in reliance upon it. In any event it will be a question of judgment as to whether it is prudent to rely upon the substantive content of the report, which may have been produced some time ago, and for different purposes. Apart from this issue, there are legal difficulties in any third party relying on the report.

The third party will not have a contractual relationship with the consultant. Any action will therefore lie in tort. Recent years have seen a drawing back from some of the innovative decisions of the 1970s and 80s and in particular from the recovery of purely economic loss in tort.[45]

---

[42] *GUS Property Management Ltd.* v. *Littlewoods Mail Order Stores Ltd.* 1982 S.C. (HL) 157 at p. 177.

[43] See also *Dunlop* v. *Lambert* (1839) 6 CL & F 600.

[44] See para. 10.10 below.

[45] See *D. & F. Estates Ltd.* v. *Church Commissioners for England* [1989] A.C. 177; *Department of the Environment* v. *Thomas Baes & Son* [1991] 1 A.C. 499; *Murphy* v. *Brentwood District Council* [1991] 1 A.C. 398.

The main potential basis for liability to a third party is that line of authority which stems from the decision in *Hedley Byrne & Co. Ltd.* v. *Heller & Partners Ltd.*[46] This involves liability for advice or opinion given in a professional capacity or in some special relationship, where it is reasonable to expect that the recipient of the information will rely on it: in such circumstances even purely economic loss can be recovered. Whether such a duty of care is owed will depend on whether the professional adviser, at the time of giving his advice, was or ought to have been aware that his advice or information would in fact be made available to and would be relied on by a particular person or class of persons for the purpose of a particular transaction or type of trans-action.[47] Where a statement put into general circulation might be relied on by a variety of third parties for a variety of purposes there will not be the requisite relationship of proximity to give rise to a duty of care.[48] There is no reason of public policy why an expert advising a local authority (or for that matter any other developer) as to soil conditions should be liable to a subsequent purchaser who has not relied on the expert's report and who, at the time of the negligent act cannot be identified other than as a member of a class of potential purchasers.[49]

It is therefore certainly arguable that a consultant who prepares a report knowing that the client requires it in connection with an imminent forthcoming sale or refinancing could be liable to the pur-chaser or bank, even though their precise identity may not be known at the date of the report. At the other exteme, in the case where the client makes available the report to a local authority, who may then be obliged to disclose the information contained in it to the general public, it seems most unlikely that any relationship of proximity would exist with those who might come upon and rely on that information. Between those two extremes there is obviously considerable room for debate and uncertainty.

It should be noted that the *Hedley Byrne* type of duty will extend only to professional relationships and to persons such as consulting engineers, architects or structural engineers[50]: it seems likely that environmental consultants will fall into this category. The duty will not apply to specialist manufacturers of equipment, even though they may give advice.[51]

---

[46] [1964] A.C. 465.
[47] *Cann* v. *Willson* (1888) 39 Ch.D. 39; *J.E.B. Fasteners Ltd.* v. *Marks Bloom & Co.* [1981] 3 All E.R. 289; *Caparao Industries plc* v. *Dickman* [1990] 2 A.C. 605.
[48] *Ibid.* See also the "masterly analysis" of Denning L.J. in *Candler* v. *Crane Christmas & Co.* [1951] 2 K.B. 164 at pp. 179–184, approved by Lord Bridge in *Caparo Industries.*
[49] *Preston* v. *Torfaen Borough Council, The Independent,* September 24, 1993.
[50] *Pirelli General Cable Works Ltd.* v. *Oscar Faber & Partners* [1983] 2 A.C. 1.
[51] *Nitrigin Eireann Teoranta* v. *Inco Alloys Ltd.* [1992] 1 All E.R. 854.

It is also important to note that it is open to the consultant to attempt to negate any duty to third parties by way of express disclaimer, such as a statement on the face of the report that it is not intended to be relied on by any third party. Any such disclaimer may well be regarded as a notice which excludes liability for negligence which would have arisen but for the notice.[52] As such it may be subject to the test of reasonableness under The Unfair Contract Terms Act 1977.[53] However, the counter argument (unsuccessful on different facts in *Smith* v. *Eric S. Bush*)[54] is that the disclaimer is an important evidential consideration in determining whether a special relationship of reliance existed at all under the rule in *Hedley Byrne* v. *Heller*.

Extension of duty to third parties

In view of the inherently uncertain position as to the ability of third **10.10** parties to rely on a consultant's report, the issue is frequently addressed by creating a direct contractual relationship between the consultant and third party. This may involve the report being re-issued in the name of the third party, or by a letter or agreement acknowledging that the third party may rely on the report; or by a formal collateral warranty. These matters should ideally be addressed at the time of the consultant's initial appointment.[55] The consultant will want to be clear as to whom he may be required to extend his duty of care and understandably may be unwilling to go beyond the first purchaser or tenant. No consultant is likely to relish the idea of extending the duty to a large number of tenants in a case where the development is to be let. From the client's point of view, where the intention is to use the report in financing a project, the possibility of a number of financial institutions being involved will need to be catered for.

From the third party's point of view, the desired objective is a clear contractual relationship with the consultant; this will not necessarily be achieved simply by the consultant acknowledging in writing that a duty exists. The preferred option will thus probably be a collateral warranty agreement by way of deed, which will avoid any arguments as to consideration and will provide a 12-year limitation period. The essence of the agreement will be a warranty by the consultant that it has exercised all reasonable care, skill and diligence in the production of the report and the work leading up to it. Difficulties are most likely to arise

---

[52] See Unfair Contract Terms Act 1977, s.11(3).
[53] *Smith* v. *Eric S. Bush*; *Harris* v. *Wyre Forest District Council* [1990] 1 A.C. 831, especially *per* Lord Griffiths at pp. 856–7. See also para. 10.06 above.
[54] See n.11 above.
[55] See para. 10.06.

where the draftsman attempts to impose on the consultant more onerous liabilities than were owed under the original contract:[56] the consultant will wish to see any limitations or exclusions from the main contract carried over into the collateral warranty. The consultant will also wish to see a suitable "other parties" clause to ensure that it is not held solely liable where the negligence of other professionals is also involved. The issue of professional indemnity insurance should also be addressed.

A precedent for an agreement dealing with those issues is given below.[57]

Sub-contractors

10.11   The consultant may in practice make use of sub-contractors in the course of his work: the obvious example is the sub-contracting of the analysis of soil samples to a laboratory. This situation may give rise to a number of potential difficulties.

The first issue is whether the consultant is entitled to delegate performance of the agreed work. In *Moresk Cleaners Ltd.* v. *Hicks*[58] it was held that an architect is not entitled to delegate the design of a building to a sub-contractor; however it is arguable that this principle is limited to the function of design, where the client may reasonably expect that the architect he has chosen will actually do the work.[59]

Secondly, whilst a professional person may be free to sub-contract the actual performance of their work to another, they may not necessarily be free to delegate responsibility: regardless of the care which they took themselves in selection and supervision, they will be liable for the negligence of the sub-contractor.[60]

Thirdly, the position will naturally be otherwise where the consultant's role is to recommend to the client the appointment of independent specialists: here the consultant's responsibility is limited to care in recommendation and supervision.[61]

Finally, where the consultant employs the laboratory or other sub-contractor, the client will of course have no direct contractual relationship with the subcontractor. Any attempts to construct or spell out a

---

[56] Winward Fearon & Co., *Collateral Warranties* (Oxford, 1990) pp. 120 *et seq.*
[57] App. A.
[58] [1966] 2 Lloyd's Rep. 338.
[59] *Investors in Industry Ltd.* v. *South Bedfordshire District Council* [1986] 1 All E.R. 787, p. 807.
[60] A.M. Dugdale and K.M. Stanton, *Professional Negligence* (2nd ed.), 1988, p. 391.
[61] See para. 10.07 above.

contractual relationship are likely to be fraught with difficulty,[62] so the client will have to fall back on arguing the existence of a duty of care in tort. This may be easier said than done in the case where a laboratory is simply analysing a batch of samples with no knowledge of the context or the reliance to be placed on the results.

From the point of view of all concerned it is therefore important to be clear as to the relationship between the parties: either the consultant should be responsible to the client for lack of care on the part of the laboratory, or alternatively (and perhaps preferably from the consultant's point of view) there should be a separate contract for analysis between the client and laboratory. This second alternative may be unsatifactory to the client in that it may not be straightforward to establish whether the fault lay with the consultant or the laboratory; on the other hand, many major laboratories may be more substantial than some small consultancies.

Insurance

The general difficulties relating to insurance of environmental risks are **10.12** discussed elsewhere.[63] However, in dealing with consultants it is important to be aware of the difficulties which they are currently facing in relation to professional indemnity insurance. Both insurers and reinsurers are currently "risk averse" to possible claims involving environmental damage and this is reflected in the increasing withdrawal of cover or liability caused by seepage, pollution or contamination, with the exception of sudden, unintended and unexpected happenings. It appears that insurers may now be going even further in excluding cover for any loss arising from claims for bodily injury or property damage directly caused by the insured arising out of the actual, alleged or threatened discharge, dispersal, release or escape or pollutants. Even more sweeping exclusions may apply in relation to claims in respect of North American jurisdiction. Such exclusions are potentially very serious for consultants engaged in environmental work, and for their clients and others who may seek to rely on their work.

Coupled with this, the overall capacity of the professional insurance market has contracted, and many consultants may find it difficult to maintain previous levels of cover, at least without paying very large

---

[62] See *e.g.*, *Scuttons Ltd.* v. *Midlands Silicones Ltd.* [1962] A.C. 446; *Morris* v. *C.W. Martin & Sons Ltd.* [1966] 1 Q.B. 716; *New Zealand Shipping Co. Ltd.* v. *A.M. Satterthwaite & Co. Ltd. The Eurymedon* [1975] A.C. 154; *Salmond and Spraggon (Australia) Pty Ltd.* v. *Port Jackson Stevedores Pty Ltd., The New York Star* [1979] 1 Lloyd's Rep. 298.

[63] See App. F.

premiums for the higher layers. The problems are compounded by the fact that many environmental consultancies do not have a major capital base.

Whereas in the past cover was generally written on each and every claims basis with no upper aggregate limit, coverage may now only be provided on an aggregate basis,[64] and thus consultants can be understandably reluctant to commit a major proportion of their yearly cover to a particular project. Clients and their lawyers will therefore need to take a realistic approach to what can be demanded in terms of insurance cover.

The fact that professional indemnity insurance needs to be renewed annually and that it is written on a claims made basis means that it is very difficult for the consultant to guarantee that any specific level of cover will be maintained, given the vagaries of the market, for periods such as six or twelve years.[65] The underwriting will depend on the nature of the services provided, and the fee income of the business. The answer may be a warranty to use best endeavours to obtain cover, provided it is available in the market at reasonable rates. In any event it must be questionable how an absolute obligation to maintain insurance would ultimately protect the client if the consultant did fall into breach of it.[66]

Finally, the insurance aspects will be important in relation to collateral warranties, since most policies will exclude any claim arising out of a specific liability assumed under contract which increases the insured's standard of care or measured of liability above that normally assumed.[67] Mindful of that exclusion, many consultants will wish to obtain their insurer's approval to the terms of any proposed warranty.

Many of these problems also apply to analytical laboratories and to remediation contractors, probably a smaller proportion of which will be insured for professional negligence. Where a contractor is carrying out remediation activities, it should be remembered that unless a specific environmental impairment liability policy has been obtained, the general public liability policy of the contractor will now generally not cover gradual pollution.[68]

---

[64] Digby C. Jess, *The Insurance of Professional Negligence Risks* (2nd ed.), 1989, p. 194.
[65] Winward Fearon & Co., *Collateral Warranties* (Oxford, 1990) p. 138.
[66] *Ibid.*, p. 139.
[67] Jess, *op. cit.*, p. 155.
[68] See App. F.

438

Chapter 11

PROPERTY TRANSACTIONS

Introduction

The possibility or reality of land being contaminated may impact **11.01** upon property transactions in various ways. The fitness of the land for its current or intended purpose may be affected, requiring expenditure to rectify the problem: how much expenditure depends, in part, on how law and policy on clean-up standards develop. In the absence of any provision to the contrary, such a problem will lie where it falls, with the current owner. Contaminated land may also involve actual or contigent liabilities. Whilst a transfer of the ownership or occupation of contaminated land will not rid the transferor of liability which has already accrued, for example in respect of water pollution, the transferee may find himself liable for the future as owner or occupier.[1] Finally, the potential problems of fitness for purpose and liability may be subject to market perception in such a way as to have a serious blighting effect on the property and its value, irrespective of the actual scale of the risks.[2]

These issues may be considered in the context of three main types of transaction, each of which raises its own particular problems:

(a) sale;
(b) lease; and
(c) mortgage or charge.

Essentially, there are two main concerns: (i) the provision or acquisition of information; and (ii) the contractual allocation of risk.

The key issues are summarised below with references to the relevant text.

---

[1] For example, for an ongoing common law or statutory nuisance: see Chap. 2.
[2] Valuation of contaminated land is considered at Annex B.

Party	Concern	Reference
Vendor	Price obtainable Avoidance of future liability	para. 11.12
Purchaser	Fitness for purpose Effect on value Future liability Future saleability/mortgagability	para. 11.02
Landlord	Prevention of contamination by tenant Allocation of liability between landlord and tenant(s) Effect on rental stream	para. 11.14
Tenant	Avoidance of exposure to liability for clean-up costs Fitness for purpose	para. 11.14
Mortgagee	Effect on value of security Avoiding contamination by mortgagor Possible liability on exercising security	para 11.20

SALE

Generally

11.02   The purchaser of land should be concerned to ensure that it is not subject to such contamination as may:

(1) affect its fitness for the intended purpose;

(2) diminish its value unacceptably; or

(3) carry with it hidden liabilities.

Ways of guarding against these risks are essentially;

(a) the obtaining of information about the land's conditions; and

(b) contractual provisions shifting the risk from the purchaser to the vendor.

So far as information is concerned this may be obtained from three sources: (i) the purchaser's own investigations (considered at Chapter 4); (ii) regulatory and local authorities (considered generally at Chapter 3); and (iii) the vendor. Contractual provisions can take a wide variety of forms: some, such as indemnities, may be apt mainly to address the risks of liabilities, whereas others—for example a reduction or retention in price—may be best suited to deal with issues such as fitness for purpose and diminution in value.

Information: generally

The issues of information and investigation are considered at Chapters **11.03** 3 and 4, which should be read in conjunction with this chapter. Two specific information issues are considered in this chapter, in that they arise particularly within the context of property transactions. These are:

(a) local authority enquiries; and

(b) pre-contract enquiries of the vendor.

The exercise of obtaining information, particularly where professional assistance is involved, has implications in terms of cost and time, particularly for smaller value transactions. There may therefore be difficult practical issues to be faced in deciding how far to go in seeking information. The problem can be particularly acute in the case of domestic property, where even the costs of a basic investigation may be regarded as prohibitive, yet the subsequent discovery of contaminative problems may have disastrous personal consequences for the purchaser.

The section 143 registers, had they been introduced,[3] would at least have provided an obvious search which could have been undertaken in all cases; yet it is doubtful how useful the bare information on the register would have been to the purchaser or their solicitors, given the experience and further investigations required to interpret and appraise it.[4] The Construction Industry Research and Information Association[5] has commissioned a project to write guidance on the sale and transfer of land which may be affected by contamination—it may be that in due course this guidance will help to provide some measure of consistency in approach.

In the meantime all that can be said is that solicitors should be aware of the potential problems and exercise vigilance: remembering in particular that the size of the transaction is no indication of the size of the risks, and the fact that a bank or building society is willing to advance money on the security of the property is no guarantee that it is problem-free.[6] At least the solicitor should be aware of those sources of information which are available free, by way of register or direct enquiry. Suitable additional enquiries may be asked of the local authority and of the vendor.

[3] See generally Chap. 3.
[4] S. Tromans, *Blundell Memorial Lecture*. 1993.
[5] See App. E.
[6] See para. 11.21.

Local authority enquiries

11.04   Very few of the enquiries contained in Parts I and II of the standard form of Enquiries of Local Authorities (form CON 29 (1991)) are of relevance to contaminated land. Enquiry 7 deals with entries in the Register of planning applications and permissions, referred to above, and the somewhat ineptly worded enquiry 16 also asks whether the property is "included in the Register of contaminated land" (*sic*).[7] Enquiry 33, in the optional Part II section of the form, asks for details of entries on the Register relating to hazardous substance consents maintained under section 28 of the Planning (Hazardous Substances) Act 1990: this will indicate whether land has been used for the storage of certain specified quantities of a number of hazardous substances.[8]

However, it is possible to raise supplementary questions of the authority if it is thought appropriate to make enquiries not contained in the printed form: conventionally this is done by way of questions typed in duplicate on separate sheets and attached to form CON 29.[9] Precedent enquiries can be found at Appendix A, below. An authority is under no statutory obligation to answer such enquiries, whether on the standard form or otherwise, and given the potential liability involved for negligent answers many authorities may be reluctant to respond.[10] However, so far as regards environmental information in its possession an authority may now have no option but to respond in view of public rights of access to certain information.[11] It may, in responding, attempt—subject to the provisions of the Unfair Contract Terms Act 1977—to exclude or limit its liability.

The authority may be placed in a particularly difficult dilemma where the information in its possession is essentially of a speculative nature, for example where the authority is still in the course of investigating or inspecting a site, or is monitoring it, and is asked to disclose whether they are carrying out any such activities. A positive response may be extremely damaging to the owner, whereas failure to disclose the position may be seen as quite wrong from the point of view of the prospective purchaser: either way it is conceivable that litigation could arise. Giving an accurate picture of the position regarding a particular

---

[7] It is understood that the question is to be removed from the next revision of CON 29 to be published during 1994. Rewording of the question is at the time of writing under discussion between the local authority associations, the Law Society and the Department of Environment.

[8] See para. 3.10 above.

[9] Frances Silverman, *Searches and Enquiries—A Conveyancer's Guide* (2nd ed.), 1992, p. 90.

[10] *Ibid.*, p. 14.

[11] See Chap. 3 generally.

site may not be easy: the relevant information may be uncollated and may be spread between a number of departments of the authority. Some authorities may be understandably reluctant to disclose damaging information: such was the attitude of one authority in responding to an approach by Friends of the Earth in 1992 for information on gas in landfills when it stated that it was ". . . effectively debarred from disclosing information of a sensitive nature which would give rise to blight or public alarm."[12]

Ultimately, the safest course for an authority is probably to follow as closely as possible the Environmental Information Regulations 1992,[13] to exercise restraint in disclosing information outside the ambit of the Regulations and extreme caution in cases where one of the exemptions to the Regulations may apply.

Enquiries of other bodies

In addition to searches and inspections of the various public registers, **11.05** and enquiries of local authorities, it may be necessary to try and elicit information from other bodies, who may have knowledge of material facts in relation to contamination. These include:

(a) the Nature Conservancy Councils for England and Scotland and the Countryside Council for Wales to establish whether there are any sites of special scientific interest in the vicinity which might be affected by contaminants migrating off-site;

(b) where the site is in proximity to a canal, the British Waterways Board or other owner (*e.g.*, the Manchester Ship Canal Company) to establish whether there have been any problems with contamination from the site;

(c) the Health and Safety Executive to establish whether they have been consulted or have exercised any of their statutory powers in relation to contamination;[14]

(d) in certain areas, mining searches may be appropriate as a matter of good conveyancing practice: these include coal mining enquiries of British Coal, tin and arsenic mining searches in Cornwall and South-West Devon, searches with the Mining Records Office for abandoned mines, and limestone mining enquiries in areas of the West Midlands.[15] Such searches and enquiries are mainly for the purpose of detecting possible

---

[12] ENDS Report, April 1992, p. 12.
[13] See Chap. 3.
[14] See Chap. 5.
[15] Frances Silverman, *Searches and Enquiries—A Conveyancer's Guide* (2nd ed.), 1992, pp. 238–254.

problems of land instability,[16] but it should be remembered that abandoned mines can also present serious problems of environmental contamination and that it was not an uncommon practice in the past for old mineshafts to be filled with industrial waste;

(e) the Ministry of Defence in relation to former military land which may be contaminated with munitions or explosives[17];

(f) the Ministry of Agriculture, Fisheries and Food (and also local environmental health departments) as to the location of diseased animal carcasses[18];

(g) British Rail (or, after privatisation, the British Railways Board or Railtrack as former or current owner of the infrastructure) in relation to operational or former railway land;

(h) the National Rivers Authority in relation to pollution of ground and surface water and the location of licensed sources of abstraction; local environmental health departments for data on private (unlicensed) wells.[19]

Such enquiries may be made by way of letter, or by personal telephone enquiry. In practice, the helpfulness of organisations and individuals may vary widely; there may, however, in some cases be an obligation to disclose information in the case of a body with public responsibilities for the environment.[20] The purchaser's solicitors should in all cases bear in mind the possible sensitivity of such contact with regulatory or other interested parties so far as the vendor is concerned, and it may be necessary to tread very delicately.

Disclosure of information by the vendor

11.06   The general principle is that a vendor is under no obligation to the purchaser to disclose information as to the physical condition of the property, even in the case of defects which are not readily apparent, yet are known to the vendor. It is for the purchaser, if he does not protect himself by an express warranty, to ". . . satisfy himself that the premises are fit for the purposes for which he wants to use them, whether that fitness depends on the state of their structure or the state of the law or any other relevant circumstances."[21]

---

[16] PPG 14, *Development on Unstable Land* (1990).
[17] See para. 7.25.
[18] See para. 7.26.
[19] See Chap. 6.
[20] See generally Chap. 3.
[21] *Edler* v. *Auerbach* [1950] 1 K.B. 359, 374; *Hill* v. *Harris* [1965] 2 Q.B. 601. See also *Turner* v. *Green* [1895] 2 Ch. 205, *Greenhalgh* v. *Brindley* [1901] 2 Ch. 324.

This general principle can be qualified in certain circumstances:

(1) Defective premises

The vendor who is also the builder of a house may have liability at common law and under the Defective Premises Act 1972 in relation to some defects of a physical nature.[22]

(2) Misleading Statements

Whilst there may be no obligation to disclose a physical defect, failure to do so may make what *is* stated about the property false or misleading so as to constitute misrepresentation.[23]

Such statements if made in the course of an estate agency business or property management business, can also constitute a criminal offence under the Property Misdescriptions Act 1991. The Act applies to statements about the fitness for purpose of the land itself and the historical use of the land.[24] The term "statement" is given a very wide meaning for the purpose of this legislation, including the spoken and written word and non-verbal means of communicating information, such as pictures. There is, however, a statutory defence that "all reasonable steps" and "all due diligence" were exercised to avoid committing the offence.

(3) Concealment of defects

Deliberate concealment of a physical defect (for example, in one case[25] the covering up of dry rot) can be equated to fraudulent misrepresentation. This could apply for example, where a vendor takes steps to conceal signs of contamination, such as covering up discoloured soil.

---

[22] *Hancock* v. *Brazier (Anerley) Ltd.* [1966] 1 All E.R. 901. Under the Defective Premises Act, and the standard N.H.B.C. agreement, the question would probably be whether the house had not been built in a workmanlike manner and was not fit for human habitation: the wording is not entirely apt to cover problems with contaminated land. However, *Hancock* v. *Brazier* was in fact a case involving the adverse effects of a chemical on the structural integrity of foundations.

[23] *Nottinghamshire Patent Brick and Tile Co.* v. *Butler* (1886) 16 Q.B.D. 778 (statement that the vendor is not aware of restrictive covenants was literally true, but misleading because no check had been made on the relevant documents).

[24] The Property Misdescription (Specified Matters) Order 1992 S.I. 1992 (No. 3834), Sched., paras. 8 and 13.

[25] *Gordon* v. *Selico Ltd.* [1986] 1 E.G.L.R. 71.

(4) Negligent works by vendor

A vendor may potentially be under a duty of care to the purchaser in relation to defective improvements or other works carried out to the property.[26] Conceivably, this principle could apply where a vendor carries out defective reclamation or remediation works which present a hazard to future occupiers or users of the property.

(5) Misdescription

Where a misdescription of the property, though not fraudulent, is such that it affects the subject-matter of the contract so that the purchaser can reasonably be said to be not getting what he contracted for then the contract may be avoided.[27] It is possible that a serious physical defect in the property could fall within this principle, as in one case where property described as "valuable prospective building element" and "suitable for development" was seriously affected by an underground culvert.[28] The potential application of such cases to soil contamination remains to be explored.

(6) Notices and disputes

There is some authority to suggest that substantial undisclosed liabilities arising from disputes with third parties or from the exercise of statutory powers may be matters affecting the title to property and hence give rise to the remedy of recission.[29]

Pre-contract enquiries

11.07 Whilst it is standard practice to elicit information from the vendor as to the state and condition of the property, by enquiries directed through his solicitor,[30] the common form printed standard enquiries do not address squarely the issue of potential contamination.[31] It will therefore be necessary for the purchaser's solicitor to devise their own enquiries. If these are to elicit useful and sensible answers, then it is important that

---

[26] *Hone* v. *Benson* (1978) 248 E.G. 1013 (defective heating system).
[27] *Flight* v. *Booth* (1834) 1 Bing. N.C. 370.
[28] *Re Puckett and Smith's Contract* [1902] 2 Ch. 258.
[29] *Re Englefield Holdings Ltd. and Sinclair's Contract* [1962] 1 W.L.R. 1119 (certificate of disrepair); *Carlish* v. *Salt* [1906] 1 Ch. 335 (party wall award); *Beyfus* v. *Lodge* [1925] 1 Ch. 350 (tenants' notices requiring repairs); *Citytowns Ltd.* v. *Bohemian Properties Ltd.* [1986] 2 E.G.L.R. 258 (local authority dangerous structure notice). See also para. 11.08 below on contractual conditions.
[30] See I.R. Storey, *Conveyancing* (3rd ed.), 1990, p. 38.
[31] See [1986] Conv. 70.

the enquiries are sensibly and realistically drafted and are sufficiently precise. Enquiries as to present or past use or storage of undefined "hazardous substances" on the property are unlikely to be helpful. The key questions which the purchaser should ask are as follows, although more specific questions may be useful in relation to particular kinds of property:

(1) Has the vendor himself carried out any investigations as to potential contamination, or does the vendor hold any such reports commissioned by a third party, or is he aware of the existence of such reports? If so, sight of such reports should be requested;

(2) Is the vendor aware of any previous or current uses on the property which are such as to present a risk of contamination? It will probably be helpful, in this regard, to attach, without limitation, a list of the most commonly recognised contaminative uses;

(3) Is the vendor aware, either during his current ownership or during any previous ownership, of incidents such as leaks or spills on the site which may have led to soil contamination? This is not an enquiry necessarily to be confined to commercial or industrial property; it has been known for serious soil contamination to occur in the case of domestic properties from the storage of oil for domestic heating;

(4) Where the property is one on which potentially contaminative materials are or have been kept, have all proper precautions (so far as the vendor is aware) been observed against soil contamination? This is an issue where to some extent the purchaser can rely upon his own observations when inspecting the site; such observations cannot, however, identify past defective storage practices which have subsequently been rectified;

(5) In a similar vein, is the vendor aware of the current or past presence of underground storage tanks or pipework under the property? This is again a matter which will not readily be ascertainable by physical inspection, but which may be within the vendor's knowledge. A positive answer will merit further investigation;

(6) Has any notice, claim or other communication been received from a public or regulatory authority, or any third party, concerning actual or possible contamination?;

(7) Is the vendor aware of any other circumstances which would indicate the presence of potentially harmful materials within the property, or on adjacent or nearby land such as to present a threat to the property? The vendor is of course likely to be wary

447

of giving any meaningful answer to this question, but there may well be matters within the vendor's knowledge (such as the presence of an old waste site near the property) which the purchaser might legitimately expect to be informed of.

Suggested forms of enquiries are given at Appendix A below.

Care should be taken in placing over-reliance on loosely-worded answers to enquiries. Whilst the question asked (and the answers to other questions) can be used as an aid to interpreting the answers,[32] careful analysis may indicate that their scope is somewhat narrower than the purchaser might wish to suggest. In one recent case,[33] answers given in relation to questions specifically on contamination and the disposal of effluent and waste were expressly warranted to be correct. It was held that none of the answers could be taken to be a warranty that the site (a former laboratory) was free from contamination, nor as a warranty that the laboratory or its drainage system had been decontaminated.

In relation to questions on possible contamination or contaminative uses, the vendor's solicitor should be wary of giving the response "Not so far as the vendor is aware" or words to similar effect. It has been held that such a statement implies that the vendor has taken reasonable steps to ascertain whether such matters as are referred to in the inquiry do in fact exist.[33a] This is particularly the case where the vendor is in a better position than the purchaser to ascertain the true facts.[33b] This may represent a heavy onus on the vendor to check for the existence of possible contamination.[33c]

Standard contract provisions

11.08   The standard form contracts of sale all adopt, by and large, the philosophy of *caveat emptor* and are not helpful in providing the purchaser of contaminated land with any redress.

In relation to the condition of the property, National Condition 13(3) states that:[34]

> "The purchaser shall be deemed to buy with full notice in all respects of the actual state and condition of the property and, save

---

[32] *Foliejon Establishment* v. *Gain S.A.* (Ch.D., July 7, 1993); see para. 11.10 below.

[33] *Ibid.*

[33a] *William Sindall plc* v. *Cambridgeshire County Council, The Times,* June 8, 1993 (see also para. 11.08), citing *Heywood* v. *Mallalieu* [1883] 25 Ch.D. 357 and *Brown* v. *Raphael* [1958] Ch. 636. See also [1994] Conv,. 85.

[33b] *Smith* v. *Land and House Property Corporation Ltd.* [1884] 28 Ch.D. 7, at p. 15.

[33c] In the *Sindall* case the vendor was held to have acted correctly by checking deeds and files, inspecting the property, and checking public records.

[34] National Conditions of Sale (20th ed.).

where it is to be constructed or converted by the vendor, shall take the property as it is."

It has been held that this type of provision does not affect the vendor's obligation to give vacant possession in a case where movable rubbish is left on the property.[35] However, in *Hynes* v. *Vaughan*,[36] where piles of rubble and other rubbish were left on a smallholding by the vendor on completion, it was held that the deposits of rubbish had lost their distinct character as movable items and thus were part of the property, which condition 13(3) obliged the purchaser to take as it was. This suggests a distinction between (for example) drums of waste, which the purchaser might well be able to compel the vendor to remove, and waste spills or deposits which have become part of the land itself, and which fall within condition 13(3).

Similarly, condition 3.3.1 of the Standard Conditions of Sale[37] provides that:

"The buyer accepts the property in the physical state it is in at the date of the contract, unless the seller is building or converting it."

Law Society[38] condition 5(2)(a) provides that the purchaser shall purchase with full notice of the actual state and condition of the property and shall take it as it stands, save where it is to be constructed or converted by the vendor. However, this provision is expressly subject to the general warranty at condition 5(1) that the vendor has disclosed to the purchaser the existence of all (*inter alia*) liabilities affecting the property of which the vendor knows or ought to know other than the existence of those known to the purchaser at the date of the contract, or which a prudent purchaser would have discovered by that date. Similarly, condition 14 of the National Conditions, by which the property is sold subject to (*inter alia*) all liabilities affecting it, is subject to "duty of the Vendor to disclose all latent easements and latent liabilities known by the Vendor to affect the property." Contamination may (but will not necessarily) involve a liability affecting the property, though it may of course be a difficult question as to whether the vendor ought to have known of the liability or whether a prudent purchaser should have discovered it. The wording of National Condition 14, with its reference to "latent liabilities" may bear further consideration in this respect as liabilities resulting from contamination may well be of a "latent" nature. Certainly the effect of National Condition 14 is not to

---

[35] *Cumberland Court Consolidated Holdings Ltd.* v. *Ireland* [1946] K.B. 264 (cement and containers left in cellar).

[36] (1985) 50 P. & C.R. 444.

[37] 2nd ed.

[38] Law Society's General Conditions of Sale (1984 revision).

expose the vendor to the risk of liabilities for which he had no knowledge or means of knowledge.[39]

The standard provisions may also be relevant where contamination leads to the service of a statutory notice (for example a statutory nuisance abatement notice).[40] In relation to any such notices or requirements after the date of the contract, the standard conditions provide that the purchaser is responsible for compliance at his own expense and is to indemnify the vendor in respect thereof: risk thus effectively passes to the buyer on exchange.[41] This may well be an unsatisfactory position from the buyer's point of view where the statutory requirement results from contamination caused by the seller either before exchange or (worse still) between exchange and completion: it should be considered whether the standard condition should be excluded or modified in these circumstances.

Warranties and indemnities

11.09   A purchaser may wish to seek comfort in relation to potential contamination by way of express warranties from the vendor as to the condition of the property, absence of hazardous substances, compliance with environmental legislation, etc. Needless to say, the vendor will usually resist giving such warranties: nonetheless there may be matters exclusively within the vendor's knowledge and on which the purchaser is relying where it is legitimate to expect a formal warranty. Warranties are in fact more commonly encountered as a component of corporate transactions and the relevant legal and drafting considerations are discussed below in that context.[42]

There may also be circumstances where it will be appropriate for the parties to a property transfer to seek indemnities against actions, claims and costs arising from contamination on the property. The indemnities which apply under the standard-form conditions of sale in relation to requirements of public authorities have already been mentioned. In the absence of an indemnity, the loss will lie where it falls: the vendor will retain any liability as the original cause of contamination, but the purchaser will assume ongoing liability as the occupier and owner of the property.[43] The purchaser's argument will be that they should not be liable for conditions originating before completion and that they should be indemnified in respect of such liabilities. The vendor, on the other

---

[39] *William Sindall plc* v. *Cambridgeshire County Council, The Times,* June 8, 1993.
[40] See Chap. 2.
[41] National Condition 16; Standard Condition 3.1.5; Law Society Condition 3(4).
[42] See Chap. 12.
[43] See Chap. 2 generally.

hand, may argue that all liabilities in relation to the property should be assumed by the purchaser, whenever the condition giving rise to the liability originated, and may indeed seek an indemnity from the purchaser in respect of any liability after completion.

There is no ready answer to this clash of views and, as always, the ultimate result will be determined by commercial considerations. These include the commercial context of the transaction, the perceived risks presented by the site, the relationship of price to risk, and the extent, if any, by which the price is being discounted to reflect risk, the respective knowledge of the parties about site conditions, the proposed future use of the site and the general approach of the parties and their advisers. Where the site has been subject to a contamination survey, the discussion is likely to be more focussed, since the results of the survey can be used as a baseline and it may be possible to confine the indemnity to specific substances or specific parts of the site which are perceived as presenting particular risks.

The problems and detailed points which arise in the drafting of indemnities are discussed below.[44]

Construction of warranties

The construction of warranties relating to environmental matters in the **11.10** context of the sale of land was considered in the case of *Foliejon Establishment* v. *Gain S.A.*[45] The defendants Gain, a company incorporated in Switzerland, owned an estate including a substantial manor house bordering Windsor Great Park, the house being used in part as a residence and in part as offices. A stable block and outbuildings were used as laboratories by a company in the defendant's group, carrying on highly specialised research in the development of high purity metal alloys. Contracts were exchanged for the sale of the estate to Foliejon Establishment S.A., a company incorporated in Liechtenstein. The contract included what was described as "an unusual provision" introduced by the purchaser at the meeting for exchange of contracts, which read as follows:

"Contamination

(A) The Vendor hereby warrants that the replies attached hereto given by its solicitors to the Enquiries attached hereto are accurate as at the date hereof and hereby undertakes that nothing shall be done on the property between the date hereof and the date of actual completion which will render such replies materially inaccurate. The Purchaser shall have the

---

[44] See para. 12.06 *et seq.*
[45] *Foliejon Establishment* v. *Gain SA* (Ch.D., July 7, 1993).

right to enter the Property prior to the Completion Date with Specialist Contractors for the purpose of carrying out an environmental audit or inspection of the property and the Vendor will if requested by the Purchaser provide details of all chemicals and similar substances which to its knowledge have been used or stored in the laboratories on the Property."

Subsequently the Purchaser instructed consulting engineers to carry out a survey of the property; their report indicated that part of the laboratories, the drainage system and surrounding land, and an adjacent stream running through the estate were seriously contaminated by radicals and a variety of heavy metals. It was alleged by the purchaser that the warranted replies to preliminary enquiries were not accurate.

Following the breakdown of negotiations as to a deduction from the purchase price, the vendor's solicitors served notice to complete. The response of the purchaser's solicitors was to require a substantial retention fund, to be released against a certificate as to completion of remedial works. The purchasers then issued a writ claiming specific performance with an abatement in the price or in the alternative damages for breach of warranty; injunctive relief was also sought by way of a Mareva injunction[46] restraining the vendors from remitting the whole of the proceeds of sale to Switzerland. Such an injunction was granted in October 1992, following which the vendors instructed their own expert and in July 1993 applied to discharge the injunction.

In part the case was concerned with technical issues of expert evidence as to the true extent of contamination; these issues are considered elsewhere.[47] It was clear, however, that there were serious deficiencies in the initial report produced by the purchaser's expert and that the problems of contamination were much less serious than was alleged by that initial report.

Several of the preliminary enquiries were directed to the state of the property and potential contamination, but a number of these were either not answered or were answered in such terms as not to constitute warranties. However, one specific enquiry asked how trade effluent was disposed of from the property and the answer given was effectively that acid waste was neutralised and thereafter disposed of through the ordinary drainage system. It was suggested by counsel for the purchasers that this amounted to a warranty that nothing went down the drain except acid waste which was then neutralised. This interpretation was rejected, on the basis that it would lead to absurd results which could not have been intended: clearly some non-acid material would have been

[46] See *Mareva Compania Naviera SA* v. *International Bulkcarriers SA* [1975] 2 Lloyd's Rep. 509.
[47] See para. 2.34.

put down the drain. It was held that the correct interpretation of the warranty was that waste which could be safely discharged down the normal drainage system was so discharged, any acid content being neutralised. It was accepted that it could be implicit in such a warranty that the normal waste outlets were properly designed and were properly maintained.

Two further enquiries related to the disposal of industrial waste; it was held that the answers to these effectively amounted to a warranty that non-trade effluent waste, whether solid or liquid, was disposed of outside the property while the laboratory was in use and that when the laboratory ceased to be used, any remaining waste was removed and disposed of outside the property.

It was held on the facts that there was no breach of these warranties. In particular, selective sampling in the laboratory had detected small isolated beads of metal or chemical debris: it was argued for the purchasers that this indicated the laboratories had not been properly "decommissioned" and that the warranties had been broken: proper decommissioning, it was said, would involve steam cleaning, stripping out of potentially contaminated sheeting, partitions or wall coverings. In the court's view it was impossible to spell out of the warranties given any warranty that the laboratories had been decommissioned in this sense: at most, the warranty was to the effect that solid waste and toxic effluent not flushed down the drain were regularly and carefully removed. There was no clear evidence that such a warranty had been broken. Similarly, the finding of contamination in various parts of the drainage system did not constitute breach of any warranty, no warranty having been given that the drainage system had been decommissioned in the sense of being cleansed of every trace of chemicals, metals or solid deposits. At most, there was a warranty that during the operation of the laboratories there had been an adequate system of disposing of effluent and waste and that it was properly maintained.

Finally, it was alleged that there was serious contamination of a filter bed forming part of the draining system, together with the bed of a nearby stream. It was found that the levels of contamination identified would not present a realistic threat to human health or plant uptake; nor was there any evidence that the stream itself was contaminated to any significant extent by substances which could be identified as possibly emanating from the processes carried on in the laboratory. The risk to human health from contamination of the irrigation or filter bed was therefore held to be remote, and there was no evidence that any regulatory body would insist that any corrective action need be taken.

In summary therefore, the claim that the vendors warranted that the laboratories and drainage system had been decommissioned—"that every particle of waste product had been removed and that every contaminated piece of absorbent material had been ripped out and taken away"—was misconceived.

A claim emerged at a late stage that there was a warranty that the system for removing waste was adequate if properly maintained to ensure that no contaminants entered the filter bed or the stream; this was held to be speculative on the basis of evidence adduced. Whilst it could not be said that it was so unarguable that it ought to be struck out, the damages recoverable if there was a breach of it were unquantified and, if quantified, were likely on the evidence to be comparatively small: the purchaser's expert had suggested that corrective action would involve the removal of a top layer of soil, but had not addressed the issue of whether much cheaper corrective action involving fixation of chemicals and covering would be sufficient. In those circumstances, the court held that the right course was to discharge the injunction.

Criticisms of the *caveat emptor* rule

11.11   The rule of *caveat emptor*, described above, has been the subject of criticisms in the context of contaminated land. The House of Commons Environment Committee was not convinced that existing principles and practice offered sufficient protection to the purchaser and found that the effect of the rule, in relation to contaminated land, was to discourage sound environmental practice and environmental responsibility.[48] The Committee recommended that the Government bring forward legislation to place upon vendors a duty to declare information in their possession about contamination on site, however caused.

Whilst apparently initially sympathetic to this issue, the Government ultimately side-stepped the recommendation on the basis that proposals for local authority registers of contaminative uses would meet most of the needs for information expressed by the Committee.[49] Reliance was placed on the recommendations of the Conveyancing Standing Committee of the Law Commission,[50] though a close reading of those recommendations indicates that the Committee saw information on public registers as preferable to reliance on disclosure by the seller, rather than totally excluding the need for disclosure. In any event, with the proposals for registers now shelved, the Government's approach requires reconsideration.

In its March 1994 consultation paper "Paying for Our Past"[50a] the Government appears to contemplate a shift in the existing balance under

[48] *Contaminated Land.* Session 1989–90 170–I, Vol. I, para. 92–95.
[49] Cmnd. 1161, para. 5.9.
[50] *Let the Buyer be Well Informed* (December 1989), para. 27.
[50a] See para. 3.07A.

the *caveat emptor* rule, at least in the domestic market and transactions involving small and mediium-sized enterprises (as opposed to "major commercial transactions"). For major commercial transactions the Government apparently considers the "existing balance of incentives to make disclosures" to work satisfactorily; a conclusion which seems debatable.

Contamination surveys

If there is to be a contamination survey then the question will arise as **11.12** to which party should carry it out. The survey may be commissioned by the vendor, perhaps preparatory to marketing the property; or the prospective purchaser may carry it out; or it may be commissioned jointly by both parties.

Each of these possible sources has potential benefits and drawbacks. There may be advantages from a vendor's point of view in taking the initiative, particularly if it is known that the site is likely to be sensitive in environmental terms: the work will be under the vendor's control and time may be saved in marketing and achieving a sale. On the other hand, any purchaser will be unwise to rely on the survey without the benenfit of a collateral warranty from the consultants, or unless the report is issued addressed to the purchaser.[51] These issues will need to be discussed with the consultants at the time of their appointment.

It is still more usual in practice for the purchaser to commission their own survey. This has the benefit of avoiding doubt as to whether the purchaser can rely on it, though there is the risk of wasted fees if the transaction does not proceed. The cooperation of the vendor will be necessary and there may well be practical and operational constraints, for example as to the location of boreholes, as well as potential problems of confidentiality. Allowing access for such a survey will present the vendor with risks. The vendor may have to live with those risks as the price for the purchaser proceeding, but a written agreement may be used to minimise the risks as far as possible, covering the following matters:[52]

1. prior approval by the vendor of the consultant/contractor. Details to be provided of their third party liability insurance;
2. prior approval by the vendor of the proposed scheme of investigation, including location of boreholes and (if permitted) trial pits;
3. an indemnity from the purchaser in respect of liability or damage arising from the investigation;

---

[51] See Chap. 10 and Precedent at App. A.
[52] A precedent is given at App. A.

4. access by the vendor to the results of the survey (which will be a vital negotiating tool) plus the ability to verify the results of any analysis;

5. a restriction on contact with regulatory authorities (and possibly others, such as employees) without the vendor's prior consent; and

6. obligations as to confidentiality in respect of the results, with an obligation to deliver up all copies of the report to the vendor forthwith in the event that the purchase does not proceed.

A solution which may be well worth considering in some cases is for an agreed consultant to be commissioned jointly by the parties to conduct the survey. This may avoid any feeling by one party of lack of objectivity where a consultant is retained by the other. Problems can of course arise if one or other party argues with the results of the joint report, and this eventuality should be addressed at the outset, either by agreeing that the report will be accepted as conclusive, or that either party will have the right to ask the consultant to reconsider certain points, or to obtain a "second opinion".

The use of conditional contracts

11.13 Where it is not possible, for whatever reason, to conduct a full contamination survey prior to exchange of contracts, the parties may consider entering into a conditional contract. Such a solution, whilst ostensibly attractive, should be treated with caution. The difficulty lies in drafting a condition which is sufficiently precise to be effective. Simply providing that the contract is "subject to a contamination survey" will almost certainly be too vague to constitute a valid condition.[53] The same may be the case if the condition refers to a survey "satisfactory to the purchaser."[54] Contamination surveys can take many forms and different methodologies will produce results of differing degrees of statistical confidence; it is common for a report to conclude by highlighting areas of uncertainty and recommending further monitoring activity. Even if the results are agreed, views can differ as to how those results should be interpreted and whether there is indeed any serious risk of liability. There may well be doubts as to whether a purchaser is acting reasonably in regarding results as unsatisfactory and, if there are unresolved questions, whether a purchaser is under an obligation to seek to clear

---

[53] *Marks* v. *Board* (1930) 46 T.L.R. 424; *Astra Trust* v. *Adams and Williams* [1969] 1 Lloyds Rep. 81.
[54] See *Lee-Parker* v. *Izzet* (*No. 2*) [1972] 1 W.L.R. 775 and *cf Janmohamed* v. *Hassam, The Times,* June 10, 1976.

them up by commissioning further (and possibly costly) work.[55] For these reasons, such conditional contracts are best avoided.[56]

LEASES

General Issues

The grant of a lease raises rather different considerations from a sale **11.14** of the freehold. Whereas on a sale the risk essentially lies with the purchaser in the absence of contractual stipulations to the contrary, in the case of a lease there are risks on both sides. The tenant will be at risk of liability as occupier in relation to pre-existing contamination; the landlord may well have concurrent liability as owner and could be prejudicially affected either during the lease or after it expires by contamination caused by the tenant.[57]

These risks can be addressed primarily through the obtaining of information before, during and on termination of the lease, and by appropriate drafting.

Selection of tenant

Some types of tenant may present a greater risk than others in terms **11.15** of contamination: the landlord would be well-advised to obtain information prior to the grant of the lease in order to be able to assess that risk. A simple standard questionnaire or checklist dealing with the following issues may be helpful:

1. *Nature of proposed use*—a list of the main potentially contaminated uses may be attached for reference;
2. *Types of substances used*—will the tenant be storing or using substances such as solvents, petroleum or other chemicals which may cause soil contamination?;
3. *Precautionary arrangements*—if suitable preventative measures are not already in place, will the tenant be installing the appropriate equipment such as bunding, impervious floor

---

[55] See *Re Longland's Farm, Alford* v. *Superior Developments* [1968] 3 All E.R. 552; *Hargreaves Transport Ltd.* v. *Lynch* [1969] 1 W.L.R. 215; *Richard West and Partners (Inverness)* v. *Dick* [1969] 2 Ch. 424; *Smallman* v. *Smallman* [1972] Fam. 25.
[56] The case of *Foliejon Establishment* v. *Gain SA* (see para. 11.10) above provides a salutary warning of the difficulties which can flow from carrying out a contamination survey *after* a contract has been entered into.
[57] See generally Chap. 2.

surfaces, interceptors, dedicated loading and unloading areas, spill detectors etc?;

4. *Personnel*—will the tenant ensure that personnel are adequately skilled and trained in the relevant procedures to avoid contamination?;

5. *Past record*—has the tenant a record of any past offences under environmental or safety legislation?

Drafting and construing leases

11.16   Even the lengthiest and most comprehensive of leases granted during the 1980s and earlier is unlikely to contain any provisions drafted with contamination specifically in mind. Various covenants and other provisions may, however, have a bearing on the issue.

(1) Repairing covenants

Whether a repairing covenant can impose an obligation to rectify a problem caused by contamination will, fundamentally, depend on the nature of the problem. There can be no liability under a covenant to repair unless the property is in disrepair[58]: unless, that is, the covenant has been extended to cover all defects whether or not manifesting themselves in physical damage.[59] Thus contamination may have serious effects—for example, gas generation—but not yet have had any adverse impact on the structure of the property. Conversely, contamination may result in disrepair, for example by attacking services or foundations. The fact that the contamination was pre-existing, or indeed that the services or foundations were already affected prior to the grant of the lease, will not of itself provide an excuse from the obligation to repair.[60] Moreover, it is arguable that work may be required going beyond simply the immediate works necessary to bring the structure into repair—for example the removal of contaminated soil or the insertion of impervious membranes—if the immediate works of repair would otherwise be rendered abortive.[61] However, where the works required are extensive and would render the premises a different thing from that demised, counter-arguments are possible.[62]

---

[58] *Post Office* v. *Aquarius Properties Ltd.* [1987] 1 All E.R. 1055; *Quick* v. *Taff-Ely Borough Council* [1986] Q.B. 809.
[59] See S. Tromans, *Commercial Leases* (1987) p. 88.
[60] *Lurcott* v. *Wakely and Wheeler* [1911] 1 K.B. 905; *Proudfoot* v. *Hart* (1890) 25 Q.B.D. 42; *Brew Bros. Ltd.* v. *Snax (Ross) Ltd.* [1970] 1 Q.B. 612.
[61] *Smedley* v. *Chumley & Hawke Ltd.* (1981) 44 P. & C.R. 50.
[62] *Ravenseft Properties Ltd.* v. *Davstone Holdings Ltd.* [1980] Q.B. 12; *Wates* v. *Rowland* [1952] 2 Q.B. 12.

(2) Service charges

Whether work required to rectify problems caused by contamination can be recovered under a service charge will be a question of construction, akin to that referred to above in relation to repairing obligations.[63] It is not inconceivable that problems of this type will arise in future, as many developments of contaminated sites for commercial purposes have been carried out on a "footprint specific" basis, with areas where contamination is worst or where contaminants are left in situ being designated as common areas such as access roads and car parks.

(3) Tenant-like use

All tenants have an implied obligation to use the premises in a tenant-like manner, including abstention from acts of wilful or negligent damage.[64] Egregious acts of contamination could well constitute a breach of this obligation: so also might failure to take obvious precautionary measures such as draining disused underground tanks.[65]

(4) Waste

Intentional or careless acts by the tenant which result in the property becoming contaminated might well fall within the tort of waste.[66]

(5) Keep premises clean and tidy

It is common for leases to contain a provision requiring the tenant to keep and yield up the premises "in a clean and tidy condition" (or words to that effect). Whilst on general principles the extent of the demise may include the sub-surface[67] it would appear extremely unlikely that such a covenant could be used to compel the tenant to clean up contaminated soil. The purpose behind such provisions is to ensure that surface buildings and structures are properly maintained.

---

[63] *Rapid Results College Ltd.* v. *Angell* [1986] 1 E.G.L.R. 53; *Mullaney* v. *Maybourne Grange (Croydon) Management Co. Ltd.* [1986] 1 E.G.L.R. 70.

[64] *Warren* v. *Keen* [1954] 1 Q.B. 15.

[65] *Ibid.*

[66] *Mancetter Developments Ltd.* v. *Garmanston Ltd.* [1986] 2 W.L.R. 871 (a case where directors of the tenant company were also personally liable); *West Ham Central Charity Board* v. *East London Waterworks Co.* [1900] 1 Ch. 624 (raising height of marsh land by 10 feet by dumping demolition and household rubbish on it held to be waste by changing nature of property, regardless of whether or not the material was offensive).

[67] *Grigsby* v. *Melville* [1974] 1 W.L.R. 80.

(6) Compliance with statutory requirements

Modern leases usually contain a covenant by the tenant to comply with all statutes, regulations and notices affecting the property. Such a covenant may well oblige the tenant to comply with a notice served as a result of contamination: for example a statutory nuisance abatement notice. It may also require the tenant to take steps to avoid contravening statutory obligations; for example, to prevent unconsented polluting matter entering controlled waters. However, in many cases there may be no specific obligation imposed by law on the tenant: rather the statutory authorities will themselves take steps to clean-up and then seek to recover their costs.[68] It is far less clear that the covenant relating to statutory requirements would apply in these circumstances, and instead the landlord may seek to rely on the other usual covenants as to payment of rates and other impositions and outgoings. There is a large and confusing body of case-law on such covenants and the tenant may contend with some force that capital expenditure to remedy contamination conditions is not covered.[69]

Where works are required under a notice by a statutory authority, there may be express power for the court to apportion those costs between the owner and occupier. For example, the Statutory Nuisance (Appeals) Regulations 1990[70] give such a power and require the court in exercising that power to have regard to the terms and conditions of any tenancy and the nature of the works required.[71] Apart from such express guidance, there is mixed authority as to whether the court has power to overthrow the terms of the bargain embodied in the lease.[72]

(7) Nuisance

There may be a covenant not to do anything on the demised premises so as to constitute a nuisance: this could be relevant in some cases.[73] Acts by the landlord or tenant which constitute a common law nuisance as against the other will be actionable in any event irrespective of the lease.[74]

---

[68] See, for example, s.161 of the Water Resources Act 1991 and s.61 of the Environmental Protection Act 1990.

[69] *Wilkinson* v. *Collyer* (1884) 13 Q.B.D. 1; *Farlow* v. *Stevenson* [1900] 1 Ch. 128; *Villenex Co. Ltd.* v. *Courtney Hotel Ltd.* (1969) 20 P. & C.R. 575.

[70] S.I. 1990 No. 2276.

[71] Reg. 2(7)(*a*).

[72] *Monk* v. *Arnold* [1902] 1 K.B. 761; *Munro* v. *Lord Burghclere* [1918] 1 K.B. 291; *Horner* v. *Franklin* [1905] 1 K.B. 479.

[73] See Chap. 2 for nuisance generally.

[74] *Manatia* v. *National Provincial Bank* [1936] 2 All E.R. 633; *Meadows and Morley* v. *Homor Properties Ltd.* (Q.B.D., February 25, 1993).

Protecting the landlord

The landlord's position can to some extent be protected by careful **11.17** drafting, but equally important will be the exercise of vigilance during and at the expiry of the lease. A number of provisions, specifically angled towards the problems of contamination, could be inserted in the lease, particularly if the tenant's intended use presents risks:

(1) a covenant as to compliance with statutory requirements as to the storage, keeping use and disposal of contaminative substances: including the obtaining, renewal and maintenance in force of all necessary licenses.[75] This might be extended to require compliance with good industrial practice;

(2) a covenant not to dispose of waste substances within the demised premises;

(3) a covenant to inform the landlord immediately of any spills or other potentially contaminative incidents on the property, to remedy the results of such incidents to the landlord's satisfaction and to indemnify the landlord against losses, costs, claims or demands resulting from any such incident;

(4) a covenant to leave the demised premises, including the sub-surface, not contaminated to any greater extent than was the case at the commencement of the term;

(5) rights of entry and inspection, including soil sampling and analysis, during the lease to determine the tenant's compliance with the covenants, and at the expiry or sooner determination of the term to determine compliance with the covenant suggested at point (4) above.

Suggested precedents for such obligations are given at Appendix A. The covenants should be subject in the normal way to a proviso as to re-entry. In the light of the powers of courts to apportion certain clean-up liabilities as between landlord and tenant, referred to above,[76] it would also be sensible to insert a proviso to make it absolutely clear that the tenant is to bear the entire cost of remedying contamination caused by the tenant.

It is possible that the type of covenants referred to above, whilst they may involve physical remedial works, will not be subject to the requirements of the Leasehold Property (Repairs) Act 1938 in relation to enforcement by the landlord or to the restriction on damages under

---

[75] This should include an obligation to renew the licence where necessary, as failure to do so may have serious consequences for the value of the property: see *Davy Ltd.* v. *Guy Salmon (Service) Ltd.*, June 9, 1993, reported *Chartered Surveyor Weekly*, July 23, 1992; a case involving a petroleum spirit licence.

[76] See para. 11.16.

section 18 of the Landlord and Tenant Act 1927.[77] In *Starrokate Ltd.* v. *Burry*[78] it was held that the 1938 Act did not apply to a covenant to cleanse the demised premises.

The landlord may also wish to exercise control over disposition by assignment or underletting from the point of view of the contamination potential of the assignee or underlessee. Provision may be made for a questionnaire[79] to be completed and provided to the landlord as part of the process of seeking consent to assign or underlet.

Fitness for purpose

11.18   From the tenant's point of view, pre-existing contamination may render the premises unsuitable for the purpose for which they were demised. In the case of leases there is no implied term as to fitness or suitability for purpose, though the position may be different in the case of a licence.[80] In *Sutton* v. *Temple*[81] a lease of pasture was granted; unfortunately the land was contaminated by poisonous flakes of paint which had been mixed into a manure heap. A number of cattle died and the tenant refused to pay a second instalment of rent which was due. It was held that the agreement was for the letting of a specified area and that nothing was agreed as to its fitness for a particular purpose: the tenant was obliged to pay the rent "whether the land answer the purpose for which he took it or not."

The prospective tenant, particularly in the case of a long-term lease, would therefore be well advised to investigate whether the premises are subject to such contamination as might affect their use; or indeed, as might give rise to potential liability. In some circumstances it might be appropriate to ask the landlord for an express warranty to that effect, for example where the landlord has constructed the premises; though most landlords are unlikely to accede to such requests without considerable argument. In an extreme case, for example failure of gas control systems, the tenant may wish to have an option to terminate the lease.[82]

The possibility or reality of contamination may have an effect on rent review valuations, though no cases have been reported on the issue.[83] The tenant should be particularly wary of the usual clause requiring the exclusion from the normal disregard of improvements, those carried out

---

[77] See generally, S. Tromans, *Commercial Leases* (1987), p. 98.
[78] (1983) 265 E.G. 871.
[79] See para. 11.15.
[80] *Wettern Electric Ltd.* v. *Welsh Development Agency* [1983] 1 Q.B. 796; *cf Morris-Thomas* v. *Petticoat Lane Rentals Ltd., The Times,* June 17, 1986.
[81] (1843) 12 M. & W. 52; [1986] Conv. 70.
[82] See para. 11.19.
[83] As to valuation of contaminated land generally, see App. B.

by the tenant pursuant to an obligation to the landlord:[84] this could potentially have the effect of the rent being increased where works required by statutory notice have been carried out at the tenant's cost.[85]

Safeguarding the tenant

Whilst as a matter of principle it may be difficult for the tenant to **11.19** argue against having to shoulder responsibility for contamination caused during the term, it is less obvious that the tenant should assume liability for pre-existing contamination. The tenant's advisers should therefore ensure, so far as possible, that the covenants in the lease do not have this effect.

One way of ensuring that the tenant is not fixed with responsibility for contamination pre-dating the lease is for a survey to be undertaken initially, and for the contaminative equivalent of a schedule of dilapidations to be prepared; this may then be compared with the results of any investigation carried out by the landlord during the lease or upon its termination. Obviously, whether the cost of the exercise can be justified within the commercial context is another matter.

The tenant should also be wary of the possibility of being held liable for contamination found on the demised premises during or at the end of the lease which has migrated there from other premises; any drafting should at least retain the ability for the tenant to demonstrate that the pollution arose from external sources outside the tenant's control, and thereby avoid liability.

Where it is known that the demised premises have been constructed on or near problematic land, it will be prudent from the tenant's point of view to make provision for the eventuality that the remedial or precautionary measures taken in developing the site may prove to have been inadequate. The tenant may wish, for example, to reserve a break clause in the event that the premises become incapable of beneficial use or occupation. Such a provision may also deal with suspension of rent in that event and make it clear that the tenant is under no obligation to rectify, or contribute to the cost of rectifying, such defects. The terms may be extended, as appropriate, beyond contaminative effects to problems of ground conditions generally, such as slip, subsidence or heave.[86]

---

[84] See *e.g.*, s.34 of the Landlord and Tenant Act 1954, often incorporated by reference.

[85] *Forte & Co. Ltd.* v. *General Accident Life Assurance Ltd.* [1986] 2 E.G.L.R. 115.

[86] A precedent is given at App. A.

MORTGAGES

Generally

11.20   The concerns of a secured lender in a sense combine those of the purchaser with those of the landlord: the lender's position may be prejudiced by the state of the property at the time the mortgage is granted but, equally, it may be worsened by the use or abuse of the property by the borrower. Essentially the concerns are threefold[87]:

(1) the effect of liability for contamination and its consequences on the ability of the borrower to service the loan;

(2) the effect of contamination on the value of security; and

(3) the possibility of primary liability on the part of the lender.

The first two problems speak for themselves; the third requires some further explanation. So long as the lender takes no steps to enforce the security, the risks are relatively slight, on the current state of the law. However, once the mortgagee seeks to exercise its security, whether by foreclosure, or possession, or by exerting influence over the actions of borrower, the risks inevitably increase. In particular, there is the risk that a lender could be liable by virtue of the degree of control which it exerts, or by being regarded as "owner". Even in the absence of occupation or control, it is arguable that receipt of rent, or the right to receive rent, may give rise to liability as owner.[88] For this reason, taking an assignment of rents, or reserving the right to do so, may be prejudicial. Being a "mere conduit" for the transmission of rental income is not, however, of itself enough.[89]

It is obviously helpful that, where a receiver is appointed under the Law of Property Act 1925, the receiver will be regarded as the agent of the mortgagor rather than the mortgagee. However, excessive practical control by the mortgagee over the actions of the receiver may result in the loss of this protection.[90] Moreover, in most cases the mortgagee will have given an indemnity to the receiver; this, combined with the receiver's personal exposure, presents real risks for the mortgagee.[91]

---

[87] See generally, S. Tromans, *The Relevance of Environmental Law for Banks* [1990] 11 J.T.B.L. 433; Jarvis & Fordham, *Lender Liability: Environmental Risk and Debt* (Cameron May, London, 1993); Fordham [1993] N.L.J. 750.

[88] *Maguire* v. *Leigh-on-Sea Urban District Council* (1906) 95 L.T. 319; *Solomons* v. *Gerzenstein* [1954] 2 Q.B. 243; *Midland Bank Ltd.* v. *Conway Corporation* [1965] 1 W.L.R. 1165; see also Chap. 12, generally.

[89] *Midland Bank Ltd.* v. *Conway Corporation* (n.88 above).

[90] See *Standard Chartered Bank* v. *Walker* [1982] 1 W.L.R. 1411.

[91] See generally Chap. 12.

Lending policy

With these considerations in mind, lenders may need to reconsider **11.21** their standard due diligence procedures, applicable both before granting a loan facility and before taking steps to enforce a loan against security.

The United Nations Environment Programme has issued a statement by banks, *Banking and the Environment*, to which many banks subscribe: it contains the following statement:[92]

> "We recognise that environmental risks should be part of the normal checklist of risk assessment and management. As part of our credit risk assessment, we recommend, when appropriate, environmental impact assessments."

Notwithstanding such general statements, the inevitably subjective impression at the time of writing is that there are enormous variations of awareness and sophistication as between financial institutions as to environmental risk.

Any checklist for a lender is likely to combine the investigations of the site and its history appropriate to a purchaser with the scrutiny of a landlord as to the likely and ongoing activities of the borrower. Reference should therefore be made to the preceding sections.[93] A suggested questionnaire is given later,[94] which can form the basis of an informed decision by the lender as to what further investigations may be required. Vigilance is required not only before granting the loan but also during the loan and, critically, before taking steps to exercise security: at which point it may be sensible to require the completion of a further checklist or questionnaire.

Mortgage Documentation

As with standard leases, traditional mortgage documents make little **11.22** specific provision as to contamination problems, though general provisions on repair, inspection, and care of the property may well be relevant. It is suggested that the following types of provision could be of benefit to a lender:

(1) an obligation on the borrower to disclose the existence of contamination, however arising, affecting the property;
(2) reservation of the right to inspect and monitor the site during the term of the mortgage, including the right to production of relevant authorisations, licences, notices, etc;

---

[92] See also the similar recommendations of the Financial Sector Working Group of the Advisory Committee on Business and the Environment (1993).
[93] See in particular paras. 11.03 and 11.15.
[94] See App. A.

465

(3) reservation of the right to limit uses, types of equipment and substances on the property, particularly in relation to sites with very sensitive neighbouring uses and potential pathways of pollution;

(4) a general covenant not to use the site so as to contaminate it or to give rise to liability arising from the condition of the property, including the sub-surface;

(5) a requirement of notification in the event of any spills or other incidents which might give rise to contamination, changes in operations such as to increase the risk of contamination, complaints, claims, investigations and prosecutions;

(6) an obligation on the mortgagor to supply such information, or to carry out such monitoring, as the mortgagee may require— including an obligation to complete regular questionnaires on request;

(7) an obligation to remedy, to the lender's satisfaction, contamination conditions affecting the property, however arising;

(8) an indemnity against any liability, costs, claims or demands affecting the lender, preferably supported by directors' or parent company guarantees;

(9) a requirement to maintain insurance in respect of own-site clean-up and contamination-related liabilities, to the extent such cover is available from time to time on the market; and

(10) provisions giving adequate flexibility in the appointment of receivers; for example allowing certain property to be excluded if the mortgagee so wishes.

At the more general level, rates of interest may be set so as to reflect the lender's perception of environmental risk; the training of credit officers should also be considered, so that they are alert to identify and respond to environmental warning signs, both at the time of the credit application and subsequently during the term of the loan.

Chapter 12

CORPORATE TRANSACTIONS AND INSOLVENCY

Corporate transactions: general issues

The potential scale and unpredictability of environmental liabilities **12.01** makes it essential for those dealing with company transactions to be alert as to likely difficulties and risks. Where a business is being sold as a going concern, whether by acquisition of the company or of its assets, pre-existing problems of contamination may potentially have a serious impact upon the ability to make optimum use of those assets, and consequently their value. There may also be actual or contingent liabilities arising from past activities of the company, or from the continuing state of the assets, if contaminated.

In this sense, contaminated land is but one of a number of issues of environmental compliance which should be investigated thoroughly in company transactions. Its importance relative to other potential environmental problems will depend upon the nature of the target company or assets, but certainly in most cases it is likely to be amongst the significant and problematical issues.

A distinction needs to be drawn at the outset between the sale of shares and sale of assets. This distinction is of significance in relation to the type of liabilities which will effectively be transferred to the purchaser as a result of the transaction. Environmental liabilities can be broadly categorised into three types:

(a) *Liability as the originator of contamination or the polluter.* Where shares in a company are being sold, the company will carry with it any such liabilities. These may relate not only to currently operational sites and assets of the company, but also to property no longer owned by the company. In the case of a sale of assets such liabilities will not pass, though effectively the purchaser may be at risk where that liability results from the condition of the assets being transferred and that condition is of an ongoing nature: in such circumstances the purchaser may very soon themselves become liable for continuing the pollution.

467

(b) *Liability as occupier.*   In relation to both company sales and sales of assets, this liability will pass in relation to the assets being transferred. The difference is that where a company is being sold, there may be actual or contingent liability as an occupier of premises previously disposed of by the company, whereas of course there could be no question of this passing in the case of a sale of assets.

(c) *Liability as the owner of property.*   The position is effectively the same as in relation to liability as occupier above: a transfer of assets will transfer the liability with it and in addition the sale of a company may involve a transfer of liability which accrued during the ownership of the former assets.

Thus to summarise, there are two significant areas of risk which will apply to the purchaser in the case of a company share sale which will not apply in the case of an assets transaction. These are, first, liability as the originator of pollution which has ceased prior to completion and, secondly, liability as polluter, occupier or owner which has accrued before completion in respect of properties previously disposed of and therefore not forming part of the transaction. Liability should not be envisaged solely in the sense of liability to third parties or regulatory authorities: contamination can cause losses in the sense of self-imposed clean up costs and diminution in value. These potential problems also need to be considered carefully. They will of course naturally follow the assets and are therefore purchaser's rather than vendor's risks.

The additional risks inherent in a company sale can to a large extent be safeguarded against by the device (which may be expedient in any event for tax or other reasons) of transferring the target assets into a new and "clean" company, which is then sold to the purchaser.

Investigations and information

12.02 As with property transactions, which are considered in the previous chapter, it will be important for the purchaser to make adequate investigations as to potential contamination and associated liabilities. As with property transactions the sources of information are essentially threefold: public sources, the vendor, and the purchaser's own enquiries. Reference should be made to earlier chapters for further details on such investigations.[1]

In the context of company transactions the equivalent of pre-contract enquiries is the usual information request forwarded to the vendor. This may be used to elicit information as to environmental matters, and a

[1] See Chaps. 3, 4 and 11.

suggested precedent is given at Appendix A. The practice of seeking warranties from the vendor is another, indirect, means of eliciting information, in that the vendor will disclose against the warranties any matters which would otherwise result in misrepresentation. The issue of warranties is further considered below.[2]

Solutions to identified problems

Assuming that problems are identified in the course of investigations, **12.03** various possible solutions are open, including:

1. warranties;
2. indemnities;
3. restructuring of the deal, for example as an assets rather than a company sale, or by excluding certain "problem" assets;
4. price adjustment, though this can be risky even when problems are known, given the uncertainty which often surrounds clean-up costs;
5. a retention in price against the cost of rectifying identified problems;
6. postponement of completion to allow further investigations to proceed, or perhaps making completion conditional on problems being rectified; or
7. some form of "put" option, by which the purchaser can require the vendor to buy back problematic assets.

Of these, the issue of warranties and indemnities require further explanation.

Risk allocation

However much is known about a property—or even if some remedial **12.04** works have been undertaken—there will always be an element of risk. No investigation can guarantee to identify all problems, which may become apparent later; sometimes many years later. The issue of risk allocation between vendor and purchaser therefore needs to be addressed, and that allocation should be agreed before discussion on detailed drafting begins.

Many factors will influence the negotiations on risk allocation, though ultimately the most important will usually be bargaining power and relative risk-sensitivity. It is by no means always the case that the vendor will accept all the risk for historic contamination. There may well

[2] See para. 12.05.

be cases where the purchaser will accept a significant measure of risk or indeed the entire risk. Examples of such situations are where the purchaser knows of the risks and is taking the asset "as seen"—for example in a management buy-out or where the purchaser has conducted a thorough pre-acquisition audit. A purchaser who is acquiring assets for development may also in practice be prepared to accept a measure of environmental risk, as one of the general risk factors involving development.

Warranties

12.05   The practice of seeking warranties on an acquisition of a company is a response to the fundamental principle of *caveat emptor*, which applies with all its force in relation to such transactions.[3] The length and breadth of warranties in typical acquisition agreements has expanded over the years, and environmental liabilities are simply one further factor which needs to be reflected in the range of such warranties. Warranties on a company sale serve a dual function. First, they will bring to the attention of the vendor those matters which are likely to be of concern to the purchaser; in turn, this will force the issue of potential problems to the attention of the vendor who will wish to avoid exposure by way of disclosing potential liabilities. This should mean that both parties' minds will be concentrated on the problem, so that a negotiated solution results. Secondly, the object of environmental warranties is to obtain redress against the vendor in the event that these prove to be problems of the kind referred to in the warranties. To that extent warranties are a device for allocating risk between the parties.

It is unusual to give warranties in two cases: first, cases where the purchase consideration is satisfied wholly or partly by the allotment of shares in the purchaser and, secondly, bids for listed companies.[4] As has been pointed out by various commentators,[5] there is no practical logic in this distinction drawn between private and listed companies, or any logical reason why the purchaser of a listed company should be prepared to accept the risk of undisclosed liabilities which the purchaser would

---

[3] W. J. L. Knight, *The Acquisition of Private Companies* (6th ed.), 1993, p. 99; Neil Sinclair, *Warranties and Indemnities on Share Sales* (3rd ed.), 1992. S.47 of the Financial Services Act 1986 provides that it is a criminal offence for any person to induce or attempt to induce another to enter into an agreement for the acquisition of securities by dishonest concealment of material facts; however it does not appear that any civil remedy based on the section has yet been awarded by the courts; *Securities and Investment Board* v. *Danfell SA* [1991] 4 All E.R. 883, 887.

[4] Sinclair, *op. cit.*, p. 2.

[5] *Ibid.*

not be prepared to countenance if purchasing a private company. Nonetheless, the distinction is well accepted in practice.

The drafting of warranties relating to contamination and other environmental matters requires careful consideration. A number of the issues arising are common to other types of warranty—for example clear procedures for notification of claims and tax treatment of payments. Other issues relate specifically to the nature of environmental liabilities, and to the effects of standard drafting in the context of such liabilities. Detailed issues of drafting are considered below.[6]

It is standard practice to disclose various matters against warranties and increasingly frequently such disclosures relate to environmental matters. The purchaser needs to be wary of accepting disclosure in some cases, where the information may be insufficient to give a true picture of the risk. Disclosure can be appropriate where a specific breach of legislation, incident, or regulatory problem can be identified. Often, however, disclosure will pose more questions than it answers, and a disclosed "one-off" problem may be symptomatic of more widespread difficulties.

Indemnities

Liability for breach of warranty is to be distinguished from liability **12.06** under an indemnity; in the latter case liability arises not because of breach of any obligation but because the parties have stipulated that one shall save another from loss in specified circumstances.[7] Also, whereas a warranty is essentially an issue between the vendor and purchaser, an indemnity may be given by the vendor in favour of the target company. Traditionally, indemnities, as opposed to warranties, have been confined to taxation liabilities. However, there is no reason why indemnities should not be given in the case of other types of liability, and indeed it appears to be standard drafting practice in the United States for environmental liabilities to be dealt with by way of indemnity rather than warranty. From the point of view of the recipient, there are significant advantages of an indemnity over a warranty. Enforcement is far simpler, with no arguments as to whether the warranty was breached. An indemnity will also avoid complex arguments which could arise over the measure of damages for breach of warranty, *i.e.* whether the cost of cure is recoverable or whether damages are limited to the difference in value of the assets between their actual value as warranted.[8] This may not necessarily equate with the direct cost of cure or out of pocket expenses which could be recovered under an indemnity.

[6] See para. 12.07.
[7] W. J. L. Knight, *The Acquisition of Private Companies* (6th ed.), 1993, p. 134.
[8] *Tito* v. *Waddell (No. 2)* [1977] Ch. 106.

Since the warranty is essentially a representation by the vendor that a particular state of affairs does or does not exist, warranties are perhaps best used where the purchaser has carried out no investigation, or where investigations have been carried out in respect of matters remaining within the exclusive knowledge of the vendor. Indemnities may be appropriate, on the other hand, where investigation has been carried out and has revealed specific problems in respect of which the vendor has agreed to take the risk. An indemnity may also be appropriate where potential liabilities have been disclosed against the warranties.[9]

There is therefore no settled rule as to the circumstances in which warranties and indemnities respectively should be used, but it will be important to ensure that, where both warranties and indemnities are given, they do not conflict. This will need careful consideration, for example, where specific environmental indemnities are given, and some extent there is overlap with matters covered in general warranties. There may be valid tax reasons why the vendor would prefer a claim to be made under a warranty rather than the indemnity, and appropriate provision should be made to as to the precedence of claims.[10] Particular care would be needed where an indemnity, for example, contains a different limitation period or maximum limit on liability from the warranties.

Similar problems arise in the drafting of indemnities to those in the case of warranties; these are considered below.[11]

Common drafting problems

12.07   Warranties and indemnities on environmental issues present a number of common drafting points. These include the following:

(1) Relationship with general provisions

Standard documentation will already contain warranties which in general terms may cover certain environmental problems: such as compliance with all laws, the absence of disputes or litigation and the condition of assets. It is possible to argue that such warranties are preferable to those specifically angled at environmental issues, in that their generality means that they should catch the widest possible range of problems. However, warranties which are more specifically aimed at particular problems of an environmental nature have considerable advantages over general warranties. First, they leave less room for

[9] See para. 12.05 above.
[10] Neil Sinclair, *Warranties and Indemnities on Share Sales* (3rd ed.), 1992, pp. 4, 24.
[11] Para. 12.07. See also App. A for precedents.

argument as to whether a specific circumstance is covered. Secondly, warranties of a general nature will not necessarily draw the vendor's attention to environmental problems; therefore the problem may remain latent and not be made known to the purchaser. In any event, general provisions of this nature can be no substitute for a specifically agreed and precisely-drafted allocation of risk. Care should be taken to ensure that general provisions do not alter the specific allocation of environmental risk which has been agreed, and it may be necessary to exclude or "carve out" environmental matters from these general provisions.

(2) Retrospective legislation

A warranty or indemnity may sometimes be inserted which relates to compliance with all environmental laws: this will usually be widely defined to include primary and subordinate legislation, requirements of public authorities and, frequently, any European Community legislation. The extent to which such provisions are appropriate will depend to a considerable degree upon the opportunities the purchaser has had to satisfy itself as to compliance: in any event it is common for many matters (often of quite trivial importance) to be disclosed against warranties as to compliance. What will be of concern is the extent to which such provisions could relate not only to current laws, but also future legislation and especially to that applying retrospectively. It is usual to find a definition provision to the general effect that references to enactments are to be construed as a reference to the enactment as amended or re-enacted or as modified by other provisions. Care is needed here on the part of the warrantor or indemnifying party, since the effect of such general provisions could be to throw onto them the risk of liability from retrospective legislation. This would be inconsistent with the normal principle that, as from the exchange of contracts or at least from completion, the business of the target company is conducted at the risk of the purchaser.[12] The risk for the warrantor may be reduced by providing that legislative modifications after the date of completion are excluded or, alternatively, by excluding any amendment or modification enacted after completion which would materially extend or increase the liability of the warrantor. A slight twist upon this problem relates to the increasingly prevalent legislative practice of enacting provisions which may remain on the statute book for a considerable time before being brought into force (if ever) by a commencement order. It should be made clear which party is to bear the risk in this case: at least the nature

---

[12] Sinclair, *Warranties and Indemnities on Share Sales* (3rd ed.), 1992, p. 28.

of the liability can be appreciated at the outset, although it is not certain as to when that liability may become a reality.[13]

(3) Presence of "hazardous substances"

It is common practice in the US for environmental warranties and indemnities to refer to the presence of "hazardous substances" on relevant land. This is a reflection of the scheme of liability under relevant US legislation,[14] and it may not be at all appropriate in the UK context. It can be said that any substance may be "hazardous" if present at the wrong place in the wrong quantities at the wrong time, and many warranties relating to "hazardous substances" could be taken as requiring disclosure of the presence of substances such as milk, apple juice or common cleaning fluids. The warrantor or indemnifier should seek to have the provision limited to an appropriate range of specified substances, if there is genuine concern as to the presence of those substances on the company's property.

(4) Problems not caused by the vendor

Problems of contamination may be the results of the vendor's own activities or may be due to other causes, for example historical activities on the land, or the migration of contamination from other land. The vendor may be unwilling to accept the risk of liability for contamination other than that which he has caused himself. The issue can be heated, as often the risks of historic contamination are significant. From the purchaser's point of view, the origin of the risk may be seen as irrelevant; also it can be argued that the vendor as owner of the land is currently subject to those risks, as much as to the risks of contamination arising from the conduct of the vendor's business. Ultimately the issue will be determined by bargaining power rather than strict logic.

(5) Vendor's knowledge

It is common for some warranties to be qualified so as to apply only to the best of the knowledge and belief of the warrantor. Since many environmental problems, in particular contamination, may not be readily apparent it would be easy for the warrantor to avoid liability simply by not looking for problems. It is therefore particularly important that,

---

[13] In some cases, however, the extent of the risk or liability may not be apparent from the face of primary legislation and will only be clear when implementing secondary legislation is enacted; an excellent example is s.143 of the Environmental Protection Act 1990 providing for registers of contaminative uses, the description of those uses being left to subsidiary legislation.

[14] See App. C.

where the warranties are so limited, there is the usual provision that the warrantor has made full enquiry into the subject matter; and that it is not a defence that the warrantor did not appreciate the relevance or significance of any particular matter. Similar issues can arise where it is sought to limit an indemnity to matters known to the indemnifying party.

(6) Time limitations

It is usual for time limitations to be placed upon warranties and indemnities within which claims must be notified. What may be an appropriate limitation period for some types of provision may not necessarily be appropriate in the case of environmental liabilities, which of their nature may not be apparent for many years. Consideration therefore needs to be given as to whether a different limitation period can be negotiated and specified in relation to environmental liabilities. From the purchaser's point of view, too short a period can present difficult problems in that it may be necessary to investigate immediately to establish whether there are any problems giving rise to possible grounds for claim. Negotiation of an unreasonably short period may therefore be something of a mixed blessing for the vendor. The issue of time limitations is closely linked to that of the conditions to be satisfied for a claim, considered below.

(7) Maximum limit on liability

It is common for the vendor to seek a maximum figure for liability under warranties: often the amount of consideration paid for the target company. It is a truism that environmental liabilities do not necessarily bear any relation to the amount of consideration paid for the "asset" which gives rise to the liability and therefore it can be argued that it is not necessarily appropriate to cap liability at this figure. The usual justification given for such limitation is that, if major liabilities do become apparent, then the purchaser may avoid further liability by the expedient of allowing the target company to be placed in solvent liquidation. This, however, is not necessarily a sound argument in general, since there may be very good reasons why a purchaser would not wish to abandon the target to its fate in this way.[15] Environmental liabilities in particular, for example those relating to a badly contaminated site, may not be susceptible to being packaged up and disposed of in so neat a way.

---

[15] Sinclair, *op. cit.*, p. 23; W. J. L. Knight, *The Acquisition of Private Companies* (6th ed.), 1993, p. 132.

(8) Effect of post-completion events

Environmental liabilities may be of an on-going nature spanning both the period before and after completion. Whilst warrantors and indemnifiers may be willing to accept the risk in relation to liabilities arising after completion as the result of a pre-existing condition of contamination, they are much less likely to welcome the idea of assuming liabilities caused by activities after completion. This will be particularly important where a business is being sold as a going concern or where a site forming part of the assets is to be developed. Provisions are therefore sometimes limited so as to provide that the warrantor or indemnifier shall not be liable for any claim which would not have arisen but for an act, event, omission or default occurring after completion. Care needs to be taken as to how this standard wording might apply in the context of a contaminated site. In particular, use of the words "omission or default" could imply that a purchaser would not be able to claim on a warranty where the purchaser has failed to take action to rectify some pre-existing state of contamination.[16]

(9) Indemnities and negligence

A point related to post-completion events is that of negligence by the indemnified party. On ordinary principles an indemnity will be construed against the person in whose favour the indemnity is given and will not cover loss due to a person's own negligence or that of his servants unless adequate and clear words were used, or unless the indemnity could have no reasonable meaning unless so applied.[17] In particular, where the loss in question arises concurrently from breach of statutory duty and negligence the indemnity may be construed as not extending to the negligence.[18] These principles could potentially be very difficult to apply in cases where it is alleged that the post completion actions (or inaction) of the purchaser have exacerbated a pre-existing problem, or have turned a possible liability into an actual one.

(10) Cross indemnities

It is important to achieve as full an allocation of risk as possible. For example, where a vendor agrees to indemnify a purchaser in respect of environmental liabilities up to a maximum of £5,000,000, does this imply that the purchaser is accepting all other risks? If so then, bearing in mind that the vendor retains residual risk as original polluter, logically

[16] Sinclair, *op. cit.* p. 31.
[17] *Canada Steam Ship Lines Ltd.* v. *The King* [1952] A.C. 192; *Walters* v. *Whessoe* [1960] 6 B.L.R. 35.
[18] *E. E. Caledonia Ltd.* v. *Orbit Valve Company Europe* Q.B.D., May 28, 1993; *cf. Smith* v. *South Wales Switchgear* [1978] 1 W.L.R. 165.

the purchaser should indemnify the vendor against all liability in excess of that figure.

(11) Conditions of claims

Clear conditions and procedures need to be laid down for claims under warranties or indemnities. Conditions which are excessively onerous can substantially negate or diminish the protection of such provisions. Various conditions or combinations of conditions can be expressed, for example:

(a) the existence of relevant contamination;
(b) the existence of actual claims by third parties or regulatory authorities; or
(c) expenditure being incurred on clean up.

From a vendor's point of view, they will not wish liability to be triggered simply by the discovery of contamination. Many sites are contaminated without imposing any liabilities or costs on the owner. On the other hand, a purchaser may not wish the ability to claim to be restricted to situations where a third party sues or a regulatory authority seeks clean-up: for one thing the purchaser may wish to put the problems right before that happens, and for another delays in a third party or regulatory authority discovering the problem and deciding to take action may take the claims outside any agreed time limit for the indemnity. Out of pocket expenditure by the purchaser on clean-up could be used as the trigger for a claim, but the vendor will need protection against costs being incurred unnecessarily or against unreasonable expenditure. It may be possible to limit such circumstances to cases where contamination would or could result in liability or have a material adverse effect on the conduct of the business by the purchaser. However, there are inherent uncertainties for the parties in both of these formulations. From the point of view of a company's finance director, it is a question of the size of any provision to be made in reserves on the balance sheet, the date at which payments may have to be made and the spread of such payment; any tax consequences may also be important.

It will also have to be established whether costs of investigating possible contamination or actual or potential claims is covered within any indemnity: such costs can of course be very considerable.

(12) Mechanics of claims

Clear procedures should exist for the making of claims and the conduct of claims. Where the indemnity is against third party liability or regulatory claims, the indemnifying party may wish to have the right to take over the conduct of the action or response to the claim. There should be provisions for mutual cooperation, assistance and exchange of information in relation to any claims, and the ability of one party to settle or compromise the claim without the consent of the other may need to be restricted.

(13) Date of application of warranties or indemnities

Provision should be made in relation to any interval between exchange of contracts for purchase of the target company and the date of completion. Where the vendors are continuing to run the target company in that interim period, the purchaser may wish to make provision as to the way in which the business should be run so as to lessen the risk of contamination occurring during that interim period.[19] Additionally, the purchaser will wish the warranties to apply both to the date of exchange of contracts and at completion, and for any relevant events in the interim period (such as spills or the discovery of contamination) to be disclosed.

(14) Loss of profits

The first priority of an indemnity will probably be to cover third party liabilities and the direct costs of on-site clean-up or statutory claims relating to such clean-up. It is more unusual for indemnities to address expressly the indirect costs of such operations, such as loss of profit. Yet such costs, may in fact present a considerable burden. In some cases, elaborate formulae have been devised, limiting the indeminity in relation to such profits by reference to earlier profits, and avoiding any obligation to indemnify in respect of unusual profits or lost contracts.

Practical problems with warranties and indemnities

12.08   Aside from the drafting problems mentioned above, both warranties and indemnities share the common problem that they are only as good as the financial strength of the warrantor or covenantor, respectively. Additionally, claims under indemnities and more especially warranties in relation to pollution problems can be costly, protracted and difficult to make out: for example, it may be very difficult to establish whether or not pollution or contamination (or damage thereby caused) took place before or after completion, or both.

For these reasons it is generally preferable in practice to discover as much as possible about the assets before completion, enabling the risk to

---

[19] The issues are similar to those as between vendor and purchaser in many respects: see para. 11.08.

be reflected in the purchase price. Nonetheless, even following such investigations, warranties and indemnities must still have an important role, in that there will still be residual risk which needs to be allocated. The existence of data about the contaminative state of the property will in that event be useful to provide a "baseline" as at the date of exchange or completion, thereby reducing uncertainty as to where the risk falls under the contractual provisions.

Company accounts and listing particulars

Liabilities arising from contaminated land may be sufficiently serious **12.09** to require reference in listing particulars or company accounts. In relation to company accounts the key principles are that the company accounts must present a true and fair view and that only material amounts need be shown or disclosed.[20] The Companies Act 1985, Schedule 4, requires provision to be made for liabilities or loss which are either likely to be incurred or certain to be incurred but are uncertain as to amount or as to the date on which they will arise. In the case of a contingent liability not provided for in the accounts, the amount or estimated amount of that liability must be disclosed, together with its legal nature and whether any valuable security has been given by the company in connection with the liability.[21] "True and fair view" though referred to in statute,[22] is not defined and ultimately can only be authoritatively interpreted by a court, which would doubtlessly look for guidance to the ordinary practices of professional accountants.[23] Whilst the meaning of "true and fair" remains the same, the content given to the concept can change over time[24]: this is important to bear in mind in the context of contaminated land, which may now have an impact on the valuation of assets and liabilities far greater than could have been foreseen when many standards of accounting practice were developed.

The issue of what should be disclosed can also arise in relation to listing particulars. Section 146 of the Financial Services Act 1986 contains the general duty that any listing particulars submitted under section 144 shall contain all such information as investors and their professional advisors would reasonably require, and reasonably expect to find there, for the purpose of making an informed assessment of:

[20] Jenny Bough, *Company Accounts* (1987), p. 4.
[21] Companies Act 1985, Sched. 4, para. 50.
[22] Companies Act 1985, s.228(2).
[23] See the joint opinion of Leonard Hoffman Q.C. and Mary Arden, quoted at Bough, *op. cit.*, p. 197, and the subsequent opinion by Mary Arden Q.C. (taking into account the changes made by the Companies Act 1989) which was issued as an Appendix to the Foreword of *Accounting Standards—Statements of Standard Accounting Practice* of the Accounting Standards Board.
[24] *Ibid.*

(a) the assets and liabilities, financial position, profits and losses, and prospects of the issuer of the securities; and

(b) the rights attaching to those securities.

A similar general duty of disclosure applies in relation to company prospectuses under section 163 of the Financial Services Act 1986 (not yet in force). In practice the existence of such a duty may be very important because a high proportion of companies will have land assets, which may well have been subject to one or more contaminative uses.

It may well be that liabilities for contaminated land or the effect of contamination on the value of assets is of such a scale as to be included within the information investors and their professional advisors would require for the purpose of making an informed assessment. It should be noted that by section 146(2) of Financial Services Act the information to be included shall be not only that which is within the knowledge of the person responsible for the listing particulars, but also that which it would be reasonable for him to obtain by making enquiries.

CORPORATE INSOLVENCY

Receivership

12.10   A receiver may be appointed out of court either under an express power contained in the security document, or alternatively by a mortgagee under the statutory powers of the Law of Property Act 1925. Commonly in practice a debenture holder will appoint under an express power contained in the mortgage deed, and a mortgagee will appoint under the statutory powers contained in the Law of Property Act.

In relation to the first category of receiver, the Insolvency Act 1986 confers special powers and status upon a receiver or manager of the whole (or substantially the whole) of the company's property. This distinction is capable of presenting a difficulty in a case where part of the company's assets are subject to potential environmental liabilities: the lender may wish to exclude the problematic property from the receivership, but doing so may result in the receiver failing to be appointed in relation to the whole or substantially the whole of the company's property, and consequently not having the special powers of Schedule 1 of the Insolvency Act. The problem is perhaps in practice theoretical rather than real, since nowadays most debentures and fixed charges will contain extensive powers removing the need for reliance on Schedule 1. Indeed in practice the debenture holder will not wish the receiver to be an administrative receiver under Schedule 1 because of the extra expense involved.

There are a number of pertinent points to note about the position of an administrative receiver, or receiver and manager, in relation to contaminated land and environmental liability. First, in relation to a receiver appointed under a debenture, the receiver will have the power to carry on the day to day process of realisation and management of the company's property without interference from the board of directors, who are effectively displaced by the receiver's appointment.[25] This may entail responsibility under environmental legislation or common law on the part of the receiver. Interference with the rights of third parties, however innocent, may be actionable in tort:[26] the extent to which a receiver may be responsible for the acts of employees of the company probably depends on his degree of personal conduct and culpability in the same way as a director of the company, since the employees are not employees of the receiver himself.[27] As mentioned below, the position may change dramatically if the company should go into liquidation.

One Canadian case[28] suggests that where certain properties managed by the receiver are subject to environmental liabilities under statute, an administrative order may be addressed to the receiver rather than the company and indeed that this may involve application of proceeds or profits from other, non-problematic, assets managed by the receiver. It was suggested that the receiver cannot pick and choose between assets so as to walk away from liability on problematic assets, saying simply that remedial action would diminish distribution to secured creditors.

Secondly, the receiver, whether appointed under a debenture or under the Law of Property Act 1925, may potentially be liable in his capacity as occupier for breaches of legislative requirements. In one case, *Lord Advocate* v. *Aero Technologies (in receivership)*,[29] injunctive relief was obtained against a receiver to prevent explosive materials being left in an insecure condition, in breach of the Explosives Act 1875, which applies to the occupier of a factory. In another case, *Meigh* v. *Wickenden*,[30] a receiver was held liable for contravention of Factories Act requirements as the

---

[25] *Gomba Holdings Limited* v. *Homan* [1986] 1 W.L.R. 1301 at 1306.

[26] See *Kerr on Receivers and Administrators* (17th ed.), 1989, p. 376.

[27] *Ibid.*, p. 377.

[28] *Panamericana de Bienes y Servicios, SA* v. *Northern Badger Oil and Gas Ltd.* (1991) 81 D.L.R. (4d) 280. See also the earlier Ontario Court of Appeal decision in *Canada Trust Co.* v. *Bulora Corpn. Ltd.* (1980) 34 C.B.R. (NS) 145; affirmed 39 C.B.R. (N.S.) 152. But compare *A.G. (Ontario)* v. *Tyre King Tyre Recycling Ltd.* (1992) 8 C.E.L.R. (NS) 202 and *Re Lamford Forest Products Ltd.* (1992) 86 D.L.R. (4th) 434; also the 1992 Bankruptcy and Insolvency Act which makes it clear that trustees have no personal liability in respect of environmental conditions arising before their appointment, save where the condition arose as a result of due diligence on their part: [1993] Env. Liab. 86.

[29] 1991 S.L.T. 134 (Outer House).

[30] [1942] 2 Q.B. 160.

occupier; the receiver in question had no practical or technical expertise in running a factory, and left these matters in the hands of the directors. Nonetheless, it was held, the receiver "was complete master of the affairs of the company" and "had absolute and complete power to manage the property of which he took possession."[31] The argument that he was agent of the company did not alter this: nonetheless, certainly for rating purposes a receiver will not be regarded as displacing the company as occupier, his occupation being treated as that of the company.[32]

Thirdly, the fact that the receiver may be in receipt of rents from the property, or would be entitled to be in receipt of such rents were any payable, may result in the receiver being regarded as "owner" of the property and consequently liable under any environmental legislation which bites upon the owner.[33] The question is in what capacity the receiver is receiving the rents; on general principles, so long as the receiver is acting as the agent of the company, he ought not to be regarded as receiving rents in his own right.

Fourthly, and perhaps most importantly, a receiver will be regarded as an agent of the company, rather than the lender, either by virtue of express provisions in the debenture, or under the statutory presumption of agency by section 44(1)(a) of the Insolvency Act 1986. The effect of the presumption will be to insulate the debenture holder from the consequences of wrongful acts committed by the receiver.[34] It follows from this that actions of the receiver may have adverse consequences for the company and it has been suggested in one case that a receiver may not exercise his discretion so as to lead to the commission of an offence by the company[35]: This may have important implications in the case where property is subject to a statutory notice or other requirement, failure to comply with which constitutes an offence.

It should also be remembered that the appointment of a receiver is no bar to the company being wound up, and the effect of winding-up will be that the receiver will no longer be agent of the company, now in liquidation. He will either need the approval of the debenture holders to act as their agent, or he will be acting as principal. Thus the receiver's position is fundamentally different before and after liquidation.

The power of a receiver to carry out a clean-up operation in relation to the property will depend upon the terms of the debenture or mortgage,

---

[31] *Ibid.* at p. 168.

[32] *Ratford v. Northavon District Council* [1987] Q.B. 357.

[33] See *Backup Corporation v. Smith* [1890] 44 Ch.D. 395; *Solomons v. Gertzensten Limited* [1954] 2 Q.B. 243; *Midland Bank v. Conway Corporation* [1965] W.L.R. 1165.

[34] *Re Simms* [1934] Ch. 1. It does not apply where the receiver is appointed by the court, in which case he acts as principal, subject to an implied right of indemnity in respect of liabilities properly incurred.

[35] *Re John Willment (Ashford) Limited* [1979] 2 All E.R. 615.

and upon any statutory powers. It seems likely that the extent of statutory powers applying to administrative receivers under Schedule 1 of the Insolvency Act 1986 could be sufficient to allow such clean-up costs to be incurred; it is much less likely that more limited powers of a Law of Property Act receiver under section 109 of the Law of Property Act would be wide enough for this purpose. One potential difficulty could be whether powers which are related to the carrying on of the company's business would necessarily apply to all clean-up costs.

Unlike a liquidator, a receiver has no power to disclaim onerous property, and therefore will need to persuade the lender to release problematic properties from the receivership or, as a matter of last resort, the receiver can resign. It will be appreciated that a receiver of a property which turns out to be contaminated may be in an exposed position; this risk being made all the worse by the speed with which a receiver is required to accept appointment.[36] It is for the receiver to protect his or her own position by obtaining an appropriate indemnity from the lender as a condition of appointment. Save in the case of the clearing banks such an indemnity is standard practice: but the receiver should be wary that the indemnity (whether express or inplied by common law) may not extend to negligence or unlawful or improper conduct on his part. The right to an indemnity against tort damages or fines may therefore depend on whether the receiver acted properly and with due care.[37] The common law indemnity will be limited to the assets,[38] whereas environmental liabilities may be of such a scale as to exceed the value of those assets, particularly if those assets comprise contaminated land.

Insolvency Act administrators

An administrator under the Insolvency Act 1986 is in essence a **12.11** receiver and manager of the company, appointed by an administration order to facilitate one or more specific purpose, to be achieved by taking the affairs of the company out of the control of its directors to be entrusted to the administrator.[39] As a recent creature of statute, there is less case law to indicate the position of administrator; however, it would not appear to be substantially different to that of the receiver or manager

---

[36] Before the end of the next business day after receiving the letter of appointment; Insolvency Act 1986, s.33. In practice however, the receiver will previously have investigated the situation on behalf of the lender.

[37] The standard of care required is probably that of a reasonably prudent man of business: *Speight* v. *Gaunt* (1883) 9 App. Cas. 1, at p. 19.

[38] See *Boehm* v. *Goodall* [1911] 1 Ch. 155; *Johnston* v. *Courtney* [1920] 2 W.W.R. 459.

[39] Kerr on *Receivers and Administrators* (17th ed.), 1989, p. 261.

as described above. The administrator has the power to do all such things as may be necessary in the management of the affairs, business and property of the company and has also all the powers statutorily conferred upon an administrative receiver.[40] Also, like a receiver, the administrator is deemed to act as the company's agent.[41] However, unlike a receiver who may ask the lender to release properties from the receivership, the administrator has no obvious means of getting rid of environmentally problematic properties; nor does the administrator have an appointor as such, from whom an indemnity may be obtained.

Liquidators

12.12   There are significant differences between the position of a liquidator and that of a receiver or an administrator. The powers of liquidators are more rigidly confined within the framework of the Insolvency Act 1986: there is no obvious power to conduct remedial or clean up operations in relation to contaminated property, though this may well be implied within the statutory power under Schedule 4 of the Insolvency Act to do all things as may be necessary for the winding up of the company's affairs and distribution of its assets.

The basic duty of the liquidator on a compulsory liquidation under section 143 of the Insolvency Act is to secure the assets of the company and get in, realise and distribute them to the company's creditors and, if there is a surplus, to the persons entitled to it; thus the obligation is to realise the assets as efficiently as possible and to satisfy the liabilities in so far as the realised assets permit. Generally, there would appear less scope for personal liability on the part of a liquidator in relation to environmental problems, though this possibility cannot be precluded. Certainly in practice a liquidator is less likely than a receiver or administrator to run a business on an ongoing basis.

The liquidator is not an agent of a company, and therefore the arguments which apply in the case of receivers and administrators as to the exercise of powers so as to avoid the company committing an offence may be of less force in relation to a liquidator faced with a statutory notice requiring remedial measures. Indeed to prefer such a notice to claims of other creditors, in the absence of any statutory preference or priority given to the notice, would appear to run counter to the liquidator's general duties. However, whilst it is true that a liquidator is not an agent of the company, his status is in practice similar as the company can only act through him. For example, the liquidator might procure that certain assets of the company are put up for sale. To the

---

[40] Insolvency Act 1976, s.14(1) and (2).
[41] Insolvency Act 1986, s.14(5).

extent that the liquidator incurs liability in realising those assets, or needs to expend money in realising them, then this will be a proper expense of the liquidation which he may quite properly pay out in preference to the claims of ordinary creditors. The crucial question in relation to contaminated land will usually be what liabilities and costs were reasonably and necessarily incurred to achieve proper realisation of the asset.

Another significant point of difference is the liquidator's express powers to disclaim onerous property under sections 178–182 of the Insolvency Act 1986. Under section 178(2) the liquidator may, by giving prescribed notice, disclaim any onerous property notwithstanding that he has taken possession of it, endeavoured to sell it, or otherwise exercised rights of ownership over it. The property which may be disclaimed includes property which is not readily sellable, or is such that it may give rise to a liability to pay money or perform any other onerous act: this would appear to be clearly applicable to property which is found to be contaminated and subject to liabilities at common law or under statutory provisions. The effect of disclaimer under section 178(4) is to terminate the rights and liabilities of the company in the property disclaimed—it does not beyond this affect the rights and liabilities of any other person.

However, it should be noted that under the Insolvency Act section 178(6): "Any person sustaining loss or damage in consequence of the operation of a disclaimer under this section is deemed a creditor of the company to the extent of the loss or damage and accordingly may prove for the loss or the damage in the winding up." Thus the cost of environmental clean up measures at one of the company's properties, even if disclaimed so as not to be recoverable as a liquidation expense, could ultimately increase the company's liabilities, possibly to a significant extent.

Chapter 13

CONTAMINATED LAND LEGISLATION
IN OTHER JURISDICTIONS

A. Scotland
B. United States
C. Canada
D. The Netherlands
E. Germany
F. Denmark
G. Australia

A.   SCOTLAND*

13.01   Whilst in many respect the statutory framework for contaminated land is the same for Scotland as for England and Wales, in other important respects there are differences. The main points of distinction are listed and considered below.[1]

Civil remedies

13.02   The Scots law of delict will be relevant to many contaminated land situations; in particular the doctrine of nuisance. The remedies of damages and interdict correspond to the equivalent English remedies of damages and injunction: there is also the possibility (though the law is undeveloped) of the remedy of specific implement, which corresponds to a mandatory injuction. Specific implement is generally available as an alternative to damages without special circumstances needing to apply

---

* The assistance of Charles Smith of Brodies W.S., Edinburgh, is gratefully acknowledged.
[1] The best summary of the Scottish position is *Scots Law and the Environment: Liability for Contaminated Land* written by Brodies Solicitors in association with Lanarkshire Development Agency, T&T Clark, 1992.

as in English law. However, in the context of nuisance there may be problems with the remedy if, for example, the only way to remedy a relatively minor polluting incident is by disproportionately large expenditure, or where a remedy is impossible.[2] No distinction is drawn in Scots law between private and public nuisance.

One important difference is that that rule of strict liability in *Rylands* v. *Fletcher* has been held not to apply in Scotland.[3] Thus fault or negligence *(culpa)* will need to be proven in an action for damages, though not where interdict is the remedy sought.[4] However, the escape of a dangerous substance or thing, or the creation of some other danger that would not have been there but for the act of the defender, will give rise to a strong presumption of fault or negligence (effectively the doctrine of the *res ipsa loquitur*).[5]

English and Scots law share the doctrine of interference with riparian rights to unpolluted water,[6] though it is not wholly clear whether the doctrine is part of the law of nuisance in Scotland (and so dependent on *culpa*), or is a branch of the law in its own right.[7] It is by no means clear that a Scots court would follow the decision of the House of Lords in *Cambridge Water Co. Ltd.* v. *Eastern Counties Leather plc*[7a] on the issue of strict liability for interference with groundwater abstraction rights: if interference with water rights is indeed part of the law of nuisance, or otherwise depends on *culpa*, then that may make it more difficult for the courts to follow the decision.

---

[2] In *Hugh Blackwood (Farms) Limited* v. *Motherwell District Council* 1988 G.W.D. 30–1290, the Outer House appears to envisage that an order for specific implement might be made simply requiring damage to be rectified without necessarily specifying how or at what cost.

[3] *R. H. M. Bakeries (Scotland) Ltd.* v. *Strathclyde Regional Council* 1985 S.L.T. 214.

[4] *Logan* v. *Wang (UK) Limited* 1991 S.L.T. 580 (Outer House) is authority that it is not necessary to plead fault or negligence for an award of interdict.

[5] *Kerr* v. *Earl of Orkney* (1857) 20 D. 298—The principle is in many senses akin to *Rylands* v. *Fletcher* in that it applies where the defendant voluntarily brings onto or creates on his land some *novum opus*, creating a danger not naturally there. The distinction is that there must be a finding of fault, though that finding is lightly inferred from an especially heavy duty of care in the absence of any exculpating explanation from the defendant: ". . . A dam that gives way in a night's rain is not such as the maker was bound to erect. The fact that it gives way is a proof that his obligation was not fulfilled, and that the protection was not afforded which he was bound to provide" (1857) 20 D. 298 at 302. See also *Tennent* v. *Earl of Glasgow* (1864) 2 M. (H.L.) 22, 26; *Caledonian Railway* v. *Greenock Corporation* 1917 S.C. (H.L.) 56, 60, 63, 65; *Campbell* v. *Kennedy* (1864) 3 M 121.

[6] *Young* v. *Bankier Distillery Co.* [1893] A.C. 691; (1893) 20 R. (H.L.) 76; 1 S.L.T. 204.

[7] See D.M. Gordon, *Scottish Land Law*, p. 164, n. 7, *Duke of Buccleuch* v. *Cowan* (1866) 4 M. 475; *Montgomery & Fleming* v. *Buchanan's Trustees* (1853) 15 D. 853; *Noble's Trustees* v. *Economic Forestry (Scotland) Ltd.* 1988 S.L.T. 662.

[7a] [1994] 2 W.L.R. 53; see generally Chap. 2.

The principles of the law of negligence are broadly the same in both jurisdictions.

Water pollution

13.03   Water pollution is still governed by the Control of Pollution Act 1974, Part II, though the provisions on criminal liability are substantially the same in effect. Section 46(4) of the Control of Pollution Act gives to River Purification Boards broadly the same powers of remedial and preventative anti-pollution measures as are available to the NRA under section 161 of the Water Resources Act 1991.

Statutory nuisance

13.04   Statutory nuisances in Scotland are dealt with by environmental health authorities (District or Islands Councils) under the Public Health (Scotland) Act 1897 (as amended by section 83 of the Environmental Protection Act 1990). Section 16 of that Act defines the categories of statutory nuisance in terms similar, but not identical, to Part III of the Environmental Protection Act. In *City of Glasgow District Council* v. *Carroll*[8] it was held by a Sheriff Court that the first and general head of nuisance (premises in such a state as to be a nuisance or injurious or dangerous to health) should not be pleaded where the nuisance was such as to fall clearly within one of the more specific heads; there is some doubt as to whether the decision would be followed by a higher court.

Another Sheriff Court decision, *Clydebank District Council* v. *Monaville*,[9] involved an action for abatement of a statutory nuisance against the innocent purchaser of a site contaminated by asbestos. It was held that an abatement notice could validly be served on the purchaser: this follows from the definition in section 3 of the 1897 Act of the "author of the nuisance" which includes "the person through whose act or default the nuisance is caused, exists, or is continued, whether he be the owner or occupier or both." In addition a notice under section 20 of the 1897 Act (like its counterpart under the Environmental Protection Act 1990) is expressly stated to be capable of service on an owner or occupier of land if the author of the nuisance cannot be found.

The procedure under sections 20–22 of the 1897 Act differs from that for abatement notices under the Environmental Protection Act: the

---

[8] *Glasgow District Council* v. *Carroll* 1991 S.L.T. (Sh.Ct.) 46.

[9] *Clydebank District Council* v. *Monaville* 1982 S.L.T. (Sh.Ct.) 2; referring to two Inner House authorities, *Cadder Local Authority* v. *Lang* (1879) 6 R. 1242 and *Govan Police Commissioners* v. *Mackinnon* (1885) 22 S.L.R. 843.

authority must first serve notice, then in the event of non-compliance must petition the Sheriff for a decree requiring compliance and finally, if compliance is still not forthcoming, apply to the Sheriff for a warrant authorising the authority to take the necessary action, in which case the expenses would be recoverable from the author, occupier or owner.

Section 146 of the 1897 Act (as amended by the Local Government Finance Act 1992, Schedule 13, paragraph 2) contains a procedure whereby a group of 10 non-domestic ratepayers or Council Tax payers, or the local procurator fiscal, having given 14 days' notice in writing to the authority, may petition the Sheriff for a decree requiring the authority to inspect land or to take action against a statutory nuisance.

Property rights

The Scottish system of real property is of course very different to that **13.05** of England and Wales and consequently a different interpretation may be given to the term "owner" where it appears in legislation such as section 61 of the Environmental Protection Act 1990. For the purpose of establishing ownership of land recourse must be made to the Land Register or Register of Sasines, which are open to the public. The owner of land has essentially similar natural rights to those enjoyed in England. Scots law acknowledges "the undoubted right of the proprietor to the free and absolute use of his own property, but there is this restraint or limitation imposed for the protection of his neighbour, that he is not so to use his property as to create that discomfort or annoyance to his neighbour which interferes with his legitimate enjoyment."[10]

A lease in Scotland, as in England, is capable of creating a real interest in the land, but it is arguable whether a Scots Court would regard the tenant as being the "owner" for the purposes of statutory provisions. It remains to be determined to what extent the Scots Courts would be notivated by other definitions of the word "owner" in other UK statutory provisions as a primary determinant of the liability question, rather than by having regard to pure feudal theory (by virtue of which non-one-subject to certain esoteric exceptions—owns land outright).

While the system of taking security is radically different in Scotland from that which applies in England, the issue of the possible liability of lenders, receivers, liquidators and administrators for breaches of environmental legislation is probably to be approached in a similar way. It has been held in *Lord Advocate* v. *Aero Technologies Ltd.*[11] that receivers may be jointly liable with the company or occupiers for the purposes of the Explosives Acts 1875 and 1923.

[10] *Fleming* v. *Hislop* 1886 13 R. (H.L.) 43, at p. 48 *per* Lord Fitzgerald.
[11] 1991 S.L.T. 134.

B. USA*

Legislative development

13.06   The lynch-pin of the US System for the investigation and clean-up of sites at which hazardous substances have been released into the environment is the Comprehensive Environmental Response, Compensation, and Liability Act of 1980 (CERCLA) as amended in 1986 by the Superfund Amendments and Reauthorisation Act (SARA). The legislation is known collectively as the federal "Superfund" law, because a key component of the Act is the so-called Hazardous Substance Superfund, which is available to finance the cleaning-up of hazardous waste sites.

During the 1950s and 1960s a number of important federal statutes dealt with environmental problems such as clean air and water and the disposal of solid wastes. However, no legislation specifically addressed the problem caused by improper disposal of hazardous wastes: legislation on waste, such as the Solid Waste Disposal Act of 1965 and the Resource Recovery Act of 1970, were concerned primarily with unsightly and unsanitary refuse disposal and with the promotion of recycling. Pressure for legislative action grew with the accumulation of evidence as to the risks of past and current hazardous waste disposal practices, in particular the contamination of drinking water. The first measure enacted as a response to the problem was the Safe Drinking Water Act of 1974 which authorised the US Environmental Protection Agency (EPA) to regulate public water systems, to develop drinking water standards and to protect underground sources of drinking water. The more direct response to the hazardous waste problem was, however, the Resource Conservation and Recovery Act of 1976 (RCRA).

RCRA instituted "cradle to grave" regulation of hazardous wastes. EPA is required to compile and maintain a list of such wastes, or criteria for identifying such wastes, which when so identified, may be stored or disposed of only at sites holding operating permits and which satisfy EPA regulations. Generators and transporters are placed under duties as to safe packaging and labelling, record keeping and reporting under the "manifest system". RCRA also establishes a specific programme for regulating and undertaking corrective actions of underground storage tanks. However, RCRA was essentially preventative rather than curative legislation and with the exception of one section, creatively interpreted

* The assistance of Jeffrey B. Groy of Stoel Rives Boley Jones & Grey, Salt Lake City, Utah and Lee E. Braem, Senior Counsel of Schering-Plough Corporation, Kenilworth, New Jersey is gratefully acknowledged.

by the courts,[12] did not make provision for the clean up of problems caused by past practices.

The immediate impetus for further action was provided by the Love Canal incident[13] though as the underlying congressional Committee reports of CERCLA demonstrate, there had been other incidents which were almost equally worrying—the contamination of the James River by kepone, the contaimination of the Hudson River by PCBs, and the ingestion of PCBs by livestock in Michigan. CERCLA was enacted following consideration of various other similar bills in December 1980, just after the defeat of Jimmy Carter in the presidential election: it has been described as having been enacted in a "lame duck" administration "in a situation which allowed for no amendments".[14]

Very broadly, CERCLA has three main aspects[15]:

(a) a comprehensive federal-state mechanism for a rapid response to releases or threatened releases of hazardous substances into the environment at facilities where the owner or operator is unwilling or unable to do so;

(b) a federal trust fund, financed in the main by private industry, to pay the cost of response actions by federal or state agencies or private "volunteers"; and

(c) a federal cause of action for recovery of costs incurred for responses to hazardous substances releases from four categories of person—current owners and operators, owners and operators at the time of disposal, generators of the hazardous substances, and transporters who selected the facility.

It is of course this final aspect of CERCLA the liability scheme, which has proved to be immensely complex and controversial.

Identification of sites

The crucial concept under CERCLA is the release of a hazardous **13.07** substance: such substances are designated under the Act, but the term does not include petroleum, natural gas and their fractions. Under

[12] Section 7003, 42 U.S.C. $6973 which was interpreted in *United States* v. *Price* 688 F. 2d (3rd Circ. 1983) as authorising governmental injunctive action against the leaking of wastes formerly deposited at a landfill; see also *United States* v. *Northeastern Pharmaceutical & Chemical Co., Inc.* 810 F. 2d 726 (8th Cir. 1986).

[13] See Preamble n.3.

[14] Frank P. Grad, "A legislative History of the Comprehensive Environmental Response, Compensation and Liability ("Superfund") Act of 1980" [1982] Columbia Journal of Environmental Law 1.

[15] See Bradford F. Whitman, "Superfund Law and Practice," (ALi-ABA, 1991), p. 14.

section 103 of CERCLA there are various reporting requirements, backed by severe civil and criminal sanctions, which apply to operators of facilities from which a hazardous substance is released in a reportable quantity; this includes an obligation for initial reporting by June 1981 of the existence of facilities at which hazardous substances had been stored, treated or disposed of. The term "release" is broadly defined to mean any spilling, leaking, pumping, pouring, emitting, emptying, discharging, injecting, escaping, leaching, dumping, or disposing into the environment, including the abandonment or discarding of barrels or other containers containing any hazardous substance, pollutant, or contaminant.

Section 104 of CERCLA gives EPA broad powers of access to property and to records for the purpose of gathering information: the Agency is required to perform a preliminary assessment (PA) on all sites listed in CERCLA Information System, CERCLIS, its data-base of potentially contaminated sites. Under s.105(a)(8)(A) the EPA is under a detailed obligation to establish criteria "for determining priorities among releases or threatened releases throughout the United States for the purpose of taking remedial action and, to the extent practicable taking into account the potential urgency of such action, for the purpose of taking removal action." This obligation is met by the EPA's Hazard Ranking System based on three factor categories,[16] which calculates a site's ranking on a score between one and 100; a score of 28.50 or more will justify a site's inclusion on the National Priorities List (NPL).

Quite separately to this assessment, the Department of Interior will investigate the issue of damages to natural resources. Section 107 gives rise to liability (as distinct from liability for removal and remedial response costs) for damages for injury to, destruction of, or loss of natural resources,[17] and s.107(f) makes the U.S. and state governments trustees for this purpose.

Response by EPA

13.08   Action taken by the EPA in relation to sites can be divided into two categories: short term removal actions in response to emergency circumstances and the selection of long-term remedial actions.

---

[16] The three factors relate to risks from:
  (a) the likelihood of a release of hazardous substances from the site;
  (b) flammability, explosive or toxicity characteristics of the hazardous substances; and
  (c) the pathways of exposure.
EPA's use of the HRS has been attacked as arbitrary, capricious and an abuse of power, but has been upheld: *Eagle-Pitcher Industries* v. *EPA* 759 F. 2d 905 (D.C. Circ. 1985).
[17] Defined as land, fish, wildlife, biota, air, water, groundwater, drinking water supplies and other natural resources.

"Removal action" can be taken in relation to releases or threatened releases even before a site is placed on the NPL: the term "removal" is defined broadly to include clean-up or removal of hazardous substances from the environment, monitoring, assessment and evaluation, and any other actions necessary to prevent, minimise or mitigate damage to the public health or welfare, or to the environment. If the removal action is funded by the Hazardous Substance Superfund, action is subject to financial and time limitations ($2 million and 12 months), but these limitations can be surpassed—and often are—where there is an emergency situation or where continued action is appropriate and consistent with the long-term remedial action to be taken.[18]

Remedial action, as distinct from removal action, is defined as actions consistent with permanent remedy. Section 101(24), in defining the term, and section 121(b) indicate a preference for on-site treatment, disposal or disposition of hazardous substances, in that off-site options are only included if they are more cost-effective or are necessary to protect public health, welfare or the environment, or where off-site disposal will create new capacity to manage hazardous substances. Action can include the cost of permanent relocation of residents, businesses and community facilities. Remedial action cannot be undertaken until various procedural and substantive requirements have been fulfilled: these include publicity, a public meeting, and responses to all comments made by the public. This process—which may take a period of years—results in a "record of decision". The procedure is known as the remedial investigation/feasibility study (RI/FS); it may be undertaken either by the Government alone or with the participation of those potentially responsible for the clean up costs.

In order for a site to qualify for remedial action financed by the Fund, it must be on the NPL (see above). Entry on the NPL is not, however, necessary in order for injunctive action or cost recovery proceedings to be taken against potentially responsible parties. Nor can Superfund resources be expended on remedial action until the relevant state enters into a cooperative agreement with EPA: such agreements may relate to participation by the state in the remedial action, or may guarantee the cooperation and assistance of the state in various respects.

A crucial section in relation to selection of remedial action and standards of clean-up is section 121. Cost is an issue to be taken into account, but a strong preference is expressed for the use of technologies that "will result in a permanent and significant decrease in the toxicity, mobility or volume of the hazardous substance pollutant or contami-

---

[18] S.104(c)(1); 42 U.S.C. 9604 (c)(1).

nant". Compliance is to be achieved with any Federal or state environmental law containing standards or criteria as to the substance (*e.g.*, maximum contaminant level goals under the Safe Drinking Water Act and water quality criteria under the Clean Water Act).

Enforcement and liability

13.09 The EPA has an extensive armoury of enforcement options under CERCLA. These are:

    (a) administrative orders and injunctions under section 106 directing or compelling responsible parties to take action where "there may be imminent and substantial endangerment to the public health or welfare or the environment":

    (b) action under section 106 to enforce administrative orders where these are not complied with wilfully and without sufficient cause. Sanctions include penalties for contempt of court, fines of up to $25,000 dollars per day on non compliance, and clean up by EPA itself followed by action for recovery of its own costs plus punitive damages of up to three times that amount;

    (c) actions under section 107 to recover the costs of investigation and clean up, plus interest. This is the remedy which has been subject to the greatest volume of litigation;

    (d) actions under section 107 to recover natural resource damages. It has been held that to recover such damages the plaintiff must prove by a preponderance of the evidence that releases from the facility were a contributing factor to the damage: if so, then the defendant is jointly and severally liable for all the injury unless it can prove the injury is divisible;[19] and

    (e) federal liens under section 107(1) (added by SARA in 1986) applying to all rights in the entire property on which response action is taken. Such liens may be enforced by an action *in rem* directly against the property in the relevant Federal District Court.

A key feature of CERCLA is the wide range of potentially responsible parties under section 107 against whom clean up costs actions and natural resource damages actions may be pursued. These are:

---

[19] *In Re Achusnet River and New Bedford Harbor: Proceedings Re Alleged PCB Pollution (Achusnet VIII)* 725 F. Supp. 1264 (D. Mass. 1989).

1. owners and operators[19a] of a vessel or facility;
2. persons who owned or operated a vessel or facility at the time of disposal there;
3. generators[20] of hazardous substances who arranged for treatment of disposal directly or through a transporter; and
4. transporters of hazardous substances who selected the facility from which there is a release of hazardous substances.

The section does not state that such parties are jointly and severally liable, although the early draft bills did confirm such a provision. Notwithstanding the omission, joint and several liability has been implied by the courts as consistent with the intention of Congress:[21] The rule is based on the Restatement (Second) of Torts section 433B and provides for apportionment only if the defendant can demonstrate that the harm is divisible.[22] Nonetheless, volumetric apportionment is frequently used on negotiating voluntary settlements under CERCLA.

Questions have arisen as to how far the limits of the categories of potentially responsible parties can be pushed. EPA has for example taken the view that it will seek to impose liability on shareholders, particularly in situations involving parent/subsidiary relationships: this strategy has met with mixed success in the courts.[23]

Successor corporations to former owners, transporters, generators, etc., have been held liable by the courts on public policy grounds.[24] More controversially, secured lenders may in some circumstances find them-

---

[19a] Different approaches have been adopted to the issue of whether a corporation can be regarded as an "operator" in relation to the activities of other corporations. One test is that of actual control by involvement in policy and day-to-day operations: see *US* v. *Kayser-Roth Corp.* 910 F. 2d 24 (1st Cir. 1990), cert. denied 498 US 1084 (1991) and *Lansford-Coaldale Joint Water Authority* v. *Tonolli Corporation* 4 F.3d 1209 (3rd Cir. 1993). A harsher test is that of capacity or authority to control: see *Nurad, Inc.* v. *William E. Hooper & Sons Company* 966 F. 2d 837 (4th Cir. 1992), cert. denied 113 S.Ct. 337 (1992).

[20] Proof of personal ownership or physical possession of the substance is not necessary: *United States* v. *Northeastern Pharmaceutical and Chemical Co.:* 810 F. 2d 726 (8th Cir. 1986). However, the section is not applicable to hazardous substances supplied as finished products (*e.g.* transformers containing PCBs): *Florida Power & Light Co.* v. *Allis-Chalmers Corp.* in 893 F. 2d 1313 (11th Cir. 1990).

[21] *O'Neil* v. *Picillo* 883 F. 2d 176 (1st Cir. 1989); *US* v. *Stringfellow* 661 F. Supp. 1053 (C.D. Cal. 1987).

[22] *US* v. *Mirabile* 15 Envtl. L. Rep. 20, 994 (E.D. Pa. Sept. 4, 1985); *US* v. *Dickerson* 640 F. Supp. 448 (D. Md. 1986).

[23] *Cf, Idaho* v. *Bunker Hill Co.* 635 F. Supp. 665 (D. Idaho 1986) and *Joslyn Mfg. Co.* v. *T.L. James & Co., Inc.* 893 F. 2d 80 (5th Cir. 1990), *cert. denied* 111 S. Ct. 1017 (1991).

[24] *Smith Land & Improvement Corp.* v. *Celotex Corp.* 851 F. 2d 86 (3rd Cir. 1988), *cert. denied,* 488 US 1029 (1989).

selves liable.[25] Section 101(20)(A) of CERCLA effectively creates an exemption for a lender who does not participate in the management of the facility and holds indicia of ownership primarily to protect his security interest in the property: it is relatively easy, however, for a lender to step inadvertently outside this exemption, though administrative guidance has now provided greater clarity. Contractors employed to excavate or grade sites may also be at risk as "operators".[26] Liability has even been imposed on a corporate trustee holding property in a fiduciary capacity, even though the trustee did not engage in any wrongdoing and despite the fact that the trust no longer exists and cannot indemnify the trustee.[27]

The fact that liability under CERCLA is not dependent upon traditional concepts of causation[28] but rather on strict and retroactive liability leaves a purchaser of a site subject to past releases of hazardous substances in a highly exposed position.

One of the very few statutory defences provided by CERCLA is the case where the release can be shown to have resulted solely from an act or omission of a third party other than an employee or agent of the defendant or someone whose act or omission occurs in connection with a direct or indirect contractual relationship with the defendant, if the defendant can establish that he exercised that he exercised due care with regard to the hazardous substance and took precautions against foreseeable acts or omissions of the third party and the consequences that could foreseeably result from them.[29] Since section 101(35)(A) defines contractual relationships as including land contracts, deeds or other instruments

---

[25] *United States* v. *Maryland Bank & Trust Co.* 632 F. Supp 573 (D. Md. 1986); *United States* v. *Fleet Factors Corp.* 901 F. 2d 1550 (11th Cir. 1990), *cert. denied*, 111 S. Ct. 752 (1991). A greater, though not absolute, degree of certainty was temporarily provided by the issuance of an administrative rule by EPA: the rule was cited successfully by secured lenders in some recent cases such as *Waterville Industries, Inc.* v. *Finance Authority of Maine* 984 F. 2d 549 (1st Cir. 1993) and *Ashland Oil, Inc.* v. *Sonford Products Corp.* 810 F. Supp. 1057 (D. Minn. 1993). However, the rule was struck down in *Kelley* v. *EPA and others* 1994 W.L. 27881 (D.C. Cir., February 4, 1994) on the basis that the EPA had no delegated authority to enact such a rule, the interpretation of the statute being a matter for the courts rather than the Agency.

[26] *Kaiser Aluminium and Chemical Corp.* v. *Catellus Development Corp.* 92 Daily Journal D.A.R. 13871 (1992); the limited indemnity rules applicable to such contractors under administrative guidelines are seen as unsatisfactory given the high risk nature of the work—see P. Tunnicliffe and C. Kiely, Environment Risk, April 1993, p. 39.

[27] *Phoenix* v. *Garbage Services Company*, US District Court for District of Arizona, April 16, 1993.

[28] *State of New York* v. *Shore Realty Corp.* 759 F. 2d 1032 (2nd Cir. 1985), *aff'd* 861 F. 2d 15 (7th Cir. 1988).

[29] S.107(*b*)(3).

transferring possession, a purchaser will not generally be able to rely on this "third party" defence. However, section 101(35)(A)(i) effectively creates an "innocent purchaser" defence by excluding from the contractual relationship category cases where at the time the defendant acquired the facility he did not know and had no reason to know of the disposal of the hazardous substance there: this involves establishing that the purchaser undertook "all appropriate inquiry . . . consistent with good commercial or customary practice."[30] Attempts to invoke the defence have led to an increase in the numbers of environmental audits undertaken, but have met with limited success in the courts.[31]

Private actions, citizens suits and contributions actions

A number of provisions of CERCLA in particular sections 107, 113(*f*) **13.10** and 310, create important rights of action for private citizens, including municipalities and other local governments. Some of these provisions have been interpreted as allowing one potentially responsible party to bring a contribution action for necessary response costs against another: thus alleviating somewhat the broad scope of CERCLA liability.[32] Citizen suits under section 310 may be brought against EPA for breach of the legislation or failure to perform any duty. In fact very few such actions have been brought, but their possibility no doubt encourages stringent enforcement efforts.

Settlements

In practice there are frequently good reasons why potentially respon- **13.11** sible parties (PRPs) should enter into settlements with each other and with EPA, not least the draconian sanctions ultimately available to EPA and the fact that the PRPs may at least be able to exert some influence over the clean up strategy selected. Section 122 confers express authority to enter into settlements and indeed provides that such agreements are to be facilitated whenever practicable and in the public interest. Settlements can include "mixed funding" whereby EPA reimburses

---

[30] S.101(35)(B); relevant factors include specialised knowledge of the defendant, purchase price, commonly known or readily ascertainable information and the ability to detect the contamination by appropriate inspection.

[31] *US* v. *Pacific Hide & Fur Depot, Inc.* 716 F. Supp. 1341 (D. Idaho 1989) (acquisition by involuntary gift); *US* v. *Serafini* 706 F. Supp. 346 (M.D. Pa 1988); 711 F. Supp. 197 (M.D. Pa 1988) (acquisition 20 years earlier).

[32] For example *Emhart Indus. Inc.* v. *Duracell Int'l, Inc.* 665 F. Supp 549 (M.D. Tenn. 1987) —action by buyer against seller.

parties to the agreement in respect of some actions they undertake or where EPA undertakes a portion of the response action, subject to EPA making all reasonable efforts to recover from other parties: the objective of such agreements is to encourage settlement even where some PRPs are unknown, insolvent or recalcitrant. There is also the possibility of EPA issuing non-binding preliminary allocations of responsibility (NBARs) informing PRPs of their likely position and that of others, and so facilitating settlements. Agreement may be reached specifically with *de minimis* PRPs (typically those who individually have contributed between 0.2 per cent. and 1 per cent. of total waste volume at the site): this allows such PRPs, usually on payment of a premium, to obtain an early release from further proceedings. Once a party has settled with the Government, section 113(*f*)(2) provides for contribution protection.

Superfund and its financing

13.12   Governmental and private party claims for reimbursement of response costs can be made against the Hazardous Substance Superfund. The initial monies for the Fund came predominantly (87.5 per cent.) from taxes on petroleum and certain feedstock chemicals. The Fund is supplemented by amounts recovered under CERCLA including penalties and punitive damages; continued funding also comes from the Tax on Certain Important Substances and a general Corporate Environmental Tax.

The future of Superfund

13.13   Superfund has been criticised as being excessively bureaucratic and wasteful of resources: the pace of clean-up is slow, too much money is spent on legal and consultancy fees, and vast expenditure on some clean-ups produces relatively tiny benefits in risk reduction.[33] Whilst performance has improved with recent programmes such as the Superfund Accelerated Clean-up Model, dealing with sites on the NPL remains a vastly daunting task. In May 1993, 26 more sites were added to the NLP, making a total of 1,256 final and proposed sites: it has been estimated that this may grow to 2,000 sites by the year 2000. Total costs are estimated to range from $25 billion to over $120 billion and indeed the Office of Technology Assessment has estimated a figure of between $300 billion and $700 billion (10 per cent. of annual US GNP) for the total national effort to clean up toxic waste.[34] The single most damning

---

[33] See *Superfund: EPA Success, National Debacle* by E. Donald Elliott, Natural Resources and Environment, Vol. 6, No. 3, 11 (1992).

[34] Including other programmes such as on underground storage tanks, abandoned mines, asbestos and state programmes.

statistic has been said to be the fact that it takes, on average, 10 years to clean-up each site, of which only three years is actually spent on physical remediation measures.

The existing programme expires in 1994 and it seems likely that the debate on re-authorisation will be acrimonious. The Clinton Administration has expressed itself to be committed to a new Superfund legislation that protects human health and the environment more efficiently and fairly than does the current law, and to achieve this goal is guided by four objectives: (i) reduce the time and costs needed to clean-up sites; (ii) make the liability scheme more fair and efficient; (iii) greater involvement of communities that live near sites in Superfund decisions; and (iv) remove impediment to economic redevelopment of contaminated properties.[34a] A legislative proposal incorporating these objectives, the Superfund Reform Act of 1994, was submitted to Congress in February 1994. Key features of the proposal include the following:[34b]

- a requirement for the involvement of the affected local community in all phases of response action, with creation of Community Working Groups to act as clearing-houses for information and provide recommendations as to remediation and future land-use (Title I).
- powers for the EPA Administrator to delegate to states the authority to carry out response and enforcement actions for facilities listed, or proposed for listing, on the NPL. Regulations are proposed as to the criteria for such delegation, requiring states to demonstrate they have the necessary capability and resources. Delegated states would be eligible for Superfund monies and the Administrator would retain significant powers of review (Title II).
- establishment of programmes to assist states and municipalities in developing voluntary response programmes—a number of states already have voluntary response programmes which allow parties to remediate sites with minimal state oversight (Title III).
- significant amendments to the liability and allocation scheme. These include the exemption from liability of *de micromis* parties (arrangers and transporters of less than 500 pounds of municipal solid waste or less than ten pounds of materials containing

---

[34a] Statement of Carol M. Browner, Administrator, US EPA, before the Sub-Committee on Transportation and Hazardous Materials of the Committee on Energy and Commerce, US House of Representatives, February 3, 1994.

[34b] This summary is based on material provided by the US law firms Latham & Watkins and Jenner & Block, which is gratefully acknowledged.

hazardous substances; also exempted would be "bona fide prospective purchasers" who can demonstrate they have exercised due care to address and limit adverse impacts of contaminants. The EPA is given express powers to issue regulations defining and interpreting the limitations on liability of lenders, financial service providers, transfers and other fiduciaries (effectively reversing the decision in *Kelley* v. *EPA*[34c]) (Title IV). Many other procedural reforms are suggested, all with the aim of increasing fairness and reducing transaction costs, particularly in the area of allocation, where a new and expedited settlement system with substantial incentives to settle is proposed; these include final covenants by the Administrator resolving all present and future liability.

- requirement of promulgation of national goals and national generic clean-up levels, which reflect reasonably anticipated future land uses and concentrations below which a response action is not required. Power to rely on site-specific risk assessment standards rather than national generic standards is also provided. The requirement that preference be given to "permanent" remedies is to be deleted (Title V).

- establishment of an environmental insurance resolution fund to settle CERCLA claims brought against insurers by policy-holders. The settlement fund, to be financed by a tax on insurers (including a tax on net premiums received from 1971–1985), would provide settlements for "eligible costs" incurred by "eligible persons" at "eligible sites". Acceptance of an offer of costs from the Resolution Fund would entail a waiver of all claims against insurers; the proportion of costs recoverabale would be set on the basis of the laws of the relevant state in relation to policy wordings. A stay on claims would be imposed, to be lifted only if a policyholder requested, then refused, a settlement offer from the fund. Policyholders refusing such an offer would be penalised on costs in certain instances where a later claim results in a lower final judgment than the offer (Title VIII).

State legislation

13.14   In addition to the federal Superfund law, a number of states have developed their own "mini-Superfund" systems of clean-up and liability

---

[34c] See n.25 above.

for sites contaminated by hazardous substances. Notable amongst these is New Jersey, a state with perhaps the greatest environmental problems in terms of hazardous waste disposal: the New Jersey legislation has provided a model for some other states in their own legislative programmes. States like Connecticut, Illinois and California have adopted similar transaction-based laws designed to force sellers or buyers of contaminated property to remediate such property at their own expense, thus avoiding clean-ups funded by taxpayers.

In particular, the New Jersey Environmental Clean-up Responsibility Act of 1983 (ECRA) is triggered not by a release or threatened release, but by a business decision to close or transfer specified industrial facilities ("Covered Transactions"). ECRA applies to the "closing, terminating or transferring" of operations, including a change in ownership: sales of stock or of controlling shares are included within this category. Before such transactions can take place, the current owner/ operator must demonstrate to the State Department of Environmental Protection and Energy that the property is clean, or must develop and implement a clean-up plan. As well as monetary sanctions for non-compliance, the State can—and has done so—void the sale or transfer. The delays inherent in formulating monitoring schemes and submitting them to the State authorities have had serious consequences for commercial transactions; sale documentation involving New Jersey property will typically contain lengthy and complex provisions on cross-indemnities, options to repurchase, and mechanisms for establishing between the parties when contamination occurred. New Jersey amended ECRA in June 1993 by the Industrial Site Recovery Act—primarily in response to much criticism that ECRA was unworkable and was damaging the State's economy. The 1993 statute sets out nine factors to be taken into account in choosing appropriate remedial action: for example, that remediation will not be required below the concentration of a contaminant which is consistently present in the environment of the region of the site and which has not been influenced by localised human activities (the regional natural background). The Act also provides for the creation of an exemption relating to historic fill material—non-indigenous material used to raise the topographic elevation of the site, the fill having been contaminated prior to its placement. An innocent landowner defence—though strictly limited in its nature—is also introduced.

Another statute, the New Jersey Spill Compensation and Control Act of 1977, pre-dates CERCLA by a considerable period, and is the prime means by which the state deals with abandoned hazardous waste sites, both on and off the NPL. The Act is similar in concept to CERCLA, though different in some significant details.

New Jersey, along with a few other states,[35] has adopted a system of "Superliens". These provisions have the common feature that clean-up costs take priority over prior mortgages and all other liens, with exception of tax liens. Such provisions are a matter of major concern to lenders, but have survived judicial challenge on the ground of non-constitutionality and uncompensated taking.[36]

Oil pollution

13.15   As mentioned above, hazardous substances under CERCLA do not include petroleum. However, the Oil Pollution Act of 1990 (OPA)[37] establishes a comprehensive liability scheme for oil spills, which in many ways is analogous to the CERCLA provisions. A "responsible party", which generally includes the owner and operator of a facility or vessel, is strictly, jointly and severally liable for the removal costs and a wide range of damages resulting from a discharge of oil (not limited to petroleum) onto or into navigable waters, adjoining shorelines or the exclusive economic zone. Removal costs include all costs to remove the oil or to prevent, minimise or mitigate the threat of discharge. Categories of damage compensable include injury to property, loss of use of property, injury to or loss of use of natural resources, loss of taxes, rents and royalties, loss of income and costs incurred in providing additional public services.

Regulation of PCBs

13.16   Section 6(e) of the Toxic Substances Control Act[38] mandated the EPA within six months from January 1, 1977 to promulgate regulations to (*inter alia*) prescribe methods for the disposal of PCBs, require PCB items to be marked with clear and adequate warnings and provide instructions with respect to their processing, distribution in commerce, use, or disposal. Pursuant to this obligation, EPA promulgated comprehensive

---

[35] Connecticut, Maine, Massachusetts and New Hampshire. Other states, such as Arkansas, Ohio, Oregon and Tennessee, have statutes that provide for liens to the extent of clean-up costs expended by the state on property owned by the liable party, without affording the liens any special priority.

[36] *Kessler* v. *Tarrats* 194 N.J. Super. 136, 476 A. 2d 326 (N.J. Super. Ct. App. Div. 1984).

[37] 33 U.S.C. §§ 2701–61; for a description of the Act and previous law, see J.B. Ruhl and M.J. Jewell, "Oil Pollution Act of 1990: Opening a New Era in Federal and Texas Regulation of Oil Spill Prevention, Containment and Clean-up, and Liability", 32 South Texas L. Rev. 475 (1991).

[38] 15 U.S.C. § 2605(e).

regulations[39] which are similar to many of the R.C.R.A. regulations applicable to hazardous waste: the regulations on PCBs are broader in scope, however, in that they apply to PCBs in use, for example in transformers, before they become waste. The regulations include very detailed requirements for PCB spill clean-up, such as reporting, decontamination of surfaces and standards for removal and replacement of contaminated soil.

[39] 40 C.F.R. Part 761; the regulations generally regulate materials containing PCBs in excess of 50 parts per million.

C. Canada*

13.17   As a federal state, Governmental authority for environmental matters is divided in Canada between the national government and the regional governments of the ten provinces and two territories. At federal level, the emphasis is placed upon controls based on designated substances,[40] or upon harmful environmental effects which impact upon matters of federal jurisdiction, such as fisheries.[41]

Contaminated sites are seen as matters of property and civil rights, and accordingly jurisdiction rests at provincial level. The provincial governments have not, as yet, adopted the model of the US for clean-up, save for the most industrialised of the provinces, Ontario; sections 16 and 17 of the Ontario Environmental Protection Act[42] provide for preventative and remedial administrative orders to study the effect of a discharge of a contaminant into the environment and to repair any injury or damage.

Section 16 applies where a contaminant has been discharged into the natural environment and the discharge has damaged or endangered land, water, property, human health or safety, or animal or plant life, or is likely to do so. The order may be directed to any person who causes or permits the discharge, irrespective of whether or not that person is a present or former owner of the property.

Section 17 is of a preventative nature, and applies where a contaminant is present which if discharged would be likely to have an adverse effect and where preventative measures are necessary and advisable to reduce the risk of discharge or to minimise an adverse effect. Such order may be directed against present or former owners or any person who has or had management or control of the undertaking or property; the section was amended in 1990[43] to extend liability to previous owners or occupiers. Unlike the equivalent US provisions, liability does not attach to transporters of waste, or persons arranging for such transportation; nor is there any equivalent of the US "innocent purchaser" defence.

Section 17 (prior to its 1990 amendment) was given a narrow interpretation in the case of *Northern Wood Preservers* v. *Ministry of the Environment*.[44] The case concerned a property in northern Ontario owned

---

* The assistance of Roger Cotton of Fasken Campbell Godfrey, Toronto (known internationally as Fasken Martineau) is gratefully acknowledged.
[40] Canadian Environmental Protection Act S.C. Ch. 22 (1988) (Can.) as amended.
[41] Fisheries Act R.S.C., Ch. F–14 (1985) (Can.) as amended.
[42] R.S.O., Ch. 141 (1980) (Ont.).
[43] Bill 220: An Act to Amend the Environmental Protection Act and the Ontario Water Resources Act.
[44] May 3, 1991, Div. Ct. Ontario.

by a subsidiary of Canadian National Railways and occupied under a sub-lease by Northern Wood Preservers. The soil was heavily contaminated with preservatives which were leaching into surface waters. It was held by the Ontario Divisional Court that Canadian National Railways was the owner of the soil, but that this was equated to the "natural environment" into which the contaminant was discharged so that CNR was not within the ambit of the section; notwithstanding the fact that the contaminant was leaching through the soil owned by CNR into other property. Secondly, it was held that the owner of a mortgage or headlease, having the right to enter and take possession of the contaminating operation in the event of default, did not have sufficient management or control to be caught by the section: the judgment suggests, however, that the position could be different where the mortgagee takes active steps with a view to taking control. The issue of the liability of secured lenders has also been considered in a decision of the Alberta Court of Appeal,[45] where a receiver appointed by the court was held to be liable for the costs of "abandonment" of oil wells as required by the relevant regulatory authority. The reasoning would appear to apply equally to clean-up orders in the case of contaminated sites.

As well as the Environmental Protection Act, other Ontario legislation has relevance to contaminated land, in particular two acts concerned with groundwater protection, the Ontario Water Resources Act[46] and the Gasoline Handling Act.[47] These acts are concerned with both prevention and remediation and, as in the UK, there is considerable scope for overlap in the applicability of legislation.

Canada has suffered a number of serious incidents of groundwater contamination requiring the use of statutory powers. Examples include the contamination of the drinking water supply of Port Loring, Ontario by petroleum from an underground storage facility: the company responsible, Gulf Oil, was required by the Ministry of Environment to construct and operate a new central water system for the community to replace the contaminated wells. In another incident, very serious chemical contamination of groundwater occurred at Elmira, Ontario, including dioxin and other carcinogens from a plant operated by Uniroyal Chemical Co. prior to 1970. A proposed solution of pump and treat was abandoned and instead administrative orders were issued relating to the waste deposits which were the source of the problem. Ultimately

[45] *Panamericana de Blenes y Servicos, SA* v. *Northern Badger Oil and Gas Ltd.* (1991) 81 DLR (41) 280. Contrast, however *Att.-Gen. (Ontario)* v. *Tyre King Tyre Recycling Ltd.* (1992) 8 C.E.L.R. (NS) 202 and *Re Lamford Forest Products Ltd.* (1992) 8 C.E.L.R. (2d) 186.
[46] R.S.O., 1990 Ch. E.19 (1990) (Ont.) as amended.
[47] R.S.O., 1990 Ch. G.4 (1990) (Ont.).

Uniroyal appealed an order requiring the removal of some 11,000 cubic yards of soil from the site and litigation still continues. Costs have included a $20 million remediation study and the cost of a new seven mile water supply pipeline and the distribution of bottled water to the township while the pipeline was being constructed.

Various provinces have formulated guidelines as to soil quality standards and clean-up—these include the MoE Guidelines for the decommissioning and Clean up of Sites in Ontario (1990—providing criteria for some 22 compounds),[48] Quebec's MENVIQ Guidelines, Alberta's MUST Guidelines, and also national guidelines prepared by the Canadian Council of Ministers of the Environment.

Two other features of Canadian environmental law may be mentioned in conclusion. Firstly, it is a common feature to impose an obligation on companies as to the reporting of spills.[49] Secondly, recent decisions have indicated a strict attitude towards corporate officers implicated in environmental offences committed by their companies.[50]

---

[48] Para. 7.5 of the Guidelines states that in general remedial action is required where contaminants are present at a site at concentrations above "background levels": defined as the ambient level of a contaminant in the local area. However, more stringent criteria may be required to deal with aesthetic parameters such as odour.

[49] For example s.92 of the Ontario Environmental Protection Act, s.30(2) of the Ontario Water Resources Act, Pt. II of the Canadian Environmental Protection Act.

[50] In particular, *R. v. Bata industries et al* (1992) 9 O.R. (3d) 329 (see also *R. v. Bata Industries Ltd., Douglas Marchant and Keith Weston* (1994) J.E.L. Vol. 6, No. 1, p. 107; K. Kwan); *R. v. Blackbird Holdings Ltd.* (1991) 6 C.E.L.R. (N.S.) 138; *R. v. Erie Battery Inc. Taylor George Gordon and Joseph Ted D'Amico* (April 1992, unreported); *R. v. Varnicolor Chemical Ltd. Severin Argenton and Tri-Union of Elmira, Inc.* (September 1992, unreported).

D.   THE NETHERLANDS*

The Soil Clean-up (Interim) Act 1982 (Interim Wet Bodemsane Ring)

This Act was a somewhat hurried response to the incident of soil **13.18** pollution at Lekkerkeck, near Rotterdam, where toxic chemicals found their way into drinking water serving a housing development.[51]

Section 2 of the Act requires provincial authorities to draw up each year a clean-up programme to deal with soil contamination; the programme must indicate those cases within the province where the soil is contaminated or is in danger of becoming contaminated so as to pose a serious threat to health or the environment. The programme must specify details of investigations or remedial measures to be carried out.

By section 11, the provincial authority has extensive rights of entry and investigation for the purpose of implementing the programme; the authority may also order any person whose activities it considers wholly or partly responsible for causing contamination to suspend the activities in question or to suspend them if specified requirements are not met.[52]

In the case of sites designated for clean up, an order may be made by the Minister of Housing, Physical Planning and Environment against the person with rights to the property on which the source of contamination is situated, to take appropriate measures to eliminate that source or to restrict the contamination or its effects so far as possible.[53] By section 17 if the recipient of such an order is likely to suffer financial loss or damage which he cannot reasonably be expected to bear in whole or in part, the provincial authority or Minister shall grant him indemnification to be fixed equitably, insofar as reasonable indemnification has not or cannot be provided by other means.[54] Under section 33(1) any person contravening an order under section 12 is liable to a term of imprisonment not exceeding six months or a fine not exceeding 10,000 guilders; greater penalties apply under section 33(2)—one year's imprisonment or a fine not exceeding 25,000 guilders—for any person committing an act knowing and having reasonable grounds for assuming that it carries with it a significant risk of soil contamination.

The way in which it was originally envisaged that the Act would work was by the provincial authorities undertaking clean-up operations, funded by the municipalities and by central government.[55] Legal pro-

[51] See Preamble, n.2.
[52] S.11(2).
[53] S.12(1). To date, no order has been issued under the section.
[54] S.17(1).
[55] Ss.18–20.

ceedings under section 21 of the Act would then follow against the person whose unlawful act had caused the contamination in question, to recover costs incurred by the State. However, as the following section indicates, the Act has not worked in this way in practice.

Proceedings by the State

13.19   The first decision on liability under the 1982 was *State* v. *Van Amersfoort* (Dutch Supreme Court, February 21, 1990). It was held that section 21 did not set aside the normal requirements of the law of tort—in particular, a duty owed to the State—as a precondition for recovery.

The requirements for liability were subsequently clarified in *State* v. *Akzo Resins* (Supreme Court, April 24, 1992) where it was held that as from January 1, 1975 it was foreseeable to operators who contaminated their own soil that the government would have to take remedial measures: thus from such a date there is a duty of care owed to the State. This ruling presents practical difficulties of apportionment in cases where the pollution in question occurred both before and after the 1975 date; this was the case in *State* v. *van Wijngaarden,* a Supreme Court decision at the same time as *Akzo Resins,* which was referred back to the court of appeals to determine that issue. The decision absolved *Akzo Resins* of liability completely, as the pollution concerned spillages of resin solvents between 1954 and 1967.

The *Akzo* and *van Wijngaarden* cases concerned own-site contamination, and there remains doubt as to the application of these principles to off-site disposal of wastes: *Staat & Gemeente Ouderkerk* v. *Shell Nederland Raffinaderij BV & Shell Nederland Chemie BV* (Court of Appeal, The Hague November 19, 1992); *State* v. *Philips Duphar* (Court of Appeal Amsterdam, December 1992). In the *Shell-Gouderak* case, the soil in a residential area appeared to be seriously polluted by "drin" pesticides originating from Shell in the 1950s. The contamination was such that a number of houses on the site had to be demolished. In the subsequent claim by the State for clean up costs from Shell, it was held that the principles of the *Azko* case were not relevant to the situation here where the contamination resulted from the transport of wastes for disposal off-site. On the basis of what was known and what could have reasonably been anticipated in the 1950s when the wastes were consigned, Shell was found not to be liable. In the *Duphar* case, it was found that Duphar ought to have been mindful, in the period prior to 1975, of the risks of disposing of chemical waste at a landfill site, but that there was no evidence that this either had been or should have been the case prior to 1970.

The Soil Clean Up (Interim) Act in practice

By 1992 some 155 legal actions for cost recovery at contaminated sites **13.20** had been launched by the Dutch Environment Ministry (VROM). The total costs sought amount to Fl 940 million ($520m). Current estimates suggest that there are 120,000 contaminated sites in the Nederlands, of which between 30,000 and 60,000 will require some degree of clean up.[56] The *Akzo* case, in particular, presents the Government with difficulties in obtaining redress in relation to older historic contamination.

As a matter of practice, however, many clean-ups are carried out "voluntarily" by owners or occupiers under threat of state action, under the supervision of the authorities. There are some tax advantages to this couse.

Proposed Legislation

Proposals have been submitted by the Dutch Government for amend- **13.21** ments to the 1982 Act regime by inserting new provisions into the Soil Protection Act 1986 *(Wet Bodembescherming)*. The essential nature of the proposed amendments is to allow investigation and clean-up orders to be made against current owners as well as polluters. Unlike section 21 of the 1982 Act, the new provisions will contain no requirement for the Government to prove its interest in the clean-up— the so-called "relativity" principle—thus effectively overruling the *Akzo* and *van Amersfoort* cases.

The proposal has been heavily criticised by the business community in view of the strict and retrospective nature of liability. The Government agreed to modify the rigour of the proposals in relation to the owner by providing that the owner will be held liable only if no polluter with sufficient financial resources can be found, and then subject to a defence where:

(1) the owner has not himself caused any pollution;
(2) the owner had no legal relationship with the polluter at the time of the pollution; and
(3) at the time the owner acquired the property he did not know of the contamination nor should he have known of it.

Further amendments were made to the legislation following fierce debate in the Lower House. Powers to issue orders requiring temporary measures were introduced, together with power to issue orders against

[56] See also "Soil Protection in the 90s: 10 year planning scenario with specific reference to industrial sites" (Lower House of the States-General 1989–90 Session, 21 557, No. 1).

current and former users of property. Apart from the "innocent owner" defence, a defence was introduced for owners who did not have a considerable share in the pollution; under the defence they may avoid orders on condition that they are prepared to pay a proportional contribution (based on their part of the pollution) to the clean-up costs. These legislative proposals are anticipated to come into force early in 1994. Other legislation is being prepared to prohibit the transfer of contaminated sites and to place obligations on sellers to carry out clean-up operations at the time of transfer, or alternatively to give secured undertakings for clean-up at some date. This legislation is not expected to come into force before the end of 1994.

Against the background of this new legislation, there is considerable activity involving cooperation between industry and Government in voluntary investigation and clean-up—the so-called BSB operation. The advantage for industry of such a scheme lies in the ability to exert influence over timing, strategies and costs. The objective of the scheme is to achieve voluntary clean-up of contaminated sites by industry with the aim of having all such sites cleaned-up within a period of 25 years.

The Government's Committee on Clean-up of Industrial Sites was established in 1988 and published its final report on the plan for clean up in June 1991: this involves investigation and prioritisation of sites in actual use.

Clean-up criteria and soil protection guidelines

13.22   The Soil Clean-Up (Interim) Act 1982 itself contains no criteria for remedial operations. However, immediately after the Act became law, the Environment Ministry issued *Guidelines on Soil Clean-up* which established the well-known A, B and C levels for the assessment of contamination by a range of substances.

The 'A' Level (or refence value) constitutes the natural or background level of substances in clean soil.

The 'B' Level indicates a situation requiring investigation to determine the extent and location of contamination.

The 'C' Level indicates that clean-up is necessary.

The Guidelines still currently apply, though they have been renamed "Guidelines for Soil Protection" to accord with the approach of the Soil Protection Act 1986. The standards have been reconsidered in the light of recent scientific studies and it is proposed to change the system by abolishing 'B' values and by replacing 'A' and 'C' values with "target levels" and "intervention levels" respectively.

Whilst the basic principle of the Dutch approach is that of multifunctionality[57] (that is, restoring soil to a level of cleanliness to enable it to be

---

[57] See Chap. 1 generally.

used for any purpose) the rule is not applied inflexibly and in practice the levels for remediation will vary on public health, environmental protection and site specific criteria, *i.e.* specific characteristics of the soil and the current and future use of the site. It is anticipated that sites previously used for industry will only have to be cleaned up to 'B' level in order to make the programme successful and workable.

E. GERMANY*

Federal legislation

13.23 German law provides no uniform nationwide scheme for the regulation of contaminated land.[58] Federal control over waste disposal sites is provided by the Waste Disposal Act of 1972 *(Abfallgesetz* or *AbfG)*. This Act is concerned primarily with the regulation of waste disposal practices, rather than the clean up of old sites; though control does extend to the securing and aftercare of currently operational sites. Moreover, the Act's definition of waste refers to "movable things", and so the provisions are of limited application to wastes which have penetrated into the soil so as to lose their movable character.

A second federal statute of potential application is the Waste Management Act of 1960 *(Wasserhaushaltsgesetz* or *WHG)*. As well as provisions on control of pollution, the Act imposes liability in certain cases for damage caused by the emission of substances into ground and surface waters from premises used for the production, processing, storage, deposit, transportation or discharge of the substance. However, the Act applies only to contamination intentionally or knowingly caused: *i.e.* by deliberate discharges or failure to abate an ongoing known discharge.

Thirdly, the new Environmental Liability Law of 1991 *(Umwelthaftungsgesetz* or *Umwelt HG)* provides a statutory mechanism for compensating the victims of environmental damage.[59] The basic scheme is one of strict liability for specified types of establishment: liability is triggered if there is an impact on the environment from the establishment which causes death, personal injury or damage to property.[60] However, the Act is concerned primarily with providing civil remedies rather than ensuring that contaminated sites are remedied on a precautionary basis.

The common problem shared the AbfG, the WHG and the Umwelt HG is that of retrospectivity: none of the statutes apply to contamination arising before the Act came into force. The ability to use the Acts as a means of achieving clean-up of old waste sites and other historically contaminated land *(altlasten)* is thus limited.

---

* The assistance of Dr. Birgit Spiesshofer, MCJ, formerlyof Feddersen Laule Scherzberg & Ohle Hansen Ewerwahn, Frankfurt, is gratefully acknowledged.
[58] See the synopsis by Dr. V. Jesch and I. Winterstein at *Environment Risk*, November 1992.
[59] See the article by Professor Dr. Günter Hager [1993] Env. Liab. 41.
[60] S.6(I).

State legislation

The various federal states, or länder, have all enacted their own **13.24**
detailed legislation on water and waste within the framework of the
federal laws: such legislation generally shares the shortcomings of the
federal law in its relation to contaminated land.

The main state legislation used to deal with the problem in practice
are the general state police laws: these are based on concepts dating back
to the last century and in many cases are patterned on a Uniform Draft
Police Act, and as such they are not entirely suited to dealing with the
problems posed by contaminated sites. Such laws are designed to
address hazards to "public security and order" such as public health
risks: equating to some extent to the UK provisions on statutory
nuisances. What constitutes a sufficient hazard in individual cases is a
matter for debate. Some courts have taken the view that any threat to
groundwater resources can be equated to a threat to human health;
others have followed the narrower approach that there must be a risk to
immediately recognisable resources, such as a reservoir. The federal
privatisation agency or *Treuhandanstalt* (see below) generally differs from
the state agencies in requiring some imminent danger. In some quarters
an approach is advocated which relates the degree of risk required to the
perceived importance of the threatened object or sector.

The first question to be determined in relation to a site is whether
there is sufficient danger to warrant further action: this is usually
regarded as the task of the state authorities and there is a divergence of
opinion as to whether the costs of this first stage investigation can
lawfully be passed back to potentially responsible parties. If there is a
sufficient degree of hazard then administrative orders can be issued
requiring a potentially responsible party to carry out further investigations to determine the nature and extent of contamination: This equates
in some ways to the RI/FS stage of action under the US "Superfund"
legislation,[61] though there is no opportunity for public involvement in
setting the clean up strategy—the issue being one for the PRP and the
state authority.

The detail of the process varies between states: in Hessen, for
example, the order will typically require the PRP to establish a clean up
plan to be approved by the state. In all cases orders may be subject to
challenge on public law grounds if they fail to specify with sufficient
clarity what is requited of the PRP. Failure to comply is a criminal
offence, and the authority may also take steps to comply with the order
itself, or engage a third party to do so, and then recover the costs from
the PRP.

[61] See p. 13.08 above.

The legislation recognises two distinct categories of potentially responsible party: the person primarily responsible is the one who naturally caused the contamination (the "*Verhaltensstoerer*").[62] Where that party no longer exists or cannot be traced, the owner or possessor of the property can be (the "*Zustandsstoerer*"). The latter category of liability is irrespective of fault and an innocent purchase can consequently be at risk: that risk is compounded by the absence of statutory defences and contribution rights against other PRPs, coupled with the fact that selection of the PRP is entirely at the discretion of the state authority. Frequently a single PRP will be held liable for the entire costs, as a matter of administrative convenience.

The state police laws constitute a relatively blunt, though effective, instrument and are subject to review in the light of the historical problems faced by the new (former GDR) states. In some cases steps have been taken towards adopting more sophisticated systems (see below).

Identification of sites

13.25 The process of identifying contaminated or potentially contaminated sites rests with the discretion of individual states, often under their state waste disposal law: there is no coherent federal approach or national priority list.[63] However, in most *Länder* there exist *Verdachtsflachenkartien* ("Card files on Suspected Areas") and *Atlastenregister* ("Registers on Old Pollution"). Such records are based on information collected from subordinate state authorities such as records of old landfills and former industrial sites.

The criteria for effectiveness of clean-up is the removal of identified hazards; however, remedial action does not result in the deregistration of the site. Rather, the site remains on the register of old pollution, but with an entry referring to the clean up. In general, the authorities will not provide any binding confirmation as to the effectiveness of clean-up measures, and thus the authorities are not precluded from further or fresh action if it subsequently transpires that hazards remain on a remediated site.

There is little correlation between this information and the exercise of development and building control functions: to obtain building permission a developer must submit a report on ground conditions, but this is concerned principally with stability rather than contamination. There

---

[62] This category can include, for example, a landlord who causes contamination by failing to exercise proper care and control over the selection of industrial tenants.
[63] However, the Treuhandanstalt is pressing for the completion of such a list.

have been examples of public authorities being held liable to the owners of properties built on contaminated sites designated for development by the authority.

The former GDR[64]

Problems of soil contamination are particularly acute in the former **13.26** GDR territories: around 50,000 sites have been identified in the new Federal Länder as likely to be contaminated, such that closer examination is required to determine whether they present a risk to human health or the environment. Some 23,000 of these are the sites of waste deposits and 27,000 are abandoned industrial sites; to these must be added contaminated military sites.[65] Relatively few have as yet been subject to detailed investigation and risk assessment.[66]

This presents a problem for the Treuhandanstalt (the Federal Trust Agency for the Privatisation of Former State-owned Assets) in trying to attract purchasers and investors. The problem is addressed in various ways: in March 1993 the Federal Government announced a budget of DM 15 billion (£6.3 billion) for clean-up, targeted at the triangle linking Halle, Leipzig and Bitterfeld, former centres of chemical production and lignite mining areas.[67] Such supraregional assistance seems likely to be essential for some time to come and is seen as justified in the light of job-creation opportunities.[68]

Secondly, the Treuhandanstalt addresses the problem through the terms of the sale contracts it negotiates which define the risk undertaken by the purchaser and allocate the risk not assumed by the purchaser to the Federal Government and Länder. In each case the matter is one for negotiation between the parties; it is common for the statutory limitation period for warranties relating to real estate (one year) to be extended by agreement.

---

[64] See the article by Dr. Sterzinger at *Environmental Risk*, November 1992.
[65] Figures presented by Dr. Urban Rid at IBA "Conference on Contaminated Land in Property Transactions" Berlin, November 1992.
[66] "Ecological Reconstruction Basic Guidelines for Ecological Recovery and Development in the New Länder", Federal Ministry of the Environment, November 1991.
[67] *Financial Times*, March 18, 1993; "Ecological Recovery and Development Concept: Leipzig/Bitterfeld/Halle/Merseburg," Rhineland Technical Inspection Service (TÜV) and Institute for Environmental Protection and Energy Technology, December 1991.
[68] "Action Programme: Ecological Reconstruction," Federal Ministry for the Environment, March 1991.

Finally, certain exemptions have been provided by statute: under the 1991 Law on Removal of Disincentives[69] it was possible to obtain an exemption from liability for "old pollution" caused prior to July 1, 1990. The time limit for such applications was March 28, 1992. Whether such dispensation is given rests with the discretion of the Länder: Since the effect of giving such dispensation is to place future costs of remedial measures with the Länder, many states have delayed, so as to place pressure on the Treuhandanstalt to assume a share of the problem contractually. Arrangements have been reached between the Treuhandanstalt and Länder that, subject to the exclusion of costs which exceed one billion DM ceiling, and the assumption of at least 10 per cent. responsibility by the purchaser, costs will be shared in a 60:40 ration between the Treuhandanstalt and the state: effectively, in a limited and indirect way, this amount to a sort of "superfund".

Some states have also tried to address the problem: the state law of Saxony[70] provides for an extended exemption applying to soil pollution occurring before July 1, 1990 at a time when the owner had no actual control over the property: the decision as to whether the exemption shall apply is made by the Länder authorities. The state of Thuringia has adopted relatively sophisticated legislation going beyond the general police law model and defining various categories of potentially responsible party: owners of polluting facilities; producers and transporters of waste; other persons causing contamination; and present and former landowners. Additionally, provision is made for contribution actions between potentially responsible parties and a state "superfund" financed primarily by waste producers.

---

[69] Law on the Removal of Disincentives in the Privatisation of Enterprises and for the Promotion of investments, March 22, 1991, s.12; see also the *Umweltrahmengesetz* (Environmental Master Act) which applies existing German environmental legislation to the new Länder.

[70] First law of Waste Management and Protection of soils in the Free State of Saxony, August 12, 1991, Art. 10.

F. DENMARK

The Danish Waste Deposits Act 1990[71] deals with the identification **13.27** and clean-up of sites used for the deposit of chemical waste up to 1976, those used for the deposit of oil wastes before November 1, 1972 and generally sites established before October 1, 1974 and not in operation after September 1, 1990. Some 2200 waste deposit sites have been recorded, with a total of 7,000 anticipated ultimately and clean-up expected to take between 30 and 100 years at a cost of DKr eight billion (US $1.3 billion).[72] Once registered, no building may take place on a site without application to, and investigation by, the local county council or National Agency for Environmental Protection *(Miljostyrelsen)*, or (at his own cost) by the owner. Assessment of sites and remediation measures are based on the proposed end use.[73] Provision has been made, by amendments to the Waste Deposits Act, for the development of regis-tered sites under exceptional circumstances and with agreement of the Minister of the Environment without the requirement of prior investiga-tion and remedial measures.[74] It must be demonstrated that the develop-ment will not make future investigation and remedial measures impossible or substantially more expensive; the object of the amend-ments is to reduce the blighting effect on property values. The Minister of the Environment has also issued a statutory order requiring technical surveys to be carried out before sites are registered, and limiting registration to cases where the waste deposits are giving rise to pollution or the risk of pollution.[75]

Liability issues have arisen where the local and national agencies have funded clean up and have then pursued potentially responsible parties under general liability principles. In the *Rockwool case*[76] of 1991 the Danish Supreme Court considered contamination discovered in 1987 which pre-dated the company's acquisition of the site in 1962. It was held that in the absence of clear legislative intention liability should be based on an evaluation of culpability and that a current owner with no knowledge should not be liable. However, since 1986 proposals have been under consideration for the imposition of strict liability for environ-

---

[71] Act No. 420 of June 13, 1990. See generally the helpful concise summary by Prof. Ellen Margrethe Basse of the University of Aarhus at [1993] Env. Liab. CS 20.

[72] Report of the National Agency for Environmental Protection (No. 1/1992).

[73] National Agency for Environmental Protection "General Guidelines on Remedial Activities on Polluted Soil" (No. 3/1992).

[74] Act No. 213 of April 28, 1993; see Prof. E.M. Basse [1993] Env. Liab. CS54.

[75] Statutory Order No. 17 of January 12, 1993 and *General Guidelines on Registrations, etc.* (No. 1/1993; Basse, *ibid*).

[76] Danish Weekly Law Report 1991.674H.

mental damage on heavily polluting enterprises. The report of the relevant committee, published in 1992,[77] endorses such a proposal, and legislation is anticipated.

The Danish Courts have also considered the issue of limitation periods and retrospectivity. The case, *Cheminova II*,[78] involved contamination of soil and groundwater caused between 1944 and 1954 at a pesticide production site near Copenhagen. The clean-up operation cost DKr 20 million, split between central and local government. In a subsequent action against Cheminova the question was whether the general 20-year limitation period under the 300–year old act of King Christian V applied. At first instance the western district superior court ruled that the limitation period did not apply, because the plaintiff authorities were not in a position in the 1950s to know of the damage ensuing from the spillages of pesticide residues. This decision was reversed by the Danish Supreme Court on the basis that ignorance by the injured party was not relevant: indeed, such ignorance should favour the defendant company, who should be judged against the standards applying at the time of the contamination originally occurring. The proposed new strict liability law referred to above would, however, impose a limitation period of 30 years from the time of the tortious occurrence, with the requirement that this be not more than five years from such time as the injured party became aware of the pollution.

[77] Report No. 1237/1992 on "Liability for Environmental Damage"—Committee constituted by the Danish Ministry of Justice.
[78] Danish Weekly Law Report 1992.575H.

G. Australia*

Introduction

In Australia there is no federal legislation dealing with contaminated **13.28** land. Each State enacts its own legislation to cover site contamination. Queensland is the only state which has enacted legislation specifically directed to contaminated land, in the Contaminated Land Act 1990.

NSW, Victoria and Western Australia however have legislation which covers contaminated land and clean up of contaminated sites. The other States do not specifically cover contamination; however other legislation such as the relevant Health Acts, Clean Air or Clean Waters Acts may require clean up of sites which have become contaminated.

New South Wales

The remediation of contaminated land in NSW is governed by the **13.29** Environmentally Hazardous Chemicals Act 1988 and the Unhealthy Building Land Act 1990.

The Environmentally Hazardous Chemicals Act defines "contaminated site" broadly and allows the Environmental Protection Authority (EPA) to deem a site to be contaminated if it is unsafe or unfit for habitation or occupation, if it is degraded in its capacity to support plant life, or is otherwise environmentally degraded. The EPA may issue clean up notices to occupiers of the land or to any person who is in control of the contaminated site.[79] A person "in control" may include the owner of the site and can also extend to lenders such as a mortgagee in possession of the site. A lessor, if it is deemed to have control over the site, may also be held liable.

A clean-up notice can only be issued if the EPA has reasonable grounds to believe that the site has become contaminated. The notice may order remedial action to be taken: however this must be reasonable in the circumstances and must be specified in the notice. The notice may also require investigation to be conducted on the site to establish the level of contamination and preparation of a remedial action plan and possibly a long-term management plan. The Act specifies certain time limits within which the prescribed remedial action is to be taken, or alternatively, where the Minister is satisfied that urgent action is required, the notice may require action to be taken forthwith.

---

* This summary is based on a paper by Mr. John Taberner of Freehill, Hollingdale & Page, Sydney which is most gratefully acknowledged, as is the assistance of Mr. Andrew Poulos of Clayton Utz, Sydney.
[79] S.35(1).

As well as issuing clean-up notices, the EPA may itself enter and clean up the site if it has reasonable grounds to believe that the site is contaminated. Such remedial action may also be taken by other public authorities if they have the consent of the EPA. An occupier of the site is liable for the cost of the remediation by the EPA or other public authority. This is so even if it is not the occupier who caused the contamination. There is no provision under the Act for the occupier to be indemnified by the party which actually caused the contamination.

Clean-up notices may also be required if the use of the premises is to be changed and the owner wishes the site to be re-zoned. The council may require an environmental audit to be conducted and a clean-up to be carried out as a precondition to the re-zoning of the land.

Under the Unhealthy Buildings Act 1990 the EPA may, by notice in the NSW Gazette, declare that land is "unhealthy building land". The notice must be served on the owner of the land together with a report setting out the EPA's opinion and the reasons for its opinion. The EPA may specify the remedial action which is required to be taken in the notice. The EPA keeps a register of notices and will issue certificates indicating whether particular land is subject to a declaration that it is "unhealthy building land". Once the site has been cleaned up then a further notice is published in the Gazette that the land has ceased to be unhealthy. The Act makes it an offence for an owner to erect or complete the erection of a structure on unhealthy land unless the construction was without the knowledge or consent of the owner, or with the prior approval of the EPA and in accordance with conditions set by the EPA.

The EPA is preparing a Contaminated Sites Register which will be available through the NSW Land Title Office.

In NSW other legislation such as the Clean Air Act, Clean Waters Act, Environmental Offences & Penalties Act, Pollution Control Act, Dangerous Goods Act, and Radiation Control Act may require an owner or occupier to clean-up a site.

Queensland

13.30   The Contaminated Land Act 1991 came into force on January 1, 1992 and provides for the identification, classification and clean-up of land which is contaminated with hazardous substances.[79a] A "hazardous substance" includes any substances which may pose a hazard to human health or to the environment if it is inadequately or improperly managed. "Contaminated Land" includes land that is affected by a hazardous substance so that it causes other land, water or air to be a

---

[79a] See the summary by Nicolette Rogers [1994] Env. Liability 22.

hazard. The Act requires owners or occupiers to report contamination to the chief executive of the Department of the Environment within 30 days of becoming aware of the contamination or the likelihood of contamination. Therefore it is not necessary that the owner or occupier knows definitely that the land is contaminated.

A local authority or government department is also under an obligation to report contamination or likely contamination of land within its jurisdiction. The Contaminated Land Regulations (made under the 1991 Act) provide that land is deemed to be contaminated if it has been used for one of the purposes set out in Schedule 1 to that Regulation. Such activities include asbestos production and manufacture, drum reconditioning, wastes, chemical manufacture and formulation, metal sprayers, sanitary landfill sites, smelting and refining, etc.

The chief executive may issue notices requiring preparation of a site investigation report to the owner, occupier or any other suspected on reasonable grounds to have caused or permitted contamination of a site. When the site investigation report indicates that the land is contaminated, a further notice (a remediation notice) may be issued requiring specified clean-up measures to be taken.

The owner has a defence if they can claim that the contamination conformed with the lawful and accepted practices at the time that it occurred, that the contamination occurred before the commencement of the relevant provision of the Act and therefore it would be unreasonable for the person to be required to comply with the Act, or the person is unable to pay the costs of a report.

The chief executive may also clean-up the site itself, if events occur such as the discharge of hazardous substances. The costs of such clean up are recoverable from the owner or occupier. The chief executive may recover such costs by exercising its power of sale over the site. The chief executive has priority over all other parties, except the local authority in respect of rates and charges, or a registered mortgagee if the mortgagee was registered prior to the classification of the land as contaminated. If the chief executive cannot recover the costs, then these are to be paid by the local authority in which area the land is situated and by the department, in shares agreed by the Minister.

There is a Contaminated Sites Register which specifies six different classes of land. These classes are:

1. a possible site;
2. a probable site;
3. a confirmed site;
4. a restricted site;
5. a former site; and
6. a released site.

An owner or occupier may also be required to clean up a site under the Clean Waters Act, the Health Act, the Radioactive Substances Act,

521

the Pollution of Waters by Oil Act or The Workplace Health & Safety Act.

Victoria

13.31   The legislation which deals with contaminated sites in Victoria is the Environmental Protection Act 1970. It is administered by the Victorian Environmental Protection Authority (EPA).

The Act provides that a person shall not pollute land so that the condition of the land is so changed as to make or be reasonably expected to make the land or its produce noxious or poisonous, harmful or potentially harmful to humans, flora and fauna, obnoxious or unduly offensive to human senses, or detrimental to any beneficial use made of the land.[80]

A party may be required by notice issued by the EPA to clean up a contaminated site under the Act where that party:[81]

(a) is the occupier of premises from which pollution occurred; or

(b) caused or permitted pollution to occur; or

(c) appears to have abandoned or dumped any industrial waste or potentially hazardous substance; or

(d) handles industrial waste or potentially hazardous substances in a manner likely to cause an environmental hazard.

The EPA may clean-up a site and recover the costs from the occupier. There is provision for the occupier to seek a court order to recover these costs from anyone else who may be responsible for the pollution. In addition to the costs of clean up, there are also penalties set for breaches of the Act. The EPA may also issue pollution abatement notices which require the owner or occupier to modify or cease certain operations. The Act presumes that the pollution is caused by the occupier and therefore the onus is on the occupier to show that they did not cause the pollution.

The Victorian legislation is at present unique in that it confers power on the EPA to require the occupier of premises to conduct an environmnental audit and to publish the results of that audit.[82] Clean-up notices may also be issued under Acts such as the Radiation Control Act or the Dangerous Goods Act.

---

[80] S.45(1). S.45(2) of the Act sets out the circumstances in which a person shall be deemed to have polluted land.

[81] S.62A(1).

[82] S.31C, introduced pursuant to amendments made in 1989.

Western Australia

The Environmental Protection Act 1986 provides that a party may be **13.32** required to clean up a site if they were the occupier at the time of the discharge or if they caused or allowed the discharge to occur. The EPA may clean up the site itself and recover costs.

Pollution abatement notices may also be issued to occupiers and owners requiring them to take such steps as are specified to prevent the discharge of waste. Such a notice, while it is current, may bind successive owners of the land.

There are also clean-up provisions under the Health Act, Metropolitan Water Supply Sewerage & Drainage Act, the Radiation Safety Act and the Explosives and Dangerous Goods Act. A party may also be required to clean up other property which has become contaminated as a result of its activities.

South Australia

There is no specific legislation dealing with contaminated sites; **13.33** however a clean-up notice may be issued under legislation such as the Clean Air Act, Dangerous Substances Act, Radiation Protection & Control Act, Public and Environmental Health Act, Waste Management Act and Water Resources Act. If a clean-up notice is not complied with, then the governmental agency involved may clean up the site and recover its costs.

ACT

There is no legislation directed generally at site contamination; **13.34** however clean-up notices may be issued under the Air Pollution Act, the Water Pollution Act, the Dangerous Goods Ordinance, the Public Health Act, and the Radiation Ordinance.

Northern Territory

Once again there is no specific legislation, however the Dangerous **13.35** Goods Act, Water Act, Public Health Act, and Radiation (Safety Control) Ordinance provide mechanisms which can be used for the clean-up of sites.

Chapter 14

RECOMMENDATIONS

Generally

14.01   It is apparent that the law relating to contaminated land is at a formative stage both in the UK and within the EC. Even in jurisdictions where the law is far more advanced, progress towards a workable and effective system of liability which is also perceived as equitable by the business and commercial sector has been far from easy. At the time of writing the Government's further proposals on liability for contaminated land are awaited, and the Royal Commission on Environmental Pollution is embarking upon a wide-ranging study of soil protection, to include contamination from all sources, reclamation and the relationship with groundwater.[1] it is unusual for a work of this nature to contain the authors' recommendations for future action, but we feel in this case that it may be useful to conclude with a brief perspective of how the law in this area might be developed to best advantage.

Identification of contaminated land: generally

14.02   Any attempt to address the problems caused by contaminated land must begin with the process of identification of contaminated sites and the risks they pose. Otherwise no prioritisation is possible and gross anomalies or wastage of resources may result. The proposed registers under section 143 of the Environmental Protection Act 1990 were at least a first step towards this process. The problem was that the further steps were not laid out clearly at the same time, the logical next steps being the identification of actually (as opposed to potentially) contaminated land, the assessment of the seriousness or otherwise of the contamination and its likely consequences, and a clear liability regime for allocating the cost of the measures necessary to manage, reduce or remove the risk to an acceptable level. Realistically, it probably must be accepted that:

[1] Royal Commission on Environmental Pollution, News Release July 9, 1993.

(*a*) a larger number of sites will become entered on the register than might originally have been anticipated; and

(*b*) that for psychological reasons there will inevitably be some blighting effect resulting from entry on the register.[2]

Identification of contaminated land: procedure

The question then arises of what is the most appropriate method of **14.03** identifying contaminated land; any system should ideally be cost effective, consistent and fair. It should also encourage responsible behaviour on the part of landowners. A considerable amount of data is already within the possession of public authorities, and the proposed creation of a unified Environmental Protection Agency represents a valuable opportunity to bring together disparate information currently held by the NRA, waste authorities, HMIP, and local environmental health, planning and building control departments.

One of the Government's objections to creating a register of actual, as opposed to potential, contamination was the cost to local authorities of investigating potentially contaminated sites. However, it is by no means self-evident that this would have to be a cost falling on the public purse. There seems no reason why the responsibility for establishing whether his land represents a threat to its occupiers, neighbours or the environment generally should not lie with the landowner. Where on the basis of information available to the relevant regulatory authority it appears that there is the possibility that land is contaminated, the authority should be given power to require the landowner to produce the necessary monitoring or other data to enable the authority to assess whether the site presents risks to human health or to the environment. It should be possible to frame the power in such a way as to prevent the landowner being faced with unreasonable demands in this respect.

Prioritisation of sites

It is essential to have a fair and objective means of prioritising sites as **14.04** the basis for further action. There is a sensible distinction to be drawn between (*a*) sites where there is existing harm to health or the environment, or an imminent risk of harm, sufficient in either case to render immediate remedial action necessary; and (*b*) on the other hand, sites which do not require immediate remedial action but which it may be

---

[2] Both of these phenomena were certainly the experience in Denmark, where it was initially thought that about 500 sites would required registration; the final figure is now estimated at about 10,000.

desirable to clean up in a phased manner. The approach to the two types of site may be quite different. Soil standards such as thresholds may be a helpful part of that process, but should not be conclusive; ultimately the process should be driven by sound principles of risk assessment. It is important that an efficient and robust screening and ranking process is evolved: lack of such a process is one of the defects of the US Superfund system. The programme to clean up sites which fall into the second category and do not require immediate remedial action may extend over many years.[3]

Spill reporting and response

14.05   As matters stand in UK law, it is not illegal to contaminate your own land, unless that contamination has other consequences, such as water pollution. Nor is there any general obligation to report spillages, releases or other activities or incidents which contaminate land. It is surely axiomatic that the creation of further contaminated land is undesirable, even if it happens to be the polluter's own land. Land is a limited natural resource, the quality of which should be protected. There should therefore be an obligation on a person whose activities or operations have contaminated any land to report the fact to the relevant regulatory authority. Such an obligation should be backed by criminal sanctions and should apply only to spills or other incidents occurring after the relevant date, *i.e.* on a prospective rather than retrospective basis. The regulatory bodies should be given power to require the polluter to remedy the consequences of that contamination. The polluter could be adequately safeguarded by reasonable rules as to the standard of clean-up required (see below). Compliance with statutory requirements should be a defence, *e.g.* the emplacement of waste in the ground under a waste management licence. Such a regime, combined with sensible precautionary legislation, *e.g.* on standards of storage installation, *etc.*, could effectively deal with new contamination.

Past contamination

14.06   Inevitably, the most difficult problems are presented by historically contaminated sites. As mentioned above, the first step should be to identify and prioritise such sites.

---

[3] See the Report of the Select Committee on the European Communities of the House of Lords, "Remedying Environmental Damage" (Session 1993–94, 3rd Report, H.L. Paper 10) para. 45, suggesting that a phased national programme might extend over several decades.

Where a site is causing immediate or imminent harm to human health or to the environment, the first step ought to be to reduce the risk to acceptable levels. The polluter and the current owner may or may not be the same person. If they are different persons it may or may not be possible to identify the polluter; indeed there may be a number of polluters whose actions together have contributed to the problem. Essentially the options as to who might be liable to carry out or to pay for the necessary costs of clean-up are:

(1) the original polluter(s) if identifiable—where there is more than one, liability may be pro rata or may be joint and several;
(2) the owner of land (however that term is defined);
(3) some form of joint compensation fund; or
(4) the public purse.

Choice of the liability regime may be motivated by various considerations ranging from expressing disapproval of irresponsible behaviour through to ensuring that the desired standard of clean-up is achieved at the minimal cost to the public purse. Our view is that the primary consideration should be whatever system is most effective in achieving the desired goals of removing unacceptable risks. In some cases speedy action may be necessary, and who pays may be a secondary consideration in terms of relative importance: this fact should be recognised when designing any liability system.

The polluter

Fixing the original polluter with liability for past contamination **14.07** inevitably involves some element of retrospectivity: the focus is on the past acts which gave rise to the problem rather than on the current situation. The original polluter will no longer necessarily be in a position to exert control over the problem or implement possible solutions—they may no longer own or occupy the land in question. Additionally, in many cases the original polluter may no longer be available as a source of funding for clean-up. It is thus unlikely that any workable regime can function effectively solely by attributing liability to the original polluter. But nonetheless, the original polluter would be regarded by most people as the natural primary focus for liability—the "first port of call." The main objection to such liability in the case of past contamination runs essentially as follows: the damage has already been done, therefore imposing retrospective liability serves no deterrent purpose in modifying the behaviour which gave rise to the problem. Linked with this, it can be perceived as unfair to impose or increase the liabilities of parties for actions which at the time they were carried out were not illegal, negligent or deficient when compared with the then current industry or

527

commercial practice. Finally, it can be said that in some cases the polluter will simply not be able to bear the costs, and the resultant liquidation of his business and unemployment will generate further costs for the public purse, which money would better have been spent on the pollution problem in the first place. On the other hand there may be cases where the pollution is relatively recent, was caused by unsatisfactory (though not illegal) standards of environmental management, has serious environmental consequences which were foreseeable, and where the polluter has the necessary funds to clean up. Between the two extreme situations there are obviously a multitude of circumstances which could exist. This tends to indicate that dogmatic and legalistic black and white situations such as "polluter pays" are not the way forward in relation to past contamination of land. A more pragmatic and flexible approach is required, and we discuss how this might work below.

The owner

14.08   Another possible focus for liability is the current owner of the land, by which we mean not only the owner of the freehold, but anyone with a sufficient interest, however that is ultimately defined. The owner may in some cases be the original polluter, but in many cases they will be different persons. Attention here centres not upon the past acts which caused the pollution, but rather the continuing state of the land and the person who currently has control of it. Liability is therefore retrospective only to the extent that the person in question may have acquired their interest in the land some years ago, before the development of current environmental standards of due diligence. Here the choice of liability regime can help to modify commercial practice, for example by providing the person who unwittingly acquires contaminated property or collateral with a due diligence type of defence. Conversely, the wrong choice of liability regime could have serious consequences for the marketability of property; rendering the contaminated land unsaleable or unmortgageable is of itself no help whatsoever to the environment, indeed quite the reverse. Our view is that the benefits of a due diligence defence in encouraging responsible practice for the future would outweigh the disbenefit of those cases where as a result of the defence, the cost of remedial action had to fall on the public purse. In any event, the scope to invoke such a defence will decrease over time as standards of due diligence become more stringent. What is clear is that to absolve owners entirely from liability for contamination which was not of their making would not encourage a responsible attitude; indeed the transfer of land would be seen as an easy way to pass the burden to the taxpayer. Inevitably, there will be difficult cases; land held by trustees, charities or donees; banks exercising their security, and the like. Again this tends to suggest that, as with the original polluter, there is no easy single answer; a responsive and flexible regime is required which will reward responsible behaviour and will facilitate the sale and transfer of land through the operation of the market. Lender liability is a specific problem which must be addressed expressly and in sufficiently clear terms to allow lenders to operate their normal lending procedures with confidence. In our view any definition of "owner" ought to be phrased in such a way that lenders will only be liable if they take a conscious decision to exercise control over the relevant assets: this is most likely to be at the stage of exercising security. Clarification will be required as to what is meant by control in this context, and steps should be taken in conjunction with the financial services sector to establish a code of good banking practice dealing with environmental issues such as due diligence. This would be relevant in determining whether a bank in control would be able to rely on a due diligence defence, or whether the problems affecting the property should be regarded as attributable to the bank's failure to act responsibly.[4]

Joint compensation funds

The EC Green Paper on repairing damage to the environment **14.09** contains considerable, though ultimately inconclusive, discussion on joint compensation mechanisms on an industry sector basis.[5] Whilst it is conceivable that such arrangements might be feasible on a narrow sectoral basis, e.g., the waste sector or the petroleum sector, it has to be doubted whether they can ever provide a complete solution to problems of historically contaminated land. The interests and problems of the potentially liable parties are likely to be too divergent for any such system to work on a voluntary basis. Also there is a fundamental difference between a fund set up to deal with future contingencies such as oil spills, from one designed to fund the clean-up of pollution which has already occurred. Any such fund would therefore need to be instituted by the state, based on taxes or levies on certain sectors. Such a system would at least have the advantage of allocating the costs of historic pollution to the broad industry sector which originated the problem, rather than the cost falling to taxpayers at large. In this way such funds might form a component of a long-term remedial strategy: the structure and application of any such fund would however need to be

[4] See the evidence presented to the Select Committee (n. 3 above) by the British Bankers' Association (pp. 83–88).
[5] A more helpful discussion is provided in the Report by Professor H. Bocken of the University of Ghent to the OECD Environment Directorate—Group of Economic Experts (Paris, May 2, 1989, ENV/ECO 89.8).

very carefully thought out if it is to be effective. A great deal of contaminated land may not be readily attributable to any specific industry sector, and there is a danger of burdening unfairly those sectors which are currently high profile, such as chemicals and oil. On the other hand, the existence of a fund would go a long way to solving the common complaint of regulatory bodies that they cannot be expected to outlay significant sums in clean-up with ultimately no certain prospect of recouping that cost. We believe that the Government should therefore look closely at the possible advantages of creating such funds, in the recognition that they are unlikely to come about voluntarily.

The taxpayer

14.10   However sophisticated the regimes of liability which may be established in relation to contaminated land, there is no doubt that ultimately some residual costs will fall to the taxpayer. Apart from anything else, some of the more serious cases of contamination are likely to be the result of previous Government activity, *e.g.* Ministry of Defence land. Also, liability mechanisms will fail where no responsible party with sufficient funds is available, even if there is such a party it may not, as explained above, be equitable or appropriate to charge that party with the full costs of remediation. In the absence of some fully comprehensive scheme of joint liability funds (which is unlikely), it therefore seems inevitable that some cost will fall to the taxpayer.

Contingent problems

14.11   As mentioned above, there is a need to identify those sites which present unacceptable risks in their immediate condition and use. Beyond this category, there will be sites where the risk is contingent, *i.e.* the problems will arise only when the site is developed or if it is put to a more sensitive use. Here the problem will need to be approached in a phased manner. It may need to be tackled in the context of a specific proposal for development, or perhaps sooner in the interests of restoring flexibility of possible uses and serving urban regeneration. As well as rendering a site acceptably safe for continuation in its current use, any system ought to seek to maximise to the fullest practicable extent the range of realistic possible future land uses that can be achieved without excessive cost.[6] The most appropriate way in which to deal with these

---

[6] See the Discussion Paper of the Australia and New Zealand Environment and Conservation Council, "Financial Liability for Contaminated Site Remediation" (June 1993) p. 7. The same view is expressed in the Select Committee Report (n. 2 above) at para. 45.

problems is in the context of development. It should become mandatory to produce a contamination survey to the local planning authority when seeking planning permission (certain forms of minor development could be excluded by regulations). This survey would then form part of the planning history of the site. Planning authorities should be given guidance as to the importance of addressing contamination issues fully at this stage, and the desirability of remediation to the appropriate level (see below) should be a material consideration, reflected in development plan policies. In this way, we believe that significant improvements in land quality could be made with relatively little pain. In some cases, it may not be acceptable for the problem to be addressed only in the context of a specific development site when (if ever) development proposals come forward. The Urban Regeneration Agency could be given the role of identifying and promoting strategic schemes for clean-up on urban regeneration grounds under a rolling programme and in close consultation with the relevant environmental protection authorities. The allocation of the cost of remediation could be considered globally within the context of that scheme (see paragraph 14.13 below).

How clean is clean?

So far as the remediation of contaminated land is concerned this is **14.12** perhaps the single most crucial issue. It is intimately linked with the question of what degree of environmental damage, impairment or risk will trigger requirements for clean-up and consequent liability. But it also goes to the issue of the nature and scale of the remedial work required. There is much to be learnt here from the mistakes made in the US in terms of risk assessment. In particular it is essential that unrealistic exposure scenarios are avoided, that a site specific approach is so far as possible adopted, that preference is not automatically given to inflexible requirements for a "permanent solution", that assumptions made as to site use are reasonable, and that standards or requirements set for other purposes (*e.g.*, drinking water) are not automatically used as standards to be met on clean-up, irrespective of their necessity or achievability. Unless caution in relation to these matters is exercised the mistakes and problems which have occurred in the US will be repeated. As one US commentator has put it:[7]

> "Companies have been asked to pump and treat contaminated groundwater as if there is a time when it can be determined that the pumping and treating can be stopped. Potentially responsible

[7] Randy B. Mott [1992] *Environment Law Reporter, p. 1301, August 28, 1992.*

parties (PRPs), under the threat of penalties and horrendous press coverage, have taken the course of least resistance and agreed to turn on the pumps with no understanding of when, if ever, they will be turned off. Consent decrees over the last several years have legally committed the unwary to the pursuit of the impossible. It is now time to reconcile the commitment of massive amounts of public and private funds to the realities of ground water remediation."

Part of the problem in the US is that very little guidance has been provided by Congress as to how to balance the conflicting pressures of permanence of solutions against cost; consequently Federal agencies have broad discretion and have tended towards a bias in favour of high cost "permanent" remedies. Site-specific risk assessment is not always used as effectively as it might be to counteract that tendency. The UK Government should provide a clear framework and guidance for assessing remedial or clean-up strategies and the criteria to be met by those strategies. Such guidance need not (indeed should not) take the form of hard trigger or threshold levels, though such levels can be helpful if provided on an indicative basis as flags and signposts. There is also however a need for a degree of finality, in the sense that future liability should be discharged by complying with current standards of clean-up as to soil or groundwater quality: this is critical to the commercial success of many reclamation and regeneration schemes.[8] If standards subsequently change then it is the taxpayer who should bear the cost of achieving them.

The decision making process

14.13   The key to a successful strategy for addressing contaminated land lies in our view in the arrangements for decision making: when action is necessary, what action is necessary, to what standard clean-up is to be carried out, and who (and in what proportions) it is to bear the cost. Particularly when dealing with past contamination, a strict judicial process based on notions of civil liability is unlikely in our view to be effective: the courts are simply not the correct forum to deal with such matters, the essence of which is the exercise of discretion within a policy framework. In our view, the process would be far better served by a system more akin to planning inquiries, with the use of technical assessors and with a procedure consisting of exchange of statements and proofs, rather than pleadings. We would suggest that such a forum would also serve the legitimate public interest and concern in ensuring

[8] See P. Boyle and J. Finnecy, *Waste Environment Today (News J.)*, Vol. 6, No. 19, October 1993.

that contaminated land is dealt with adequately. The tribunal we are proposing could operate within a framework of Government guidance, but would have a large degree of discretion to determine which potentially responsible parties should pay for what and over what time scale, and the extent to which public funds should be committed, possibly by way of an interest free or low-interest loan to the liable party. The main objective should be to get the contamination remedied to acceptable levels as cost effectively and as efficiently as possible. There should be a broad power of apportionment between all responsible parties and state funds, taking into account all relevant factors including past conduct, current resources, and hardship.

There will inevitably be hard cases, such as trustees, donees, owners of domestic property, and those whose land has become contaminated by adjoining land, whose circumstances will need to be weighed and taken into account. Specific provision or guidance may be required for the owners of domestic property affected by contamination.[9] Quite apart from such hard cases, the approach which could be adopted might be a mixture of fault-based and risk-based liability, *i.e.* potential liability would rest on the contribution to risk as polluter or owner, rather than on fault; the relevance of fault, together with other relevant factors, would lie in the share of the costs which the responsible party was expected to bear.

We believe that such a system could work, and indeed that it may represent the only feasible way forward in countering the UK's historical legacy of contaminated land.

Anti-avoidance measures

Any scheme of liability will need to be sufficiently robust to prevent **14.14** liability being avoided or circumvented by technical means such as transfers of land, the use of subsidiary companies, or insolvency. Broad powers of piercing the corporate veil by reference to benefit, economic control and other suitable tests will be required. The liability regime may need to be given dominance over current rules on corporate and individual insolvency.

---

[9] It is interesting to note the solution being proposed in Denmark, whereby innocent owners of private houses on contaminated land may get the site cleaned up by the Government on payment of a fee of DKr 60,000 (approximately £600), a figure which corresponds to 10–15 per cent. of average clean-up costs. Such a solution may be attractive to affected home-owners in the UK if it results in property which was blighted becoming saleable once again.

Avoiding the mistakes of the US

14.15   The importance of avoiding mistakes made in the US on clean-up standards has already been mentioned. Another area requiring caution is the treatment of multi-party waste disposal sites, the typical Superfund site to which many waste producers may have consigned their wastes. It appears that the US system is unusual in placing continuing liability on waste generators for the clean-up of a site to which they sent their waste and over which they have never had control.[10] Any such liability, should it be imposed in the UK, should be imposed only a prospective basis and in our view only where the waste producer was at fault in consigning waste to an unlicensed facility or in failing to exercise the relevant standards of due diligence demanded by his duty of care as a waste producer: such a system could in fact have the benefit of providing a strong incentive for responsible behaviour.

Another key feature of the US system to be avoided is that of joint and several liability which potentially makes the waste producer responsible for costs entirely disproportionate to his own contribution to the problem. The importance of retrospective joint and several liability as a generator of clean up funds can be judged by the fact that currently around 30 per cent. of clean-up costs are met from the Federal Trust Fund—the rest comes from potentially responsible parties. It has been estimated that if all producers who deposited wastes at Superfund sites before January 1981 (when the statute was enacted) were released from liability and if the resulting "orphan" shares were transferred to the fund rather than subsequent consignees of waste, then the Fund's share of cost would rise to 68 per cent.[11] Notwithstanding the fearsome efficacy of these provisions for allocating costs to private parties rather than the public purse, we would not advocate that the American solution should be adopted.

---

[10] See *A Comparison of Superfund with Programmes in Other Countries* (The Business Roundtable, Washington D.C., September 1993).

[11] *Assigning Liability for Superfund Cleanups: An Analysis of Policy Options* K. N. Probst and P. R. Portney (Resources for the Future), 1992, ELR 004, December 1993, p. 11.

Appendix A

Precedents

The following precedents for dealing with contaminated land in **A.01** various commercial contexts are given in this Appendix. A variety of drafting styles are offered. Whilst it is hoped that these precedents will provide guidance and ideas, they should not be used dogmatically: practice in the area of contaminated land is evolving gradually and a degree of flexibility on the part of the draftsman is required.

1. Enquiries of the local authority regarding possible contamination;
2. Enquiries of the vendor in property transactions;
3. Indemnity on sale of land;
4. Access agreement for site investigations;
5. Letter to environmental consultant requesting proposal;
6. Agreement appointing environmental consultant;
7. Collateral warranty by environmental consultant;
8. Covenants on sale of part of land;
9. Landlord's environmental questionnaire;
10. Leasehold covenants;
11. Landlord's protection clause: pre-existing contamination;
12. Tenant's protection clause: pre-existing contamination;
13. Provision in lease giving the tenant the right to terminate the lease in the event of contamination problems and excluding tenant's liability to contribute to such matters;
14. Acquisition of a company—information request relating to environmental matters;
15. Acquisition of a company—environmental warranties;
16. Acquisition of a company—environmental indemnities;
17. Company or assets acquisition—contaminated land indemnities;
18. Provisions for inclusion in loan facility letter;
19. Covenants by mortgagor.

A.02 **PRECEDENT** 1: ENQUIRIES OF THE LOCAL AUTHORITY REGARDING POSSIBLE CONTAMINATION

1. Has the property or any nearby property been monitored by the authority or by any person on the authority's behalf in relation to possible soil contamination? If so, please provide details of such monitoring and whether the results of such monitoring are open to inspection.

2. Has the authority been supplied with information by any other authority or person in relation to possible soil contamination on the property or any nearby property? If so, please provide details of such information and whether such information is open to inspection.

3. Has the authority carried out any investigation in relation to contaminative uses on the property or any nearby property for the purpose of compiling any register (whether statutory or non-statutory) of potentially contaminated land? If so, please provide details of such investigation and whether the register and/or the information used in compiling it is open to inspection.

4. Has the authority received any complaint relating to contamination or the effects of contamination on the property or on any nearby property? If so, please provide details of such complaint and of any action taken in response.

5. Has the authority ever been asked to advise in relation to public or environmental health, building or planning control in relation to contamination or its effects on the property or any nearby property? If so, please give details of such advice.

NOTE:
See para. 11.04.

PRECEDENT 2: ENQUIRIES OF VENDOR IN PROPERTY **A.03**
TRANSACTIONS

1. Please confirm that the Property has not been used at any time for any of the following purposes or operations:

   - burial of diseased livestock;
   - the extraction, handling or storage of coal, petroleum or similar materials;
   - the extraction, handling or storage of mineral ores;
   - gasworks or coal carbonisation plants;
   - plants for the treatment of coal, oil or similar materials;
   - power stations;
   - electricity sub-stations;
   - metal production, processing and finishing;
   - storage and handling of scrap metals;
   - production and processing of mineral products;
   - asbestos works;
   - chemical works;
   - engineering;
   - shipbuilding;
   - explosives or ordnance manufacture or testing;
   - electrical and electronic component manufacture;
   - manufacture of pet foods or animal feedstuffs;
   - processing of animal by-products;
   - paper and print works;
   - chemical treatment or coating of timber or timber products;
   - tanning or leatherworks;
   - fulling, bleaching or dyeing;
   - carpet or floor covering manufacture;
   - processing of natural or synthetic rubber;
   - marshalling, dismantling, repairing or maintaining railway rolling stock, road transport vehicles, vessels, or aircraft;
   - sewage treatment;
   - storage, treatment or disposal of sludge;
   - treating, keeping, disposing of or depositing waste;
   - storage or disposal of radioactive materials;
   - dry cleaning;
   - educational or research laboratories.

2. If the Property has been used in whole or in part for any of the purposes referred to at (1) above, please provide details of such use.

3. Please confirm that properties adjoining or neighbouring the Property, in sufficient proximity to effect the Property, have not

537

been used for any of the purposes referred to at (1) above. If they have been so used, please provide details.

4. Please confirm that no noxious or polluting substances are present in, on or under the Property so as to present a risk of harm to human health or pollution of the environment.

5. If unable to give the confirmation requested at (4) above, please supply details as to the substances, the risks presented by them and any steps taken to remedy the same.

6. Please confirm that there are not and have not been any under-ground storage tanks or underground pipework at the Property used to store or transport substances which may cause harm to human health or pollution of the environment.

7. If the confirmation requested at (6) above cannot be given, please supply full details of:

   (a) the location of such tanks and pipework;
   (b) the types of substances stored and transported;
   (c) whether the tanks or pipework are currently in use;
   (d) if not currently in use, when the use ceased and any steps taken to drain and decontaminate the tank or pipework; and
   (e) any known or suspected escapes of substances from the tank or pipework.

8. Please confirm that the use and condition of the Property complies in all respects with legislation for the protection of human health and the environment and with any orders, notices or directions made or given under such legislation, and that all necessary licences, authorisations and consents have been obtained and remain in effect. Please supply copies of all current licences, authorisations and consents relating to the Property.

9. Please confirm that no notices, orders, claims or demands have been made or given in respect of the Property as a result of the condition of the Property or non-compliance or alleged non-compliance with any legislation as referred to at (8) above and that none are anticipated. If this cannot be confirmed, please provide full details.

10. Please confirm that no waste materials or substances have been disposed of at the Property. If such confirmation cannot be given, please provide full details of the location and date or dates of disposal and of the nature of the materials or substances and of the disposal operations.

11. Please provide details of how waste, including liquid wastes and effluent, produced on the Property is disposed of.

12. Please confirm that there are no closed or operational waste disposal sites or proposed waste disposal sites within 250 metres of the Property.

13. Please state whether any environmental audit or assessment or site investigation has been undertaken in respect of the Property. Please supply full details of any such investigation which has been undertaken and copies of any reports or results which are in the possession of the Vendor.

14. Please state whether any works have been carried out to treat, remove, isolate or immobilise contamination on the Property or on adjoining or neighbouring property. Please supply full details of any such works and any documentation or contracts in relation thereto which are in the possession of the Vendor.

NOTE:
See para. 11.07. The list of uses at enquiry (1) is drawn from the first and most comprehensive list of contaminative uses published by the DoE at Annex C to its Consultative Paper of May 3, 1991.

A.04 PRECEDENT 3: INDEMNITY ON SALE OF LAND

1. The Vendor agrees with the Purchaser to indemnify and hold harmless the Purchaser against:

   (a) all claims, judgments, damages, costs, penalties, expenses, losses, demands and actions asserted against or imposed upon the Purchaser at common law or under any Environmental Law arising from or in respect of Contamination;

   (b) all costs incurred by the Purchaser in complying with any notice, order, direction, injunction or other requirement of any court or any competent authority arising from or in respect of Contamination and made or given under common law or any Environmental Law; and

   (c) all costs incurred by the Purchaser as are reasonably necessary to remove, neutralise or isolate any Contamination so as to cause the Property to be in compliance with the minimum requirements of any Environmental Law.

   [in each case where notice of the claim, judgment, damages, costs, penalties, expenses, losses, demands or actions is given to the Vendor in writing before the [   ] anniversary of Completion].

2. Within [   ] working days of receiving notice of any claim, judgment, damages, costs, penalties, expenses, losses, demands or actions as referred to at paragraph 1 above, or receiving any notice, order, direction, injunction or other requirement as referred to at paragraph 1 above, or at least [   ] working days before incurring any costs as referred to at paragraph 1 above the Purchaser shall notify the Vendor in writing and shall provide the Vendor with full details thereof, including copies of all related correspondence and reports of any environmental consultants or similar experts.

3. Upon receiving notice under paragraph 2 above, the Vendor shall have the right at any time, but not the obligation, to defend any claim, to contest or comply with any notice, order, direction injunction or other requirement, or to incur any costs, and the Purchaser shall afford the Vendor all assistance as may be reasonably necessary in respect thereof.

4. If the Vendor elects not to act under paragraph 3, the Purchaser shall on a timely basis keep the Vendor informed of the conduct and progress of all claims and of all costs incurred or proposed to be incurred by the Purchaser and shall provide the Vendor with

copies of all data, reports, records, pleadings and correspondence in respect thereof, and in particular shall not settle or compromise any claim without giving the Vendor at least [10] working days prior notice after which the Vendor has either given its written consent to such settlement or has not within such notice period elected to take over the conduct of the claim.

[5. The maximum amount payable in aggregate under the indemnity contained in paragraph 1 shall not exceed [£   ]].

Definitions

"Environmental Law" means any act or regulation or any notice, direction, imposition, or requirement issued, imposed or directed by any competent authority which relates to the protection of human health or protection of the environment and which is applicable at the date of Completion including any modification or re-enactment thereof [but not to the extent that such modification or re-enactment introduces materially more onerous or stringent requirements in respect of Contamination].

"Contamination" means contamination of the Property by any substance which, in the quantities or concentration at which it is present on the Property, presents a risk of harm to human health or of pollution of the environment, [ALTERNATIVELY, SPECIFIC SUBSTANCES MAY BE IDENTIFIED] [provided that]:

[(a) the Contamination was present on the Property [before the date of Completion] or [as a result of the acts or omissions of the Vendor]; [and

(b) the effects of or risks presented by the Contamination have not been materially increased by the positive acts of the Purchaser or the Purchaser's agents.]

NOTE:
This precedent is intended as an example of an indemnity which may be used on the sale of property. It has been deliberately kept as simple as possible and such indemnities are likely to vary considerably in their scope, effect and sophistication. It covers not only claims by third parties but also own-site clean-up costs reasonably incurred by the Purchaser. Care will need to be taken to establish exactly what type of contamination is covered and whether the indemnity extends to costs incurred as a result of legislative requirements which become more onerous after Completion. There may be great difficulties in establishing what degree of contamination was present on the property at Completion, and if the indemnity is worded in such a way that requires this to be determined, then provision for determination by an expert in default of agreement may well be desirable.

A.05 **PRECEDENT** 4: ACCESS AGREEMENT FOR SITE
INVESTIGATIONS

THIS AGREEMENT dated [DATE] is made between:
1. [   ] ("the Owner") and
2. [   ] ("the Interested Party")

Recitals

1. The owner is the owner of land at [DETAILS OF LAND] ("the Property").
2. The Interested Party has expressed an interest in buying/leasing/lending against the Property and has requested access to the Property for the purpose of carrying out investigation as to ground conditions at the Property.
3. The Owner is willing to allow such access by the Interested Party subject to the terms and conditions of this Agreement.

IT IS AGREED AS FOLLOWS:

1. The Owner shall permit [NAME OF INTERESTED PARTY'S CONSULTANT] ("the Consultant") on behalf of the Interested Party to enter the Property on 2 (two) days' notice to the Owner for the purpose of inspecting the Property and of taking samples of soil, strata, building materials, contaminants, groundwater and surface water upon the following terms.

2. The samples shall be taken by the Consultant by means of boreholes [and/or trial pits] at the agreed locations shown on the plan annexed hereto.

3. The Consultant shall exercise the permission to enter the Property and to take samples so as to cause as little damage and disruption as possible and in particular:

   (a) the Interested Party shall make good all damage caused to the Property by the Consultant; and
   (b) neither the Consultant nor the Interested Party shall communicate with any employee of the Owner nor with any person exercising a regulatory function in relation to the Property without the Owner's prior written consent.

4. The Interested Party shall indemnify and hold harmless the Owner against all costs, claims, damages, expenses and loss arising from or in the course of the activities of the Consultant.

5. The Interested Party shall provide the Owner with a copy of the Consultant's report in draft form and shall give the Owner the

opportunity (within a period of [ONE WEEK] from being provided with the draft report) to make comments or representations upon it. The Interested Party shall provide the Owner with a signed copy of the final report.

6. The Interested Party shall exercise strict control over all copies of the Consultant's draft and final reports and shall ensure that such reports and all related information held by the Consultant and the Interested Party are used solely for the purpose of deciding whether and upon what terms to proceed with the proposed transaction. In particular:

   (a) no more than [NUMBER] copies of any draft or final report shall be produced, each of which shall be numbered consecutively on its face and no further copies shall be made without the prior written consent of the Owner;
   (b) the Interested Party shall not without the prior written consent of the Owner make available to any third party any draft or final report or information contained in or used in the preparation of such report, nor indicate to any third party the existence of any such report or information;
   (c) the Interested Party shall in all other respects treat such reports, draft reports and information as confidential.

7. In the event that proposed transaction with the Interested Party does not proceed for any reason (whether at the decision of the Owner or the Interested Party) the Interested Party shall forthwith deliver to the Owner all copies of final and draft reports of the Consultant, all information in tangible form used in the preparation thereof and all samples of soil or water taken from the Property. The Interested Party shall also ensure that all computer disks containing such reports and information are erased and shall provide the Owner with written confirmation to that effect.

NOTES:
1. The main purpose of this agreement is to protect the position of the Vendor of Property where a prospective purchaser or other interested party is allowed to conduct physical investigations.
2. It assumes that the Consultants who will carry out the investigations have been appointed by the interested party. However, in some cases there may be advantages in the parties making a joint appointment.

A.06 **PRECEDENT** 5: LETTER TO ENVIRONMENTAL
CONSULTANT REQUESTING PROPOSAL

Dear [CONSULTANT]

Re: Pre-acquisition Contaminated Land Survey
[IDENTIFY PROPERTY]

[NAME OR PURCHASER/TENANT] is currently in negotiation to acquire the [freehold/leasehold] of the property located at [IDENTIFY PROPERTY].

We believe that the current use of the property as [CURRENT USE] has existed since [DATE] when the site was redeveloped by [NAME]; or

The property is currently being developed for [INTENDED USE] by [DEVELOPER] and the development is scheduled to be completed by [DATE].

[PURCHASER/TENANT] wishes to appoint an experienced environmental consultant to undertake an independent investigation into the site's history and condition and provide [PURCHASER/TENANT] with an assessment of the potential environmental liabilities associated with acquisition or funding of the property. In this context [PURCHASER/TENANT] considers environmental liabilities to include the potential for any costs, fines or penalties imposed for breaches of environmental legislation, any third party claims for damage caused as a result of the condition of the property either from individuals or regulatory agencies, any costs which could be recovered by any regulatory body with powers to undertake remedial or mitigation works at the property, and any significant capital expenditure which would need to be incurred to upgrade or change plant, equipment or practice on the site in order to prevent or remedy these types of potential environmental liabilities.

[PURCHASER/TENANT] would like to invite you to submit a Proposal for this work which addresses the matters set out below. Following [PURCHASER'S/TENANT'S] acceptance of the Proposal a formal letter of appointment will be issued.

[PURCHASER'S/TENANT'S] solicitors will be making preliminary enquiries before contract requesting copies of all relevant environmental documentation from the Vendor. However, at this point [PURCHASER/TENANT] have identified the following documents which may be relevant to the preparation of the Proposal:
[LIST DOCUMENTS]
Copies of these documents are enclosed herewith. For the avoidance of any doubt, these documents are being provided to you on a strictly

confidential basis on the understanding that they will be returned to [PURCHASER/TENANT] forthwith if [PURCHASER/TENENT] does not accept your Proposal.

The Proposal should address the following issues:

1. Scope of work

Identification and review of existing information on the history of the site and its surrounding area including geological, hydrogeological, hydrological, geotechnical, use history data, development documentation and information provided from meetings or discussions with the [engineers/architects/other] for the development. A site visit and walk-over survey by suitably qualified personnel should also be undertaken.

The consultant's report should provide [PURCHASER/TENANT] with an opinion on the following issues:

(a) the likely existence and extent of any contamination of soil or waters at the property or in the surrounding area;

(b) whether in the consultant's professional opinion there are any environmental risks associated with any such contamination or other releases to the environment from the site itself or from adjacent land which could result in [PURCHASER'S/TENANT'S] non-compliance with environmental law or exposure to any significant environmental liability;

(c) whether any site practices in relation to waste management or storage or use of hazardous substances might give rise to future contamination of the site and/or the surrounding area;

(d) wherever possible provide written confirmation of the approach or views of any regulatory authorities (including the National Rivers Authority, local authority health and planning departments, waste regulatory authority, HMIP) about the property and the surrounding area; and

(e) that it is either not necessary or appropriate to undertake a further phase of site investigations or, if this is not the case, indicate the nature and cost of any recommended sampling, testing or other investigations necessary or appropriate to enable the consultant to provide the opinions set out above.

The foregoing is provided as guidance as to [PURCHASER'S/TENANT'S] minimum requirements for a pre-acquisition contaminated land survey. However, [PURCHASER/TENANT] will be relying on the consultant's experience and judgment about the necessary or appropriate investigations or techniques for this site and the Proposal should address the issue in full. For the avoidance of any doubt, although the activities mentioned above do not include sampling and analysis or monitoring, if on the basis of the information already provided you feel

545

that it is necessary and/or appropriate for any such provision to be included in the Proposal at this stage there should be no hesitation in doing so.

[PURCHASER/TENANT] accepts that in undertaking the work you will need to rely from time to time upon work undertaken by others. Whilst it will be acceptable to [PURCHASER/TENANT] for information to be accepted as accurate without further verification, the consultant will be expected to exercise professional judgment in the interpretation of an an assessment of the reliance which can be placed upon such information. The consultant will be required to identify to [PURCHASER/TENANT] as soon as possible any deficiencies or difficulties with such information in order for the situation to be addressed within the overall timescale for the acquisition.

2. Timing and Capacity

[PURCHASER/TENANT] will require at least [seven] clear working days prior to the exchange of contracts to review the final draft of the report. The final draft report (including plans, photos, attachments, etc.) must therefore be in [PURCHASER'S/TENANT'S] and its solicitors' hands by the close of business on [DATE]. We should be grateful if the Proposal could confirm that you will be able to comply with this timetable.

The Proposal should also indicate the individuals who it is proposed will carry out the work and an indication of their experience in this area.

The Proposal should also indicate which laboratories you would consider acceptable for conducting any analysis of samples should that prove necessary.

3. Production and Form of Report

[PURCHASER/TENANT] would be grateful if you could include in the Proposal an indication of a suggested format for the report.

The consultant will be required to provide a very brief written interim report on [DATE]. However, if during the course of carrying out the work the consultant reaches a definitive view on whether a further phase of investigations will be required or if the accuracy of existing data cannot be safely assumed this should be communicated to [PURCHASER/TENANT] at the earliest opportunity.

Copies of all relevant correspondence and draft reports should be sent to [NAME] at [PURCHASER'S/TENANT'S ADDRESS] and its solicitors [NAME AND ADDRESS OF SOLICITORS] the attention of [NAME]. In the case of the final draft report [PURCHASER/TENANT] may request that it be forwarded directly to [three] other parties.

4. Costs

Please indicate the total cost of carrying out the works indicating the level of your fees, expected level of expenses, costs of any equipment hire, laboratory analysis charges and any other anticipated disbursements.

5. Terms and Conditions

[The work would be undertaken subject to the standard [modifications to your] terms and conditions agreed between [PURCHASER] and yourselves in the letter dated [DATE] a copy of which is attached.]
or
[IN THE CASE WHERE A CONSULTANT WITH WHOM THERE ARE NO EXISTING ARRANGEMENTS IS BEING CONTACTED]
[We would be grateful if you could forward to us a copy of your standard terms and conditions as soon as possible. You should be aware that the following terms and conditions will be unacceptable to [PURCHASER/TENANT]:

- Professional indemnity coverage of less than [£1,000,000] for each occurrence to be maintained for a period of less than [six] years;
- Total exclusion of liabilities on the part of the consultant including liability for breach of contract or limitations of the amount of liability to the amount of the consultant's fees;
- Provisions requiring [PURCHASER/TENANT] to indemnify the consultant for losses associated with the work;
- Any further fee for extending reliance on the report to the first purchaser, first tenant or any financial institution with an interest in the Property. In this regard [PURCHASER/TENANT] will require execution of a collateral warranty under seal in favour of each of the foregoing in the form of the relevant draft annexed hereto.
- Exclusion of any warranty that in performing the services the consultant has exercised such reasonable skill, care and diligence as may be expected of a properly qualified and competent environmental consultant experienced in carrying out work of a similar nature.]

Please do not hestitate to contact [NAME] should you require any further information or wish to discuss the details of this letter.

As timing is quite critical we look forward to receiving a Proposal from you by [DATE]. If you are unable to submit a Proposal for any reason we would be grateful if you would let us know as soon as possible to enable us to make other arrangements.

Yours faithfully

[PURCHASER/TENANT]

NOTE:
See para. 10.04. This precedent is intended as an example of a letter inviting a consultant to submit a detailed proposal for a site investigation; it indicates the essential nature of the client's requirements. It can be used either with consultants where agreement has already been reached on contractual terms of engagement or with consultants where there are no existing arrangements. It may be necessary to agree in advance the terms on which collateral warranties will be given by the consultant, and a precedent warranty should be annexed for this purpose (see Precedent 7). The requirements as to terms and conditions of appointment may be controversial, and (depending on the nature of the work) the details given here may not be acceptable to all consultants. Professional indemnity insurance is a particularly difficult area (see generally Chap. 10 and Appendix F).

PRECEDENT 6: AGREEMENT APPOINTING ENVIRONMENTAL **A.07**
CONSULTANT

THIS AGREEMENT made the [   ] day of [   ] 199[   ]
BETWEEN
(1) [CLIENT] ("the Client"); and
(2) [CONSULTANT] ("the Consultant")

WITNESSES as follows

Appointment

1. The Client engages the Consultant to provide in relation to the property briefly described in the First Schedule ("the Site") the professional services briefly described in the Second Schedule ("the Normal Services") and the Consultant agrees to provide the Normal Services and the Additional Services mentioned below (together "the Services") subject to and in accordance with the terms of this Agreement.

Care and diligence

2.1 The Consultant has had an opportunity of inspecting the physical conditions (including the sub-surface conditions) and other conditions of or affecting the Site and shall be deemed to have fully acquainted himself with the same and to have obtained all necessary information as to risks, contingencies and all other circumstances which may influence or affect the execution of the Services and no failure on the part of the Consultant to discover or foresee any such condition, risk, contingency or circumstance (whether the same ought reasonably to have been discovered or foreseen or not) shall entitle the Consultant to an addition to the fee stated in the Third Schedule or the addition of fees for Additional Services or to an extension of time and the Consultant should not and shall not be entitled to rely upon any survey report or other document prepared by or on behalf of the Client regarding any such matter as referred to in this clause and the Client makes no representation or warranty as to the accuracy or completeness of any such survey report or document and the Client shall have no liability arising out of or in relation to any such survey, report or document or from any representation or statement whether negligently or otherwise made therein contained.

2.2 The Consultant shall exercise all the skill, care and diligence in the discharge of the Services to be expected of an appropriately

549

qualified and competent environmental consultant experienced in carrying out services of the relevant nature.

Assignment or transfer

3. The Consultant shall not without the prior written consent of the Client (which consent shall be at the absolute discretion of the Client) delegate any of its obligations in relation to the Services or any part thereof and the Consultant shall be responsible for the acts of any party to whom the Consultant's obligations (or any of them) are delegated whether or not the requisite consent of the Client has been obtained and in particular without limitation the Consultant shall be responsible for the work of any laboratory or other sub-contractor used by the Consultant and approved by the Client and the Client may assign or transfer all or any of the benefit of this Agreement and/or any part share or interest therein.

Normal Services

4. As part of the Normal Services the Consultant shall give to the Client such advice and assistance within the field of its qualifications and competence as may be reasonably required in connection with the Services from time to time by the Client.

Additional Services

5. The Consultant shall if requested by the Client provide in relation to the Site any additional services ("the Additional Services") of reasonably the same nature as the Normal Services.

Fees

6. The sum payable by the Client to the Consultant for the Normal Services shall be the fee stated in the Third Schedule and the Client shall pay the Consultant reasonable additional fees for Additional Services and all fees shall be payable after submission for the Consultant to the Client of the Consultant's final report and satisfactory completion of all the Services.

Expenses and disbursements

7. Unless otherwise expressly agreed in respect of particular expenses and disbursements the fees shall be in full satisfaction of the Client's liability to the Consultant in respect of expenses and disbursements incurred in the provision of the Services.

Period for payment and interest

8. All sums properly due from the Client to the Consultant in accordance with this Agreement shall be paid within thirty working days of the submission by the Consultant of its accounts to the Client and any sums remaining unpaid at the expiry of such period of thirty working days shall bear interest after that time such interest to accrue from that time at the rate of [three] per centum per annum above the sterling base lending rate of [NAME OF BANK] from time to time in force.

Value Added Tax

9. All sums due from the Client to the Consultant in accordance with this Agreement are exclusive of Value Added Tax, the amount of which at the rate and in the manner prescribed by law shall be paid by the Client to the Consultant.

Final report and Consultant's documents

10. The Consultant shall submit its final report to the Client in five copies and each copy of the final report shall include such information, date, drawings, reports, specification, calculations and other similar material as is necessary to enable a reader fully to comprehend the report without reference to any other documents and promptly after completion of the Services the Consultant shall deliver to the Client free of charge one copy of all completed drawings, reports, specifications, calculations and other similar documents relevant to the Services in its possession.

Copyright

11. The copyright in all drawings, reports, specifications, calculations and other similar documents provided by the Consultant in connection with this Agreement shall to the extent they are vested in the Consultant remain vested in the Consultant but the Client and its appointee shall have a royalty-free non-exclusive licence to copy and use such drawings and other documents and to reproduce any designs contained in them for any purpose related to the Site including but without limitation the construction, completion, maintenance, letting, promotion, advertisement, reinstatement, repair and/or extension of the Site and/or of any works or structures for the time being on the Site and the Consultant shall, if the Client so requests and undertakes in writing to pay the Consultant's reasonable copying charges, promptly supply the Client with further conveniently reproducible copies of all such drawings and other documents.

Confidentiality

12. The Consultant shall keep this Agreement and its terms strictly confidential and shall not without the written consent of the Client disclose the existence of this Agreement or any of its terms to anyone and any information concerning this Agreement and/or the Site obtained either by the Consultant or by any person employed by the Consultant in connection with this Agreement is confidential and shall not be used or disclosed by the Consultant or by any such persons except for the purposes of this Agreement.

Professional indemnity insurance

13.1 The Consultant shall maintain professional indemnity insurance covering (inter alia) all liability hereunder in respect of neglects, errors and omissions upon customary and usual terms and conditions prevailing for the time being in the London insurance market and with reputable insurers lawfully carrying on such insurance business in the United Kingdom in an amount of not less than [AMOUNT] pounds for any one occurrence or series of occurrences arising out of any one event for a period beginning now and ending 12 (twelve) years after the completion of the Services provided always that such insurance is available at commercially reasonable rates and the said terms and conditions shall not include any term or condition to the effect that the Consultant must discharge any liability before being entitled to recover from the insurers or any other term or condition which might adversely affect the rights of any person to recover from the insurers pursuant to the Third Parties (Rights Against Insurers) Act, 1930 or any amendment or re-enactment thereof and the Consultant shall not without the prior approval in writing of the Client settle or compromise with the insurers any claim which the Consultant may have against the insurers and which relates to a claim by the Client against the Consultant or by any act or omission lose or prejudice the Consultant's right to make or proceed with such a claim against the insurers.

13.2 Any increased or additional premium required by insurers by reason of the Consultant's own claims record or other acts omissions matters or things particular to the Consultant shall be deemed to be within commercially reasonable rates.

13.3 If such insurance ceases to be available at commercially reasonable rates the Consultant shall promptly notify the Client.

13.4 The Consultant shall fully co-operate with any measures reasonably required by the Client including (without limitation) completing any proposals for insurance and associated documents maintaining such insurance at rates above commercially reasonable rates if the Client undertakes in writing to reimburse the Consultant in respect of the net cost of such insurance to the Consultant above commercially reasonable rates or if the Client effects such insurance at rates at or above commercially reasonable rates reimbursing the Client in respect of what the net cost of such insurance to the Client would have been at commercially reasonable rates.

13.5 As and when reasonably requested to do so by the Client the Consultant shall produce for inspection documentary evidence (including if required by the Client the originals of the relevant insurance documents and/or a letter from the insurer confirming that the policy is in existence and that any policy contains no unusual limitations) that the required professional indemnity insurance is being maintained.

13.6 The above obligations in respect of professional indemnity insurance shall continue notwithstanding termination of this Agreement for any reason whatsoever including (without limitation) breach by the Client.

Collateral warranties

14.1 The Consultant shall within 7 (seven) working days of the Client's request so to do execute in favour of any persons who have entered or shall enter into an agreement for the provision of finance in connection with the Site or any part thereof and/or in favour of any persons who have acquired or shall acquire any interest in or over the Site or any part thereof a Deed in the form annexed as Annex 'A' or a similar form reasonably required by the Client and deliver the same to the Client.

14.2 The above obligation for the provision of a Deed shall continue notwithstanding termination of this Agreement for any reason whatsoever including (without limitation) breach by the Client and any such Deed given after such termination shall be amended by the Client so as to refer to the fact and date of such termination and to omit any obligation to continue to exercise skill care and diligence after such termination.

Proper law and jurisdiction

15. The construction validity and performance of this Agreement shall be governed by English law and the parties agree to submit to the non-exclusive jurisdiction of the English courts.

IN WITNESS whereof the parties have executed this deed in duplicate on the date first stated above

FIRST SCHEDULE
The Site

SECOND SCHEDULE
Normal Services

[As described in:

- the Client's request for the Consultant's Proposal dated [   ] 199[   ]; and
- the Consultant's Proposal dated [   ] 199[   ];

copies of which are annexed.]

THIRD SCHEDULE
Fees for Normal Services

NOTE:

This Precedent gives a form of agreement appointing an environmental consultant to carry out agreed works of investigation. Such agreements may be under hand or made by an appointment under seal, as is provided here.

The agreement refers to agreed "Normal Services" but provides the flexibility to incorporate such further work (the "Additional Services") as may become necessary or advisable during the course of the investigation.

An agreement appointing the Consultant may contain provisions for the execution of collateral warranties whereby the Consultant will warrant the results of his environmental investigation to any lender of the property and/or any person acquiring an interest in the site.

PRECEDENT 7: COLLATERAL WARRANTY BY ENVIRONMENTAL CONSULTANT   A.08

THIS AGREEMENT is made the [   ] day of [   ]
BETWEEN
(1) [CONSULTANT] ("the Consultant")
(2) [PURCHASER] ("the Purchaser")
   WHEREAS

   A. The Consultant carries on business as [Environmental Consultants] [Structural and Civil Engineers] and has been appointed as such by [DEVELOPER] ("the Developer") by an agreement ("the Appointment") for the purpose of investigating the history and condition of site of the Development (as hereinafter defined), assessing the nature and extent of contamination and advising on remedial and precautionary measures in relation to such contamination.

   B. The Developer [has constructed] [has entered into a building contract with [CONTRACTOR] ("the Contractor") under which (inter alia) the Contractor is to design and build] [DESCRIPTION OF THE DEVELOPMENT] ("the Development")

   C. The Purchaser has entered into an agreement with the Developer whereby the Purchaser agrees to purchase the Development from the Developer.

NOW IT IS HEREBY AGREED as follows:

1.1 The Consultant warrants to the Purchaser that it has exercised [and will continue to exercise] reasonable skill care and diligence in the performance of its services to the Developer under the Appointment PROVIDED THAT [the Consultant's liability to the Purchaser under this Agreement for economic and consequential losses suffered by the Purchaser in relation to the Development shall be limited to the reasonable costs of remedying any damage to or defects in the Development which are directly caused by the Consultant's failure to exercise the aforesaid skill care and diligence together with any consequential loss and costs directly attributable to such defects or remedy of such defects and further that] the Consultant shall be entitled in any action or proceedings by the Purchaser under this Agreement to rely on any limitation in the Appointment and to raise the equivalent rights and defence of liability as it would have under the Appointment.

[1.2 The Consultant's liability for costs under this Agreement shall be limited to that proportion of such costs which it would be just and

555

equitable to require the Consultant to pay having regard to the extent of the Consultant's responsibility for the same and on the basis that [NAME OF OTHER CONSULTANTS] shall be deemed to have provided a contractual undertaking to the Purchaser in respect of the performance of their services in connection with the Development and shall be deemed to have paid to the Purchaser such proportion which it would be just and equitable for them to pay having regard to the extent of their responsibility.]

2. The Consultant acknowledges and covenants with the Purchaser that it has exercised all reasonable skill and care in the exercise of its duties and responsibilities in investigating the site for the suitability of the Development and in the preparation of the report entitled [TITLE, DATE AND NUMBER OF REPORT] pursuant to the Consultant's appointment by the Developer and that the Purchaser has relied upon and may continue to rely upon the said report provided that the Consultant shall have no greater duty of care to the Purchaser by virtue of this clause than it would have had if the Purchaser had been named as the Client under such appointment [and provided further that the Consultant's liability to the Purchaser under this clause for economic and consequential losses suffered by the Purchaser in relation to the Development shall be limited to the reasonable costs of remedying any damage to and/or defects in the Development and/or the rebuilding and/or reconstruction of the Development together with any consequential loss and costs directly attributable to any of the aforesaid matters].

3.1 The Consultant shall maintain professional indemnity insurance in the amount of not less than [AMOUNT] for any one occurrence of series of occurrences arising out of any one event for a period of 12 years from the date of [this Agreement] [practical completion of the Development under the said building contract] provided always that such insurance is available at commercially reasonable rates.

3.2 The Consultant shall immediately inform the Purchaser if such insurance ceases to be available at commercially reasonable rates in order that the Consultant and the Purchaser can discuss means of best protecting the respective positions of the Purchaser and the Consultant in the absence of such insurance.

3.3 As and when it is reasonably requested to do so by the Purchaser the Consultant shall produce for inspection documentary evidence that such professional indemnity insurance is being maintained.

3.4 This agreement may be assigned [once by the Purchaser by way of absolute legal assignment to another person taking an assignment of the Purchaser's interest in the Development] without the consent of the Consultant being required [and thereafter may be assigned on one further occasion with the prior written consent of the Consultant (such consent not to be unreasonably withheld or delayed)] and written notice of such assignment shall be given to the Consultant.

4. No action or proceedings for any breach of this Agreement shall be commenced against the Consultant after the expiry of 12 years from the date [of this Agreement] [practical completion of the Development under the said building contract.]

IN WITNESS whereof the Consultant has executed this Agreement as a Deed the day and year first above written.

THE COMMON SEAL of
[CONSULTANTS]
was hereunto affixed
in the presence of:
     Director

     Secretary

NOTE:
See para. 10.10. This is an example of a collateral warranty given by a consultant under seal in favour of a purchaser. It contains various optional limitations and alternatives for use where the Development is being sold in the course of construction. It also contains various provisions which the consultant's advisers might seek to have inserted for the protection of the consultant.

A.09 PRECEDENT 8: COVENANTS ON SALE OF PART OF LAND

The Purchaser hereby covenants for itself and its successors in title with the intention to bind the Property and each and every part thereof for the benefit of the Vendor's Retained Land and each and every part thereof as follows:

1. Not to use the Property or any part of it for any purpose which may be or become a nuisance (whether or not amounting to a legal nuisance) or an annoyance or obnoxious to the Vendor or its successors in title (including tenants and occupiers) to the Retained Land or any part of it or which tends to diminish or lessen the value of the Retained Land or any building erected on any part of it.

2. Not to deposit on the Property any controlled waste as defined in the Environmental Protection Act 1990 or special waste as defined in the Control of Pollution (Special Waste) Regulations 1980 or radioactive waste as defined in the Radioactive Substances Act 1993 (or any re-enactment thereof) or any other substance (whether from premises used for agriculture within the meaning of the Agriculture Act 1947 or from other sources) which may produce concentrations or accumulations of noxious gases or noxious liquids which may cause pollution of the environment or harm to human health.

3. To take all practicable precautions to ensure that no noxious substances are spilled or deposited on the Property or the Retained Land and that contamination of the Property or the Retained Land does not occur.

4. To indemnify and keep indemnified the Vendor against all damage caused directly or indirectly by the activities of the Purchaser or by the use of the Property to the Vendor's Retained Land or the Vendor's use of the Retained Land and against all actions claims and demands made against the Vendor in respect of damage to or pollution of the environment or damage to property or harm to human health caused directly or indirectly by the use of the Property or by any substance thereon whether in liquid or solid form or in the form of gas or vapour.

5. To indemnify the Vendor and its successors in title for the benefit of the Vendor's Retained Land and each and every part thereof against all losses costs expenses claims actions liabilities damages demands proceedings and orders (whether of a statu-

tory or civil nature) which may at any time hereafter arise (whether or not they arise out of an act omission or negligence preceding the date of this Deed) in relation to any matter concerning the state and condition of the Property and adjoining property or any surrounding air space or the substratum of the Property or any adjoining property or any claim direction order or fine imposed under any legislation for the protection of human health or the environment (including without limitation the Control of Pollution Act 1974, the Environmental Protection Act 1990, the Water Resources Act 1991, the Water Industry Act 1991 and the Radioactive Substances Act 1993) or any statute modifying amending adding to or replacing the same.

6. Not to discharge or allow to be discharged into any pipe or drain serving the Property and the Vendor's Retained Land in common any oil grease deleterious or other harmful matter or substance which might be or become a source of danger or injury to any person or damage the said pipes or drains or any part thereof.

NOTE:
These covenants may be imposed where the Vendor retains adjoining land in order to provide protection against contamination arising from the Purchaser's future activities. They may be supplemented by specific restrictions on certain potentially contaminative activities or the use or storage of certain contaminative substances, if so desired. The Purchaser may, of course, seek reciprocal covenants from the Vendor.

A.10 **PRECEDENT 9**: LANDLORD'S ENVIRONMENTAL QUESTIONNAIRE

1. Please provide a full description of the nature of your proposed business.

2. Does the business involve any form of industrial process? If so please provide details of how the process operates and the nature of the raw materials, products, by-products and waste produced.

3. How will wastes, gases and liquid effluents arising from your proposed business be disposed of? Please provide full details.

4. Does your business involve the use, handling, storage or keeping of any of the following?

   - asbestos;
   - PCBs or PCTs;
   - chlorinated solvents;
   - oil, petroleum or other hydrocarbons;
   - scrap metal;
   - waste materials;
   - any substance classified as hazardous or dangerous by law, including the Control of Pollution (Special Waste) Regulations 1980, the Classification, Packaging and Labelling of Dangerous Substances Regulations 1984, the Control of Substances Hazardous to Health Regulations 1988 or the Planning (Hazardous Substances) Act 1990.

   Please provide full details of the circumstances in which such materials or substances will be used, handled, stored or kept including the quantities likely to be kept, the proposed location on site, the means of containment and the proposed precautions to prevent their release or escape.

5. Please provide copies of:

   - your corporate environmental policy;
   - any documentation relating to your internal environmental management systems;
   - your proposed safe operating procedures and emergency or contingency plans;
   - your current insurance policy in respect of third party liability and (if any) environmental impairment liability.

6. Do any of your proposed activities require any licence, authorisation or other consent? If so, please provide full details and provide confirmation as to what steps you have taken or intend to take in order to obtain such consent.

7. Have you, or any parent, subsidiary or associated company of yours, or any director of such company, been convicted of any offence relating to protection of the environment, whether in the UK or elsewhere? If so, please provide details.

8. Have you, or any parent, subsidiary or associated company of yours, been the subject of any notice, action or claim relating to pollution or contamination, whether in the UK or elsewhere? If so, please provide details.

9. Do you, or an parent, subsidiary or associated company of yours, operate any similar process to that which you propose elsewhere in the UK or abroad? If so please provide details, including the name(s) and address(es) of the landlord(s) where such operations are conducted from leasehold property.

NOTE:
This questionnaire may be used by a landlord to obtain relevant information relating to a prospective tenant.

A.11 PRECEDENT 10: LEASEHOLD COVENANTS

1. Reservations

The following rights are reserved:

(a) the right to commission at the Tenant's expense an environmental investigation ("the Second Investigation") similar in nature to the investigation carried out for the purposes of the preparation of the report annexed to this Lease ("the Report") and to be carried out on the Property in the last six months of the term;

(b) the right to enter onto the Property with environmental consultants appointed by the Landlord with or without vehicles and appropriate equipment and machinery on giving reasonable notice for the purpose of carrying out tests and examinations necessary for the preparation of the Second Investigation (the Landlord making good any damage caused thereby) and specifying the remediation works (if any) required to restore the Property to the state and condition specified in the Report.

2. Tenant's Covenants

The Tenant covenants as follows:

(a) to maintain the Property in no worse state and condition than that specified in the Report and to take all practicable precautions to ensure that no noxious substances are spilled or deposited on the Property and that contamination of the Property does not occur.

(b) within one month after service upon the Tenant of notice of remediation to carry out the remediation works (if any) specified in the Second Investigation and if the Tenant shall not within one month after service of such notice or (in case of emergency) immediately after service of such notice commence and thereafter proceed diligently with the execution of such remediation works then to permit the Landlord and all persons authorised by it to enter upon the property and to execute the necessary remediation works the cost of which shall be paid by the Tenant on demand and if not so paid the cost shall be a debt due from the Tenant to the Landlord and be forthwith recoverable by action notwithstanding the expiration or sooner determination of this Lease.

(c) not to deposit on the Property any controlled waste as defined in the Environmental Protection Act 1990 or special waste as defined in the Control of Pollution (Special Waste) Regulations 1980 or Radioactive Waste as defined in section 18 of the

Radioactive Substances Act 1993 or any re-enactment thereof or any other substance (whether from premises used for agriculture within the meaning of the Agricultural Act 1947 or from other sources) which may produce concentrations or accumulations of noxious gases or noxious liquids which may cause pollution of the environment or harm to human health.

(d) within 14 days of the occurrence of a Notifiable Event to inform the Landlord of its occurrence and to permit the Landlord to enter and inspect the Property. "Notifiable Event" means the spilling or deposit on the Property of any noxious substance in a quantity which would cause serious damage to or pollution of the environment or serious damage to property or serious harm to human health.

(e) not to discharge or cause to be discharged into any pipe or drain serving the Property any oil, grease, deleterious or other harmful matter or substance which might cause damage to the environment or be or become a source of danger or injury to those pipes or drains or any part thereof.

(f) to indemnify and keep the Landlord indemnified against all actions, claims, costs, damages, judgments, penalties, expenses, losses, and demands in respect of damage to or pollution of the environment or damage to property or harm to human health caused by the Property or any substance thereon whether in liquid or solid form or in the form of gas or vapour.

NOTES:
1. So far as the landlord is concerned, the terms of the following usual clauses should be considered carefully so as to protect the reversionary interest:
    (1) ensure that the terms of the user covenant are suitable and sufficiently restrictive and include, if appropriate, a restriction on the use and types of equipment on the site;
    (2) ensure that there is a sufficient covenant to comply with the provisions of every enactment, instrument, regulation and by-law and notice, order or direction, etc., and that the right to production of copy notices, etc. includes a right, without limitation, to production of IPC, NRA, water company,and waste disposal authority licences (although these will be in the public domain);
    (3) rights of entry and inspection.
2. In particular, where actual contamination is likely it may be useful to have a soil survey carried out before execution of the lease. The survey report would be attached to the lease like a schedule of repair. The precedent assumes that such an investigation has been carried out. A second investigation can be carried out at the expiration of the lease to assess whether the tenant has caused contamination. The landlord then requires restoration/clean-up on the expiration of the term and the tenant is bound to bring the site up to the standard it was at the beginning of the term. Such provisions will not be suitable for all leases, but may be particularly useful in the case of leases of industrial premises, oil depots and the like.

3. Sub-clause (g) attempts to reverse the effect of section 81B of the Environmental Protection Act 1990 which gives the tenant the power to deduct from rent expenses recoverable from him to relation to statutory insurance. Whether such a provision is contrary to public policy is arguable: see *Johnson* v. *Moreton* [1980] A.C. 37.

> (g) where expenses for clean-up costs on the Property become a charge on the Property under section 81A of the Environmental Protection 1990 ("the 1990 Act") and such expenses are recovered by the local authority from the tenant under section 81B of the 1990 Act, to waive its statutory right to deduct such expenses from the rent due to the landlord and to pay to the local authority all outstanding clean-up costs as demanded by the local authority in full settlement of such demands irrespective of the amount of rent due to the landlord at any given time.

PRECEDENT 11: LANDLORD'S PROTECTION CLAUSE— A.12
PRE-EXISTING CONTAMINATION

1. The Tenant agrees that except as expressly provided in this Lease no representations by or on behalf of the Landlord have been made to the Tenant as to the condition of the Demised Premises, or the applicability or otherwise to the Demised Premises of any requirements under environmental law, or the suitability of the Demised Premises for any purpose whatsoever.

2. The Tenant represents to the Landlord that the Tenant has made its own independent investigation of the Demised Premises and is relying solely on such investigations.

3. The Tenant acknowledges that the Landlord has no experience concerning environmental matters or the requirements of environmental law and that the Tenant is not relying on any representation or assurance by the Landlord with regard to such matters as they affect the Demised Premises.

4. The Tenant unconditionally releases the Landlord from and against any and all liability, whensoever arising, in respect of any liabilities, damage, costs or claims suffered or incurred by the Tenant as a result of the condition of the Demised Premises including, without limitation, the presence of contaminating substances in, on over or under the Demised Premises or any part thereof whether before or during the term hereby granted or any lawful extension thereof and the Tenant covenants to indemnify and hold harmless the Landlord against all liabilities, damages, costs or claims suffered or incurred by the Landlord as a result of such condition of the Demised Premises.

5. It is agreed that the Tenant shall not be excused or released from performance of any of the Tenant's covenants contained in this lease where the performance of such covenants involves work or expenditure to make good, rectify, remove, treat or render harmless contaminating substances present in, on, over or under the Demised Premises (whether before or during the term hereby granted or any lawful extension thereof) or to make good any damage caused by such substances whether on the Demised Premises or elsewhere.

NOTE:
The object of this provision is to throw the risk of liability arising from the pre-existing soil contamination wholly onto the tenant. Whether it is reasonable to do this will depend on the circumstances, including the length of the term.

A.13 PRECEDENT 12: TENANT'S PROTECTION CLAUSE—
PRE-EXISTING CONTAMINATION

1. Notwithstanding the Tenant's covenants in this Lease, the Tenant shall have no liability, in respect of the terms of this Lease or otherwise, as a result of the presence in, on, over or under the Demised Premises or any adjoining or neighbouring property at the date of this Lease of contaminative substances ("Contamination") or as a result of such previous uses of the Demised Premises or any adjoining or neighbouring property as have resulted in the release of contaminative substances ("Contaminative Uses").

2. It is agreed that, without prejudice to the generality of clause 1, the Tenant shall not be required by any of the Tenant's covenants contained in this lease to make good or rectify (or pay to make good or rectify) any defect or want of repair resulting from Contamination or Contaminative Uses (whether at the Demised Premises or elsewhere), nor shall the Tenant be required to rectify, remove, treat or render harmless Contamination or rectify any damage or other adverse consequences of any Contaminative Use.

3. The Landlord shall indemnify and hold harmless the Tenant against all liabilities, damage, costs or claims whensoever arising resulting from Contamination or Contaminative Uses.

NOTE:
This provision affords the Tenant protection against being held liable (under the terms of the Lease or otherwise) to clean-up or make good pre-existing contamination. The Tenant should be aware that liability in respect of contamination can arise in various ways, for example direct covenant, covenant to comply with stature, covenants as to repair, decoration, service charges etc. Provisions throwing the risk of such matters on to the Landlord may have a significantly adverse effect on the value of the reversion and may therefore be strongly resisted.

PRECEDENT 13: PROVISION IN LEASE GIVING TENANT   **A.14**
THE RIGHT TO TERMINATE THE LEASE IN THE EVENT OF
CONTAMINATION PROBLEMS AND EXCLUDING TENANT'S
LIABILITY TO CONTRIBUTE TO COSTS IN SUCH AN EVENT

1. Exclusion of liability to repair

1.1 In this Clause and the following Clause only the following words shall have the following meanings:

"Emissions" shall mean emissions of methane or other gases from the soil of the Estate.

"Ground Faults" shall mean landslip, subsidence, settlement or heave.

"Excluded Occupation" shall mean the Demised Premises are in such a state or condition due to Emissions or Ground Faults that the Tenant cannot make beneficial use or maintain beneficial occupation of the Demised Premises and that such condition is likely to continue for a period in excess of 12 months without remedial works being carried out which are in excess of the Tenant's repairing obligations hereunder as may be varied by this Clause.

"Occupation Notice" shall means a notice in writing given by the Tenant to the Landlord that there exists a state of Excluded Occupation.

"the Landlord's Works Option Period" shall mean the period of three months commencing with the date of receipt of the decision of the person appointed in accordance with Clause 1.2 or the date of an agreement between the parties in lieu of reference to the Arbitration Procedure relating to Excluded Occupation.

1.2 Notwithstanding anything elsewhere in this Lease contained it is hereby agreed and declared between the parties that:

   1.2.1 during the period of the first twelve years of the Term the Tenant shall not save to the extent hereinafter in this Clause provided be under any liability to the Landlord or to any other person to carry out or contribute towards the cost of carrying out any works to the Demised Premises or the means of access thereto or to the Estate or to anything therein or serving the same which is attributable to Emissions; and

   1.2.3 during the Term the Tenant shall not be under any liability or obligation to carry out or contribute towards the cost of carrying out any works of repair to the Demised Premises or the Estate made necessary or caused by Ground Faults.

PROVIDED THAT:

1.3 Nothing herein contained shall exclude or excuse or prevent the Tenant from complying with its obligations herein contained as to the normal maintenance and repair of the Demised Premises and the equipment installed therein for the protection of the Demised Premises from Emissions; and

1.4 Such exclusion hereinbefore contained from the Tenant's liability to repair or contribute to repairs shall not affect the Tenant's obligations to carry out repairs to existing systems, structures or works within the Demised Premises which are designed to protect the Demised Premises or the Estate from Emissions and which are in the nature of routine maintenance works.

2. Tenant's Option to Break

2.1 If during the first 12 years of the Term there exists a state of Excluded Occupation and the Tenant shall give the Landlord an Occupation Notice within three months of the coming into existence of the state of Excluded Occupation THEN unless Excluded Occupation is brought about as a result of the Tenant's failure to observe and perform its obligations hereunder the following provisions shall apply:

2.2 Either the Landlord or the Tenant may require a certificate from an independent surveyor to be agreed upon or appointed in accordance with the Arbitration Procedure certifying whether or not Excluded Occupation exists.

2.3 If the surveyor shall certify that Excluded Occupation exists or the Landlord and the Tenant shall agree that the Excluded Occupation exists the Landlord shall within the Landlord's Works Option Period notify the Tenant in writing whether or not it will carry out such works as may be necessary to end Excluded Occupation.

2.4 If the Landlord shall elect to carry out such works the Landlord shall commence and proceed diligently with such works as soon as practicable thereafter and shall use all reasonable endeavours to complete the same within 12 months.

2.5 If the Landlord shall decline to carry out such works as aforesaid the tenant may by notice in writing at any time within three months after the Landlord's notification under clause 2.1 determine this Lease on giving not less than 14 days' written notice to the Landlord and upon the expiry of such notice this Lease shall cease and determine but without prejudice to the rights and remedies of either party against the other in respect of any antecedent claim for breach of covenant.

2.6 During the period of the Excluded Occupation commencing with the service of the Occupation Notice until the Demised Premises are again rendered fit for occupation and use or until (as the case may be) determination of the Lease the rent payable hereunder or a fair proportion thereof according to the extent to which the Tenant shall have been deprived of occupation shall be suspended and cease to be payable.

2.7 If the Tenant shall not have exercised its option to determine the Landlord may at any time thereafter serve notice upon the Tenant requiring the Tenant to determine the Lease within one month of receipt of such notice and if the Tenant shall not have determined the Lease within such period of one month then upon the expiry of the said period of one month the yearly rent shall thereafter continue to be payable notwithstanding the provisions of clause 2.6.

2.8 If the Tenant shall so determine the Lease the Lease shall cease and determine as provided in clause 2.4 hereof.

3. Relationship to repairing obligations

For the avoidance of doubt nothing in the foregoing clauses 1 and 2 shall be construed as increasing the repairing obligations of the Tenant under this Lease beyond those which would have existed had those clauses not been included herein.

NOTE:
Such a provision may be useful where, for example, offices or retail premises are constructed on or near a reclaimed waste site. The tenant is allowed to break if the Premises become unusable due to gas emissions or subsidence during the first 12 years of the term and the landlord does not carry out the works necessary to restore them to good order (with rent suspension in the meantime, during such works). The provision also makes it clear that the tenant is not liable to contribute towards any costs arising in respect of subsidence, landslip, settlement or heave.

A.15 **PRECEDENT** 14: ACQUISITION OF A COMPANY— INFORMATION REQUEST RELATING TO ENVIRONMENTAL MATTERS

In respect of the Company and each of the Subsidiaries please supply the following particulars:

(a) The full postal addresses of all sites owned or occupied by the Company or any of its Subsidiaries, in each case identified by means of a plan and with details as to the nature of the activities, operations or processes carried on at the site.

(b) So far as is known, the full postal addresses of sites owned or occupied by the Company or any of its Subsidiaries within the last 30 years, in each case identified by means of a plan and with details as to the nature of the activities, operations or practices carried on at each site during the ownership or occupation of the Company or its subsidiaries.

(c) Copies of all statutory authorisations held by the Company and any of its Subsidiaries together with details of any such authorisations applied for.

(d) In relation to all such authorisations, copies of any correspondence with the relevant authorities, notices received from the relevant authorities and any information supplied to the relevant authorities in support of the application for such authorisations.

(e) With regard to all wastes produced by the Company and any of its Subsidiaries, whether solid, liquid or gaseous, particulars of the means by which such wastes are disposed of, including: (i) the names and addresses of the waste carriers and disposal contractors and the sites to which such wastes are disposed of; (ii) details (if known) of the carriers, the contractors and the sites to which such wastes have been disposed of in the past; (iii) copies of existing waste disposal contracts.

(f) Copies of any statements of corporate environmental policy and operating procedures and copies of any environmental audit, investigation or report carried out in relation to the activities, operations and processes of the Company and any of its Subsidiaries, or in relation to any former or existing sites owned or occupied by the Company or any of its Subsidiaries.

NOTE:
See para. 12.02.

PRECEDENT 15: ACQUISITION OF A COMPANY—   **A.16**
ENVIRONMENTAL WARRANTIES

1. Authorisations, etc.

(a) Full particulars are given in the Disclosure Letter of all authorisations, permissions, consents, licences and agreements held by the Company as are necessary to enable the Company to carry on its business lawfully and effectively in the places and in the manner in which such business is now carried on as specified in the Disclosure Letter and in particular (but without limitation) as are necessary: (i) to make all relevant abstractions of water; (ii) to keep, store or hold all relevant substances whether as raw materials, products or wastes; (iii) to carry on all relevant processes; (iv) to construct and maintain all relevant buildings, plant and equipment; and (v) to hold, treat, manage, consign and dispose of all waste materials, substances, gases and effluents in the relevant manner. All such authorisations, permissions, consents, licences and agreements have been lawfully obtained and are in full force and effect. No further authorisations, permissions, consents, licences or agreements are necessary.

(b) Save as stated in the Disclosure Letter the Company has complied at all times with all conditions attaching to the authorisations, permissions, consents, licences and agreements referred to above (whether such conditions are imposed expressly or are implied by statute) and the Vendor is not aware of any circumstances which would render it impossible for the Company to comply with such conditions in the future.

(c) The Company has received no notice, correspondence or communication in any other form in respect of any of the authorisations, permissions, consents, licences or agreements referred to above revoking, suspending, modifying or varying the same and is not aware of any circumstances which might give rise to such notice being received or of any intention on the part of any relevant authority to give such notice.

(d) The Vendor will use all reasonable endeavours to ensure that all relevant authorisations, permissions, consents, licences or agreements are (where necessary) transferred to the Purchaser or, as the case may be, renewed. In particular, but without limitation, the Vendor shall assist the Purchaser in making application to or providing information to any relevant authority for the purpose of such transfer or renewal.

571

2. Compliance with Environmental Protection Laws

(a) Save as stated in the Disclosure Letter neither the Company nor any of its officers, agents or employees have committed, whether by act or omission, any breach of statutory requirements for the protection of the environment or of human health or amenity, and have acted at all times in conformity with all relevant codes of practice, guidance, notes, standards and other advisory material issued by any competent authority.

(b) The Company has not received any notice, order or other communication from any relevant authority in respect of the Company's business, failure to comply with which would constitute breach of any statutory requirements or compliance with which could be secured by further proceedings. The Vendor is not aware of any circumstances which might give rise to such notice, order or other communication being received or of any intention on the part of such authority to give such notice.

3. Civil Liability

(a) The Company is not aware of any actual or potential liability on the part of the Company arising from (i) any activities or operations of the Company; or (ii) the state or condition of any properties now or formerly owned or occupied by the Company or facilities now or formerly used by the Company. In particular (but without limitation) such liability includes liability for: (i) injury to persons, including impariment of health or interference with amenity; (ii) damage to land or personal property; (iii) interference with riparian or other proprietory or possessory rights; (iv) public or private nuisance; (v) liability for waste or other substances; and (vi) damage to or impairment of the environment including living organisms.

(b) The Company is not engaged in any litigation, arbitration or dispute resolution proceedings relating to such actual or potential liability and the Vendor is not aware of any such litigation or proceedings pending or being threatened nor of any circumstances or facts likely to give rise to such litigation or proceedings.

(c) The Company is not subject to any injunction or similar remedy or order by a court of competent jurisdiction, or to any undertaking given to such court, in respect of matters referred to in paragraph (a) of this warranty. The Company has not been subject to any such injunction, order or undertaking during the period of [20] years prior to Completion, save as fully particularised in the Disclosure Letter.

(d) Full particulars are given in the Disclosure Letters of all claims made or matters notified (or which should have been notified) to the Company's insurers during the period of [twenty] years prior to Completion in respect of such liability or potential liability as is referred to in paragraph (a) of this warranty.

4. *Management, Consignment, and Disposal of Wastes*

(a) The Company has at all times taken all necessary steps to ensure proper keeping, treatment, management, consignment and disposal of wastes produced in the course of the Company's business so as to comply with all relevant statutory requirements and duties and in accordance with all relevant codes of practice, guidance notes, notes, standards and other advisory material issued by any relevant authority. For the purposes of this warranty "wastes" includes materials and substances which are wastes to the Company notwithstanding that they may be of value or utility to some other person.

(b) Without prejudice to the generality of the previous words of this warranty, the Company has taken all necessary steps to ensure: (i) that all such wastes are consigned only to a properly authorised disposer or carrier for disposal at a facility licensed to receive such wastes; (ii) that all such wastes have been properly described; and (iii) that adequate contractual rights of indemnity exist so as to enable the Company to obtain indemnity for any claim arising against the Company in respect of such wastes by reason of breach of statutory duty, lack of due care, or malpractice on the part of the disposer or carrier. Full particulars of all relevant contracts, registrations and licences are given in the Disclosure Letter.

(c) Save as stated in the Disclosure Letter no dispute, claim, or proceedings exists between the Company and any disposer or carrier with regard to the Company's wastes, whether or not yet consigned to such disposer or carrier, and the Vendor is not aware of any circumstances which are likely to give rise to such dispute, claim or proceedings.

5. *Condition of Sites and Other Land*

(a) All sites owned or occupied by the Company are free from any contamination which could give rise (whether on the relevant site or on other land) to any of the following risks: (i) harm to human health or safety; (ii) damage to property; or (iii) pollution of surface or groundwater or soil. All sites formerly owned or occupied by the Company within the period of [30] years prior to completion were free of such contamination at the time when they ceased to be owned or occupied by the Company.

(d) The Vendor is not aware of any circumstances which are such as to require expenditure (whether by the Company or by any other person or authority) on cleaning up or decontaminating any sites owned or occupied by the Company in order to prevent, reduce or mitigate any of the risks referred to in paragraph (a) of this warranty, including investigatory, monitoring, precautionary or remedial engineering measures.

(c) The Vendor is not aware of any circumstances which might give rise to a claim against the Company in respect of expenditure for cleaning up or decontaminating any sites formerly owned or occupied by the Company during the period of [30] years prior to Completion.

(d) Save as stated in the Disclosure Letter no notice or other communication has been received from any relevant authority relating to the physical condition of any site now or formerly owned or occupied by the Company nor is the Vendor aware of any circumstances likely to give rise to the service of such notice or communication.

(e) No notice or other communication has been received from any relevant authority as to a proposal for the inclusion of land owned or occupied by the Company within any register of contamined or potentially contaminated sites and the Vendor knows of no intention on the part of any relevant authority to give such notice or communication nor of any investigations by any competent authority which might give rise to such an intention.

(f) No site owned or occupied by the Company has been used for the deposit of controlled waste during the ownership or occupation of the Company and the Vendor is not aware of any such prior use.

(g) No site owned or occupied by the Company is situated in proximity to other land the condition of which is such as could in relation to that site give rise to any of the risks referred to in paragraph (a) of this warranty.

6. Plant and Equipment

All structures, machinery, plant and equipment, whether movable or fixed, provided in connection with the activities, operations and premises of the Company for the protection of human safety, health and amenity, property and the environment, including (without limitation) those for the abatement, arrestment or treatment of polluting substances or emissions, the containment of substances and the prevention of spillages and contamination:

(a) are in good repair and condition and satisfactory working order;
(b) conform with all statutory and other legal requirements;
(c) are capable and will be capable, without further expenditure, of fulfilling the function for which they are designed or intended for the period of six (6) years from Completion.

7. Environmental Information

The Company has at all times supplied to the competent authorities such information and assessments as to the Company's processes, substances, discharges, wastes and effluents as is required by law to be supplied; all such information given (whether under a legal obligation or otherwise) was correct at the time the information was supplied and so far as the Vendor is aware all information contained on public registers relating to such matters is correct.

8. Internal Policy Assessments and Plans

(a) The Company has complied with any statements of corporate environmental policy and operating procedures.
(b) The Company has properly carried out and made all such assessments or plans as are required by law in relation to the Company's substances, processes operations and wastes (including without limitation those relating to hazardous substances, accident hazards, releases to the environment and noise); proper records have been kept of such assessments and plans and the Vendor knows of no subsequent circumstances which would render such appraisals or plans incorrect or subject to revision.

NOTE:
This precedent is of general company warranties, some of which cover wider issues than contaminated land. Given the general nature of many warranties, it is difficult and possibly dangerous to try and isolate those dealing specifically with contaminated land. However, where specific indemnities are given, care will be needed to ensure general warranties do not cut across them.

A.17 PRECEDENT 16: ACQUISITION OF A COMPANY— ENVIRONMENTAL INDEMNITIES

The Vendor covenants with the Purchaser (for itself and as Trustee for all others being the owner for the time being of the shares of the Company which trusteeship the Purchaser acknowledges) and as separate covenants with the Company to indemnify the Company and the Purchaser and hold them harmless against the following:

1. Fines or penalties whenever imposed in respect of any breaches prior to Completion by the Company or its officers, agents or employees of any statutory requirements for the protection of the environment or of human health or amenity.

2. Liability (whenever arising) resulting from; (a) any activities or operations of the Company prior to Completion or; (b) the state or condition prior to Completion of any properties now or formerly owned or occupied by the Company or facilities now or formerly used by the Company. In particular (but without limitation) such liability includes liability for: (i) injury to persons including impairment of health or interference with amenity; (ii) damage to land or personal property; (iii) interference with riparian or other proprietory or possessory rights; (iv) public or private nuisance; (v) liability for waste or other substances; and (vi) damage to or impairment of the environment including living organisms.

3. Losses and costs arising from any order or notice received from a competent authority or made by a court of competent jurisdiction in either case whether before or after Completion in respect of: (a) any activities or operations of the Company prior to Completion; and (b) the state or condition before or after completion of any properties now or formerly owned or occupied by the Company or facilities now or formerly used by the Company insofar as the state or condition prior to Completion was such as to justify such order or notice being given. Such losses and costs include in either case (without limitation): (i) the cost of steps reasonably taken to comply with such order or notice; (ii) losses arising from disruption of the business of the Company including loss of profits; and (iii) the cost of steps reasonably taken to investigate and defend any such order or notice.

4. Expenditure incurred by any authority or any person other than the Purchaser whether before or after Completion in taking remedial or preventive measures in respect of any state of affairs

arising from: (a) any activities or operations of the Company prior to Completion; or (b) the state and condition whether before or after Completion of any property now or formerly owned or occupied by the Company or any facility now or formerly used by the Company insofar as the state or condition prior to Completion was such as to justify such expenditure which and where in either case the Company is subsequently required by law to reimburse such expenditure in whole or in part.

5. Liability whether arising before or after Completion in respect of personal injury, damage to land or personal property, interference with riparian or other proprietory or possessory rights and damage to or impairment of the environment caused in any case by wastes produced by the Company and disposed of by the Company prior to Completion and irrespective of whether such wastes were the sole cause of the injury, damage, interference or impairment (as the case may be).

6. The cost of reasonable measures taken in respect of sites owned or occupied by the Company to prevent or mitigate any risk presented by such site to human health or safety, property, surface or groundwater or soil by reason of contamination of the site which arose prior to Completion and including, without limitation, investigatory and monitoring measures.

7. Any reasonable costs, charges and expenses incurred by the Purchaser or Company in connection with any of the above matters or in connection with any action taken in avoiding, verifying, reducing, resisting or settling any such fine, penalty, liability, order, notice, loss, cost or claim.

[Optional Limitation Provisions]

PROVIDED THAT:

(a) The liability of the Vendor under this provision shall apply for the period of [   ] years from Completion and after that period shall cease but without prejudice to any rights on the part of the Purchaser or Company which shall have arisen during that period;

(b) The maximum amount of the Vendor's liability under this covenant shall be limited to [£   ] OR the following percentage of the relevant amount;

For the first twelve months after Completion: [   ] per cent
For the second twelve months after Completion: [   ] per cent

For the third twelve months after Completion: [   ] per cent
For the fourth twelve months after Completion: [   ] per cent

and thereafter shall cease.

NOTE:
This is a precedent for indemnities in a general form, as with Precedent 15 dealing with wider matters than simply contaminated land (though specific reference to the issue is included). The person giving the indemnity will wish to see provisions included as to the giving of notice of claims under the indemnity, the right to take over defence of claims etc., as to which see Precedent 3.

PRECEDENT 17: COMPANY OR ASSETS ACQUISITION— A.18
CONTAMINATED LAND INDEMNITIES

1. Definitions

Environmental Law   means all present and future rules of common law, acts, regulations, standards or codes having the force of law, applicable rights or obligations under European Community Law, and any notices, directions, impositions or requirements issued, imposed or directed by any competent authority relating to the protection of human health and safety, the protection of property and proprietary rights, or the protection of the environment [and for the avoidance of doubt it is expressly agreed that the term shall include any law introducing materially more onerous or stringent requirements than were applicable at the date of Completion.]

Environmental Conditions   means the state and condition of soil, other strata, surface or sub-surface water, groundwater, all surface and sub-surface structures including, without limitation, mines, adits, drains and sewers, all tips, lagoons, spoil heaps, waste disposal sites whether closed or operational, made ground, and all contaminative or polluting substances and shall include, without limitation, the presence of any Regulated Substance in any environmental medium.

Regulated Substance   means any substance or compound, in whatever form and including commixed substances and waste materials, the presence of which may give rise to requirements for removal, abatement, immobilisation, neutralisation, containment, rendering harmless, or any other form of treatment, remediation or clean-up under any Environmental Law.

Onsite claims   means all losses, claims, judgments, damages, penalties, fines, costs, liabilities, obligations, liens, out of pocket costs or expenses including, without limitation, the costs of investigating or defending any prosecution or claim imposed on, incurred by or asserted against the Purchaser under any Environmental Law and arising from Environmental Conditions at the Property at the Date of Completion.

Clean-up Costs   means all reasonable costs incurred by the Purchaser in remedying Environmental Conditions at the Property as at the date of Completion including, without limitation, the removal, isolation, neutralisation or other treatment of regulated Substances [and including the reasonable cost of investigating such Environmental Conditions] PRO-VIDED THAT such costs shall be limited to those necessary in order:

579

(i) to avoid Onsite Claims arising;

(ii) to render the Property fit for use as [STATE USE];

[(iii) to avoid the risk of harm to the Purchaser, the Purchaser's employees and invitees and the Purchaser's property];

[(iv) to render the Property saleable upon reasonable commercial terms].

2. Indemnity

The Vendor covenants to indemnify and hold harmless the Purchaser against:

(a) Onsite Claims; and

(b) Clean-up Costs

arising within the period of [PERIOD] from the date of this Agreement up to a maximum of [AMOUNT] in aggregate for all such Claims and Costs within that period.

3. Indemnity Provisions

3.1 The Purchaser shall notify the vendor in writing of all Onsite Claims made or asserted against the Purchaser. Such modification shall be made as soon as reasonably practicable after receipt of any notice of claim and shall be accompanied by all correspondence and documentation relating thereto. The Vendor may, within six weeks of such notification (or any shorter if necessary to allow the Purchaser adequate time to respond to the claim) elect to conduct the response or defence to the claim. The party conducting such response to defence shall keep the other informed of the progress of the claim and shall supply copies of all relevant documents. The other party shall offer all reasonable assistance and cooperation as is necessary for the proper response or defence to the claim. The Purchaser shall not admit liability or compromise the claim without the written consent of the Vendor, such consent not to be reasonably withheld or delayed.

3.2 Prior to incurring any Clean-up Costs the Purchaser shall notify the Vendor of the Purchaser's intention to do so, together with details of the Costs proposed to be incurred and copies of all relevant reports, data, recommendations, correspondence or other documentation. Within 14 days of receiving such notification the Vendor shall either:

(a) notify the Purchaser in writing that the Vendor approves the proposed Clean-up Costs; or

(b) notify the Purchaser in writing that the Vendor objects to the proposed Clean-up Costs and requires the matter to be referred to arbitration in accordance with the provisions of clause 3.3

3.3 Where the Vendor objects to the proposed Clean-up Costs in accordance with Clause 3.2(b) then the issue of whether the Vendor is obliged to indemnify the Purchaser against all or part of the Proposed Clean-up Costs shall be referred to an appropriately qualified expert (who shall act as an expert and not as arbitrator) to be agreed by the parties or in default of agreement to be appointed by the President of the Institute of Civil Engineers. [ADD FURTHER STANDARD DISPUTE RESOLUTION PROVISIONS, AS REQUIRED].

NOTE:
This indemnity is closely focused on contaminated site conditions than the more general indemnity at Precedent 15. It covers not only claims or actions against the Purchaser relating to pre-existing contamination, but also clean-up costs incurred by the Purchaser for certain specified purposes.

A.19 PRECEDENT 18: PROVISIONS FOR INCLUSION IN LOAN FACILITY LETTER

The obligation of the Bank to allow drawdown hereunder is subject to the fulfilment of the following conditions precedent:

1. The Bank being satisfied that the Borrower has a good and marketable title to the Property free from any matter or restrictions which in the opinion of the Bank materially affect its value as security and that all usual searches and enquiries in relation thereto have been made and that specific enquiries have been made of the Vendor as to the presence in, on or under the Property of noxious substances in such concentrations as may cause pollution of the environment or harm to human health and as to the legality of the operations being carried out on the Property and specific enquiries have been made of the local authority as to the registration or likelihood of registration of the Property on any register made pursuant to section 143 of the Environmental Protection Act 1990 or any similar register of contaminated land or of contaminative uses and the Bank having no reasonable objection to the replies thereto and the Borrower having deposited with the Bank all deeds and other documents of title (if any).

2. The Borrower having commissioned an environmental investigation of the Property on terms approved in advance by the Bank by consultants approved in advance by the Bank and the Bank being satisfied, having been sent copies of all reports, in draft and in final form, prepared by the consultants in relation to the Property at the same time as such reports are sent to the Borrower, that the reports do not reveal the existence of any circumstances which would materially affect the value of the Property as security.

Note:
The object of this provision is to make it clear that the drawdown of the loan is conditional upon appropriate investigations relating to (inter alia) possible contamination.

582

PRECEDENT 19: COVENANTS BY MORTGAGOR   A.20

The Mortgagor covenants with the Bank as follows:

1. From time to time and, in any event, within seven days of service by the Bank on the Mortgagor of written notice of investigation, to commission an environmental investigation of the Mortgaged Property on terms approved in advance by the Bank by consultants approved in advance by the Bank and to instruct the consultants to forward to the Bank copies of all reports, whether in draft or in final form, prepared by the consultants in relation to the Mortgaged Property at the same time as such reports are forwarded to the Mortgagor and to implement forthwith all reasonable recommendations made by the consultants as to operational procedures and remediation works and further investigations on the Mortgaged Property and to pay the professional fees of the consultants.

2. To permit the Bank and such consultants as the Bank from time to time in writing for that purpose appoint at all reasonable times during business hours and on 24 hours' written notice to the Mortgagor to enter into and upon the Mortgaged Property with or without vehicles and appropriate equipment and machinery for the purpose of carrying out environmental investigations and forthwith after the service by the Bank of notice of works to implement the reasonable recommendations as to operational procedures and remediation works on the Mortgaged Property made by the consultants and to pay the professional fees of the consultants.

3. Within three days of its occurrence to give full particulars to the Bank of any release, spill or deposit on the Mortgaged Property of any noxious substance in a quantity which would cause serious damage to or pollution of the environment or serious damaged to property or serious harm to human health.

4. Within seven days of receipt or notification to give full particulars to the Bank of any correspondence or communication, whether written or verbal, received from any competent authority in connection with any environmental matter including, without prejudice, any notification as to inclusion or possible inclusion of the Mortgaged Property on any part thereof or any register or list of land which is or may be contaminated or which has been or is subject to any contaminative use.

5. The Mortgagor is unaware of any actual or potential liability on the part of the Mortgagor in respect of the activities carried on

at the Mortgaged Property for breach of any legislation having amongst its objectives the protection of the environment or of any actual or potential civil or criminal liability on the part of the Mortgagor for harm to persons or property, nuisance or impairment of the environment resulting from any activities or operations of the Mortgagor or the state or condition of the Mortgaged Property or of any circumstances which might give rise to any such liability in the future.

NOTE:
These covenants, for inclusion in a mortgage or charge, are intended to protect the interests of the Lender, by requiring the provision of relevant information by the lender, and by giving rights and obligations as to investigation for contamination and appropriate remedial action. The mortgagee should, however, be aware of the enhanced risk of lender liability which may result from becoming involved in decisions as to clean-up or other remedial action: see Chap. 12 generally.

Appendix B

VALUATION OF CONTAMINATED LAND

Generally

Whilst many valuers and their clients recognise the potential impact of **B.01**
contamination on the value of the property there is, as yet, little
consensus as to how that impact is to be adequately and accurately
factored into the valuation process. This lack of common ground appears
from a survey of one hundred leading valuation practices carried out by
the Environmental Assessment Group.[1] The dilemma is neatly summed
up by one of the respondents to that survey as follows:

> "The difficulty we, and presumably many other practitioners, have
> in dealing with environmental matters and contamination issues in
> the context of valuation reports, is knowing precisely how far a
> general practice survey is expected to go in giving advice, when
> these are really outside our normal field of expertise. While
> acknowledging that these are questions which must be addressed, it
> is important not to mislead clients by purporting to have specialist
> knowledge on environmental matters when we, like many other
> firms, have no specialism and as such there is, as we see it, an
> inherent danger in attempting to say too much."

In the absence of employed staff with specialist knowledge of contamination problems, a valuer will therefore need to recommend to his
client that a specialist consultant be retained; the problem is that the
willingness of the client to pay for such additional and specialist input
depends upon the appreciation that this cost should be seen against the
magnitude of possible liabilities rather judged against the value of the
site or the size of the loan.[2]

The assistance and advice of Mr. Martin Sheard of Matthews & Son,
Chartered Surveyors, and of Mr. Philip Wilbourn of Philip Wilbourn and
Associates, Urban Regeneration and Environmental Property Consultants, are
gratefully acknowledged.
[1] Mark Day [1993] *Estates Times*, p. 1181.
[2] *Ibid.*

585

Having established the nature, extent and risks of contamination on a site, its potential costs will need to be considered and taken into account by the valuer. These include:

(a) the cost of any necessary further investigative measures;
(b) the physical cost of clean-up;
(c) any necessary temporary measures to avoid further contamination pending clean-up;
(d) on-going management and monitoring costs, such as ground-water pumping and gas control;
(e) the possible need to redesign the layout and built form of the development, together with any constraints on end use which that may present;
(f) any possible contingent environmental liabilities in respect of contamination;
(g) provision in respect of the risk of liabilities, for example third party insurance (if available) and self insurance or the provisions of a contingency fund;
(h) any necessary works to isolate the site, either to avoid migration of contamination offsite, or to prevent the ingress of contaminants from adjacent land; and
(i) on the positive side, the availability of any grants or other financial incentives.

It is of course also important to consider the proposed end use of the property and the extent to which contamination affects the fitness for that use: the effect of contamination on existing use value may differ markedly from the effect on alternative use value. There is also the most nebulous factor, that of "blight" or market perception, the extent of which depends upon the perceived risk of increased future standards for the condition of land and more stringent liability regimes.[3]

Application of existing valuation methods

B.02   Generally used techniques can be applied to contamination problems. For example, open market value principles may be applicable, though in assessing the "best price" there may be difficulties in relation to the assumption of the "idiot bid" from a reckless or naive purchaser who would pay more than the properly advised purchaser would pay. Logically, if the market in fact comprises such bidders, there is no reason why this evidence should be excluded from the valuer, however misguided their bids might be.[4]

---

[3] Tim Stapleton, *Blundell Memorial Lecture,* June 14, 1993.
[4] See E. Martin Sheard, *Valuing Contaminated Land: Asset or Liability?* Land Reclamation and Contamination, 1993, Vol. 1, No. 1, p. 9.

For specialised properties, where an open market value is not possible, the depreciated replacement cost (DRC) basis may be applicable. This involves estimating the replacement cost of the asset, *e.g.* a factory. If the asset is constructed on contaminated land then it will be a difficult issue how clean-up costs (and to what standard) are to be built into the replacement cost: the cost of meeting such requirements could easily fully outweigh or at least make very significant inroads into the total value.[5]

Contaminated land may well lend itself to the residual method of appraisal based on essentially two questions:

   (i) what will be the cost of work to clean-up the land; and
   (ii) what will the land be worth when the work is completed?

Neither of these questions is easy or straightforward. For the first, the valuer must depend on the expertise of other specialists. It is very difficult to obtain accurate figures in advance for decontamination; this is particularly problematic in the case of grant applications where there will be no "second bite of the cherry". Other factors which will need to be built in include appropriate sums for contingencies, the cost of finance and the developer's profit figure. As to the "after" value, it has to be accepted that even if it is cleaned up to acceptable contemporary standards, the land is still not virgin land and the price it can command will probably reflect this. Some discount is likely to reflect factors such as less flexibility in terms of future uses, the risk of environmental standards changing or of the treatment failing, and general adverse perceptions. Ongoing costs of monitoring and control may be involved and will need to be capitalised. Taking the cost of clean-up and after value together may quite conceivably result in a negative value, depending on market conditions and current perception.

Valuing let property will also be difficult, particularly given the doubt as to how many common lease terms might operate to allocate liability for contaminative problems.[6] If the legal position is not clear then some allowance for risk will need to be made, whichever interest is being valued.

Liability of valuers

Failure to take account of the possibility of contamination in the **B.03** context of a property survey or valuation will raise the question of professional negligence. Whilst many surveyors will not have specialist expertise in the field of contaminated land, it is clear that the risks and

---

[5] *Ibid.*
[6] See Chap. 11 generally.

effects of such contamination are generally well-known,[7] and on that basis a surveyor who does not at least alert his client to the need for additional specialist advice or explicitly limit the scope of his survey must be at risk.

It appears that no court has yet had to consider the issue of damages where a surveyor is found to be negligent in relation to the identification of contamination. However, on general principles, the correct test to apply is the difference between what the purchaser has paid for the property on the basis of the negligent advise and that sum which the purchaser would have paid had correct advice been given; it is not correct to assess damages on the basis of the cost of works to put the property in the state it would have been in, had the valuation been correct.[8] This difference of approach may be important, since it is quite conceivable that two tests could produce a widely different result. In many cases the cost of remedial works may greatly exceed the actual effect upon the value of the property, depending upon factors such as the general state of the market and proposed end use. On the other hand, the value test will take into account contingent liabilities (which may result in property having "negative" value) in a way in which the simple cost of remedial works test would not.

In the case of negligent valuations given in the context of loan advances, the leading case is *Swingcastle* v. *Gibson*.[9] Following that case, it is necessary to distinguish two situations: first, where the lender would have lent nothing had the valuation been carried out properly; and, secondly, where the lender would have advanced a lesser amount had the valuation been carried out properly. Either situation may of course apply in the case of contaminated land, depending largely upon the nature of the contamination and its contingent risks and liabilities. In the first case, where the lender would have lent nothing, the damage to be compensated is the difference between the amount of the advance and any capital recovered on repayment or sale, together with consequential expenses such as repossession proceedings against the borrower, and interest at an appropriate rate to reflect the loss of use of the capital sum advanced, credit being given for any interest payments received by the borrower.[10]

In a case where the effect of a negligent valuation is that the lender advanced more than would otherwise have been the case, it will be necessary to establish the difference in amount, and the lender's damages will be assessed on that basis.[11] It will be for the lender to

[7] See the section on RICS caveats below.
[8] *Philips* v. *Ward* [1956] 1 W.L.R. 471; *Watts* v. *Morrow* [1991] 1 W.L.R. 1421.
[9] [1991] 2 A.C. 223; overruling *Baxter* v. *F. W. Gapp & Co.* [1939] 2 All E.R. 752.
[10] The notional rate of interest was set at 12 per cent. in *Swingcastle:* (see [1991] 2 A.C. 223 at 239).
[11] *Corisand Investments Limited* v. *Druce & Co.* (1978) 248 E.G. 315.

furnish evidence to prove its case on the correct basis, and this may involve evidence as to the attitude of the lender had it known of the contamination, or possibly by calling evidence from the borrower to show that, had the lender been willing to advance a smaller sum, this would not have been sufficient to enable the borrower to proceed to take up the loan and proceed with the transaction.

RICS valuation guidelines

The RICS has published draft guidance for valuers, prepared through **B.04** a working party, and which is intended finally to become a chapter in the *Manual of Valuation Guidance Notes* ("the White Book"). The guidance, published in March 1993,[12] proceeded on the assumption that section 143 of the Environmental Protection Act 1990 would be implemented; the draft also anticipates the imminent publication of the new RICS/ISVA Homebuyers Survey and Valuation Scheme. The draft guidance refers to the facts that may be relevant in the valuation of potentially contaminated land, problems with contaminative or harmful building materials, and the issue of current use.

As to the valuation basis, the general principle is stated as being that the valuer should reflect all relevant issues in his or her valuation and in particular should not automatically assume that the property is uncontaminated. If instructed to report on that basis, for which there may be a quite proper reason, the valuer may do so, but should insert into the report Caveat 1 referred to below; even in that case, the valuer should undertake normal enquiries and report on possible contamination which has not been reflected in the valuation. This advice is stated specifically not to apply to residential services—*i.e.*, the valuation of residential properties for mortgage purposes and the RICS/ISVA Homebuyers Survey and Valuation Scheme. In all other cases, unless instructed otherwise, the valuer should cause to be made such enquiries as in his or her professional judgment are necessary to establish any existence and the probable extent of contamination, the likelihood of inclusion on the section 143 register, and should consider the likely effect on value of the contamination or the inclusion or possibility of inclusion in the register. Guidance is given as to the type of enquiries and sources of information which may be consulted.

The guidance envisages a number of possible outcomes of these investigations:

    (a) Cases where there is no evidence of contamination: the property should then be valued on that basis subject to Caveat 2 (see

---

[12] *General Practice*, March 1993, p. 2.

 below). It is suggested that this will apply to the vast majority of reports;

(b) Cases where there is no evidence of contamination but the property for historical reasons is or is likely to be included in the section 143 register. This should be reported and any effect reflected in the valuation;

(c) Cases where there is evidence of contamination and the cost of rectification has been estimated by experts with appropriate experience, having regard to the relevant use. This can then be reflected in the valuation, having particular regard to the data being used, any assumptions, the likely effect of statute and the perception of the market. A suitable caveat (Caveat 3 below) should be adopted;

(d) Cases where there is evidence of contamination, but its extent cannot be established for reasons such as absence of technical skills, the time available, or costs. The valuer in this circumstance may either decline the instruction, or negotiate an acceptable basis for undertaking the work. Such a basis may include the agreement of specific assumptions or estimates and reporting the contamination but valuing on the assumption that it does not exist, and recommending subsequent suitable investigation after which the valuation should be reviewed.

The draft guidance states that any apparent evidence of possible contamination arising from adjacent property should be noted and considered and that in all cases, the valuer is under a duty to advise the client if an issue has been identified which is outside the valuer's competence. In this context, the valuer should be particularly wary of responding to questions in standard form presented by lenders as part of the valuers instructions.

The draft guidance also points out that contamination issues are likely to have a particular effect on valuations on a DRC basis where "environmental obsolescence" would mean that a replacement building would not be permitted if current standards and controls were to apply; further, a site value may well be negative. it is also suggested that contamination issues may affect both rental valuations and the valuation of freeholds in respect of leases which subsist, together with the valuation of leasehold interests themselves. Valuations in such cases need to reflect the respective responsibilities of the parties and the likely action of the other in case of breach of those responsibilities. Particular attention will need to be paid to repairing and service charge provisions, covenants requiring compliance with statutory provisions, and rent review clauses.[13]

[13] See generally Chap. 11.

RICS caveats

Following introduction of the Environmental Protection Act 1990, the **B.05** RICS and Incorporated Society of Valuers and Auctioneers drafted a form of caveat for valuations which was agreed with the Council of Mortgage Lenders. This was a fairly crude caveat simply stating that the valuer had not investigated whether or not the site is or had been in the past contaminated and whether or not it is or is to be placed on section 143 register; it also stated that the legal advisers of the clients should investigate this matter and that the valuation was on the assumption that the land was not contaminated and was not or would not be on the Register.

The draft RICS guidance referred to above adopts a somewhat more sophisticated approach by proposing three forms of caveat reflecting the instructions, the nature of the property and the sources and quality of information.[14]

Caveat 1

This is suggested where an approach of total disregard of contamination is adopted and reads:

> "We are not aware of the content of any environmental audit or other environmental investigation or soil survey which may have been carried out on the property and which may draw attention to any contamination or the possibility of any such contamination. In undertaking our work, we have been instructed to assume that no contaminative or potentially contaminative uses have ever been carried out on the property. We have not carried out any investigation into past or present uses of either the property or of any neighbouring land to establish whether there is any potential for contamination from those uses or sites to the subject property and have therefore assumed that none exist, nor have we had regard to the contents of the register of land which may be subject to contamination. Should it however be established subsequently that contamination exists at the property or on any neighbouring land or that the premises have been or are being put to a contaminative use, or that the property is on the register, this might reduce the values now reported."

It is stated, however, that if despite instructions, assumptions or caveats, the valuer's enquiries reveal probable contamination, this

---

[14] The caveats given in the draft guidance are stated to be subject to the receipt of legal advice and full consultation with the insurance industry.

should be reported in a similar way that any significant physical building defect would be reported, even though a structural survey had not been undertaken.

Caveat 2

This Caveat is intended for use where enquiry is made but reveals no evidence of contamination:

> "Our enquiries have not revealed any contamination affecting the property or neighbouring property which would affect our valuation. Should it, however, be established subsequently that contamination exists at the property or on any neighbouring land or that the premises have been or are being put to any contaminative use, this might reduce the values now reported."

Caveat 3

This Caveat is intended for use where there is evidence of contamination and the cost of rectification has been estimated:

> "We have made enquiries and have been supplied with information [source] which has identified contamination [specified]. Our valuation for the relevant use has had regard to the estimated costs and likely liability for treatment, as advised by [name of consultant] and our opinion of the market's likely perception of the issues involved. Should it however be established subsequently that further contaminants exist at the propery or on any neighbouring land, or that the premises have been or are being put to any other contaminative uses, or placed on the register, this might reduce the values now reported."

Lands Tribunal cases

B.06   Issues valuing contaminated land have on occasion been considered by the Lands Tribunal. In *Proudco* v. *Department of Transport*[15] the Department compulsorily purchased for the purposes of a road scheme the freehold interest in an area of land forming part of the site of a former chemical works. The claimants sought compensation for the land acquired. As at the valuation date (November 1, 1985) the whole site was contaminated by chemical pollution and some radioactivity. It was

[15] Ref/82/1989; (1991) R.V.R. Vol. 31, No. 5, p. 103 (V. G. Wellings, Q.C., President).

agreed as a fact that the cost of decontaminating the site (inclusive of fees) could be taken to be £9,900,000. The approach of the Lands Tribunal was to assess the value of the freehold site by means of comparables, ignoring contamination, and then to deduct the agreed cost of decontamination. In relation to a claim for use and occupation of one of the site areas occupied by the Department for 775 days, it was argued by the District Valuer on behalf of the Department that this area could not have been put to any beneficial use, except for the the special needs of a Department of Transport which were to be ignored. On that basis, in his opinion, the plot had no market value in that it could not have been developed by the owner during the priod of occupation because removal of the contamination was necessary before development could be carried out. On that basis the District Valuer valued compensation at a spot figure of £1,000. The Lands Tribunal disagreed, on the basis that compensation for use and occupation is not based on the value to the owner, but rather on the basis of a reasonable compensation to the owner for the occupation. In that case, compensation for the area, contaminated as it was, as to be assessed on a daily basis at a nominal rent of £15 per day, resulting in a sum of £11,625.

In *Haddon* v. *Black Country Development Corporation*[16] the Lands Tribunal considered the amount of compensation payable on the compulsory acquisition of some six hectares of vacant freehold land at Wednesbury, West Midlands, previously used for the extraction of furnace ash and the deposit of industrial waste materials. From about 1900 to the 1980 the site had been used for the surface tipping of ash from foundries and iron works. During the 1980s ash was extracted for sale and some 200,000 cubic metres of non-toxic industrial waste were deposited on the site, followed by a degree of levelling and surface covering. It was agreed as a fact that the void created by the proposed extraction of ash and other saleable materials from the site would be sufficient to receive 175,000 cubic metres of compacted non-hazardous waste, that it was a practical proposition to re-work the land for ash and that the further void space could therefore be created; and that the estimated cost of £227,778 for the long term monitoring of landfill gas emanating from the site was sufficient. The principal elements of the claimant's suggested figure of £5,760,400 included the value of ash to be extracted, the value of the newly created void which would result from that extraction for waste disposal, and the value for open storage use of the surface which would be created by waste disposal. A section 17 certificate was obtained which included a condition requiring that remedial measures to counter the hazards from any contamination and/or the emission of gases be carried out before any part of the development was commenced.

[16] Ref/166/1991; March 15, 1993, unreported (T. Hoyes, F.R.I.C.S.).

The main forms of contamination highlighted in the expert evidence to the Tribunal related to the pollution and seepage of groundwater and the production of methane gas; it was not disputed that some remedial works were needed if the site was to be reused, both as a practical matter and as a requirement of the section 17 certificate. The real issue between the opposing experts was not so much the degree and technical nature of contamination but whether there was a remedy for it, and if so the cost, immediate and recurring, of effecting that remedy. It was ultimately accepted that despite the past use of the site it did not inhibit the ultimate use for open storage, subject to remedial works being carried out, including ventilation trenches, impermeable capping, treatment of mineshafts, an improved surface water drainage system, long term gas monitoring and continuing maintenance of the ground surface against water penetration and gas leaks.

In terms of the general characteristics of the land, it was noted that the site had the advantage of being some 250 metres distant from the nearest dwellings and that it was adjacent to uses which themselves might be regarded as unneighbourly.

The ultimate decision of the Tribunal in relation to site contamination and remedial measures was that the land was not contaminated to such an extent that the remedial work proposed could not render it fit for open storage use. The "reworking" of the site as proposed was a practical alternative to immediate use for open storage; a new waste repository to current regulations and standards could be formed from on-site materials. However, a prudent purchaser would include a contingency sum in case the clays on site needed supplementing as to quality for the lining of the repositories; this provision should be about 20 per cent. and there should be included a further 10 per cent. for further possible cost overruns or unforeseen circumstances. The claimant's estimated costs for remedial or safeguarding works were generally accepted, subject to a slight uplift. In relation to the proposed revenues to be achieved from extraction of ash and waste disposal, deductions of 30 per cent. were made in each case to reflect the fact that ash extraction and solid waste reception could not be regarded as a "risk free activity". The final amount of compensation determined by the Tribunal was £1,463,000, the acquiring authority to pay the claimant's costs of the reference.

Conclusions

B.07   It is difficult at this stage to assess the impact of possible contamination on land values. Even without the introduction of section 143 registers it has been suggested that uncertainty as to potential liabilities under existing legislation is already having a profound effect, with effect on value being equated to clean-up costs in a fairly simplistic way.[17] However, there are conflicting signs. Research carried out at the end of 1992 among the main U.K. institutions and property companies indicates that the majority (72 per cent.) had an environmental policy and that the discovery of contamination would not necessarily preclude an acquisition.[18]

It is probably also the case that initial perception of a general problem may induce a substantial loss in value ("dread factors"): as understanding increases, so values may rise again to a point where they relate to logical factors such as clean-up costs, control measures, delay and contingent liabilities.[19] It is probably always the case however, that the public or an investor will not necessarily agree with the scientists, resulting in long-term residual uncertainty and stigma.[20] Finally, not all purchasers will be equally risk-sensitive: a lender or investor with local knowledge may be prepared to bid more for a remediated contaminated site than an institution.[21]

[17] Grimley J. R. Eve, "Contaminated Land — The Implications for Values" (unpublished, 1992).
[18] M. F. Creamer, "Contaminated Land and Capital Value," (Hillier Parker, 1992, unpublished).
[19] Ibid.
[20] Ibid.
[21] Ibid.

Appendix C

INFORMATION SOURCES

1: Table 1 from BSI DD 175: 1988.
(See para. 4.06 of text.)

C.01

Readily accessible documented information for the preliminary investigation of contaminated sites		
Type of information	**Principal characteristics**	**Sources**
Maps, plans and charts Ordnance survey topographical maps	**Large scale maps** a. 1:1250 scale (50.668 in to one mile); cover major urban areas in Great Britain. b. 1:2500 scale (25.344 in to one mile) from 1853; cover the remainder of Great Britain, apart from areas of mountain and moorland. c. 1:10560 scale (six in to one mile) from 1840; cover the whole of Great Britain, but are being replaced by maps at the 1:10000 scale.	Early maps, early editions of OS maps and plans are available for reference at the locations listed as notes 1, 2 and 3 at the end of the table. Local and national libraries; British Library Map Library; County Record Offices.
	Small-scale maps a. 1:25000 scale: The first series covered the whole of Great Britain except the Scottish Highlands and Islands. The second series, which includes the Scottish Highlands and Islands, is gradually replacing the first. b. 1:50000 scale, first and second series; these maps have replaced one into one mile (1:63360) maps. c. 1:250000 scale; the series popularly known as 'quarter-inch' maps. d. 1:625000 scale; specialist maps on this scale are available on such subjects as route planning, administrative areas, archaeology and geology.	All types of printed maps and plans are listed in the British Museum Catalogue which may be consulted in university and other large libraries.
OS special maps, plans and books	a. Geological maps for the British Geological Survey (note 4); mostly small scale (1:63360 or 1:50000) in solid and drift editions. b. Soil survey maps for The Soil Survey of England and Wales (note 5), and The Soil Survey of Scotland (note 6). c. Archaeological and historical maps and texts.	Catalogues of OS maps and publications, and information about services and copyright, are available from the Ordnance Survey (notes 7 to 11).

596

Table 1. *(continued)*

Type of information	Principal characteristics	Sources
OS special maps, plans and books— *cont.*	d. Professional papers, Gazetteer, place names on maps of Scotland and Wales.	
Other maps and plans	a. Tithe Survey maps (usually 1:4752 or 1:2736) 1836–60, for rural and urban areas; also enclosure maps.	County Record Offices; House of Lords Record Office (for plans deposited as part of Acts of Parliament); Public Record Office; local and national reference libraries, British Coal.
	b. Plans of public and statutory undertakings, *e.g.* canals, railways, gas and water undertakings.	
	c. Insurance plans for 46 major towns, 1885–1940, published by Chas. E. Goad Ltd., Scale 1:480, listed in [7].	
	d. Land use survey maps, *e.g.* Second Land Utilisation Survey of Britain (1:25000) (note 12).	
	e. Survey of Contaminated Land, Welsh Office (note 13).	
	f. Admiralty charts and hydrographic publications (tide tables etc.).	
		Hydrographic Department Ministry of Defence (note 15).
Meteorological and hydrological records	a. Weather observations (temperature, rainfall, sunshine, evapotranspiration) from selected locations in the UK; for various time periods; collated statistics.	Meteorological Office (note 15).
	b. Surface water run-off data; groundwater level data.	Regional Water authorities; private water undertakings; Institute of Hydrology (note 16).
Air and ground-based photographs	a. Vertical air photographs (from about 1945 onwards), oblique air photographs (various periods). Mostly black and white but more recent surveys may be on colour film. Some special surveys using remote sensing techniques may also be available.	Central Registers of Air Photographs (notes 17 to 19); County planning offices; Ordnance Survey (post-1970); Commercial air survey companies.
	b. Ground-based photographs of building, structures, industrial operations, etc.	Local collections; owners; occupiers; libraries, etc.
Local and topographical literature	a. Victoria County History series.	Local libraries; reference libraries.
	b. Local histories; local newspapers; proceedings and publications of local societies (*e.g.* history and archaeology; industrial archaeology).	Local libraries; local societies; industries.
Directories	a. Local street directories (1850 onwards) *e.g. Kelly's town and country directories* and *Post Office London Directories* (note 20), for example see.	Local libraries.
	b. Trade and business directories, *e.g.* collieries, mines, quarries, for example see.	Various publishers and trade associations.

Table 1. *(continued)*

Type of information	Principal characteristics	Sources
Technical and professional literature	a. Details of industrial processes; descriptions of particular sites and plants, b. Site records of owners, occupiers and operators, in private hands, record offices or libraries. Information on the location of manuscript material relating to the site may be available from the National Register of Archives (note 21).	Reference libraries; professional institutions; local companies and industries; Open University (History of Chemistry Research Group).

NOTES

1. The British Library Map Library, Great Russell Street, London WC1B 3DG (Telephone 071-636 1544).
2. The Department of Maps, Prints and Drawings, National Library of Wales, Aberystwyth SY23 3BU (Telephone 0970 3816).
3. The Map Room, National Library of Scotland Annex, 137 Causewayside, Edinburgh EH9 1PH (Telephone 031–667 7848).
4. British Geological Survey, Nicker Hill, Keyworth, Nottingham NG12 5GG (Formerly the Institute of Geological Sciences).
5. Soil Survey of England and Wales, Rothamsted Experimental Station, Harpenden, Herts AL5 2JQ.
6. Soil Survey of Scotland, Macaulay Institute of Soil Research, Craigiebuckler, Aberdeen AB9 2QJ.
7. For all parts of Great Britain. Ordnance Survey, Romsey Road, Maybush, Southampton SO9 4DH.
8. For Northern Ireland. The Chief Survey Officer, Ministry of Finance, Ordnance Survey, Ladas Drive, Belfast BT6 9FJ.
9. For the Irish Republic. Ordnance Survey, Phoenix Park, Dublin, Irish Republic.
10. For the Channel Islands. Ordnance Survey publishes a three inch map of Guernsey. Further enquiries should be directed to the authorities in Guernsey, Jersey, Alderney or Sark, as appropriate.
11. For the Isle of Man. For maps having scales larger than one inch, enquiries should be made to the Isle of Man Government Board, Murray House, Douglas, Isle of Man.
12. Obtainable from the Director of the Land Use Survey, Kings College, London WC2 or from Edward Stanford Ltd., 12–14 Long Acre, London WC2.
13. Welsh Office, Cardiff, CF1 3NQ.
14. Hydrographic Department, Ministry of Defence, Taunton, Somerset (Telephone 0823 87900; Telex 46274).
15. The Director General, Meteorological Office, London Road, Bracknell, Berks RG12 2SZ.
16. The Institute of Hydrology, Wallingford, Oxon OX10 8BB (Telephone 0491 38800).
17. For England. Ordnance Survey, Romsey Road, Maybush, Southampton SO9 4DH (Telephone 0703 775555 Ext. 584).
18. For Scotland. The Central Register of Air Photography, Scottish Development Department, Room 1/21 New St Andrew's House, St James Centre, Edinburgh EH1 3SZ (Telephone 031–556 8400 Ext. 4766).
19. For Wales. The Central Register of Air Photography, Welsh Office, Room 0–003 Crown Offices, Cathays Park, Cardiff, CF1 3NQ (Telephone 0222 823815).
20. Kelley's Directories Archives Division, IPC Business Press Ltd., Quadrant House, The Quadrant, Sutton, Surrey. (Telephone 081–661 3500).
21. The National Register of Archives, Quality House, Quality Court, Chancery Lane, London WC2A 1HP (Telephone 071–242 1198).

2. Annex F from DoE Consultation Paper, May **C.02**
(1991, see para. 4.06 of text.)

LIST OF SOURCES

NOTE: This list is provisional. Sources and organisations listed are still in the process of confirmation.

F.1 Principal sources

The Government strongly recommends that the following sources should be consulted:

MAPS: All editions of the following series:

OS County Series 6 inch and 1:10,000

Lancashire and Yorkshire were surveyed at the six inch scale between 1840 to 1854; maps for other counties were produced by photographic reduction from the 25 inch scale bearing the same date of survey. The replacement series is 1:10,000. Coverage: all of Great Britain. For rural and semi-rural areas, these maps will locate almost all industrial sites, but they are less helpful for densely developed areas. Identification of operations on six inch series varies between counties; on the 1:10,000 series all industrial sites are described as works or factories.

OS County Series 25 inch (1:2,500)

From 1854, with first edition complete by 1893. First revision started with 1891 resurvey of London, Middlesex and Surrey; second revision started in 1904. Coverage: all of Great Britain except (i) urban areas covered by 1:1,250 series since 1945 and (ii) areas of mountain and moorland covered only 1:10,000 series.

OS 50 inch (1:1250)

Begun after 1945. Coverage: urban areas only (about six per cent. of Great Britain). Essential source for densely developed areas.

COLLATED SOURCES

Derelict and Despoiled Land Survey (England and Wales only)

First compiled 1973, updated 1981 and 1988. Surveys are undertaken by local authorities for DoE/WO. Further updating scheduled for [1993]. The survey covers all of England and Wales but data on previous uses of sites is often imprecise. A disadvantage is that reclaimed sites are removed from the records.

Waste disposal site licences and licence applications (where available)

Records are held by Waste Disposal Authorities and their successor Waste Regulation Authorities. Licensing began in 1976, although records for closed sites are not stored indefinitely. They identify sites and types of waste permitted. Data for registers must be extracted empirically.

Records of premises regulated under the Radioactive Substances Act 1960 [now 1993]

Records held by HMIP of premises on which radioactive material is kept or used, and on or from which accumulation and disposal of radioactive waste takes place.

Registers of Premises

Registers compiled by Environmental Health Departments. These only give addresses for active sites, but records are comprehensive and accessible.

Surveys of mineral workings

Survey of all workings between 1947 and 1982 carried out in 1982 by local authorities in England and Wales on behalf of DoE and the Welsh Office to identify land permitted to be used for mineral workings. Updated 1988 to cover mineral activities 1982–88.

HMIP public registers

Authorisations under the Environmental Protection (Prescribed Processes and Substances) Regulations 1991 (S.I. 1991 No. 472).

Statutory planning registers

Registers of planning applications and decisions kept by local planning authorities under the Town and Country Planning General Development Order 1988.

National Archaeological Record and National Building Record

These records are held by the Royal Commission on Historical Monuments of England. The NAR has details of some 150,000 archaeological sites in England (including industrial and military sites) and will eventually cover all such sites up to 1945. The NBR includes the National Records of Industrial Monuments. Computerised statutory lists of buildings of architectural or historic interest are currently being compiled.

Dedicated sites for sludge disposal

Dedicated sites used for the disposal of sludge under the Sludge (Use in Agriculture) Regulations 1989, kept by Water Companies.

F.2   Other sources

Authorities may find the following sources provide useful supplementary information: **C.03**

Maps

1:500 Town Maps

Most towns and cities mapped only once, ca 1863–93. A useful cross-check because of detailed information on sites.

Other maps based on Ordnance Survey

British Geological Survey series: mostly small scale (1:63,360 or 1:50,000), but may show details of military installations which are blank on other OS maps.

Soil Survey and Land Research Centre: maps of all of England and Wales at 1:25,000 and parts at 1:25,000. Show boundaries of built-up areas at time of survey and of disturbed land in rural areas (the nature of the disturbance is indicated on some maps). Published and unpublished data archives.

Land use survey

Archaeological and historical series published by OS in conjunction with the Royal Commission on Historical Monuments of England and other bodies.

Maps other than Ordnance Survey

Tithe Survey maps: 1836–60, usually 1:4752 or 1:2736. Three copies were made, one each for the Tithe Commissioners and the relevant diocese and parish. The master copies formerly held by the Tithe Redemption Commission are now in the Public Record Office. Other copies are now normally held by local record offices.

Enclosure Plans

Settlement Plans

Early County Maps

Parish and Ward Maps

Specialised Town Plans, *e.g.*, public health maps

Plans of public and statutory undertakings, *e.g.*, canals, railways, gas and water installations. Railways have been very well mapped (*Jowett's Atlas* is the most complete source). Canal records and plans are held by the British Waterways Board Archives. The House of Lords Record Office holds records of Private Bills referring to proposed, railways and other public undertakings; duplicate copies are normally held by local record offices.

Industrial maps

Fire Insurance plans for 46 major towns, 1885–1940, 1:480, published by Chas. E. Goad Ltd.

Aerial and satellite photographs

Aerial photographs

C.04   Coverage of most of Britain from 1946 onwards. The most complete collections are those of the National Library of Air Photographs, held by the Royal Commission on Historical Monuments for England (over 3.5 million photographs giving full coverage of the landscape since 1939) and the Air Photographs Units of the Welsh Office. An important source of data on past and present industry and disturbed land, but some training and experience is needed to interpret photographs.

Satellite imagery

Only recommended if authority already has images and has personnel skilled in interpreting them.

Collated sources

DoE 1973/74 Survey of landfill sites

C.05   Desk study by the Institute of Geological Sciences (now the British Geological Survey) on behalf of DoE in co-operation with local authorities, of landfill sites to assess potential risks of groundwater and surface water contamination—the subject of articles by the "Observer" newspaper in February 1990. Covered some 2,500 sites then active in England, Scotland and Wales. Not all L.A. areas covered.

Records of burial sites of diseased animals

Water companies may hold records of burial sites of herds or flocks slaughtered because of notifiable diseases. Local authorities are responsible for disposal of carcasses of animals infected with anthrax.

Records of the former Regional Water Authorities and statutory water supply companies

These are held by the National Rivers Authority or by Water Companies, though many older records have been deposited in local authority record offices. They may have information on waste sites before the introduction of registration under CoPA. Industrial effluent discharge consents may also help to locate contaminative processes.

Directories

Local street directories were published from about 1850, *e.g.*, *Kelly's town and county directories, Post Office London directories*. A collection covering the whole country is available at the Guildhall Library, London.

Many trade associations and other publishers also issued trade and business directories.

Local archives and societies

Local history collections containing books of local interest, maps, photographs, street directories etc.

Local museums sometimes hold material on local industries.

Historical archives and societies exist in most areas, and are worth consulting selectively. The network of Industrial Archaeology Panels convened by the Council for British Archaeology should be consulted as the main coordinating bodies for industrial archaeology in their areas.

Industrial sources

Company histories may contain plans of sites and other useful information. A major collection of company histories is available at the Business Archives Council, but local firms may be covered by local libraries. Archives of firms that have ceased trading may be deposited in the Local Authority Record Office.

Local knowledge

Many individuals, such as former or current employees of the industries concerned or of the local authority, may have information about sites or records.

F.3 Organisations from which information or advice can be obtained

C.06 *Note:* Profiles of contaminative processes will indemnify sources of information on specific industries.

The organisations listed below may charge a fee for information.

(1) Association of Independent Museums, Dundee Industrial Heritage, 26 East Dock St, Dundee DD1 9HY.

(2) Association for Industrial Archaeology, The Wharfage, Iron-bridge, Telford TF8 7AW. (The Association has no full time staff but may be able to offer contact addresses for specialist societies or individuals).

(3) British Geological Survey, Nicker Hill, Keyworth, Nottingham, NG12 5GG.

(4) British Library Map Library, Great Russell St, London, WC1B 3DG.

(5) Business Archives Council, 185 Tower Bridge Road, London, SE1 2UT.

(6) Chas. E. Goad Ltd., 8–12 Salisbury Square, Old Hatfield, Herts, AL9 5BR.

(7) County Record Offices.

(8) Department of Maps, Prints and Drawings, National Library of Wales, Aberystwyth, SY23 3BU.

(9) Director of the Land Use Survey, Kings College, London, WC2.

(10) Geological Museum, Exhibition Road, London SW7 2DE.

(11) Kelly's Directories Archives Section, IPC Business Press Ltd, Quadrant House, The Quadrant, Sutton, SM2 5AS.

(12) Local libraries and museums (listed in "Record Repositories in Great Britain: A Geographical Directory", 9th edition (in preparation), published by HMSO for the Royal Commission on Historical Manuscripts).

(13) Mining Records Office, HM Inspectorate of Mines, Health and Safety Executive, St Annes House, University Road, Bootle, L20 3RA.

(14) National Association of Mining History Organisations, c/o Dr. R. Burt, Department of Economic and Social History, University of Exeter, Amory Building, Rennes Drive, Exeter, EX4 7RH.

(15) National Register of Archives, Quality House, Quality Court, Chancery Lane, London, WC2A 1HP.

(16) National Rivers Authority. Regional Offices:
Kingfisher House, Goldhay Road, Orton Goldhay, Peterborough, PE2 0ZR.
Richard Fairclough House, Knutsford Road, Warrington, WA14 1HP.
Guildbourne House, Chatsworth Road, Worthing, BN11 1LD.
Nugent House, Vastern Road, Reading, RG1 8DB.
Rivers House, East Quay, Bridgewater, TA6 4YS.
Eldon House, Regent Centre, Gosforth, Newcastle upon Tyne, NE3 3UD.
Sapphire East, 550 Streetsbrook Road, Solihull, B91 1QT.
Manley House, Kestrel Way, Exeter, EX2 7LQ.
Rivers House, St Mellons Business Park, St Mellons, Cardiff, CF3 0EG.
21 Park Square South, Leeds, LS1 2QG.

(17) Ordnance Survey, Romsey Road, Maybush, Southampton, SO9 4DH.

(18) Royal Commission on the Historical Monuments of England, Fortress House, 23 Saville Row, London, W1X 2JQ.

(19) Royal Commission on the Historical Monuments of Wales, Crown Building, Plas Crug, Aberystwyth, SY23 2HP.

(20) Royal Geographical Society, 1 Kensington Gore, London, SW7 2AR.

(21) Soil Survey of England and Wales, Silsoe Campus, Silsoe, MK45 4DT.

(22) Subterranea Britannica, 96a Brighton Road, South Croydon, CR2 6AD.

Appendix D

ASSESSMENT OF CONTAMINATION

(See para. 4.17 of text)

D.01   Paragraph 33–39 and Tables 3 and 4 of ICRCL Guidance Note 59/83 (Second Edition, July 1987), *Guidance on the Assessment and Redevelopment of Contaminated Land.*

33.   Careful assessment of the significance of contamination and of the importance of the risks disclosed by the site investigation is crucial. Because the risks posed by contamination are difficult to quantify, an indirect method based on "threshold" and "action" trigger concentrations has been devised to assess the findings of site investigations. Their purpose is to assist in selecting the most appropriate use for the site and in deciding whether remedial action is required.

34.   The trigger values define three possible concentration zones (see Fig. 1)* for each contaminant. The concentrations actually present on the site will fall within these zones:

> (i) In the first zone, a contaminant is found only in relatively low concentrations. These can usually be disregarded, because there is no significant risk that the hazard(s) will occur. As the concentration increases, a value is reached at which the risk begins to become significant. The concentration at which this occurs is defined as the threshold trigger concentration for that contaminant. Since not all site uses are at equal risk from the hazards, it follows that the threshold trigger value varies with the actual or proposed use of the site. Below the threshold trigger value the site can be regarded as uncontaminated for that end use, and therefore no remedial action is needed even though the concentrations present may be above the normal background values typical for the area.
>
> (ii) In the second, intermediate, zone the concentration of the contaminant is between the threshold value and the upper trigger concentration. Even though the threshold trigger value is exceeded, this does not automatically mean that the risk of the

---

* Reproduced at para. 4.17.

606

hazard is significant: merely that there is need to consider whether the presence of the contaminant justifies taking remedial action for the the proposed use of the site. If such considerations suggest that some action is justified, then it should be taken: the decision to do so is therefore based on informed judgement.

(iii) In the third zone, where the concentration is equal to or greater than the action trigger value, the risks of the hazard(s) occurring are sufficiently high that the presence of the contaminant has to be regarded as undesirable or even unacceptable, *i.e.* the site has to be regarded as contaminated. Action of some kind, ranging from minor remedial treatment to changing the proposed use of the site entirely, is then unavoidable.

35. For the purpose for setting trigger concentrations, contaminants can be divided into three categories:

(i) Those which may present a hazard even in very low concentrations: examples are methane, and asbestos. For these, any measurable concentration requires action to be considered or taken. Their threshold concentration is, therefore, effectively zero.

(ii) Those for which a given concentration in the soil produces a measurable effect on a "target": examples are sulphate (attack on building materials); phenol and organic compounds (contamination of water supplies) (Table 4); phytotoxic metals (*e.g.* zinc, copper and nickel — see Table 3, Group B); and cyanide (toxic through ingestion); and

(iii) Those for which no "dose-effect" relationship between the concentrations in the soil and the effects has been determined experimentally. Most of the contaminants of importance to man's health, whether through uptake by plants or by direct ingestion, fall within this category. There is at present insufficient evidence to specify precise trigger values for these contaminants, although for certain metals Group A Table 3 indicates concentrations above which the need for remedial action should be considered.

36. In both Tables 3 and 4, the tentative trigger values are based on professional judgement after taking into account the available information. *They are only applicable when used in accordance with the conditions and notes specified in the Tables, most especially only after an adequate investigation of the site. They do not apply to sites which have already been developed.*

37. These assessments are seldom simple. As may be seen from Tables 3 and 4, trigger concentrations are available only for a limited range of contaminants, though these are generally the most important. For most contaminants, it is very difficult at present to set upper values at which the concentration would automatically be considered undesirable or unacceptable. Given the paucity of information about some contaminants and the difficulty of obtaining it for others, it is unlikely that some of these values could ever be derived experimentally. The assessment of risks and of the need for remedial action must therefore depend instead on subjective or qualitative criteria.

38. Trigger concentrations only apply before a decision to develop has been taken, *i.e.* to sites being considered for development. They do not apply to sites already in use, nor to those in the course of development, and must certainly not be regarded or used as standards which all sites must meet. This restriction is very important. Trigger concentrations have been set on the basis of an implied economic condition. The cost of taking remedial action, which normally incrases development costs and extends the time required, has to be weighed against the likely risks. Where the risks are judged to be high, then remedial action will be necessary unless the original proposals are to be abandoned. The cost of abandoning a completed building which is already in use is likely to be judged high, and the practical constraints on designing and implementing remedial measures will certainly be much greater than before development started. The risks might, in these circumstances, have to be regarded as acceptable: in the case of a site still to be developed, this judgement might well be different.

39. The following working rule is suggested with the aim of reducing the risks as low as is reasonably practicable:

(i) where the source of the contamination has ceased and the site investigation has shown that the contamination is no worse than that of surrounding areas in similar use or equivalent areas elsewhere, then at worst the risks and the assocaiated hazards and consequences at this site can be no greater than at other sites in use; but
(ii) nonetheless, when an opportunity arises to take action to clean the site, or in some way reduce the risks, this should be done.

ICRCL 59/83 (SECOND EDITION): **D.02**
TABLE 3   TENTATIVE "TRIGGER CONCENTRATIONS"
FOR SELECTED INORGANIC CONTAMINANTS

Conditions

1.   This table is invalid if reproduced without the conditions and footnotes.
2.   All values are for concentration determined on "spot" samples based on an adequate site investigation carried out prior to development. They do not apply to analyse of averaged, bulked or composited samples, nor to sites which have already been developed. All proposed values are tentative.
3.   The lower values in Group A are similar to the limits for metal content of sewage sludge applied to agricultural land. The value in Group B are those above which phytotoxicity is possible.
4.   If all sample values are below the threshold concentrations then the site may be regarded as uncontaminated as far as the hazards from these contaminants are concerned and development may proceed. Above these concentrations, remedial action may be needed, especially if the contamination is still continuing. Above the action concentration, remedial action will be required or the form of development changed.

Contaminants	Planned Uses	Trigger Concentrations (mg/kg air dired soil) Threshold	Action
Group A: Contaminants which may pose hazards to health			
Arsenic	Domestic gardens, allotments	10	*
	Parks, playing fields, open space	40	*
Cadmium	Domestic gardens, allotments	3	*
	Parks, playing fields, open space	15	*
Chromium (hexavalent) (1)	Domestic gardens, allotments	25	*
	Parks, playing fields, open space		
Chromium (total)	Domestic gardens, allotments	600	*
	Parks, playing fields, open space	1,000	*
Lead	Domestic gardens, allotments	500	*
	Parks, playing fields, open space	2,000	*
Mercury	Domestic gardens, allotments	1	*
	Parks, playing fields, open space	20	*
Selenium	Domestic gardens, allotments	3	*
	Parks, playing fields, open space	6	*
Group B: Contaminants which are phytotoxic but not normally hazardous to health			
Boron (water-soluble) (3)	Any uses where plants are to be grown (2, 6)	3	*
Copper (4, 5)	Any uses where plants are to be grown (2, 6)	130	*
Nickel (4, 5)	Any uses where plants are to be grown (2, 6)	70	*
Zinc (4, 5)	Any uses where plants are to be grown (2, 6)	300	*

NOTES:
*   Action concentrations will be specified in the next edition of ICRCL 59/83.
1.   Soluble hexavalent chromium extracted by 0.1M HCl at 37°C; solution adjusted to pH 1.0 if alkaline substances present.
2.   The soil pH value is assumed to be about 6.5 and should be maintained at this value. If the pH falls, the toxic effects and the uptake of these elements will be increased.
3.   Determined by standard ADAS method (soluble in hot water).
4.   Total concentration (extractable by $HNO_3/HClO_4$).
5.   The phytotoxic effects of copper, nickel and zinc may be additive. The trigger values given here are those applicable to the "worst-case": phytotoxic effects may occur at these concentrations in acid, sandy soils. In neutral or alkaline soils phytotoxic effects are unlikely at these concentrations.
6.   Grass is more resistant to phytotoxic effects than are most other plants and its growth may not be adversely affected at these concentrations.

D.03 ICRCL 59/83 (SECOND EDITION):

TABLE 4   TENTATIVE "TRIGGER CONCENTRATIONS" FOR
CONTAMINANTS ASSOCIATED WITH FORMER COAL
CARBONISATION SITES

Conditions

1. This table is invalid if reproduced without the conditions and footnotes.
2. All values are for concentration determined on "spot" samples based on an adequate site investigation carried out prior to development. They do not apply to analyses of averaged, bulked or composited samples, nor to sites which have already been developed.
3. Many of these values are preliminary and will require regular updating. They should not be applied without reference to the current edition of the report "Problems Arising from the Development of Gas Works and Similar Sites".
4. If all sample values are below the threshold concentrations then the site may be regarded as uncontaminated as far as the hazards from these contaminants are concerned and development may proceed. Above these concentrations, remedial action may be needed, especially if the contamination is still continuing. Above the action concentration, remedial action will be required or the form of development changed.

Contaminants	Proposed Uses	Trigger Concentrations	(mg/kg air-dired soil)
		Threshold	Action
Polyaromatic hydrocarbons (1, 2)	Domestic gardens, allotments, play areas.	50	500
	Landscaped areas, buildings, hard cover.	1000	10000
Phenols	Domestic gardens, allotments.	5	200
	Landscaped areas, buildings, hard cover.	5	1000
Free cyanide	Domestic gardens, allotments, landscaped areas.	25	500
	Buildings, hard cover.	100	500
Complex cyanides	Domestic gardens, allotments.	250	1000
	Landscaped areas.	250	5000
	Buildings, hard cover.	250	NL
Thiocyanate (2)	All proposed uses.	50	NL
Sulphate	Domestic gardens, allotments, landscaped areas.	2000	10000
	Buildings (3)	2000(3)	50000(3)
	Hard Cover	2000	NL
Sulphide	All proposed uses.	250	1000
Sulphur	All proposed uses.	5000	20000
Acidity (pH less than)	Domestic gardens, allotments, landscaped areas.	pH5	pH3
	Buildings, hard cover.	NL	NL

NOTES

NL: No limit set as the contaminant does not pose a particular hazard for this use.
1. Used here as a marker for coal tar, for analytical reasons. See "Problems Arising from the Redevelopment of Gasworks and Similar Sites" Annex A1. (1)
2. See "Problems Arising from the Redevelopment of Gasworks and Similar Sites" for details of analytical methods. (1)
3. See also BRE Digest 250: Concrete in sulphate-bearing soils and groundwater. (4)

Appendix E

CURRENT RESEARCH

There are two main UK research programmes relevant to contami- **E.01** nated land: one managed by the Department of Environment's Contaminated land Branch and the other by the Construction Industry Research and Information Association.

Details of each programme, as provided by the Department of Environment, are set out below:

Department of Environment: Contaminated Land Research Programme

The research programme managed by the Department of the Environment Contaminated Land Branch (CLL1) supports development of policy and the provision of technical guidance on the assessment and treatment of contaminated land. The programme largely follows the commitments given in the Government's response to the Environment Select Committee (Cm 1161) and subsequently in the White Paper "This Common Inheritance" (Cm 1200) and subsequent annual reports. Expenditure in the financial year 1993/94 is expected to be around £1.5 million.

The principal areas of research are:

- Information to help to identify contaminated land;
- Development of Guidelines for investigating sites and assessing risk;
- Reviews of and guidance on treatment techniques;
- Monitoring and quality assurance.

Details of commissioned projects and planned work are given in the Environmental Protection Group Research Newsletter, available each year from the DoE Chief Scientist Group.

The programme complements other Government research. DoE programmes include work on other aspects of environmental protection, planning, land reclamation and construction; details of these are given in "DoE Research Market 1992", Science and Technology Information

Note 1/92, available from the DoE Chief Scientist Group. CLL is also secretariat for the Inter-Departmental Committee for Redevelopment of Contaminated Land (ICRCL), through which other Departments and agencies liaise on relevant research.

The Programme Officer for this research area is:

> Miss J. M. Denner
> Head of Contaminated Land Branch (CLL1)
> Directorate of Pollution Control and Wastes
> Room A228, Romney House
> 43 Marsham Street
> London, SW1P 3PY

Contact points:

> Mark Sumner 071 276 8751
> Colin Grant 071 276 8481

E.02 Contaminated Land Research Programme: Current Projects

(Source: DoE Environmental Protection Group Research Newsletter, June 1993).

Information requests

1. Using documentary sources to identify industrial sites
Guidance on local authority systems for information on land where contamination is known or suspected.

2. Information systems for contaminated land
Guidance on local authority systems for information on land where contamination is known or suspected.

3. Industry profiles (I)
Editing of profiles and preparation for publication.

4. Industry profiles (II)
Editing of profiles and preparation for publication

5. Blight and communication of risks from contaminated land
Analysis of blight problems which may arise when land is known or suspected to be contaminated and of requirements for information and communication of risks.

6. Factors affecting saleability and value of land which may be contaminated
Assessment of factors influencing saleability and value of land which is known or suspected to be contaminated, and recommendations on measures to counteract such effects.

7. Sale and transfer of land which may be contaminated
Guidance on procedures for the sale and transfer of land which is known or suspected to be contaminated.

Risk assessment

8. Coordination of contaminated land risk assessment research
Review and co-ordination of research on development of guidance on assessment of risks from contaminated sites.

9. Framework for risk assessment
A framework for an integrated approach to the assessment and management of the risks associated with contaminated land.

10. Risk assessment and categorisation procedure for sites
Development of a structured risk assessment procedure to categorise sites which may be contaminated.

11. Preliminary site inspection
Guidance on preliminary site inspection techniques.

12. Sampling strategies for contaminated land
Guidance on a cost-effective sampling strategy to provide assurance that significant contamination is not overlooked.

13. Framework for assessment of impact of contaminated sites on water environment
A framework for assessing the pollution potential of contaminated land on ground and surface waters.

14. Generic guideline values for contaminants
A computer model to assess the pathways for human exposure to contaminants, from which generic guidelines can be derived for contaminants in soil.

15. Collation of toxicological data
A critical review of published toxicological standards relevant to their use in derivation of guidelines values for contaminated soil.

613

16. Effects of chemicals in contaminated land on materials
Research into the effects of chemical contaminants in soils on building materials and structures, including evaluation of protective measures and resistance of materials.

17. Review of research on chemicals in contaminated land
Review and assessment of the DoE programme of research on the effect of chemical contaminants in soils on materials used in construction and remedial works on contaminated land.

18. Analysis of asbestos in soils and loose aggregates
Guidance on site assessment for asbestos, including sampling and analytical procedures for asbestos fibres in soils.

19. Laboratory methods for testing contaminants in soils
Critical review of testing methods for contaminants in soils used in laboratories in European countries, particularly those published or under consideration by national and international standard organisations, and of their relationship to guideline values for site assessment.

20. Ingress of landfill gas to buildings
Development of models for ingress of landfill gas to buildings and evaluation of preventive and remedial measures.

21. Fire and explosion hazards
Assessment of possible hazards to buildings from landfill gas and combustible material, and guidance on mitigation of such hazards.

Remedial technologies

22. Remedial technologies for treatment of contaminated land
Review of international technology developments of those suitable for UK use and development of an integrated treatment approach.

23. Protection of housing on contaminated land
Guidance for the construction industry on the selection measures to remove threats to existing and proposed housing and associated developments from solid and liquid contaminants.

24. Selection of remedial measures for contaminated land
Development of a system for selecting remedial treatments for contaminated land.

25. Evaluation of monitoring technologies
Review and evaluation of monitoring technologies for contaminated land.

Planned projects

26. Protection of commercial and industrial development on contaminated land

Guidance for the construction industry on the selection of measures to remove threats to existing and proposed commercial and industrial developments from solid and liquid contaminants.

Note: other projects may be developed from work currently in progress.

E.04 Construction Industry Research and Information Association (CIRIA)

CIRIA manages a number of projects as part of the CLL Programme. The CIRIA Programme *Building on Derelict Land* comprises three main areas: Safe Working Practices, The Contaminated Land Programme, and Methane and Associated Hazards to the Construction Industry. The scheme of research can be shown as follows:

Building on derelict land (1991)

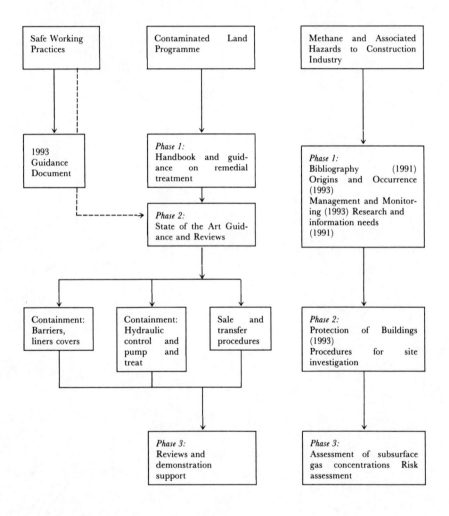

Projects managed by CIRIA   E.05

Sale and transfer of land

Sale and transfer of contaminated land
McDowells

Methane

Methane bibliography
Building Research Establishment

Nature, origins and occurence of methane
British Geological Survey

Methods of detection, sampling, measurement and monitoring methane
Fire Research Station

Priorities for research and information needed by the construction industry in relation to methane hazards
Wardell Armstrong

Protection of new and existing developments from methane and associated gases in the ground
Frank Graham and Partners

Procedures for the investigation of sites for methane and associated gases in the ground
W. S. Atkins

Interpretation of subsurface gas concentrations
Wimpey Environmental

Assessment of degree of risk
Ove Arup

Building on contaminated land

Safe working practices for contaminated sites
W. S. Atkins

Assessment and remedial treatment of contaminated land
ECOTEC

Remedial treatment of contaminated land: in-ground barriers, liners and cover systems
Edmund Nuttall

Remedial treatment of contaminated land: hydraulic control and pump and treat
Scott Wilson Kirkpatrick

617

Contact   Dr. Simon Johnson
point: Construction Industry Research and Information
            Association
            6 Storey's Gate
            London SW1P 3AU

            Telephone: 071 222 8891
            Fax: 071 222 1708

Appendix F

INSURANCE

Generally

Insurance currently offers little comfort to those concerned about **F.01** liability for contaminated land. This is partly a reflection of the general situation for pollution risks coverage, and more specifically the result of the particular problems which contaminated land poses for insurers and underwriters. Insurance is based on the principle of fortuity; that is, the coverage of risks which may or may not occur, rather than inevitable consequences. Writing cover in relation to historic problems which are known to have affected a site is hardly then an attractive insurance proposition. Also, there are often grave difficulties in the case of contaminated land in determining the precise event which triggers any coverage there may be. The build-up of contaminants may take place over a long period, as may their migration towards the target or receptor; there may be a delay before there is any perceptible effect, or before the harm occurs or is discovered; further delay may occur before any claim is made. There is thus much scope for disagreement as to whether a particular claim falls within the relevant policy period.

Public liability indemnity policies

Most companies will carry public liability insurance (usually known in **F.02** the USA as Comprehensive General Liability Insurance, or CGL), Often such cover is part of a composite policy including also Employer's Liability and Product Liability. Initially such policies were written on an occurrence basis, (*i.e.*, occurrences within the policy period, whether the claim was made during the policy period or thereafter) and without any form of pollution exclusion. Despite the absence of any express pollution exclusion, the usual policy wording presents certain difficulties in the case of pollution liabilities:

    (a) The policy will generally be worded so as to indemnify the insured against sums the insured becomes legally liable to pay in respect of claims made against the insured arising from bodily injury or disease, or damage to persons or property. Whilst pollution may have these effects, an equally substantial risk is the imposition of clean-up costs under statutory provisions. Such costs would probably not constitute a third party claim.

(b) Cover is restricted to harm occurring accidentally. This may present great difficulties in that pollution may arise from accidents such as spillages, but equally may be the result of deliberate and conscious acts such as the infilling of land or the discharge of effluent.

(c) Insurance is subject to the general principle that the insured must make full disclosure of all facts known to the insured which are material to the insurer's appraisal of the risk.[1] The test of materiality is whether the circumstance would influence the judgement of a prudent insurer in fixing the premium or determining whether he will take the risk; it is not necessary for the insurer to show that the underwriter's final decision would have been different if the circumstances had been disclosed.[2] An insured who was aware of the possible contamination of a site by whatever means could therefore find that the insurer attempts to avoid liability on the ground of non-disclosure.

Despite these potential difficulties for insureds, the traditional public liability or CGL policy left insurers in an untenable position as pollution-related claims began to increase dramatically in the U.S. in the 1970s and 80s. In particular the issue of cover on an occurrence basis left open the possibility of long-tail exposure, long after the expiry of the policy period and in relation to policies written long before pollution claims could have been foreseen by the underwriters.

Pollution exclusion provisions

F.03   The response of the insurance industry, first in the U.S. and subsequently in the UK, has been to attempt to control the risks referred to above by way of specific policy wordings. The approach adopted initially in the US was to restrict claims relating to gradual pollution. However, it rapidly became apparent that it was difficult to distinguish between gradual pollution and sudden and accidental pollution. This led to a

---

[1] *Carter* v. *Boehm* (1766) 3 Burr. 1905.
[2] *Container Transport International Inc. and Reliance Group Inc.* v. *Oceanus Mutual Underwriting Association (Bermuda) Limited* [1984] 1 Lloyd's Rep. 476; *Highlands Insurance Comany* v. *Continental Insurance Company* [1987] 1 Lloyd's Rep. 109; *Pan Atlantic Insurance Company Ltd. and Another* v. *Pine Top Insurance Co. Ltd.* [1992] 1 Lloyd's Rep. 101.

multitude of inconsistent decisions amongst US courts, with protracted litigation which in many cases involved courts straining policy wordings to reach decisions favourable to the insured. The US market ultimately responded by placing total pollution exclusions (not confined to gradual pollution) on CGL policies. The UK market has not progressed (yet) to total exclusion of pollution cover but rather has evolved a form of wording which restricts pollution cover to "sudden unexpected and unintended" pollution incidents which "take place in their entirety at a specific time and place during the policy period": pollution or contamination which arises out of one incident being deemed to have occurred on the date the insured first becomes aware of circumstances which have given or may give rise to such pollution or contamination.[3]

The UK courts have not had occasion as yet to interpret such wording, but it can be anticipated that similar arguments may be raised as in the US context in due course.

Professional indemnity cover

The flight away from pollution cover in the context of public liability **F.04** policies has been mirrored in professional indemnity policies. PI policies for solicitors and, more seriously, for environmental consultants may now contain exclusions relating to claims for pollution other than the sudden and accidental variety. Exclusions for claims within the US jurisdiction are likely to be substantially wider. Such exclusions present a very serious problem for those seeking to rely on professional advice whether, under a direct appointment or through the medium of a collateral warranty.[4]

Similarly it has recently been announced that insurers of chartered surveyors are to restrict PI cover in relation to advice on contamination, unless the surveyor can demonstrate proven specialist ability in that area.

Environmental impairment liability insurance (EIL)

Insurance products specifically targeted at pollution liability have **F.05** been on the market for some years, though without great success. The market for EIL insurance suffered a collapse in the US in the 1980's.

However, the continued existence of such products, albeit on a limited basis, is perhaps indicative that a market is perceived for them. A

[3] See also Chemical Industries Association, *Liability Insurance: Model Policy Wordings and Guidance Notes* (2nd ed.), 1989.
[4] See Chap. 10.

number of such schemes are currently (November 1993) marketed in the UK, by a Lloyd's syndicate, by two US companies, and by two Swiss companies.[5] The basic approach to such cover is fairly similar, namely:

(a) aggregate limits for all the policyholder's locations;
(b) cover is provided on a named site specific basis only after a stringent surveying and underwriting process (usually at the expense of the proposer);
(c) own site clean up is excluded but is available as a separate product;
(d) no distinction is drawn between gradual and sudden and accidental pollution;
(e) known non-compliance with regulatory standards and "deliberate" acts are excluded;
(f) cover excludes circumstances known to the insured prior to the inception of cover;
(g) a high self insured excess may be applied to each claim; and, most importantly
(h) cover is written on a claims made basis, extending only to claims within the policy period (usually no more than 2–3 years).

Of particular importance to the insurer is the claims made basis, avoiding "long tail liability" and allowing for regular re-appraisal of the risks.

From the point of view of the insured coverage is relatively limited, in some cases only £2 million. As yet the relevant insurers appear unwilling to pool resources so as to offer a more meaningful capacity on a co-insured basis, possibly because of disagreements as to the exact breadth of cover and the relevant policy wordings. The stringent underwriting and surveying procedures also result in the slightly paradoxical situation that those to whom insurance is available are those who probably have relatively little need of it. Within the context of a contaminated site the process of obtaining cover would undoubtedly involve a stringent site investigation and quite possibly the expenditure of substantial sums on precautionary measures. Fresh data would have to be submitted regularly to obtain renewal of the policy, and in the event that such data indicated a failure of containment or control systems, renewal might not be obtainable without further substantial work.

Insurance archaeology

F.06 Coverage under policies written prior to the imposition of pollution exclusions on an "accident" or "occurrence" basis may be extremely valuable to companies faced with environmental claims. Such policies

[5] Some of those products are confined to specific sectors, *e.g.*, chemical industry and waste disposal facilities.

also often included within cover the cost of defending claims as a separate item to the maximum cover. There has thus grown up the practice of "insurance archaeology", of seeking to find old policies which may have been lost or overlooked by the insured.

Having located the policy or series of policies, the difficulty for the insured then lies in proving that the loss falls within the policy. In the UK the onus is on the insured to prove (on the balance of probabilities) that it has suffered a loss covered by the policy, by adducing sufficient evidence to show that the loss is covered by the policy.[6]

This includes establishing the date on which the accident or occurrence took place, which in pollution cases may be very difficult. The US courts have developed a variety of alternative approaches to the triggering of coverage:[7] these include the actual date of injury or damage, the period of exposure to a potentially harmful event, the time at which injury or damage manifest itself, and what is called "the continuous trigger" or "triple trigger" theory whereby all policies in effect from the date of the first exposure to the date of manifestation of injury are obliged to respond to a claim.

Courts in the UK have not been called upon to examine the coverage trigger in pollution cases. The word "occurrence" was considered in the case of *Kelly* v. *Norwich Union Fire Insurance Society Ltd.*[8] where a major water leak before the inception of the relevant policy resulted in damage some years later, during the policy period. It was held that the relevant occurrence was the original leak and not the later damage: the consequential damage was not an "event" to which the policy was required to respond.

The future

It is not clear where the developments described above will lead. If **F.07** anything, the attitudes of insurers to pollution risks are likely to harden.[9] Insurers and indeed reinsurers are reappraising the way in which even "sudden and accidental" pollution cover is provided. Some insurers are precluded by their reinsurance treaties from covering "toxic waste"

---

[6] *Munro, Brice & Co.* v. *War Risks Association Limited* [1918] 2 K.B. 78; *Regina Fur Company Limited* v. *Bossom* [1958] 2 Lloyd's Rep. 425.

[7] This section relies heavily on a paper by Mr Oliver J. Kinsey, Simmons & Simmons, on *Insurance Coverage Issues,* given at the 4th Annual Conference on the Insurance Aspects of Pollution, Environmental Improvement and Waste (June 30, 1992).

[8] [1989] 2 All E.R. 888.

[9] This section relies heavily on a memorandum by Syndicate 386/683, Underwriters at Lloyd's (Michael Payne & Others) produced as evidence to House of Lords Sub-Committee C (Environmental and Social Affairs) in relation to the EC Green Paper on Remedying Environmental Damage.

disposal, and some major insurers may take unilateral decision to abstain from certain areas of business. Another aspect of the problem is that most reinsurance capacity comes from continental European reinsurers, who may favour their own domestic insurers so far as providing EIL capacity is concerned.

What is clear is that even if a system of compulsory insurance for certain types of activities were to be introduced, there is no guarantee whatsoever that insurers and reinsurers would respond to that requirement: thus leaving industry in the difficult position of having to achieve some form of mutual self insurance management. Indeed insurers would not welcome a compulsory system for two reasons: first, it would encourage the tendency to see such insurance as being predominantly there for the benefit of the injured party rather than the insured and, secondly, it would cast insurers in the role of unwilling licensors of the operations of certain sectors of industry.

The overall message, therefore, is that at the present time and for the foreseeable future insurance offers little comfort in relation to liability for contaminated land.

INDEX

(All references are to paragraph numbers)

ABATEMENT NOTICE
see also Abatement of nuisance
appeal against, 2.68, 2.71
execution of works, 2.68
liability, 2.71
joint and several, 2.71
"person responsible", 2.71
local authority, duty to serve, 2.68
requirements of, 2.68
Scotland, in, 13.04
statutory nuisance, 2.02, 2.68
summary proceedings, 2.68
by persons aggrieved, 2.70, 2.71
suspension of, 2.68
ABATEMENT OF NUISANCE
see also Abatement notice
entry onto neighbours land, 2.39
generally, 2.39
local authority, by, 2.69
cost recovery, 2.69, 2.71
Scotland, in, 13.04
works of
neighbours land, on, 2.39
one's own land, on, 2.39
ABATTOIRS, EFFLUENT FROM, 5.38
ABBEYSTEAD PUMPING STATION, LAN-
CASHIRE, 2.28
ABSTRACTION LICENCE, 6.04, 6.34,
6.35
see also Abstraction of water
application for, 6.34, 6.35
boreholes, construction of, 6.34
effect of, 6.34
pollution and, 6.35
riparian owners, 6.34
ABSTRACTION OF WATER
see also Abstraction licence
generally, 6.34
information on abstraction
sources, 6.36
landowners' right of, 2.22, 6.34
interference with, nuisance, as,
2.23

ABSTRACTION OF WATER—*cont.*
percolating water, 2.22
ACCEPTABLE DAILY INTAKE (ADI),
4.22
ACCESS AGREEMENT FOR SITE INVES-
TIGATIONS, A–05
ACCESS TO ENVIRONMENTAL INFORMA-
TION *SEE* INFORMATION
ACCIDENTAL SPILLAGE
active, 2.03
passive, 2.03
water pollution by, 2.48
ACID WORKS, CONTAMINATION FROM,
4.04
ACIDS
concrete foundations, aggressive
effects on, 1.02
contamination by, 1.02, 4.04
skin, contact with, 1.02
special waste, as, 5.32
"ACTION FOR CITIES" INITIATIVE,
9.01, 9.09
ADVICE, PROFESSIONAL *see*
CONSULTANTS
AESTHETIC EFFECTS, SOIL CONTAMINA-
TION, OF, 1.02
AGGRESSIVE CHEMICAL EFFECT, BUILD-
ING MATERIALS AND SERVICES, ON,
1.02, 4.12, 4.19
AGRICULTURE
abattoirs, effluent from, 5.38
activities of, controls over, 5.01
animal carcases, disposal of, 5.39
animal processing wastes, 5.38,
5.39
anthrax contamination, 7.26
Code of Good Agriculture Practice for the Protection of Soil,
5.39
contaminative use, as, 3.03

AGRICULTURE—*cont.*
Control of Pollution (Silage, Slurry and Agricultural Fuel Oil) Regulations 1991, 5.01, 5.38, 6.10
European Agricultural Guidance and Guarantee Fund (EAGGF), 9.27
fuel oil
Control of Pollution (Silage, Slurry and Agricultural Fuel Oil) Regulations 1991, 5.01, 5.38, 6.10
storage of, 5.39
generally, 5.38
milk and dairy products, disposal of, 5.39
nitrates, 5.38, 5.39, 6.03
pesticides, 5.38, 5.39
sensitivity of site use, 4.09
sewage sludge, 1.01, 5.38, 6.40
DoE Code of Practice, 5.38
storage of, 5.39
sheep dip, disposal of, 5.39
silage, storage of, 5.39
Sludge (Use in Agriculture) Regulations 1989, 5.38
storage installations and stores, 5.38
waste from, 5.25, 5.38, 5.39
AIR POLLUTION
air pollution control, 5.15
registers relating to, 3.10
Indoor Air Pollution, 1.07
receptor group, identification of, 4.22
AIRBORNE PARTICULATE MATTER, 1.01, 2.03, 2.43
lead, 2.56, 7.23
AIRFIELDS, CONTAMINATION FROM, 4.04
ALDRIN, 5.14
ALKALI WORKS, CONTAMINATION FROM, 4.04
ALKALIS
contamination by, 4.04
earth metals and their oxides, prescribed for release to land, 5.14
metals and their oxides, prescribed for release to land, 5.14
special waste, as, 5.32
ALLOTMENTS, SENSITIVITY OF SITE USE, 4.09

ALUMINIUM SULPHATE, DRINKING WATER, IN, 2.37, 6.31
AMBER VALLEY, DERBYSHIRE, *Preamble*, 1.05
AMENITY, CONDITION OF LAND ADVERSELY AFFECTING, SECTION 215 NOTICES, 2.73–2.77
AMENITY AREAS
contaminated soil in, 4.12
sensitivity of site use, 4.09
AMMONIA, BATHING WATER, IN, 6.41
AMMONIUM ION, BUILDING MATERIALS AND SERVICES, AGGRESSIVE EFFECTS ON, 4.12
ANIMALS
burial sites
diseased animals, where, records of, C–05
groundwater protection zones and, 6.14
carcases, disposal of, 5.39
fluoride, ingestion of, 5.39
ingestion of contaminants by, 1.02, 5.39
processing of
prescribed processes in, 5.12
waste from, 5.38, 5.39
ANTHRAX, 7.26
ANTIMONY AND ANTIMONY COMPOUNDS, SPECIAL WASTE, AS, 5.32
APPRAISAL *see* INVESTIGATION AND APPRAISAL
AQUATIC ENVIRONMENT, POLLUTION OF, EC DIRECTIVE ON, 6.03, 6.08
AQUIFER
see also Groundwater
chalk, contamination of, 2.34, 2.50
contamination of, 1.02, 2.26, 6.01
chalk aquifers, 2.34, 2.50
chlorinated hydrocarbons, by, 2.55n
damages for, 2.36
joint and several liability, 2.40
solvents, by, 2.23, 2.55n, 6.20
definition, 6.07
major, 6.14
minor, 6.14
receptor group, identification of, 4.22
ARCHITECTS, CLEAN-UP OPERATIONS AND, 7.37
ARMLEY, LEEDS, 1.05

ARSENIC, 1.02, 1.05, 4.12
  compounds of, special waste, as, 5.32
  dangerous substance, as, 6.25
  dust, absorption into skin, 7.18
  food plants and crops, accumulation in, 1.02
ASBESTOS, 1.01, 1.05, 4.04, 4.12
  Asbestos (Licensing) Regulations 1983, 7.22
  blue, 1.05
  clean-up operations, 7.22
  Control of Asbestos at Work Regulations 1987, 7.22
  demolition, from, 2.56
  dust, 1.05, 7.18
  effluent containing, 6.38
  HSE Approved Code of Practice on Control of Asbestos at Work, 7.22
  ICRCL Guidance Note on, 4.19
  inhalation of, 1.02
  manufacture of
    contamination from, 1.01, 1.05, 4.04
    contaminative use, as, 3.03, 4.04
  products of, manufacture of, contaminative use, as, 3.03
  railway-carriage breaking, from, 2.56
  ship-breaking, from, 2.56
  special waste, as, 5.32
ASPHYXIATION, RISK OF, AT WORK, 7.18
ASSOCIATIONS FOR THE PROTECTION OF THE ENVIRONMENT, COUNCIL OF EUROPE CONVENTION AND, 2.83
ATMOSPHERIC POLLUTION see AIR POLLUTION
ATRAZINE, 5.14
AUSTRALIA
  ACT, 13.34
  contaminated land in, 13.29–13.35
  New South Wales, 13.29
  Northern Territory, 13.35
  Queensland, 13.30
  South Australia, 13.33
  Victoria, 13.31
  Western Australia, 13.32
AZIDES
  prescribed for release to land, 5.14
  special waste, as, 5.32

AZINPHOS-METHYL, 5.14

"BAD EGGS" see HYDROGEN SULPHIDE
BARIUM COMPOUNDS, SPECIAL WASTE, AS, 5.32
BATHING WATER
  contamination of, 6.41
  pH value of, 6.41
  quality of, EC directive on, 6.03, 6.41
BATNEEC, 5.13, 5.14
BEACHES, CONTAMINATION OF, 6.41
BENTLEY MILL LANE, WALSALL, 1.02N, 2.55N, 6.01
BENZENE, 4.04
BENZO-PYRENES, EXPOSURE TO, 7.18
BERYLLIUM AND BERYLLIUM COMPOUNDS, SPECIAL WASTE, AS, 5.32
BEST AVAILABLE TECHNIQUES NOT ENTAILING EXCESSIVE COST (BATNEEC), 5.13, 5.14
BIOCIDES, SPECIAL WASTE, AS, 5.32
BIOREMEDIATION, 7.07
BIRMINGHAM HEARTLANDS, 9.06
BITUMEN
  contamination by, 4.19
  processes, prescribed processes in, 5.12
BITUMINOUS MATERIAL, MANUFACTURE OF, CONTAMINATIVE USE, AS, 3.03
BLACK COUNTRY DEVELOPMENT CORPORATION, 9.06
BLIGHT, 1.06, 3.01, 11.01
BLUE ASBESTOS, 1.05
  see also Asbestos
"BLUE BILLY" GASWORKS WASTE, 1.05, 7.18
BOILLY LANE, KILLAMARSH, SHEFFIELD, 1.05
BOLSOVER, DERBYSHIRE, 1.05
BOREHOLES
  abstraction licence, 6.34
  contamination of, 1.05, 2.03, 2.22
  joint and several liability, 2.40
  organic solvents, by, 2.55n
BORON
  compounds of, special waste, as, 5.32
  phytotoxic effects of, 1.02
  soil, in, 1.02
BREACH OF CONDITION NOTICES, REGISTER OF, 3.10
BRISTOL DEVELOPMENT CORPORATION, 9.06

BRITISH COAL, 1.05, 2.46, 9.27

BRITISH STANDARDS INSTITUTION, DRAFT FOR DEVELOPMENT DD 175: 1988, *CODE OF PRACTICE FOR THE IDENTIFICATION OF POTENTIALLY CONTAMINATED LAND AND ITS INVESTIGATION*, C–01, 4.02, 4.03, 4.04, 4.07, 4.09, 4.10, 4.12, 7.17, 10.07

BRITISH WATERWAYS BOARD, ENQUIRIES OF, 11.05

BROMOXYNIL, GROUNDWATER, IN, 6.09

BROMOXYNIL OCTANOATE, GROUNDWATER, IN, 6.09

BUILDING CONTRACTS
architects, 7.37
design and build contracts, 7.41
engineers, 7.38
generally, 7.35
insurance, 7.44
JCT '80, 7.42
  contractor's obligation under, 7.39
  development under, 7.36
  variations, 7.40
effect on payment, 7.40
JCT '81, 7.41, 7.43
  insurance, 7.44
  variations, 7.42
cost effects, 7.42

BUILDING CONTROL *see* BUILDING REGULATIONS 1991

BUILDING MATERIALS AND SERVICES, AGGRESSIVE CHEMICAL EFFECT ON, 1.02, 4.12, 4.19

BUILDING REGULATIONS 1991, 1.09, 8.16
dangerous and offensive substances, 8.16
preparation of site, 8.16

BUILDING RESEARCH ESTABLISHMENT (BRE), 1.07, 4.19

BURIAL SITES
animals, of *see* Animals
cemetries *see* Cemetries and graveyards

BUSINESS ARCHIVES COUNCIL, C–05

CABLES, UNDERGROUND, FIRE AND, 1.02

CADMIUM, 1.02, 1.05, 4.04
compounds of
  prescribed for release to water, 5.14

CADMIUM—*cont.*
compounds of—*cont.*
  special waste, as, 5.32
drinking water, in, 6.30
food plants and crops, accumulation in, 1.02
prescribed for release to water, 5.14
sewage sludge, in, 5.38
soil, in, 1.02, 4.12, 5.38
special waste, as, 5.32

CALLYWHITE LANE INDUSTRIAL SITE, DRONFIELD, 1.05

CAMBOURNE, CORNWALL, 1.05

CAMELFORD, CORNWALL, 2.37, 6.31

CANADA, CONTAMINATED LAND IN, 13.17

CANALS, CONTAMINATED DREDGINGS FROM, 2.56

CANCER
carcinogens, skin absorption of, 7.18
pitch residue dusts and, 7.18
substances causing, 7.18

CAR PARKS, SENSITIVITY OF SITE USE, 4.09

CARBON DIOXIDE, LANDFILL SITES, FROM, 1.05

CARBON MONOXIDE, NATURALLY OCCURRING, 1.07

CARCINOGENS *see* CANCER

CARDIFF DEVELOPMENT CORPORATION, 9.06

CATCHPITS, CONSTRUCTION OF, WATER UNDERTAKERS, BY, 2.53

CATTLE *see* ANIMALS; LIVESTOCK

CEMETRIES AND GRAVEYARDS
development relating to use of land as, 6.15
groundwater protection zones and, 6.14

CENTRAL DIRECTORATE OF ENVIRONMENTAL POLLUTION, 1.09
Contaminated Land Branch, 1.09

CENTRAL MANCHESTER DEVELOPMENT CORPORATION, 9.06

CERAMICS MANUFACTURE, CONTAMINATIVE USE, AS, 3.03

CERTIFICATE OF LAWFULNESS OF EXISTING USE OR DEVELOPMENT, REGISTER OF, 3.10

CERTIFICATE OF LAWFULNESS OF PROPOSED USE OR DEVELOPMENT, REGISTER OF, 3.10

CESSPITS, LEAKAGE INTO WATER SUP-
PLIES, 6.01
CHALK AQUIFERS, CONTAMINATION OF,
2.34, 2.50
CHANGE OF USE, 5.01, 5.08
CHATHAM NAVAL DOCKYARDS, WASTE
FROM, 1.05
CHEMICAL INDUSTRY
contamination from, 1.01, 1.04,
4.04
contaminative use, as, 3.03
prescribed processes in, 5.12
CHEMICAL RELEASE INVENTORY, PRO-
POSED, 5.16
CHEMSTAR SITE, GREATER MANCHES-
TER, 1.05, 9.12
CHIEF INSPECTOR
powers of entry, 2.43
prohibition notices, 2.43
radioactive waste, site records of,
5.37
CHILDREN
soil, ingestion of, 1.02, 4.12
special waste, ingestion of, 5.32
trespassers, as, 2.33
CHLORATES, SPECIAL WASTE, AS, 5.32
CHLORIDES, AGGRESSIVE EFFECT ON
BUILDING MATERIALS AND SER-
VICES, 1.02, 4.12
CHLORINATED HYDROCARBONS, CON-
TAMINATION BY, 2.55N
CHLORINATED SOLVENTS, 1.05, 2.03,
2.22, 2.49, 2.50, 6.01
organic, 6.01
CHLORINE, DRINKING WATER, DISINFEC-
TION OF, 6.28
CHLORPYRIFOS, GROUNDWATER, 6.09
CHOLOROFORM, EFFLUENT CONTAINING,
6.38
CHROME WASTE, CONTAMINATION BY,
2.55N
CHROMIUM
contamination by, 4.04
dangerous substance, as, 6.25
hexavalent chromium com-
pounds, special waste, as,
5.32
sewage sludge, in, 5.38
CITY ACTION TEAMS (CATs), 9.09,
9.18, 9.20
CITY CHALLENGE, 9.01, 9.09, 9.20

CITY GRANT, 9.01, 9.09, 9.16, 9.20
derelict land grant
compared with, 9.17
relationship with, 9.11
intention of, 9.16
payment of, 9.16
projects covered by, 9.16
CIVIL LIABILITY
Building Regulations, breach of
duty imposed by, 8.16
cause of contamination, 2.03
generally, 2.03
nature of damage, 2.03
nature of, 2.02
negligence see Negligence
nuisance see Nuisance
"polluter pays" principle, 1.06,
2.02, 9.12
EC and, 1.10, 2.81, 2.82, 2.83,
9.26
Rylands v. Fletcher, rule in see
Rylands v. Fletcher, rule in
Scotland, in, 13.02
statutory duty, breach of see Statutory duty, breach of
trespass see Trespass
CLEAN WATER SUPPLY, 6.27–6.36
water undertakers, 6.27
CLEAN-UP
anthrax, 7.26
asbestos, 7.22
bioremediation, 7.07
building contracts see Building
contracts
buried explosives, 7.25
cleanliness, standards of, 7.15,
14.12
construction and, 7.17
contaminated soil
excavation of, 7.02, 7.03
mixing with uncontaminated
soil, 7.28
duty of care
generally, 7.31
nature of, 7.32
transfer documentation, 7.33
electro-kinetic techniques, 7.09
encapsulation, 7.05
explosives, buried, 7.25
funding of see Funding
groundwater, contaminated, 7.13
health and safety law, 7.18–7.27
contaminated land, development of, 7.18

CLEAN-UP—*cont.*
  health and safety law—*cont.*
    contractual matters and design
      and management, 7.27
    general statutory duties, 7.19
    risk assessment, 7.20
  in-situ vitrification, 7.10
  isolation, 7.05
  land values and, 7.01
  lead, 7.23
  methodologies, 7.01–7.17
  monitoring, 7.16
  NRA policy, 6.19
  off-site disposal, 7.04
  problems of, 8.15
  purposes of, 7.01
  radioactive contamination, 7.24
  radioactive waste, 7.30
  remedial action, forms of,
    7.02–7.17
  soil vapour extraction, 7.06
  soil washing, 7.08
  special waste, 7.29
  stabilisation and solidification,
    7.12
  standards of cleanliness, 7.15
  techniques, selection of, 7.14
  thermal methods, 7.11
  urban commons and, 8.15
  validation, 7.16
  waste brokers and dealers, regis-
    tration of, 7.34A
  waste carrier registration, 7.34
  waste management licence *see*
    Waste management licence
  wildlife habitats and, 8.15
CLEANLINESS, STANDARDS OF, 7.15,
  14.12
CLEARANCE *see* DEMOLITION AND
  CLEARANCE
COAGULANTS, DRINKING WATER, TREAT-
  MENT WITH, 6.28
COAL
  bituminous material from, manu-
    facture of, contaminative use,
    as, 3.03
  carbonization plants, contamina-
    tion from, 4.04
  mines
    see also Mining
    gas from, 1.05
COALITE CHEMICAL WORKS, BOLSOVER,
  DERBYSHIRE, 1.05

COASTAL WATERS
  see also Water
  contamination of, 1.02, 6.41
  controlled waters, as, 2.45
  quality of, 6.26
COATINGS
  manufacture of, prescribed pro-
    cesses in, 5.12
  metals used in, contaminants, as,
    4.04
  protective, aggressive chemical
    effect on, 1.02
CODE OF PRACTICE FOR THE IDENTI-
  FICATION OF POTENTIALLY CON-
  TAMINATED LAND AND ITS
  INVESTIGATION, BRITISH STAND-
  ARDS INSTITUTION, 4.02, 4.03,
  4.04
COKE
  manufacture of
    contamination from, 1.04
    contaminative use, as, 3.03
  particles, flammable nature of,
    1.02
  underground fires caused by, 7.18
COLIFORMS, BATHING WATER, IN, CON-
  TROL OF, 6.41
COLLECTION AND DISPOSAL OF WASTE
  REGULATIONS 1988, 5.25, 5.38,
  7.28A
  waste management licensing,
    exemptions from, 7.18A,
    7.28B
COMBUSTIBLE SUBSTANCES, 1.02, 4.04,
  4.12
  see also Coal; Coke; Fire
  development on sites containing,
    8.08
COMBUSTION PROCESSES, PRESCRIBED
  PROCESSES IN, 5.12
COMMERCIAL BUILDINGS
  aggressive chemical effect on, 4.12
  sensitivity of site use, 4.09
COMMERCIAL CONFIDENTIALITY, 3.15
COMMERCIAL CONTAMINATIVE USE
  SEARCHES, 4.06A
COMMERCIAL RISK ASSESSMENT, 4.24
COMMERCIAL WASTE
  final deposit of, contaminative
    use, as, 3.03
  treatment by chemical or thermal
    means, contaminative use,
    as, 3.03

COMMITTEE OF EXPERTS ON COMPENSA-
TION FOR DAMAGE CAUSED TO THE
ENVIRONMENT (CJ-EN), 2.83
COMMONS ENVIRONMENT COMMITTEE
see HOUSE OF COMMONS
ENVIRONMENT COMMITTEE
COMMUNITY SUPPORT FRAMEWORKS,
9.27
COMPENSATION, JOINT COMPENSATION
FUNDS, 14.09
COMPENSATION ORDERS, 2.78
appeal against, 2.78
damages and, 2.78
CONCRETE FOUNDATIONS
aggressive chemical effect on
acids, 1.02
chlorides, 1.02, 4.12
sulphate, 1.02, 4.12, 4.19
CONSTRUCTION (DESIGN AND MANAGE-
MENT) REGULATIONS AND
APPROVED CODE OF PRACTICE,
PROPOSED, 7.27
CONSTRUCTION INDUSTRY RESEARCH
AND INFORMATION ASSOCIATION
(CIRIA), E–04–E–05, 1.06,
11.03
Building on Derelict Land, E–04
CONSTRUCTION WORK, CONTACT WITH
CONTAMINANTS DURING, 4.12
CONSULTANTS, 10.01–10.12
additional services, A–07
appointment of
agreement, A–07
solicitor, role in, 10.05
breach by, damages for, 10.08
brief for, 10.04
collateral warranties, A–07, A–08
confidentiality, A–07, 10.06
contract, terms of, 10.06
confidentiality, 10.06
implied, 10.07
codes of practice, 10.07
cost, estimation of, 10.07
design, 10.07
legal issues, 10.07
site investigation, 10.07
specialist advice, 10.07
indemnity, 10.06
insurance, 10.06
liability, exclusion or limitation
of, 10.06
reliance on report
client, 10.08

CONSULTANTS—*cont.*
contract, terms of—*cont.*
reliance on report—*cont.*
third party, 10.06, 10.09
site conditions and safety, 10.06
sub-contractors, 10.06
third parties, 10.06
damages for breach by, 10.08
documents, copyright, A–07
drawings
copyright, A–07
provision of, A–07
expenses and disbursements,
A–07
fees, A–07
period for payment and interest, A–07
VAT and, A–07
indemnity, A–07
information on, sources of, 10.03
insurance, A–07, 10.12
negligence, 10.07
Normal Services, A–07
period for payment and interest,
A–07
professional indemnity insurance,
A–07, 10.12
proposal
costs, A–06
report, production and form of,
A–06
request for, A–06
scope of work, A–06
terms and conditions, A–06
timing and capacity, A–06
report, A–07
copyright, A–07
production and form of, A–06
reliance on
client, 10.08
third party, 10.06, 10.09
selection of, 10.02
sources of information on, 10.03
standard of care, A–07, 10.07
sub-contractors, 10.06, 10.11
third parties
extension of duty to, 10.10
reliance on report, 10.06, 10.09
warranties, collateral, A–07, A–08
CONTAMINATED LAND, REPORT OF THE
HOUSE OF COMMONS ENVIRON-
MENT COMMITTEE, 1.04, 1.07,
1.11, 7.01

CONTAMINATED LAND
defining
  Discussion,, 1.04
  harm test *Discussion*
  NATO Committee on Challenges to Modern Society (CCMS), *Discussion*
  derelict land distinguished, *Discussion*
  harm test, *Discussion*
identifying, 1.06, 1.08
  procedure, 14.03
  recommendations, 14.02
institutions dealing with, 1.09
policy approaches, 1.06
valuation of *see* Valuation of contaminated land
CONTAMINATION
assessment of, D–01–D–03
consequences of, 1.02
historic, 2.43, 2.48
  old landfills, 2.55
investigation of *see* Investigation and appraisal
naturally occurring, 1.07
pollution distinguished, *Discussion*
CONTAMINATIVE USE, 3.03
commercial searches, 4.06A
potential, 3.10
CONTRIBUTORY NEGLIGENCE, NUISANCE AND, 2.20
CONTROL OF ASBESTOS AT WORK REGULATIONS 1987, 7.22
CONTROL OF LEAD AT WORK REGULATIONS 1980, 7.23
CONTROL OF PESTICIDES REGULATIONS 1986, 5.01, 5.38, 6.11
CONTROL OF POLLUTION ACT 1974 (COPA), 5.20
consents under, 41
controlled waste, definition, 5.21
exemptions, 5.21
shortcomings of, 5.22
site licensing system, 5.20, 5.22, 5.23
special waste, 5.31
CONTROL OF POLLUTION (SILAGE, SLURRY AND AGRICULTURAL FUEL OIL) REGULATIONS 1991, 5.01, 5.38, 6.10
CONTROL OF POLLUTION (SPECIAL WASTE) REGULATIONS 1980, 5.01, 5.31, 5.32, 5.33, 7.33

CONTROL OF POLLUTION (SUPPLY AND USE OF INJURIOUS SUBSTANCES) REGULATIONS 1986, 7.22N
CONTROL OF SUBSTANCES HAZARDOUS TO HEALTH REGULATIONS 1988 (COSHH), 7.21
CONTROLLED WASTE
see also Special waste
definition
  COPA, in, 5.21
  EPA, in, 2.56, 2.60, 5.24
  exceptions to, 5.25
deposits of
  control over, 5.01, 5.20
  noxious gases or noxious liquids caused by, 2.60
duty of care, 5.01, 5.30
exemptions from licensing, 5.25
keeping of, 2.65
  control over, 5.01
old landfill, in, 2.60
treatment of, control over, 5.01
CONTROLLED WATERS
definition, 2.45
pollution of, 2.44
  see also Water pollution
  monitoring of, 3.09
  prevention of, 5.01
  sewage effluent, by, 2.44, 2.47
  trade effluent, by, 2.44, 2.47
quality objectives for, 6.12
CONVENTION ON CIVIL LIABILITY FOR DAMAGE RESULTING FROM ACTIVITIES DANGEROUS TO THE ENVIRONMENT, 2.83
CONVEYANCING, LAW COMMISSION STANDING COMMITTEE ON CONVEYANCING, 1.06
COPPER, 1.02, 4.04, 4.12
compounds of, special waste, as, 5.32
dangerous substance, as, 6.25
drinking water, in, 6.30
food plants and crops, accumulation in, 1.02
phytotoxic effects of, 1.02
sewage sludge, in, 5.38
watercourse, contamination of, by, 2.55n, 6.01
CORPORATE INSOLVENCY
Insolvency Act administrators, 12.11

CORPORATE INSOLVENCY—*cont.*
liquidators, 12.12
receivership, 12.10
CORPORATE TRANSACTIONS
assets, sale of, 12.01
company accounts, 12.09
generally, 12.01
indemnities, 12.03, 12.06
contaminated land indemnities,
precedent, A–18
cross-indemnities, 12.07
date of application, 12.07
drafting problems, 12.07
environmental indemnities, precedent, A–17
negligence and, 12.07
practical problems with, 12.08
information, request for, 12.02,
A–15
investigations, 12.02
liability
company accounts, reference in,
12.09
listing particulars, reference in,
12.09
polluter, of, 12.01
listing particulars, 12.09
originator of contamination,
liability of, 12.01
parties to, 1.03
polluter, liability of, 12.01
risk allocation, 12.04
shares, sale of, 12.01
warranties, 12.02, 12.03, 12.05,
A–16
date of application of, 12.07
drafting problems, 12.07
practical problems with, 12.08
CORROSIVE SUBSTANCES
eyes, contact with, 1.02
skin, contact with, 1.02, 7.18
COST RECOVERY
abatement by local authority,
2.69, 2.71
owner, from, 2.63, 2.69
section 215 notices, 2.76
waste regulation authorities, by,
2.58, 2.63
water undertakers, by, 2.53
COUNCIL OF EUROPE CONVENTION ON
CIVIL LIABILITY FOR DAMAGE
RESULTING FROM ACTIVITIES
DANGEROUS TO THE ENVIRON-
MENT, 2.83

COUNCIL OF MORTGAGE LENDERS
(CML), 3.05
COUNTRYSIDE COUNCIL, ENQUIRIES OF,
11.05
COUNTRYSIDE FOR WALES, 6.11
COVENANTS OF SALE ON PART OF LAND,
A–09
CRIMINAL COURTS
see also Criminal liability
powers of
compensation orders, 2.78
appeal against, 2.78
damages and, 2.78
confiscation of proceeds of
offence, 2.80
depriving offender of property,
2.79
CRIMINAL LIABILITY
see also Criminal courts
failure to prevent escape, for, 2.65
generally, 2.02
water pollution, for, 2.44–2.49
see also under Water
CROPS
uptake of contaminants by, 1.02,
4.12, 5.39
see also Phytotoxicity
CRYPTOSPORIDIOSIS, 6.31
CYANIDES
bathing water, in, 6.41
clean-up of
electro-kinetic techniques, 7.09
soil washing, 7.08
exposure to, 7.18
ground and surface water, in, 4.12
inorganic, special waste, as, 5.32
soil, in, 4.12
waste, 5.19

DAMAGES
aggravated, 2.37
aquifer pollution cases, 2.36
compensation orders and, 2.78
consequential, 2.36
consultant, breach by, 10.08
continuing nuisance, 2.36
cost of reinstatement, 2.04
death, 2.36
development potential of land,
2.36
diminution in value of property,
2.04, 2.36
exemplary, 2.37

DAMAGES—*cont.*
  foreseeability and, 2.36
  injunction, in lieu of, 2.36
  migration of pollutants, 2.36
  negligence, 2.36, 2.37, 2.41
  nuisance, 2.23, 2.36, 2.37, 2.41
  personal injury, 2.36, 2.41
  point at which material damage
    occurs, 2.36
  property
    damage to, 2.36
    development potential, 2.36
    diminution in value, 2.04, 2.36
  public nuisance, 2.37
  Rylands v. *Fletcher*, 2.36, 2.37
  statutory duty, breach of, 2.37,
    2.41
  trespass, for, 2.04
DANGEROUS SUBSTANCES, 2.83, 6.25
  aquatic environment, discharge
    into, 6.25
  black list, 6.25
  Building Regulations 1991 and,
    8.16
  EC directives on, 6.25, 6.38
  grey list, 6.25
  Red List, 6.25, 6.38
DDT, ISOMERS OF, 5.14
DECOMMISSIONING OF INDUSTRIAL
    FACILITIES, CONTAMINATION
    CAUSED BY, 1.01
DEMOLITION AND CLEARANCE
  asbestos released by, 2.56
  contact with contaminants dur-
    ing, 4.12
  industrial facilities, of, contamina-
    tion caused by, 1.01
  sampling, in process of, 4.11
DEMOS, 9.25
DENMARK
  identification of sites, 13.27
  liability issues, 13.27
  limitation periods and retrospec-
    tivity, 13.27
  National Agency for Environmen-
    tal Protection, 13.27
  register of contaminated land,
    3.02
DENSE NON-AQUEOUS PHASE LIQUIDS
    (DNAPLS), WATER POLLUTION
    BY, 6.01

DEPARTMENT OF ENVIRONMENT
    (DoE), 1.09
  Code of Practice, agricultural use
    of sewage sludge, 5.38
  contaminated land, defining
    Discussion
  Contaminated Land Research
    Programme, E–01, E–02
  derelict land, estimates of, 1.04
  environmental assessment, guide
    to, 8.06
  funding from, 9.01
  Grants in Urban Areas, 9.09
  groundwater protection, 6.11
  information
    freedom of access to, Guidance
      on, 3.13, 3.14, 3.15
    sources of, C–02
  landfill sites, survey of, C–05
  planning appeals, 6.11
  Private Water Supplies, 6.32
  waste management licences,
    appeals on, 6.11
DEPARTMENT OF TRADE AND INDUSTRY
    ENVIRONMENT UNIT, 9.22
  Demos Scheme, 9.23
DEPOSIT OF POISONOUS WASTE (NOTI-
    FICATION OF REMOVAL OR
    DEPOSIT) REGULATIONS 1972,
    5.19
DERELICT LAND, 1.06, 7.18
  *Assessment of the Effectiveness of Der-
    elict Land Grant in Reclaiming
    Land for Development*, 9.11
  contaminated land distinguished,
    Discussion
  definition, *Discussion*
  Derelict Land Survey 1988, 1.04
  DoE estimates of, 1.04
  extent of, 1.04
  Government definition, *Discussion*,
    9.11
  grant aid
    see also Derelict land grant
    Discussion, 5.06
  *Proposals to Prevent Land Becoming
    Derelict*, 1.06, 2.77, 5.05
  reclamation of, 1.06, 8.14
  trespassers on, occupiers' liability
    to, 2.33
DERELICT LAND GRANT, 9.01, 9.04,
    9.09
  amount of, 9.14

DERELICT LAND GRANT—*cont.*
application for, 9.15
availability of, 9.13
City Grant
compared with, 9.17
relationship with, 9.11
contaminated land and, 9.12
costs eligible for, 9.12, 9.14
green-field state, definition, 9.11
legal basis, 9.10
policy, 9.11
"polluter pays" principle and, 9.12
restrictions on, 9.13
Urban Programme Grant, relationship with, 9.11
DERELICT LAND SURVEY 1988, 1.04
DEVELOPMENT
building control *see* Building Regulations 1991
clean-up, problems of, 8.15
environmental assessment, 8.06
groundwater, protection of, 8.11
health and safety law relating to, general requirements, 7.18
landfill sites, on *see* Landfill sites
"overall advantage" issues, 8.14
plan *see* Development plan
planning conditions *see* Planning conditions
planning obligations *see* Planning obligations
planning permission, need for, 8.02
policy guidance on, 8.03
potential for, interference with, damages for, 2.36
proposed
certificate of, register of, 3.10
consultation requirements, 6.15
notice of, 3.10
sites containing combustible materials, 8.08
town and country planning controls, 8.02–8.15
water protection issues, 8.11
wildlife habitats, 8.15
DEVELOPMENT CONTROL SYSTEM, 5.05
DEVELOPMENT PLAN
NRA policies and, 6.18
policies, 5.04, 8.04
examples of, 8.05
waste policies and, 5.09

DI-ISOCYANATE PROCESSES, PRESCRIBED PROCESSES IN, 5.12
DIBENZODIOXINS, 7.22A
DIBENZOFURANS, 7.22A
DICHLOROETHANE, 1, 2-DIC-HLOROETHANE, 5.14
DICHLORVOS, 5.14
DIELDRIN, 5.14
DIESEL OIL
contamination by, 4.19
leakage of, 2.49
DIOXINS
see also PCBs
contamination by, 1.05
dibenzodioxins, formation of, 7.22A
dibenzofurans, formation of, 7.22A
persistence of, 7.22A
"DIRECTIVE WASTE"
see also Waste framework directive
definition, 5.24
generally, 5.24
DIRECTOR GENERAL OF WATER SER-VICES, 6.05, 6.27, 6.31, 6.37
DISCHARGE CONSENT, 2.44, 6.04
DISTILLING, TAR RESIDUES FROM, SPE-CIAL WASTE, AS, 5.32
DNAPLS (DENSE NON-AQUEOUS PHASE LIQUIDS), WATER POLLUTION BY, 6.01
DOCKS
see also Naval yards
contaminative use, as, 1.01, 4.04
dredgings from, 2.56
filled dock basins, 1.01
DOMESTIC WASTE
discharge into sewers, 6.38
flammable nature of, 1.02
putrescible, 2.55
DRAINS
see also Sewage; Sewers
construction of, 2.53
matter likely to damage, dis-charge of, 6.38
powers to open up, 2.53
records of, 3.10
DREDGINGS, DEPOSITS OF, 1.01, 7.28B
DRINKING WATER
chlorine, treatment with, 6.28
coagulants, treatment with, 6.28
disinfection of, 6.28
nitrates, removal of, 6.28

DRINKING WATER—*cont.*
ozone, treatment with, 6.28
pollution of, 2.52
see also Water pollution
aluminium sulphate, 2.37, 6.31
DNAPLS, 6.01
EC directives on, 6.29
phenols, 6.30
phenols, by, 1.02
powder-activated carbon, treatment with, 6.28
quality of, 6.28
EC directives on, 6.03, 6.29,
6.30
private supplies, 6.32
public supplies, 6.31
taste of, 6.28
treatment of, 6.28
DRINKING WATER INSPECTORATE, 3.09,
6.31
powers of, 3.09
DRY-CLEANING, CONTAMINATIVE USE,
AS, 3.03
DUST
asbestos, 1.05
escape of, 1.01
inhalation of, 1.02
DYES
contamination by, aesthetic effects
of, 1.02
manufacture of
contaminative use, as, 4.04
prescribed process in, 5.12

EASEMENTS, INTERFERENCE WITH, 2.13,
2.15, 2.36
EDUCATIONAL LABORATORIES, CON-
TAMINATIVE USE, AS, 3.03
ELECTRICAL EQUIPMENT
PCB waste from, 7.22A
repair of, contaminative use, as,
3.03
ELECTRO-KINETIC REMEDIATION TECH-
NIQUES, 7.09
ELECTRONICS MANUFACTURING FACIL-
ITIES, CONTAMINATION FROM, 4.04
ELECTROPLATING, ANODIZING AND GAL-
VANIZING WORKS, CONTAMINATION
FROM, 4.04
ENDOSULFAN, 5.14
ENDRIN, 5.14
ENERGY INDUSTRY, CONTAMINATIVE
USE, AS, 3.03, 4.04

ENFORCEMENT NOTICES
failure to comply with, 2.43
register of, 3.10
service of, 2.43
special, register of, 3.10
ENGINEERING PROCESS
contamination from, 4.04
contaminative use, as, 3.03
ENGINEERS, 2.34, 7.38
ENGLISH ESTATES, 9.05
ENGLISH NATURE, 6.11
ENGLISH PARTNERSHIPS, 3.08, 9.01
see also Urban Regeneration
Agency
ENNERDALE ROAD, DONCASTER, 1.05
ENTERPRISE ZONES, 9.09
ENTRY
powers of, 3.09
Chief Inspector, 2.43
EPA, under, 2.67
Her Majesty's Inspectorate of
Pollution, 3.09
section 215 notices, under, 2.76
waste regulation authorities,
2.61
ENVIREG, 9.28
ENVIRONMENT COMMITTEE *see* HOUSE
OF COMMONS ENVIRONMENT
COMMITTEE
ENVIRONMENTAL AGENCY, 3.08, 6.04
ENVIRONMENTAL ASSESSMENT, 4.01,
8.06
ENVIRONMENTAL AUDIT, 4.01
ENVIRONMENTAL CONSULTANTS *see*
CONSULTANTS
ENVIRONMENTAL INFORMATION REGU-
LATIONS 1992 *see* *under*
INFORMATION
ENVIRONMENTAL PROTECTION ACT
1990 (EPA)
abatement notices, 2.69
air pollution control, 5.15
controlled waste, 5.24
exceptions, 5.25
enforcement notice, 2.43
entry, powers of, 2.67
integrated pollution control, 1.06,
5.11
investigation, powers of, 2.67
local authorities, duty to inspect
and investigate, 2.67
non-controlled waste, 5.26
Part I, liability under, 2.43

ENVIRONMENTAL PROTECTION ACT 1990 (EPA)—*cont.*
prohibition notice, 2.43
register of contaminated land, proposed, 1.06, 3.10, 11.03, 14.02
alternative proposals, 3.05
consultation and abandonment, 3.03
criticisms, 3.04
Paying for Our Past and, 3.08
review of, 3.06–3.07
statutory framework, 3.02
sampling, powers of, 2.67
section 143 *see* register of contaminated land, proposed *above*
section 59 *see* waste unlawfully deposited *below*
section 61 *see* waste regulation authorities *below*
special waste, 5.31
statutory nuisances, 2.66–2.72
abatement by local authorities, 2.69
cost recovery, 2.69
abatement notice, liability, 2.71
duty to inspect and investigate, 2.67
entry, powers of, 2.67
liability, 2.71
Scotland and, 2.72
summary proceedings, 2.68
by persons aggrieved, 2.70
testing, powers of, 2.67
waste, definition of, 5.24
waste management authorities
licencing conditions, 5.10
supervision of licensed activities, 3.09
waste management licence, 5.23
conditions, 5.28
exemptions from, 5.25
"fit and proper person", relevance of, 5.27
surrender of, 3.09, 5.29
waste regulation authorities
cost recovery, 2.63
duty to avoid pollution or harm, 2.62
duty to inspect, 2.61
guidance by Secretary of State, 2.64
harmful waste deposits, 2.60

ENVIRONMENTAL PROTECTION ACT 1990 (EPA)—*cont.*
waste regulation authorities—*cont.*
registers, maintenance of, 3.10
waste unlawfully deposited, removal of
notice, 2.57
non-compliance with, 2.57, 2.59
problems, 2.59
recovery of costs, 2.58, 2.59
summary power, 2.58
ENVIRONMENTAL PROTECTION (DUTY OF CARE) REGULATIONS 1991, 7.33
ENVIRONMENTAL PROTECTION (PRESCRIBED PROCESSES AND SUBSTANCES) REGULATIONS 1991, 5.12, 6.04
ENVIRONMENTAL QUALITY OBJECTIVES (EQSs), 6.24
ENVIRONMENTAL RISK ASSESSMENT, 4.23
ENVIRONMENTAL TECHNOLOGY INNOVATION SCHEME (ETIS), 9.01, 9.23
ERITH QUARRY, BEXLEY, 8.07
ESTABLISHED USE CERTIFICATES, APPLICATIONS FOR, REGISTER OF, 3.10
ESTUARIES
see also Water
contamination of, 1.02
proposals leading to increased industrial discharge into, 6.15
quality of, 6.26
EUREKA, 9.24
EUROPEAN AGRICULTURAL GUIDANCE AND GUARANTEE FUND (EAGGF), 9.27
EUROPEAN COMMUNITY, 1.10
bathing water, quality of, directive on, 6.03, 6.41
Committee of Experts on compensation for damage caused to the environment (CJ-EN), 2.83
Community Support Frameworks, 9.27
construction sites, minimum health and safety requirements at, directive on, 7.27

EUROPEAN COMMUNITY—*cont.*
Convention on Civil Liability for Damage Resulting from Activities Dangerous to the Environment, 2.83
Council of Europe Convention, 2.83
Dangerous Substances Directive, 6.25, 6.38
"directive waste", 5.24
Drinking Water Directives, 6.03, 6.29, 6.30
Envireg, 9.28
environmental action programmes, 1.10
environmental liability, proposals on, 2.82
European Regional Development Fund, 9.01
fresh waters, quality of, directive on, 6.03
funding from, 9.01
    Envireg, 9.28
    European Investment Bank (EIB), 9.28
    European Investment Fund (EIF), 9.28
    LIFE Programme, 9.26
    structural funds, 9.27
Green Paper, 2.82, 14.09
groundwater, policy on, 1.10, 6.03, 6.08
UK implementation of, 6.09
hazardous waste, directive on, 5.40
information, public access to, directive on, 3.01, 3.11, 3.12, 3.17
integrated pollution control, proposals for, 5.17
joint compensation funds, 14.09
landfill, proposed directive on, 5.41
LIFE Programme, 9.26
Maastricht Treaty, 1.10
PCBs, disposal of, directive on, 7.22A
PCTs, disposal of, directive on, 7.22A
"polluter pays" principle, 1.10, 2.81, 2.82, 2.83, 9.26
precautionary principle, 1.10
preventative action, 1.10

EUROPEAN COMMUNITY—*cont.*
public access to information, directive on, 3.01, 3.11, 3.12, 3.17
rectification of damage at source, 1.10
shellfish waters, quality of, directive on, 6.03
structural funds, 9.27
Surface Water Directive, 6.29
toxic and dangerous waste, directive on, 5.31
Urban Waste Water Treatment Directive, 6.03, 6.37, 6.38, 6.40
waste framework directive, 5.05, 5.24, 5.40
exclusions under, 5.25
waste legislation, 5.40
waste, liability for
"producer", meaning of, 2.81
proposals on, 2.81
EUROPEAN INVESTMENT BANK (EIB), 9.28
EUROPEAN INVESTMENT FUND (EIF), 9.28
EUROPEAN REGIONAL DEVELOPMENT FUND (ERDF), 9.01, 9.27
EUROPEAN SOCIAL FUND (ESF), 9.27
EUTROPHICATION OF WATERS
fertilizers and manures, by, 5.39
nitrogen, by, 6.40
phosphorus, by, 6.40
EWELME LANDFILL, OXFORDSHIRE, 2.55N
EXCAVATIONS
asphyxiation/gassing during, 7.18
release of contaminants by, 2.03
EXEMPLARY DAMAGES *see* DAMAGES
EXISTING USE OR DEVELOPMENT, CERTIFICATE OF LAWFULNESS OF, REGISTER OF, 3.10
EXPLOSIONS
contamination caused by, 1.01
hazardous substances, 3.10, 4.12
HSE guidance and, 7.18
landfill gas, caused by, 1.04
migrating gases, caused by, 1.02
risk of, investigation where, 4.12
EXPLOSIVE GASES
see also Gas
generation of, 1.02, 2.66

EXPLOSIVE SUBSTANCES, PRODUCTION OF, 4.04

EXPLOSIVES
buried, 7.25
munitions production and testing sites, contamination from, 4.04
Royal Ordnance factory, former site of, 1.05
waste, 5.25

EXPLOSIVES ORDNANCE DISPOSAL UNIT, 7.25

EXTRACTIVE INDUSTRY, CONTAMINATIVE USE, AS, 3.03

EYES
contact with contaminants, 1.02
special waste, 5.32

FELLMONGER SITES, ANTHRAX CONTAMINATION FROM, 7.26

FENITROTHION, 5.14

FERTILIZER
manufacture of, contaminative use, as, 4.04
phosphorus in, 5.39
waste used as, 3.03

FIBROUS CONTAMINANTS, INHALATION OF, 1.02

FILLED DOCK BASINS, 1.01

FINLAND, REGISTER OF CONTAMINATED LAND, 3.02

FIRE
contamination caused by, 1.01
flash fires, 2.27
gas liberated by, 1.02
landfill gas and, 1.04
liberation of toxic substances by, 1.02
PCBs, equipment containing and, 7.22A
sites presenting fire hazards
development on, 8.08
ICRCL guidance on, 4.20, 8.08
investigation, 1.02, 4.12
tyre dump, at, 1.02, 1.05
underground, 1.02, 1.05, 7.18
buried power cables, 1.02
microbial activity, heating effect of, 1.02
persistent, 1.02

FISH FARMING, DEVELOPMENT FOR PURPOSES OF, 6.15

FISH LIFE, WATERS SUPPORTING, PROTECTION OF, EC DIRECTIVE ON, 6.03

FISHING, PROFIT A PRENDRE OF, INTERFERENCE WITH, 2.21

FLAMMABLE GASES, GENERATION OF, 1.02, 2.66

FLAMMABLE MATERIALS, PRODUCTION OF, 1.02, 4.04

FLASH FIRES see FIRE

FLOOD PROTECTION, 6.18

FLOODS, CONTAMINATION BY, 1.01, 6.15

FLUORIDE, INGESTION OF, ANIMAL HEALTH AND, 5.39

FLUORINE
food plants and crops, accumulation in, 1.02
soil contamination by, 1.02

FOOD
contamination of, 1.02
Steering Group on Chemical Aspects of Food Surveillance, 5.38
water used in preparation of, 1.02, 2.52, 6.30, 6.32

FOOD PLANTS
uptake of contaminants by, 1.02, 4.12, 5.39
see also Phytotoxicity

FOOD PROCESSING INDUSTRY, CONTAMINATIVE USE, AS, 3.03

FORESHORE, CONTAMINATION OF, 6.41

FOUL WATER SEWAGE
contamination by, prevention of, 6.37
discharge into sewers, 6.38
treatment of, 6.37
Urban Waste Water Treatment Directive, 6.37

FOUNDATIONS, CONCRETE, AGGRESSIVE CHEMICAL EFFECT ON, 1.02, 4.12, 4.19

FOUNDATIONS FOR THE PROTECTION OF THE ENVIRONMENT, COUNCIL OF EUROPE CONVENTION AND, 2.83

FOUNDRIES, CONTAMINATION FROM, 1.05, 4.04

FOUNDRY SAND, "MADE GROUND", USE IN, 2.56, 7.28

FRESHWATERS
Freshwater Quality, report of the Royal Commission on Environmental Pollution, 6.01
matter discharged into, 2.44
protection of, EC directive on, 6.03
FUEL OIL
agricultural *see* Agriculture
heavy, contamination by, 4.19
FUEL PRODUCTION PROCESSES, PRESCRIBED PROCESSES IN, 5.12
FUEL STORAGE DEPOTS, CONTAMINATION FROM, 4.04
FUNDING, 1.06, 2.02, 9.01–9.28
"Action for Cities" initiative, 9.01, 9.09
City Challenge, 9.01, 9.09, 9.20
city grant *see* City grant
derelict land grant *see* Derelict land grant
DoE, from, 9.01
EC, from *see* European Community
local authorities, credit approvals for, 1.06, 9.01
new technologies, for *see* New technologies
owner, by, 14.07, 14.08
polluter, by 14.07, *see also* "Polluter pays" principle
taxpayer, by, 14.10
Urban Development Corporations, from *see* Urban Development Corporations
Urban Programme Grant, 9.01, 9.11, 9.19
Urban Regeneration Agency *see* Urban Regeneration Agency
Welsh Development Agency, 9.08

GALLYWHITE LANE INDUSTRIAL SITE, DRONFIELD, 1.05
GARAGES, CONTAMINATION FROM, 4.04
GARDENS
domestic
contaminated of, *Discussion,,* 1.05, 4.12
sensitivity of site use, 4.09
landscaped, sensitivity of site use, 4.09

GAS
asphyxiating, 1.02, 7.18
coal mines, from, 1.05
explosive, generation of, 1.02, 2.66
fire, liberated by, 1.02
flammable, generation of, 1.02, 2.66
landfill sites, from *see* Landfill gas
manufacture of, contaminative use, as, 3.03
methane *see* Methane
migration of, 1.02, 1.05, 2.41
mineral extraction, produced by, 4.04
noxious, deposits causing, 2.60
premises, emitted from, 2.66
putrescible matter, from, 1.02, 1.05
radioactive, 1.07
toxic *see* Toxic gases
GAS-MANTLE FACTORY, CONTAMINATION FROM, 1.05
GASOLINES, CONTAMINATION BY, 4.19
GASWORKS
contamination from, 1.01, 1.04, 4.04
"blue billy" waste, 1.05, 7.18
residues, 1.05
redevelopment of, ICRCL guidance on, 4.20
GELATIN PRODUCTION, ANTHRAX CONTAMINATION FROM, 7.26
GENETICALLY MODIFIED ORGANISMS, 2.83
GERMANY
contaminated land in, 13.23–13.26
register of, 3.02
former GDR, 13.26
identification of sites, 13.25
legislation
federal, 13.23
state, 13.24
register of contaminated land, 3.02
GLASS MAKING, CONTAMINATIVE USE, AS, 3.03
"GLORY HOLE" SITES, CONTAMINATION FROM, 1.05
GRANTS IN URBAN AREAS, DoE GUIDE, 9.09
GRAVEYARDS *see* CEMETRIES AND GRAVEYARDS

GREAT CAMBRIDGE ROAD, ENFIELD, 1.05
GREEN-FIELD STATE, DEFINITION, 9.11
GROUNDWATER, 6.07–6.22
  see also Aquifer
  classification of, 6.14
  clean up operations, 6.19
  controlled waters, as, 2.45
  development and, 8.11
  EC policy on, 1.10, 6.03, 6.08
    UK implementation of, 6.09
  exploitability of, 6.07
  landfill, pollution from, 1.05
  meaning, 6.07
  migration by flow of, 2.23
  PCBs in, 7.22A
  pesticides in, 6.08, 6.09
  planning applications affecting, 6.15, 6.16
  Policy and Practice for the Protection of Groundwater (NRA), 5.03, 6.10
  pollution of, 1.02, 2.21, 4.12, 7.18
    see also Water pollution
    Canada, in, 13.17
    contaminated land, from, 2.44
    continuing, 2.41
    control and, 2.24
    DNAPLS, 6.01
    EC directive on, 6.03
    industrial areas, 6.20
    industrial solvents, by, 2.26
    landfill, from, 1.05
    nuisance, as, 2.22
    PCBs, 7.22A
    solvents, by, 2.26
  protection of
    DoE, responsibilities of, 6.11
    EC policy on, 1.10, 6.03, 6.08
    UK implementation of, 6.09
    Her Majesty's Inspectorate of Pollution, responsibilities of, 6.11
    legislation, 6.10
    Ministry of Agriculture, 6.11
    NRA, responsibilities of, 6.10, 6.11
    planning permission, application for, where, 8.11
    planning system, use of, 5.03
  protection zones, 6.14
  quality objectives for, 6.12

GROUNDWATER—cont.
  receptor group, identification of, 4.22
  Source Protection Zones, 6.14
    development in, 6.22
  treatment of, contaminated, where, 7.13
  vulnerability and risk, 6.14
GYPSUM, DEPOSIT OF, 3.03

HALOGENS
  compounds containing, inorganic, special waste, as, 5.32
  and covalent compounds of, prescribed for release to land, 5.14
  organic compounds of, special waste, as, 5.32
HARWELL LABORATORY UK ATOMIC ENERGY AUTHORITY LANDFILL, OXFORDSHIRE, 2.55N
HAYLE, CORNWALL, 1.05
HAZARDOUS SUBSTANCE CONSENTS, 3.10
  register of, 3.10
HAZARDOUS WASTE, DIRECTIVE ON, 5.40
HEALTH
  accumulation or deposit prejudicial to, 2.66
  Control of Substances Hazardous to Health Regulations 1988 (COSHH), 7.21
  harm to
    condition of land causing, 2.60
    duty to avoid, 2.62
  premises, state of, and, 2.66
  skin see Skin
HEALTH RISK ASSESSMENT, 4.22, 7.20
  Acceptable Daily Intake (ADI), 4.22
  consequences to human health, 4.22
  exposure, assessment of, 4.22
  human exposure pathways, potential, identification of, 4.22
  potentially problematic contaminants, identification of, 4.22
  receptor or "target" group, 4.22
HEALTH AND SAFETY
  contaminated land, development of, 7.18
  general statutory duties, 7.19

HEALTH AND SAFETY EXECUTIVE, 1.09
Anthrax, pocket card on, 7.26
Approved Code of Practice on Control of Asbestos at Work, 7.22
Code of Practice for the Protection of Workers, 7.25
enquiries of, 11.05
Guidance on Protection of Workers, 7.21, 7.22, 7.23, 7.27
Protection of Workers and the General Public during the Development of Contaminated Land, 7.18
radioactive materials, safe removal of, 7.24
HEAVY ENGINEERING INSTALLATIONS, CONTAMINATION FROM, 1.01, 4.04
HEAVY FUEL OILS, CONTAMINATION BY, 4.19
HEAVY METALS
bathing water, in, 6.41
clean-up of
electro-kinetic techniques, 7.09
soil washing, 7.08
contamination by, 1.05, 5.39
HER MAJESTY'S INSPECTORATE OF POLLUTION (HMIP), 1.04, 1.09, 6.38
groundwater, protection of, 6.11
powers of, 3.09
entry, 3.09
water pollution, prevention of, 6.02, 6.04
radioactive material, safe removal of, 7.24
HEXACHLOROBENZENE, 5.14
HEXACHLOROBUTADIENE, 5.14
HEXACHLOROCYCLOHEXANE, ISOMERS OF, 5.14
HIGHER KILN LANDFILL, DEVON, 2.55N
HIGHWAYS, LANDFILL SITES, ON, 8.07
HISTORICALLY CONTAMINATED SITES *see* PAST CONTAMINATION
HOUSE OF COMMONS ENVIRONMENT COMMITTEE, 1.09
Contaminated Land, 1.04, 1.07, 1.11, 7.01
contaminated land
defining, *Discussion*
register of, 3.02
contaminating land use, 1.01

HOUSE OF COMMONS ENVIRONMENT COMMITTEE—*cont.*
Indoor Air Pollution, 1.07
radon contamination, 1.07
remedial techniques, views on, 7.02
Toxic Waste, 5.18, 5.41
HOUSE OF LORDS SELECT COMMITTEE ON SCIENCE AND TECHNOLOGY, 5.19, 5.22
HOUSEHOLD WASTE
final deposit of, contaminative use, as, 3.03
treatment by chemical or thermal means, contaminative use, as, 3.03
HOUSEHOLDERS GUIDE TO RADON, THE, 1.07
HOUSING DEVELOPMENTS
contamination of, 1.05, 2.08, 4.12
landfill sites, on, 8.07
sensitivity of site use, 4.09
HUMAN HEALTH *see* HEALTH
HYDROCARBONS, 4.04, 6.01
compounds of, special waste, as, 5.32
dangerous substances, as, 6.25
drinking water, in, 6.30
petroleum hydrocarbons, 7.08
storage tanks for, groundwater protection zones and, 6.14
HYDROGEN SULPHIDE
generation of, 1.02
igniting of, 7.18
inhalation of, 7.18
HYDROLOGICAL RECORDS, SOURCE OF INFORMATION, AS, 4.06

ICRCL *see* INTERDEPARTMENTAL COMMITTEE ON THE REDEVELOPMENT OF CONTAMINATED LAND
IMPOUNDMENT LICENCES, 6.04
IN-SITU VITRIFICATION, CONTAMINATED SOIL, OF, 7.10
INCINERATION, CONTAMINATED SOIL, OF, 7.11
INCINERATION OF WASTE, DANGEROUS ACTIVITY, AS, 2.83
INDOOR AIR POLLUTION, 1.07
INDUSTRIAL BUILDINGS
aggressive chemical effect on, 4.12
decommissioning and demolition of, contamination caused by, 1.01

INDUSTRIAL BUILDINGS—*cont.*
sensitivity of site use, 4.09
INDUSTRIAL WASTE
chemical or thermal treatment of, contaminative use, as, 3.03
definition, 7.28
estuaries, discharge into, 6.15
final deposit of, contaminative use, as, 3.03
groundwater, contamination of, 2.26, 6.20
lagoons, 1.01, 2.56
NRA policy, 6.21
rivers, discharge into, 6.15
slag heaps, 2.56
triazines, 2.34
INDUSTRY, SITING OF, NRA POLICY, PREFERRED LOCATIONS, 6.22
INFORMATION, 3.01–3.18
see also Investigation and appraisal
abstraction sources, on, 6.36
access to
DoE Guidance on, 3.13, 3.14, 3.15
EC directive on, 3.01, 3.11, 3.12, 3.17
blighting effects of, 3.01
categories of, 3.01
collated data sources, 4.06
commercial confidentiality, 3.15
commercial contaminative use searches, 4.06A
contaminated land, on, holdings of, 1.06
Council of Europe Convention and, 2.83
DoE guidance on, 3.13, 3.14, 3.15
Environmental Information Regulations 1992, 3.01, 3.12–3.14
commercial confidentiality, 3.15
exceptions, 3.12
"information", definition of, 3.13
information covered by, 3.12
internal communications, 3.14
local government meetings, information on, 3.18
personal information, 3.17
"records", definition of, 3.13
scope of, 3.12
statutory restrictions, relationship with, 3.16

INFORMATION—*cont.*
Environmental Information Regulations 1992—*cont.*
unfinished documents, 3.14
volunteered information, 3.17
European Directive on, 3.01, 3.11, 3.12, 3.17
hydrological records, 4.06
interpretation of, 4.08
land values, effect on, 3.01
legal documents, from, 4.06
local authorities
enquiries of, 11.04
meetings of, 3.18
local history, 4.06
local knowledge, 4.06
maps, C–02, C–03, 4.06
meteorological records, 4.06
national defence, relating to, 3.12
organisations, list of, C–06
personal, 3.17
photographs, 4.06
aerial and satellite, C–04
powers to obtain, 3.09
property transactions, 11.03–11.07
local authority enquiries, 11.04
public access to, 3.11–3.14
DoE Guidance on, 3.13, 3.14, 3.15
EC directive on, 3.01, 3.11, 3.12, 3.17
public authorities, information held by, 3.11
registers of *see* Registers
sources of, C–01, 4.06
statutory restrictions, 3.16
street directories, C–05
street names, from, 4.06
trade directories, from, 4.06
under-used land, on, 9.21
unused land, on, 9.21
volunteered, 3.17
INGESTION
contaminants, of, livestock, by, 1.02, 5.39
lead, of, 7.23
soil, of, 1.02, 2.33
children, by, 1.02, 4.12
pica, 1.02
special waste, of, 5.32
toxic substances, of, 1.02, 7.18

INHALATION
asbestos, of, 1.02
fibrous or particulate contaminants, of, 1.02
hazardous substances, of, 3.10, 7.18
lead, of, 7.23
receptor group, identification of, 4.22
special waste, of, 5.32
toxic substances, of, 1.02
INJUNCTION, 2.38
damages in lieu of, 2.36
mandatory, 2.38, 2.39
Scotland, in, 13.02
nuisance, where, 2.13
quia timet, 2.38
INLAND WATERS, CONTAMINATION OF, 1.02
INSOLVENCY *see* CORPORATE INSOLVENCY
INSPECTORATE OF POLLUTION *see* HER MAJESTY'S INSPECTORATE OF POLLUTION
INSTITUTE OF PETROLEUM, 4.19
INSTITUTION OF ENVIRONMENTAL HEALTH OFFICERS, 3.05
INSTRUMENT-DIAL MANUFACTURE, RADIOACTIVE CONTAMINATION FROM, 1.05, 5.36
INSURANCE
archaeology, F–06
building contracts, 7.44
JCT '81, 7.44
consultants, A–07, 10.12
environmental impairment liability insurance (EIL), F–05
future of, F–07
generally, F–01
pollution exclusion provisions, F–03
professional indemnity cover, F–04, A–07, 10.12
public liability indemnity policies, F–02
INTEGRATED CIRCUIT, MANUFACTURE OF, CONTAMINATION FROM, 1.01
INTEGRATED POLLUTION CONTROL (IPC), 1.06, 2.43, 5.01, 5.11–5.17
air pollution control, 5.15

INTEGRATED POLLUTION CONTROL (IPC)—*cont.*
authorisations
need for, 5.12
objectives of, 5.13
chemical release inventory, 5.16
EC proposals, 5.17
prescribed processes, 5.12
prescribed substances, 5.14
process, registers relating to, 3.10
soil contamination and, 5.14
INTERDEPARTMENTAL COMMITTEE ON THE REDEVELOPMENT OF CONTAMINATED LAND (ICRCL), 1.02, 1.09, 6.19
guidance notes, 4.02, 4.03, 4.17, 4.19, 4.20, 7.02, 8.07, 8.09
trigger concentrations, D–01–D–03, 1.06, 4.09, 4.17
INVESTIGATION AND APPRAISAL
see also Information
access agreement, A–05
analysis, 4.13
reports on, 4.14
selection of contaminants for, 4.12
assessment of findings, 4.16
Code of Practice for the Identification of Potentially Contaminated Land and its Investigation (BSI DD 175), 4.02, 4.03, 4.04, 4.07, 4.09, 4.10, 4.12
commercial contaminative use searches, 4.06A
computer records, 3.09
consultants, implied terms of contract, 10.07
developed sites, 4.15
documents, power to compel, legal professional privilege, 3.09
environmental assessment, 4.01
environmental audit, 4.01
existing owners, by, 4.01
findings, assessment of, 4.16
guidance, sources of, 4.02
health risk assessment *see* Health risk assessment
information
interpretation of, 4.08
sources of, 4.06

INVESTIGATION AND APPRAISAL—*cont.*
Interdepartmental Committee on the Redevelopment of Contaminated Land (ICRCL), guidance notes, 4.02, 4.03
limitations on investigative powers, 3.09
local and other statutory authorities, by, 4.01
main steps in, 4.03
Phase I audit, 4.01
Phase II audit, 4.01
preliminary investigation
  interpretation of information, 4.08
  methodology, 4.05
  relevant information, 4.05
prospective purchaser/lenders, by, 4.01
reasons for, 4.01
reports on sampling and analysis, 4.14
risk assessment *see* Risk assessment
sampling *see* Sampling
self-incrimination, 3.09
site history, 4.04
  information on, sources of, 4.06
site reconnaissance, 4.07
site sensitivity, 4.09
sources of guidance, 4.02
summary of process, 4.25
trigger concentrations, ICRCL Guidance, 4.17
IONISING RADIATION REGULATIONS 1985, 7.24
IPC *see* INTEGRATED POLLUTION CONTROL
IRON, DRINKING WATER, IN, 6.30
IRON AND STEEL WORKS, CONTAMINATION FROM, 1.01, 1.05, 4.04

JOINT COMPENSATION FUNDS, 14.09
JOINT AND SEVERAL LIABILITY, 2.35, 2.40
abatement notices, 2.71
aquifer, contamination of, 2.40
boreholes, contamination of, 2.40
Netherlands, in, 2.35
soil contamination, 2.35
United States, in, 14.15

JOINTING SEALS, AGGRESSIVE CHEMICAL EFFECT ON, 1.02

KEROSENE, CONTAMINATION BY, 4.19

LABORATORIES
chemical waste from, special waste, as, 5.32
contaminative use, as, 3.03
LAGOONS, FOR INDUSTRIAL WASTE, 1.01, 2.56
LAKES
controlled waters, as, 2.45
discharge of sewage or trade effluent into, 2.44
LAND POLICY, CONTAMINATED LAND AND, 2.01
LAND USE SURVEY, C–03
LAND-SCAPED GARDENS, SENSITIVITY OF SITE USE, 4.09
LANDFILL GAS, 1.04, 1.05, 2.55, 4.19, 5.28, 8.07
Building Regulations 1991 and, 8.16
carbon dioxide, 4.19
generation of, 1.04, 1.05, 2.55, 4.19
liability for, 2.27
Loscoe, Derbyshire, *Preamble*, 1.05
methane, 1.05, 2.06, 2.08, 2.27, 2.55
LANDFILL SITES
see also Waste disposal sites
Bentley Mill Lane, Walsall, 1.02n, 2.55n, 6.01
Building Regulations 1991 and, 8.16
closed, 2.60
combustible materials in, 8.08
contamination from, 1.01, 4.04, 6.01
control over, 2.24
development near, 8.07
development on, 8.07
  combustible materials, where, 8.08
  commercial uses, 8.07
  highways, 8.07
  housing, 8.07
  ICRCL guidance on, 4.20
  pre-stabilisation use, 8.07
  DoE survey of, C–05

LANDFILL SITES—*cont.*
Erith Quarry, Bexley, 8.07
Ewelme Landfill, Oxfordshire, 2.55n
gas generated by *see* Landfill gas
groundwater, pollution of, 1.05
Harwell Laboratory UK Atomic Energy Authority Landfill, Oxfordshire, 2.55n
Higher Kiln Landfill, Devon, 2.55n
information regarding, 3.10
leachate from, 2.47, 5.28
licences, 2.55
methane from, 1.05, 2.06, 2.08, 2.55
liability for, 2.27
nuisance caused by, 2.13
liability for, 2.17
old sites, problems of, 2.55
Pakefield, Suffolk, 6.09
PCBs disposed to, 7.22A
proposed Directive on, 5.41
radioactive waste, 5.36
water pollution from, 1.05, 2.55
LANDS TRIBUNAL, VALUATION OF CONTAMINATED LAND CASES, B–06
LAPORT WORKS, ILFORD, 1.05
LATENT DAMAGE
knowledge of, 2.42
limitation of actions, 2.42
LAW COMMISSION STANDING COMMITTEE ON CONVEYANCING, 1.06
LAW SOCIETY, 3.05, 3.08
LAW SOCIETY OF SCOTLAND, 3.05
LEACHATE
acid leachate, contamination by, 1.05
formation of, 2.60
landfill, from, 2.47, 5.28
mineral extraction, generated by, 4.04
trade effluent, as, 2.47
trespass by, 2.04
LEAD, 1.02, 1.05, 4.04
airborne particulate, 2.56
protection of employees from, 7.23
alloys of, 7.23
manufacture of, contaminative use, as, 3.03
clean-up of, 7.23

LEAD—*cont.*
compounds of, special waste, as, 5.32
Control of Lead at Work Regulations 1980, 7.23
dangerous substance, as, 6.25
drinking water, in, 6.30
food plants and crops, accumulation in, 1.02
fumes, inhalation of, 7.18
ingestion of, 7.23
inhalation of, 7.23
manufacture or refining of, contaminative use, as, 3.03
medical surveillance of employees, 7.23
sewage sludge, in, 5.38
soil, in, 1.02, 4.12, 5.38
LEAKS, STORAGE TANKS AND DRUMS, FROM, 1.01
LEASES
construing, 11.16
drafting, 11.16
duty to repair, 2.19
fitness for purpose, 11.18
generally, 11.14
keeping premises clean and tidy, 11.16
landlord
environmental questionnaire, A–10
protecting, 11.17
protection clause, pre-existing contamination, A–12
leasehold covenant, A–11
nuisance, 2.19, 11.16
pre-existing contamination protection clause
landlord, A–12
tenant, A–13
repairing covenants, 11.16
exclusion of, A–14
selection of tenant, 11.15
service charges, 11.16
statutory requirements, compliance with, 11.16
tenant
leasehold covenant, A–11
option to break, A–14
protection clause, pre-existing contamination, A–13
right to terminate lease, A–14

LEASES—*cont.*
  tenant—*cont.*
    safeguarding, 11.19
    selection of, 11.15
    tenant-like use, 11.16
    waste, tort of, 11.16
LEATHER TANNING WORKS *see* TANNERIES
LEEDS DEVELOPMENT CORPORATION, 9.06
LEGAL DOCUMENTS, SOURCE OF INFORMATION, AS, 4.06
LEKKERKERK, *PREAMBLE, see ALSO* NETHERLANDS
LEPTOSPIROSIS (WEIL'S DISEASE), 7.18
LIABILITY
  anti-avoidance measures, 14.14
  causation, 2.34, 2.48
  civil liability *see* Civil liability
  clean-up costs, 2.02
  concurrent causes, 2.35
  consultants, of, exclusion or limitation of, 10.06
  corporate transactions and, 12.01
  criminal *see* Criminal liability
  criminal courts, powers of *see* Criminal courts
  EC proposals on *see* European Community
  effect of contamination, 2.02
  environmental harm, for, EC and, 1.10
  EPA, Part I, under, 2.43
  expert evidence, 2.34
  joint and several *see* Joint and several liability
  limitation of actions *see* Limitation of actions
  "long tail", 2.01
  migrating contaminants, for, 2.01
  nature of contamination, 2.02
  nature of, 2.02
  occupier, of *see* Occupier
  originator of contamination, of, 12.01
  owner, of *see* Owner
  past contamination *see* Past contamination
  Paying for Our Past, in, 3.08
  polluter, of, 12.01
  "polluter pays" principle, 1.06, 2.02, 2.81, 2.82, 2.83

LIABILITY—*cont.*
  proof, 2.34
  retrospective, 2.01, 2.83
  strict *see* Strict liability
  uncontained contaminants, for, 2.01
LIFE PROGRAMME, 9.26
LIMITATION OF ACTIONS, 2.41
  latent damage, 2.42
    knowledge of, 2.42
  Limitation Act 1980, 2.41
  negligence, 2.42
  nuisance, 2.42
LIQUIDATORS *see* CORPORATE INSOLVENCY
LIQUIDS
  escape of, 1.01, 2.56
  industrial waste, 2.55
  noxious, deposits causing, 2.60
LIVESTOCK, INGESTION OF CONTAMINANTS BY, 1.02, 5.39
LOCAL AUTHORITIES
  abatement notice, duty to serve, 2.68
  abatement of nuisance by, 2.69
    cost recovery, 2.69, 2.71
  clean-up, credit approvals for, 1.06, 9.01
  complaints, investigation of, 2.67
  contaminated land, register of, 3.02
  derelict land, grant assistance for, 1.06
  enquiries of, property transactions and, A–02, 11.04
  investigations by, 4.01
  meetings of, access to information on, 3.18
  reclamation works, 9.07
    funding of, 9.01
  statutory nuisances, duty to inspect and investigate, 2.67
LOCAL AUTHORITIES ASSOCIATION, 3.05, 3.08
LOCAL GOVERNMENT (PUBLICATION OF INFORMATION ABOUT UNUSED AND UNDER-USED LAND) (ENGLAND) REGULATIONS 1992, 9.21
LOCAL HISTORY, SOURCE OF INFORMATION, AS, C–05, 4.06
LOCAL KNOWLEDGE, SOURCE OF INFORMATION, AS, C–05, 4.06

LOCAL PLANNING AUTHORITY, 14.11
see also Development plan; Local plan
contamination, responsibilities in respect of, 6.15
execution of works by, 2.76
cost recovery, 2.76
NRA, consultation of, 6.15
section 215 notices see Town and Country Planning Act 1990
LOCAL PLANS, 5.04, 6.18
waste local plan, 5.09
LOCAL WASTE REGULATION AUTHORITIES, 1.09
LOCK JAW (TETANUS), 7.18
LONDON DOCKLANDS DEVELOPMENT CORPORATION, 9.06
LOSCOE, DERBYSHIRE, Preamble, 1.05
LOVE CANAL
see also United States
Preamble, 13.06
LUBE OILS, CONTAMINATION BY, 4.19
LUMSDEN ROAD, PORTSMOUTH, 1.05

MAASTRICHT TREATY, 1.10
"MADE GROUND", 2.56, 7.28
contamination by, 1.01
MAINS, DETERIORATION OF, 1.02
MALALTHION, 5.14
MALKINS BANK, CHESHIRE, 5.19
MANAGEMENT OF HEALTH AND SAFETY AT WORK REGULATIONS 1992, 7.20
MANHOLES, ASPHYXIATION/GASSING IN, 7.18
MANUFACTURING PROCESS, CONTAMINATIVE USE, AS, 3.03
MANURE
see also Fertilizer
phosphorus in, 5.39
MAPS, SOURCE OF INFORMATION, AS, C–02, C–03, 4.06
MEDICINAL PRODUCTS, SPECIAL WASTE, AS, 5.32
MERCURY, 1.02, 1.05, 5.14
compounds of
prescribed for release to water, 5.14
special waste, as, 5.32
dangerous substance, as, 6.25
drinking water, in, 6.30
sewage sludge, in, 5.38

MERSEYSIDE DEVELOPMENT CORPORATION, 9.06
METAL CARBONYLS, 5.14
METALS
alkali, and oxides of, 5.14
alkaline earth, and oxides of, 5.14
electroplating, anodizing and galvanizing works, contaminative use, as, 4.04
finishing of, contamination from, 1.01, 4.04
foundries, contamination from, 1.05, 4.04
inhalation of, 1.02
mining of, contamination from, 4.04
non-ferrous metals processing, contamination from, 1.01
paint pigments or coatings, used in, 4.04
production of, contaminative use, as, 3.03
production and processing of, prescribed processes in, 5.12
sludges, in, 4.04
smelting, contamination from, 1.05, 4.04
soluble, ground and surface waters, in, 4.12
toxic, contamination by, 1.02, 1.05
waste, contamination by, 1.04
METEOROLOGICAL RECORDS, SOURCE OF INFORMATION, AS, 4.06
METHANE, 1.02, 2.14, 4.04, 4.12
Building Regulations 1991 and, 8.16
CIRA projects, E–05
igniting of, 7.18
landfill sites, from, 1.05, 2.06, 2.08, 2.55
liability for, 2.27
naturally occurring, 1.07
liability for failure to foresee, 2.28
phytotoxic effects of, 1.02
putrescible waste, from, 1.02
reservoir methane, 2.28
stress methane, 2.28
MICROBIAL ACTIVITY, HEATING EFFECT OF, 1.02

MICROELECTRONICS MANUFACTURING FACILITIES, CONTAMINATION FROM, 4.04
MICROORGANISMS, CONTAMINATION BY, 4.04
MIGRATION OF POLLUTANTS, 1.01
  damages for, 2.36
  flammable gases, 1.02
  foreseeability of, 2.23
  gases, 1.02, 1.05, 2.41
    flammable, 1.02
  groundwater flow, by, 2.23
  liability and, 2.01
    joint and several liability, 2.40
  PCBs, 7.22A
  plastic pipes, through, 1.02
  trespass, as, 2.04
  water, by, 2.23, 2.39
MILITARY LAND, CONTAMINATION FROM, 4.04
MILK AND DAIRY PRODUCTS, DISPOSAL OF, 5.39
MINERAL EXTRACTION *see* MINING
MINERAL OILS
  bathing water, in, 6.41
  building materials and services, aggressive effects on, 4.12
  drinking water, in, 6.30
  persistent, dangerous substances, as, 6.25
  refining or storing, development for purposes of, consultation requirement, 6.15
MINERAL PLANNING POLICY GUIDANCE NOTE PPG 14: DEVELOPMENT ON UNSTABLE LAND, 4.05
MINERAL WORKINGS, SURVEYS OF, C–02
MINERALS INDUSTRY, PRESCRIBED PROCESSES IN, 5.12
MINERALS PLANNING GUIDANCE MPG12: TREATMENT OF DISUSED MINE OPENINGS AND AVAILABILITY OF INFORMATION ON MINED GROUND (1944), 4.05
MINING
  abandoned mines, water pollution from, 2.46
  coal mines, gas from, 1.05
  contamination from, 1.05, 4.04
  development including, consultation requirements, 6.15

MINING—*cont.*
  gas from, 1.05
  metalliferous, restoration and aftercare of sites for pasture and grazing, ICRCL guidance on, 4.20
  metals, of, contamination from, 4.04
  searches, property transactions, in, 11.05
  surface collapse due to, 9.07
  tin mines, water pollution from, 1.05
  waste from, 5.25
  water pollution from, 2.46, 6.01
  zinc mines, contamination from, 1.05
MINISTRY OF AGRICULTURE, GROUNDWATER, PROTECTION OF, 6.11
MORTGAGES
  covenants by mortgagor, A–20
  documentation, 11.22
  generally, 11.20
  lending policy, 11.21
  loan facility letter, provisions for inclusion in, A–19
MUNITIONS PRODUCTION AND TESTING SITES
  see also Explosives
  contamination from, 4.04
  Royal Ordnance factory, former site of, 1.05

NAMAS (NATIONAL MEASUREMENT ACCREDITATION SERVICE), 4.13
NAPTHYLAMINES, EXPOSURE TO, 7.18
NATIONAL ARCHAEOLOGICAL RECORD, C–02
NATIONAL BUILDING RECORD, C–02
NATIONAL MEASUREMENT ACCREDITATION SERVICE (NAMAS), 4.13
NATIONAL PARK AUTHORITIES, 6.11
NATIONAL RADIOLOGICAL PROTECTION BOARD (NRPB), 1.07
NATIONAL RIVERS AUTHORITY (NRA), 1.09, 5.29
  see also Rivers
  abstraction licences, 6.04, 6.35
  abstraction sources, information on, 6.36
  anti-pollution works and operations, 2.50

NATIONAL RIVERS AUTHORITY
(NRA)—*cont.*
clean up operations, 6.19
controlled waters, monitoring extent of, 3.09
corporate body, as, 6.04
development plans, 6.18
discharge consents, 6.04
enforcement policy, 2.51
enquiries of, 11.05
flood defence functions, 6.04
functions of, 6.04
groundwater, protection of, 6.10, 6.11, 6.16, 8.11
Guidance Notes for Local Planning Authorities on the Methods of Protecting the Water Environment through Development Plans, 6.18
impoundment licences, issue of, 6.04
industry
discharges from, 6.21
industrial areas of widespread contamination, 6.20
preferred locations, 6.22
local planning authorities, consultation by, 6.15
major incidents, 2.51
minor incidents, 2.51
monitoring pollution of controlled waters, 3.09
organisation of, 6.04
planning permission
consultation requirements, 6.15
high risk of contamination and, 6.16
Policy and Practice for the Protection of Groundwater, 5.03, 6.10, 8.11
powers of, 3.09
water pollution, prevention of, 6.02
prohibition notices, 2.44
quality objectives, 6.26
samples taken by, register of, 3.10
significant incidents, 2.51
surface water, policy on, 6.26
waste regulation authorities, consultation with, 2.62, 6.09, 7.28A
water pollution, prevention of, 6.02

NATIONAL RIVERS AUTHORITY
(NRA)—*cont.*
water quality
control of, 6.04
objectives, 6.26
water resources, conditions and agreements to protect, 6.17
NATO COMMITTEE ON CHALLENGES TO MODERN SOCIETY (CCMS), CONTAMINATED LAND, DEFINING, HARM TEST *Discussion*
NATURALLY OCCURRING CONTAMINATION, 1.07
NATURE CONSERVANCY COUNCILS, ENQUIRIES OF, 11.05
NAVAL YARDS
see also Docks
waste from, 1.05
NEGLECTED LAND
Discussion
regeneration of, 9.02
funding for, 9.01
local authorities and, 9.07
NEGLIGENCE
conduct of defendant, 2.29
consultants, 10.07
contaminated water, injury or damage suffered from, 6.27
damages for, 2.36, 2.37, 2.41
duty of care, 2.25
failure to take steps, 2.29
foreseeability and, 2.26, 2.28
generally, 2.03, 2.24, 2.25
landfill gas, liability for, 2.27
limitation of actions, 2.42
natural methane, failure to foresee, 2.28
nuisance and, 2.03, 2.20
release of pre-existing contaminants, 2.29
res ipsa loquitur, doctrine of, 13.02
Rylands v. *Fletcher* and, 2.03
Scotland, in, 13.02
spillages, liability for, 2.26
NESTON TANK CLEANERS, QUEENSFERRY, 1.05
NETHERLANDS
clean-up criteria, 13.22
contaminated land in, 13.18–13.22
register of, 3.02
Dutch National Institute for Public Health and Environmental Protection (RIVM), 6.08

NETHERLANDS—*cont.*
joint and several liability, 2.35
Lekkerkerk, *Preamble*, 13.18
multifunctional approach, 1.11
National Institute of Inland Water Management and Waste Water Treatment (RIZA), 6.08
proposed legislation, 13.21
register of contaminated land, 3.02
Soil Clean-up (Interim) Act 1982, 13.18
in practice, 13.20
proceedings by the state, 13.19
proposed amendments, 13.21
soil contamination incidents, 1.11
soil protection guidelines, 13.22
soil quality, A, B and C Guidelines, 4.18, 7.15, 13.22
NEW SOUTH WALES, CONTAMINATED LAND IN, 13.29
NEW TECHNOLOGIES
Demos, 9.25
Environmental Technology Innovation Scheme (ETIS), 9.01, 9.23
Eureka, 9.24
funding of, 9.01, 9.22, 9.23
NICKEL, 1.02, 4.04, 4.12
compounds of, special waste, as, 5.32
dangerous substance, as, 6.25
drinking water, in, 6.30
phytotoxic effects of, 1.02
sewage sludge, in, 5.38
special waste, as, 5.32
watercourse, contamination of, 2.55n, 6.01
NITRATE SENSITIVE AREAS, 5.38, 6.11
NITRATE SENSITIVE AREAS (DESIGNATION) ORDER 1990, 5.38
NITRATES
agricultural sources, from, 5.38, 5.39
biological dentrification, removal by, 6.28
clean-up of, 7.09
EC directives on, 6.03, 6.10
ion exchange, removal by, 6.28
NITROGEN, EUTROPHICATION OF WATERS BY, 6.40

NON-FERROUS METALS PROCESSING, CONTAMINATION FROM, 1.01
NON-METALS AND PRODUCTS OF, PRODUCTION OF, CONTAMINATIVE USE, AS, 3.03
NORTHERN TERRITORY, AUSTRALIA, CONTAMINATED LAND, IN, 13.35
NOTICES OF PROPOSED DEVELOPMENT, REGISTER OF, 3.10
NOXIOUS GASES *see* GAS
NOXIOUS LIQUIDS *see* LIQUIDS
NUISANCE
accumulation or deposit causing, 2.66
act of trespasser, 2.18, 2.20
care and skill, exercise of, 2.20
coming to, 2.20
contaminated water, injury or damage suffered from, 6.27
continuing pollution, foreseeability and, 2.24
contributory negligence, 2.20
damages for, 2.23, 2.36, 2.37, 2.41
defences, 2.20
disposal of property, 2.19
easement, interference with, 2.13, 2.15
enjoyment of land, interference with, 2.13
exercise of care and skill, 2.20
foreseeability, 2.13, 2.22, 2.23, 2.36
continuing pollution and, 2.24
generally, 2.03, 2.13
groundwater, pollution of, 2.22
injunctions, 2.13
interest in land, interference with, 2.13
knowledge or means of knowledge of risk, 2.14, 2.18
landfill site, operation of, as, 2.13
liability for, 2.17
leases, 11.16
limitation of actions, 2.42
naturally occurring, 2.18
nature of, location, 2.15
negligence and, 2.03, 2.20
occupier, liability of, 2.18, 2.19
originator, liability of, 2.17, 2.21
owner, liability of, 2.18, 2.19, 2.21
physical harm to persons or property, 2.13, 2.15, 2.36

NUISANCE—*cont.*
  predecessor in title, caused by, 2.18
  premises, state of, 2.66
  profit à prendre, fishing, from, interference with, 2.21
  property, disposal of, 2.19
  public, 2.14
    damages, 2.37
  regulatory authority for, 2.20
  risk, knowledge or means of knowledge of, 2.14
  Rylands v. *Fletcher*, rule in and, 2.10
  Scotland, in, 13.02
  statutory *see* Statutory nuisance
  surface waters, pollution of, 2.21
  title to sue, 2.16
  trespasser, act of, 2.18, 2.20

OCCUPIER
  see also Premises
  liability of
    corporate transactions, 12.01
    degree of control, 2.32
    nuisance, 2.18
    "occupier", identifying, 2.32
    trespassers, duty to, 2.33
    visitors, duty to, 2.32
    warning signs or notices, 2.32
  section 59 notices, 2.59
ODOURS, PRODUCTION OF, 1.02
OFFICES, SENSITIVITY OF SITE USE, 4.09
OIL POLLUTION, UNITED STATES, IN, 13.15
OIL REFINERIES
  see also Petroleum refineries
  contamination from, 1.01, 4.04
OILS
  aggressive effects of, 1.02, 4.12
  contamination by, 1.02, 1.05, 4.19
    aesthetic effects of, 1.02
    eyes, contact with, 1.02
  flammable nature of, 1.02
  heavy fuel oils, contamination by, 4.19
  industrial, storage of, groundwater protection zones and, 6.14
  lube oils, contamination by, 4.19
  skin, contact with, 1.02, 7.18
  storage facilities, pollution from, 6.21

OILS—*cont.*
  waste, 2.47, 2.55n
  water-borne, 2.56
1, 2-DICHLOROETHANE, 5.14
ORGANIC COMPOUNDS, SPECIAL WASTE, AS, 5.32
ORGANIC MATERIALS, INHALATION OF, 1.02
ORGANIC SOLVENTS *SEE* SOLVENTS
ORGANO-METALLIC COMPOUNDS, 5.14
ORGANOCHLORINE COMPOUNDS, DRINKING WATER, IN, 6.30
ORGANOCHLORINE SOLVENTS, 2.07
OWNER
  "for the time being", 2.63
  liability of
    corporate transactions, 12.01
    nuisance, 2.16, 2.18
    past contamination, 2.16, 14.08
    Paying for Our Past, in, 3.08
  rack rent, receiver of, as, 2.63, 2.69
  recovery of costs from, 2.63, 2.69
OXIDISING AGENTS, 5.14
OXYGEN, DEPLETION OF, IN SOIL, 1.02
OZONE, DRINKING WATER, TREATMENT WITH, 6.28

PAINT
  metals used in, contaminants, as, 4.04
  works, contaminative use, as, 4.04
PAKEFIELD, SUFFOLK, 6.09
PAPER INDUSTRY
  contamination from, 1.01, 4.04
  contaminative use, as, 3.03
  prescribed processes in, 5.12
PARKING, SENSITIVITY OF SITE USE, 4.09
PARKS, SENSITIVITY OF SITE USE, 4.09
PARTICULATE CONTAMINANTS
  accumulation of, 2.56
  airborne, 1.01, 2.03, 2.43
  arsenic dust, 7.18
  asbestos dust, 1.05, 7.18
  inhalation of, 1.02
  lead, 2.56, 7.23
PAST CONTAMINATION, 2.43, 2.48
  see also Site history
  liability for, 14.06
    former owner, 2.16, 14.07
    "long tail", 2.01
    polluter, 14.07

PAST CONTAMINATION—*cont.*
present owner, 14.08
old landfills, 2.55
PAYING FOR OUR PAST, 1.04N, 1.06, 2.02N, 3.08
liability, on, 3.08
markets, supplying information to, on, 3.08
overview, 3.08
policy objectives, 3.08
public sector bodies, other roles for, on, 3.08
statutory framework, 3.08
common law, relationship with, 3.08
strict liability, possible extension of, on, 3.08
PBBs, 7.22A
PCBs, 4.04, 7.22A
see also Dioxins
clean-up of
electro-kinetic techniques, 7.09
soil washing, 7.08
disposal of
EC Directive on, 7.22A
Waste Management Paper No. 6, 7.22A
EC directive on, 7.22A
fire and, 7.22A
groundwater, in, 7.22A
landfill, disposed to, 7.22A
migration of, 7.22A
monitoring of, 7.22A
phasing out of, 7.22A
prescribed for release to water, 5.14
sources of, 7.22A
surface water, in, 7.22A
United States, regulation of, in, 13.16
waste, 7.22A
PCNs, 7.22A
PCTs, 7.22A
disposal of, EC Directive on, 7.22A
PEMBREY COUNTRY PARK, LLANELLI, 1.05
PENTACHLOROPHENOL AND COMPOUNDS OF, 5.14
PERCHLORATES, SPECIAL WASTE, AS, 5.32

PERCOLATING WATER
no proprietary rights in, 2.22
right to abstract, 2.22
PEROXIDES, SPECIAL WASTE, AS, 5.32
PESTICIDES
bathing water, in, 6.41
bromoxynil, 6.09
bromoxynil octanoate, 6.09
chlorpyrifos, 6.09
clean-up of, soil washing, 7.08
Control of Pesticides Regulations 1986, 5.01, 5.38
definition, 5.14
drinking water, in, 6.30
groundwater, in, 6.08, 6.09
manufacture of, contaminative use, as, 4.04
prescribed for release to land, 5.14
sale, supply, use and application of, control over, 5.38
water pollution from, 1.05, 6.08, 6.09, 6.30
PETERBOROUGH, CAMBRIDGESHIRE, 1.05
PETROCHEMICAL INDUSTRY, CONTAMINATION FROM, 4.04, 4.19
PETROL STATIONS, CONTAMINATION FROM, 1.01
PETROLEUM
contaminant, as, 4.19
hydrocarbons, 7.08
Institute of Petroleum Code of Practice, 4.19
manufacture, refining or recovery of, contaminative use, as, 3.03
storage of, contaminative use, as, 3.03, 4.04
tank farms, contamination from, 4.04
PETROLEUM PROCESSES, PRESCRIBED PROCESSES IN, 5.12
PETROLEUM REFINERIES
see also Oil refineries
contamination from, 1.01, 1.04
pH VALUE
bathing water, of, 6.41
sewage sludge, of, 5.38
soil, of, 4.12, 5.38
PHARMACEUTICALS
manufacture of, contaminative use, as, 4.04
special waste, as, 5.32

PHASE I AUDIT, 4.01
PHASE II AUDIT, 4.01
PHENOLS, 1.02, 4.04, 4.12
  bathing water, in, 6.41
  building materials and services, aggressive effects on, 4.12
  drinking water, in, 1.02, 6.30
  ground and surface water, in, 4.12
  vapours generated by, 7.18
PHOSPHATES, CLEAN-UP OF, 7.09
PHOSPHORUS
  compounds of, special waste, as, 5.32
  eutrophication of waters by, 6.40
  fertilizers, in, 5.39
  prescribed for release to land, 5.14
PHOTOGRAPHS
  aerial and satellite, C–04
  source of information, as, C–02, C–04, 4.06
PHYTOPHARMACEUTICAL SUBSTANCES, SPECIAL WASTE, AS, 5.32
PHYTOTOXICITY, 1.02, 4.12, 5.38
  definition, 1.02
PICA, 1.02
  see also Soil
PIGMENTS
  contamination by, aesthetic effects of, 1.02
  metals used in, contaminants, as, 4.04
PIPEWORK
  aggressive chemicals effect on, 1.02
  migration of substances through, 1.02
  records of, 3.10
PITCH RESIDUE DUSTS, LUNG CANCERS AND, 7.18
PLANNING, 5.02–5.10
  see also Town and Country Planning Act 1990
  development plan see Development plan
  Government policy, 5.05
  local plans, 5.04, 6.18
  waste local plan, 5.09
  water resources, protection of, in, 5.03
PLANNING APPEALS
  decisions, examples of, 8.10
  DoE and, 6.11

PLANNING APPLICATIONS
  appraisal report, proposed, 3.05
  environmental assessment, 8.06
  information on, 3.10
  Register of, C–02, 3.10
    RICS proposals, 3.05, 3.08
  responsibilities of applicant, 6.15
PLANNING CONDITIONS, 5.06, 8.12
  Grampian conditions, 8.12
  waste disposal and, 5.10
PLANNING OBLIGATIONS, 5.06, 8.13
  waste disposal and, 5.10
PLANNING PERMISSION
  applicant, responsibilities of, 6.15
  consultation requirements, 6.15
  development of contaminated land, 8.02
  landfill sites, 8.07
  water protection issues, 8.11
PLANNING POWERS, SECTION 215, UNDER see TOWN AND COUNTRY PLANNING ACT 1990
PLANTS
  food, uptake of contaminants by, 1.02
  inhibition of growth of, 1.02
  see also Phytotoxicity
  sensitivity of site use, 4.09
PLASTIC
  aggressive chemical effect on, 1.02
  flammable nature of, 1.02
  pipework, migration of substances through, 1.02
PLYMOUTH DEVELOPMENT CORPORATION, 9.06
POLICY AND PRACTICE FOR THE PROTECTION OF GROUNDWATER (NRA), 5.03, 6.10
POLLUTER, LIABILITY OF 14.07, SEE ALSO "POLLUTER PAYS" PRINCIPLE
"POLLUTER PAYS" PRINCIPLE, 1.06, 2.02
  derelict land grant and, 9.12
  EC and, 1.10, 2.81, 2.82, 2.83, 9.26
POLLUTION
  see also Contaminated land; Contamination
  contamination distinguished, Discussion
  environment, of, definition, 2.60
  water, of see Water pollution

POLYAROMATIC HYDROCARBONS (PAHs), 7.08

POLYBROMINATED BIPHENYLS (PBBs), 7.22A

POLYCHLORINATED BIPHENYLS *see* PCBs

POLYCHLORINATED DIBENZO-P-DIOXIN AND CONGENERS, 5.14

POLYCHLORINATED DIBENZOFURAN AND CONGENERS OF, 5.14

POLYCHLORINATED NAPTHALENES (PCNs), 7.22A

POLYCHLORINATED TERPHENYLS *see* PCTs

POLYCYCLIC AROMATIC HYDROCARBONS, DRINKING WATER, IN, 6.30

POLYHALOGENATED BIPHENYLS, 5.14

POLYHALOGENATED NAPHTHALENES, 5.14

POLYHALOGENATED TERPHENYLS, 5.14

POLYMERIC MATERIALS, AGGRESSIVE CHEMICAL EFFECT ON, 1.02

POLYNUCLEAR AROMATIC HYDROCARBONS, 4.12

PONDS
controlled waters, as, 2.45
discharge of sewage or trade effluent into, 2.44
effluent ponds, 2.56

POTABLE WATER *see* WATER

POVERTY BOTTOM, SEAFORD, 2.49

POWDERS, SPILLAGE OF, 2.56

POWER CABLES, BURIED, FIRE AND, 1.02

POWER STATIONS, CONTAMINATION FROM, 1.01, 4.04

POWYS, WALES, 1.05

PRAIRIE (POLLUTION RISK FROM ACCIDENTAL INFLUXES INTO RIVERS AND ESTUARIES) SOFTWARE, 6.13

PRELIMINARY INVESTIGATION *see* INVESTIGATION AND APPRAISAL

PREMISES
see also Occupier
defective, liability for, 11.06
fumes or gases emitted from, 2.66
registers of, C–02
state of, prejudicial to health, where, 2.66

PRESCRIBED PROCESSES, 5.12, 6.04, 6.38

PRESCRIBED SUBSTANCES, 5.14, 6.25, 6.38

PREVENTION, 5.01–5.41

PRINTING INDUSTRY
contamination from, 1.01, 4.04
contaminative use, as, 3.03

PRINTING INK, MANUFACTURE OF, PRESCRIBED PROCESSES IN, 5.12

PRIORITISATION OF SITES, RECOMMENDATIONS, 14.04

PRIVATE WATER SUPPLIES, DoE CIRCULAR, 6.32

PRIVATE WATER SUPPLIES REGULATIONS 1991, 3.09, 6.32

PROFESSIONAL ADVICE *see* CONSULTANTS

PROFIT Á PRENDRE, INTERFERENCE WITH, 2.21, 2.36

PROHIBITION NOTICES
Chief Inspector, 2.43
EPA, under, 2.43
NRA, 2.44

PROPERTY RIGHTS, SCOTLAND, IN, 13.05

PROPERTY TRANSACTIONS
aesthetic effects of soil contamination, 1.02
blight, 1.06, 3.01, 11.01
British Rail, enquiries of, 11.05
British Waterways Board, enquiries of, 11.05
caveat emptor rule, criticisms of, 1.06, 3.08, 11.11
conditional contracts, use of, 11.13
contamination surveys, 11.12
covenants of sale on part of land, A–09
development potential, interference with, damages for, 2.36
diminution in value, 1.02, 2.03, 11.02
damages for, 2.04, 2.36
fitness for purpose and, 11.01, 11.02
generally, 11.01
HSE, enquiries of, 11.05
indemnities, A–04, 11.09
information on, 11.03–11.07
disclosure by vendor *see* vendor *below*
public access to, land values, effect on, 3.01
investigations, 4.01
leases *see* Leases

PROPERTY TRANSACTIONS—*cont.*
liability and, 11.01, 11.02
loan facility letter, provisions for inclusion in, A–19
local authority enquiries, A–02, 11.04
mining searches, 11.05
Ministry of Agriculture, enquiries of, 11.05
MoD, enquiries of, 11.05
mortgages *see* Mortgages
Nature Conservancy Councils, enquiries of, 11.05
NRA, enquiries of, 11.05
nuisance and, 2.19
pre-contract enquiries, 11.07
sale
generally, 11.02
information on, 11.03
searches, 11.04–11.05
standard contract provisions, 11.08
valuation of contaminated land *see* Valuation of contaminated land
vendor
disclosure of information by, 11.06
concealment of defects, 11.06
defective premises, 11.06
misdescription, 11.06
misleading statements, 11.06
negligent works by vendor, 11.06
notices and disputes, 11.06
enquiries of, A–03
pre-contract enquiries, 11.07
warranties, 11.09
construction of, 11.10
PROPOSALS TO PREVENT LAND BECOMING DERELICT, 1.06, 2.77, 5.06
PROPOSED DEVELOPMENT *see* DEVELOPMENT
PROTECTION OF WORKERS AND THE GENERAL PUBLIC DURING THE DEVELOPMENT OF CONTAMINATED LAND, 7.18
PROTECTIVE COATINGS, AGGRESSIVE CHEMICAL EFFECT ON, 1.02
PUBLIC NUISANCE *see* NUISANCE
PUBLIC REGISTERS *see* REGISTERS
"PUMP AND DISPERSE" SYSTEM, 1.05
"PUMP AND TREAT" METHOD, 7.13

PUTRESCIBLE WASTES
domestic, 2.55
gas produced by, 1.02, 1.05, 8.07

QUARRY
contamination from, 4.04, 6.01
infilled, 1.05
waste from, 5.25
QUAYS
see also Docks
contamination from, 4.04
QUEENSLAND, CONTAMINATED LAND IN, 13.30
QUIA TIMET INJUNCTION *see* INJUNCTION

RADIOACTIVE MATERIALS, 1.05, 5.35–5.37
application of control, 5.36
contact with during demolition/clearance/construction, 4.12
contamination by, 1.01, 1.05, 4.04, 7.24
Ionising Radiation Regulations, 7.24
exposure to, trespassers, 2.33
groundwater, discharge to, 6.11
instrument-dial manufacture, 1.05, 5.36
keeping and use of, control over, 5.01
premises kept or used on, records of, C–02
site records, 5.37
RADIOACTIVE WASTE, 5.25
accumulation and disposal of, control over, 5.01
clean-up operations and, 7.30
landfill, 5.36
liquid, discharge to sewer, 5.36
methods of disposal, 5.36
special waste, as, 5.32
RADIUM 226, CONTAMINATION BY, 1.05
RADIUM
contamination by, 1.05
radon produced by, 1.07
RADON
Building Regulations 1991 and, 8.16
naturally occurring, 1.07
The Householders Guide to Radon, 1.07

RADON AFFECTED AREAS, 1.07
  "directed" surveys, 1.07
  "on demand" surveys, 1.07
RAILWAY LAND, CONTAMINATION FROM,
  1.01, 4.04
RECLAMATION, FUNDING OF see
  FUNDING
RECREATIONAL LAND
  contaminated soil in, 4.12
  sensitivity of site use, 4.09
REFINERIES see OIL REFINERIES;
  PETROLEUM REFINERIES
REGENERATION, FUNDING OF see
  FUNDING
REGIONAL WATER AUTHORITIES, 6.27
  records of, C–05
REGISTERS, C–02, 3.01
  abstraction licences, of, 6.36
  air pollution control, of, 3.10
  breach of condition notices, of,
    3.10
  certificate of existing use or
    development, of, 3.10
  certificate of proposed use or
    development, of, 3.10
  contaminated land, of, proposed,
    1.06, 4.02, 14.02
    section 143, under, 3.02–3.08,
      3.10, 11.03
    alternative proposals, 3.05
    criticisms of, 3.04
    review of, 3.06–3.07
    statutory framework, 3.02
  development, proposed, of, 3.10
  enforcement notices, of, 3.10
  established use certificates, appli-
    cation for, of, 3.10
  hazardous substance consents, of,
    3.10
  impounding licences, of, 6.36
  information held on, 3.10
  IPC process, of, 3.10
  local authority air pollution con-
    trol, of, 3.10
  planning applications, of, C–02,
    3.10
    RICS proposals, 3.05, 3.08
  premises, of, C–02
  proposed development, of, 3.10
  section 143 see contaminated land,
    of above
  sewers, records of, 3.10

REGISTERS—cont.
  sludge, use of, 5.38
  special waste, of, 5.34
  stop notices, of, 3.10
  trade effluent discharge, consents
    and agreements to, of, 3.10
  under-used land, of, 9.09, 9.21
  unused land, of, 9.09, 9.21
  waste management licences, of,
    3.10
  water discharge consents, of, 3.10
  water pollution control, of, 3.10
  waterworks, records of, 3.10
REMEDIATION see CLEAN-UP
RESEARCH AND DEVELOPMENT SITES,
  CONTAMINATION FROM, 4.04
RESEARCH LABORATORIES, CONTAMINA-
  TIVE USE, AS, 3.03
RESERVOIR METHANE see METHANE
RESERVOIRS, MANAGEMENT OF, 6.04
RESIDENTIAL DEVELOPMENT, SEN-
  SITIVITY OF SITE USE, 4.09
RIPARIAN OWNERS, 2.03, 2.21
  abstraction licence, 6.34
  rights of, 6.27
    interference with, Scotland,
      13.02
RISK ASSESSMENT, 4.21
  see also Investigation and
    appraisal
  commercial, 4.24
  environmental, 4.23
  health see Health risk assessment
RIVER FAL WATERWAY SYSTEM, POLLU-
  TION OF, 1.05
RIVER PURIFICATION AUTHORITIES
  (SCOTLAND), 1.09, 2.43, 3.10
RIVER TAME, POLLUTION OF, 6.01
RIVERS
  see also National Rivers Authority
    (NRA)
  artificial, controlled waters, as,
    2.45
  controlled waters, as, 2.45
  development including operations
    in, 6.15
  proposals leading to increased
    industrial discharge into,
    6.15
  restocking of, 2.62
  water quality objectives for, 6.12,
    6.26

ROYAL COMMISSION ON ENVIRONMEN-
    TAL POLLUTION, 6.01, 6.26
ROYAL INSTITUTE OF CHARTERED SUR-
    VEYORS (RICS), 3.05, 3.08
  valuation
    caveats, B–05
    guidelines, B–04
RUBBER
  aggressive chemical effect on, 1.02
  flammable nature of, 1.02
  processes involving, prescribed
    processes in, 5.12
  works, contamination from, 3.03,
    4.04
RUBBLE, "MADE GROUND", USE IN, 2.56
RUN-OFF, NEW DEVELOPMENTS, FROM,
    6.15
RYLANDS v. *FLETCHER*, RULE IN, 2.03,
    2.05, 2.24
  bringing and accumulation on
    land, 2.06
  damages, 2.36, 2.37
  escape, 2.09
  foreseeability, relevance of, 2.10
  future of, 2.11
  harmful propensities, 2.08
  natural and anticipated con-
    sequences, liability for, 2.10
  negligence and, 2.03
  "non-natural" use, 2.05, 2.07
  nuisance and, 2.10
  requirements for liability under,
    2.05
  Scotland and, 2.12, 13.02
  strict liability, 2.05, 2.11, 13.02
  subsequent owners or occupiers
    and, 2.06
  things "not naturally there", 2.07
  use for general benefit of com-
    munity, 2.07

ST MARY'S ISLAND, RIVER MEDWAY,
    1.05
SAMPLING
  EPA, powers under, 2.67
  evidential conditions, 3.09
  procedures, 4.11
    avoidance of damage, 4.11
    confidentiality, 4.11
    demolition and clearance, 4.11
    health and safety, 4.11
    sample preservation, 4.11
    site security, 4.11

SAMPLING—*cont.*
  procedures—*cont.*
    visual observations, 4.11
  programme, 4.10
    background samples, 4.10
    number of sampling points,
      4.10
    number of stages of sampling,
      4.10
    off-site sampling, 4.10
    on-site testing, 4.10
    sampling methods, 4.10
    sampling patterns, 4.10
  reports on, 4.14
  selection of contaminants for anal-
    ysis, 4.12
SAWSTON MILL, CAMBRIDGESHIRE,
    1.05
SCAVENGING, DISTURBANCE OF CON-
    TAMINANTS BY, 2.33
SCOTLAND
  abatement notices, 13.04
  civil remedies, 2.12, 13.02
  contaminated   land   in,
    13.01–13.05
  nuisance, 13.02
  property rights, 13.05
  riparian owners, interference with
    rights of, 13.02
  river purification authorities, 1.09,
    2.43, 3.10
  Rylands v. *Fletcher*, rule in and,
    2.12, 13.02
  statutory nuisance, 13.04
  water pollution, 13.03
SCOTTISH HOUSEBUILDERS FEDERA-
    TION, 3.05
SCOTTISH OFFICE, 1.09
SCRAP METAL
  reduction plants, contaminative
    use, as, 4.04
  sites
    contamination from, 1.04, 4.04
    redevelopment of, ICRCL guid-
      ance on, 4.20
  storage of, contaminative use, as,
    3.03
  waste, as, 2.56
SEA
  sewage effluent, discharge into,
    2.44
  trade effluent, discharge into, 2.44
SEALS, JOINTING, AGGRESSIVE CHEMICAL
    EFFECT ON, 1.02

SEASHORE, CONTAMINATION OF, 6.41

SECTION 143 REGISTERS *see* REGISTERS

SECTION 215 NOTICES *SEE* TOWN AND COUNTRY PLANNING ACT 1990

SELENIUM AND SELENIUM COMPOUNDS, SPECIAL WASTE, AS, 5.32

SEMI-CONDUCTORS, MANUFACTURE OF, CONTAMINATION FROM, 1.01

SENSITIVITY SCALES, 4.09

SEPTIC TANK
leakage into water supplies, 6.01
sludge, 5.38

SERVICE CONDUITS, AGGRESSIVE CHEMICAL EFFECT ON, 1.02

SERVICE PIPES, RECORDS OF, 3.10

SEWAGE
coliforms in, control of, 6.41
disposal of, control over, 5.01
effluent
definition, 2.47
discharge of
controlled waters, into, 2.44, 2.47
lakes, into, 2.44
ponds, into, 2.44
sea, into, 2.44
farms
foul water sewage from, 6.37
redevelopment of, ICRCL guidance on, 4.20
foul water *see* Foul water sewage
retention, treatment or disposal of, development relating to, 6.15
sludge *see* Sludge
statutory undertakers, 6.02
treatment of, 6.40
Urban Waste Water Treatment Directive, 6.03, 6.37, 6.40
works
contamination of land by, 1.01, 4.04, 6.37
effluent from, water pollution by, 2.47, 6.02
foul water sewage from, 6.37
groundwater protection zones and, 6.14
redevelopment of, ICRCL guidance on, 4.20

SEWERAGE UNDERTAKERS
appointment and regulation of, 6.05
duties of, 6.37

SEWERAGE UNDERTAKERS—*cont.*
functions of, 6.02, 6.37
registers of consents and agreements to discharge trade effluent, 3.10
sewers and drains, records of, 3.10

SEWERS
construction of, 2.53
contaminated land, under, 3.10
damaged, where, leakage of contaminated sub-surface water into, 6.39
discharge into, 6.38
radioactive waste, 5.36
leakage into water supplies, 6.01
matter likely to damage, discharge of, 6.38
powers to open up, 2.53
radioactive waste discharged to, 5.36
reclamation schemes and, 6.39
records of, 3.10
sub-surface water, discharge of, into, 6.39
surface water, discharge of, into, 6.39
trade effluent input, 5.38

SHEEP *see* ANIMALS; LIVESTOCK

SHEEP DIP, DISPOSAL OF, 5.39

SHEFFIELD DEVELOPMENT CORPORATION, 9.06

SHELLFISH WATERS, QUALITY OF, EC DIRECTIVE ON, 6.03

SHIPBREAKING
contamination from, 4.04
asbestos, 2.56

SHIPBUILDING, CONTAMINATION FROM, 4.04

SHIPHAM, SOMERSET, 1.05

SILAGE
Control of Pollution (Silage, Slurry and Agricultural Fuel Oil) Regulations 1991, 5.01, 5.38, 6.10
storage of, 5.39

SILVER
compounds of, special waste, as, 5.32
dangerous substance, as, 6.25

SIMAZINE, 5.14

SITE HISTORY
see also Past contamination
problematic uses, 4.04
sources of information on, 4.06

SITE INVESTIGATIONS *see* INVESTIGA-
    TION AND APPRAISAL
SITE SENSITIVITY, 4.09
SKIN
    absorption of materials by, 7.18
    contact with contaminants, 1.02
        special waste, 5.32
    penetration of materials into, 7.18
SLACKY LANE, WALSALL, 1.02N, 6.01
SLAG
    deposits of, 3.03
    heaps, industrial, 2.56
    "made ground", use in, 2.56, 7.28
SLUDGE
    agricultural land, application
        onto, 1.01, 5.38, 6.40
    agricultural land, disposal to, EC
        directive on, 5.38
    Department of Environment Code
        of Practice, 5.38
    disposal of, registration and
        authorisation, 6.40
    metals in, contamination by, 4.04
    PCBs in, 7.22A
    pH of, 5.38
    register of use, 5.38
    retention, treatment or disposal
        of, development relating to,
        6.15
    septic tanks, from, 5.38
    ships, dumping from, 6.40
    storage of, 5.39
    surface water, disposed to, 6.40
    testing of, 5.38
    trade effluent, effect of, 5.38
    Urban Waste Water Treatment
        Directive, 6.37, 6.40
SLUDGE (USE IN AGRICULTURE) REGU-
    LATIONS 1989, 5.01, 5.38
SLURRY
    Control of Pollution (Silage,
    Slurry and Agricultural Fuel Oil)
        Regulations 1991, 5.01, 5.38,
        6.10
    retention, treatment or disposal
        of, development relating to,
        6.15
SMELTING, CONTAMINATION FROM,
    1.05, 4.04
SOCIAL FUND *see* EUROPEAN SOCIAL
    FUND
SOIL
    analysis, 4.13

SOIL—*cont.*
    Code of Good Agriculture Prac-
        tice for the Protection of Soil,
        5.39
    contaminated, 1.02, 2.56, 4.12
    aesthetic effects of, 1.02
    clean-up of *see* Clean-up
    domestic gardens, in, *Discussion*,
        1.05, 4.12
    expert evidence, 2.34
    food plants grown in, 1.02,
        4.12, 5.39
    integrated pollution control,
        relationship with, 5.14
    liability for *see* Liability
    livestock grazing on, 1.02, 5.39
    mixing with uncontaminated
        soil, 7.28
    property values and, 1.02
    water pollution and, 1.02
    ingestion of, 1.02, 2.33, 4.12
    pica, 1.02
    pH of, 4.12, 5.38
    receptor group, identification of,
        4.22
SOIL VAPOUR EXTRACTION, 7.06
SOIL WASHING, 7.08
SOLICITOR, APPOINTMENT OF CONSUL-
    TANT, ROLE IN, 10.05
SOLIDIFICATION OF CONTAMINATED
    SOIL, 7.12
SOLVENTS, 1.02, 1.05, 4.04
    aquifer, contamination of, 6.20
    aquifer, in, 2.23, 2.55n
    benzene, 4.04
    chlorinated, contamination by,
        1.05, 2.03, 2.22, 2.49, 2.50,
        6.01
    groundwater, contamination of,
        2.26
    organic, 2.55n, 5.14
    organochlorine, 2.07
    spillage of, 2.18, 2.23
        liability for, 2.26
    toluene, 4.04
    trade effluent, as, 2.47
SOUTH AUSTRALIA, CONTAMINATED
    LAND IN, 13.33
SPECIAL CATEGORY EFFLUENT, CONSENT
    FOR, 6.38
SPECIAL ENFORCEMENT NOTICES, REGIS-
    TER OF, 3.10

SPECIAL WASTE
  clean-up operations and, 7.29
  consignment notes, 5.33, 7.29
    register of, 5.34
  control over, 5.01
  Control of Pollution (Special
    Waste) Regulations 1980,
    5.01, 5.31, 5.32, 5.33, 7.33
  "dangerous to life", 5.32
  definition, 5.32
  documentary tracking of, 5.33
  generally, 5.31
  ingestion of, 5.32
  licensing and, 7.28B
  medicinal products as, 5.32
  radioactive waste as, 5.32
  registers, 5.34
  regulation of, 5.33
  site records, 5.34
SPECIAL WASTE REGULATIONS 1980,
  4.18, 5.19
SPILLAGE
  accidental
    active, 2.03
    passive, 2.03
    water pollution by, 2.48
  liability for, 2.26
  liquids, of, 2.56
  powders, of, 2.56
  reporting and response, recom-
    mendations, 14.05
  solvents, of, 2.18, 2.23
  storage tanks and drums, from,
    1.01
SPOIL HEAP, CONTAMINATION FROM,
  4.04
STABILISATION OF CONTAMINATED SOIL,
  7.12
STANDING   LOCAL   AUTHORITY
  OFFICERS' PANEL   ON   LAND
  RECLAMATION, 3.05
STATUTORY DUTY, BREACH OF, 2.03
  damages, 2.37, 2.41
  general principles, 2.30
  particular class of persons, benefit
    of, 2.30
  public right, creation of, 2.30
  special damage, 2.30
  unlawful waste deposits, 2.31
  wholesome water, supply of, 6.27
STATUTORY NUISANCE, 2.66–2.72
  abatement notice see Abatement
    notice; Abatement of
    nuisance

STATUTORY NUISANCE—cont.
  detection of, 3.09
  duty to inspect and investigate,
    2.67
  health, premises, state of and,
    2.66
  investigation of complaints, 3.09
  premises, state of, 2.66
  Scotland, in, 13.04
  summary proceedings, 2.68
    by persons aggrieved, 2.70
STATUTORY   NUISANCE   (APPEALS)
  REGULATIONS 1990, 2.68
STEEL
  alloys of, manufacture of, con-
    taminative use, as, 3.03
  manufacture or refining of, con-
    taminative use, as, 3.03
STEERING   GROUP   ON   CHEMICAL
  ASPECTS OF FOOD SURVEILLANCE,
  5.38
STOP NOTICES, REGISTER OF, 3.10
STREAM
  development including operations
    in, 6.15
  pollution of, 2.21
STREET NAMES, SOURCE OF INFORMA-
  TION, AS, 4.06
STREET WORKS, WATER UNDERTAKERS'
  POWERS TO UNDERTAKE, 2.53
STRESS METHANE see METHANE
STRICT LIABILITY
  possible extension of, Paying for
    Our Past, in, 3.08
  Rylands v. Fletcher, rule in, 2.05,
    2.11, 13.02
  water pollution, 2.50
STRUCTURAL FUNDS (EC), 9.27
STRUCTURE PLANS, 5.04, 5.09
SUB-CONTRACTORS, CONSULTANTS, USE
  BY, 10.06, 10.11
SUB-SURFACE   WATER,   SEWERS,   DIS-
  CHARGE INTO, 6.39
SULPHATES, 4.04
  concrete, aggressive effect on,
    1.02, 4.12, 4.19
  ground and surface water, in, 4.12
SULPHIDES, BUILDING MATERIALS AND
  SERVICES, AGGRESSIVE EFFECT ON,
  4.12
SULPHUR
  compounds of
    contamination by, 4.04

SULPHUR—*cont.*
compounds of—*cont.*
inorganic, special waste, as, 5.32
construction, use in, 4.12
SULPHUR DIOXIDE, INHALATION OF, 7.18
SURFACE WATER
classification of, 6.24
EC directive on, 6.03, 6.29
environmental quality objectives (EQOs), 6.24
NRA policy, 6.26
pollution of, 1.02, 4.12
contaminated land, from, 2.44
nuisance, as, 2.21
PCBs, 7.22A
protection of, planning system, use of, 5.03
quality of, 6.23–6.26
EC directive on, 6.03, 6.29
environmental quality objectives (EQOs), 6.24
quality objectives, 6.24
receptor group, identification of, 4.22
sewers, discharge into, 6.38, 6.39
sludge disposed to, 6.40

TANK FARMS, CONTAMINATION FROM, 1.05, 4.04
TANNERIES
anthrax and, 7.26
contamination from, 1.01, 2.07, 4.04
water pollution by, 1.05, 2.03, 2.55n
TARS AND TARRY MATERIALS
aggressive effects of, 1.02, 4.12
building materials and services, aggressive effect on, 4.12
contamination by, 1.02, 1.05, 4.12
aesthetic effects of, 1.02
distilling, from, 1.05, 4.04
special waste, as, 5.32
eyes, contact with, 1.02
flammable nature of, 1.02
PCBs in, 7.22A
processing, prescribed processes in, 5.12
refining, from, special waste, as, 5.32
skin, contact with, 1.02, 7.18
underground fires caused by, 7.18

TEESIDE DEVELOPMENT CORPORATION, 9.06
TELLURIUM AND TELLURIUM COMPOUNDS, SPECIAL WASTE, AS, 5.32
TERRITORIAL WATERS, CONTROLLED WATERS, AS, 2.45
TETANUS, 7.18
TEXTILE INDUSTRY
contamination from, 1.01
contaminative use, as, 3.03
THALLIUM AND THALLIUM COMPOUNDS, SPECIAL WASTE, AS, 5.32
THAMESMEAD, GREENWICH, 1.05
THE HOUSEHOLDERS GUIDE TO RADON, 1.07
THERMAL DESORPTION, CONTAMINATED SOIL, OF, 7.11
THIRD INTERNATIONAL MINISTERIAL CONFERENCE ON THE PROTECTION OF THE NORTH SEA 1990, 7.22A
THIS COMMON INHERITANCE: BRITAIN'S ENVIRONMENTAL STRATEGY, 1.04, 2.01, 3.01
THORIUM, RADIOACTIVE, CONTAMINATION BY, 1.05
TIMBER INDUSTRY
contamination from, 1.01
contaminative use, as, 3.03
prescribed processes in, 5.12
TIN MINES, WATER POLLUTION FROM, 1.05
TIPS, CONTAMINATION FROM, 1.01
TOLUENE, 4.04
TORT *see* NEGLIGENCE; NUISANCE; *RYLANDS* V. *FLETCHER*, RULE IN; STATUTORY DUTY, BREACH OF; TRESPASS
TOWN AND COUNTRY PLANNING ACT 1990
change of use, 5.08
development, definition of, 8.02
engineering operations, definition of, 8.02
established use certificates, applications for, register of, 3.10
planning applications, 6.17
register of, 3.10
planning conditions, 8.12
planning obligations, 8.13
planning permission, 8.02
registers maintained under, 3.10
section 215

TOWN AND COUNTRY PLANNING ACT
1990—*cont.*
  section 215—*cont.*
    entry, powers of, 2.76
    industrial dereliction, combating, 5.07
    notices, 2.73–2.77
      appeals, 2.75
      cost recovery, 2.76
      execution of works, 2.76
      proposed extension of powers, 2.77
      sanctions, 2.74
    waste disposal, 5.08
TOWN AND COUNTRY PLANNING (GENERAL DEVELOPMENT) ORDER 1988, 6.15
TOWN AND PLANNING (ASSESSMENT OF ENVIRONMENTAL EFFECTS) REGULATIONS 1988, 8.06
TOXIC GASES, 1.02
  see also Gas
  fire, liberated by, 1.02
  generation of, 1.02, 2.66
TOXIC SUBSTANCES
  generation of, 4.04
  ingestion of, 1.02
  inhalation of, 1.02
  liquids, fire, liberated by, 1.02
  metals, contamination by, 1.05
TOXIC WASTE, EC DIRECTIVE ON, 5.31
TOXIC WASTE (SECOND REPORT OF THE HOUSE OF COMMONS ENVIRONMENT COMMITTEE), 5.18, 5.41
TRADE DIRECTORIES, SOURCE OF INFORMATION, AS, 4.06
TRADE EFFLUENT
  consents and agreements to discharge, register of, 3.10
  control over disposal, 5.01
  discharge of
    controlled waters, into, 2.44, 2.47
    lakes, into, 2.44
    ponds, into, 2.44
    sea, into, 2.44
    sewers into, 5.38, 6.38
  leachate as, 2.47
  meaning, 2.47
  sewers, in, 5.38, 6.38
  solvents, 2.47
  Urban Waste Water Treatment Directive, 6.37
  waste oils, 2.47

TRADE EFFLUENT NOTICE, 6.38
TRADE EFFLUENT (PRESCRIBED PROCESSES AND SUBSTANCES) REGULATIONS 1989, 6.25, 6.38
TRADE WASTE, RETENTION, TREATMENT OR DISPOSAL OF, DEVELOPMENT RELATING TO, 6.15
TRAFFORD PARK DEVELOPMENT CORPORATION, 9.06
TRANSFER NOTE, WASTE, FOR, 7.33
TRANSFER STATIONS, UNLICENSED TEMPORARY DEPOSITS OF WASTE, 2.59
TRESPASS, 2.03, 2.04, 2.36
  back washes, matter deposited by, 2.04
  damages, measure of, 2.04
  direct injury, 2.04
  title to sue, 2.04
  undercurrents, matter deposited by, 2.04
  underlying strata, to, 2.04
TRESPASSERS
  children as, 2.33
  nuisance arising from act of, 2.18, 2.20
  occupiers' duty to, 2.33
TRIAZINES, 2.34
TRIBUTYLTIN COMPOUNDS, 5.14
TRICHLOROBENZENE, ISOMERS OF, 5.14
TRIFLURALIN, 5.14
TRIGGER CONCENTRATIONS (IRCRCL), D–01–D–03, 1.06, 4.09, 4.17
TRURO, CORNWALL, POLLUTION OF RIVER FAL, 1.05
TRYPHENYLTIN COMPOUNDS, 5.14
TYNE AND WEAR DEVELOPMENT CORPORATION, 9.06
TYRE DUMPS, FIRES AT, 1.02, 1.05

UNDER-USED LAND
  Discussion
  information on, 9.21
  regeneration of, 9.02
    funding for, 9.01
  register of, 9.09, 9.21
UNDERGROUND FIRES *see* FIRE
UNDERGROUND SERVICES, AGGRESSIVE CHEMICAL EFFECT ON, 1.02
UNDERGROUND WORKS, RECORDS OF, 3.10
UNITARY DEVELOPMENT PLAN (UDP), 5.04

663

UNITED STATES
citizens suits, 13.10
clean-up costs, 14.15
clean-up standards, 14.15
contaminated land in, 13.06–13.16
contamination incidents, 1.11
contributions actions, 13.10
Environmental Protection Agency (EPA), 13.06, 13.07
action by, 13.08
enforcement and liability, 13.09
Hazard Ranking System, 13.07
settlements with, 13.11
Toxics Release Inventory, 5.16
Hazardous Substance Superfund see Superfund Programme below
identification of sites, 13.07
joint and several liability, 14.15
legislative development, 13.06
state legislation, 13.14
Love Canal, *Preamble*,, 13.06
multi-party waste disposal sites, 14.15
National Priorities List (NPL), 13.07, 13.08
oil pollution, 13.15
PCBs, regulation of, 13.16
potentially responsible parties (PRPs), 13.11, 14.12
private actions, 13.10
remedial action, 13.08
settlements, 13.11
non-binding preliminary allocations of responsibility (NBARs), 13.11
state legislation, 13.14
Superfund programme, 1.11, 13.12, 14.15
financing of, 13.12
future of, 13.13
UNSIGHTLY LAND
regeneration of, 9.02
funding of, 9.01
local authorities, 9.07
UNUSED LAND
Discussion
information on, 9.21
regeneration of, 9.02
funding for, 9.01
register of, 9.09, 9.21

URANIUM
processes involving, prescribed processes in, 5.12
radon produced by, 1.07
URBAN COMMONS, 8.15
URBAN DEVELOPMENT CORPORATIONS, 1.09, 9.05, 9.06
funding from, 9.01, 9.06
objectives of, 9.06
powers of, 9.06
Urban Regeneration Agency, as agent of, 9.03
URBAN PROGRAMME, 9.09, 9.19
URBAN PROGRAMME AREAS, 9.01
URBAN PROGRAMME GRANT, 9.01, 9.19
derelict land grant, relationship with, 9.11
URBAN REGENERATION, 2.01
funding, 9.01
URBAN REGENERATION AGENCY, 1.09, 9.01, 9.02–9.05, 14.11
financial assistance, provision of, 9.04
powers of, 9.03
role of, 9.05
urban development corporation as agent of, 9.03
URBAN WASTE WATER TREATMENT, EC DIRECTIVE ON, 6.03, 6.37, 6.38, 6.40

VACANT LAND
Discussion
regeneration of, 9.02
funding for, 9.01
VALUATION OF CONTAMINATED LAND
existing methods, application of, B–02
generally, B–01
lands tribunal cases, B–06
liability of valuers, B–03
RICS
caveats, B–05
guidelines, B–04
valuers, liability of, B–03
VANADIUM COMPOUNDS, SPECIAL WASTE, AS, 5.32
VEGETABLE MATTER
treatment and processing of prescribed processes in, 5.12
waste from, 5.39

VEHICLE BUILDING AND MAINTENANCE WORKSHOPS, CONTAMINATION FROM, 4.04
VEHICLE PARKS, SENSITIVITY OF SITE USE, 4.09
VETERINARY PRODUCTS, SPECIAL WASTE, AS, 5.32
VICTORIA, AUSTRALIA, CONTAMINATED LAND IN, 13.31
VISITORS, OCCUPIERS' DUTY TO, 2.32
VITRIFICATION, CONTAMINATED SOIL, OF, 7.10
VOLATILE AROMATICS, VAPOURS GENERATED BY, 7.18
VOLATILE ORGANIC COMPOUNDS (VOCs), REMOVAL OF, 7.06

WALES
  see also Welsh Development Agency; Welsh Office
  contaminated land in, 1.04
WALTHAM PARK, WALTHAM ABBEY, 1.05
WASTE
  beneficial use of, 7.28
  commercial
    deposit of, contaminative use, as, 3.03
    treatment by chemical or thermal, contaminative use, as, 3.03
  contamination by, 2.54–2.65
  controlled see Controlled waste
  definition, 7.28
    COPA, in, 5.21
    EPA, in, 2.56, 5.24
  deposit of
    deliberate, 2.03
    development involving use of land for, 6.15
    unlawful see unlawful deposits below
  domestic
    discharge into sewers, 6.38
    flammable nature of, 1.02
    putrescible, 2.55
  duty of care, 2.65
  fertiliser, use as, 3.03
  harmful deposits, 2.60
    cost recovery, 2.63
    duty to avoid pollution or harm, 2.62
    duty to inspect, 2.61

WASTE—cont.
  harmful deposits—cont.
    guidance by Secretary of State, 2.64
  household
    deposit of, contaminative use, as, 3.03
    treatment by chemical or thermal means, contaminative use, as, 3.03
  incineration of, dangerous activity, as, 2.83
  industrial
    chemical or thermal treatment of, contaminative use, as, 3.03
    deposit of, contaminative use, as, 3.03
  keeping of, 2.65
  plans, 5.09
  poisonous, deposit of, 5.19
  policies, 5.09
  spreading of, 7.28B
  toxic, EC directive on, 5.31
  transfer note, 7.33
  trespass of, 2.04
  unlawful deposits
    liability for, 2.31
    removal of, 2.57
  section 59
    notice, 2.57
  non-compliance with, 2.57, 2.59
    problems with, 2.59
    recovery of costs, 2.58, 2.59
    summary power, 2.58
  waste local plan, 5.09
WASTE BROKERS AND DEALERS, REGISTRATION OF, 7.34A
WASTE CARRIERS REGISTRATION, 5.30, 7.34
  applications for, 7.34
  exemptions, 7.34
  refusal/revocation of, 7.34
WASTE COLLECTION AUTHORITIES, 2.57
WASTE DISPOSAL
  contaminative use, as, 3.03
  planning conditions or obligations and, 5.10
  prescribed process, as, 5.12
WASTE DISPOSAL LICENCE, 2.34
  records of, C–02
WASTE DISPOSAL SITES
  see also Landfill sites

WASTE DISPOSAL SITES—*cont.*
breach of licence conditions, 2.31
closed, retrospective liability and, 2.83
contamination from, 1.01, 4.04
operation of, dangerous activity, as, 2.83
WASTE FRAMEWORK DIRECTIVE, 5.05, 5.24, 5.40
exclusions under, 5.25
WASTE LAND, *Discussion*
WASTE LOCAL PLAN, 5.09
WASTE MANAGEMENT LAW, 5.18–5.30
WASTE MANAGEMENT LICENCE, 2.65
appeals on, DoE and, 6.11
applications for, register of, 3.10
breach of conditions, 2.31
Collection and Disposal of Waste Regulations 1988, 5.25, 5.38, 7.28A
conditions, 5.28
directive waste, 7.28
EPA and, 5.23
exemptions, 5.25, 7.28A, 7.28B, 7.28
soil, contaminated
clean-up operations, 7.28
mixing with uncontaminated soil, 7.28
surrender of, 3.09, 5.29
trade effluent, discharge of, 2.44
variation of, groundwater, protection of, 6.09
waste, definition of, 7.28
WASTE MANAGEMENT LICENSING REGULATIONS 1994, 5.05, 5.06N, 5.23N, 5.24, 5.28, 5.38, 6.09, 7.28B, 7.28
waste brokers and dealers, 7.34A
WASTE METAL SITES, CONTAMINATION FROM, 1.04
WASTE RECYCLING, PRESCRIBED PROCESS, AS, 5.12
WASTE REGULATION AUTHORITIES, 2.57, 2.60, 5.10
cost recovery, 2.58, 2.63
duty to avoid pollution or harm, 2.62
duty to inspect, 2.61
entry, rights of, 2.61
guidance by Secretary of State, 2.64

WASTE REGULATION AUTHORITIES—*cont.*
inspection of land
waste deposited without licence, where, 3.09
waste management licence, application to surrender, following, 3.09
NRA, consultation with, 2.62, 6.09, 7.28A
powers of, 3.09
records of, source of information, as, C–02
waste management licence
application to surrender, inspection of land following, 3.09
monitoring of, 3.09
WASTE SITE LICENCE, 2.61, 5.20
conditions, 5.10, 5.20, 6.38
COPA and, 5.20, 5.22
WATER
abstraction of *see* Abstraction of water
anti-pollution works and operations, 2.50
chlorine, treatment with, 6.28
coagulants, treatment with, 6.28
coastal waters, contamination of, 1.02
controlled waters *see* Controlled waters
disinfection of, 6.28
domestic purposes, for
see also Drinking water; Food
contamination of, 2.52, 6.33
drinking, for *see* Drinking water
EC directives on *see under* European Community
estuarial waters
contamination of, 1.02
quality of, 6.26
food preparation, used in, 1.02, 2.52, 6.30, 6.32
groundwater *see* Groundwater
human consumption, for *see* Drinking water; Food
ozone, treatment with, 6.28
percolating *see* Percolating water
pollution of *see* Water pollution
potable, 1.02, 2.51, 2.55
prescribed substances, 5.14, 6.25, 6.38

WATER—*cont.*
  private supplies
    monitoring of, 3.09
    quality of, 6.27
  quality of, 6.28
    monitoring of, 6.30
    NRA objectives, 6.26
    private supplies, 6.27
    statutory water quality objectives, 6.12
  resources, protection of, planning system, use of, 5.03
  service mains, deterioration of, 1.02
  sources, contamination of, 6.33
  substances prescribed for release to, 5.14, 6.25, 6.38
  supplies, wholesomeness of, 3.09
  surface waters *see* Surface waters
  undertakers *see* Water undertakers
WATER DISCHARGE CONSENTS, REGISTER OF, 3.10
WATER MAINS, RECORDS OF, 3.10
WATER POLLUTION, 1.02, 1.05, 2.44–2.53
  aluminium sulphate, by, 2.37
  anti-pollution works and operations, 2.50
  chlorinated solvents, 1.05
  contaminated land and, 6.01
  controlled waters, 2.44
    monitoring of, 3.09
    sewage effluent, discharge into, 2.44, 2.47
    trade effluent, discharge into, 2.44, 2.47
  criminal liability for, 2.44–2.49
  dense non-aqueous phase liquids (DNAPLS), 6.01
  domestic purposes, water for, 2.52
  drinking water, 2.52
    aluminium sulphate, 2.37, 6.31
    DNAPLS, 6.01
    EC directives on, 6.29
    phenols, 1.02, 6.30
  EC directives on *see under* European Community
  food manufacture, water for, 2.52
  groundwater *see* Groundwater
  human consumption, water for *see* Drinking water
  landfill sites, from, 1.05, 2.55
  liability for, criminal, 2.44–2.49

WATER POLLUTION—*cont.*
  major incidents, 2.51
  migration of pollutions through pipework, 1.02
  minor incidents, 2.51
  offences, 2.44–2.49
    causing and knowingly permitting, 2.48
    contamination of water sources, 2.52
    controlled waters, 2.45
    major incidents, 2.51
    minor incidents, 2.51
    penalties, 2.49
    poisonous, noxious or polluting matter, 2.46
    sewage effluent, 2.47
    significant incidents, 2.51
    strict liability, 2.50
    trade effluent, 2.47
  penalties, 2.49
  pesticides, 1.05, 6.08, 6.09, 6.30
  plastic pipes, migration of pollutants through, 1.02
  prevention of, 5.01
  Scotland, in, 13.03
  significant incidents, 2.51
  soil contamination and, 1.02
  strict liability, 2.50
  surface waters, 1.02, 2.44, 4.12
    nuisance, 2.21
    PCBs, 7.22A
    PCBs in, 7.22A
  tin mine, from, 1.05
WATER PROTECTION ZONES, 1.06, 6.13
WATER RESEARCH CENTRE, 6.01
WATER SERVICES
  Director General of Water Services, 6.05
  provision of, 6.05
WATER SUPPLIES, CONTAMINATION OF, 1.02
WATER SUPPLY AND SEWERAGE SERVICES (CUSTOMER SERVICE STANDARDS) REGULATIONS 1989, 6.27
WATER SUPPLY UNDERTAKERS
  contamination, powers to deal with, 2.53
  drains and sewers
    construction of, 2.53
    powers to open up, 2.53

WATER SUPPLY UNDERTAKERS—*cont.*
powers of, 2.53
street works, powers to undertake,
2.53
water supply, monitoring of, 3.09
watercourses, construction of,
2.53
WATER SUPPLY (WATER QUALITY)
REGULATIONS 1989, 3.09, 6.05,
6.31
WATER TABLE
meaning, 6.07
proposals leading to increased
drainage problems, 6.15
WATER UNDERTAKERS, 6.02, 6.27
abstraction licences, 6.35
appointment and regulation of,
6.05
records kept by, 3.10
reservoirs, management of, 6.04
water quality, statutory duties,
6.28
WATERCOURSES
construction of, 2.53
contamination of, 2.55n, 6.01
controlled waters, as, 2.45
WATERWORKS
contamination from, 4.04
contamination of, 6.33
maps of, 6.36
meaning, 2.52, 6.33
records of, 3.10
WEIL'S DISEASE, 7.18
WELLS
pollution of, 2.22
chlorinated hydrocarbons, by,
2.55n

WELLS—*cont.*
receptor group, identification of,
4.12
WELSH DEVELOPMENT AGENCY
(WDA), 3.08, 9.08
function of, 9.08
funding from, 9.01, 9.08
funding of, 9.08
powers of, 9.08
WELSH OFFICE, 1.04, 1.09
environmental assessment, guide
to, 8.06
WESTERN AUSTRALIA, CONTAMINATED
LAND IN, 13.32
WHARF
see also Docks
contamination from, 4.04
WHEAL JANE TIN MINE, POLLUTION
FROM, 1.05
WILDLIFE HABITATS, 8.15
WOOD PRESERVATIVES, INDUSTRIES
MAKING OR USING, 4.04
WOOD TREATMENT PLANTS, CON-
TAMINATION FROM, 4.04
WORKSHOP, VEHICLE BUILDING AND
MAINTENANCE, CONTAMINATIVE
USE, AS, 4.04

ZINC
compounds of, special waste, as,
5.32
contamination by, 1.02, 1.05,
4.04, 4.12
dangerous substance, as, 6.25
drinking water, in, 6.30
mines, contamination from, 1.05
phytotoxic effects of, 1.02
sewage sludge, in, 5.38